GREAT JOY UNDER HEAVEN

GREAT JOY UNDER HEAVEN
天下大悦
Wildlife in China

Nathan Morehart

2024

First edition December 2024

Library of Congress Control Number: 2024922993

ISBN: 979-8-9914042-0-4 : cloth hardcover

ISBN: 979-8-9914042-1-1 : paperback

ISBN: 979-8-9914042-4-2 : ebook

ISBN: 979-8-9914042-5-9 : Kindle ebook

The Chinese seal script included in the cover design is in
Chong Xi Small Seal font (崇義篆體) from Academia Sinica (中央研究院).
(CC BY-ND 4.0) https://xiaoxue.iis.sinica.edu.tw/chongxi/copyright.htm.

For my parents

堯舜既沒聖人之道衰暴君代作
壞宮室以爲汙池民無所安息棄
田以爲園囿使民不得衣食邪說
暴行又作園囿汙池沛澤多而禽
獸至及紂之身天下又大亂周公
相武王誅紂伐奄三年討其君驅
飛廉於海隅而戮之滅國者五十
驅虎豹犀象而遠之天下大悦

孟子·滕文公下

The sagely way was abandoned after the deaths of Yao and Shun. Successive tyrants tore down houses to build ponds and lakes, leaving the people no quiet place to repose. They turned fields into gardens and parks, depriving the people of clothes and food. Corruption and oppression spread, gardens, parks, ponds, lakes, and marshes proliferated, and birds and beasts became many. Upon the arrival of the tyrant Zhou, there was great turmoil under heaven. The Duke of Zhou aided King Wu, killing Zhou and attacking Yan, slaying its ruler after three years. He drove Fei Lian to the sea and there slew him. He destroyed fifty states. **He drove off the tigers, panthers, rhinoceroses, and elephants, and there was great joy under heaven.**

Mencius, Book 3B

CONTENTS

Political Map of Mainland China

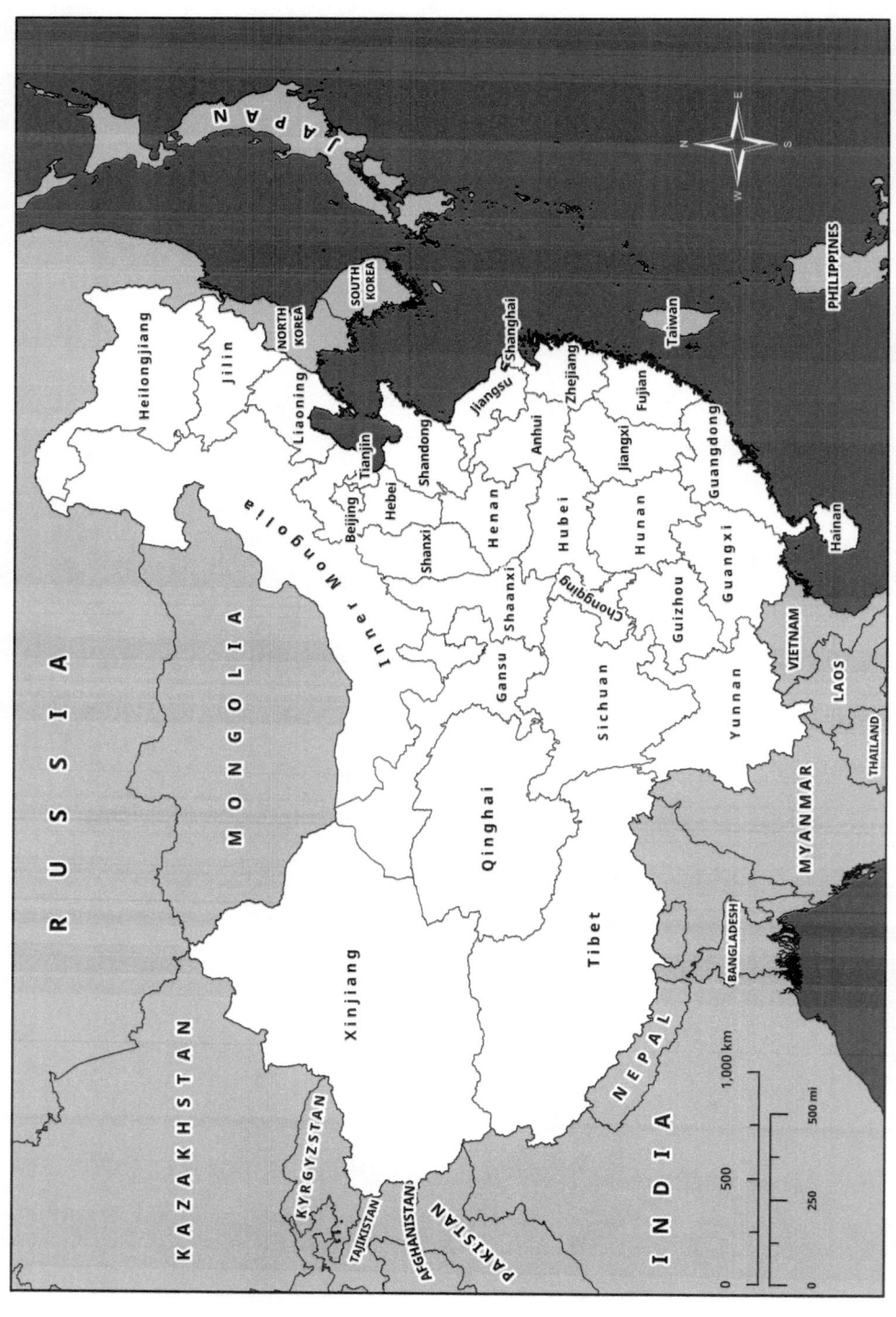

LIST of MAPS

All maps made by author using data from Natural Earth
(https://www.naturalearthdata.com/).

Map of Terrain of Mainland China

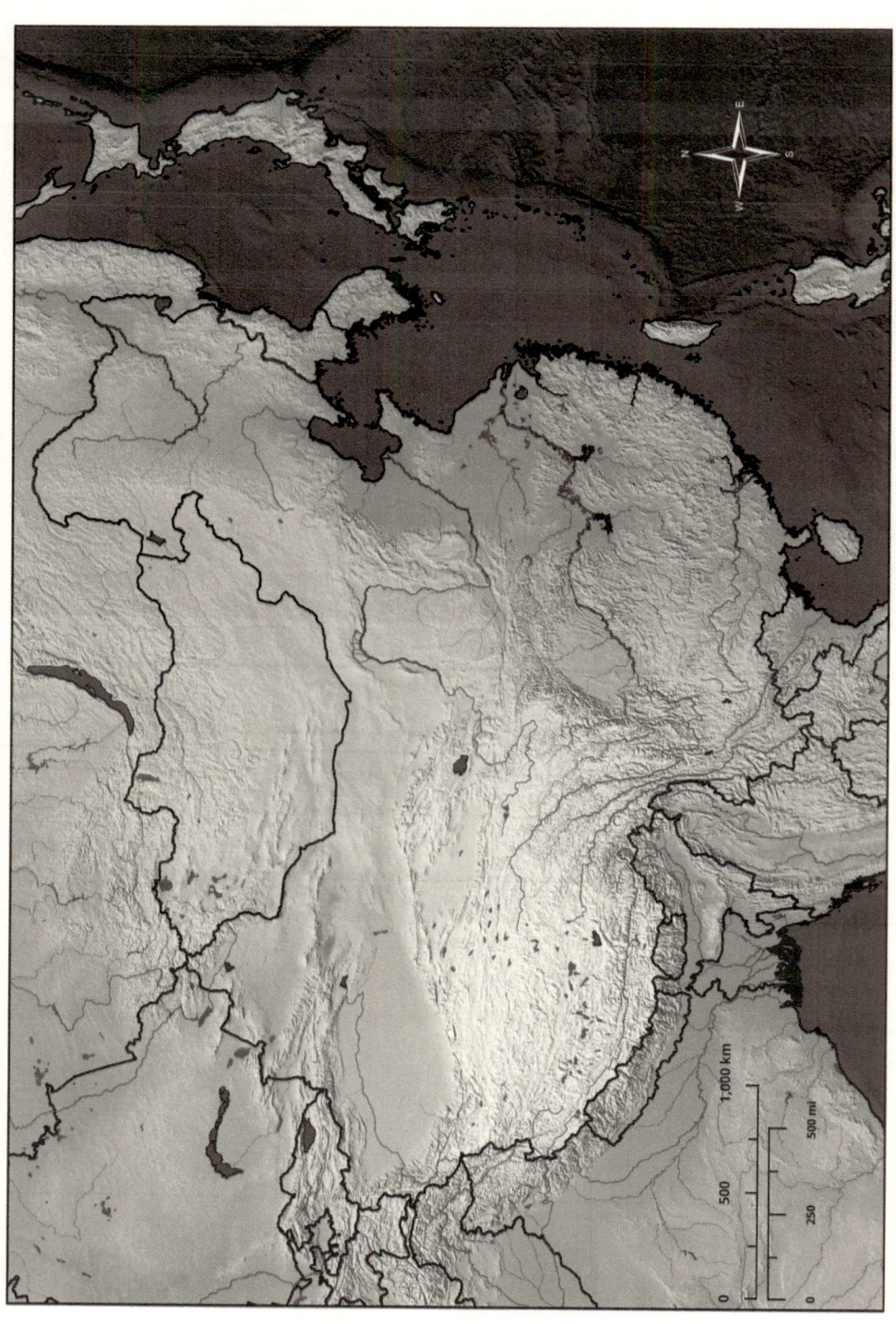

PREFACE

My interest in animals began as early as any other, an interest in China only developing much later. Even after living in the country for several years, it took me several years longer to bring the two together. At some point I can't pin down I read Mark Elvin's *The Retreat of the Elephants*, a first taste of China's environmental history. But it was a few years more before I turned in earnest to learning about China's wildlife. After finally visiting a few reserves in mountainous Sichuan, I began to delve into the history of how the biodiversity of China—and of the wider world—reached its present diminished state. For an overview of China's environmental history, I was able to turn to Robert B. Marks' *China: Its Environment and History*. For its wildlife history, there was no such volume.

This is not work of original research but instead a synthesis and distillation of existing scholarship—limitations of time, access, ability, and patience have deterred me from attempting to produce original scholarly work. Instead this is meant as an accessible account of how China's flora and fauna have fared over the last few thousand years. Books of every level of erudition cover the historical dynamics of America's wildlife, and similar accounts have been written for India, Madagascar, Australia, New Zealand, and much of Europe. For China, however, the information is scattered. Plenty has been written on the topic—just see the preposterously long bibliography at the back—but learning the known history of more than a handful of species was impossible without leafing through a hefty stack of books and papers. This book was written to serve as single source for those few who wish to know the overarching story.

ACKNOWLEDGMENTS

First and foremost I owe my gratitude to all the authors and researchers who produced the corpus of historical and scientific knowledge on which this book relied. If I have misunderstood or misrepresented any of their works, the fault is wholly my own.

For providing corrections and suggestions I am indebted to David Bello, Maarten J. M. Christenhusz, Chris Coggins, Charlotte Hacker, Donald Harper, Richard B. Harris, Thomas A. Jefferson, Anna Jemmett, Brian Lander, Li Juan, Ian M. Miller, Andrew T. Smith, E. Elena Songster, Roel Sterckx, Terry Townshend, Yifu Wang, Wei Qiwei, and Daniel Winkler.

My thanks to Nicole M. Wong for her excellent Tibetan fox illustration. Also to Pat Polansky of the University of Hawai'i at Mānoa Library for help obtaining the nesting storks illustration.

To Katie and Jessie, thanks for the feedback on the cover design and typesetting.

And of course, to my family, thank you for all the support and encouragement you have given me.

HISTORY of CHINA

This text covers the historical changes in population and distribution that various wildlife species within the present-day bounds of the People's Republic of China. The human history of that territory is long and immensely complex. The timeline below offers a glimpse of this complexity, depicting the major periods of Chinese history. It shows only the major dynasties and states, smoothing over the maddening intricacies that confront serious students of the subject.

The timeline also ignores the many city-states, kingdoms, and empires that came and went in the regions surrounding Chinese empires. Often the elites of these polities adopted Chinese customs and governmental structures, becoming highly Sinicized though maintaining their independence. For others Chinese cultural influence was far weaker—Tibetans maintained a distinct culture that took inspiration from India and Nepal in equal if not greater measure than China. Similarly, the mix of states that existed in present-day Xinjiang typically resembled those of Persianate Central Asia more than their contemporaries in China.

Timeline of Major Chinese States

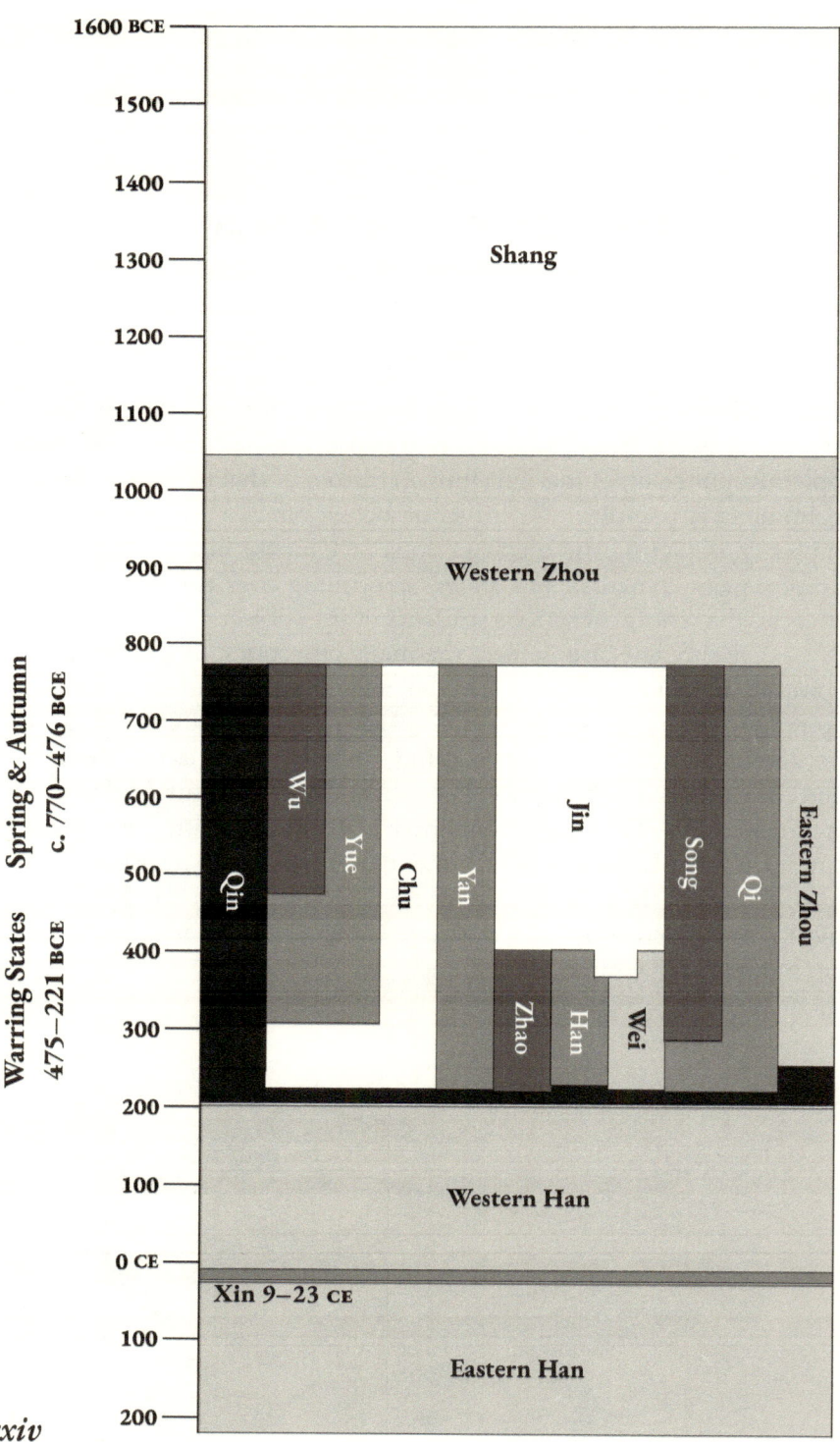

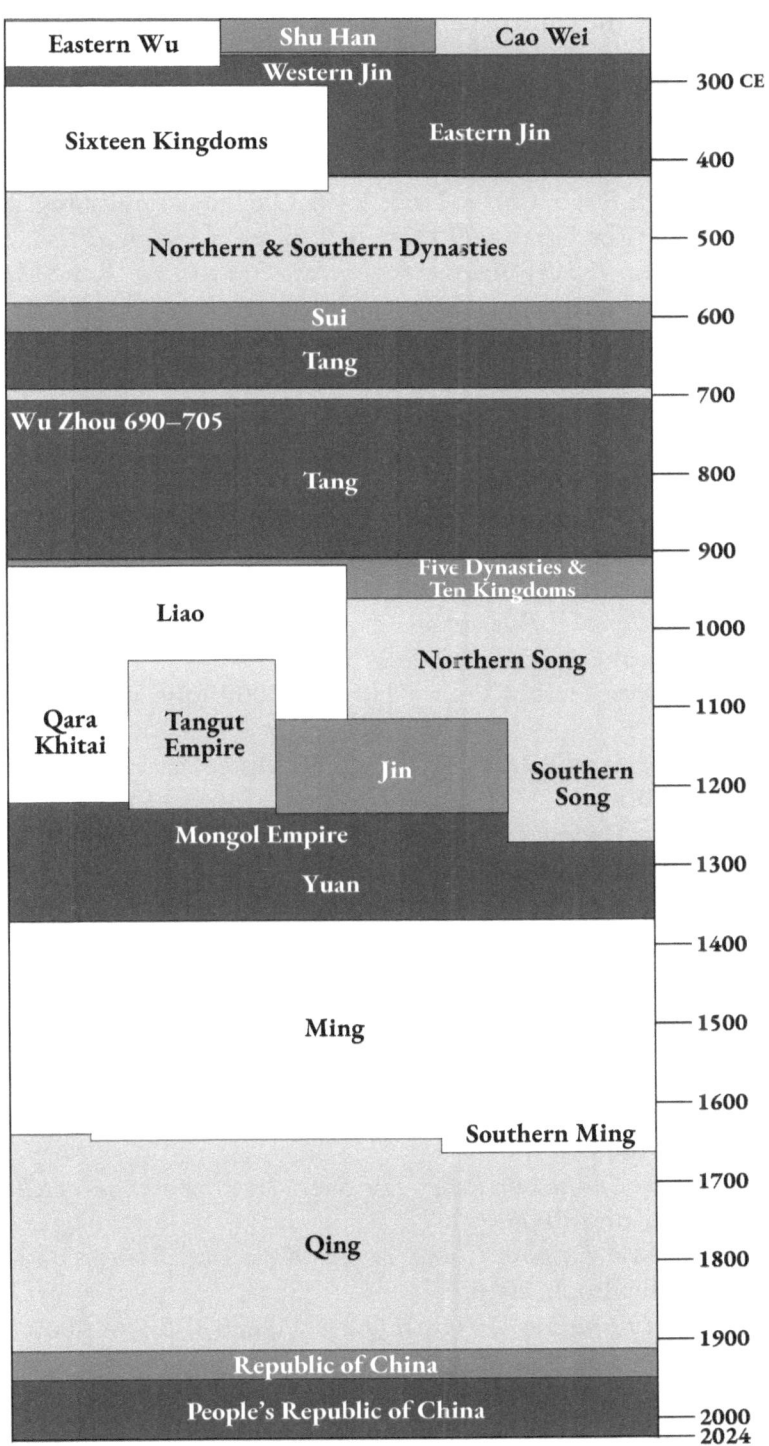

A firm grasp of China's past is helpful but not necessary to understanding the contents of this book. For those who wish to learn more of the historical background, a list of recommended books is provided below:

Quick Reads:

The Shortest History of China. Linda Javin. Old Street Publishing, 2021.

This Is China: The First 5,000 Years. Berkshire Publishing, 2010.

Modern China: A Very Short Introduction, 2nd edition. Rana Mitter. Oxford University Press, 2016.

China in the 21st Century: What Everyone Needs to Know, 3rd edition. Jeffrey N. Wasserstrom and Maura Elizabeth Cunningham. Oxford University Press, 2018.

General Histories of China:

The Cambridge Illustrated History of China, 3rd edition. Patricia Buckley Ebrey. Cambridge University Press, 2022.

China: A History. John Keay. Basic Books, 2009.

The Story of China: A Portrait of a Civilisation and Its People. Michael Wood. Simon & Schuster, 2020.

China: A History. Harold Tanner. Hackett, 2009. (also available in two volumes)

Imperial China, 900–1800. Frederick W. Mote. Harvard University Press, 2000.

The Search for Modern China, 3rd edition. Jonathan D. Spence. W. W. Norton & Company, 2012.

History of Imperial China. Timothy Brook, editor. Belknap Press. (six-volume series)

> *The Early Chinese Empires: Qin and Han*. Mark Edward Lewis. 2007.
>
> *China Between Empires: The Northern and Southern Dynasties*. Mark Edward Lewis. 2009.
>
> *China's Cosmopolitan Empire: The Tang Dynasty*. Mark Edward Lewis. 2009.
>
> *The Age of Confucian Rule: The Song Transformation of China*. Dieter Kuhn. 2009.
>
> *The Troubled Empire: China in the Yuan and Ming Dynasties*. Timothy Brook. 2010.
>
> *China's Last Empire: The Great Qing*. William T. Rowe. 2009.

People's Republic of China:

Mao's China and After: A History of the People's Republic, 3rd edition. Maurice J. Meisner. Free Press, 1999.

The Tragedy of Liberation: A History of the Chinese Revolution 1945–1957. Frank Dikötter. Bloomsbury Press, 2013.

Mao's Great Famine: The History of China's Most Devastating Catastrophe, 1958–1962. Frank Dikötter. Walker & Company, 2010.

The Cultural Revolution: A People's History, 1962–1976. Frank Dikötter. Bloomsbury Press, 2016.

Mao's Last Revolution. Roderick MacFarquhar and Michael Schoenhals. Belknap Press, 2006.

China Under Mao: A Revolution Derailed. Andrew G. Walder. Harvard University Press, 2015.

Never Turn Back: China and the Forbidden History of the 1980s. Julian Gewirtz. Belknap Press, 2022.

China After Mao: The Rise of a Superpower. Frank Dikötter. Bloomsbury Publishing, 2022.

Tibet:

Tibet: A History. Sam Van Schaik. Yale University Press, 2011.

The Dragon in the Land of Snows: A History of Modern Tibet Since 1947. Tsering Shakya. Columbia University Press, 1999.

Xinjiang:

Eurasian Crossroads: A History of Xinjiang, Revised and Updated. James A. Millward. Columbia University Press, 2021.

A NOTE on LANGUAGE

Names and words in Chinese are primarily in Mandarin, with romanizations in the pinyin system except for a select few terms for which alternative spellings remain commonly used in English. When Chinese text is provided, both the traditional and simplified characters are used in different circumstances. Roughly, traditional characters are used when referring to people, places, or events prior to 1949 in mainland China, for passages from texts written before the same year, and for anything involving Hong Kong, Macao, or Taiwan where traditional characters remain the standard. For anything concerning mainland China after 1949, simplified characters are used.

In the past few years there has been an intensifying push within China to Sinicize minority groups. This has involved not only the push to force the use of Mandarin and to replace minority language names with Chinese ones, but also to use Chinese names in English, e.g. "Xizang" in place of "Tibet" or "Nei Menggu" instead of "Inner Mongolia" or the earlier-favored hybrid "Nei Mongol." I do not wish to be a party to such efforts, and so for names of non-Han people, places, etc., I have mostly chosen to provide the names in the native language and text instead of in Chinese.

For any readers who wish to attempt to read out the handful of Tibetan words in the text, be warned that they are written according to the Wylie transliteration system, which does not typically reflect modern pronunciation of Tibetan. This is because native Tibetan writing itself does not accurately reflect pronunciation, as it adheres to an orthography set in the eleventh century and has not evolved with changes in the spoken language.

The text is peppered with words in several scripts representing multiple languages. The meanings of most of these can be found either in the glossary or in the list of section breaks in the appendices.

INTRODUCTION

Map of Major Geographical Features of Mainland China

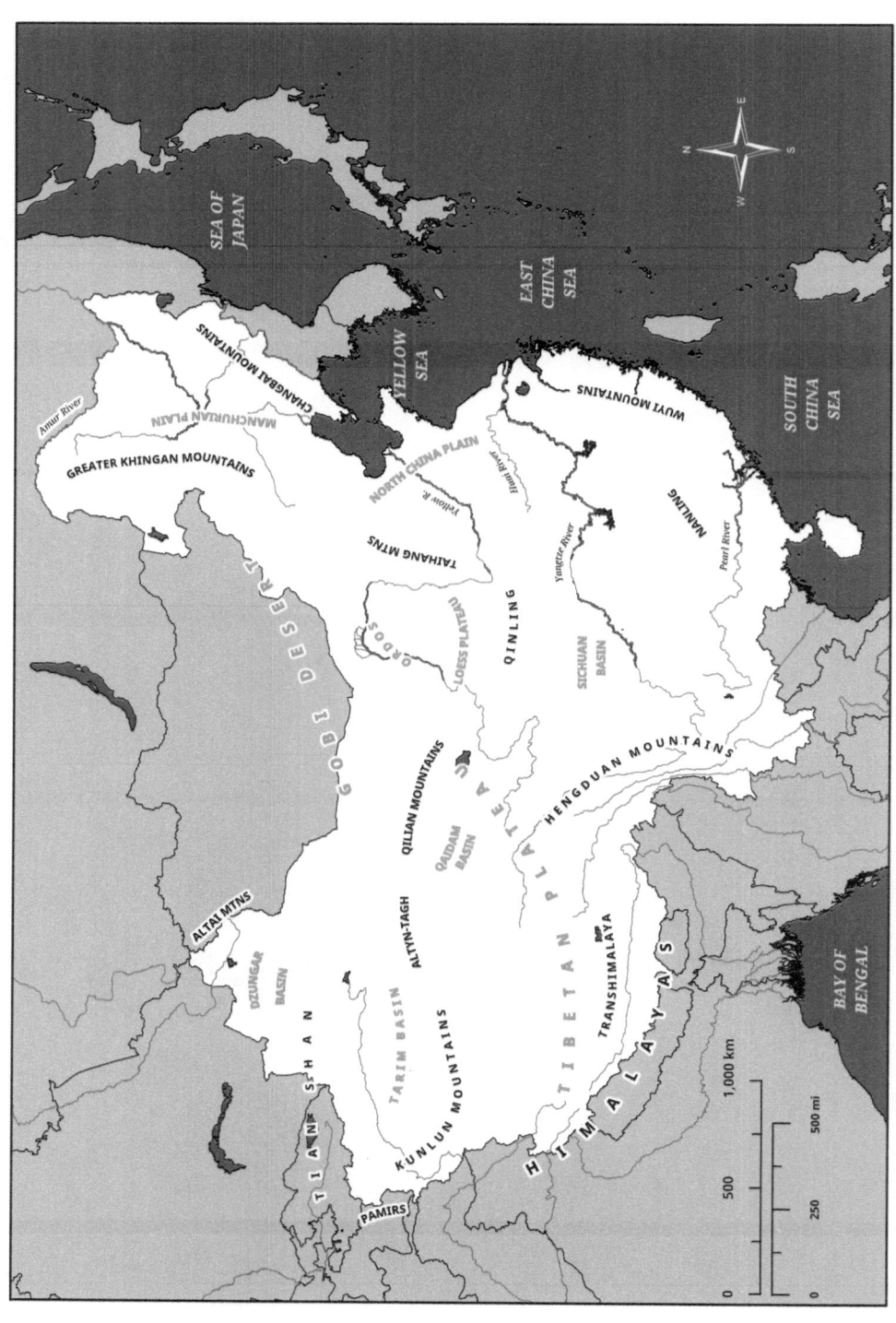

CHINA today is a massive state that boasts among the world's greatest geographic and human diversity.[1] It contains not only the densely packed ancestral homelands of the Han Chinese majority, but also frozen taiga, expansive grasslands, deserts both hot and cold, high mountains, rugged forests, and tropical jungle. Among the most biologically diverse countries on Earth, it is roughly the same size as the United States of America, but hosts an even greater array of plant and animal life, much of it found nowhere else.[2]

Wild things and wild places do not first spring to mind at the mention of China. As with practically everywhere on Earth, millennia of human activity and climatic fluctuations have left a changed and much reduced flora and fauna. Nonetheless, while it is true that the rich grasslands, forests, and wetlands of the north and east are largely gone and no longer teem with tigers, leopards, rhinos and elephants—nor with many other long expelled species—the country is still home to an extraordinary breadth of life. Yet despite a welcome and sorely needed leap in efforts to protect China's many species, some continue to dwindle and disappear.

China hosts not only a great array of creatures, but a large number of endemic species, those found nowhere else on Earth. Many such plants and animals were forced into their current ranges millennia ago in response to the great climate shifts of the ice ages. Others, such as the Chinese alligator, Yangtze sturgeon, and giant panda, retreated far more recently when faced with human encroachment. Some, such as the hot-spring snakes *Thermophis* of the Tibetan Plateau and Hengduan Mountains, are highly specialized and can survive only in a small number of locations. Their restricted distributions mean endemics can be especially vulnerable to extinction, and many of China's endemic species are indeed now endangered.

Wildlife in China is found primarily in the vast open spaces and high, rugged mountains of the western regions, as well as in the densely forested hinterlands of the northeast and southwest. Those are the lands most inhospitable to humans, historically home to pastoralists, hunters and fishermen, or slash-and-burn agriculturalists. The great majority of China's people live in the country's eastern half, where the largest and wealthiest cities, and the richest agricultural lands are found. No matter how remote or uninhabitable, however, humanity's influence has long stretched to even the farthest flung patches of land and water.

The world is often seen as split between man and nature. The natural environment is separated from humankind's built environment, and further categorized according to its degree of desolation or despoliation, from wilderness to cityscape. But there is nothing unnatural about the act of remaking our surroundings. Humans are hardly alone in radically reshaping the world. Through sheer size, number, or industry, many species bring about large alterations of their habitats, even if few can quite match the extent of our efforts. Our own transformation of the world began long before we first built homes or ploughed the earth.

Humanity's reworking of the world's landscapes began in the deep past—perhaps prior to the evolution of modern humans. Our distant ancestors and other hominids learned to forage, hunt, form tools, and manipulate fire before the emergence of *Homo sapiens*.[3] Today's threatened species have faced millennia of human impact. Although the more than 200 year-old debate continues, scientific option increasingly leans towards singling out humans as the primary driver of the great wave of megafaunal extinctions over the last 50,000 years.[4] The loss of so many megafauna led to wide-ranging and complex changes to Earth's natural systems, the echoes of which are felt to this day.[5] Globally, millennia of increasing human growth and action have resulted in a stunning collapse of wild plants and animals.[6] Compared to millennia past, we now live in a biologically impoverished world.

We cannot restore the Earth to its former state, but knowing how the world once looked can give us a better idea of what it might become. The historical memory of what the world once looked like is typically lost from generation to generation. Our expectations of what constitutes a normal landscape and mix of wildlife shift over the years until the sight of anything beyond songbirds and squirrels becomes exceptional. Learning the historical ecology of the world can help us reset our expectations, and our goals for preserving what remains and for rewilding what has been destroyed. It can extend our ambitions and illuminate possibilities we might not otherwise consider.

Between our distant ancestors' initial reshaping of the world and the onset of the Industrial Age, agriculture was the greatest source of ecological destruction. Wherever humans could find a way to grow crops, they did. They felled forests, plowed grasslands, drained wetlands, and irrigated deserts. Those same societies placed myriad other demands on their environments. Forests were felled to build cities and fuel fires. Animals were hunted for their meat and skins, or simply because they were pests.

Settled agrarian societies have an innate need for large swathes of land, placing them in direct conflict with many wild species. Successful communities grow enough food to support an expanding population, but even the most advanced premodern societies faced hard material constraints on their growth. Traditional agricultural systems could not match modern yields, meaning that practically all arable land was put to use. Wildlife was thus pushed into the lands humans considered marginal or useless, with the exception of those few species that found a niche in human landscapes. This remained true until the advent of chemical fertilizers and other fruits of the Industrial Revolution.

The Chinese excelled in transforming natural landscapes into cultivated fields and paddies, and in driving away the native wildlife, but they were hardly unique. Iron Age population growth in the Levant led to the disappearance of hartebeest, aurochs, hippopotami, and elephants.[7] In Europe deforestation for agriculture began around 6,000 years ago, and—as in China—continued for millennia, pausing only during periods of immense upheaval and human population decline.[8] Different species began to decline and even disappear over a broad range of times. Those least suited to living in agrarian landscapes began to fade even before our earliest histories were written.[9] By Aristotle's time (384–322 BCE) the Greeks had pushed lions from southern and central Greece, and the big cats could only be found in a small area of the north, where they had harassed Xerxes' armies during the second Persian invasion (480–479 BCE).[10] Ancient Roman demand for animals to slaughter in *venationes* caused the decline and even extirpation of numerous species within the empire and its surroundings.[11] Removal and destruction of wildlife were traits shared widely across civilizations.

In the historical period climate change has primarily had an indirect impact on wildlife's fortunes. Until recent decades, changes in climate—both regional and global—were the result of natural processes and not human action. Over the course of its history China has experienced several periods of both comparative warmth and cold, with often drastic effects on the people of the time. Warm periods tended to allow greater agricultural yields, ultimately stimulating population and societal growth. More favorable conditions also allowed agriculturalists to push into previously unsuitable lands, opening the prospect of colonial expansion. These trends would reverse when climatic conditions turned cooler, leading to resource shortages and social crises.[12]

Such pressures sometimes played a major role in the collapse of dynasties.[13] Plants and animals would have responded to changes in climate at their own accord, but for many populations the expansion and contraction of human activity—primarily through habitat alteration—would have likely had the greatest impact on their numbers. Many species are now beginning to feel the effects of human-induced climate change—for some it is a existential threat, while for others it will open new expanses of habitat.

Texts are the foundation of our knowledge of China's wildlife history. The Chinese literary corpus is among the world's largest, oldest, and richest. Even though many texts have been lost, and others exist only in fragments, what remains nonetheless offers an excellent basis for determining how China's faunal and floral communities have changed. Much of the immense task of sifting through over two millennia of literature has been done. There remains, however, plenty of lingering uncertainty over what much of it means. Precisely what creatures past authors were writing about it often far from clear, and whether many stories were honestly reported or merely fabrications is frequently impossible to discern. Beyond Chinese, other written languages (e.g. Manchu, Mongolian, Tibetan, Turkic) have not yet been so thoroughly mined, and may yet offer up new clues.

Old arts and handicrafts, too, sometimes offer hints at animals people encountered centuries ago. Unwritten knowledge handed down over generations—in academia known as traditional ecological knowledge (TEK)—is especially valuable when gathering evidence from communities without longstanding literary traditions. Zooarchaeology—the study of animal remains found in archaeological sites—has shown not only how past humans related to the fauna around them, but has even revealed the existence of previously unknown—and sadly now extinct—species.[14] Genetic analysis of ancient DNA has revealed hints of the population histories of species far beyond what any textual or even zooarchaeological evidence can provide. Many suffered severe losses in the distant past, especially during the Last Glacial Maximum (c. 26,000–20,000 years ago) when glaciers and permafrost covered much of China's west and north. Of course, as with written sources, all these, too, come with their own caveats and uncertainties. Nonetheless, it is these methods that will likely provide the greatest new insights. Whatever the weakness of individual sources, taken together they provide enough solid evidence to be confident in the trends that emerge.

China spans over such a broad range of species and biomes, and its history stretches back so far that there is no simple, neat way to divide it up. I have chosen what seems the least muddled method, touring the country by geographic region. Many species are spread across multiple regions, meaning a handful appear several times throughout the text. Each entry is of the length and detail that available resources allow, be it a mere paragraph or a full chapter. Unsurprisingly, the creatures that attract the most attention and are easiest to study are best represented in the literature and consequently here.

This is not a straightforward narrative history, but it is not quite a reference or textbook either. The contents are intended to be read in order, but each chapter or section should be largely comprehensible on its own. The text is divided into ten parts, each of which opens with a brief introduction of the regional biogeography and history. Within each part are chapters divided along broadly thematic lines, which are further subdivided according to species or topic. A familiarity with Chinese history and culture is helpful but not necessary to follow the text. The same is true for relevant scientific fields, namely biogeography, ecology, evolution, and genetics.

Part I focuses on North China, the heartland of China's earliest dynasties, centered on the Yellow River Basin. Once covered with forests and grasslands, the regions lowlands hosted tigers, rhinos, gazelle, water buffalo, and a long list of other species that were pushed out centuries ago. Today the species that hold out are restricted to remnant forests in the mountains, and the lowlands are given over to farmland and sprawling cities.

Part II shifts to China's northeast, otherwise known as Manchuria. Although the southern portion of the region passed in and out of Chinese control over the centuries, the densely forested reaches to the north long remained separate. Valued as a source of natural riches such as ginseng, sable, and pearls, the opening of Manchuria to migrants from the south in the second half of the nineteenth century marked the beginning of decades of deforestation and the near extirpation of many of its animal species.

Part III covers the vast steppes, once the home of feared horsemen who traded and battled with Chinese dynasties for nearly two millennia. Mongols and other nomads moved with their livestock over the region, sharing it with immense herds of gazelles and bulbous-nosed saiga antelope that once criss-crossed the grasslands, wolves close in step. Yet the mass slaughter of wild grazers and their predators, and attempts to fix the nomads in place and fence in their herds, have left the steppe ecosystems deeply disrupted.

Part IV shifts from the grasslands into the deserts. The deep desert of the far west hosts some of the few remaining wild camels on the planet, hardy creatures that have survived even the fallout from China's nuclear weapons testing. They share the harsh landscape with wild asses, gazelles, and wolves, while to their north China's only populations of beavers eke out a living near the Mongolian border.

Part V climbs into the mountains and plateaux of the west, peaking at Mount Everest on the Nepali border. The denizens of these cold and windswept highlands have adapted over millennia to the thin air and sparse vegetation. Tibetan foxes, wild yak, and black-necked cranes live on the alpine steppe, while above in the rocky peaks live wild sheep and the snow leopards that prey upon them.

Part VI arrives finally at the home of China's most famous and beloved animal, the giant panda. They live in the bamboo forests of the

Qinling and Hengduan mountains, a region that hosts the spectacularly golden-coated takin. Three species of snub-nosed monkey are also spread across the mountain ranges, and the crested ibis—once on the cusp of extinction—began its long recovery here.

Part VII moves down the Yangtze River exploring the life in the waters and surrounding lands of its middle and lower reaches. Once among the richest fishing grounds in the world, the Yangtze and its tributaries have reached a dire state. Dams, overfishing, pollution, and a myriad of other ills have caused the extinction of the baiji—China's only river dolphin—and the Chinese paddlefish, while leaving others— among them the Chinese alligator and Yangtze sturgeon—on the brink.

Part VIII explores the forests of the south, home to many ancient plant species that found refuge there during the ice ages, as well as animals greatly valued for the purported medicinal benefits their parts confer, such as the pangolin and musk deer. Subjected to intense hunting and poaching over the course of the twentieth century, many species are only now beginning to recover.

Part IX explores the tropical southern edges of China. Only a small percentage of the country, the tropics host an outsize share of China's biodiversity. Many species typical of South and Southeast Asia are found here, such as elephants, clouded leopards, gibbons, and green peafowl. Having suffered for decades from overhunting and the loss of their forests, many now barely hang on within China.

Part X traces the lands and waters of China's long coastline, from the Yellow Sea down to the disputed waters of the South China Sea. Decades of breakneck coastal development and intensive fishing of the waters have left many of the resident species drastically reduced. Many have endured to the present, although a handful have been wiped out within Chinese waters.

Following the conclusion is an appendix of the species mentioned in the text, which includes their most commonly used scientific names, English names, as well as their names in simplified and traditional Chinese characters, along with pinyin romanizations. A glossary is also included, providing translations and romanizations of the decorative text sprinkled along the outer margins of the book. Words in Manchu, Jurchen, Khitan, Tangut, and Mongolian are included. Explanations of the text featured as section breaks are found in the List of Section Breaks. Image credits and explanations are in the List of Illustrations.

NORTH CHINA

Map of North China

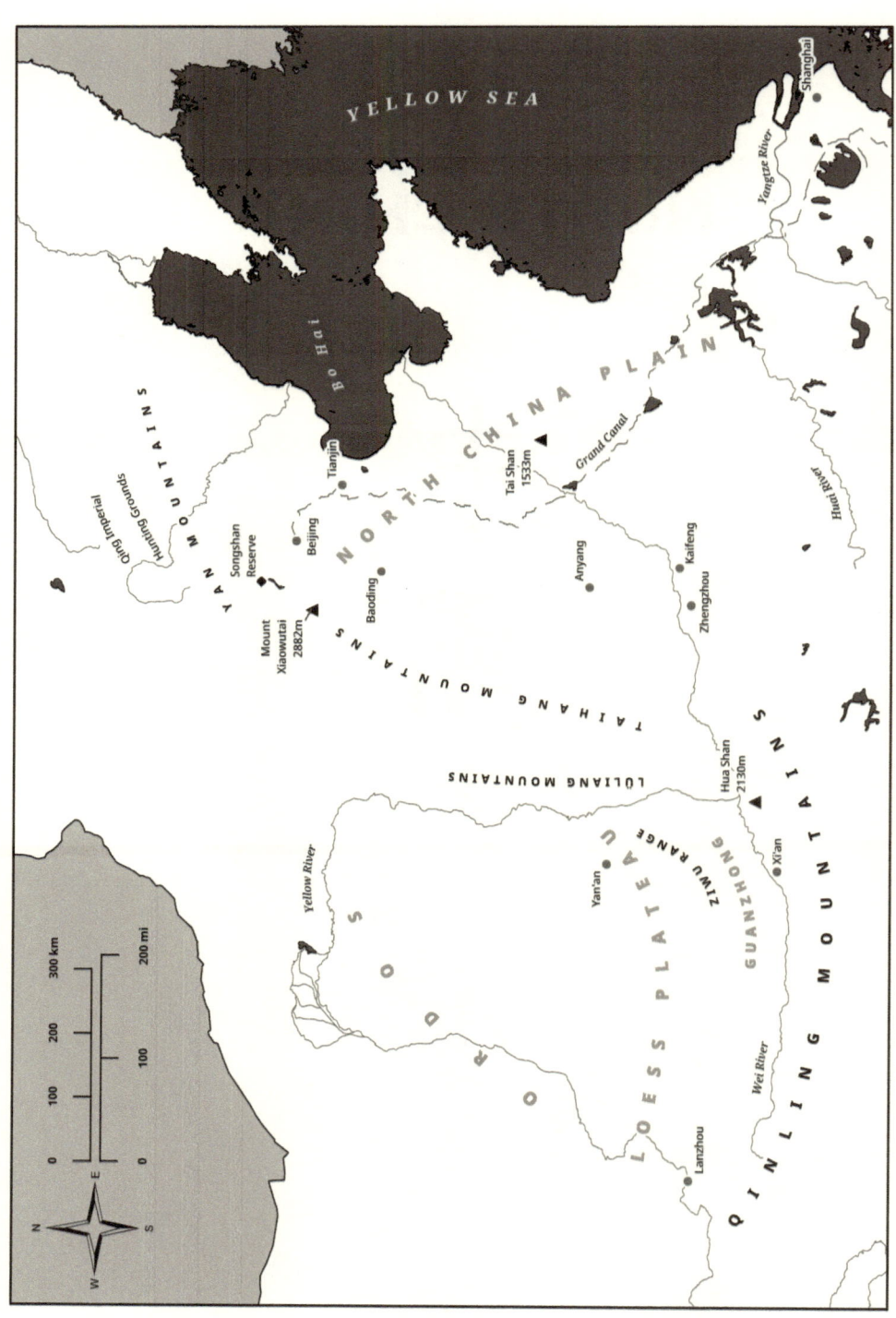

Nᴏʀᴛʜ China, centered on the Yellow River Basin, is in some ways a curious place to begin a survey of China's wildlife. The region is home to vanishingly little in the way of natural habitat or wild creatures.[1] The plains that stretch from Beijing south nearly to the Yangtze and west to the ancient capital of Xi'an are covered solid with cultivated fields, many tended for centuries or millennia. Anything larger than a hare is difficult to find outside of the few last patches of mountain forest. Yet once this was a place of woodlands and savanna, teeming with deer, rhinos, wolves, tigers, and much more.

The history of North China's transformation from a landscape rich in wild fauna and flora to an empty expanse of farmland is in many ways a distillation of China's broader wildlife history. The destruction of the region's biodiversity came earlier and has been more complete than the rest of China, but the patterns that played out across the Yellow River Basin replayed again and again as Han Chinese culture spread from its heartland. In its simplest form it was a pattern that repeated not only in China but around the world. Humanity advanced and wildlife retreated.

Roughly, North China encompasses the plains and hills of the Yellow River Basin. This has long been considered the birthplace of Chinese culture, and was the cultural, political, and economic center of the earliest dynasties.[2] The landscape is dominated by two formations and the interactions between them: the Yellow River and the Loess Plateau through which it flows.

The Yellow River begins in the Bayan Har Mountains of Qinghai in China's west and flows southeast into northern Sichuan before doubling back to the northwest and then again to the east into Gansu. Past the city of Lanzhou it bends north and flows through the desert and plains of the Ordos. Eventually it turns east and then again south, forming the Great Bend and entering the Loess Plateau.[3] It is the loess, a fine, dusty soil blown in from the Gobi, that here erodes into the river in astounding abundance and shades it yellow. East of the imperial capital of Xi'an, past the sacred mountain of Hua Shan, the Yellow River merges with the Wei. At this point it makes an abrupt turn eastwards, and enters the Central Plains of Henan. As the river reaches the Shandong border it shifts course again and winds northeast to the coast of the Bo Hai north of the Shandong Peninsula.[4]

The Central Plains were the heartland of the ancient dynasties, from the Shang (1600–1046 BCE) until the Northern Song (960–1127 CE), when the Han lost control of North China to the Jurchen, who swept south from the northeast to establish the Jin dynasty (1115–1234 CE), decisively shifting the center of Chinese culture and wealth south to the Yangtze Valley.[5] The Central Plains form the southwestern quarter of the larger North China Plain, which extends north past the Taihang Mountains in the west to the Yan Mountains beyond Beijing. In the east it stretches to the coast of the Bo Hai and the rocky hills of the Shandong Peninsula, and in the south to northern Anhui and Jiangsu.

The North China Plain is now a monotonous expanse of farm fields, with practically no natural habitat. It is one of the world's great agricultural centers, but that belies the harshness of the landscape. The region is infamous for the Yellow River's cataclysmic floods, but in fact a lack of water has been the more constant danger. Rainfall is scarce, and drought has been a regular threat to harvests throughout the millennia.[6] The seasons, too, can be cruel, with hot summers and frigid winters. Even the soil, the alluvial runoff rich with loess and easy to till, is far from ideal for crops, and requires the extensive use of fertilizers. Until recent decades that meant manure (primarily human, as livestock were scarce), grass stalks, and any other organic material that could be found. In spite of these obstacles hundreds of generations of farmers have transformed the plain from a mix of forest and grassland into a never-ending patchwork of plowed fields. The only great changes of recent decades are the additions of modern roads, railways, factories, and sprawling cities.

Biologically, the landscape is practically a desert. This is by design, the desired result of a total transformation of the North China Plain over the course of many centuries. The early Han Chinese who settled North China found expansive woodlands and savanna, filled with rhinos, deer, tigers, wolves and dozens of other species, large and small. Practically all are now gone, some extinct. The few that remain have taken refuge in the rugged mountains that rise from the plains, and even there struggle to survive. For the Chinese, ancient to modern, this was not a loss, but an improvement. In driving out the beasts and turning the wasteland into fields of wheat, barley, and sorghum, they reordered the world to fit their needs and ideals.

Wildlife in Chinese Thought

W ESTERNERS faintly aware of the basic tenets of Daoism and Buddhism, yet unfamiliar with China's environmental history, often attribute to Chinese civilization a greater respect and care for the natural world than its Western counterpart has ever managed.[1] Pithy aphorisms from the *Dao De Jing* or Buddhist injunctions against harming animals are taken as evidence of an ecologically friendly vein of Eastern belief that—by logical extension—must have led to a more harmonious coexistence between man and nature.[2]

A deeper reading of the ancient sages quickly shatters this illusion, and even a cursory look through the Chinese past reveals the yawning gap between the stated ideal and the reality of lived experience.[3] Just as other peoples across the world and throughout history, the Chinese— ancient and modern—have sought to conquer nature and shape it to their wants and needs. To the ancient Han two of the great symbols of the natural world—forests and the animals within them—were not to be cherished and protected but removed and replaced. The Zhou dynasty (c. 1046–256 BCE) had no love of forests, and during the centuries of their reign much of the North China Plain was stripped of its trees. Wild animals were pests to be killed and expelled. These actions were not merely admirable but were essential conduct for righteous rulers. Mencius, the great successor of Confucius, in comparing the Duke of Zhou, the revered early regent of the Zhou dynasty, to the loathsome, defeated final Shang king, praised the Duke for "driving out the tigers, leopards, rhinoceroses, and elephants," at which "all under heaven rejoiced."[4]

The mention of rhinos and elephants may seem bizarre, but both species did in fact once live far to the north of their present limits. The Sumatran rhinoceros *Dicerorhinus sumatrensis*, now restricted to small patches of Sumatra and Borneo, once ranged through Southeast Asia and north to the Yellow River Valley.[5] Ancient records place rhinos through much of the north, from the Taihang Mountains in Shanxi to the Shandong Peninsula, and noted that the animals were hunted for their hides, which were used to make armor. Hunting and agricultural expansion pushed the rhinos from the north sometime before the beginning of the Common Era, though they persisted in the south of China for centuries after.[6]

Asian elephants, *Elephas maximus*, are often cited as another species that lived in North China into the Shang and Zhou periods. It is certain that elephants and their proboscidean kin and ancestors inhabited the region before the Holocene (the current geological epoch, which began roughly 11,650 Before Present), yet there is no solid evidence that they persisted there into the early eras of Chinese history.[7] Elephant remains have been excavated north of the Yellow River, at Anyang in northern Henan, but these were likely remnants of animals brought from the south to be kept captive at the Shang court. Bronzes depicting elephants have also been found in the Yellow River Valley, but there is not nearly enough evidence to conclude elephants roamed the North China Plain within the last several thousand years, though the occasional wanderer may have moved north from the Huai River Valley.[8]

That the ancient Chinese eagerly drove out and hunted large animals to extinction is not to say that China had no tradition of valuing or protecting the natural world. For the Chinese, as opposed to the Western view, humankind and the rest of nature were inextricably intertwined, inseparable and interdependent. Humans were not apart from but a part of nature. Yet they were the greatest part, superior to other beasts, if not inherently. It was man's moral nature that set him apart from other animals, and only through the development of morality could he rise above them. Indeed without superior morals a man was simply another beast. This comes through most strongly in the writings of the Confucian scholars that became dominant over the course of the Han dynasty (202 BCE–220 CE) and remained preeminent through to the end of the imperial period. Confucian thought has little regard for the natural world beyond its relation and utility to man, and on those rare occasions when Confucian thinkers turned their attentions towards animals, they considered them in the same moral terms in which they viewed mankind. It therefore comes as no surprise that for the length of Chinese intellectual history animals were considered primarily in moral terms, as a mirror of human society and not as creatures in their own right, deserving of study on their own terms.[9]

Some of the ancient sages did urge benevolence towards animals and lamented the rapacity of their fellow man towards the forests and beasts. There is ample evidence of taboos and royal decrees meant to protect nature—or more appropriately natural resources. For that is how nature was valued. Though some expressed a general appreciation for the natural world removed from the trappings of human civilization, the overwhelming sentiment was that things in nature had value only so far as they were useful to man. The Chinese were by and large profoundly utilitarian. Nature was to be bent to the will and needs of humans, and flora and fauna were protected only to prevent their hasty exhaustion and to preserve their utility over the *longue durée*.[10] These efforts, whether simple admonitions or vigorously enforced decrees, inevitably met resistance from both poor and privileged and rarely achieved their intended ends.[11]

As the ancient heartland of Han culture, the landscape and wildlife of North China has been subjected to the result of these views for millennia—a total absence of primeval habitat or wilderness. Wilderness, popularly perceived in the American mind as a place absent of permanent human presence and noticeable human impact, does not exist in China. The idea of the wild—places beyond cultivation and culture—has always been anathema to the Chinese, as it was to Western peoples until it was spun into a romantic ideal in the nineteenth century.[12] For the Chinese both people and the land could be divided along the same lines—the wild and the cultivated. Those who followed the proper customs and observed the rites of civilized (i.e. Han Chinese) society were cultivated, cultured human beings, no matter their ethnic origins. Those who failed to adhere to those practices were uncivilized.[13] For the land the division was agricultural. Good land was tilled and cultivated, productive and habitable. Wilderness was wasteland, not yet cleared, plowed, and sown. In modern Chinese the word for wilderness is *huāngyě* 荒野, literally "uncultivated wasteland." Except for the occasional Daoist or Buddhist recluse seeking beatific peace in the mountains, in the Chinese mind the wild—and all the creatures in it—was a foreboding place waiting to be tamed and bettered.[14] Certainly there existed no notion of valuing and preserving it for its own inherent worth.[15]

There was little change to the place of nature in Chinese thought until the late Qing dynasty (1636–1912) when Western influence began to seep in. After British and French guns forced China open in the mid-nineteenth century, Western visitors spread across the empire to collect and catalogue the rich and—to them—new and undiscovered array of plant and animal life.[16] Amateur and professional naturalists brought with them the Linnaean system of taxonomy and early forms of the modern natural sciences. These outside influences were slow to take hold, however. Even after Western naturalists had been roaming across China on collecting expeditions for decades, natural history and zoology had yet to take hold in Chinese society. China's own community of trained natural scientists only began to take shape in the 1920s and 1930s, and then only slowly. When the Chinese-American adventurer Quentin Young decided to teach himself zoology while living in China around 1930, he had no choice but to read only English and Japanese texts, as there were no modern Chinese-language works on China's own natural history.[17] While the works of Linnaeus and Darwin reshaped the thoughts of China's educated classes, at the lower level Christian missionaries worked to break villagers' beliefs in taboos and superstitions, including those concerning animals.[18]

The total effect, though impossible to measure, was not salutary to the health of China's wildlife. Wildlife science of the late-nineteenth and early-twentieth centuries was profoundly utilitarian, and openly hostile to any species deemed harmful to human endeavors, especially large predators. The result was a weakening of traditional restraints on harming and exploiting some habitats and species, coupled with reinforcement of those utilitarian strains of Chinese thought that had long ago led to the destruction of much of China's natural heritage. These trends only quickened, often to extreme ends, with the Communist victory and subsequent flood of Soviet intellectual influence.[19]

At the end of the civil war in 1949 Chinese society became increasingly aggressive in its treatment of the natural world. The Maoist drive to speed headlong into industrialization melded with rigid Marxist dogma and the traditional need to conquer and control nature, forming a potent militancy that aimed to utterly reshape the natural world to man's benefit. Mao Zedong, from peasant stock but of a bookish bent and with little knowledge of farming or nature, treated the natural world with the same cold utilitarian contempt he treated

China's own people. Believing that anything could be achieved through the use of mass human labor and sheer will, Mao and the Party launched a sustained series of campaigns to transform the Chinese landscape into a modern, industrialized, Communist utopia.[20]

This Maoist war on nature unleashed a wave of devastation over the whole of China's natural environment, and few species escaped unaffected. In North China, where wild animals were already scattered and dwindling, the greatest impact came from extermination campaigns. The most infamous of these was the 1958–1962 drive to wipe out "the four pests"—mice and rats, flies, mosquitos, and sparrows.[21] Running parallel to efforts to destroy small pests was a nationwide drive to eliminate predators. Bears, wolves, tigers, leopards, and others were all condemned as unwanted restraints on progress in New China.[22] Professional hunters, teams of villagers, and military units were enlisted to hunt down any predators they could find and to bring them in for a bounty.[23] In this way the beasts made their contribution to advancing the nation—their bodies were exported for foreign exchange to help pay down the national debt.[24] Smaller predators such as foxes and mustelids were hunted out over much of the country as well, less because of any threat they posed to humans or livestock than for their valuable furs. A common consequence of this removal of small predators was for rodent populations to surge, leading to massive crop losses.[25]

Another major change in the Maoist years has had increasingly damaging and widespread effects to the present. Animals have been used in Chinese medicine since before the earliest medical texts.[26] This is no surprise, as animal parts have been a common ingredient in medical traditions around the world, including in Western practice until the rise of modern pharmaceuticals in the nineteenth century.[27] Indeed China's ancient and medieval *materia medica* feature an impressive array of animal medicinals—Chinese doctors seemingly never found a creature they couldn't or wouldn't use to heal. Many of these ingredients' purported qualities were purely magical, and while many traditional uses were dismissed by the mid-twentieth century, others remained widespread.

Yet not only did Chinese medicine retain many animal ingredients, it greatly expanded their use from the late 1950s to today. Some were ancient treatments that had once been purely local but spread across the nation, some were rare and expensive treatments that were industrialized into mass-produced goods, others were wholly new inventions. The result was an explosion in the medicinal use of animals that led to the slaughter of wild populations and the rise of China's massive wildlife farming industry, in which dozens of species—from deer and tigers to turtles and snakes—are bred and harvested like sheep or cattle.[28]

In part this was due to the desperate state of China's public healthcare in the early decades of the Communist period. Anything—however dubious—that promised to heal the people was worth trying. Additionally, the mad drive to industrialize combined with the Maoist contempt for expertise and Marxist certainty in working-class superiority to push for extensive and creative use of all available resources. This led to workers—even the untrained and uneducated—devising new therapeutic uses for animals. Market reforms in the 1980s and 1990s then gave further impetus to the liberal use of wildlife in medicine, as the profit motive sparked a new rush of creativity and quackery. The result was the four hundred species listed in the classic sixteenth-century *Compendium of Materia Medica* ballooned to 832 in the state's official 1979–1983 listing, and to 2,341 by 2013.[29] Tragically this medicinal demand for animals has contributed to the devastation of the wildlife of the wider world, from rhinos and reindeer to lions and pangolins.[30]

The Maoist drive to conquer and reshape nature morphed into an all-out effort to squeeze the natural world of all its resources. The basic utilitarian assumptions—that the world existed for the benefit of humanity and could be shaped to our will—did not change, but the catalyst of profit motive was added onto them. Though the dominant Confucian literati strata of imperial China looked down upon traders as morally inferior, the Chinese nonetheless possessed a thriving entrepreneurial culture until it was crushed under the Maoist project. Suppressed for three decades, Deng Xiaoping's opening of the economy to animal spirits unleashed a torrent. In spite of the general turmoil of the Maoist years, China had made many developmental advances. Yet much of the population remained mired in poverty, and few were satisfied with their lot in life. The freedom to pursue individual and familial betterment led to likely the greatest leap in human welfare and prosperity in history. For wildlife it was a disaster.

The turn to a market economy led to a dramatic increase in the exploitation and destruction of China's natural habitat and wildlife.

Forests fell with increased rapidity, and ever-expanding herds of livestock razed the grasslands. The increased flows into government coffers allowed for the realization of long-delayed gargantuan engineering projects. Animals were targeted for the wealth they could bring, dead or alive. A massive market for game meat soon grew—the consumers were centered in South China, but their tastes reached across the country. When wild populations began to dwindle, the forward-looking established wildlife farms, and took as many of the remaining wild individuals they could find to be their founding stock. Other species were taken for their hides, horns, or bones—the rest of their bodies were often left to rot.

Even among wildlife professionals there was precious little concern for animals as anything but a resource. Writings of the time, whether from academic or government sources (they were often the same), invariably described animals as living sources of potential wealth, and often described them by listing which parts could be used and how. Protection was—and often still is—explained as merely a precondition for rational use.[31] Wildlife researchers and workers often had no personal interest in the creatures they were to study and protect. The government had assigned their field of study and work without regard for their own curiosities and hopes. Stuck in professions they did not care for, receiving inadequate pay, and often separated from their homes and families, many showed little enthusiasm for their work.

Recent decades have seen a welcome sea change in China's relationship with its wildlife.[32] With increasing affluence has come increasing care for the natural environment and the plant and animal life within it. Awareness of and concern for China's own fauna, once largely exclusive to the giant panda, has expanded to cover more and more species, from the chiru to the once persecuted wolf.[33] With openness to foreign ideas, new generations have studied and trained in the latest theory and practice of wildlife science, providing China with a growing cadre of wildlife professionals.[34] As both the general populace and the party-state give greater concern to protecting their natural heritage, the prospects for China's wildlife grow brighter.

A World Made for Farming

THE Yellow River Basin was one of the world's first agricultural centers. Although in popular Western imagination rice is the universal staple of Chinese cuisine, in North China this is not so. Millet was the first staple grain cultivated there, perhaps as far back as 8500 BCE, but with more certainty by about 6000 BCE in the Lower Yellow River, and for millennia afterwards it was the foremost grain of the region.[1] Wheat arrived from Central Asia sometime later and during the Han dynasty overtook millet as the preferred grain, giving rise to the wheat-flour staples still seen today: noodles, dumplings, and breads (steamed or griddled more often than baked).[2] Agricultural success allowed for the gradual expansion of the population, and in time the development of more complex societies and technologies, eventually giving rise to the literate civilization of the Shang, to which subsequent Chinese have long looked as the fount of their culture.[3]

The Shang—just as subsequent dynasties in China and many other agriculturally-based states throughout history—encouraged the clearance of forests and drainage of wetlands for conversion into cropland. This served the state's interests in two crucial ways. More land under cultivation provided more food, which in turn could support a growing population. More subjects and greater yields in turn supported larger armies and provided a larger tax base for the state. Thus for Chinese dynasties throughout history—which until only the last few decades derived the bulk of their wealth from agriculture—the expansion of agricultural land was fundamental to the power of society and state. Given such powerful cultural and material incentives, the destruction of nature in North China was seemingly only a matter of time.

The North China of today bears no resemblance to its ancient past—outside of the hills there is little other than cities and farmland. In those times it was widely forested and hosted a rich complex of fauna and flora. The prehistoric landscape of North China was not uniform. The dry Guanzhong Plain was predominantly grassland, dotted with trees and woodlands.[4] The larger North China Plain was largely covered with spacious deciduous woodland, the trees growing denser on the foothills before turning to coniferous forests farther up the slopes.[5] This landscape hosted a rich mix of species, the flora closing resembling the forests of eastern North America, except a richer, more diverse assemblage. The animal life was similar to that now found in the Terai of northern India and southern Nepal—water buffalo, rhinos, deer, and tigers—as well as species more typical of the steppes to the north— wild horses and gazelles.[6]

The trees, grasslands, and scattered wetlands have all but disappeared, cleared to advance human civilization. By far the greatest driver was agriculture. Agriculture is the great foundation of settled existence, but it is in turn the great destroyer of wild flora and fauna. No human pursuit, even to this day, is so destructive to our fellow species as agriculture. The success of North China's earlier settlers led to the growth of their numbers, and as they multiplied they expanded their reach, clearing the trees and the savanna to plant their crops. Removing the flora pushed out the fauna. Those animals that stood their ground were left with little forage, so they fed on the farmers' crops, and in turn the farmers killed them as pests. The settlers replaced the wild creatures with domesticated ones, and if predators remained they preyed on the tame pigs and sheep until they too were killed or driven away as vermin.

This process of taming the land for human use was hardly unique to North China, but there it happened earlier and more thoroughly than nearly anywhere else. Trees were not cleared solely to make way for crops. The timber had many uses, foremost for construction and fuel. The homes of the ancient peasantry were not primarily made of wood, but the great structures of the ruling classes and of the cities were. As the palaces, temples, and cities of the region became ever grander from the Shang to the Tang, more and more of North China's timber disappeared until the region could no longer meet demand.[7] Other trees and smaller woody plants provided fuel for fire, be it for warmth, cooking, or industry. Myriad other demands also ate away at the northern woods, and even as early as the Shang the forests were clearly losing ground. The process continued through the Zhou and into the imperial period so that by the fourth century CE "much of north China had been deforested to become one large farm."[8]

Deforestation was slowed and even reversed at times, most often after wide swathes of country were depopulated in the aftermath of war and its fellow horsemen. People would flee but eventually return, whether after months or decades. On rarer occasions the threat of invasion prompted dynasties to rework entire landscapes. The Song dynasty (960–1279) bordered a hostile northern neighbor, the Khitan Liao dynasty (916–1125), and faced the intractable problem of having no great natural or manmade barriers to impede their armies of mounted archers. The Song decided to make the landscape itself into an obstacle. Over the course of decades, the Song transformed part of the northern Hebei borderland into a string of ponds and other watery obstacles, a Great Ditch in place of a Great Wall.[9] East of the Great Ditch to the Bo Hai coast, and west to the Taihang Mountains, the Song planted dense forests of elm and willow to stymie the advance of Khitan cavalry. The reworked landscape helped deter the Liao, but did not save the Song. After the Jurchens rebelled against their Khitan masters, the Song allied with the rebels to destroy their old enemy. The northbound Song army cleared the forest to hasten their way, only for the Jurchens to ride south through the empty landscape a few years later. They sacked the capital at Kaifeng and drove the Song south of the Huai River.[10] The Great Ditch slowly faded away as the Jin let the ponds dry up and farmers reclaim the land.[11]

Until the rise of the modern state in Europe, China stood out for the size and sophistication of its state bureaucracy. The educated, literate classes of Chinese dynasties were far larger and more influential than their counterparts in the rest of the world. This class put its own special demands on the environment, notably in the form of ink. The finest ink was made with pine soot, and therefore pine forests were targeted not simply for timber and firewood, but also for ink production. The expanding bureaucracies had an unquenchable thirst for pine soot ink. As a result, Shandong was bereft of its pines by the Tang dynasty (618–907), and those of the Taihang Mountains in Shanxi and Hebei followed. By the Song dynasty, with the north's pine forests exhausted, ink production had come to rely on vegetable and mineral oils instead.[12]

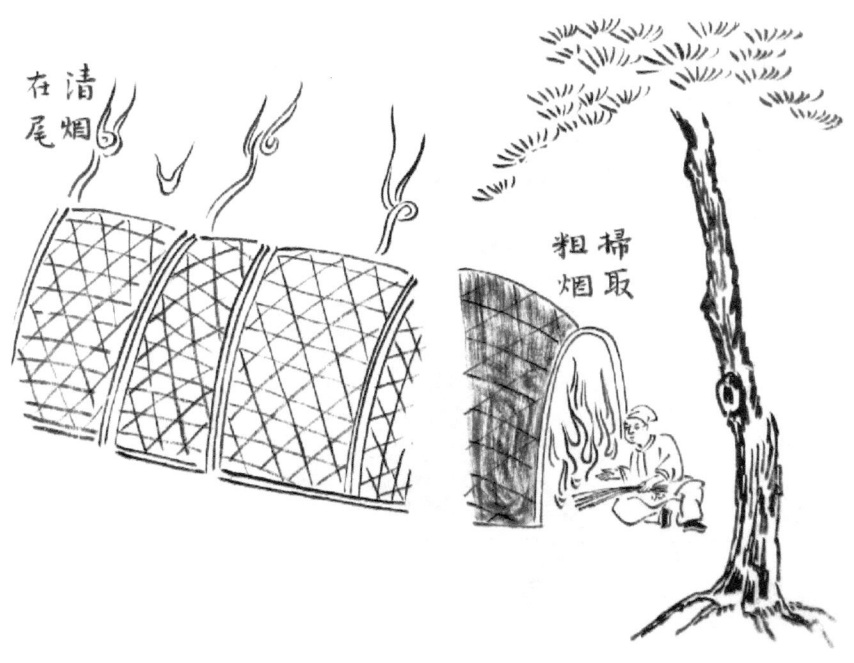

China's population fluctuated greatly throughout history, but the centuries from the Shang to the Han were a time of growth. More people required more land, and as the best and most easily cleared and cultivated tracts were settled, people inevitably pushed into less and less favorable territory. These marginal lands served first as sanctuaries for wildlife forced from their former homes, but in time they too were cleared and transformed into cropland. Eventually the only lands safe for wild animals were the most rugged and unwelcoming to cultivation—the rough and steep terrain of the mountains and the swamps of the lowlands. Before long men learned how to drain the marshes and turned those too into fields. They pushed higher into the hills as well, yet it was not until the arrival of New World crops that they made their last great advance, with the imperial government prodding them on. In the end only the most inhospitable stretches of the mountains hosted large animals such as deer and leopards. By the early twentieth century the lowlands were so completely transformed that the North China Plain "was entirely free from any tree or shrub, every available inch being taken up by the cultivation of cereals."[13] There was little animal life other than "hares, hedgehogs, and bats."[14]

The destruction of forests and wetlands in ancient and medieval North China was so extensive that some species disappeared entirely. Just what species and how many is a mystery, but recent zooarchaeological work has brought to light at least one case: a gibbon species named *Junzi imperialis*. *J. imperialis* is known only from bones found in a Warring States-era (475–221 BCE) tomb in Shaanxi, possibly belonging to Lady Xia (夏姬, c.300–240 BCE), grandmother of Qin Shi Huang, the First Emperor (秦始皇, 259–210, r. 221–210 BCE).[15] The gibbon was likely a pet, and though it could have been transported from farther south, the fact that the many other species of wildlife found in the tomb all still reside—or did until recent decades—in the region strongly suggests that *J. imperialis* was a native. That later records tell of gibbons living near medieval Chang'an into the tenth century and in other regions of Shaanxi into the eighteenth century only strengthens this conclusion. Southern Shaanxi is at the northern limit of gibbons' potential range, yet the extent of human destruction of their forest habitat points to man as the likeliest culprit in *J. imperialis'* extinction.[16] This discovery brings to light the distinct possibility that future investigations will uncover other recently extinct species in China—lost trees endemic to the lowlands of North China are among the likeliest candidates.[17]

One forest animal that held on in North China into modern times was the tiger. Tigers appear in the earliest writings, and Shang oracle bone inscriptions tell of royal tiger hunts.[18] But tigers are primarily forest cats and as the forests retreated so did the tigers. Reports of man-eating tigers from the fifth century suggest by that time the cats had too little forest and too little prey to survive without making use of humans as a food source. As deforestation continued through the Sui dynasty (581–618) and into the Tang, tigers disappeared from more and more of the region. By the Song they existed only in isolated patches of remnant forest.[19] The descendants of some of those holdouts somehow managed to persist into the Qing.[20] The naturalist Arthur de Carle Sowerby (1885–1954)—born and raised in Shanxi to British missionary parents—saw what he took to be tiger tracks in the former Imperial Hunting Grounds in Hebei and again in western Shanxi in the 1910s, and knew of the capture of another tiger in the south of the province in the early 1930s.[21] These were some of North China's last tigers, and by 1950 the region's cats were—if not gone—already doomed.

Controlling the Waters

C HINA has perhaps the most intensely modified and managed water system of any large country in the world, a result of millennia of work.[1] Water control was central to ancient Chinese civilization, a fact illustrated by the reverence for the sage-king Yu the Great of Chinese legend. Yu is credited with successfully establishing a flood control system for Guanzhong and the Central Plains, a feat so great that the reigning emperor, Shun, named Yu his successor, making him founder of the Xia dynasty (c. 2070–c. 1600 BCE).[2]

Much of China's efforts at hydraulic control have focused on its river systems, none more so than the Yellow.[3] The Yellow River contains the highest concentration of sediment of any river in the world, a fact that has been both blessing and curse to the people of the river basin.[4] The sediment provided abundant alluvial soil on the floodplain for farming, but the excessive load in the water caused the riverbed to rise, leading people to build dikes to hold back the waters. This only worked for so long, and periodically the river would break through and cause horrendous devastation to wide swaths of North China, at times even radically shifting its course.[5]

This dramatic and dangerous cycle was in fact a result of human action. The Yellow River had taken in sediment from the Loess Plateau for millennia, but it was not until the large-scale arrival of Han agriculturalists that erosion reached astounding levels and turned the river yellow.[6] The imperial regimes of the Qin and Han, and later the Tang, Northern Song, Ming, and Qing sent massive waves of settlers to the Loess Plateau to claim and secure the territory against rival powers, most often nomadic peoples such as the Xiongnu and later the Mongols. The fragile ecosystem was unsuited to intensive agriculture, and over decades and centuries the farmers devastated the landscape. With the natural vegetation stripped away, seasonal rains eroded the fine soil, sending immense volumes of loess into the waterways. Thus it was that over the centuries the Han created the conditions that wreaked so much destruction on the floodplain.[7]

Siltation was a problem the imperial regimes never solved, but could only ever hold off for a time. It was not solely the Yellow River that carried a massive silt load, but many of the region's waterways. One attempt during the Qing to clear the rivers of the Beijing region led to the demise of North China's last great swamps. The muddy waters of the rivers were diverted to run into the Eastern and Western swamps, stretching over hundreds of square kilometers south of Beijing, between the coastal city of Tianjin and Baoding to the west in Hebei. The swamps were home to probably the region's greatest collection of wildlife, from wolves and large cats and their ungulate prey to a great variety of waterfowl and other birds. In diverting the rivers the engineers hoped the silt would settle in the swamps and flow out clear. Silt did settle, so much so that over the years dry land began to form, which peasants soon claimed and farmed. Eventually the swamps disappeared entirely, along with the animals that had found a last refuge there.[8]

Wetlands were not merely potential filters for river sediment, but more often were seen as obstacles to expanding settlement. Agriculturalists worldwide have always shunned swamps and marshes. Both reservoirs of disease-carrying insects and unsuitable to agriculture, wetlands are considered wasteland, though they may provide some goods such as reeds and serve as fishing and hunting grounds. For an agricultural society such as China's the ideal solution is to drain the marshes and turn them into tillable land. Over time, this is exactly what happened across North China, so that now there are nearly no natural wetlands.

Wetlands are some of the most biodiverse habitats on the planet, and their disappearance from North China was a major blow to the region's wildlife. Dozens of species of birds, resident and migratory, rely on wetlands for their survival, and it is certain that the region's avian diversity suffered terribly as their habitat disappeared. So too did North China's aquatic life, including plants, insects, fish, and amphibians. The destruction of wetlands spread throughout China, although in the south many were replaced not with dry land but flooded paddies, allowing some of the native fauna to survive in a fully manmade landscape.

A peculiar deer, the elaphure, suffered grievously from the loss of North China's wetlands. Of all the region's wildlife there is perhaps none with a more extraordinary story than the elaphure or Père David's deer *Elaphurus davidianus*. Also known by its Mandarin name *mílù* 麋鹿, the elaphure is of decidedly strange appearance. Known since ancient times as "the four unlikes" (*sì bú xiàng* 四不像), the elaphure is said to have the hooves of a cow, the neck of a camel, the antlers of a deer, and the tail of a donkey.[9] The milu's hooves do in fact strongly resemble cattle hooves, being noticeably longer and more splayed than typical of other deer. This is likely an adaptation to their native wetland habitat, where their large, wide feet allow them greater stability.[10] Even the antlers are strange—unlike most deer, elaphure grow their antlers in autumn and shed them in winter, and, uniquely, the tines point backward. They have long, sloping, equine faces, and unlike other cervids their tails are long and tipped with a black tassel of hair similar to a horse or donkey.[11]

The milu is the example par excellence of a species expelled from its range by the relentless march of Chinese agriculture. Elaphure were once abundant in North China, where they lived in the wetlands of the Yellow River Basin and likely north into the river valleys of present-day Liaoning and Jilin.[12] The deer were a favorite hunting target of the Shang and Zhou kings—if their claims are to be trusted they captured thousands of elaphure in the course of some hunting expeditions. An incomplete tally of oracle bone records from the reign of the Shang king Wu Ding (武丁, r. 1250–1192 BCE)—the earliest Chinese sovereign whose existence is confirmed by contemporary records—totaled 1,179 deer.[13] The Zhou were just as fond of hunting and eating the milu, but the destruction of North China's forests and wetlands, which gradually deprived the deer of their habitat, was all but certainly the foremost cause of their disappearance from the region.

By the beginning of the Han elaphure were still found in the Lower Yangtze Valley, but there is nothing to indicate wild herds still survived in the north. The only milu that remained in the region were kept within hunting reserves, captive if not tamed. There the emperors of successive dynasties continued to hunt the deer—the Kangxi Emperor (康熙帝, 1654–1722, r. 1661–1722) killed fourteen in 1719. By the time of the Tongzhi Emperor (同治帝, 1856–1875, r. 1861–1875) the only remaining northern herd lived within the walled hunting garden of Nanhaizi south of the capital Beijing.[14] All this time the elaphure remained unknown to the outside world, until the arrival of one of the great Western naturalists to roam China in the late nineteenth century.

Père Armand David (1826–1900), a Lazarist priest from France's Basque country, sailed to China to save souls but instead was soon devoted to exploring and collecting its natural history. An unsuccessful missionary, his natural history work proved a triumph. Père David was not only the first Westerner to discover the elaphure, but far more famously the giant panda, as well as hundreds of other plants and animals, many of which—*E. davidianus* included—still bear his name.

Through his network of contacts Père David heard rumor of a strange deer that lived within Nanhaizi. Unable to enter himself— trespassers were to be executed—he managed to bribe a guard to smuggle him a hide and bones. These were enough to convince him that the rumored deer did indeed exist, and furthermore was unknown to science. This discovery of a strange cervid unique to a single park in Beijing and with only a few dozen individuals remaining set off a scramble to acquire specimens for European collections. The head of the British legation secured a pair for the London Zoo in 1868, and two years later the French ambassador managed to persuade the Imperial court to part with three more live deer, but the trio did not survive the siege of Paris during the Franco-Prussian War (1870–1871).[15]

These first deer sent out of China never bred, but in 1876 a hart and two hinds arrived in Berlin and became the founders of all surviving elaphure.[16] Their kin in Beijing died out over the following decades. A flood in 1894 breached the park's walls and many of the deer escaped, only for the nearby common folk to promptly kill and consume them.

Within the park the remaining elaphure succumbed to the depredations of soldiers stationed there during the First Sino-Japanese War (1894–1895).[17] A few remained in scattered menageries in China until they too all died out by 1921.[18] In Europe the elaphure were spread across several menageries until Herbrand Russell, the 11th Duke of Bedford, brought the last eighteen to his estate at Woburn Abbey in Bedfordshire. There the herd grew over the decades, with some sent to zoos and reserves around the world.[19]

For decades after the disappearance of China's last elaphure around 1920 there was no prospect of the deer returning to their ancestral land. The unrest that wracked the country—constant warfare until the establishment of the People's Republic in 1949, followed by the turmoil of the Maoist years—meant that conservation was no priority for a still poor country. After Deng Xiaoping instituted reform and opening in the late 1970s, wildlife began to attract more care, and soon plans were afoot to bring back the milu. Although it is a wetland species better suited to the marshes of the Yangtze Valley, the elaphure first returned to their former home at Nanhaizi. In 1985 the first twenty deer arrived at the park, with more added a few years later. There they multiplied as Beijing grew to swallow up the park. Once surrounded by countryside, the former hunting garden now has housing complexes on all sides. Because the resident elaphure have long since exceeded the park's capacity to accommodate them, the park now keeps about 200 milu and sends the extra to offshoot herds that have been established around China, from the northeast to the Yangtze Valley.[20]

Another denizen of North China's wetlands disappeared centuries ago, but sadly there is no chance North China's short-horned water buffalo *Bubalus mephistopheles* will ever return. *B. mephistopheles* died out in the distant past, likely sometime during the Zhou. The short-horned water buffalo were larger than the domesticated species still common far to the south. Like their wild cousins that still live in India, and the extinct aurochs with which they shared their habitat, they likely lived in herds in the plains' wetlands. They featured prominently in Shang and Zhou bronze art, but in time their homes were drained and they themselves fell to the arrows of the kings and nobles until they disappeared entirely.[21]

The Difficulties of Coexistence

NOT all animals simply flee in the face of human encroachment. Many try to hold on to their claim as the land and vegetation is transformed around them. More often than not this leads to clashes with their new human neighbors. Once the landscape is domesticated, herbivores must make do with a new floral community on which to feed. With the supply of wild plants reduced or eliminated, they turn to crops. Farmers have little tolerance for what they deem thievery, and so drive off or kill crop raiders. Such efforts, and the fear it instills in wildlife, often leads to increasing attacks on humans as hungry and frightened animals become increasingly desperate.

Wild boar are an especially persistent nuisance to farmers throughout much of China, just as they are elsewhere in the world. In some of North China's rural uplands they remain so to this day. In the early twentieth century Western naturalists and hunters noted that farmers struggled to scare off the swine. While keen to end crop raiding and add pork to their larders, farmers' simple muskets were little threat to wily droves of pigs.[1] Westerners with modern rifles and shotguns were thus happily welcomed to shoot as many of the animals as they could.[2] Disease was ultimately a more effective check on the wild swine, with epidemics periodically killing off large numbers, saving the farmers much trouble and providing them with stores of pork.[3]

A similar pattern of conflict is seen between humans and predators. As wild prey disappears, predators become more and more reliant on what remains—primarily domesticated animals, at times even humans. Farmers are no more tolerant of the loss of their animals than of their crops. The results are predictable. Not only do large predators maim and kill livestock, they inspire fear and ultimately persecution.[4] Yet sometimes farmers find in carnivores welcome allies against the depredations of crop raiding herbivores. Until the introduction of rabies led to a spate of attacks on humans, farmers in the mountains of central Honshu, Japan viewed the native wolves as beneficent crop guardians who kept away marauding boar, deer, and macaques.[5] The Chinese rarely regarded wolves or any other predators with such benevolence, yet farming communities often managed an ambivalent coexistence with neighboring carnivores.

視

In North China wolves were still numerous in the mountains into the middle of the twentieth century. They rarely formed packs, instead hunting alone or in small groups of two or three; still they were a constant terror to villagers.[6] During harsh winters or famine years wolves would even come down into the plains to search for food, and finding little else available they inevitably targeted villager's pigs or the villagers themselves. Wolf attacks were apparently widespread and frequent. Local gazetteers and Western travelers regularly recorded attacks on livestock and even humans, particularly children.[7] Sowerby, China's preeminent naturalist during the first half of the twentieth century, attested to many tales of ravaging wolves he heard from central Shanxi villagers, and more viscerally to the wolf-scarred faces of children who grew up with him.[8]

The predators that survived in heavily farmed areas of China often did so in spite of their depredations on farmers and livestock. This was due to a combination of folk beliefs and the simple difficulty of hunting and killing large, dangerous animals. Many communities throughout China formed powerful taboos around the killing of particular species, and the superstitions could act as a check against the wanton destruction of wildlife, even those that caused great hardship for people.

For many villagers there was a fatal resignation that nothing could be done to stop predator attacks. If anything was more dangerous than living with tigers, leopards, and wolves, it was venturing into the woods to hunt them. Villagers, even into the early twentieth century, were rarely equipped with anything more powerful than primitive and unpredictable muskets, so if neither poisoning nor trapping worked, and no professional hunters were on hand to try their luck, people would often choose to stoically endure periodic attacks. When given the opportunity, however, such fatalistic souls eagerly embraced the chance to rid themselves of their animal enemies. Many Western travelers in the late nineteenth and early twentieth centuries, who often carried guns for hunting, discovered this firsthand. As word of their armament spread ahead of them, they frequently found themselves beseeched to eliminate some or another hated beast as they neared a new village.

Wolf numbers had begun to thin in Hebei and Shandong by the 1920s, but it was the predator extermination campaigns of the Maoist years that wiped wolves from North China. Along with tigers and dholes, their disappearance left the leopard the region's last surviving large predator. The North China leopard *Panthera pardus japonensis*, considered its own subspecies, was long ago pushed out of the lowlands and into the hills along with its fellow predators.[9] Through to the end of the Qing and even into the early years of the People's Republic, leopards remained in the mountains around Beijing and west into the Taihang and Qinling ranges. This comes as no surprise, for leopards are the most adaptable of the big cats and, from Africa to India, have shown themselves remarkably adept at making their homes amidst dense human settlements inhospitable to other large predators.[10]

North China's leopards did not take up residence in the cities, if for no other reason than China's urban areas are utterly bereft of prey. Few cities have anything larger than squirrels (and many do not even have those), a rare exception being the raccoon dog which can be found in Shanghai and a few other metropolises.[11] Instead leopards survived in the hills where there was still sufficient prey. In some districts locals killed the cats for their furs, shipping them to markets in Beijing or farther afield. Few Chinese at the time were properly equipped to hunt leopards, so instead they poisoned carcasses of prey, a method with the added benefit of leaving the leopards' pelts undamaged.[12] In some districts, at least into the 1920s and 1930s, leopards enjoyed large enough populations of wild prey that they rarely ventured onto farms or into villages to snatch livestock.[13] They remained widespread into the 1950s, but in that decade the leopard and other large predators were deemed intolerable pests that held back the grand Maoist project from achieving its full potential. Villages—and later communes—formed teams to track down and kill the predatory pests, and army units were sent to help. After millennia of uneasy coexistence, and centuries after having pushed them into the marginal lands of the mountains, China had finally launched a campaign to exterminate its predators.

Over the next three decades nearly all of North China's remaining leopards were killed. As agriculture expanded into ever more marginal lands, and as their prey base was hunted out for the pot or the market, the cats increasingly turned to livestock for their sustenance. Such attacks gave further impetus to the predator exterminators, and over the course of the 1950s and 1960s at least 100 leopards were killed in the mountains surrounding Beijing alone. Farther west, in Shaanxi, leopards were more numerous, but they could not hold out against the onslaught either. In a single county through the 1960s and 1970s five to ten leopards were killed every year until by 1980 there were thought to be only about ten remaining. Some cats escaped death, destined instead to supply the region's zoos.[14]

Exterminating leopards—and tigers—not only removed an unwanted drain on livestock, but provided the Chinese medical community with a precious resource: bones. In Chinese medicine the bones of large cats—most especially tigers but also leopards, whether common, clouded, or snow—have been a coveted source of strength and healing since time immemorial. After 1949 the rapid expansion and industrialization of Chinese medicine—and its aggressive inclusion of parts from nearly any wildlife species—led to increased demand for such ingredients. Shanxi alone saw the sale of 5,947 kg (13,110 lb) of leopard bones in the 1960s and 1970s, though it is always uncertain how many of these were indeed leopard bones, as fraud has always been rife in the medicinal trade in animal parts.[15] Leopards are now a protected species in China, yet their bones—imported instead of from China's own cats— remain a legal ingredient in a range of patent medicines.[16]

With the increased interest in wildlife conservation that marked the post-Mao years, leopards finally received a reprieve. The few that were left were increasingly protected instead of persecuted, though they by no means escaped the rampant poaching and habitat destruction that accompanied the period. While the law and government cadres might have switched from calling for the death of all leopards to admonishing for their protection, the cats received little in the way of actual safeguards.[17] The last two decades have finally seen North China's leopards stabilize and begin to recover. They live now only over a tiny percentage of their ancient range, most of them in Shanxi's Taihang Mountains and on the slopes of neighboring Shaanxi's Ziwu Range, southwest of the Communist Party's wartime refuge, Yan'an. Smaller populations live in Hebei and Henan, and cat conservationists are now hopeful that leopards will migrate east into Beijing in the near future.[18]

Putting Animals to Use

A LONG with humankind's remaking of the landscape, hunting has been, for some species, a major cause of decline. The pre-agricultural peoples of China relied heavily on wild game for their sustenance, but the domestication of pigs and bovids led to a marked decrease in the killing of wildlife for food.[1] Nonetheless, subsistence hunting continued up until the end of the twentieth century. Hunting—often illegally—for wild game continues, yet doing so to fill empty stomachs is now a rarity. Judging from the scattered evidence available, subsistence hunting was rarely a threat to wildlife populations unless they had already suffered severe declines due to other factors, such as habitat loss or disease.

In contrast to the diffuse and small-scale effects of subsistence hunting, the grand hunting excursions of the elite regularly involved the mass killing of wild animals, as noted above with the Shang kings' enthusiasm for shooting down elaphure and other deer. Just what impact these hunts had on North China's wildlife is unclear. Many hunts were conducted within large hunting parks, walled and landscaped enclosures well stocked with game and sometimes exotic species from afar.[2] The early dynasties, from the Shang to the Han, were all enthusiastic hunters, and the tradition reached even greater popularity during the Tang, when the cultural influences of Central Asia held great sway over the upper crust of society.[3]

Later dynasties showed varying degrees of enthusiasm for the royal hunt. The Song—remembered as a dynasty of great cultural and scientific achievement but martial weakness—preferred to use their parks as relaxing pleasure gardens instead of hunting grounds. The Yuan (1271–1368), the Mongol dynasty that conquered and replaced the Song, were far more eager for the chase.[4] The succeeding Ming (1368–1644) marked a restoration of Han Chinese dominance, and is remembered as a return to Han traditions after decades of Mongol rule. Nonetheless, the Ming continued the Mongol hunting tradition, holding large expeditions to demonstrate their martial prowess. This lasted for several generations until the literati class turned against such displays.[5] The Manchu Qing eagerly returned the royal hunt to prominence and conducted massive hunting campaigns involving thousands of troops as a form of military training.[6]

Once Confucianism became the dominant ideology during the Han dynasty, it became a regular refrain of dissatisfied court advisers and the wider Confucian commentariat to beseech the ruler and nobility to refrain from frequent hunting excursions. These protests had little or nothing to do with a concern for the preservation of wildlife. Confucian thinkers in fact had no objection to hunting per se, which they often praised as an excellent way to cultivate one's character. Instead their complaints were barely cloaked admonishments against indulgence in frivolous pleasures and were meant to encourage the restraint expected of a Confucian ruler, as an emperor enmeshed in a life of adherence to Confucian ritual by necessity ceded much of his power to his ministers.[7]

The elaphure, with its reliance on wetland habitat, disappeared from North China before the region's other cervids, but no species of deer escaped the unwanted attention of man. Along with the milu, the sika *Cervus nippon* was the favored game of the Shang and their successors.[8] The Shang were enthusiastic hunters and carnivores, and no doubt enjoyed large amounts of sika venison. Chinese medicine makes thorough use of the deer—from antlers and their velvet, to the blood, penis, and placenta. It is not, however, clear just when medicinal consumption of deer parts began.[9]

Millennia before the first dynasties deer were a crucial resource for the inhabitants of North China. The earliest agriculturalists of the Neolithic period had relied on sika and other deer not only for meat but also for hides, antlers, bones and other parts. Late Stone Age settlers frequently burned vegetation to open up farmland, but because the plots were small and the clearance moderate, the numbers of deer species that favor mixed habitats along the edges of human settlements and fields, such as sika and water deer, would have risen, a fact people no doubt realized and encouraged. By the late Neolithic the human impact on the landscape had started to become more severe, and as fields and cities expanded, the deer and other species that had once shared space with humanity began to dwindle.[10]

The arrival of domesticated livestock from West Asia roughly 5,0000 years ago helped free North China's early agriculturalists from their reliance on wildlife. With cattle, goats, and sheep added to the pigs and dogs they already possessed, they now had a ready source of not only animal goods but extra labor. Humans turned more of the landscape over to supporting themselves and their animals, replacing the mixed habitats the deer favored with larger and larger stretches of open fields. Deer gradually became scarcer and scarcer across the North China lowlands until they became so few that the Zhou kings had to build hunting parks to ensure themselves a population of game to hunt. Over the following centuries deer could only recolonize the lowlands in the wake of human depopulation due to devastating war and disease, times that never lasted long.[11]

Deer, and sika in particular, were domesticated early, no later than 370. Domesticated deer were kept all through the succeeding centuries, but deer farming did not become a large-scale enterprise until the eighteenth century. What began as breeding operations to supply menageries eventually expanded into supplying antlers and venison to the wider market. These farms began in the northeast and the practice later spread to the rest of the country, mostly using the Manchurian subspecies *C. n. hortulorum* to stock their herds.[12]

By the early twentieth century the sika of North China were nearly gone. Wild herds remained only in the mountains of Shanxi and in the former Imperial Hunting Grounds in northern Hebei, north of the Qing eastern tomb complex and bordering Inner Mongolia. These preserves enjoyed strict protection until the fall of the Qing, at which point the soldiers stationed there turned to hunting the game themselves. Other hunters soon followed, and in a short time many of North China's last wild sika were wiped out. The deer in western Shanxi did not last much longer.[13]

Other ungulates, such as the Siberian roe deer *Capreolus pygargus*, the Chinese goral *Naemorhedus goral*, and the ubiquitous wild boar *Sus scrofa*, have persisted into the present, although only by keeping to the rugged mountains where human impact has been comparatively light.[14] Like the region's deer, goral—gray-brown, goat-like animals distantly related to the North American mountain goat or European chamois— have been hunted for their meat and horns, but now the remaining populations suffer most from the fracturing of their habitat. The region's few goral live in the rural, mountainous districts of Beijing Municipality and in the mountains of neighboring Hebei and west into Shanxi.[15]

More deadly to animal populations than royals and nobles were market hunters. Market demand for animal parts began early in Chinese history, and has since only grown. The wealth and size of China extended its reach far in all directions, bringing in furs from the north, musk and ivory from the south, and a constant stream of live exotic animals from the west. In North China the native deer were hunted for many parts, but demand was greatest for their antlers. In time, as deer disappeared from North China, traders had to import antlers from farther and farther afield. Other species better endured the depredations of the market, but from the late nineteenth century on, more and more species began to dwindle in the face of unrelenting pressure as China became more firmly integrated into growing global markets and technological advances allowed for improved preservation and transport of animal flesh.

Over the course of history the Han and other peoples of China have made use of seemingly every species of plant and animal known to them, to a bewildering variety of ends. Even when the Chinese have had no use for particular animal parts, they have been happy to sell them to those who do.[16] The widest and most common use for animals is as medicine, as already seen with tiger bones and deer antlers. Furs and feathers have been favorite items for clothing and accessories, with the most valuable and luxurious often restricted by law to individuals of high rank. More mundane items also relied on animal parts, from feather dusters to strings and picks for musical instruments. Like North China's pines, some animals were harvested to supply China's bureaucratic army—the pines provided ink while animals provided brushes. Fur from wild cats, red pandas, weasels, and many other animals were used to make calligraphy brushes of varying types and uses.[17] Plastics and other cheap, modern materials have largely taken the place of animal parts, while those products still made from animals now primarily come from farmed populations. Many birds have for centuries been trapped not for their feathers or flesh, but instead for their song or companionship. Fighting birds have also long been prized, and the trade in cage birds continues to present dangers to numerous species.

China has one of the world's richest array of pheasants, birds that since time immemorial have been hunted for not only their meat but their beautiful feathers. Despite the devastation wrought on the region's wildlife over the course of history, there are still a few remaining species unique to North China, foremost the brown eared pheasant *Crossoptilon mantchuricum*. Many pheasants possess long tail plumes, and in *mantchuricum*'s case these are white with black ends; from the Han to the Qing their plumes were used to decorate military headwear. Its wings and body are brown, darkening to black on its neck and head, with red skin around its eyes. White feathers cover the underside of its face and sweep back to stick up from either side of its head, as though it has grown a white beard and combed the sideburns back and up to form horns.

The brown eared pheasant is endemic to the forests of upland North China. Historical records note that *mantchuricum* were offered as tribute to the court during the Tang and Song, and occurred from east and central Shaanxi, through their heartland which covered nearly all of Shanxi, and into west and central Hebei, including a patch of what is now westernmost Beijing. As the birds' forests were felled, the pheasants disappeared from increasingly large stretches of the north. Forests were victims not only of expanding agriculture and demand for construction material and fuel, but also of the many wars that raged across the region over the course of history, with trees cut down during conflicts to supply campaigns or deprive enemies of shelter, and cut further during the ensuing peace as communities rebuilt. What little of the eastern Shanxi forests that survived into the modern era was all but cleared during the Ming and Qing. Consequently, there remains a gap between the largest concentration of birds in the Lüliang Mountains of western Shanxi and their kin on Mount Xiaowutai in Hebei.[18]

Predators dwindled and disappeared along with their prey. Small predators such as weasels and foxes, both the red fox *Vulpes vulpes* and the corsac fox *Vulpes corsac* on the steppe, were once abundant outside of the heavily cultivated plains.[19] Foxes were widely hunted—poisoned so as not to damage their pelts,[20] which were available in such numbers that even the poor could afford a foxtail neck comforter or cravat.[21] During the Maoist decades, smaller predators such as foxes and mustelids were hunted out over much of the country, as in prior times, for their valuable furs.

Across the world wildlife has had to adapt to the increasing loss of habitat not only to agriculture but to expanding cities. Many species are flatly unable to adapt to living in close proximity to dense human populations; others struggle in urban centers but can make do in more thinly developed suburbs. Even comparatively large species have managed to find their niche, such as deer in suburban America and macaques and langurs in urban India. Predators, too, can thrive in cities, from foxes in London and coyotes in Chicago to leopards in Mumbai. China remains largely bereft of urban wildlife. Certainly there are wild animals living in China's megacities, but these are with rare exception limited to such small creatures as songbirds. Strictly speaking, Beijing, Shanghai, and Chongqing are all home to larger species, however these animals are not urban-dwelling, instead restricted to the rural hinterlands of the municipalities.[22] Leopard cats, Beijing's current apex predators, reside outside the city, although some do live surprisingly close to the urban center.[23] China's cities remain urban islands—expanses of inhospitable industrial and agricultural wasteland separate them from any wildlife that might be inclined to try their luck in the steel and concrete jungles.

One predator, however, is found in many cities, Beijing included—the little, tawny-coated Siberian weasel *Mustela sibirica*. When traditional homes were still common, the weasels often lived within the rafters. A folk belief in North China held—and some still believe—that weasels are capable of seizing control of people's souls and controlling their bodies and minds; fear of the terrible soul stealing mustelids meant that the weasels were largely left alone. The disappearance of old homes means the weasels and other wildlife that had adapted to and come to rely on traditional architecture must now adapt to concrete, glass, and steel. Some will likely struggle and even disappear from the cities, but others, including hopefully the bewitching weasels, will find a way to persist.[24]

MANCHURIA

Map of Manchuria

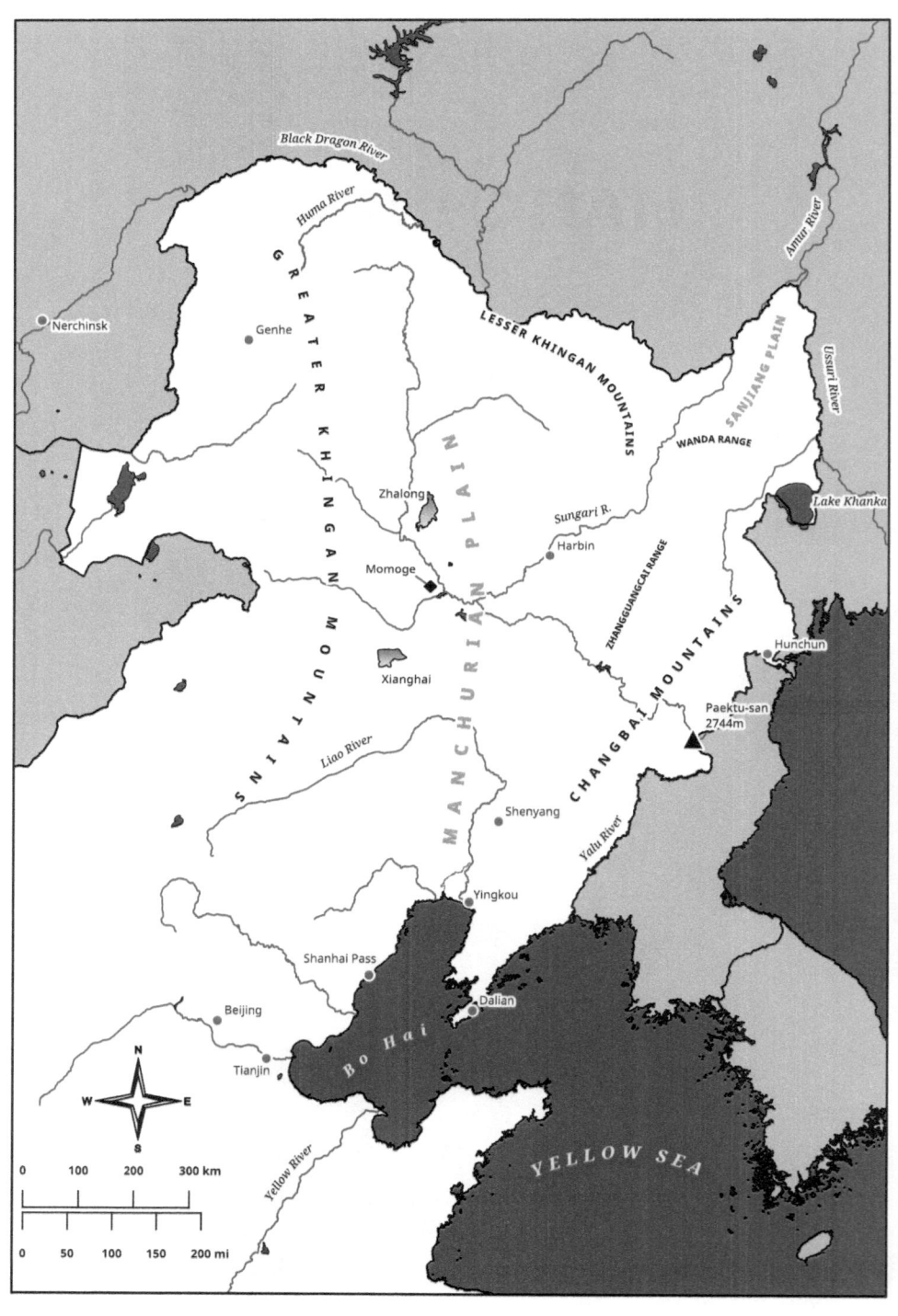

EYOND Beijing, through the Shanhai Pass, is the vast Northeast of China, better known in decades past as Manchuria.[1] With frigid winters and stifling summers, the Northeast has a harsh climate yet possesses a surprising array of wildlife. Ringed by three mountain ranges, Manchuria was formerly a land of vast and dense forests filled with tigers, sables, and ginseng, and crossed and ringed with rivers rich with salmon, sturgeon, and pearl-bearing mussels. Today it retains a shadow of its natural bounty. Many of the forests have been cleared or remade, the rivers dammed and polluted, and the wetlands and plains drained and turned to farmland. The homeland of the Manchu rulers of China's last imperial dynasty, Manchuria became a vast battleground in the early twentieth century between Russia and Japan. After decades under foreign domination, the region came under full Chinese control after the founding of the People's Republic, becoming New China's industrial heartland. In recent decades it has struggled as China's rustbelt, with a crumbling economy and fleeing population.

Geographically, Manchuria encompasses the three provinces of Liaoning, Jilin, and Heilongjiang, as well as the northernmost section of Hebei and easternmost Inner Mongolia.[2] Liaoning in the south has long supported a substantial human population, and its extensive lowlands were long ago turned over to agriculture. In Manchuria's east, along the border with Korea, rise the Changbai Shan, the Ever White Mountains, which reach their height at the sacred volcanic peak of the same name.[3] Dense forests surround the mountains, and during the Qing these were protected as the sacred homeland of the Manchu—and just as importantly as a rich source of ginseng.

To the west, running north to south, the Greater Khingan Mountains and their forests straddle the border between Heilongjiang and Inner Mongolia, and run north into Russia. These mountains contain the Northeast's only stretch of taiga or boreal forest, in China found only one other place, far to the west in Xinjiang's Altai Mountains. In the north of Heilongjiang, running east to west between the Changbai and Greater Khingan stand the Lesser Khingan. As their name suggests, the Lesser Khingans are lower mountains than the Greater Khingans, though neither range stands particularly tall, the highest peak in either stretch of mountains just exceeding 2,000 m (6,560 ft).

Manchuria's three mountain ranges form a semi-circle around the vast Manchurian or Northeastern Plain, a great, alluvial lowland blessed with a thick layer of fertile black soil. The north of the plain contained large stretches of marshland and steppe, but after the draining of the wetlands and conversion into farmland during the Maoist period, little of these natural habitats remain.

In the north the Songhua River runs from the Changbai through the Manchurian Plain, while in the south the main river is the Liao, which runs through its namesake of Liaoning and into the Bo Hai. The Northeast's greatest rivers form its northern and eastern borders. Marking the border between Jilin and Korea are the Tumen and Yalu Rivers, running to the north and south, respectively, of the Changbai Mountains. Heilongjiang has the region's largest rivers, the Ussuri on the eastern border with Russia, and the great Amur which forms the boundary to the north.[4]

Manchuria has been on the periphery of Han civilization for millennia, only recently becoming an integral piece of China. The south, the Liao River Valley and Liaodong Peninsula, was part of the Han dynasty, but later belonged to the Korean Goguryeo 고구려 (高句麗 37 BCE–668 CE) and succeeding Balhae 발해 (渤海 698–926) kingdoms, and after Balhae fell, control shifted to the Khitan and their Liao dynasty. The influence of Chinese civilization waxed and waned, but was present throughout the centuries. Chinese agriculturalists settled the fertile Liao River Valley early in history, transforming it into a matrix of cleared lands much like North China.

To the north, however, the dense forests, vast marshes, and harsh climate held off attempts to conquer and transform the landscape. There lived a variety of Tungusic peoples in smaller populations, some of them hunter-gathers, some semi-nomadic pastoralists, others small-scale agriculturalists. None of the land was without people, yet their numbers were few and they lived thinly spread across a huge swathe of territory, far to the north into present-day Russia. Their impact on the landscape was negligible compared to that of the Han agriculturalists.

The region gained its name from the Manchu, a collection of peoples brought together under the rule of the Jurchen leader Nurhaci (1559–1626) and his successors in the late sixteenth and early seventeenth centuries. The Jurchens were a loose collection of Tungusic peoples who had earlier pushed out the Khitan Liao dynasty to establish their own Jin dynasty (1115–1234) over Manchuria and much of North China. The Jurchen fell back into obscurity after their defeat at the hands of the Mongols, but by the late Ming they had regained strength, subduing the surrounding peoples and forcing the submission of Joseon Korea in 1636. In China a new dynasty, the Shun, was declared after a peasant uprising took the capital at Beijing and the Ming ruler, the Chongzhen Emperor (崇禎帝, 1611–1644, r. 1627–1644), killed himself. But the peasant leader Li Zicheng (李自成, 1606–1645) failed to gain the support of the Ming general Wu Sangui (吴三桂, 1612–1678), who guarded the Shanhai Pass to Manchuria. Under rebel attack, Wu allied with the Qing, opening China to conquest and nearly three centuries of Manchu rule.

By the time they had secured control over China, nearly all of the Manchu had left their homeland to garrison their new empire. Concerned with keeping a culturally separate homeland for themselves, the rulers of the Qing tried to close off Manchuria to Han immigrants for much of the dynasty. Despite the policy of exclusion some Han always managed to find their way in, if not in great numbers. This changed in the mid-nineteenth century as the threat of Russian encroachment and the needs of starving masses of Han farmers in North China changed the Qing's thinking.[5] Manchuria suddenly required a large settled population to provide for the region's defense, and millions of hungry peasants were desperate for land to work. Millions of men arrived from Shandong and Hebei, and though many returned home after years of work and saving, over time increasing numbers settled for good with their families. By the end of the Qing the settlers were pushing back the sea of trees that covered much of the Northeast.

Russia's construction of the Chinese Eastern Railway at the turn of the twentieth century opened the region to new levels of exploitation.[6] Large scale logging began and new settlers continued to arrive in great numbers. The Japanese takeover of Manchuria in 1931 led to increasingly intense deforestation, as Japan's wartime need for wood far outstripped what it could provide from its home islands or even its colonial possessions of Korea and Taiwan.[7] By the end of the Second World War and the subsequent Communist victory over the Nationalists, Manchuria's population was vastly larger than a century prior, and its forests much reduced if still expansive.

After the Communist victory the remaining tracts of forest were not allowed to remain standing. The leadership of the warlord era and the Japanese who ousted them had built up China's most extensive industrial base in southern Manchuria, and begun intensive logging operations in the north. The new regime expanded on their efforts, and mobilized hundreds of thousands of military veterans, and later on students and intellectuals, to log the forests, drain the marshes, and turn the sparsely populated north into a land of agricultural bounty. The forests continued their steep decline through the Maoist years, accelerating in the early years of Reform and Opening. Improved forestry practices from the 1980s onwards prevented forest cover from plummeting, but most of Manchuria's natural stands disappeared.

Since a nationwide ban on logging in natural forests was instituted in 1998, some forests have seen a measure of recovery. Much however, is replanted, often with non-native species.[8] The new habitat is not as suitable for most of the region's native wildlife as the lost natural forests. Causing further damage to the health of the forests is an aggressive policy to staunch fires, put in place after the massive Black Dragon Fire of 1987, which burned an area of over 13,000 sq km (5,000 sq mi) in the northwestern corner of Heilongjiang, reducing China's entire cover of taiga by fifteen percent.[9] The policy of fire exclusion has disrupted the natural fire regime of the forests and left them loaded with large amounts of understory brush which, when ignited, leads to hotter, more destructive burns than normal, as seen in recent years in the American West and Australia. Without a change to the region's fire control practices, Manchuria's forests will all but certainly see more megafires in the years to come.[10]

Northeastern Treasures

THE Manchurian forests host a broad community of mustelids, from the diminutive Siberian weasel to the wolverine, all animals hunted and trapped for their valuable pelts. Even the yellow-throated marten *Martes flavigula*, found throughout the tropics and sub-tropics of Asia, reaches its northernmost distribution in the forests of eastern Manchuria and neighboring Russia. Known as the "honey rat" or "honey hound" for its uncanny ability to seek out bees' nests, in winter honey gatherers follow the martens' tracks through the snow to locate hives.[1] Historically, honey gathers were so dependent on the martens to guide them that without their tracks honey harvests would fall precipitously. In 1688 the inability to meet even half the Qing court's annual honey quota was blamed on inadequate snowfall to track the honey rats.[2]

As is common throughout the world, the native peoples of Manchuria and the Chinese have used furs since time immemorial. By the rise of the Manchu in the late sixteenth-century, however, even though elite Ming Chinese were avid wearers of fine furs, there was still a tinge of the barbarian to their use. The Manchu, conversely, took the wearing of furs as a crucial part of their culture.[3] Furs were used not only for lining or trimming coats and hats. Some had uses beyond fashion, such as the tail hairs of Siberian weasels, used for fine calligraphy brushes. The thick and oily pelts of the Asian badger *Meles leucurus* were sent south where they were valued as rugs.[4] Hunters kept some badger skins for themselves, which they fashioned into mats and fastened to hang over their rears, so they would always have a dry seat.[5] Subject to aggressive hunting, poisoning, and habitat loss from the 1960s onwards, mustelids became increasingly rare and remain far short of their former abundance.[6]

The largest of the land-living mustelids, the wolverine *Gulo gulo*, roams the northeastern forests, so far north that the first clear record of it within China was not made until 1736.[7] Within their limited range, however, they remained common into the early twentieth century.[8] Hunting and the loss of land to human encroachment shrank the range and number of Manchuria's wolverines. Like other mustelids wolverines themselves were valued for their pelts, and were also trapped live for zoo collections. The number hunted and captured was not great, but for an animal with such a low population density, it was damaging, nonetheless.[9] More devastatingly, their food supply collapsed as people hunted out both their prey and the carnivores on whose kills the wolverines scavenged. By the 1950s they had disappeared from the Changbai and Lesser Khingan ranges. The remaining population was restricted to the Greater Khingan, and by the mid-1970s they numbered fewer than 300. The construction of a logging road through their territory in 1980 bisected the Greater Khingan population, further driving down their numbers. By 1990 the wolverines reached their nadir, stabilizing at a population of perhaps 200, split in two over a territory a small fraction of their former range. With the end of commercial logging in the Greater Khingan, the northeastern wolverines may now have a chance for recovery.[10]

Far to the west in the Altai Mountains of northern Xinjiang live China's only other population of wolverines. Little is known of the Altai wolverines or their history, except that annual takes of their pelts dropped continuously from 1960 to 1985, indicating a possible dwindling of the population. They are rarely spotted and thought to number only around 100. Their true status remains a mystery, but such low numbers bode ill for their long-term survival.[11]

Furs have always been a necessity for the people of Manchuria, a crucial source of warmth and protection from the elements during the long, harsh winters. Yet fine furs have also long been a luxury, and consequently items of great political and economic importance. Until the last two centuries the far reaches of Manchuria were too distant, too difficult to traverse, and too sparsely populated for far away rulers to tightly control. Instead of building great cities or fortifications, ruling dynasts contented themselves with a thin presence and an annual presentation of tribute from their subject peoples. In Manchuria, furs formed a major part of the tribute trade, from tiger and bear skins to humble squirrel pelts.

The sable *Martes zibellina*—in Chinese the violet or black marten (*zǐdiāo* 紫貂; *hēidiāo* 黑貂)—was on of the most prized of the furbearers, its coat considered among the finest for its rich, glossy color (ranging from light to darkest brown), smooth touch, and great warmth. Small mustelids roughly the same size as ferrets, sables are creatures of the dense forests of the far north, once found as far west as Finland but now only distributed from the Ural Mountains east to Kamchatka and Hokkaido.

Tribute in sable pelts to Chinese rulers is recorded as early as the second century BCE, and trade in the furs no doubt continued through the rise and fall of dynasties.[12] The Ming maintained a large flow of sable tribute, and among the groups that supplied the furs were the Jurchens. Ming demand for furs grew over time and reached an estimated yearly tribute of ten thousand sable pelts by the end of the dynasty.[13] After the Jurchens became the Manchu and conquered the Ming, the Qing continued the practice of receiving sable tribute.

The primary importance of the tribute of furs—named "sable tribute" despite encompassing many other species—was political and cultural, not economic.[14] The furs were placed under the authority of the Qing Imperial Household Department, which oversaw the affairs of the imperial family as well as relations with the emperor's Mongolian and Tibetan subjects. The emperor and his household used many of the best furs themselves, incorporated into their clothing, furniture, and accessories. Other furs were used to maintain and strengthen political and cultural ties, gifted to elites and officials, especially to Mongol

nobles and Tibetan lamas. Sable, though not the rarest or most prized, was the standard fur in this system, and the Qing court could make use of thousands of pelts in a given year.[15]

By the end of the seventeenth century the Qing's own demand for sable, combined with Russian encroachment, led to a drop in the number and quality of pelts moving south from Manchuria. The tribes of the far north blamed the Cossacks for the fall in sable tribute. Just as there had been a sable trade to China for centuries, so too had there been a trade westward to Byzantium and the Slavic lands.[16] It was the riches of the fur trade that drew the Russians east towards the Pacific, and as they reached the edge of the Manchu realm they began to press the native tribes to provide them with sable pelts.[17] The Qing court responded to the dwindling tribute by allowing subject peoples to substitute other pelts for sable, as well as purchasing sable directly from the Russians. This lasted only until Siberia's own sable populations were exhausted and both countries turned to sea otters as a replacement.[18] The number and quality of sable pelts from the Nen River region began to fall in the later half of the nineteenth century as more of the local garrisons began turning to agriculture for their livelihoods, clearing forests for fields. By the end of the century officials were falling short of their quotas by hundreds of pelts.[19]

Despite the overharvesting of sable in the early Qing, by the end of the dynasty sable still roamed the Manchurian forests.[20] The great influx of fortune seekers into the region saw unrestricted hunting of furbearers, the sable included, and a consequent decline in their numbers and distribution.[21] By the 1950s sable still hung on throughout the region, but in the ensuing decades the combination of a warming climate and human hunting and encroachment more than halved their territory.[22] The 1980s and 1990s were especially hard on the sable, as a new wave of fortune hunters scoured the forests for anything of value. Logging destroyed much habitat and fragmented what remained. The profligate use of insecticides and rodenticides caused the unintended deaths of many carnivores, and anything with fur was trapped and hunted.[23]

Sable suffered severely, and by the mid-1990s they were difficult to find even in their last mountain redoubts.[24] Today small numbers survive only in three fragmented populations, one each in the Changbai, and Lesser and Greater Khingan Mountains.[25] Increased protections have cut down on sable poaching, but the fragmentation of the sable populations and the warming climate mean their future in China remains precarious.[26]

珠

Furs were not the only tribute items sent south from Manchuria. Pearls from the freshwater mussels of the rivers of the Amur Basin were just as crucial an accessory as sable for the decorations of Manchu nobles' cloaks and headwear. Records concerning trade in Manchurian pearls stretch back to the Khitan Liao dynasty, but it is only in the Qing that the pearl trade comes into focus. The Qing regulated the freshwater pearl trade, allowing only designated tribes to bring them to the court as tribute.[27] The number of pearls to be presented was strictly enforced, with severe penalties imposed on any pearlers who failed to meet their quotas, and even harsher punishments meted out to poachers. The quotas proved too high to sustain, with the yield from Jilin's waters dropping from a high of 2,890 pearls in 1750 to under a thousand by 1815. An annual harvest of under 3,000 pearls may seem too low to have caused damage to the mussel populations, but only about one mussel in a thousand produced a pearl, and tribute quality pearls were only a tiny fraction of all the pearls harvested. Thus to supply the court with a thousand pearls, well over a million mussels were likely taken from the rivers.[28]

The court first suspected the decline in pearl tribute was due to criminal acts of the pearlers themselves, and responded with tough discipline and attempts to maintain harvest levels. As the mussel beds continued to disappear, the court began to enact pearling moratoriums. Repeated moratoriums failed to reverse the decline, and eventually the court simply refused to reopen the mussel beds to harvesting.[29] To this day the Amur Basin's wild mussel populations remain endangered, a status common to freshwater mussels throughout the world.[30] Demand for freshwater pearls is now met through artificial culturing centered in the Lower Yangtze. The future of Manchuria's freshwater mussels remains precarious, but at least they will not disappear to satisfy humanity's undying love of shiny objects.

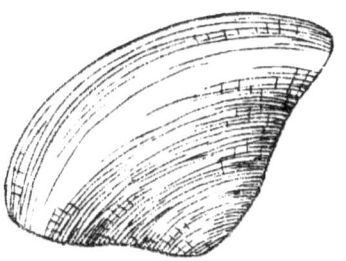

As prized as sable and pearls were, perhaps the most valuable product of the Manchurian forests was the medicinal root ginseng *Panax ginseng*. Ginseng root's perceived resemblance to the human body has led to an ancient and enduring belief in its curative efficacy, and the root has been in great demand for millennia. Ginseng has been cultivated for nearly as long, but the wild plant is considered the most potent and therefore cultivation did little if nothing to curb the harvest of wild specimens. The plant is named in early Chinese medical texts, and was found in the forests of North China, from the Taihang Mountains eastward. This ginseng was considered to be the highest quality, but in time over-harvesting and deforestation cleared it from more and more of the region. Wild ginseng crops were already dwindling during the Song dynasty, and by the end of the sixteenth century the last wild ginseng of North China had been removed from Shanxi.[31]

In the northeast ginseng first arose as a commodity with the rise of the Khitan Liao and Jurchen Jin dynasties. After the Mongols crushed the Jurchen state, Korea became the primary source for northeastern ginseng. As the Jurchens rose in power over the course of the Ming dynasty, they gradually took full control of the ginseng trade. Found throughout the forests of the region, stretching into northern Korea and what is now the Russian Far East, ginseng was a crucial source of wealth for the Jurchen, and the silver the Jurchen leader Nurhaci gathered from the ginseng monopoly fueled the expansion of Jurchen power.[32]

Ginseng's role as a major source of wealth for the Manchu emperors and the Qing state led to its gradual disappearance from the forests. Poaching was long a problem, and a source of continuing tension between the Manchu and Joseon Korea. Poaching and the even greater harvests from imperially-sponsored foraging exhausted the ginseng crops, with the plants disappearing from parts of Jilin as early as the 1680s.[33] Keen to maintain the profits that funded a substantial portion of the court budget, Qing emperors responded with reforms and restrictions to the ginseng harvest and trade.[34] Despite their attempts, overharvesting continued unabated. Even as the ginseng slowly disappeared, the Qing court continued to set high quotas to maintain the flow of revenue.[35]

At the end of the eighteenth century, over two centuries of continuous overharvesting caused ginseng yields to collapse. In 1853, despairing of ever returning to the great yields of the past, the Qing court ended the state ginseng monopoly. By then most of the ginseng forests of Liaoning and Jilin were exhausted. Only the mountains along the Korean border, long closed to legal harvest, continued to yield mature plants.[36] Farmed ginseng came to dominate the trade, and the Qing finally legalized ginseng cultivation in 1881.[37] By that time wild specimens were extremely rare, and plants yet to reach maturity were carefully nurtured and guarded.[38] Today ginseng cultivation continues to thrive, but the wild plants have never recovered, and remain exceedingly rare and are eagerly collected when found.[39]

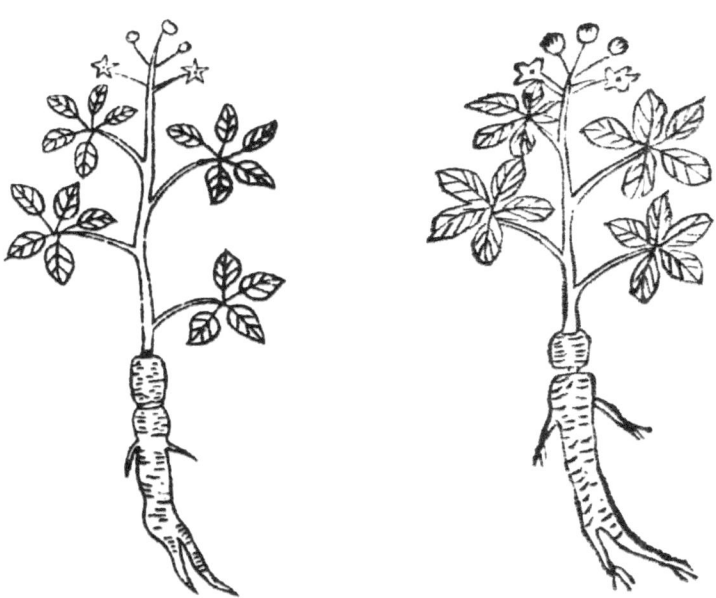

麋鹿

白鹿

Antlers & Tusks

MANCHURIA'S forests have a rich collection of deer species, from the towering moose to the diminutive Siberian musk deer.[1] Today none of the region's cervids are faring well. Deer were abundant until the great influx of settlers began in the mid-nineteenth century. Human expansion drove them ever deeper into the forests, as the settlers cleared woodland, and more and more hunters sought antlers and venison. Antlers were the strongest pull for hunters, and those of the sika deer commanded the highest prices. Sika have been valued since ancient times, kept as curiosities in menageries and within hunting estates as game. Within China the deer were domesticated on a small scale by the fourth century CE, but the practice did not expand into a commercial enterprise until the early eighteenth century.

The use of velvet antlers as a medicinal ingredient is an ancient practice, dating back to at least the Qin, and sika velvet is considered the finest available. Though sika were kept in captivity, hunters, not deer farmers, met the bulk of demand for antlers. As the demand for velvet grew in the late-Qing, sika farms multiplied and began to provide the market not only live deer but also antlers and meat.[2] Most of the farmed deer were captives taken from the wild, depleting the free-roaming populations. Despite the success of the farms, demand outstripped what they could supply, and as fortune-seekers flooded into Manchuria to hunt the deer and hack off their antlers, the sika population crashed.[3] By the beginning of the twentieth century wild sika were already rare.[4]

Beliefs about the efficacy of sika antlers encouraged cruel hunting methods. Antlers were considered most potent in summer, and particularly when engorged with blood. To maximize the value of their catch, hunters would provoke their quarry to flight, hoping the fear-driven rush of adrenaline would fill the antlers with blood. Once the deer was wounded and within range, hunters would rush to decapitate the animal before it could thrash about and damage its antlers in its death throes. The final touch was to swing the rack back and forth for a long while to ensure an even distribution of blood.[5]

Deer hunting was gruesome for the deer, but was also frequently a deadly affair for the hunter. In the closing decades of the Qing and early years of the Republic, much of the forested land of the northeast was the lawless preserve of hardy woodsmen and roving outlaws known as *hóng húzi* 紅鬍子, meaning red beards. The

Russians and Japanese kept tight control of the rail corridors, and Chinese government troops went out on periodic bandit suppression campaigns, but the forests remained a dangerous place. Trappers and hunters had to be wary not only of the dangers of the forest but of thieves, both Chinese and Russian, ready and willing to murder for pelts and antlers.[6]

At the advent of the People's Republic deer farming remained the preserve of small farms. Large-scale operations were soon established as Soviet advisors brought their own practice of wildlife farming to China.[7] Northeastern deer farms provided velvet and other deer parts to the rest of the country and for export, earning precious foreign currency for the nation. The Great Leap Forward accelerated deer farming, as it did wildlife exploitation more broadly. As the practice expanded, so did the number of uses for deer parts. The pursuit of ever-increasing production drove deer farms and pharmaceutical companies to market seemingly every part of the animals for a wider and wider range of ailments. Many of the deer parts and many of the purported health benefits were new inventions, with at best tenuous connection to traditional practice.[8]

The expanded deer farming industry was a further burden for the wild sika. Still unsuccessful in breeding enough captive deer to meet demand, farms continued to rely on a constant influx of wild deer to maintain their herds. At the turn of the millennium wild Manchurian sika were in dire straits, a few hundred remaining only due to a trickle of sika dispersing from Russia. Sika remain only in a small fraction of their former range, mostly in Jilin along the Russian border, with a few dozen in neighboring counties of Heilongjiang.[9] Along with roe and red deer, their numbers have struggled to grow even with an end to logging and increased protections. The usual mix of threats all share some blame; poaching, however, remains the main brake on Manchuria's deer populations. Until the forests are cleared of snares, the deer will struggle to multiply.

After the sika, the antlers of the Manchurian red deer or wapiti *Cervus canadensis xanthopygus*, cousin to North America's elk, were the most valuable.[10] Consequently they, along with sika, were most heavily persecuted, and by the fall of the Qing red deer were increasingly rare, limited to the deepest stretches of forest in Jilin and Heilongjiang, though many others were alive but trapped on deer farms.[11] Red deer survived but gradually dwindled until the 1990s. The increased human intrusion into the remaining forests and proliferation of cheap wire snares finally caught up to the wapiti. Within the decade the largest remaining population, in the Lesser Khingan, had dropped by up to forty percent.[12] There are positive signs, however, as recent surveys have found that the red deer population in the southern Greater Khingan is recovering.[13]

Another deer, the Siberian roe deer *Capreolus pygargus*, was the region's most widespread cervid, ranging not only in the forests but also into open spaces. A medium-sized deer, roe deer have smaller antlers than the sika or wapiti, and because their antlers were not valued as medicine they largely avoided the overhunting that decimated the larger species. The arrival of settlers to the valleys and wetlands of the region pushed out the roe deer, and though they remain in the forests, their numbers are now extremely low.[14]

The moose or elk *Alces alces* is also found in the far north, in both the Greater and Lesser Khingan ranges. Some early Western accounts suggest moose were once found far to the south in North China, yet there is no solid evidence to support the claims. Certainly by the 1920s *Alces* was restricted to Manchuria, but even then the towering cervids were neither widespread nor numerous.[15] With the rapid spread of roads and human settlements, moose numbers nearly halved over the course of the 1970s and 1980s, while their range collapsed by nearly 80%, a trend that continued through the following decade.[16] Now the moose face the impacts of climate change. By the middle of the twenty-first century moose range within Manchuria is expected to shrink by at least half, and under the worst case scenario may decrease by over ninety percent by century's end. In the 1980s and 1990s it was confirmed that, like the sable and wolverine, a second, small population of moose live in the Altai of northern Xinjiang, but they remain little studied.[17] If the moose do survive within China into the next century, they are likely to be only a few holdouts at the southern edge of a shrinking range.[18]

An unexpected denizen of the Inner Mongolia forests is the reindeer *Rangifer tarandus*. China's reindeer are in fact not natural residents, but arrived from the highlands of Siberia, east of Baikal, in the mid-seventeenth century. They came with a branch of the Evenk, a Tungusic, reindeer-herding people now split between China and Russia. There they remained on what would become the Sino-Russian border for three centuries to tend their herds of semi-wild reindeer.[19]

Beginning in 1957, official disquiet with their nomadic ways and distrust of their connections to their kin across the Soviet border led the government to force the Evenks to stay in permanent settlements. Within a few years they were twice uprooted and moved south, though their reindeer continued to migrate seasonally. The Evenks and their herds were collectivized along with the rest of the country during the Great Leap Forward, and after a second southward move in 1965 an antler processing factory was opened to meet demand for medicinal goods. State livestock policies pushed reindeer numbers to a peak of 1,080 in the 1970s, but a succession of policy changes through the 1980s and 1990s led to a decrease in the number of Evenks still herding reindeer and in the number of deer as well.[20]

A final migration south came in 2004, after the Chinese government decided the Evenks should be moved farther from the newly protected forests of the Greater Khingan. Both the reindeer and the Evenks suffered from the "ecological migration." The reindeer adapted poorly to being kept in enclosures, and the new township, on the outskirts of the small city of Genhe, did not host the lichen on which they fed. Many reindeer fell ill and even died. Before long some of the Evenk herders took their reindeer and returned north to the mountains, although they were restricted to movement between a handful of camps over a small area.[21] Other Evenks stayed within the settlement, and with fewer herders watching over the reindeer they became more vulnerable to natural predators and poachers.[22]

After the final southward move in 2004, the reindeer were split into eight separated populations, hovering between a total of 700 and 800. The Evenks and their reindeer are now struggling to adapt to their new circumstances.[23] The eight groups of reindeer no longer interbreed and have suffered a worrying drop in genetic diversity.[24] The Evenks have attempted to commercialize their herds, continuing to sell the antlers for medicinal use and turning the deer into a tourist draw, neither with much success.[25] Not truly wild, the survival of the reindeer depends on the survival of the traditional Evenk way of life, and allowing the herds to range more widely and freely. If the Evenks cannot find a way to continue to live off their herds, the future of China's reindeer may be in doubt.

Of all the animals in Manchuria coveted for their supposed medicinal potency, the most widespread and abundant was once the Siberian musk deer *Moschus moschiferus*. Much smaller than the true cervids and with tusks instead of antlers, the Siberian musk deer only reaches weights of up to 17 kg (37 lb). Once found throughout Manchuria and west across North China, now *moschiferus* is found only in the mountain forests of the northeast, Shanxi, and the Altai Mountains of Xinjiang, as well as neighboring Russia, Mongolia, and the Koreas.[26]

Like velvet antlers, musk has been used in Chinese medicine for over two thousand years. Musk is found only in the musk pod of adult male musk deer, and so hunters have long eagerly sought *moschiferus* and its congeners. Too small, nocturnal and cryptic to stalk, the deer were easiest to catch with traps.[27] Luckily for the deer, they mature quickly and breed prolifically, allowing them to withstand the constant losses. However, the persistent and increasing pressure eventually took its toll. By the early twentieth century the musk deer were becoming harder to find.[28] Despite the persistent drain on their numbers, the musk deer remained widespread in the northeastern forests into the 1960s.[29]

With the end of the Maoist era the northeast's *moschiferus* populations finally collapsed. Intensified hunting and deforestation sent their numbers crashing. The population in Jilin's Changbai range dropped precipitously under heightened hunting pressure, falling over eighty percent between 1976 and 1986.[30] They are now extremely rare in the Changbai forests; the sight of two deers' tracks in 2019 is one of the only recent indications the species still survives there.[31] The musk deer in Heilongjiang were the next to go. On top of poaching and the myriad ills of deforestation, the Black Dragon Fire gutted the deer community of the Greater Khingan in 1987, leaving the population less than a quarter of its already small size. Efforts to farm the Siberian musk deer took many more individuals from the wild, yet ultimately all attempts to breed *moschiferus* failed.[32] Today both the Changbai and Lesser Khingan forests are too fragmented for *moschiferus*, leaving only the Greater Khingans with enough suitable habitat to support the recovery of musk deer.[33]

The only caprine, indeed the only bovid, of the Manchurian forests is the Amur or long-tailed goral *Naemorhedus caudatus*. Creatures of cliffs and ridges, the gorals make their homes in rocky uplands within the forests, surveying the world below by day and descending at dawn and dusk to feed on the slopes and amongst the trees. Hunters coveted the goat-antelopes for their soft pelts, meat, and their horns, which were used in medicine.[34]

Once spread extensively through eastern Manchuria, Korea, and the Pacific provinces of Russia, the Amur gorals have suffered badly across their range in the past century due to hunting, habitat loss, and the expansion of livestock into their homes.[35] The goral survived in the Changbai Shan into the 1970s, but after the 1980s all trace of them disappeared, the last hunted out for their horns and meat. Very few are left anywhere in Manchuria.[36]

Wild boar, those great generalists, thrived in the region's forests, remaining abundant well into the twentieth century. They could be found in droves of dozens to a hundred, and Sowerby noted they were so fecund that only periodic waves of disease kept them from overrunning the region.[37] Hunters targeted the swine in early spring, after they had fattened themselves at the end of winter.[38]

An immensely difficult animal to eradicate, wild boar endured the worst effects of rampant hunting and human encroachment into the lowlands and forests. Their numbers dropped during the most intense years of persecution, but with the removal of their natural predators they quickly bounced back once hunting pressure eased. Their rebound has led to increased tension with farming communities, as boar cause millions of dollars in crop damage each year.[39] Boar continue to fall prey to poachers' snares, and when combined with competition with humans over important food sources such as pine nuts and the loss of habitat to expanding commercial activity, their numbers have recently dropped in some areas.[40] Still, if any animal can weather such difficulties, it is the wild boar.

Puren Ambani

Among all the animals of the Manchurian forest, the native Tungusic peoples most revered the Amur tiger *Panthera tigris altaica*.[1] The northernmost of the tiger subspecies, the Amur tiger is most clearly distinguished by its thick, luxuriant coat, at its most magnificent in winter.[2]

Tigers prowled throughout Manchuria at the beginning of the Qing dynasty, found on "every mountain" even in the most populous area around the regional capital of Shengjing.[3] The early Qing emperors conducted large hunts north of the Great Wall most autumns to test and train their Manchu soldiers. Tigers, among many other animals, were regular victims of these great expeditions, and over the course of fifty-eight years the Kangxi Emperor himself killed 135 tigers. In the course of his 1682 tour of Manchuria, he and his party killed over sixty tigers. His grandson, the Qianlong Emperor (乾隆帝, 1711–1799, r. 1735–1796), killed fifty-seven tigers over a span of fifty years.[4]

The Qing court not only hunted tigers in their ancestral homeland but demanded a steady supply of live tigers brought to the capital. The cats were captured live and carted south for display in menageries and for use as formidable prey in military training exercises; the court continued to bring live tigers to Beijing even after ending the live capture of other wildlife in 1822.[5] Yet by the middle of the nineteenth century the nearly two centuries of imperial demand for tiger trophies had seemingly not greatly affected the Manchurian cats, as tigers were still present wherever forest remained.[6]

As with all of Manchuria's wildlife, increasing immigration from North China sparked the steep decline of the region's tigers. The legal opening of the forest frontier and increasing demand for tiger parts led to a swift trade in the cats. Skins went to the great market centers south of the Great Wall or were sold to foreign buyers. Bones went to Chinese medicinal markets domestic and foreign. In 1896 alone 1,633 kg (3,600 lbs) of tiger bones—representing a rough estimate of between 165 and 180 tigers—passed through the region's then primary port of Newchwang (now Yingkou). Undoubtedly the bones of many more tigers left the region undocumented.[7]

Tiger blood, hearts, livers, eyes, and genitals were all used in Chinese medicine, those from adult males deemed the most potent and therefore valuable. Even their whiskers were coveted; the longest two whiskers from each tiger were worn as amulets or sewn into suit lapels, rumored to thereby give men power over women. Claws were protective talismans, while finger bones brought good fortune in business. Seemingly every part of the tiger possessed some power, even tiger scat, dried and used as a tonic for gastric illness.[8]

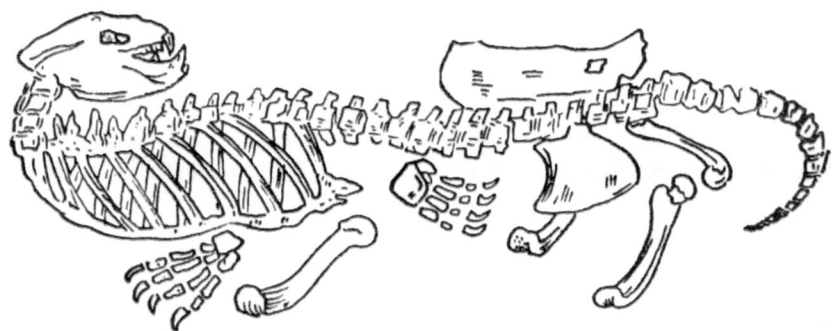

The increasing human population and its encroachment on tiger habitat led inevitably to more and more tiger attacks. Travelers in the region regularly reported attacks, sometimes on people, in other instances on their work animals.[9] Tigers responded to the coming of the railroads with equal violence. The construction and operation of the Chinese Eastern Railway deforested large stretches of land—forest was cleared to lay the track, and more trees were felled to serve as fuelwood. The railroad opened the land to increased human settlement, and the new arrivals cut down more trees for construction and charcoal. Tigers killed railway laborers and settlers so widely and frequently during construction that a Cossack regiment was dispatched to guard the workers.[10]

The completion of the Chinese Eastern Railway proved devastating. Russian soldiers and adventurers of many nations enthusiastically took to tiger hunting. Professional and hobbyist hunters sought the tigers for profit or adventure, while soldiers sought to test their mettle like the Manchu bannermen of times past, or merely out of boredom. Once the rail line fell under Japanese control in the 1930s, a dramatic expansion in logging along the railway caused extensive deforestation.[11]

The raw number of tigers killed each year was seemingly low, estimated at between fifty and sixty.[12] Yet for a large, slow-breeding apex predator this was an unsustainable rate. Amur tigers likely never numbered more than several thousand over the entirety of their range, and well over a thousand were lost to hunters alone over the course of the first decades of the twentieth century. Combined with the overhunting of their prey and the rapid loss and fragmentation of their habitat, tiger numbers collapsed and they began to disappear from large stretches of the region.

By the 1920s tigers were gone from Liaoning and the northernmost stretches of Hebei. In the same decade, far to the north in the Greater Khingan, tigers were already rare, but a few managed to hold out until the 1960s. China's last tiger in those mountains was spotted in 1962 swimming the Huma River; five years later the range's last tiger was killed on the Soviet side of the border. In the Lesser Khingan *altaica* held on into the 1980s, the last spotted in 1984. In eastern Heilongjiang tigers lingered in the Wanda and Zhangguangcai Ranges in dwindling numbers until the 1990s, but a 1999 field survey failed to find evidence of the cats in either range.[13]

At the founding of the People's Republic in 1949 tigers were still present over much of forested Manchuria, but their numbers were fast dwindling. By the time of early surveys in the mid-1950s only two hundred were thought to remain in China.[14] During these years *altaica* came under the same persecution that so many other species faced. Hunting intensified with the onset of the predator extermination drives, the tigers' bones going to pharmaceutical companies and the skins to export. In the second half of the decade an average of fifty tigers were killed each year.[15] The results of such overhunting were predictable. After two decades the last surveys of the Mao era revealed a grim state of affairs. The Heilongjiang survey in 1974 found just over eighty tigers in the province, with only four in the Lesser Khingan. The next year forty-eight cats were reported in Jilin.[16]

The forests of the Changbai Mountains provided the last refuge for Manchuria's tigers. The region was once a favorite for state pharmaceutical companies in search of tiger parts. They suffered the same persecution as tigers elsewhere in the region over the twentieth century, but enough habitat remained—particularly in the Hunchun area along the Russian and North Korean borders—to support a few survivors. By the end of the 1980s the area's population of *altaica* was split amongst several fragmented patches of habitat, rapidly facing extirpation due to a litany of dangers. Along with a few other cats scattered to the north, only an estimated thirty-five wild Amur tigers remained in China.[17]

The Amur tiger was seemingly never entirely removed from China, however the subspecies ultimately only survived in the wild due to its last relative safe havens in Russia.[18] Russia's own tigers had nearly been wiped out in the early Soviet decades, reaching a nadir in the 1930s.[19] Tigers disbursing from China helped secure their recovery.[20] Decades later the Russian tigers returned the favor, sustaining China's struggling populations and eventually helping them to grow.

After falling to barely over a dozen cats, China's Amur tigers slowly began to rebound after the turn of the millennium. The end of large-scale logging and the confiscation of firearms were critical to allowing this recovery, though a badly fragmented landscape, the continued widespread use of wire snares, and a terminally meager prey base have not made it easy. The connections with the Russian populations have and will remain crucial, as the combined remaining habitat in both countries can only support several hundred tigers. With extensive and joined tracts of protected land straddling the border, and dedicated protections offered from both national governments, wild Amur tigers have an increasingly secure future. Whether they will ever regain something of their past range and numbers, or instead persist as an isolated relict population, is far less certain.[21]

豹

The fate of Manchuria's second, smaller big cat, the Amur leopard *P. pardus orientalis*, is closely tied to that of the tiger. Distinguished from other leopards by its thick luxuriant coat, *orientalis* is one of the world's most endangered cats, with a wild population barely over a hundred and a range only three percent of its historical extent.[22] Amur leopards were once spread over Manchuria, the Russian Far East, and down the Korean Peninsula, and into the late Qing they were common throughout the Manchurian forest lands. Like tigers they were hunted for their pelts and captured live to supply the emperors' menageries.[23]

When Westerners began to travel into the region in the late 1800s, leopards remained common in Jilin and Heilongjiang, but in the first decades of the twentieth century they were all but gone from southern Manchuria. This southern population succumbed to not only the destruction of its habitat and market hunting, but also retaliatory killings; leopards share with tigers a taste for domestic dogs, a habit local villagers did not appreciate.[24]

Just as tigers, Manchuria's leopards were hunted as pests and perhaps more eagerly for the immense value of their bodies—bones for Chinese medicine and pelts for export. Hunters continued to bring in dozens of pelts a year into the 1960s, but the leopards could not withstand the losses forever. From the 1970s leopard numbers began to plummet, and the cats started to disappear from large swathes of territory.[25] As late as the 1986–1990 Five-Year Plan, Jilin's provincial government still considered its few dozen remaining leopards (as well as tigers) an economic resource to be exploited—dead, not alive.[26]

China's population of Amur leopards reached its nadir in the late 1990s and early 2000s, when fewer than ten cats were thought to remain, some in the Changbai Mountains with perhaps a few more in eastern Heilongjiang.[27] As with the tigers, the saving grace for the cats came with increasing protections in China and especially Russia, which acted as their last refuge.[28] Several dozen leopards now live in China or split their time between both countries, and after years of conservation work their numbers are growing. Their survival seems increasingly secure, but they face the looming constraints of both inadequate habitat and prey.

The Eurasian lynx *Lynx lynx* also prowls the forests, careful to avoid its larger cousins just as the leopard avoids the tiger.[29] Lynx are found across much of China but have attracted little scientific study.[30] During the Qing lynx pelts were a status symbol among the Manchu, reserved for the highest ranks of the nobility.[31] The fur trade did not seem to have had a dramatic impact on the cats' population, however, and prior to the twentieth century lynx were present across the whole of Manchuria. Yet from the late Qing, as settlements expanded in Liaoning, the lynx disappeared, first from the Liaodong Peninsula and by 1950 from the remainder of Liaoning and the Manchurian Plain.[32] Hunters targeted lynx for their fur, with 801 pelts officially taken in Heilongjiang in the decade from 1971. Nonetheless the snowshoed cats remained common in the mountains until the 1980s, but then increasing hunting and habitat loss caused their numbers to fall. A survey across Jilin over the winter of 1986–1987 found evidence of only seven cats.[33] Continuing deforestation deprived them of habitat, and the widespread use of snares intended for deer and other ungulates proved devastating. By 2017 sightings of lynx had declined over eighty-five percent from the 1950s.[34] The cats are now restricted to the relative safety of the deepest reaches of the mountains and protected reserves.

The region's smallest felid is the leopard cat *Prionailurus bengalensis*, a ubiquitous species found as far south as the Malay Peninsula and west to Afghanistan. Though less desirable than those of the lynx or big cats, until very recently leopard cats were hunted for their skins.[35] More deadly in recent decades has been the wanton use of pesticides and rodenticides, the prevalence of which has unintentionally led to the widespread poisoning of leopard cats and many other predators and scavengers.[36]

The northeastern forests once hosted several species of canids, but now only the red fox and raccoon dog remain. Foxes have always been much sought after for their pelts, and fox furs were so numerous in the late-Qing markets that even the poor could afford fox tail neck warmers.[37] Foxes, along with the similarly persecuted raccoon dog *Nyctereutes procyonoides*, still roam the forests, and though there are millions of both species packed into fur farms, the status of their wild populations is poorly understood.[38] Both have suffered large drops in number, but of what severity is unclear. Sowerby noted in the 1930s that the fur trade had decimated raccoon dogs in the Amur region, but elsewhere in China they seemed plentiful.[39] The mix of habitat loss and hunting has no doubt played a large role, but so have outbreaks of disease such as rabies and mange. The combined force of these factors has led to localized collapses, leaving areas such as the Changbai forests devoid of foxes.[40]

Wolves were present in the past, but it is difficult to know how common they were within the forests. There are records of wolves throughout the region, but there is some confusion over how often they were mistaken for dholes and vice versa. Sowerby, China's premier naturalist at the time, sighted no wolves in the course of his travels through the Manchurian woodlands between 1913 and 1915.[41] The reason is that tigers do not tolerate the presence of wolves, and, consequently, wolf numbers are low in tiger territory.[42] Humans ultimately proved more dangerous than tigers, finally killing off the last of the forests' wolves in the 1970s.[43]

More common and more feared was the dhole or Asiatic wild dog *Cuon alpinus*. A red-coated canine, typically smaller than the gray wolf, the dhole was once found across much of Siberia and into the Korean Peninsula. Today it has all but certainly disappeared from its northern ranges. Much despised throughout Chinese history as a cruel and parasitic hanger-on to larger and fiercer predators, the dhole is a common character in Chinese idioms, none of them laudatory.[44] Its foul reputation may have been why it was one of the few animals that was considered of no medicinal benefit to humans, though its flesh was deemed effective in calming horses and cattle.[45]

Dholes were common in the Manchurian forests into the early twentieth century. The wild dogs were much feared, as they lived and roamed in large clans, their numbers giving them the power to hunt and kill humans and, on rare occasion, even tigers. Not only farmers but hardened hunters and woodsmen alike all dreaded encountering a wild dog clan.[46]

What caused the disappearance of Manchuria's wild dogs is something of a mystery. Dholes were seen less and less by the middle of the twentieth century, and in some areas such as the Changbai range vanished around the 1950s.[47] Across the whole of Manchuria there have been no confirmed sightings of dholes in over thirty years.[48] Retaliatory killings for livestock degradation, loss of habitat, the depletion of their prey base, and the extended predator extermination campaigns of the Maoist era no doubt all contributed. Whether such a combination was enough to extirpate the dholes from the region, or whether a silent, undetected epidemic sped them to their end is unclear.[49] No one was paying attention until the dholes had already vanished.

Two species of bear live in the northeastern forests, the smaller and more numerous of which is the Asiatic black bear *Ursus thibetanus*, also known as the moon bear for the white patch across its chest. The Manchurian subspecies, the Ussuri black bear *U. t. ussuricus*, is the largest of the species, but on average *thibetanus* is smaller than the American black bear *U. americanus*, and sports distinctly larger ears. Despite their large size and formidable armament of teeth and claws, the black bears must be wary of brown bears and tigers, both of which may attack and—in the case of the tiger—kill and eat them. Cubs are especially vulnerable, subject to predation from smaller carnivores such as leopards, lynx, and—before their extirpation from the region—wolves and dholes.

For a time black bears held out against the great mid-nineteenth century influx of migrants that pushed so many species out of the lowlands. Along with roe deer they adapted to the replacement of woodland with crop fields, the bears happy to take their share from farmers' maize fields.[50] Eventually human encroachment proved overwhelming, as the disappearance of large trees with cavernous denning spaces deprived the bears of crucial winter shelter.[51]

Aside from the loss of habitat, China's black bears have long been eagerly sought for their paws and gallbladders. The Chinese have consumed bear parts for millennia, yet Manchuria's populations of bears, both black and brown, remained widespread into the 1960s. Hunting increased through the 1970s, but it was in the following decade that the full power of the market reached the bears as demand and prices for paws and gallbladders rose to irresistible heights.[52] The newfound and spreading wealth of the reform era sparked the hunting of immense numbers of bears. In the late 1980s restaurants in the far northern city of Harbin served over two tons of bear paws each year, a trade that legal protection bestowed upon the bears in 1989 did little to slow. Paws fed not only the Chinese but were also smuggled to bear-hungry diners in South Korea and Japan.[53]

Most famously, bears in East Asia, especially *thibetanus*, are valued for the medicinal effects of their bile. Records of using bear bile in Chinese medicine reach back to the seventh century CE, and it was undoubtedly in use long before.[54] Unlike many animal parts used in

Chinese medicine, bear bile has been scientifically proven to be an effective medication for dissolving gallstones, on account of the presence of ursodeoxycholic acid, although in Chinese medicine it is prescribed for a greater range of afflictions. Ursodeoxycholic acid can be synthesized without any use of bears, but lingering popular belief that live, and particularly wild, animals produce the most potent medicine has kept demand for bear bile high.

By necessity bear bile was traditionally taken only from dead bears. Extraction of bile from live bears was first developed in North Korea and spread to neighboring Jilin in the early 1980s, and then to Heilongjiang and Liaoning.[55] This led to the establishment of a bear farming industry in which captive bears regularly had their bile extracted. For the bears the bile farms were a catastrophe. Those condemned to live on the farms were subjected to abhorrent conditions. Bile bears were forced to endure repeated surgeries, or instead the permanent implantation of a tube or catheter to allow for daily bile drainage.

Touted as a means of meeting demand without harming wild bears, the farms did exactly the opposite. The insatiable demand for bile, combined with the difficulties of breeding bears, who do not multiply as quickly as pigs or cattle, led bile farmers to seek bears from the wild to boost their stocks. To worsen matters, wildlife scientists who would otherwise have studied wild bear populations shifted their attention to improving farming operations. Many of the scientists and their sponsoring institutions—both state agencies and universities— took direct stakes in the farms, and, eager to maximize profit, they vastly expanded the range of uses and products for bear bile.[56]

As the number of captive bile bears ballooned the wild population shrank. The black bears of Jilin's Changbai region collapsed by over ninety percent between the mid-1980s and 2010, with not a single cub or juvenile detected in the final ten years of that period.[57] The region is thought to now host at most 1,500 black bears, a number barely higher than those of the brown bears they once vastly outnumbered.[58]

Far more feared but historically far less common than the black bear is the brown bear *U. arctos*, the same species as North America's grizzly. Brown bears are also found in China's western reaches, but the Manchurian subspecies, the Ussuri brown bear *U. a. lasiotus*, is the country's largest. Except for the bears of Kamchatka, they are the largest in Eurasia. Much larger than the black bear and therefore requiring far more nourishment, the brown bear is naturally the less numerous of the two species. Like *thibetanus*, *arctos* was widely hunted, for its paws and gallbladders, but particularly for its skin.[59] Despite being prey to human hunters, the bears were greatly feared, and indeed were the only animals in the forests that could stand alone against the tiger.[60]

Since the nineteenth century hunting and habitat loss have pushed the brown bears from most of Manchuria. Sowerby noted they were already becoming rare in the 1930s.[61] Hunting became especially severe in the 1960s and continued without relent for decades. The species is likely gone from Liaoning, and few survive in Jilin. Most that remain are restricted to the Greater and Lesser Khingan ranges, likely connected to and in part sustained by Russian bears across the Amur. The number of remaining brown bears is far from clear, with only rough guesses available. Estimates in the early 1990s reached up to 2,500, but were down to only 1,000 by the end of the decade.[62] Habitat loss and demand for paws and gallbladders have been enough to devastate brown bear numbers, but the loss of pine nuts to human collectors and of acorns to felled oaks has also deprived the bears of crucial foods needed to prepare for hibernation.[63] With better protections the bears may eventually rebound, perhaps helped along by arrivals from Russia, but to date there is little sign of recovery.

閩門泊
東嶼

Fowl & Fin

MANCHURIA hosts not only some of China's most extensive forests, but also some of its most biodiverse wetlands. The two large plains of Heilongjiang and Jilin, the Songnen Plain in the west and the Sanjiang Plain in the east, hold the remnants of once vast marshlands. Both are crucial breeding and stopover sites for a host of migratory birds, many of which, such as the red-crowned crane and oriental stork, are now endangered and reliant on Manchuria's wetlands for their continued survival. To the great misfortune of the wetlands' wildlife, the marshes overlay some of China's most fertile soils. The drainage of the marshes from the 1950s onwards— predominantly a deliberate act of man, but exacerbated by a warming climate—has reduced them dramatically.

The Sanjiang Plain is China's largest area of freshwater marsh, and one-third of the plain was marshland in 1950. By 2005 nearly eighty percent of this was lost, most converted to dry farmland and paddy fields.[1] The Songnen Plain, including the critical crane habitat within Zhalong Marsh, suffered similar devastation, and the lands of both plains are now predominantly cultivated.[2] The loss of wetlands has slowed over time, but so long as the two plains remain a crucial source of China's grain supply, there is little chance of the marshes expanding to anything like their former extent.

The most famous denizen of the marshes is the red-crowned crane *Grus japonensis*.[3] Mostly covered in snow white feathers, red-crowned cranes are easily confused with Siberian cranes *Leucogeranus leucogeranus* and best distinguished by their black faces and necks, as well as the red patch of skin atop their heads for which they are named. They are large even for cranes, typically standing about 154 cm (5 ft) tall, with males only slightly larger than females. The secondary feathers on their wings are black, and when their wings are folded back the feathers rest so that it appears they have black tails, though in fact their tails are white.

In traditional Chinese thought the red-crowned crane holds the highest status of all birds, second in prestige only to the mythical *fènghuáng*, often called the phoenix.[4] Symbols of longevity, the crane is perhaps the most commonly depicted bird in Chinese art, and Chinese rulers kept captive sedges from the earliest dynasties. Manchuria contains most of the red-crowned cranes' remaining breeding grounds on mainland Asia and is therefore crucial to their survival. Traditionally they have bred in wetlands from Dalai Nor and Xianghai in Inner Mongolia, east to Lake Khanka straddling the Sino-Russian border, and south to the Liao River estuary.[5]

Red-crowned cranes appeared in Chinese art and literature as early as the Shang, as well as in the works of regional states such as Goguryeo.[6] Their breeding grounds in Manchuria have been known since at least the fifteenth century, and for hundreds of years live birds were caught and sent south to live in captivity.[7] Into the early twentieth century red-crowned cranes were still common in Manchuria, and as the region's marshlands remained largely untouched until the 1950s, their breeding grounds suffered little damage until after the foundation of the People's Republic.

Earlier efforts to settle the Songnen and Sanjiang Plains had largely failed, but the demobilization of soldiers in the late 1950s began the decades-long destruction of the cranes' wetland habitat. Sent to the Great Northern Wilderness (*Běidàhuāng* 北大荒), tens of thousands of Peoples Liberation Army veterans undertook the grueling work of clearing the forests and draining the marshes to transform the plains into the Great Northern Granary (*Běidàcāng* 北大仓).[8] The Maoist predilection for the maximal exploitation of natural resources, and the desperate search for wild food sources during the famine years of the Great Leap Forward exacerbated the threat to the cranes and other wildlife. By the early 1960s the loss of cranes to hunting had begun to worry authorities, and the 1963 edition of *Economic Avian Fauna of China* cautioned that egg collecting should be banned and hunting strictly controlled to prevent the birds' extirpation.[9]

The cranes' numbers fell rapidly in response to the shrinking of their marshland home, as well as to the increase in other human activities such as reed harvesting. The draining of the wetlands not only directly deprived the cranes of habitat, but led to an increase in fires which destroyed nesting habitat, eggs, and hatchlings. The fish populations on which the cranes fed dwindled as the hydrology changed and people caught them for their own purposes. A further danger came from the use of fertilizers and pesticides, leading to increasing pollution of the ecosystems and poisoning of animals. The first survey of the breeding red-crowned cranes in 1975–1976 estimated 1,310 birds in Heilongjiang; five years later the total in all of China reached only 1,300 and dropped to 520 in 1986.[10] By 1992 the official tally stood at 542.[11]

Conservation efforts over the last few decades have attempted to reverse the fall in crane numbers, but so far the slide has merely slowed.[12] A disconnect between the recommendations of scientists and conservationists and the actions of policymakers has meant the wetlands have seen little to no improvement. This has coincided with a long dry spell as the region's thirty-year rainfall cycle runs its course.[13] The cranes have begun to disappear from many wetlands, the survivors concentrating in fewer and smaller areas, with Zhalong Marsh remaining the most crucial.[14] At the latest count of the wintering population to the south in 2019–2020, China's red-crowned cranes numbered only 353 birds.[15]

Impending climate change only further stacks the odds against the cranes. The rising temperatures will make much of what little habitat remains unsuitable. Zhalong, which contains over sixty percent of the cranes' remaining breeding ground, is expected to remain their most critical refuge, but will lose around forty percent of its suitable crane habitat. With such restricted space in which to breed, the cranes will find it extremely difficult to increase their numbers, no matter the protections they are offered.[16]

H.D. ASTLEY

The Amur Basin has the world's greatest assemblage of cranes, hosting six Eurasian species and regular visits from North America's sandhill crane *Antigone canadensis*.[17] The great majority of Siberian cranes stopover in the region's wetlands on their way from their breeding grounds in the Russian Arctic to their winter refuge in the Yangtze Basin. A few non-breeding Siberians may even spend the summer in Manchuria. In the 1980s the Siberians preferred to stopover at Zhalong, but more recently they shifted to the Etoupao wetlands of Jilin's Momoge Reserve and nearby marshes.[18]

Aside from the red-crowned and Siberian cranes, the common crane *Grus grus*, demoiselle crane *G. virgo*, white-naped crane *G. vipio*, and hooded crane *G. monacha* all stopover in Manchuria during their migrations. The white-naped cranes prefer shallower waters than the red-crowned, which means that though they suffer from the same threats as *japonensis*, their response is sometimes different, particularly in regards to changes in the physical landscape of the wetlands.[19] Most hooded cranes breed in Russia, but two flocks of about 500 pairs breed in Heilongjiang's Lesser Khingans. Their preference for taiga bogs and mountain valley wetlands has so far offered them more protection from human encroachment than the red-crowned and white-naped cranes.[20] The common and demoiselle cranes are primarily grassland birds more common to the steppe, but some breed at Zhalong along with their congeners.

Another large migratory bird, the Oriental white stork *Ciconia boyciana*, shares the Sanjiang wetlands with the cranes. Covered in white feathers except for its black wings, and sporting a formidable black bill and bright red skin around its eyes, the Oriental stork is nearly as striking as the Gruidae. Storks, both *boyciana* and the black stork *C. nigra*, are mentioned in some of the earliest extant Chinese texts and were recorded over most of present-day China at some point in history.[21] During the early Qing dynasty the storks were sought for their black pinions, the long, outermost flight feathers. Ten hunters were to supply the court with 150 birds each year, but by 1673 they brought only 112, the next year forty-three, and in 1675 a mere twenty-three.

Despite the court's efforts to pressure the hunters to bring in more storks to make up for the repeated shortfalls, they could not find enough to meet their quotas. After years with no improvement in stork numbers, their capture was finally suspended in 1682, allowing the birds to escape local extinction.[22]

At present the storks suffer from many of the same impacts as the cranes, losing much of their aquatic food supply with the conversion of wetlands to croplands. Unlike the ground-nesting cranes, the storks nest in tall trees and so have struggled to find adequate nesting space as the expansion of farmland and the falling water table have led to the death or removal of suitable trees. They do their best to make do with telephone poles and electricity pylons, though recent efforts to install purpose-built nesting boxes have shown promise.[23]

Up to the 1960s the Oriental storks remained widespread in the region's marshes, but since the start of intensive wetland drainage and conversion, which unluckily coincided with a general warming of the regional climate, their numbers have been in terminal decline, only recently turning around. Now nearly all of the surviving storks breed in the Manchurian wetlands with a few just across the border in Russia. About half the population flies to Poyang Lake along the Yangtze River for winter, the other half preferring the Korean Peninsula.[24] Their numbers seem to be increasing, with the latest winter count coming to approximately 7,500 storks at their wintering grounds in the Middle and Lower Yangtze.[25] This growing number of birds must make do with dwindling stopover habitat in coastal Tianjin, where they have become dependent on fish from aquaculture ponds. Fearing for their livelihoods, fish farmers have responded with firecrackers and other deterrents, leading to numerous stork deaths.[26]

The Amur and its tributaries, notably the Ussuri and Sungari Rivers, host two members of the sturgeon family, the Amur sturgeon *Acipenser schrenckii* and the kaluga *Huso dauricus*. As with most sturgeons, both species are large and heavy fish, but the kaluga is truly massive. While not as large as its congener the beluga sturgeon *Huso huso*, the kaluga has been measured up to 5.6 m (18 ft 4 in) long and 1,000 kg (2,205 lb) in weight. Known as a formidable adversary for fisherman, the Kangxi Emperor eagerly sought to catch a kaluga from the Sungari River during his 1682 tour of Manchuria, but the spring melt had turned the river too dangerous, and the emperor left without his prize.[27]

As with other species of sturgeon, the Amur sturgeon and kaluga are valued for their flesh and especially for their roe, which is cured to make caviar. Neither species is considered a source of the finest grades of caviar, although, as the closest relative to the most highly prized beluga, kaluga caviar nonetheless attracts a high price. This demand, especially since the 1980s, has led to the collapse of sturgeon numbers in the Amur.

The populations of both species began to drop at the beginning of the twentieth century due to Russian overfishing. At that time the Chinese fishing fleet was negligible, but commercial fishing from the Russian shores and tributaries of the Amur saw a drop in catch from 595 tonnes of kaluga and 607 tonnes of Amur sturgeon in 1891 to only 61 tonnes and 4.2 tonnes, respectively, in 1948. The Soviet Union banned the fishing of both species in 1958 in an effort to allow the populations to rebuild.[28]

As the Russians ended their fishing of the Amur's sturgeons, the Chinese expanded their own efforts. And as the population along the river grew, so did the fishing fleet. The Chinese brought in an average of over forty tonnes annually between 1957 and 1977, but, as was so often the case, it was the reform era that saw the greatest increase in exploitation. China's opening to the global market brought in caviar traders, and the high prices on offer drove up the catch. By 1987 the combined catch of *dauricus* and *schrenckii* peaked at 452 tonnes and averaged over 320 tonnes until 1991. By the end of the century annual hauls had fallen below 150 tonnes, clear indication that populations of both species were but fractions of their former abundance.[29]

Both the kaluga and Amur sturgeon continue to struggle. The demand for caviar continues to threaten the fish, as poachers—Russian and Chinese—pluck breeding females from the waters, leaving the remaining population younger, more male, and less fecund.[30] Efforts to restock their numbers through the release of hatchery-raised fry initially yielded no discernible improvements, and few adult fish could be found outside of the Amur's estuary.[31] The most recent survey in 2021, however, determined that both species are showing signs of recovery. New Russian restrictions on salmon fishing have allowed sturgeon restocking efforts to bear fruit. If kept in place for up to another decade, the sturgeons may make a lasting rebound.[32]

FERRIER

C. BERJEAU. DEL

STEPPES

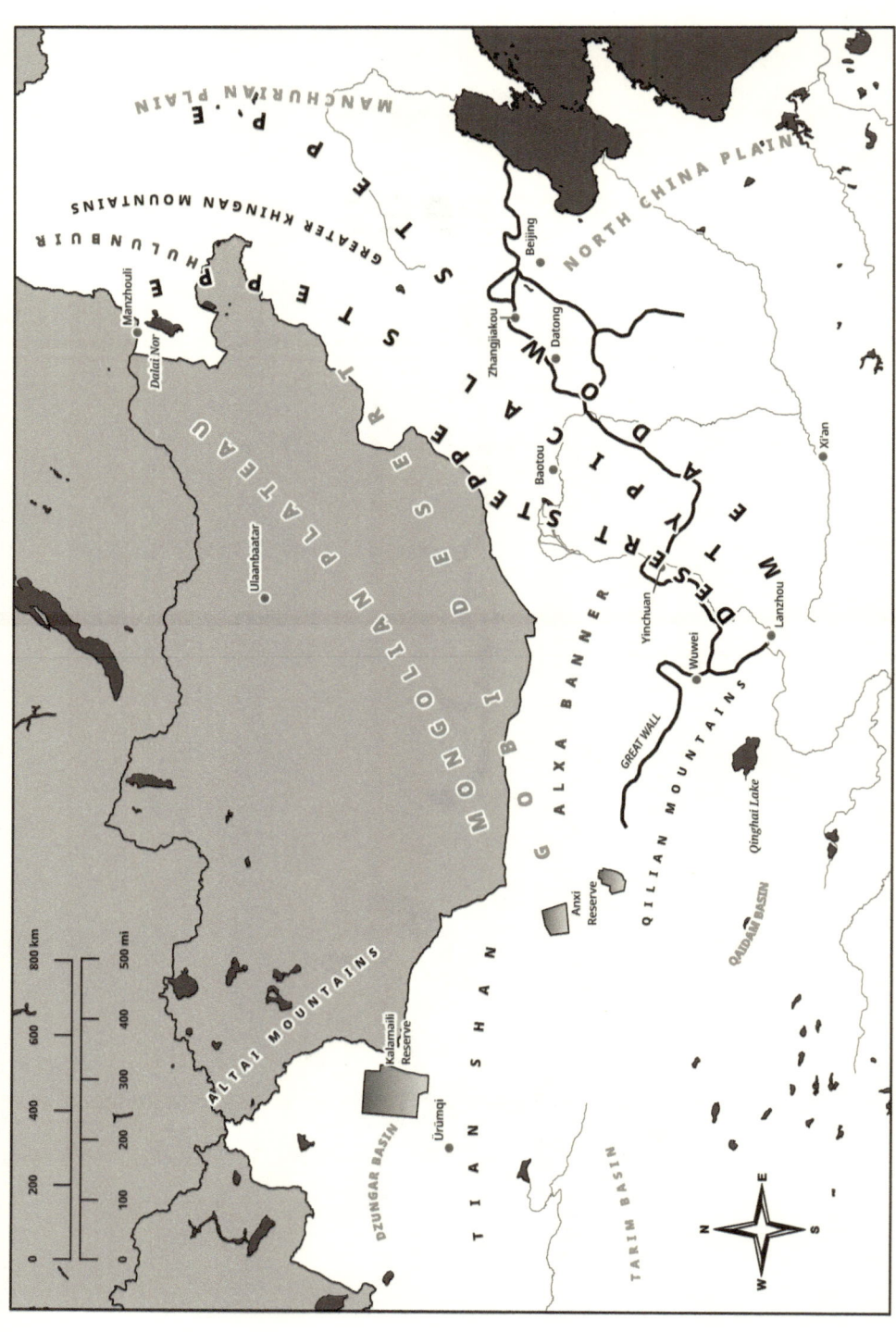

CHINESE culture and history have always centered on the agricultural lowlands, first in North China and over time expanding to the Yangtze Valley and the coastal lands of South China. Since the earliest dynasties, the steppe lands to the north, uncultivated and sparsely populated with nomadic horsemen, have stood as the great, looming other threatening Han Chinese civilization. Unsuitable for intensive agriculture in the Han mold, for most of history the steppe has existed beyond the grasp of Chinese dynasts. Only when the Han learned to fight like the nomadic cavalrymen, such as under Emperor Wu of Han (漢武帝, 156–87 BCE, r. 141–87 BCE) or Emperor Taizong of Tang (唐太宗, 598–649, r. 626–649), or when the steppe lords themselves conquered China, were the grasslands brought under unified rule with the agricultural plains.[1] The Manchu brought vast swathes of steppe into the Qing realm, and with the exception of Mongolia, most of those lands remain part of the People's Republic. These additions were so expansive that grasslands are now in fact the single most extensive type of land in China, covering a third of the country.[2]

China's grasslands can be broadly divided into four types: steppe, meadow steppe, desert steppe, and alpine steppe. The meadow steppe, the southernmost type, is found on either side of the Greater Khingan Range in Manchuria and stretches southwest to Gansu, roughly following the Great Wall. The meadow steppe receives the most rain of the four types, and therefore has the tallest grasses and supports the largest populations of wildlife. North of the meadow steppe is the steppe, where shorter grasses grow. This type of grassland is also predominant in the northernmost stretch of Xinjiang, along with a smaller patch of desert steppe. The desert steppe is a mixture of semi-arid grasslands, some of which receive only enough moisture to support scattered patches of thin, low-growing grasses. It is found to the north of the steppe, from Inner Mongolia to Gansu, acting as a transitional zone between the lusher grasslands and the true deserts. Alpine steppe is high-altitude grassland found on the Tibetan Plateau, and is covered in part five on the western highlands.[3]

In ancient times the steppe was populated with an ever-changing mix of nomadic peoples. New groups moved in to push their predecessors out, or to absorb them into their ranks. The first great coalition of steppe nomads was the Xiongnu, the great enemy of the Han dynasty. After Xiongnu power waned, other tribes and confederations, such as the Xianbei, Rouran, and a host of Turkic groups, arose and fell in their turn. The steppe nomads reached their apogee with the Mongols under Chinggis Khan, whose grandson Kublai founded the Yuan dynasty.

In recent centuries the Mongols moved into the steppes of western Manchuria, Inner Mongolia, and Gansu, and for a time they also inhabited the high steppe of Qinghai and the grasslands of Dzungaria in northern Xinjiang. The Dzungars—a confederation of Oirat, or westernmost Mongol, tribes—were conquered and destroyed as a people during the Qing conquest of Dzungaria in the mid-eighteenth century. Now largely gone from Xinjiang, in Qinghai the Mongols currently constitute only a tiny fraction of that province's population.[4]

During the late Qing dynasty, Han settlers moved into the Inner Mongolian steppe, cultivating the land and coming to dominate the native Mongols. Their conversion of the land to farm fields caused severe degradation to the grasslands, and intense resentment amongst the pastoralist Mongols. After the People's Republic was established, the Mongols were forced to surrender their nomadic lifestyles and settle in designated plots. The continuous concentration of their livestock in closed pasturelands quickly led to severe degradation of the landscape, which has contributed to the erosion of the topsoil and expansion of the bordering deserts. More recent fencing of the grasslands into private plots has further damaged the landscape, fragmenting the steppe and cutting off many species from their migratory pathways.

In the west, Kazakh and Kyrgyz pastoralists live on the western grasslands of Xinjiang, the Kazakhs in the north and the Kyrgyz in the far west. Many Kazakhs moved into Dzungaria after the destruction of the Dzungar Mongols, while more Kazakhs as well as Kyrgyz arrived in Xinjiang in the early twentieth century to escape Russian and Soviet persecution. They found little peace in China, for years facing violence from authorities of both the Republic and People's Republic; many eventually fled back to the Soviet Union.[5]

Grassland Herbivores

UNTIL recent decades the most numerous large wild animal on the steppe was the Mongolian gazelle or dzeren *Procapra gutturosa*.[1] In times past the gazelles were spread over a wide swathe of territory, grazing the steppe belt from Kazakhstan in the west, east through Mongolia and China, and north into Russia. Within China they ranged over plains stretching from Gansu east to Heilongjiang, and as far south as northern Hebei, just beyond the Great Wall.

A gregarious, migratory species, dzeren gather in herds of a few dozen to well over 1,000 animals, and move often in search of good pasture. Roughly the size of domestic goats, dzeren have reddish-yellow coats in summer, in winter lightening to yellow, the color which lends them their name in Chinese, *huáng yáng* 黃羊, "yellow goat."[2] Their bellies are white, and on their rumps they have a heart-shaped white patch. Females are hornless, but males have lyre-shaped horns and, during the rut, enlarged throats.

There are few records of the gazelles before the writings of Western observers. Early observations came from a French Jesuit, Jean-François Gerbillon (1654–1707), who frequently spotted the gazelles on his journey to and from the northern frontier of the Qing Empire.[3] Gerbillon reported that the "yellow goats" were seen in "droves of one or two thousand" and were a favorite quarry of the Manchu nobles and the Kangxi Emperor.[4] The Russian geographer and explorer Colonel Nikolay Przhevalsky (1839–1888) noted they were common on the flat plains of the Gobi and its surroundings, found usually in groups of fifteen to forty.[5]

Early accounts of the dzeren all noted how fearful of humans the gazelles were, and how challenging this made them to hunt. The animals were extremely difficult to approach, and their great speed made them all but impossible to pursue. This was no doubt on account of how commonly hunted they were, as dzeren were not only favorite targets of Manchu and Mongol lords but also of common herders. The gazelles were sought in late summer when they were at their fattest and most flavorful. Their skins, too, were valued, not for personal use but as market goods sold to Russian traders.[6] Yet ultimately the most common and persistent hunters of the gazelles were not humans but wolves, who followed the herds on their migrations.

By the turn of the twentieth century the gazelles had disappeared from the easternmost portion of their range in the Amur Basin, territory which by then belonged to Russia.[7] Yet as late as 1918 the yellow goats were still roaming the plains north of the Great Wall in great herds of a thousand or more.[8] Around the same time they were still found as far east as the plains of western Manchuria in the northeast.[9] By 1930, however, the dzeren had lost much of their range to the advance of Han settlers turning the steppe into cropland.[10] The gazelles could neither tolerate the threat of the farmers nor survive off their fields.

In time the encroachment of farmland pushed the yellow goats out of every province except Inner Mongolia. In spite of this the gazelles were still abundant, but they soon faced new and devastating threats. The construction of a railway from Beijing to the Mongolian capital of Ulaanbaatar in the early 1950s cut through the gazelles' migration route and disrupted their ranging.[11] Worse soon followed as they fell to hunters by the tens of thousands. Between 1956 and 1961 an estimated one quarter of the dzeren population was killed each year, at least 500,000 annually for a total of 2.5 million.[12]

In spite of the great numbers lost to the gun, the gazelles weathered the onslaught, but not without severe loss. As the killing continued into the 1980s, the dzeren retreated ever northward. As before, an estimated half million animals were killed every year, now a third instead of a quarter of the population. Even after the gazelles were afforded legal protection in 1989 the hunting continued. Government and party officials, military personnel, herdsmen, and others with access to firearms and motor vehicles gunned down dzeren indiscriminately during the winter rut. By the winter of 1994–1995 the population had dwindled to around 250,000.[13] At the same time the privatization and division of the grasslands into fenced pastures made migration increasingly fraught for the gazelles. The total effect was crushing. By 2000 they could only be found near the Mongolian border, and numbered fewer than 8,000.[14]

The hunting of the gazelles has largely come under control, and though the species as a whole does not face extinction, the population in China is greatly diminished, now hovering around 1,000.[15] It will take much time and effort to help the herds return to their former numbers and range. One small herd at Dalai Nor has taken seventeen years to grow from a group of eight to one of over sixty.[16] Yet so long as much of the grassland remains fenced or under the plow, the yellow goats will have to make do with the sliver of their former territory that remains open range.

馬

The steppe of China's northern and western borderlands is an extension of the great Central Asian steppe belt, where humanity first domesticated the horse. As the population of domestic horses grew and spread over the millennia, their wild cousins diminished in the face of human expansion, driven especially by their need to secure pasture for their own domesticated herds. In Asia one wild horse held on into the modern age, the takhi or Przewalski's horse *Equus ferus przewalskii*.[17] With the extinction of Europe's tarpan *E. f. ferus* in the first years of the nineteenth century, the takhi became the world's last wild horse.[18] It, too, soon became extinct in the wild, but the survival of a small captive population has allowed the species to begin the slow process of returning to its native steppe.

Przewalski's horses are small and stocky, pony-sized with uniform yellow-dun coats, cream-colored bellies, and black points at their hooves and muzzles. Their heads are especially large on account of their muscular jaws and large teeth, adaptations to their diet of tough steppe vegetation. They have manes typical of wild equids, black and upright, and in overall appearance they strongly resemble the two Asian wild ass species, the khulan and kiang.[19]

The last wild horse is named for the first Westerner to obtain a specimen, Nikolay Przhevalsky. Col. Przhevalsky was of course not the first person, not even the first Westerner, to discover the wild horse. Steppe peoples had hunted both Przewalski's horse and the tarpan for thousands of years. Despite humanity's long familiarity with the equid, the horses lived far enough removed from settled and literate civilizations that they largely escaped documentation until the modern era. Their first known appearance in writing was around 900 CE, when a monk in Tibet made note of them. They were mentioned again in *The Secret History of the Mongols*, which tells of a herd crossing paths with Chinggis Khan (c.1158–1227) in 1226 as the Great Khan set out on campaign against the Tangut Empire (1038–1227).[20]

The takhi appear again in seventeenth and eighteenth century accounts of Manchu emperors, and in a single Western account. It was not until Col. Przhevalsky's sightings and acquisition of a skull and hide in 1878 that the wild horses came to wider attention. By the time Przhevalsky and later explorers encountered them, the horses' range had already contracted from the whole of the Eurasian steppe belt to merely a few pockets of innermost Asia.[21] What caused this catastrophic decline is unclear, but the settler invasion of the steppe as the Russian and Qing empires sought to consolidate their territories and placate their growing and land-hungry populations was all but certainly a major factor.

The wild horses diminished across their entire range, and in China last survived in Xinjiang's Dzungar Basin, likely into the 1930s or 1940s. Precisely when they disappeared from China is unknown, but the last wild takhi seen anywhere was across the border in Mongolia in 1969.[22] Luckily, horses had been taken into captivity and successfully bred in Europe. In 1985 eleven takhi from the United Kingdom and East Germany arrived in Xinjiang, where they settled at a specially built breeding center. Five more horses from West Germany joined them in 1988, and that same year the first foal was born.[23]

As more foals were born and the herd grew, reintroduction into the wild was finally attempted. In 2001 twenty-seven horses were released in Kalamaili Nature Reserve in the Dzungar Basin. The horses were not given total freedom; they were allowed to roam from spring to fall, but in winter they were corralled to allow supplemental feeding and to avoid conflict with herdsmen who graze their livestock in the reserve. Conditions for the horses were poor from the outset. Heavy human activity—including coal mining and the presence of around 2,000 herdsmen and their 200,000 head of stock—led to Kalamaili's reduction from 18,000 to 12,800 sq km (6,950 to 4,940 sq mi). Just as dangerous, a highway bisects the reserve, and several horses have died due to vehicle collisions. Despite such dangers, the Kalamaili herd has bred successfully and has grown due to both natural births and the introduction of members from the captive herds.[24]

Another, smaller, semi-wild group was released into Gansu's Anxi Nature Reserve in 1997, and they have struggled ever since. Starting with a founding population of only ten, the horses have faced disease, severe wolf predation, and low fertility, all of which have contributed to a high loss of foals. Without a continuous influx of new members from the captive population, the Anxi herd will be unable to grow and become self-sustaining.[25]

Despite the difficulties, China's population of takhi is steadily growing. Intensive management of both the captive and wild herds—from careful breeding selection to supplemental feeding—have helped expand their number to over 700 horses. To truly be wild, eventually the takhi will have to be given more space and the freedom to fend for themselves through winter. Yet the horses will require careful husbandry for a long time to come, if for no other reason than the constant danger of inbreeding. The current population—descended from only fifteen founders—has worrisomely low genetic diversity.[26] Nonetheless, their success to date is an encouraging sign that wild horses may once again roam the steppes of far western China.

The most peculiar denizen of the steppe is the saiga *Saiga tatarica*, a small, goat-sized antelope with a chestnut-yellow coat and a white underside. The distinguishing feature of the saiga is its pair of bulbous, downward-facing nostrils. These huge nasal cavities help filter the large amounts of dust the herds kick up in the summer, and warm the frigid air in winter. Females are hornless, but males sport wax-colored, ringed horns.

Saiga congregate in massive herds and migrate back and forth across the steppe. In the distant past they ranged across the great grasslands of the north, from England, across Eurasia and Beringia to Canada. Over the millennia their range shrank to the Central Asian deserts and dry steppes.[27] China is at the southern edge of the species' natural distribution, but the fragmentary historical record suggests there were multiple, perhaps separated, populations of saiga in Xinjiang and farther east.[28]

Like so many other animals, the saiga has been known to the Chinese for millennia but elicited little notice except for the perceived medicinal value of its horns. Saiga horns appear as an ingredient as early as the third century *Classic of Herbal Medicine*.[29] Horns came from saiga within and beyond China's shifting borders. In the nineteenth and early twentieth centuries vast numbers came from the herds of the Russian Empire, and into the 1920s and 1930s tens of thousands found their way into China's medicine markets each year.[30] The horns attracted such high prices that at one point the Chinese postal service refused to take them due to the amount of robbery the horns attracted.[31]

Into the 1950s saiga were still found from the Kazakhstan border across the Dzungar Basin into the northernmost sliver of Gansu and westernmost Inner Mongolia. Saiga are migratory animals, but the herds were soon cut off from their lands and relatives in Kazakhstan when fences went up along the border. In the same years the new

Communist regime settled large numbers of Chinese, including many soldiers, to help secure and develop the region. Their plows destroyed swathes of grassland, and access to motorized vehicles and semi-automatic weapons made the saiga easy sources of meat and horn. It was a catastrophe. Surveys from the 1960s onwards found no living saiga, only skulls.[32]

After nearly three decades without saiga, China decided to reintroduce the species. From 1988 to 1991, eleven antelopes from Germany and the US came to a breeding center in Wuwei, Gansu. To date the effort has proven a challenge. The captive herd grew, but extremely low genetic diversity left its health fragile.[33] After reaching 130 members in 2013, a harsh winter, followed by an outbreak of disease, crashed the population to only twenty in 2018. Parallel efforts to reintroduce wild herds were even less successful. Of twenty-one saiga brought from Kazakhstan, only two survived the initial move and both later died; of thirty from Russia, only one survived and was eventually sent to join the captive herd.[34]

China's captive saiga are too few and too inbred to have hope of successful release into the wild. The only real hope now is for herds from Kazakhstan to migrate into Xinjiang. Yet there are too many barriers, physical and political, for the saiga to return of their own accord. If they are to recolonize Xinjiang then the two countries must jointly manage the transboundary population, a proposition fraught with difficulties. To complicate matters, suitable habitats in Xinjiang are now so small and fragmented that most are not suitable for year-round habitation, meaning that establishing a permanent saiga population in China may not be realistic. The future may prove otherwise, but the time for wild saiga in China may be past.[35]

Fang, Feather, & Fur

THE wolf is the top predator of the steppe, some roaming alone, others following the great migratory herds of gazelles. As with predators elsewhere in China, wolves were declared a pest and threat to livestock in the 1950s, and local governments were tasked with their removal. This view of wolves as damaging to pastoralists' herds and livelihoods was not baseless. Predators have always made use of livestock, whether for lack of wild prey or simply because the ease of the meal outweighs the fear of man. In just 1952 in Alxa Banner, eighty-seven families lost 120 camels, 184 horses, 95 head of cattle, and 356 sheep and goats to wolves.[1] And although the numbers of animals taken from a single herd or flock was often small, many families lived in or at the edge of poverty and could ill afford any loss. Most herders accepted wolves as an irritating but inescapable fact of life, but some were eager to rid themselves of the predators, and the authorities encouraged them with organizational help, free ammunition, and later with prizes and bounties.[2]

The campaigns were extensive, and produced quick results. In Ningxia—a small province—provincial and local governments quickly raised 231 "wolf-smashing teams" with over 4,300 members to carry out the effort.[3] Using traps, guns, poison, and any other method at their disposal, they killed 942 wolves and fifty-nine leopards by September 1952. Campaign members declared that, at an average depredation of twenty-five sheep and goats per adult wolf or leopard, this saved the province from the loss of 17,500 animals and ¥105,000. Several outstanding wolf killers were declared "wolf-smashing heroes" and held up as models for other herders.[4]

The extermination campaigns continued into the 1970s, and the sustained effort nearly succeeded in removing wolves from China's grasslands and deserts. But wolf depredation never stopped. As the wolves were cleared from the steppe so were their natural prey, and as poor herding practices turned the grassland into desert there was less and less land to share. Human action had left them little choice but to raid for their meals. This phenomenon however, was not universal, and wolves survived over large, remote stretches of territory, along with their natural prey. As deadly as the extermination campaigns had been, they had relied heavily on shooting and trapping, and had largely eschewed the poisoning that had all but completely removed wolves from the contiguous United States. Many wolves escaped their hunters. Their prey, too, had never suffered so catastrophically as their North American counterparts, ultimately allowing some thousands of wolves to persist past the turn of the millennium.[5]

From the 1980s and into the 1990s as a spirit of wildlife protection formed and spread across Chinese society, wolves remained enemies of mankind, whether Han, Mongolian, or Tibetan.[6] Unlike North America where wolf attacks are vanishingly rare, wolves across China have a long history of scarring and scavenging humans. In those areas where wolves still lived during the famines of 1959–1961, many survivors witnessed the animals feeding on human corpses. Such experiences left wolves with a lingering reputation as fundamentally bad animals, and into the 1990s herders and workers would shoot wolves on sight.[7]

Eventually as attitudes towards wildlife shifted, herders and local authorities turned increasingly to nonlethal means of defending livestock from predation. The nationwide confiscation of guns also made life safer for wolves, and gradually they have begun to recolonize stretches of the steppe, reappearing in places they had not been seen for decades.[8] Official recognition of this change in attitude came in 2021, thirty-two years after the first list of protected species was issued, when wolves were finally given legal protection throughout China.[9]

The steppes and deserts of China host a great array of birds, many of them migratory visitors to wetland oases. Some however, such as the bustards, prefer dry land. Three species of bustard live in China. The largest and most widespread is the great bustard *Otis tarda*.[10] The great bustards are steppe birds found from Western Europe east to China, and as their name suggests they are the largest of the bustards.[11] Both male and female great bustards wear a drab plumage of brown and black mottled feathers on their backs with light-colored undersides. Once fully grown, the sexes are immediately distinguishable. Males on average stand about 1 m (3 ft 3 in) tall and are over twice as heavy as females, making them among the heaviest flying birds on Earth. They weigh up to 18 kg (40 lb) with a wingspan from 2.1 m to 2.7 m (6 ft 11 in to 8 ft 10 in). In addition to their greater size, males also sport beard-like, long white neck bristles in the breeding season, and as they age the feathers on their lower neck and breast turn a tawny brown.

There are two subspecies of great bustard in China, *O. t. dybowskii* in the grasslands of the northeast and North China, and *O. t. tarda* in the northwestern steppes of Xinjiang. Both subspecies are struggling, not only in China but across Eurasia.[12]

In summer *O. t. dybowskii* breeds on the steppes of Russia, Mongolia, and northeastern China, from Heilongjiang south through Jilin, Inner Mongolia and into Hebei. In winter they fly south, settling over a wide band stretching over the Qinling to the Yangtze. Genetic analysis suggests that the Chinese populations of *dybowskii* have been in continuous decline for the past four thousand years, in all probability a consequence of human destruction of bustard habitat combined with intensive hunting.[13] Their initial decline was slow, and at the turn of the twentieth century the eastern bustards remained widespread and relatively common in a few areas.[14] Bustards are exceptionally wary birds and therefore difficult to hunt,[15] but demand was such that they were a frequent sight in winter markets.[16]

In the northeast, bustards have lost much of the steppe that provided their breeding grounds, large swathes of it turned to agricultural land. To the south the bustards wintering in China began to dwindle rapidly in the 1950s and 1960s as the Maoist modernization drive reshaped the landscape. Their fall continued through the following decades, as the birds found fewer and fewer places suitable to their needs. Poyang Lake, for instance, hosted hundreds of wintering bustards even into the 1980s, but they have not been sighted there in over fifteen years.[17]

There is perhaps one bright spot for the eastern great bustards: climate change is expected to extend suitable wintering habitat within China. Although their most southerly wintering grounds at Dongting and Poyang lakes no longer fit their needs, suitable habitat on the Northeast Plain will expand, as will areas of southeast Hebei and northeast Henan. This of course depends on the goodwill and efforts of the local communities, as the bustards now heavily rely on cropland and the grain left on the fields to survive. A change in farming practices or the replacement of farmland with concrete and asphalt could negate any benefit a warming climate might otherwise bring to the bustards.[18]

In the northwest *O. t. tarda* faces a grim future. Very little is known about China's western bustards, but all evidence points to a rapid decline in numbers. The usual suspects—habitat loss and fragmentation—are the primary reasons, with other pressures such as pesticide use, poaching, egg collection and powerline collisions speeding their collapse. Farmers often destroy nesting sites when flooding fields to irrigate the land; some attempt to move the nests or eggs to safe ground, but the interference drives the female bustards to abandon their nests. A recent survey of their summer and winter ranges within Xinjiang indicated a 92% drop from the years 1988–1992, with no bustards at all found in their wintering range.[19] Followup surveys from 2014 to 2018 again found no bustards at their sole wintering site, and only a few dozen on several breeding grounds. Over 300 were spotted gathering at three sites in preparation for migration, but it is unclear how many reside in Xinjiang to breed and how many were merely transients.[20]

Along with the great bustard, China hosts breeding grounds of the Asian houbara bustard *Chlamydotis macqueenii*.[21] The Asian houbara is much smaller than *Otis tarda*, about two-thirds the size of its distant cousin. Like the great bustard, the houbara's plumage is brown on its top with a white underside. The marked differences in appearance are stripes of black feathers running down both sides of the neck, and in the males a lack of *O. tarda*'s distinctive beard bristles. Whereas the great bustard restricts itself to grassland, the houbara is equally at home on the steppe or in the desert.

The scientific community were unaware of the Chinese population of houbara until the 1980s when the birds were found in the Dzungar Basin. Early surveys estimated a small population of up to 500 birds.[22] Subsequent searches found additional houbaras littered discontinuously throughout Xinjiang and into the western reaches of Inner Mongolia and Gansu, leading to new estimates first of upwards of 2,000 birds,[23] and more recently of 6,000 to 8,000 in only the Dzungar Basin.[24] Like the great bustards, the houbaras are not resident in China year-round, but arrive in April and May to breed, then depart westwards in September to winter in southern Pakistan and Iran.[25] Research showed some populations in the Dzungar Basin suffered severe declines between 1998 and 2002, likely due to poaching and the expansion of mining, oil exploration, and agriculture into the houbara's habitat, but there has yet to be a more recent investigation into the health of China's houbaras.[26] A third bustard species, the little bustard *Tetrax tetrax*, lives in Xinjiang and Ningxia, but, other than that their range has contracted within recent decades, little is known of the birds.[27]

Whereas in the highlands of the far west pikas abound, in the lower steppes of the north and east marmots are the most common burrowing mammals. Now rare, the plains of Manchuria and eastern Inner Mongolia were once home to immense numbers of the tarbagan or Mongolian marmot *Marmota sibirica*.[28] Two thirteenth century European travelers, Marco Polo and William of Rubruck, noted the great numbers of marmots on the Mongolian plains.[29] Large, rotund rodents with rough, straw-yellow and brown fur, marmots have long been a staple food source for not only steppe nomads but carnivores such as wolves and eagles. Like prairie dogs of the American plains, marmots dig large burrows, but though they are social animals, they do not connect their burrows into sprawling towns.[30]

Aside from use as an emergency source of food, marmots found themselves inducted into Chinese medicine's long list of medicinal animals.[31] A Yuan text advised that marmot could be used to cure skin ulcers, and that a marmot skull hung beside a baby's head would cure insomnia.[32] Their skins were considered poor quality, and there was little demand for marmot furs until developments in Europe at the end of the nineteenth century.[33] A sudden spike in demand for sable coincided with the invention of new dyeing techniques which made marmot fur a viable, abundant, and cheap substitute for the more luxuriantly furred mustelids.[34]

The new demand for cheap imitation sable came just as railways opened the Manchurian and Inner Mongolian steppes and connected them to world markets. All this led to a massive influx of amateur marmot hunters, most of them Chinese farmers from Shandong with no trapping experience and desperate for any income they could find. Marmot furs entering the market spiked from a few thousand to over 2,000,000 only a few years later in 1911. The rush for furs devastated the marmot population.[35] Within only a few years marmots had been completely wiped out from most of the Manchurian steppe, and the populations in Inner Mongolia soon followed. By the mid-1920s China's marmots were practically exterminated.[36]

Although they were nearly wiped out from China, the marmots did have a small measure of revenge. The inexperienced Chinese farmers-turned-trappers, ignorant of the steppe's dangers and eager to take any and every marmot available, found on the grasslands not only furs but plague. Plague—from the bacterium *Yersinia pestis*, the same that caused the medieval Black Death in Europe—was and remains endemic in the tarbagan populations of Central Asia. Mongol hunters knew to avoid sick marmots and largely avoided the pestilence, but the unsuspecting Chinese took the sick and dying animals just as readily as the healthy ones. Scattered outbreaks had occurred for years, but in October 1910 fur hunters trading in the border town of Manzhouli fell ill, and from there the plague spread south along the railway into Manchuria.[37] Before the epidemic ended in March 1911, between 45,000 and 60,000 people were dead.[38]

There are still tarbagans in China today, yet they are few in number and have yet to recolonize most of their lost territory.[39] Continued fears of plague mean those that remain enjoy no official protections, but are instead killed to keep their numbers low.[40] Until tarbagans are treated as endangered instead of merely a reservoir of disease, there is little chance they will ever return to their former extent or abundance.

Within the People's Republic a host of fungi are held dear for their culinary or curative properties. Many have been valued for centuries or millennia, such as the *lingzhi*, the mushroom of immortality.[41] A bracket fungus of the *Ganoderma* genus, *lingzhi* was widely believed to impart great bodily and spiritual strength, and was a common motif in art. A caterpillar fungus found on the Tibetan Plateau, *yartsa gunbu*, is attributed with similar potency, and today regularly commands prices of thousands of dollars per kilogram.

Another such fungus has been at risk of overharvesting since the first half of the nineteenth century. *Leucocalocybe mongolica*, found on the grasslands from Zhangjiakou, Hebei north to Inner Mongolia between Baotou and Hulunbuir, and into Mongolia and Russia.[42] *L. mongolica* is a steppe mushroom prized as a culinary delicacy and for its purported medicinal powers. Demand for mushrooms boomed in the 1820s, leading to a surge in Chinese fortune seekers passing through the Great Wall each summer in search of the fungi. They picked swathes of grassland clean of *mongolica* and other steppe mushroom species, killing off local populations of marmots and fish to feed themselves. When the damage they caused to the land and to the local Mongols became too great to ignore, the Qing authorities forced them out, often against fierce and violent resistance. Demand for the mushrooms remained high late into the century, and even today *mongolica* is still coveted.[43] After generations of continued harvesting, combined with decades of grassland degradation, the steppe mushroom *Leucocalocybe mongolica* remains severely endangered.[44]

DESERTS

قوُملوُقى

Map of the Deserts of China

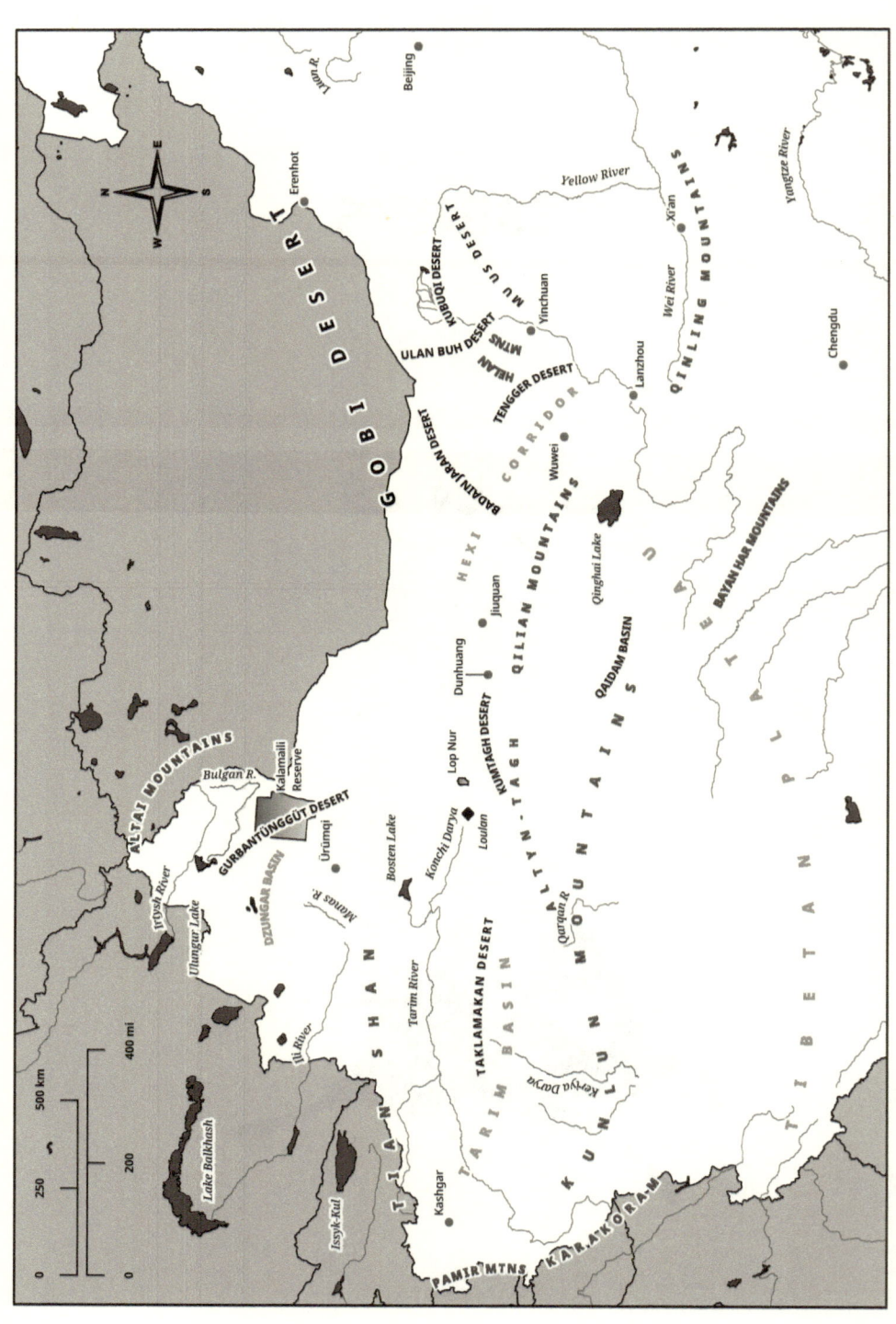

WHEN speaking of China, desert does not often come to mind, but nearly a third of the country consists of arid or semiarid land. The deserts are growing, and have been for decades as both climate change and the degradation of bordering steppe and forest allow the sands to advance.[1] China has a large number of separate deserts, stretching from eastern Inner Mongolia west to Xinjiang. Many are sandy, marked by shifting or stationary dunes, some of which, such as those in the Badain Jaran, rise to immense heights.[2] Among China's other sandy and gravel deserts are the Mu Us, Tengger, Qaidam, and Kumtagh. China's most famous desert, which it shares with Mongolia, is the Gobi, primarily a cold, rocky expanse of bare stone.[3]

Xinjiang is home to China's greatest deserts. The Tarim Basin, a dry expanse stretching over 500,000 sq km (193,000 sq mi), lies in the south of Xinjiang between the Tian Shan and Kunlun Mountains. It is home to China's largest sandy desert, the Taklamakan, an extremely hot and harsh landscape, but not completely dry. Through it run a number of rivers, most importantly the Tarim, China's longest inland river. The Tarim once terminated in a large saline lake, Lop Nur, but the lake has dried up completely due to water diversion projects along the rivers and is now an empty basin.[4] To the north, between the Tian Shan and the Altai Mountains, spreads the Dzungar (or Junggar) Basin, a smaller desert that receives more rainfall and therefore hosts a greater abundance of plant life. There are stretches of shifting sand dunes in the Dzungar Basin, yet it is primarily a rocky landscape.[5]

The deserts are home to few people, though communities and even large cities have existed in the past, only to disappear with shifts in climate and water supply. For most of history the desert regions have been outside of Han Chinese control. The Han dynasty was the first to take control of large arid areas, most notably during its expansion west into the Tarim Basin. They made efforts to secure their hold on the oases and surrounding lands through the settlement of agriculturalists—farmer-soldiers meant to protect the empire's lands while growing their own sustenance. The efforts didn't last more than a few generations, and the irrigation works likely changed the basin's hydrology so dramatically as to drain Lop Nur. The desiccation of the lake lead to the abandonment of the ancient oasis town of Loulan, which had once thrived on its banks.[6] Eventually the rivers shifted again, and the lake refilled.

Today the primary residents of the Tarim's oases are the Uyghurs, a Turkic Muslim group linguistically and culturally more closely related to other Central Asian peoples than to the Han. As during the Han and Tang dynasties, since the Communist takeover and integration of Xinjiang into the People's Republic, Han settlers have been forced or enticed into the region, and in parts of Xinjiang they now outnumber the Uyghurs and other native groups. Within the desert oases however, the majority of cities and towns remain predominantly Uyghur. How long this may last is uncertain, as in recent years the Chinese government has aggressively moved to suppress Uyghur culture and reverse their population growth, seeking—in the time-honored fashion stretching back to the Qin and Han—to erase their separate identity and subsume them into the Han cultural sphere.[7]

Although true desert creatures such as the wild camel make their homes in the most inhospitable stretches of land, much of China's steppe wildlife ranges into the deserts as well. The semi-arid desert steppes between the two biomes even host large animals such as gazelles, wolves, and Przewalski's horses.

Black Tails & Paddle Tails

SHARING the desert steppe with Przewalski's horse is another equid, the khulan *Equus hemionus hemionus*, a subspecies of the Asiatic wild ass (also known as the onager or hemione). The two are strikingly similar in appearance, and indeed Westerners' early sightings of Przewalski's horses prompted much argument over whether they were a separate species or misidentified khulan. With a similar coat coloration and pattern, the same short dark mane, and growing to a roughly equal size as Przewalski's horse, the two are difficult to tell apart at a distance. Perhaps the clearest distinguishing trait is the khulan's larger, distinctly asinine ears.

Khulan were once found across most of the arid lands of Central Asia, and within China they extended from the far northwest to the northeast. During the reign of the great expansionist Han Emperor Wu, khulan were found throughout the Hexi Corridor that runs through Gansu and connected the imperial heartland of Guanzhong with its newly acquired territories in the Tarim Basin. The Han emperor was so delighted by the arrival of a captured herd that he commemorated the event with a poem. Artistic depictions of wild ass dating to the same period have been found at sites at Wuwei and Dunhuang, major oases along the Hexi Corridor.[1]

From the Han dynasty forward khulan roamed the dry lands of northern China and Mongolia. In his *Compendium of Materia Medica* (本草綱目), Li Shizhen (李時珍, 1518–1593) noted that khulan were found as far east as the Liaodong Peninsula, and in 1762 the Qing Qianlong Emperor received tribute of khulan from Jiuquan, originally a Han dynasty frontier outpost in western Gansu.[2] The French missionary-naturalist Père Armand David noted wild asses were present north of the Great Wall in the early 1870s.[3]

There is no known record of just when or why khulan disappeared from the northeast. Han settlers began to migrate in great numbers north into Manchuria and beyond the Great Wall into the steppe of Inner Mongolia throughout the second half of the nineteenth century. Their presence and their conversion of grassland into cultivated fields may have been a major factor in driving the khulan away. Khulan have long been prized for their flesh, even prompting the adage "in heaven there is the flesh of the dragon; on earth the flesh of the wild ass."[4] As such the equines have always attracted the attention of hunters, so it is possible that hunting pressure contributed to the northeast population's disappearance, but there is little to go on except speculation.

Khulan are still present from Erenhot, Inner Mongolia in a narrow band along the Sino-Mongolian border west to the Dzungar Basin in northern Xinjiang. They were abundant in Dzungaria until they were largely hunted out over the course of the 1950s and 1960s. The drastic collapse of the population was hardly unique to China; *Equus hemionus* had been suffering grievously across the entirety of its range for centuries, eventually disappearing from the Levant and Arabia and from most of Central and South Asia. Mongolia is now home to over eighty percent of the world's remaining onagers.[5] Nonetheless, China's khulan have seen some recovery. In 1982 when researchers surveyed the Kalamaili Reserve, the equid's last stronghold in northern Xinjiang, they counted only 358 khulan in the 17,000 sq km (6,560 sq mi) of the reserve. Yet only a few years later a second survey spotted 510.[6] Over time the Kalamaili herds have grown, to around 3,200 in 2019.[7] Most recently they have faced danger from the encroachment of extractive industry into the reserve. The northeastern Dzungar Basin hosts massive coal deposits, and the local government reduced the size of the reserve to allow the coal industry to begin operating on its lands in 2006. Consequently the khulan have seen their territory reduced, and their scarce water sources either cut off or fouled. Policy shifted in 2015, and extractive activities were ended by 2018, allowing the khulan to reclaim some of their prior habitat. However, construction of a new expressway and railway, combined with the effect of the existing highway through the reserve, further fragmented their habitat and presented increased dangers to their movement.[8] To worsen matters, climate change is predicted to severely reduce the khulans' habitat within Kalamaili.[9]

China's khulan once benefited from their connection to the far larger Mongolian population, but the extensive border fencing erected in the 1980s and 1990s has all but stopped their cross-border movements.[10] The Alashan population in western Inner Mongolia was especially reliant on its connections to the Mongolian herds, and shrank to only a few dozen members.[11] It has now been years since field surveys or border guards have seen any sign of the Alashan khulan.[12] With poaching now extremely rare, the greatest threat to Inner Mongolia's khulan is fencing, not merely the border fence but also fences erected to demarcate recently privatized pastures. In the past great expanses of the steppe were long under the control of powerful families and Buddhist monasteries, yet Mongols traditionally allowed communal access to almost all pasture. Central government efforts to settle the nomadic herders entailed dividing the grasslands into fenced family plots, and despite efforts to mitigate the resultant damage, the land remains crisscrossed and fragmented with fences. The barriers constrain their movement and have isolated some populations that are so small they face the prospect of severely diminished genetic diversity, perhaps ultimately leading to their collapse and disappearance.[13]

Another hoofed desert dweller is the goitered gazelle *Gazella subgutturosa*, found across Central Asia from Iran to Mongolia and China. Medium-sized gazelles ranging from 18 to 43 kg (40 to 95 lb), *subgutturosa* sport a range of coat colors, from white or yellow to red, brown, or gray. Invariably though, their bellies are white. In Mongolian they are called *kara-sulta* "black-tailed," a feature that makes them readily distinguishable from the otherwise similar Mongolian gazelle. Males are readily discerned from females, as females do not grow horns. Males' throats also visibly enlarge during the rut, giving the species its common name.

Historical information on China's goitered gazelle is sparse, but in the 1870s Nikolay Przhevalsky noted they were found in the Ordos and Gobi west to the Helan Mountains and Qaidam Basin.[14] Later sojourners noted they were abundant in the deserts of western Gansu and Xinjiang.[15] Goitered gazelle are extremely shy of people, and keep to the most inaccessible stretches of desert where they can still find forage. This may be an artifact of human persecution, as Przhevalsky noted that where they were not hunted they were happy to graze near farming communities.[16]

China's goitered gazelles remain poorly studied, with only the vaguest information of their population and distribution available. What is known is that the gazelles have been losing both territory and numbers to the standard threats: hunting, agricultural expansion, mining, and oil extraction. Expanding herds of livestock also may threaten them, as they eat many of the same foods, which in hard winters could leave the gazelles with too little to survive.[17] They remain fairly numerous in parts of desert Xinjiang, but testing has shown they possess worrisomely low genetic diversity, lower than even the critically endangered saiga and Przewalski's gazelle.[18]

Among the most surprising inhabitants of the dry Dzungar Basin are beavers, China's only population and a unique subspecies shared with neighboring Mongolia.[19] Imaginatively, it is known as the Sino-Mongolian beaver *Castor fiber birulai*. Fossils indicate that beavers existed in much of China in the far past, but there is practically no evidence to suggest they remained widespread into historic times. Beavers were long a mainstay of the fur trade, in China as elsewhere, and the Eurasian beaver suffered such heavy hunting across the whole of the continent that the species' entire population is believed to have fallen to around 1,200 animals at the turn of the twentieth century.[20] Therefore it seems reasonable to speculate that beavers were once found over a much wider area than today, if not throughout China then at least regionally.

There are fewer than 1,000 Sino-Mongolian beavers remaining—around 500 in China and 300 in Mongolia.[21] The population is now so small that it faces the real threat of inbreeding; it already suffers from low genetic diversity.[22] The beavers are currently restricted to the Ulungur River watershed, with the largest groups in the Bulgan River, a tributary of the Ulungur that begins in the Altai Mountains of southwestern Mongolia and flows to Ulungur Lake in Xinjiang. A reserve for the beavers was established in 1980, at which point there were 162 families—the same number found in 2018. In the intervening years the total population has fluctuated to some degree, and the beavers have disappeared from some sites, but despite decades of conservation efforts their status is little changed.[23]

While Mongolia has had some success in reintroducing beavers to their former habitat, China's lone effort failed. Beavers were once also found in the Irtysh River, which runs from the Altai north of the Ulungur, through Kazakhstan and Russia to the Ob River and then to the Arctic Sea. But the beavers disappeared in the 1980s, and after a further two families of beavers were relocated to the Irtysh in 1992, a survey eleven years later found no trace of any beavers in China's stretch of the river.[24]

The beavers now face little threat from hunting. Instead they compete with the surrounding human population for wood and water. A dam on the upper Bulgan River within China has lowered the water table and blocked migration between the Mongolian and Chinese populations. Many of the poplars, on which the beavers rely for food and wood for their homes, have been cut down—much of the wood destined to fuel stoves. New trees have difficulty growing, as livestock eat up all the seedlings they find. Only the beavers within the reserve are well protected, but new efforts to enlist local support to monitor the beavers and replant trees along the waterways, if successful, could in time allow the castoridine engineers outside the reserve to finally expand again.[25] They will need the breathing room; as with so many other species, climate change threatens to shrink the little suitable habitat that remains for the beavers.[26]

In the Deep Desert

O F all the animals that live in the deserts of China and Mongolia, one of the most endangered is also one of the least known—the wild camel *Camelus ferus*. Restricted now to only a few patches of some of the most remote and inhospitable landscapes on the planet, the wild camels have weathered decades at the edge of extinction. *C. ferus* is the last wild camel species still remaining, and it is estimated that only around 700 members survive in China, with another 550 to the north in Mongolia.[1]

As is seemingly necessary for every species, there was a protracted taxonomic battle over the status of the wild camel, namely whether it was in fact an independent species or merely descended from escaped domesticated camels. There are a few physical differences between the domestic Bactrian *Camelus bactrianus* and *C. ferus*. The Bactrian is on the whole larger, with a generally heavier appearance, particularly in its two humps. The humps on *ferus* are shorter and more conical, and unlike in *bactrianus* they do not slump over when depleted of fat.[2] Wild camels also have a lighter, sandy-colored coat, less shaggy than the domestics'. Despite these morphological differences, debate over the wild camels' taxonomy did not subside until the recent development of genetic testing, which has definitively proven that the two camels are clearly distinct.[3]

Domesticated two-humped camels have been a feature of northern Chinese and Silk Road cultures for millennia. They are a particularly common motif in Tang dynasty art, when they had great importance as the "ships of the desert" that facilitated the Tang's trade with Inner Asia. The presence of camels is therefore well attested throughout the region's history. Domesticated camels can and no doubt did escape captivity to form feral populations, and from a distance or to the untrained eye, they are difficult to distinguish from their wild cousins. Nonetheless, historical records do document wild camels, and note the difference between the wild and domesticated species.

There is sparse evidence to go on, but the current best guess is that *ferus* once spread from central Kazakhstan east through Xinjiang, southern Mongolia and to the great bend of the Yellow River in China.[4] Han dynasty writings noted wild camels in Inner Mongolia, while eleventh-century records also record them spread from northern

123

Shaanxi west through Ningxia and the Hexi Corridor. As late as 1160 wild camels were even present near the headwaters of the Luan River in Hebei, north of Beijing. The Yuan period saw the camels begin to retreat west, and by the nineteenth century they were no longer found east of Lanzhou in Gansu.[5]

It was after this centuries-long retreat that the wild camels first came to the notice of the wider world. In March 1877 the Russian explorer Nikolay Przhevalsky became the first to scientifically describe the camels, after he received several skins and skulls from hired hunters who killed the animals at the edge of their refuge in the Kumtagh section of the Taklamakan Desert, southeast of Lop Nur and north of the Altyn-Tagh. Even at this time the camel population was noticeably falling. Przhevalsky's local guide told him that twenty years prior the camels had been numerous around his village by Lop Nur, and that he had seen caravans of dozens or even a hundred camels. But as the village's human population grew the camel population shrank. Village hunters killed the camels for their fat, meat, and skins, which were made into clothing. Wild camels have exceptionally acute senses, making them extremely difficult to hunt, and Przhevalsky's guide said he and the other local hunters did not set out expressly to hunt camels but only ever killed them opportunistically. Yet the guide, an old man, claimed to have killed around a hundred camels in his time, and the hunting took its toll. By the time Przhevalsky arrived, years often passed between camel sightings near the village.[6]

Subsequent European explorers in the region were eager to sight and shoot the camels, yet they were few enough that their quest for hides and bones had little impact on the animals.[7] Instead of foreign naturalists and big game hunters it was the local inhabitants that continued to stalk the camels and drive them into the deepest reaches of the deserts. In the course of his three expeditions into the wastes of Xinjiang, the Swedish explorer Sven Hedin (1865–1952) avidly sought information concerning the wild camels. On his first expedition, while following the Keriya Darya that flows from the Kunlun Mountains north into the depths of the Taklamakan, Hedin encountered a shepherd who, along with his dozen or so community members, survived primarily on camel flesh during the winters.[8] Whether such localized persecution was enough to impact the larger population is unclear. The camels are nomadic, shifting their range seasonally and in response to changes in the presence of water and humans. Hedin came across numerous places where camels had once been numerous but had since become rare, but across its range he found evidence that the camels remained relatively widespread, if few in number. He even heard that the market price for camel skins had fallen, and that consequently hunters paid less attention to the animals.[9]

After these early investigations the status of the camels again became a mystery for many decades. Soviet surveys of the Mongolian Gobi led to the establishment of protections for Mongolia's wild camels, but in China surveys had to wait until 1980–1981. The initial searches estimated up to 200 wild camels survived around the by then dry Lop Nur. The first full survey of the camels' range in China came in 1995–1996, and the results were disheartening. Camels remained in four areas and totaled an estimated 380–500 individuals.

In northwestern Gansu camels crossed back and forth into Mongolia, but military guards along the border, unpaid and isolated, hunted the camels and other wildlife for their meat.[10] To compound their troubles, a boom in mining, legal and illegal, was poisoning the land with potassium cyanide. A camel population in the central Taklamakan was facing the onslaught of an expanding petroleum industry, and a newly constructed highway bisected the camels' migration route.[11]

Even though *C. ferus* and *C. bactrianus* are separate species, they can still interbreed. This ability to hybridize has become a major threat to the survival of *ferus* as a genetically distinct species, as wild

125

camels are all too happy to mate with their domesticated counterparts. This had already become a problem for the camels in southeast Xinjiang on the north side of the Altyn-Tagh, as well as those to the north in Gansu and Mongolia.[12]

The most frightening and astounding threat to *ferus* was its subjection to nearly four dozen nuclear blasts. From China's first nuclear detonation in October 1964 to its last in July 1996, all of China's forty-seven nuclear tests were conducted at Lop Nur, over twenty of them above ground. It is unknown if the tests had any direct impacts on the camels of the area, or to what level of radiation they were exposed over the three decades of testing. Astoundingly, to this day Lop Nur's camels have shown no ill effects, their health and reproduction seemingly suffering no impact.[13]

As in the past, it was hunting that brought the greatest harm. Local hunters had continued throughout the decades to hunt the camels, but the threat they posed was soon superseded. When the government loosened its hold on society and the economy in the 1980s, many of the restrictions that had prevented mining in the desert were rescinded or simply ignored, by miners and authorities alike. Miners ventured into the most desolate and unexplored sections of desert to search for gold, armed with explosives for excavation and firearms for hunting—and for defending or seizing mines.[14] Even the military established mines, which it staffed with heavily armed soldiers.[15] The mining operations took no account of the fragility of the local ecosystems, and drained or fouled precious water sources on which desert life depended. Miners not only gunned down camels and other wildlife to eat, but used their explosives to make landmines to lay for unsuspecting animals.[16] Miners were not the only hunters. A government geological survey team that had come through the Altyn-Tagh in 1980 shot forty camels for food, a severe blow to an already small and dwindling population.[17]

Men hunted not only for food but for sport. The 1995–1996 survey team heard of police and government officials traveling from cities around Xinjiang and western Gansu to hunt camels in the desert.[18] During the 1990s this was a problem across China's west. Men in positions of authority—and with access to modern firearms—took all-wheel drive vehicles into remote landscapes to chase and gun down wildlife for sport. Others more interested in the profits from selling animal parts hired and supplied teams to do the work. Many of the targeted species, like the wild camels, where endangered and legally protected, which if anything only made them more valuable. Within the camels' range, the Altyn-Tagh was particularly rife with poachers and illegal miners. The pressure on *ferus* became so great and their survival so precarious that their natural predator, the wolf, became a mortal threat to surviving populations, forcing conservationists to contemplate culling wolves—as is done in Mongolia—to save camels.[19]

Apathetic officials were initially reluctant to act, but from the late 1990s the situation slowly began to improve. Paper preserves were gradually turned into properly staffed and protected nature reserves. The nationwide confiscation of guns helped reduce poaching. More recently, prospecting and mining within the camel's habitat are finally being stopped. Threats remain, including the continued risk of hybridization with domestic Bactrians, but on the whole the situation has greatly improved for *ferus*, and the populations in some areas are even growing.[20] The camels of the Altyn-Tagh and Kumtagh are multiplying now that they are under effective protection. Those in the Taklamakan remain subject to greater pressure from human encroachment, while the camels of the Mongolian border have disappeared, unable to survive in the area after the erection of the border fence.[21] As of late 2021, there were over 700 wild camels roaming within China.[22]

Even with the worst of the manmade threats under control, the wild camels still face the dangers of a changing climate. Already living in one of the most extreme environments on Earth, a warming planet will rob *ferus* of much of its remaining habitat. In the Kumtagh Desert alone, even a moderate change of climate is projected to reduce camel habitat by over forty percent by the 2050s.[23] If China's wild camels are to weather the changes to come they must be given not only stringent protection from human disturbance but also the freedom to roam over ever greater stretches of the desert.[24]

In Mongolia, just across the border from the camels in northern Gansu, live the last few surviving Gobi bears *Ursus arctos gobiensis,* the smallest subspecies of brown bear. Both the historical record and physical evidence are too scanty to determine whether the bears ever lived within Chinese territory, but it is possible they once did. Their population in Mongolia suffered a severe drop during the Communist era when officials drilled wells in their home range to expand livestock grazing, but any prior contraction in the bear's range is unknown. In the past decades bears have occasionally been spotted across the border: in summer 2015 one young male wandered through Chinese territory for several weeks. More bears may have made similar raids into China unnoticed; the land is so desolate and the people so few they could easily avoid detection.[25] If the bears survive the next several decades, climate change may push them southeast in search of their preferred food, perhaps into China.[26]

In ecosystems as extreme and as harsh as true desert, few species can thrive. One that does is the Xinjiang ground jay *Podoces biddulphi*, a bird endemic to the Taklamakan and neighboring arid regions of Qinghai and Gansu.[27] The Xinjiang ground jay has a sandy plumage to blend in with the desert landscape and protect it from predators, and is a common sight in those areas of the Taklamakan that support plant life. They are as widespread and ubiquitous as any bird might be in a vast sandy waste, but the scanty food base means that there are likely no more than an estimated 6,700 breeding pairs in existence. Along with the rest of the desert's wildlife, the ground jays have suffered from decades of increasing human impact, ranging from oil exploration and extraction to overgrazing. Although their population has seemingly declined in the last century, the birds do not now face any existential threats.[28]

Oases

SINCE the 1950s the massive restructuring of the Taklamakan's main waterways, the Tarim River and its tributaries, has caused severe damage to the desert's wildlife. To make the desert bloom, the rivers had much of their flow diverted to irrigation projects. As happened during the Han dynasty, the colonization of the desert with irrigated agriculture caused Lop Nur and other water bodies to shrink. The loss of water flow led to the disappearance of what remained of Lop Nur in 1970.[1]

The diversion projects were devastating for the health of the waterways and the ecosystems they supported. One of the most severely affected species was a fish unique to the Tarim River Basin, the big-head schizothoracin *Aspiorhynchus laticeps*. This endemic fish was found in most streams, rivers, and lakes in the basin, and into the early 1970s it was caught in large amounts in the basin's rivers and Bosten Lake—Bosten Lake alone saw harvests of 100 tonnes a year before the catch fell precipitously to 20 tonnes from 1965, likely a sign of overfishing. By 1974 the schizothoracin and other native fish had disappeared from the lake completely. An extensive survey in 1992–1993 validated long held worries—a total of twenty-one fish were found in three locations. The water diversion infrastructure had fragmented the waterways, preventing the big-heads and other migratory fish from reaching their spawning sites, and dooming many of the few juveniles that were born to be swept from the streams and rivers and into irrigation works. Conservation efforts to restore the schizothoracin are underway, including attempts to breed the fish, but a near total lack of understanding of the basic life history of the species make that task especially difficult.[2] The most recent research has unveiled new worries. Another fish of the Tarim Basin has been found to be a hybrid of *A. laticeps* and *Schizothorax biddulphi* the Tarim schizothoracin. Although hybridization is likely a natural occurrence, because both the big-head and Tarim schizothoracins are now endangered, extensive mixing of the two species increases the likelihood of both fish disappearing as distinct species.[3] Even if hybridization is minimized and the big-head schizothoracin adapts well to aquaculture, the wild population's prospects ultimately will not improve until the Tarim Basin's water systems are put right.

When the desert's rivers ran higher and the lakes were full, migratory birds would congregate in the water bodies and wetlands in astounding numbers. Przhevalsky reported seeing hundreds of thousands, perhaps millions of waterfowl over the course of two weeks at Lop Nur, most of them members of just over two dozen species of ducks.[4] Migrating waterfowl and other birds still find their way to the remaining desert waters, but they no longer reach the numbers of times past. Otters shared the waters with the birds, and into the nineteenth century the local inhabitants hunted them for their skins, which they sent as tribute to the Manchu court.[5] Wild boar, too, were once common in the riparian woodlands and reed beds of the lower Tarim Basin, and though they still remain their numbers are a shadow of prior times.

Red deer of several subspecies are found across much of China, from the far Northeast to the deserts of Xinjiang. Of all of them, perhaps the most exceptional and endangered are the Tarim red deer *Cervus elaphus yarkandensis*.[6] Native to the forests and reed meadows of the valleys of the Tarim River, Konchi Darya, and Qarqan River, *yarkandensis* are uniquely adapted among red deer to such extremes of aridity and heat.[7] Western adventurers in the late nineteenth and early twentieth centuries found the deer to be abundant, but hunting and the loss of habitat to agriculture and oil works has caused their numbers to decline.[8] No more than 5,000 were thought to remain in the wild in 1991, and now there may only remain three small populations of several dozen deer each.[9] There is, of course, a substantial captive population which could help to boost the wild community, though for now farmed *yarkandensis* by and large are bred not for release but for their antlers.[10]

虤

Wolves, foxes, and lynx lived in or passed through the Tarim Valley, and Pallas's cat was a commonly sighted resident, but the Caspian tiger *Panthera tigris virgata* was the apex predator of the region.[11] If the sparse historical record is any indication, the numbers and range of the Tarim Basin's tigers seemed to fluctuate. Western explorers and adventurers heard of places where tigers were once common but had become rare, and other locations where tigers had in recent years grown numerous.[12] Local herders and hunters regularly killed the tigers, whether in retaliation for snatching away members of their flocks or for their hides, which sold to Chinese buyers for a dear price.[13] The tigers lived not only in the Tarim Basin along the main waterways, but north and west, past Ürümqi through the Ili and Manas river valleys and the surrounding Tian Shan into Kazakhstan.[14] Xinjiang's tigers, likely never especially numerous, disappeared over the early decades of the twentieth century, many poisoned for depredation on livestock. Rumored sightings persisted into the early 1960s, but just when China's last Caspian tigers vanished is a mystery.[15] The remaining Caspians in Central Asia fared no better—by the 1960s the entire subspecies was extinct.[16] Yet perhaps in future tigers will return to Xinjiang. Kazakhstan is now moving ahead with plans to introduce Amur tigers—the Caspians' closest relatives—into the Lake Balkhash region roughly 550 km (340 mi) from the Chinese border.[17] It will take time to firmly establish the new population, and more time still to build a corridor of suitable habitat into China, but the return of tigers into far western China has become a real if distant possibility.

WESTERN HIGHLANDS

Map of the High Mountain West of China

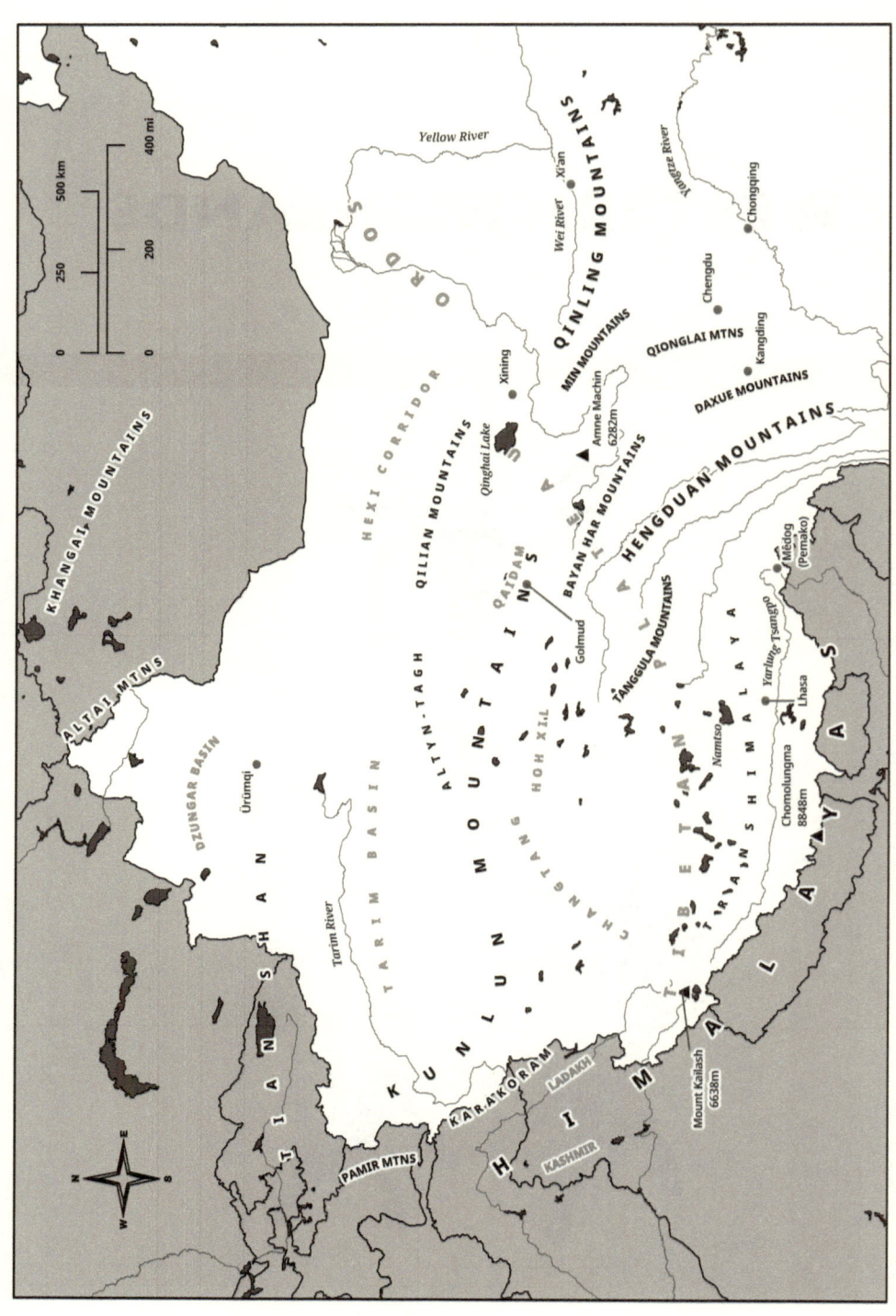

I N the far west of the People's Republic rise some of the world's highest mountain chains. For millennia the Qilian Mountains have funneled traders and armies through the Hexi Corridor between North China and Inner Asia. The Altai Mountains of Kazakhstan, Russia, and Mongolia dip into northern Xinjiang, while the Tian Shan range juts into the province farther south, separating the Dzungar and Tarim Basins. Xinjiang's southwestern border runs through the Karakoram, separating China from Kashmir.

To the south rises the immense and towering Tibetan Plateau. A jumble of peaks, valleys, and brackish lakes with forest along its southern and eastern edges, the Tibetan Plateau is a vast expanse covering 2.2 million sq km (850,000 sq mi), roughly the size of Alaska and California combined, or nine times the size of the UK. In the east the Hengduan Mountains divide the Han and Tibetan lands, while to the north the Altyn-Tagh and Kunlun ranges separate the plateau from the deserts of the Tarim Basin. In the south the Himalayas form a great wall between Tibet and the Indian subcontinent, and Mount Everest (Qomolangma ཇོ་མོ་གླང་མ in Tibetan, meaning "Holy Mother"), the world's highest peak, straddles the Sino-Nepali border.[1]

The Himalayas block the warmth and moisture that comes up from the south, leaving the Tibetan Plateau a dry and cold land of high grasslands, salt lakes, permafrost, and rocky peaks. The elevation is so high, averaging 4,000 m (13,120 ft) above sea level, and the air pressure so low that the water boils at only 80°C (176°F). Practically every animal that lives there is specially adapted for the cold and the thin air. The plateau is a windswept place, where vegetation is sparse, and trees are rarely found except in the southeast. There the elevation is lower, and the hot monsoon currents from the Indian Ocean warm the world's highest and most northerly tropical forests.[2] Large expanses of the east and south of Tibet were forested until a few thousand years ago, but whether due to shifts in climate or the arrival of herders making pasture for their livestock, those forests are long gone.[3]

The highlands are sparsely populated, and until a large influx of Han beginning in the 1950s—which accelerated in the 1990s—there were few Chinese. Instead Tibetans dominated most of the plateau, with groups of Mongols in some regions, notably around Qinghai Lake. In the high borderlands of Xinjiang, Tajiks, Kyrgyz, Kazakhs, and other minority peoples predominated, but they now face increasing pressure to assimilate to the cultural norms of the ethnic Han majority.

Throughout history the highlands have possessed a different cultural landscape from the Han-dominated lands to the east. The soil is largely unsuitable for planting, and so, with the exception of parts of southern and eastern Tibet, most of the populated lands have hosted pastoralists, some settled and others seasonally nomadic. Hunting was traditionally an integral part of not only Mongol and Kazakh, but also Tibetan culture. The Mongols and Kazakhs were known as enthusiastic huntsmen, but generally seem to have kept taboos and norms that restrained them from wiping out animal populations. For Tibetans, Buddhism has often functioned as a restraint against the overkilling of wildlife. Many monasteries still function as de facto wildlife sanctuaries, and it is a common phenomenon to find unusually abundant and tame animals living on monastery lands.[4]

Pre-Buddhist Tibetans eagerly embraced the hunt, and even after the introduction of Buddhism and subsequent efforts to impose ethical prohibitions against the killing of animals, hunting remained widespread.[5] Premodern Tibetans nonetheless had a relatively limited impact on the landscape. Long-term survival in such a harsh environment required a light touch on the grasslands and wildlife.[6] The introduction of modern firearms and integration with global markets in the nineteenth century, however, enticed extensive killing and habitat degradation.[7] Yet by and large Tibetans were restrained in their hunting, which remained a widespread pursuit until the PRC government confiscated nearly all firearms after 1998.[8]

Since the beginning of the People's Republic the greatest changes to the landscape of the highlands have come as a consequence of the increase in human population, and—even more dramatically— the rapid and massive expansion of livestock herds. Beginning in the 1960s stock numbers on the Tibetan Plateau shot up, peaking in the 1970s before decreasing slightly in the 1990s. The number of domestic animals across the plateau increased some five-fold.[9] In some localities the growth was even greater, such as around the mountain Amne Machin in eastern Qinghai, where both human and livestock populations were reported to have leapt ten-fold by the early 1980s.[10] When combined with poor management of pasturelands, such manic growth led to overgrazing and the degradation of many grasslands. The exact extent and severity of overgrazing is unclear and hotly disputed, but that many stretches of rangeland have suffered is clear enough.[11] A major factor in the uneven impacts across the region is that despite shared ethnicity and religion, Tibetans differ culturally from region to region, and grazing practices are similarly varied from place to place and even from family to family, with some more damaging than others.[12]

The Tibetan Plateau is already undergoing noticeable changes in response to a warming climate. Its many glaciers are rapidly melting, expanding the region's saline lakes and inundating pastureland. In time, however, the glaciers will disappear and the lakes will again contract. Increasing expanses of permafrost are now also melting, lowering the water table and changing the more fecund alpine meadows into sparser steppe. Springs, streams, ponds, and other surface waters found in permafrost lands are disappearing, with nearly 40% of the plateau's wetlands already lost in recent decades. This causes the ground to absorb more heat, speeding the melting of the permafrost. In the desolate Changtang region in the plateau's northwest, the warming climate has allowed herders to use some grasslands permanently instead of seasonally. And in the south and east, the tree line will slowly climb higher in both elevation and latitude in the coming years.[13]

Alpine Steppe

PERHAPS the most abundant mammal on the Tibetan Plateau is the plateau or black-lipped pika *Ochotona curzoniae*, which shares much of the uplands with its congener the Gansu pika *O. cansus*, and in the north of its range the Daurian pika *O. dauurica*. China hosts numerous pika species, but many—such as the endangered Silver or Helan Shan pika *O. argentata*—are poorly researched and little understood.[1] Pikas are small lagomorphs, relatives of rabbits and hares, but, due to their resemblance to mice, they are commonly mistaken for rodents.[2] Some species of pika, such as the two in North America and several species on the Tibetan Plateau, live in high mountain boulder and talus fields. Plateau pikas, about the same size as their American cousins *O. princeps*, instead make their homes in the high grasslands where they dig burrows much like American prairie dogs.

The the natural history of plateau pikas parallels prairie dogs in many respects: they are keystone rangeland species that cycle nutrients and aerate the soil through their digging, provide crucial shelter for numerous other small animals, and serve as a food source for nearly every carnivore found on the Tibetan Plateau.[3] Even the two animals' predators parallel each other; North America's black-footed ferret finds its Eurasian counterpart in the steppe polecat *Mustela eversmanii*.[4] Humans also dislike prairie dogs and pikas for the same reasons, complaining that they damage the grasslands, compete with livestock for forage, and that their burrows cause livestock to fall and injure themselves, or worse, that a horse carrying a rider may do so. Chinese authorities responded just as Americans had decades earlier, seeking the pikas' extermination.[5]

Zokors, small burrowing rodents analogous to moles or pocket gophers, have attracted similar ire and been targeted for eradication.[6] Five of the world's six zokor species are found in China, and the most widespread, the plateau zokor *Eospalax fontanierii*, is found not only on the high ranges of Gansu and Qinghai, but east across Inner Mongolia and into North China.[7] Whereas pika spend much of their time above ground and are consequently a favorite food source for many predators, zokor pass nearly their entire lives below the surface, ravenously consuming roots and shoots to fuel their arduous excavations.[8] Nonetheless, they too are an important food source for many species, especially in times when pika populations plummet in the face of unusually severe weather.[9]

Pikas and zokors thrive in degraded grasslands, and traditionally pastoralists have blamed the burrowers for the deterioration.[10] They expected that killing the pests would remove a ravenous competitor for forage and thereby restore the vegetation to abundance and allow their herds to thrive. Government scientists and officials concurred and initiated poisoning of small mammals in 1958, expanding initial tests into massive extermination campaigns in 1962. At the peak from 1963 to 1965, the poisoning covered an area of 130,000 sq km (50,190 sq mi).[11] The work continued over the following decades at a smaller scale until by 2006 357,060 sq km (137,861 sq mi) had been poisoned in Qinghai alone.[12]

Contrary to expectation, the extermination of pikas and zokors did not restore degraded rangelands to health, or provide livestock more forage. Pastoralists and officials had misunderstood the burrowers' ecological role. Though zokors are indeed ravenous consumers of plants, and though both they and pikas are found in great abundance on degraded land, they are rarely if ever the cause of the degradation. Instead in most instances overgrazing was to blame, and the local burrower populations exploded as a consequence.[13] Poisoning could counterintuitively even lead to a boost in burrower numbers; where pika and zokor overlap they compete fiercely for burrow space and so keep each other in check. Consequently, where both are present, removing only one releases the other to multiply.[14]

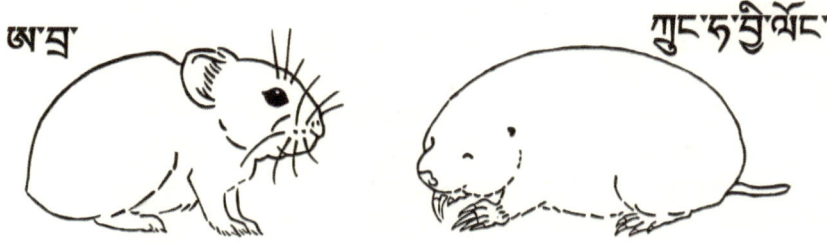

Once they are present in great densities, it may be necessary to reduce pika or zokor numbers to begin the process of restoring a grassland. However, in most circumstances their removal is damaging to the broader ecosystem. Innocuous species, such as the endangered Kozlov's pika *O. koslowi*, have fallen prey to cases of mistaken identity. The poisons first used presented dangers not only to the burrowers but also to their predators and the environment itself, prompting changes to less indiscriminate chemicals.[15] Yet even without poisoning other species secondhand, the removal of pikas and zokors has struck a blow to much of the plateau's wildlife. Species that rely on pika and zokor burrows for shelter, such as the ground tit *Pseudopodoces humilis*, have found themselves without homes, while the carnivores have been deprived of a crucial food source.[16]

After decades of attempts to clear the plateau of the burrowing mammals, and as evidence mounted that it was detrimental to the health of the broader ecosystem and brought no benefit to livestock, Chinese scientists and their foreign colleagues began to push back against the campaigns.[17] Multiple studies firmly established that high densities of pikas and zokors were primarily a consequence of overgrazing and other damaging practices. While allowing that in some strictly limited areas and circumstances burrower numbers would need to be reduced to begin the process of rangeland restoration, most scientists began to advocate against extermination.[18] Policy, however, has been slow to catch up, and although poisoning is more limited than in the past, large swathes of range continue to be poisoned.[19]

ཇེད་མོང་

The largest and certainly one of the most feared carnivores of the region is the Tibetan blue bear *Ursus arctos pruinosus*, a subspecies of the brown bear found only on the Tibetan Plateau. The Tibetan subspecies has a distinctive coat, with black legs, a cream-colored collar and muzzle, and shaggy ears.[20] Found across most of the eastern plateau, from forests in the east to alpine grasslands and high mountains, Tibetan blue bears are widespread yet few in number. The alpine grasslands and hills that cover most of their range simply do not have a natural food supply abundant enough to support large densities of bears. By necessity, bears are thinly spread, often covering large stretches of territory in continual search of sustenance.[21]

The Tibetan bears are notoriously ill-tempered and therefore much feared. The flintlock guns once common on the plateau were poor use against the bears, and until the proliferation of modern rifles in the second half of the twentieth century, the bears presented a great challenge to anyone hoping to defend against or hunt them.[22] Nonetheless, the nomadic pastoralists who most often encountered the bears largely succeeded in driving them from the grasslands where they grazed their herds. The bears do not seem to have ever been targeted for extermination, but the killings that did occur were enough to keep most surviving bears away from the herders and their livestock.[23]

Bears and herders maintained an uneasy coexistence for millennia, but radical changes to the pastoralists' lifestyles in recent decades have brought them in conflict with their ursine neighbors. The enforced settlement of the herders meant that in winter most move from their black yak-hair tents into permanently constructed homes of mud brick, departing during the warm months to take their herds to summer pastures. While away they leave behind supplies of food, including dried meats, skins of butter and cheese, and sacks of grain or flour. These attract the bears, who destructively force their way into the structures. Once inside they feast on the foodstuffs, sometimes staying for two or three days before they satisfy their appetites and depart, leaving behind piles of scat and ruinous expenses few pastoralists can afford.[24]

Unlike many bears elsewhere who are primarily herbivorous, the blue bears rely heavily on meat, particularly pika, which can make up to seventy percent of their diet.[25] Bears will devote great time and energy to the laborious task of excavating pika dens from the frozen ground for the tiny reward of a few little lagomorphs. They also feed on marmots and the ungulates of the plateau, whether hunted or scavenged. The difficulty inherent in finding adequate food makes the pastoralists' herds and foodstuffs immensely appealing to the bears.[26] If herders cannot find a way to discourage them, the bears will inevitably help themselves to the free shelter and food.

In the past herders would have responded by shooting raiding bears, which seemed an effective deterrent. But after the killing of bears was outlawed and guns were confiscated, people were left with only passive options of protection. Most of these have proven of little or no use against determined ursids, who can break through most doors and fencing, and quickly learn to ignore firecrackers, music, or other loud noises. Other social policies have compounded pastoralists' inability to deter the bears. Traditionally children provided a crucial source of labor for nomadic herders, tending to livestock and dogs and handling many other chores. Now most children must attend school, and usually at a great distance from home. This leaves little time to help with protecting animals or training guard dogs, which leaves both herds and homes more vulnerable to bears.[27]

Despite the increasing conflict between bears and herders, and the great fear and resentment caused, all told the bears are doing remarkably well. The protections they and their prey now enjoy, combined with the changes forced on the pastoralists, appear to have led to an increase in the plateau's bear population.[28] Of course, the growth in bear numbers only exacerbates the problems of ursine break-ins and attacks on livestock. More sophisticated and subtle solutions will be needed to establish a lasting, peaceful coexistence, and researchers are at work determining the best methods to keep the bears at bay.[29] Looking ahead, even with the loss of some habitat to climate change, the Tibetan blue bears seem to have a secure future.[30] Whether they will ever make good neighbors is less certain.

Sharing the high steppe with the hulking bears is the Tibetan fox *Vulpes ferrilata*, a small fox unique to the Tibetan Plateau and neighboring highlands of India, Nepal, and Bhutan. The Tibetan fox is immediately and unquestionably recognizable. Though its long, dense coat of tan and gray, and its bushy, white-tipped tail are vaguely similar to other species of fox, it is the Tibetan fox's face that is unmistakable. With extremely broad cheeks and narrowed eyes, the Tibetan fox has a look of dignified insouciance, tinged with suspicion and annoyance.[31]

Tibetan foxes live above 2,500 m (8,200 ft), with most found above 4,000 m (13,120 ft) on high-altitude grasslands where their primary prey, black-lipped pikas, are abundant. The foxes have long and warm coats to protect against the harsh winds and frigid temperatures of the plateau, but the fur is coarse and so humans do not consider Tibetan fox pelts to be of high quality. The state nonetheless purchased them until the late 1980s, and poaching has continued since, but not in such numbers as to threaten the species. A more severe danger comes from the great number of stray dogs that roam the highlands, which are known to attack and kill foxes.[32]

Tibetan foxes are sometimes seen trotting behind an unexpected companion: the Tibetan blue bear. The foxes trail behind the bears because they are after the same thing—pikas. When a bear digs into a den and flushes out a pika, the fox is waiting to pounce.[33] The little lagomorphs are essential to the fox's diet; in fact the foxes are so reliant on the burrowers for survival that they seem to be obligate pika predators, incapable of surviving solely on alternative food sources. Though there is no indication at present that Tibetan foxes are in danger as a species, their reliance on the pikas is a potentially fatal weakness. If the longstanding efforts to clear the alpine steppe of pika ever succeeds, locally or across the Tibetan Plateau, it could well lead to the collapse of fox populations.[34]

འཕར་བ་

Although gone from most of its former range across China, the dhole survives in the highlands but remains one of the region's least understood species. Despite their striking appearance and fearsome reputation, the red wild dogs do not seem to have ever attracted much attention from chroniclers of the region's wildlife. British chroniclers in the nineteenth century noted the wild dogs were found throughout the highlands of the Tibetan Plateau and South Asia, and in the early twentieth century dholes were noted to range through western Sichuan, reportedly clearing areas of prey before moving on.[35] As the dholes disappeared from most of China, and indeed most of their range throughout Asia, the highland populations also dwindled.[36] As elsewhere, the exact reasons for their decline are a mystery, because the wild dogs received no scientific attention to speak of.

By 2000 the dholes of the far west remained only in small, scattered clans. Pastoralists and wildlife professionals still spotted them occasionally, but despite their rarity and the minimal damage they caused to livestock, those who knew of their existence still considered them wholly despicable creatures.[37] Since the turn of the millennium the dogs have been sighted scattered across the highlands. People and camera traps have spotted them in Gansu's Qilian Mountains, in the Altyn-Tagh of southern Xinjiang and in Taxkorgan in the west of the province, near the borders of Pakistan, Afghanistan, and Tajikistan.[38]

Dholes have even been spotted within the past two decades in giant panda territory, from the Qinling in Shaanxi into the Min, Daxue, and Qionglai Mountains of Sichuan, though the records are so few and intermittent that it is unclear if they persist there at present.[39] In total they have been seen in seven western provinces since 2010, showing they remain widespread if precariously sparse and few.[40] Dholes, like their canid cousins the wolves, have finally received legal protection from persecution, but without immediate and intensive work to discern the extent of their numbers and range—as well as the threats they face—their future is extremely precarious.

ཤུང་གི་

The snow leopard is the apex predator of the rocks and cliffs, but on the alpine steppe the wolf and brown bear reign. Like most creatures of the plateau, the wolves and bears of Qinghai and Tibet are uniquely adapted to life above 3,000 m (9,840 ft). Unlike many high-altitude species, the region's wolves, known as Himalayan wolves, show no obvious outward adaptations, but they are genetically distinct from other wolves.[41] Himalayan wolves possess a set of genes not active in other wolves that seem to allow them to live in the low oxygen environment above 3,000 m without succumbing to hypoxia (altitude sickness).[42] Not only are they adapted to high altitude, of the world's gray wolves *Canis lupus*, Himalayan wolves are distinct enough from other wolves to certainly qualify as a subspecies *C. lupus himalayensis*, and perhaps even their own species *C. himalayensis*.[43]

Found from Qinghai Lake south to the Himalayas of Nepal, India, and Bhutan, the Himalayan wolves, like all predators of the highlands, are thinly spread. Just how many roam the steppes and mountains is unknown, but until recent years they suffered intense persecution, the same as their cousins throughout the rest of the People's Republic. Just like their pastoralist neighbors on the Mongolian steppes, the herders of the Tibetan Plateau have valid reasons to despise wolves. As other predators do, wolves sometimes take livestock for their meals. Yet Himalayan wolves in fact show a marked preference for wild prey whenever it is available, even when the numbers of domestic livestock far exceed those of wild species.[44] Nonetheless Tibetan pastoralists show the wolves little sympathy.

One incident illustrates in what low esteem wolves were once held, even amongst the Tibetans. While traveling through Qinghai in 1989, Richard B. Harris, an American wildlife biologist, spotted a pair of wolves. His traveling companions, a truckload of Tibetan pilgrims, saw the wolves as well. They stopped their truck and jumped out with rifles and pistols in hand—guns at that time still a common possession on the plateau. They all fired at the fleeing wolves, but failed to hit their targets. When Harris later recounted the episode to a Chinese zoologist to elicit his take, the man said that he too would have tried to kill the wolves. Harris assumed this was out of sympathy for local pastoralists' sensibilities and hardships. The zoologist disabused him of the notion, replying that "it has nothing to do with helping the Tibetans. I'd kill a wolf anytime I had the opportunity. Wolves are bad animals."[45]

Such a view of predators, and wolves in particular, would have earned hardy agreement from Western zoologists of previous generations, but by the close of the twentieth century had become terribly outdated. In China, however, such attitudes persisted until far more recently. Only in 2021, with the first major revision of the national list of protected animal species since 1989, did wolves receive legal protections. Once universally considered a loathsome species, the listing of wolves as protected marked a shift in the place of predators in the consciousness of Chinese policymakers and the broader public.[46]

ཁྲི་ཨེ་

The snow leopard is not the only cat of the highlands. Common leopards are still found in some of the forested mountains in the east and south, and lynx are found throughout the region. The most unusual of the cats, however, is the manul or Pallas's cat *Otocolobus manul*.[47] Found in the arid grasslands of Central Asia, throughout much of western China, and east into Hebei and formerly the Manchurian steppe, the manul is perhaps the most distinctive of the small cats.[48] Roughly the size of an average house cat, the manul has a soft, dense, long coat of drab gray, yellow, and red hues, providing both excellent insulation and camouflage. The manul's pupils, set within yellow irises, do not narrow into slits as do most small cats', but instead remain circular when contracted, the same as tigers and other big cats. With its majestic fluff, a perpetually sour countenance, and exceptional expressiveness, Pallas's cat has become a favorite source of entertainment for wildlife enthusiasts online.

The manul's voluminous coat inevitably has attracted the attention of trappers and furriers. In the 1930s several hundred manul pelts from Manchuria and Inner Mongolia passed through Harbin's markets each winter, while in the southwest the annual catch during the 1950s ranged from about 5,000 to around 10,000.[49] By 1980 hunting and other factors had caused the manul population to fall, and only about 100 pelts were registered in Sichuan that year.[50]

As mesopredators, manul must be wary of the larger carnivores that share the landscape, including their feline cousins the snow leopards. As with the Tibetan fox, feral dogs are also a threat.[51] The same as other predators of the highland steppes, manul are dependent on pikas and burrowing rodents for most of their diet, leaving them vulnerable should poisoning campaigns against the small mammals ever succeed.[52] Ultimately, however, as with so many species, habitat degradation and fragmentation are ultimately the greatest threats to the cats, who, living in such a harsh landscape, require large expanses to find sufficient food.[53]

�རྩྭ་གཡི་

Another small felid shares a swathe of the highlands with the manul, the misnamed Chinese mountain cat *Felis bieti*.[54] A denizen not of mountains but of scrublands, meadows, and forest edges, the Chinese mountain cat is unique to China, to date found only in portions of Qinghai, Gansu, Sichuan, and Tibet, typically between 2,500 and 3,500 m (8,200 ft to 11,480 ft), but sometimes at higher climes.[55] Chinese mountain cats are the size of large domestic cats, with sandy, yellow-brown coats and long, thick, black-striped tails. Their most distinguishing feature is the striking blue of their eyes, in other felids a color typically seen only in kittens.[56]

Almost nothing of substance was known of the Chinese mountain cat until the twenty-first century, including its distribution and life history, both only now becoming clear.[57] Western explorers first noted the cat as a unique species or subspecies in the close of the nineteenth-century, but for the next hundred years little information came to light. Local Tibetan herders of course knew of the cat, which they called the grass cat; they commonly valued it more dead than alive. Trapping or poisoning the cats was fairly easy: wait until snow covered the ground, follow their paw prints to a den, and there leave poisoned bait or a snare. The warm winter skins were used to make clothing, especially hats, and extra pelts were sold onward to traders or furriers.[58] The volume of the killing and associated fur trade is unclear, but as late as the turn of the millennium researchers found dozens of pelts on sale in regional markets.[59]

The Chinese mountain cats live over a relatively small territory and cannot be great in number, but they do not yet face imminent extinction. The greatest dangers to the cats are the expansion of livestock grazing which threatens to reshape their habitat, as well as the increasing number of roads criss-crossing the highlands, where more and more cats and other wildlife meet an early end. Feral and free-roaming dogs also present a constant danger for cats living near humans.[60] Perhaps the most intractable problem for the steppe cats is that they readily hybridize with the growing population of domestic cats living within their range. If extensive and prolonged enough, mating with domestic cats could see the gradual disappearance of *F. bieti* as a genetically distinct felid.[61]

Taxonomically, their status as a species is under question. One side argues that genetic evidence places the Chinese mountain cats as a mere subspecies of the Asiatic wildcat *Felis silvestris*.[62] In opposition are conservationists who worry such a move will be not only a taxonomic downgrade but in turn will lead to a loss of interest in safeguarding the cats. A third group suggests the evidence is inconclusive, and whether the cats should remain *F. bieti* or suffer demotion to *F. s. bieti* remains unclear.[63]

ཁྱུང་ཁྱུང་སྐེ་ནག

The western highlands, the Tibetan Plateau especially, is home to many beautiful and rare species of birds. Some are found across much of Eurasia, such as the golden eagle *Aquila chrysaetos*, lammergeier *Gypaetus barbatus*, and saker falcon *Falco cherrug*. Others, like the high-flying bar-headed goose *Anser indicus*, are seasonal visitors, arriving to nest before continuing to warmer climes for winter. A fewer number are restricted to the region, such as the Himalayan vulture *Gyps himalayensis*, crucial participants in the traditional Tibetan sky burial. But of the highlands' birds, the most elegant—and for many years one of the most mysterious—is the black-necked crane *Grus nigricollis*.

As their name suggests, the cranes have black necks as well as faces, with a small patch of white behind the eyes and a red cap on their foreheads. Their legs, and flight and tail feathers, too, are black, while the rest of their wings and their bodies are a light gray, nearly white on some birds.

Tibetans naturally have long been familiar with the cranes, drawn to the same scarce sources of freshwater on the plateau as the birds. There was seemingly little conflict or persecution between the two, and so the gruids became by and large tolerant of human presence. People in turn welcomed the cranes, considering them auspicious creatures.[64] Very little was known about the cranes until the end of the twentieth century; outsiders did not discover the birds until 1876. Where they bred, how many there might be, and other basic knowledge was still unknown a century later.[65] Scientists only found one of the largest wintering populations in 1979, at Caohai Lake, the Grass Sea, a lake on the Yunnan-Guizhou Plateau that had once covered over 45 sq km (17.4 sq mi), but had been drained and reclaimed for farmland during the Great Leap Forward until only 1.2 sq km (0.5 sq mi) of lake remained.[66] Luckily for the cranes, Caohai Lake has been restored to its former extent and continues to host many of the birds each winter.[67]

As late as 1987, with little concrete known about *G. nigricollis*, most scientists believed them to be highly endangered, likely one of the rarest of the world's cranes. It wasn't until foreign crane experts conducted a series of surveys from 1991 into the early 2000s that it became clear the birds were both more numerous and widespread than previously feared.[68] The researchers discovered that black-necked cranes have the smallest geographic distribution among the cranes, except for the blue crane *G. paradisea* of southern Africa. The birds spend nearly all their lives above 2,000 m (6,560 ft), breeding between 2,600–4,800 m (8,530–15,750 ft) on the Tibetan Plateau.[69] A small number—around 200—breed as far north as the Kunlun and Altyn-Tagh ranges of southern Xinjiang.[70] In autumn they fly south, and because they migrate not only from north to south but also from higher to lower altitude, they have exceptionally short migration routes; the longest only 700 km (435 mi), the shortest a mere 120 km (75 mi). Most birds follow one of three routes: the Eastern population flies to the Yunnan-Guizhou Plateau in northeastern Yunnan and northwestern Guizhou; the Central population migrates to northwestern Yunnan; and the Western population heads to the Yarlung Tsangpo valley of south-central Tibet, with some birds crossing into Bhutan.[71]

Even though the evidence is sparse, it seems certain the cranes suffered along with other wildlife during the Maoist years as they became targets for hunters and lost wetland habitat to land reclamation. The population surveyed in the early 1990s numbered 5,000 to 6,000 birds, and has since grown to over 17,000.[72] In part this was due to the cranes rebounding from the damage of earlier decades, but a significant portion of the larger count is simply due to more extensive survey work uncovering previously unknown populations. The cranes are now faring relatively well, and even seem to be increasing in number, but they still face an array of threats. Among these are changes in the agricultural practices of farmers in the Yarlung Tsangpo valley. Barley is the traditional crop there, and wintering cranes have long sustained themselves through the season by gleaning the harvested fields for leftover grains. As many farmers have begun to harvest more efficiently, less waste grain is available to the birds. Even worse, barley is increasingly replaced with crops of winter wheat, leaving the cranes with dwindling sources of food.[73]

More threatening perhaps is the warming climate. Warmer temperatures have already impacted the birds, for both good and bad. Higher temperatures have given the cranes some respite from the dangers of extreme cold, allowing more of the birds to survive through each year. Increased glacial meltwater is expanding many lakes, providing more habitat. Yet as the earth warms and permafrost degrades, shallower wetlands are beginning to disappear. As the glaciers recede and in time vanish, the short-term boom in water flow will slow and eventually end. The expanding lakes will recede again, and shrink until smaller than they were in decades past.[74] The black-necked cranes are doing well for now, but their future will be a struggle.

Upland Ungulates

T HE most endangered of all the highlands' hoofed animals is Przewalski's gazelle *Procapra przewalskii,* a small gazelle that survives only around Qinghai Lake.[1] A small, slender ungulate with the sandy body, white underside, and white rump patch typical of gazelles, Przewalski's gazelle bears close resemblance to the Mongolian gazelle of the northern steppe and the Tibetan gazelle of the high plateau. Males, darker and larger than females, are also the only sex with horns, which are ridged and curl inwards at the tips. In winter the gazelles' coats turn grayer and visibly thicken, as they lack an undercoat and must grow longer guard hairs to keep warm.

The gazelles now live only in the vicinity of Qinghai Lake (in times past better known by its Mongolian name of Koko Nor), the largest lake in China and the namesake of Qinghai Province in which it sits. A salt lake situated in Qinghai's northeast at an elevation of over 3,200 m (10,500 ft), the Blue Sea Lake hosts large communities of migratory birds. The lake itself shrank in size over most of the twentieth century, in large part due to land reclamation efforts begun in the 1950s. Over the past two decades the water area has gradually increased, as of 2023 reaching over 4,600 sq km (1,776 sq mi).[2]

Przewalski's gazelles were not always limited to a small area around Qinghai Lake. Practically no research on the species was conducted until the late 1980s when the gazelles were already restricted to the immediate lake region, so there is scarce evidence concerning their past range or habitat preferences. Colonel Przhevalsky made the first definite record of the species in 1875, but potentially earlier and many later records of the animals are ambiguous, as most observers did not distinguish clearly between the region's gazelle species. The gazelles' preferred habitat seems to be semi-arid grasslands, and they once were found from the Ordos region and Helan Mountains of Inner Mongolia and Ningxia west to the Hexi Corridor in Gansu. In fact the high grassland around Koko Nor is most likely a final safe haven on the edge of their suitable range, not a typical example of habitat best suited to the gazelles. They apparently could not tolerate the close presence of humans and their livestock, so, as pastoralists and farmers settled more and more of the species' land, the gazelles retreated until they were left with only what they have today.[3]

Humans have lived around Qinghai Lake for millennia, but the land was not intensively settled. In earlier centuries Tibetans and the Koko Nor Mongol pastoralists had grazed their herds around the lake, but this relative freedom from human disturbance came to an end in the mid-1950s when the People's Liberation Army established farms on the rangelands, expanding the area under cultivation over the ensuing decades.[4] The gazelles suffered a further blow soon after the arrival of the farms, as the threat of starvation during the Great Leap Forward forced the lake's residents to turn to the gazelles for sustenance.[5] The species garnered little attention from the outside world for years until scientists finally made a count of the gazelles in 1986; they were dismayed to find only 350 remaining.[6]

Hopes of saving the critically endangered species were soon jeopardized as the area's rangelands were divided and assigned to once nomadic families in the early 1990s. As happened on many of China's grasslands, the division of land and privatization of herds led to massive increases in livestock numbers, and subsequent overgrazing and grassland degradation. In hopes of stopping and reversing the damage, thousands and thousands of kilometers of fences were erected, crisscrossing the landscape. Several years later efforts to combat erosion and encourage forest and shrubland restoration led to even more fencing.[7]

The fences would have been an impediment to any species, but Przewalski's gazelles—whether physically incapable or evolutionarily unequipped—proved unable to safely pass most of the barriers. Much of the fencing was seemingly too high, and some of a design that led to many entanglements and deaths for those who attempted to jump over or crawl under. Consequently the gazelles would walk along the wire in search of an opening, not only losing much time and energy but leaving them extremely vulnerable to predators, particularly wolves.[8] Herders were generally sympathetic to the gazelles but were not keen to remove their fences. Many mistakenly believed gazelle numbers were increasing, and more importantly they appreciated the help the barriers brought in moving their own herds and minimizing conflicts between families.[9]

For years surveys of the gazelles' populations returned worrying figures. In 1997 a low of only 200 animals was counted, but over time the numbers ticked upwards. This was less due to the recovery of the gazelles than it was to improved surveying, which resulted in the discovery of previously unknown populations. It was not merely the low number of gazelles that was worrisome, but that they were fragmented across the landscape. Two populations existed on the eastern and western sides of Qinghai Lake, with no connections between them. Those eastern and western groups were further split in turn. Not only fencing, but also the Qinghai-Tibet railway and a major national highway were built through the gazelle's habitat, creating dangerous—and in some places impenetrable—obstacles.[10] Split into small clusters, competing with millions of head of livestock, and squeezed between humans and sand dunes, the gazelles' outlook was grim. Indeed, projections of the likelihood of their survival showed nearly all of them dying out within seventy years.[11]

By 2013, however, the estimate was more encouraging, with increases now due to expanding herds instead of improved counting. The gazelles were still limited to areas away from human settlement and activity, avoiding land close to villages, farmland, and railway stations. Nonetheless their total population had climbed over 1,300, and the next year their numbers remained steady.[12] Ongoing efforts to remove or lower hundreds of kilometers of fencing were helping the animals move more freely, and landscape restoration work was helping improve forage yields. By early 2022 the gazelles were making a notable turn around, their numbers having passed 2,800 mature individuals, with a total population of just over 4,000. Nonetheless, the improvements to the landscape have not been dramatic, and the gazelles are still restricted to fragmented patches of habitat. Consequently, not all subpopulations are faring well.[13] Przewalski's gazelles still face a difficult future, with climate change likely to deprive them of much of what little habitat they now have, but their recent rebound and ongoing and increasing conservation efforts have given them a real chance to survive far into the future.[14]

Another small antelope, the goa or Tibetan gazelle *Procapra picticaudata*, ranges the high flatlands. Males sport a pair of ridged horns that reach up before abruptly bending back almost ninety degrees. Females are hornless, but otherwise the sexes are nearly indistinguishable. The gazelles have gray-brown coats made up only of guard hairs, and which thicken very noticeably in winter. They are readily distinguished from behind, with heart-shaped patches of white covering their rumps and a short, black-tipped tail at the center. Like the chiru, goas live only on the Tibetan Plateau, ranging in elevation from 3,000 m to 5,750 m (9,840 ft to 18,860 ft).[15] Though small, the gazelles are exceptionally swift and extremely wary of humans, with excellent eyesight and hearing alerting them to far away dangers. Early Western observers marveled at both the speed and vigilance of the goas, remarking that such traits made them exceedingly difficult to hunt, and therefore excellent game for eager sportsmen.[16]

Goas have not suffered the same intensity of hunting as the larger chiru (they have the good fortune not to be considered of any great commercial or medicinal value). They are not considered unwelcome competitors with domestic livestock, nor are they as limited in habitat as the Przewalski's gazelle. Nonetheless their numbers have dropped and seem to still be dropping.[17] In some areas, such as the alpine meadows of eastern Qinghai, goas—along with most other wildlife of any size—were by and large wiped out during the relentless slaughter of the Maoist period. In other regions, despite some degree of hunting, they seem to have succumbed instead to the intrusion of pastoralists into their grazing lands.[18] Late nineteenth and early twentieth century explorers to the region noted that goas showed little fear of humans where they had long peacefully coexisted, but goas seem generally unwilling to share their habitat with humans or livestock.[19] They will, at least, soon return if humans leave, but the increase in permanent settlements has deprived the little gazelles of much prime rangeland.[20] Goas can ill afford such losses, as climate change threatens to render up to a third or more of their habitat unsuitable within the next five decades.[21]

འབྲོང་

The largest, fiercest, far and away most feared herbivore of the highlands is the wild yak *Bos mutus*. Unsurprisingly, wild yaks look extremely similar to their domesticated cousins. The most notable difference is their size; wild males reach heights of over 2 m (6 ft 6 in) at the shoulder and weights of up to 1,200 kg (2,645 lb); they noticeably loom over their more docile counterparts, though with when compared to hybrids of the two species the distinction is not always clear cut. Females are much smaller, but remain formidable animals. Yaks have distinctive long coats, with a dense skirt of undercoat at the belly hanging nearly to the ground. Unlike domesticated yaks, wild yaks are pure black, with the rare exception of a golden brown morph sometimes seen among the populations of the Changtang.[22] Black-and-white coated yaks are sometimes seen among wild herds, an indicator that some individuals are hybrid offspring of wild and domestic yaks.

    The smaller and more timid domesticated yak, along with other livestock, by and large has now supplanted the wild yak across its historic range. This process has happened not only to the yak, but to the progenitors of many other domestic species, such as the aurochs and wild horses. Unlike the aurochs, however, the wild yak's ability to find refuge in some of the planet's harshest landscapes has so far saved it from extinction, if only just. Yaks' biology restricts their distribution to high elevations, and most are found between 3,000–5,500 m (9,840–18,040 ft).[23] Wild yak once ranged from the Transbaikal (or Dauria) of Siberia south through modern Kazakhstan and Mongolia and into the highlands of Xinjiang and the Tibetan Plateau. The last wild yaks in Russia were wiped out several hundred years ago, perhaps as late as the eighteenth century. Today they are found only within the People's Republic, as well as just over a hundred yaks in India.[24]

    By the later half of the nineteenth century and into the early years of the twentieth, wild yak had been hunted and pushed from their northern reaches, yet on the Tibetan Plateau the shaggy bovids remained both common and numerous. Early Western travelers described seeing yaks frequently over most of the vast region, often gathered in great herds.[25] Some areas, however, such as southern Gansu, were already seeing the effects of overhunting.[26]

A market for yak hides existed, as yak bull leather was highly prized as among the toughest and most durable in existence.[27] Some groups, such as the Qaidam Mongols, regularly hunted yaks, eating the meat, trading the hides, spinning rope from their hairs, and using the heart and blood as medicines. The animals were often the only reliable source of meat through the long winters for those who hunted them.[28]

That the animals—especially mature bulls—were immensely strong and dangerous did much to protect them until the arrival of modern firearms. Trade caravans so feared the yaks that if they encountered one blocking a narrow pass they would simply stop and wait until the animal moved of its own accord.[29] Hunters armed with powerful and accurate modern rifles took advantage of the yak's casual bravery, easily approaching lone bulls who had no intent of ceding ground.[30] Przhevalsky and company failed to restrain themselves when presented with such easy prey, gunning down many yaks and leaving them untouched —the carcasses froze solid, and when the party returned weeks later the men found the icy yaks just as they had left them.[31]

When the British cartographer Captain M. S. Wellby (1866–1900) passed through the Yellow River headlands of eastern Qinghai in the late 1890s, he noted that wild yak were extremely abundant, describing how "On one green hill we could see hundreds upon hundreds of yak grazing; there was, I believe, more yak visible than hill."[32] The arrival of modern rifles, however, proved fatal to the region's yaks. In the 1930s when the German zoologist Ernst Schäfer (1910–

1992) crossed the same area as Wellby had, he noted yaks were already difficult to find.[33] When the American adventurer Leonard Clark passed through on his expedition to survey Amne Machin in 1949, he noted few live yaks but hundreds—even thousands—of wild yak skulls, comparing their fate to that of the American bison.[34]

The hunting frenzies that marked the Great Leap Forward and the continued hunting over the following decades were as bad for wild yak as for other large mammals of the highlands. From the late 1950s many of Qinghai's remaining wild yak were slaughtered and shipped east on the recently completed railroad.[35] Before long, except for the occasional lone bull, there were no yaks east of the Lhasa-Golmud highway, leaving most of central and eastern Qinghai empty of the long-haired bovids.[36] In western Tibet, too, most yaks were hunted out by the 1990s, their meat consumed and their horns turned into milk pails. Yaks resident in the southern section of the vast Chang Tang Reserve were also killed after the arrival of around 3,500 pastoralist families with 1.5 million head of livestock in tow.[37]

Eventually the northwestern Tibetan Plateau became the last refuge for large populations of wild yak. In the Altyn-Tagh an estimated 10,000 survived in the Altun Shan Reserve, but the intrusion of illegal gold miners in 1986 resulted in the collapse of the population, as the miners gunned down thousands of them. The intervention of government authorities ended the slaughter before all the yak were killed, but by 2008 their numbers had only recovered to 1,700 individuals.[38]

By the time the first detailed field research on wild yaks began in the 1990s, scientists found a drastically reduced population of animals that, instead of staring down entire caravans, now fled for miles at the slightest sign of humans. Once widely found in herds of hundreds, no more than 15,000 survived on perhaps half the territory they had occupied a century earlier—with nearly all their most prized habitat lost to herders.[39] Their numbers have continued to decline, yet pastoralists still view the wild yaks as a continuing menace to their own herds. Yaks and pastoralists prize the same rangelands, and where the two meet the herders by and large wish to be rid of the wild bovids. Not only do the larger and fiercer wild yaks vie for the same forage, but wild males may mate with domestic females, producing hybrid calves with the unruly, stubborn wills of their fathers—though a minority of herders in fact see benefits in having more vigorous hybrid offspring.[40] Worse, domestic

yaks may abscond to join wild herds, depriving the pastoralists—most of whom never rise far above impoverishment—of valuable property.[41] Many conservationists worry about such mixing as well, as the hybridization means a loss of the genetic distinctiveness of the wild species.[42]

The species remains little understood, with only a few decades of basic research available to inform decision making. Nor can this be easily remedied, as wild yaks are fundamentally difficult to study. Spread thinly over vast, remote, and harsh landscapes, extremely wary of humans, and physically imposing, the bovids are exceptionally challenging to observe. Further, the use of some of the best modern tools such as satellite tracking collars are forbidden on the Tibetan Plateau, the whole of which China considers militarily sensitive.[43]

Estimated at fewer than 10,000 adults in 2014, wild yak numbers now seem to be increasing.[44] With hunting now largely under control, the yaks' greatest threat comes from their continuing struggle to find undisturbed habitat. Yaks require large expanses of wilderness with little to no human presence, but their preference for pastures that pastoralists also covet has forced them into a losing contest.[45] Climate change threatens to further reduce available habitat, first bringing more glacial melt and more alpine meadows for the yaks, only to deprive them of those new pastures as the ice disappears.[46] Their future is extremely precarious, and without the cooperation and tolerance of the plateau's pastoralists, the wild yaks may diminish to a point of no return.

བོང་རྒྱུང་

Among the Tibetan Plateau's large mammals, the most curious and playful may be the kiang or Tibetan wild ass *Equus kiang*. Nearly indistinguishable to the untrained eye from its congener, the khulan, the kiang is in fact the largest of the world's wild ass species, on average not only slightly taller, but roughly thirty percent heavier than its cousin on the steppes to the north.[47] The kiang's coat is also darker than the khulan's, with a distinctive wedge of white behind the shoulders that reaches high up on the back, prominent white fur on the throat, and stripeless legs. Kiang live between 2,700 m and 5,300 m (8,860 ft and 17,390 ft) and are found over most of the Tibetan Plateau, from the Kunlun and Altyn-Tagh of Xinjiang to the foothills of the Himalayas. The vast majority of the world's kiang live within the borders of the People's Republic, but small populations are found in Pakistan, India, Bhutan, and Nepal.[48]

Kiang are usually seen in droves from as little as several individuals to up to a few dozen. Occasionally they come together in larger congregations of hundreds or well over a thousand members. Kiang live in lands that throughout human history have generally seen little settlement, with few people other than nomadic pastoralists encountering the equids. Humans have hunted kiang since first migrating onto the Tibetan Plateau, but until recent decades wolves were by far the more dangerous enemy. Many herds in fact showed no fear of humans, and it was commonly reported that kiang would approach and circle passing caravans, running in close to better inspect the strange visitors before dashing off.

Some people, such as the Koko Nor Mongols, enjoyed the meat of the kiang, prizing it especially in autumn when fattest.[49] Tibetans, however, did not generally eat kiang, though some groups did regularly hunt and consume them in the past.[50] The drokba—the pastoralists of the Changtang—refuse to eat them, even though they have ample opportunity to hunt the kiang and see them as unwelcome competitors for good forage.[51] The Muslim Hui—who live in the northern range of kiang territory—do not eat the equids either, professing a dislike for the taste.[52] There was a trade in kiang hides centered on Qinghai that persisted from at least the early Qing dynasty into the early twentieth century, but there is no evidence to suggest it was large enough to depopulate any regions of kiang.[53] Indeed, when Western travelers began to pass through in the mid-nineteenth century the "wild mules" were still abundant.[54]

When Col. Przhevalsky passed through the Koko Nor region and Qaidam Basin in the 1870s he saw many kiang; around Koko Nor they gathered in herds of several hundred.[55] In the following decades other explorers sighted hundreds and even thousands of them, near the Qilian Mountains in the north, and to the south on the vast Changtang in Tibet.[56] On the eve of the Communist takeover of the far west, kiang were still seen in large numbers. Leonard Clark (1907–1957) traveled through the Amne Machin region just before the arrival of the People's Liberation Army in late 1949, ostensibly to measure the height of the mountain, which some American fliers during the Second World War had claimed was higher than Mt. Everest.[57] While crossing eastern Qinghai Clark and his companions sighted numerous large herds of kiang, one of which he estimated at up to a thousand members. Clark traveled with a party of soldiers, and he noted that while the Tibetans among them did not shoot the kiang, the Hui killed the equids indiscriminately and for no apparent reason, leaving the dead animals untouched where they fell.[58] At nearly the same time to the west, a small party of two Americans and three White Russians traveled south from Ürümqi into the Changtang towards Lhasa, in flight from the Communists. Their small caravan would often meet herds of kiang, who in curiosity would often run rings around the men and their camels.[59]

After the start of the People's Republic, kiang remained abundant until the great wildlife slaughters began in 1958. Qinghai seems to have seen the worst of the killings, though kiang at the edges of their distribution also suffered severely; the last individuals of Taxkorgan, in the western borderlands of Xinjiang, disappeared by the end of the 1950s.[60] The highway and railroad that opened eastern Qinghai to easy exploitation led to the destruction of the region's kiang within only a few years.[61] Many places throughout the province were named for the wild equids, but over the course of the Great Leap Forward they lost the kiang for which they were named. From 1959 to 1961 multiple counties in Qinghai recorded tallies of thousands of kiang killed. In one county, a team of only three men brought in 11,500 kg (25,350 lb) of kiang meat in only half a month.[62] The region's kiang were not completely wiped out, but very few remained; decades later a month-long survey found only 186 in the vast Yellow River headlands.[63]

On the barren Changtang where Swedish explorer Sven Hedin had seen great herds in the first decade of the twentieth century, kiang fared somewhat better than to the north. The Tibetan pastoralists who expanded their grazing into the region were largely averse to eating equids. The wild asses were by no means safe from the gun, however, as local government officials sent out teams to secure yak and kiang meat; yak for local Tibetan families, and kiang for visiting Han construction crews. By the early 1990s kiang were all but gone from the eastern Changtang, but in the north and west of the region they remained numerous enough that pastoralists began to petition the government to allow culling, out of fear they would consume too much forage at the expense of domestic herds.[64]

In southern Tibet, too, the kiang faced severe persecution. They were once very common in the rangelands along the Yarlung Tsangpo, but when surveying the area in 1995 researchers heard from locals that the equids had been almost all exterminated in the previous three decades.[65] The hunting made the once curious kiang extremely wary of humans, especially of motorized vehicles. In 1986 when another group of researchers searched the Mount Kailash region for a month they found only a dozen wild asses, none of which would allow the team's vehicles to approach. On a return survey eleven years later, there were far more kiang, and the safety they had experienced in the intervening years had emboldened them enough that none showed any fear of the convoy, some even approaching the vehicles.[66]

With the end of widespread and intense hunting, kiang have rebounded in the areas where they survived, much to the consternation of many pastoralists.[67] Though kiang numbers have increased since the early 1990s, and they sometimes do gather in large herds which may strip available forage from an expanse of rangeland, they remain far less numerous than the domestic sheep and other livestock on the high plains. An occasional large herd may deprive a group of herders of good pasture, but in general complaints about the impacts of kiang are likely a mix of exaggeration and selective memory, linking the equids with degraded land for which they are not to blame.[68] With their guns taken away in the late 1990s and requests for government culls denied, pastoralists now resort to using their motorbikes to chase the kiang away.[69]

On Cliffs & Crags

ABOVE the alpine steppe live a mix of other ungulates. The red goral *Naemorhedus baileyi*, with the smallest range of all goral species, is found in the mountain forests of southeastern Tibet and western Yunnan. It is poorly studied, but is known to have suffered from the expanding agricultural and infrastructural development of the region, which has both destroyed much habitat and brought in poachers eager for goral meat, horns, and hides.[1] Sharing much of the red goral's range are the Mishmi takin *Budorcas taxicolor taxicolor* and Bhutan takin *B. t. whitei*.[2] The Mishmi takin is found south and east of the great bend of the Yarlung Zangbo and to the east in the Gaoligong Mountains of Yunnan. The lesser-known Bhutan takin is found in the lands west of the river's big bend and southwards towards Bhutan.[3] The native Mönpa hunters of the southeastern Tibetan borderlands have traditionally been eager consumers of takin meat, snaring them with woven bamboo nooses before they obtained guns. The Mönpa hunt takin on sacred lands, and believe that when killed, the takin's spirit escapes through a small hole at the tip of its horns, instantly reincarnating in a place of mystical sanctuary. This serves to reconcile their hunting with their Buddhist faith, which would otherwise preclude them from killing.[4]

གཉན་

Trophy hunters seeking prestige come from all over the globe to the mountains of Inner Asia in search of the argali *Ovis ammon*, the great spiral-horned cousin to the Caspian's mouflon *O. gmelini*, and North America's bighorn *O. canadensis* and Dall sheep *O. dalli*.[5] The largest and most prized subspecies is the Marco Polo sheep *O. a. polii*, found in the Pamirs that stretch into the far western edge of China along its borders with Tajikistan, Afghanistan, and Pakistan. Several other subspecies live throughout the ranges of the northwest, but the most widespread is the Tibetan argali *O. a. hodgsoni*, spread sparsely across most of the Tibetan Plateau.

For a long time argali were thought to be extremely scarce, largely wiped out during the Maoist period. Early Western explorers who passed through in the early twentieth century had sighted many of the wild sheep, seeing them often and in large numbers. When Western researchers first returned to the region in the 1980s and early 1990s, they revisited many of the sites mentioned from earlier texts, only to find little to no evidence of argali, and that the locals they spoke to had not seen the sheep for many years, even decades.[6]

In some of the areas, such as southeastern Qinghai, argali were indeed gone, along with most large animals. Elsewhere, though, the sparse and fragmented distribution of the wild sheep was only partly due to past overhunting. Argali are widespread but keep to a narrow ecological niche, preferring a very limited range of habitats. They require hilly terrain but do not make their homes in the steep and rugged reaches of mountains; they are tolerant of arid conditions but not true desert; they can endure chilling winters but cannot find sufficient forage in deep snow; and they are willing to cross open plains, but do not reside there, only moving between uplands. This combination of restrictions naturally requires argali to be widely spread but nowhere very abundant. The greatest impact on their numbers, greater than hunting, has likely been the expansion of pastoralists and livestock since the mid-twentieth century. Argali do not tolerate human disturbance, and unless given a wide swathe of peaceful habitat, they will struggle to return to their abundance of prior centuries.[7]

Siberian ibex *Capra sibirica*, with ridged, scimitar horns just as impressive as those of the argali, are also found in the mountains of the northwest. Most numerous in the Tian Shan, they are found in most of the ranges surrounding the Dzungar Basin.[8] However, some populations—particularly in Inner Mongolia, Gansu, Qinghai, and the eastern Kunlun—have died out as a consequence of human encroachment and hunting.[9]

A relative of the ibex, the Himalayan tahr *Hemitragus jemlahicus*, can also be found along a stretch of the frontier. Himalayan tahr are medium-sized caprids with short, light brown coats in summer that lengthen and darken for the winter season, with males growing magnificent, leonine manes. A small number, perhaps a few hundred, live in a small stretch of the southern Tibetan border, but most of the tahr's natural range is in the Indian and Nepali Himalaya.[10] Himalayan goral *Naemorhedus goral* and serow *Capricornis sumatraensis thar* are also found in the southern reaches of Tibet, but like the tahr, their small numbers and limited range at the edge of Chinese territory have discouraged thorough study, and little is known of them.[11]

གནའ་བ་

One of the snow leopard's favorite prey is the bharal or blue sheep *Pseudois nayaur*, a medium-sized caprid at home in the high craggy reaches of the mountains.[12] Today bharal are probably the most abundant large species of wildlife in the western highlands, found over a broad range and in relatively large numbers. This is in spite of several decades of intensive hunting. Bharal have long been a favored prey not only of snow leopards but of pastoralists, although such subsistence hunting was likely only ever a threat to small, localized populations. However, like the Mongolian gazelle on the northern steppes, the bharal became a target for commercial hunting for export in the late 1950s. From 1958 into the 1970s, between 100,000 and 200,000 kg of bharal meat was exported annually from Qinghai, mostly to Europe.[13] Local government agencies continued to purchase smaller amounts of bharal meat into the 1980s, some still receiving thousands of kilograms a year. The hunting proved too heavy for many bharal populations, and the caprids disappeared from numerous localities.[14] However, once hunting subsided in the 1990s, they made a quick comeback. Preferring high slopes and craggy terrain unsuited for livestock, they suffer little from competition with domestic herds.[15] They have made a strong recovery, and now only a subspecies of dwarf bharal faces is considered endangered.[16] Nonetheless, climate change may sharply shrink available habitat across the Tibetan Plateau, which the bharal may find difficult to endure if they do not have safe corridors to migrate to favorable lands.[17]

གསང་

The most elusive—and arguably the most beautiful—of the world's big cats, the snow leopard *Panthera uncia*, lives across nearly the whole of China's western highlands.[18] One of the smallest of the big cats, the snow leopard lives in the high alpine meadows and craggy peaks of the mountains, though the cats can also live at lower elevations and have even been sighted crossing open desert.[19] The snow leopard's coat is whitish-gray, tinged with faint brown and smattered with black spots and rosettes. The coat is perfect camouflage amongst the rocks and cliff sides, allowing the snow leopard to conceal itself from prey or enemies.[20] The cat has small ears to avoid losing heat in the frigid, thin air of the mountains, and wide, furry paws for walking on snow and loose, rocky terrain. Its exceptionally long tail is also unusually thick, both with stores of fat and dense fur; in the cold it can act as a blanket and warmer for the leopard's face, and as a rudder and counterbalance, especially when leaping or running downslope.[21]

Snow leopards are found only in the highlands of Inner Asia, from the mountains of Southern Siberia and Mongolia, through the Stans of Central Asia and into India, Nepal, and Bhutan.[22] China holds approximately sixty percent of the cats' entire range, covering over 1,700,000 sq km (656,370 sq mi) of the west of the country, hosting at least half of the global population. Within China snow leopards are most widespread and numerous in Xinjiang, Qinghai, and Tibet, but they are also found in the high mountains of Sichuan and Gansu, and have been sighted in Inner Mongolia, Ningxia, and Yunnan.[23] In some places at the edges of their territory snow leopards even share habitat with common leopards, and in Sichuan they live above the bamboo forests of the giant panda.[24]

The history of the snow leopard in China is extremely muddled. Some of this is due to the fact that the cats live in rugged habitat remote from settled agriculturalists. The pastoralists most familiar with snow leopards until recently lacked the literary traditions that make tracing the history of China's tigers comparatively easy. Yet even the written record that does exist is confusing. The current Chinese name for the species, *xuěbào* 雪豹, is a direct translation of the English "snow leopard," and was coined only in the 1920s.[25] Before the adoption of the new name—and widely for many years after—the species was noted under a number of different terms. These were not standardized, and when combined with frequent misidentifications, the result is that records prior to the use of the term *xuěbào* are highly unreliable. Nonetheless, the snow leopard was clearly known, certainly to the Tibetans, Mongols, and other peoples who lived in their range, but also to the Han.

References to creatures that closely fit the physical and behavioral attributes of snow leopards appear in some of the earliest extant texts. Scholars have nominated the *qiúěr* 酋耳, *mèngjí* 孟极, *zōuyú* 驺虞, *pí* 貔, and many others as possibly genuine, if somewhat fanciful, ancient references to the snow leopard.[26] Even some later records that can confidently be identified as snow leopards are not always reliable. Chinese records attest to snow leopards living in the northern reaches of Manchuria, and Arthur de Carle Sowerby also believed the cats ranged that far north and east.[27] Père Armand David even thought that the ounce—as the snow leopard was once called— lived not far north of Beijing.[28] Wen Rongsheng lists records of snow leopards in Manchuria and North China into the early decades of the twentieth century.[29] There is no reliable evidence to support such claims, however, and the terrain of the region is by and large unsuitable for the cats. Snow leopard pelts did come south through Manchuria to Beijing as trade and tribute, but these all but certainly originated much farther west, in the South Siberian Mountains or the Khangai, Sayan or Altai Ranges of Mongolia.[30]

Early twentieth century Western visitors to the highlands had no luck spotting the snow leopard alive, so instead they remarked on the pugmarks or other signs they spotted, and especially on the pelts found for sale in market centers. Snow leopard pelts were easily available on the Han-Tibetan borderlands of Sichuan, and even in western cities such as Chengdu and Chongqing.[31] In the 1920s in Xinjiang's Tian Shan, locals reported that an increase in the market price for pelts had led to heavy hunting of the range's snow leopards, causing a noticeable decline in their numbers.[32]

Market hunting for snow leopard pelts continued after the Communist takeover, though the low prices on offer restrained hunters from pursuing the species to extinction.[33] Nonetheless, the cats were targeted in the predator extermination campaigns of the era, and early surveys from years later suggested they were extirpated from many localities. Pastoralists killed the snow leopards in retaliation for preying on livestock, and took full advantage of state demand for pelts and bones.[34] Bones were by far the more valuable, worth up to ¥1,800 per cat compared to only ¥50 to ¥100 for a pelt.[35] Snow leopards were finally given legal protection in 1983, but state purchasing agents continued to buy pelts and bones for years after, supposedly due to innocent ignorance of the legal changes.[36] Such procurement programs had once been a means to fund predator control, supplying the money to subsidize guns and ammunition handed out to hunters and herders. They eventually shut up shop, in part due to changes in policy, but also because the hunters stopped bringing in their goods, instead selling on the more lucrative black market.[37]

Tibetans, Mongols, Kazakhs, and other Central Asian peoples have long both revered and made use of the snow leopard. With the general exception of Tibetans, these pastoralists traditionally used snow leopard pelts to make hats, belts, coats, or wall mountings for their homes.[38] Many herding families still possess such items and consider them precious heirlooms to be passed down the generations.[39] Tibetans used the cats as medicine—bones and teeth were the most frequently used; the canines to soothe toothaches and the bones to treat a wide variety of problems, from backaches to dog bites. Consuming snow leopard flesh was thought to drive away evil spirits and was therefore used in hopes of curing mental illness. Doctors of Tibetan medicine have stated that snow leopard parts were rarely used, however, on account of scarcity.[40]

Poaching of snow leopards for their pelts and bones continues across most snow leopard range. Some of the trade stems from retaliatory killings, when herders lose a number of livestock to a snow leopard—or at least suspect a snow leopard—and, having killed the cat, seek to gain a degree of recompense by selling the body. Others hunt the cats with the express purpose of profit, knowing bones and pelts still bring high prices.[41] The killings have declined over time, however, and since 2010 there have been far fewer cases of poaching and trade than in earlier years.[42]

Due to their cryptic nature and their remote and forbidding home terrain, wild snow leopards were little studied anywhere until the 1980s. In China the first surveys for snow leopards took place in the middle of that decade. After those early surveys research was largely restricted to neighboring countries until Chinese ornithologist Ma Ming, collaborating with foreign colleagues, began China's first in-depth research program in 2002.[43] Since then snow leopard research has rapidly grown, providing an expanding body of knowledge about the cats. One pleasant surprise has been the realization that snow leopards are more widespread and numerous than once believed. China is estimated to host between 2,500 and 4,500 snow leopards, one half or more of the global total.[44] There is however, so little historical information about snow leopards that it is impossible to say with any certainty how their numbers and distributions have changed.[45]

Although some threats such as poaching are much reduced, recent decades have brought a range of new threats. As China's government has pushed to develop its poor western regions, large infrastructure projects have sprawled across the highlands. The new roads and railways fragment the landscape, and allow more people—such as miners and tourists—easier access to what was once dauntingly remote territory. And with greater access to motor vehicles and electronics, many nomads have chosen to settle. Their new lifestyles often lead to more reliance on manufactured goods, and as they consume more they pollute more.[46] Yet the push to preserve the highland's ecosystems has led some to devote themselves to protecting nature, with a number of herders giving up their flocks to become rangers in region's reserves and newly gazetted national parks.[47]

The greatest threats to snow leopards now are their perpetual conflict with herders, and the warming of the highlands. Most pastoralists view snow leopards as relatively benign creatures, far less loathed and feared than wolves, brown bears, or even lynxes.[48] The cats do occasionally kill livestock, however, and herders respond with a range of attitudes and actions. Some are fatalistic, resigned to the belief that snow leopard predation is simply a part of the cosmic order that must be stoically endured. Others suspect they have lost livestock because they have offended the local mountain gods and must face punishment.[49] Others respond with violence of their own, killing the culprit cat—usually by poisoning the carcass of their lost livestock.

As snow leopard numbers seem to grow, they increasingly live in close proximity to large numbers of domestic livestock, far larger than the available number of wild prey. In that light it is remarkable there is not more predation of domestic herds, yet the cats have shown a marked avoidance of the pastoralists' animals. Indeed, the higher the number of livestock in a given area, the fewer snow leopards there are, likely as a consequence of a drop in wild prey numbers.[50] Like most species of large mammal in the western highlands, snow leopards face the danger of herdsmen and their flocks laying claim to the best habitat, squeezing the native species into the margins.

The warming climate will further squeeze snow leopards. As alpine meadows and wetlands dry out, and as forests climb upslope, snow leopards' prey—and consequently the cats themselves—will lose large tracts of prime habitat.[51] The cats are projected to see anywhere from fourteen to as much as forty-six percent become unsuitable by 2070. Most of their habitat in the Himalayas and Hengduan Mountains will be lost, as will much in the southeastern Tibetan Plateau. They should have refuge, however, in their territories to the north, in the Altai and Qilian Mountains, as well as the complex of the Tian Shan, Pamir, and Karakoram ranges.[52] Many local and even regional populations will be forced to migrate, or otherwise die out, yet there should be sufficient refuge for the species to survive in the western mountains far into the future.

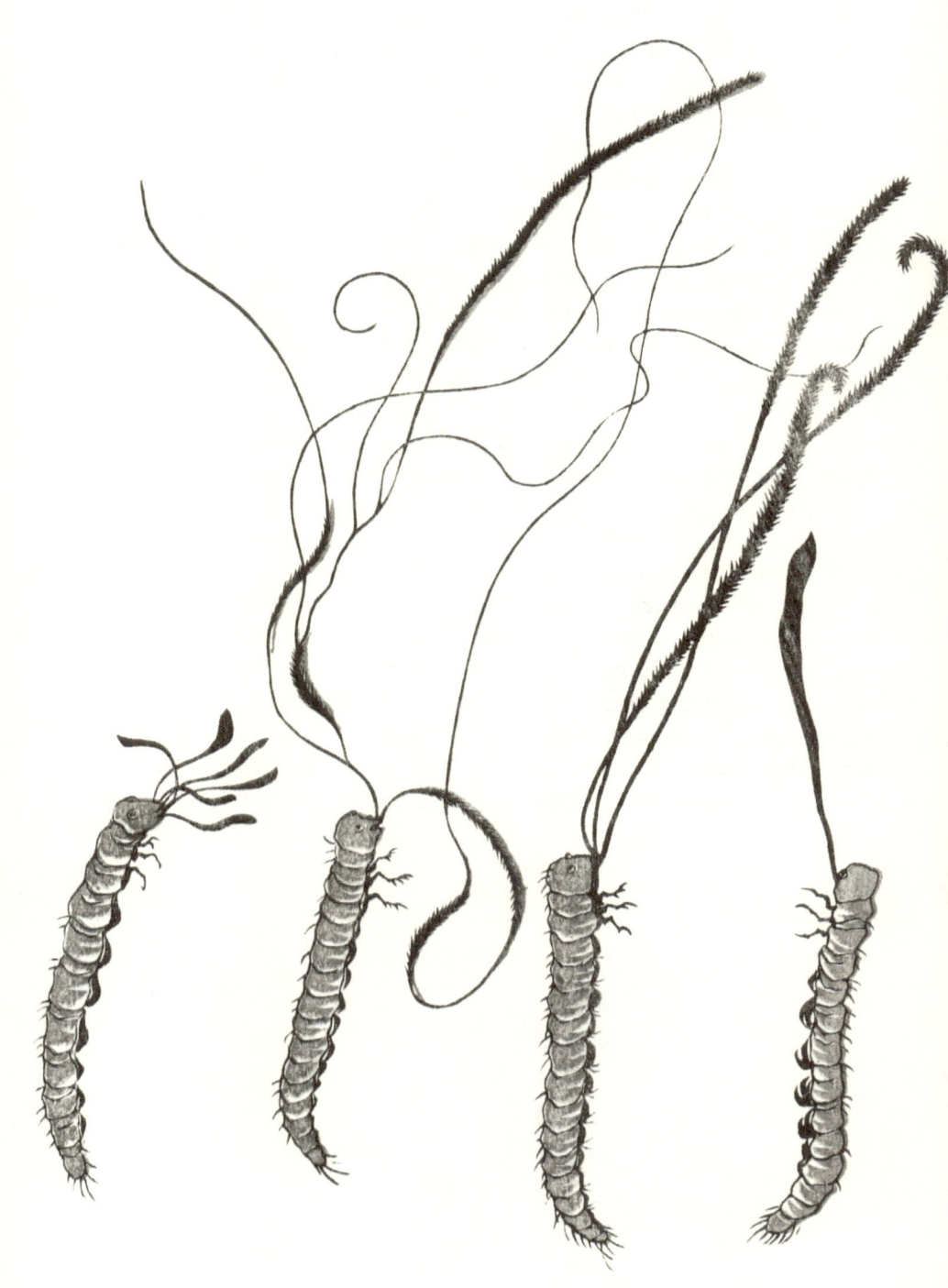

Natural Riches

THOUGH some animals such as the chiru have been used in Tibetan and Chinese medicine, few of the highlands' animal species have suffered intensive harvesting for the medicinal trade. However, the same cannot be said for their plants and fungi. Like all premodern medical traditions, Tibetan medicine relies heavily on plants and fungi. Many of the ingredients valued in Tibetan medicine found their way into the Chinese *materia medica* and have been used in both traditions for centuries. It is only in recent decades, however, with the expansion of direct Chinese administration into Tibetan lands and the explosions in demand of the Maoist and post-Mao eras, that harvests of wild medicinals has reached worrisome levels.

ཨ་རུ་རྩེ་སྨུག་ཁ་

One genus widely and intensively harvested for the Chinese medicinal trade is *Fritillaria*, members of the lily family. *Fritillaria* bulbs have been used for millennia across Eurasia, and in Chinese medicine are used to treat colds or clear the airways. Several species of *Fritillaria* are used in over 200 kinds of Chinese medicines, and the vast majority of bulbs are harvested from the wild.[1] The high demand for use within China and for export—now totaling billions of bulbs each year—has caused the value of wild *Fritillaria* bulbs to reach up to hundreds of US dollars per kilogram. Trade data from the 1950s onwards shows that annual harvests of one species, *Fritillaria cirrhosa*, have fallen over the decades, a possible indication that wild populations are slowly dwindling.[2] Recent surveys have indeed found that areas with the highest intensity of harvesting host below average densities of extant *Fritillaria* plants.[3] Harvesting of some populations of *Fritillaria delavayi* has been so intense for over long enough time to drive evolutionary changes in the plants, pushing them to change their color in the pursuit of improved camouflage.[4]

More valuable than *Fritillaria* or perhaps any medicinal plants have been a number of fungi. One of these, the matsutake mushroom *Tricholoma matsutake*, transformed entire rural communities in the 1980s and 1990s.[5] Matsutake are mushrooms that grow in temperate forests from China to North America and North Africa.[6] Found in Manchuria and the high forests of Yunnan, Sichuan, and southeran Tibet, local inhabitants did not consider matsutake to be of great interest. That suddenly changed when demand from Japan, where matsutake are a seasonal delicacy, led to a surge in the market price of the mushrooms.[7]

Matsutake only grow in tandem with trees—in Yunnan primarily pine and oak—and have so far proven impossible to cultivate. The high mountain forests of Yunnan, Sichuan, and Tibet are an ideal environment for them. Human changes to pine forests through logging and fire helped spread the pine trees matsutake need, likely expanding their territory and number over the past centuries and particularly in recent decades.[8] Despite current demand, native peoples such as the Yi and Tibetans have never considered matsutake desirable. Yi children in central Yunnan would pick and sell the mushrooms to earn spending money, but even after the Yi incorporated more wild mushrooms into their diets during the famine years of the Great Leap Forward, matsutake remained of little value.[9]

In the 1980s, Japanese taste for the mushrooms sparked a sudden change in the livelihoods of entire communities in the region. Exports began in 1985, and by the following year the trade had exploded, with hundreds of tonnes of matsutake sent to Japan every year.[10] Improvements in transportation infrastructure made it possible to ship out fresh mushrooms, bringing in even more money. The mushroom soon became Yunnan's single most valuable—and China's fifth most valuable—agricultural export, annually earning tens of millions of US dollars.[11] Oversupply eventually caused prices to fall, but in 2017 meager harvests sent them soaring again.[12]

The new mushroom market led to entire communities transforming into matsutake villages, with households sending some or all of their members into the forests to pick mushrooms. By the first years of the new millennium around eighty percent of households in matsutake producing areas of Yunnan were participating in the trade. The end of commercial logging in the region in 1998 had cut them off from what had been by far the largest local source of revenue, and the mushrooms proved lifesaving. Within a short time mushroom picking households earned between fifty and eighty percent of their income from sales of matsutake.[13] Many Tibetan families used the matsutake money to build large, beautifully appointed traditional homes, or to buy motor vehicles or open businesses.[14] In Yi regions, matsutake wealth fueled a resurgence in Yi cultural pride and expression, as members of the ethnic minority built a new industry where their own language predominated, and they used their profits to open cultural centers and restaurants, as well as to fund local festivals.[15]

The massive and sustained expansion in matsutake harvesting caused great worry amongst many conservationists, who feared the many tonnes of mushrooms removed from the forests would eventually endanger the population. Matsutake only grow under a strict set of conditions and mature slowly. Some counties have instituted protections against overharvesting, and many mushroom pickers now carefully guard and tend to the matsutake within their designated patch of forest, intent on ensuring they grow into the highest commercial grade of mushroom.[16] Despite this the mushrooms seem resilient against heavy harvesting, and face far greater dangers from the disturbance and destruction of their habitat, which the changing climate will shrink in the coming decades.[17] The effects are already being felt, as heat waves and drought in 2022 contributed to a drop in harvests of up to ninety percent.[18] Whether the matsutake are in danger of disappearing is not yet clear, but with careful management of the forests and markets, the mushrooms may remain on the menu for many years to come.

དབྱར་རྩ་དགུན་འབུ

The single most sought after species of wildlife on the Tibetan Plateau is a parasitic fungus, *Ophiocordyceps sinensis*.[19] In Tibetan *O. sinensis* is called *yartsa gunbu*, meaning "summer-grass, winter-worm," commonly shortened to "*bu*." The name is a pithy description of the fungus' life cycle. In winter caterpillars of the species *Thitarodes* burrow into the soils of the highland pastures to hibernate. Normally, once the weather warms, the caterpillars would mature into ghost moths, but those infected with spores of *O. sinensis* are instead consumed from the inside and turned into mummified shells from which the fruiting body of the fungus emerges. Thus, when dug up in summer, the sprout-like mushroom growing out of its caterpillar host makes it appear as though the insects have indeed transformed into grass.[20]

Yartsa gunbu has long been a valued ingredient in Tibetan medicine, with references to it appearing in texts as far back as the fifteenth century. The fungus was used as a potent sexual tonic, as well as treatment for a diverse array of other ailments.[21] References to caterpillar fungus may have appeared in translations of texts brought from Tibetan as early as the eighth century, and by the fifteenth century *yartsa gunbu* was passing through China and onwards to Japan. By the mid-eighteenth century the prized fungus was a regular feature of Chinese medical texts.[22] Even at that time it was exceptionally precious. In the early eighteenth century the Jesuit Father Dominique Parrenin (1665–1741) reported that it was so rare and expensive—a small amount he purchased, old and rotten, "coſt more than four times its Weight in Silver"—that it was reserved almost exclusively for the imperial court's use.[23] Called *dōngchóng xiàcǎo* 冬虫夏草 in Chinese—often shortened to *chóngcǎo*—the fungus was for a long time too rare to attract widespread attention. By the mid-twentieth century, however, harvest of the fungus had reached over 100,000 kg per year.[24] Like nearly everything else in the economy, *yartsa gunbu* collection came under state direction, and local households were obligated to provide their communes with a daily quota during the collecting season.

The market for the fungus collapsed during the Cultural Revolution, and harvest numbers dropped in turn. Prices began to rise in the 1980s with the return of a liberalized market, and though prices—as well as harvests—have always fluctuated, the retail cost of caterpillar fungus has risen to obscene heights in recent years, climbing from ¥200 per kg in 1995 to ¥250,000 ($40,000) per kg in 2012.[25] With such riches waiting to be plucked from the soils of the highland pastures, increasing numbers of rural Tibetans began to devote weeks of each year to collecting *yartsa gunbu*. Picking caterpillar fungus led to a regional economic boom, allowing once impoverished herders and farmers to build new homes and obtain the most modern amenities. Much of the wealth went into rebuilding Buddhist monasteries and cultural sites, most of which had been destroyed or repurposed during the Maoist years.[26]

The flood of harvesters also led to many problems. Turf wars broke out over fungus-bearing pastureland; litter and human waste polluted the grasslands; and careless, destructive digging damaged the soils and vegetation. All this led to worries for the long-term survival of *O. sinensis* populations.[27] Harvest totals have not been carefully tracked, and no long-term research has been conducted to determine any trends. Anecdotally, neither harvesters nor traders seem concerned about dropping output, but rather worry about increased competition.[28] This suggests that although it is conceivable that populations of *yartsa gunbu* may have fallen over time, with barely any research conducted on the species until recent years, there is too little evidence from which to judge.

Anecdotal evidence, however, supports conservationists' concerns. Long-time harvesters of *yartsa gunbu* have noticed a decline in the fungus populations over the past two decades, for which overharvesting, climate change, and annual fluctuations in weather are to blame.[29] Efforts to artificially propagate *yartsa gunbu* have been ongoing since the 1950s, yet none succeeded until recently.[30] Artificial production remains relatively small—at only fifteen to twenty tonnes in 2020, no more than a quarter of the wild harvest—and has yet to have a clear impact on the market price of wild *yartsa gunbu*.[31]

Looking ahead, the question becomes whether the new ability to artificially cultivate *Ophiocordyceps sinensis* will end the wild harvest. A collapse in demand for wild *yartsa gunbu* would relieve the wild populations from the prospect of overharvesting, but would also deprive large numbers of rural Tibetans of a major source of income. However, customers' general preference for wild over cultivated ingredients is likely to keep demand high.[32] To add further concern, except under the most optimistic projections, climate change is expected to further shrink *yartsa gunbu*'s suitable habitat.[33] If a market for caterpillar fungus is to continue indefinitely, more care must be taken to ensure harvest practices and intensity do not endanger populations of caterpillar or fungus.[34]

Many of the highlands' animals have suffered from overhunting, but only one, the chiru or Tibetan antelope *Pantholops hodgsonii*, has faced extinction as a result of the demands of fashion.[35] Medium-sized ungulates, chiru have pale to ruddy brown coats, which lighten almost to white during the rut. The fur consists of long guard hairs over an undercoat of short wool, one of the animal kingdom's finest and warmest. Males also have black faces and sport a pair of long, slender, pointed black horns which are ridged for most of their length.[36]

Until the late twentieth century, chiru lived over most of the Tibetan Plateau on flat, open steppe; their range is now reduced, with most herds found in the Changtang of northwestern Tibet.[37] Most chiru populations are migratory, moving several hundred kilometers between summer and winter grazing grounds, while females make a separate trek to congregate in their thousands at calving grounds. Except during the rut, mature males and females spend their time separately, the males in bachelor herds and the females with their young.

As is true for all species of wildlife on the Tibetan Plateau, there is little testament to the abundance and distribution of chiru prior to the arrival of Westerners in the late nineteenth and early twentieth centuries. Examination of the present chiru population's genetic profile can, however, provide a glimpse into the species' history. Approximately 5,000 years ago the chiru population decreased dramatically and rapidly, and though the reason will remain uncertain, it is very likely that hunting or the loss of habitat to newly arriving and expanding herds of livestock were major contributors.[38]

Despite such severe population decline millennia earlier, accounts from early Western observers tell of large numbers of chiru found over almost the entire Tibetan Plateau.[39] When surveying Tibet in 1896, the Irishman Henry Deasy (1866–1947) came across a stretch of plain in northwestern Tibet where "For many miles in every direction except west...in fact as far as the human eye aided by powerful binoculars could see, there were thousands of antelopes in large herds scattered about irregularly wherever there was plenty of grass." Deasy's companion estimated they saw around 15,000 chiru on the plain, and the animals were very tame and seemingly unfamiliar with humans.[40] When the British soldier Cecil Rawling (1870–1917) passed through that same area on his own survey in 1903, his party saw just as many if not more chiru, a constant stream of thousands of mothers and young migrating through.[41]

Many of the chiru populations that explorers encountered a century or more ago showed no fear of humans, yet the species was in fact widely, if not intensively, hunted. The horns were a particularly coveted item. Mongols used them to tell the future, mark the locations of Buddhist lamas' sky burials, and fashioned them into whip handles that were believed to have the power to prevent a horse from tiring.[42] Tibetans used the horns medicinally to treat a broad array of ailments.[43] Before the confiscation of firearms beginning in 1998, most nomadic Tibetan families possessed at least one matchlock rifle. To improve accuracy, the barrel had two folding prongs attached to act as a rifle rest. The long, tapering prongs were usually made from metal or wood, but their shape was clearly inspired by chiru horns, but some were instead made from chiru horns.[44]

Where nomads were present they often hunted chiru in large numbers, and consequently the animals in those regions were far warier of humans.[45] On the eve of the People's Republic, however, chiru were still widespread, numerous, and across most of the Tibetan Plateau they remained untouched and unafraid of humans.[46] Chiru undoubtedly suffered along with the rest of the highlands' wildlife during the overhunting of the Maoist period, and from the expansion of pastoralists and their herds into formerly unoccupied pasturelands. However, they seemed to fare well enough until the late 1980s when demand for an obscure wool surged in the circles of global high fashion.

Chiru were soon being slaughtered in ever greater numbers across much of their range. Conservationists at first could not discern what drove the killings, but in time it came to light that chiru are the source of *shahtoosh*, the finest and most expensive of wools. *Shahtoosh* is made from the fine undercoat of the chiru, and the lightness and warmth of *shahtoosh* shawls and scarves made them highly coveted amongst the elite of Persianate Inner Asia in centuries past. Unfortunately for the chiru, they cannot be sheared or combed for their wool; the fine undercoat hairs are too short and attached to the base of the chiru's guard hairs. Instead the chiru's hide must be taken whole, and the undercoat meticulously plucked out. To obtain the wool for a single scarf or shawl, three to five chiru must be killed.[47]

For hundreds if not thousands of years, Tibetans have hunted chiru and traded the skins, which eventually reach the *shahtoosh* weavers of Kashmir. Records of the wool go back to at least the seventh century CE, when the great Tang dynasty Buddhist monk Xuanzang (玄奘, 602–664) mentioned the wool in his account of his time passing through Kashmir. Nineteenth century British travelers also noted the fineness, expense, and rarity of "*tus.*" Consulting the traders of the raw

wool, they learned its source was a wild goat or ibex.[48] But the traders of unworked chiru wool were extremely protective of their hold on the good, and sought to obscure its origins. Knowing full well its true source, they nonetheless spun stories of it coming from tufts of wool that Tibetan ibex had rubbed off on bushes and rocks, or that it was spun from fine Siberian goose down.[49] In their own testimony, most of the spinners and weavers claimed they did not even know *shahtoosh* came from chiru, much less that the animals were slaughtered for their undercoats.[50]

The market for shahtoosh had been limited mostly to a small clientele in South Asia and the Middle East, but in the 1980s demand among the wealthy and fashion forward in the Western world caused a boom in prices, which in turn sparked a rush for more wool. The poaching quickly spread across the entirety of the chiru's range, with many thousands killed each year. Chiru numbers dropped dramatically in many regions, as people traveled from near and far to seek their fortune in chiru wool. The largest gangs came from the region's big cities and drove into the farthest reaches of the Tibetan Plateau to slaughter the animals in their hundreds. Some were groups of government, party, and military officials armed with automatic rifles. Others posed as gold miners—then still a legal practice—but arrived in convoys of jeeps and trucks, attacking at night so as to dazzle the chiru with their headlights before gunning them down.[51] Nomadic families, too, moved into chiru range in search of quick and easy riches.[52]

The official response was often nonexistent, at best ineffectual. Few reserves had the resources to stop the poachers. The Altun Shan Reserve in the Altyn-Tagh once hosted a large population of chiru, but in the early 1990s poachers decimated the herds.[53] The reserve staff, which in 1993 numbered only seventeen members to cover a territory of 45,000 sq km (17,375 sq mi), was powerless to intervene. In 1996 when officials finally rallied the strength to confront one of the gangs in the reserve, they found a stash of over 1,100 chiru hides.[54] Over the course of the 1990s, an estimated 250,000 to 300,000 chiru were killed to satiate world fashion's taste for *shahtoosh*.[55] The species was on a rapid course for extinction.

When the renowned field biologist George Schaller (1933–) uncovered the connection between the slaughter of chiru with the international *shahtoosh* trade, he and other conservationists began to rally support to end it. Trade was banned across the globe by 1998, and although a market for *shahtoosh* remains, it is greatly reduced.[56] On the Tibetan Plateau local citizens took matters into their own hands. In a vast stretch of Qinghai called Hoh Xil, Gisang Sonam Dorje (བསོད་ནམས་ རྡོ་རྗེ, 1954–1994), a local official, formed a vigilante band to stop the killing. Named the Wild Yak Brigade, the group patrolled Hoh Xil and confiscated chiru hides. The work was dangerous, and Dorje was killed in a confrontation with a poaching gang in 1994. The Brigade continued its work until the government took over in 2001.[57] After the full weight of government enforcement arrived, the worst of the slaughter was brought under control. Within a few years, surviving chiru populations began to bounce back, and in time some herds even began to lose their intense fear of humans.[58]

A more recent worry—the Qinghai-Tibet railway which cuts across a chiru migration route—proved disruptive during construction, but has since been little hindrance to the chiru, due to the inclusion of a crucial wildlife passage.[59] In fact the chiru have grown so accustomed to the railway that they will rest and forage under its bridges and power lines.[60]

Chiru have made a strong recovery. The decimated herds, such as those of the Altyn-Tagh, are steadily growing.[61] By the end of 2020 their total population within China was estimated to have reached around 300,000.[62] The speed and strength of their return, however, is unusual amongst the highlands' species. Saving chiru was a relatively simple—albeit difficult—affair. Though they suffered from the loss and degradation of habitat, it was only overhunting that presented an existential threat. Unlike most endangered animals in China, the danger to the chiru primarily came from outside the country. Once the global demand for *shahtoosh* was cut, and the laws against hunting enforced, the chiru were able to bounce back with little further help.[63] Although poaching and the *shahtoosh* trade continue, they are much reduced and no longer threaten the species' survival.[54] Barring a rampant revival of the trade, the chiru look well placed to weather the challenges of the future.

QINLING & HENGDUAN MOUNTAINS

Map of the Qinling Mountains

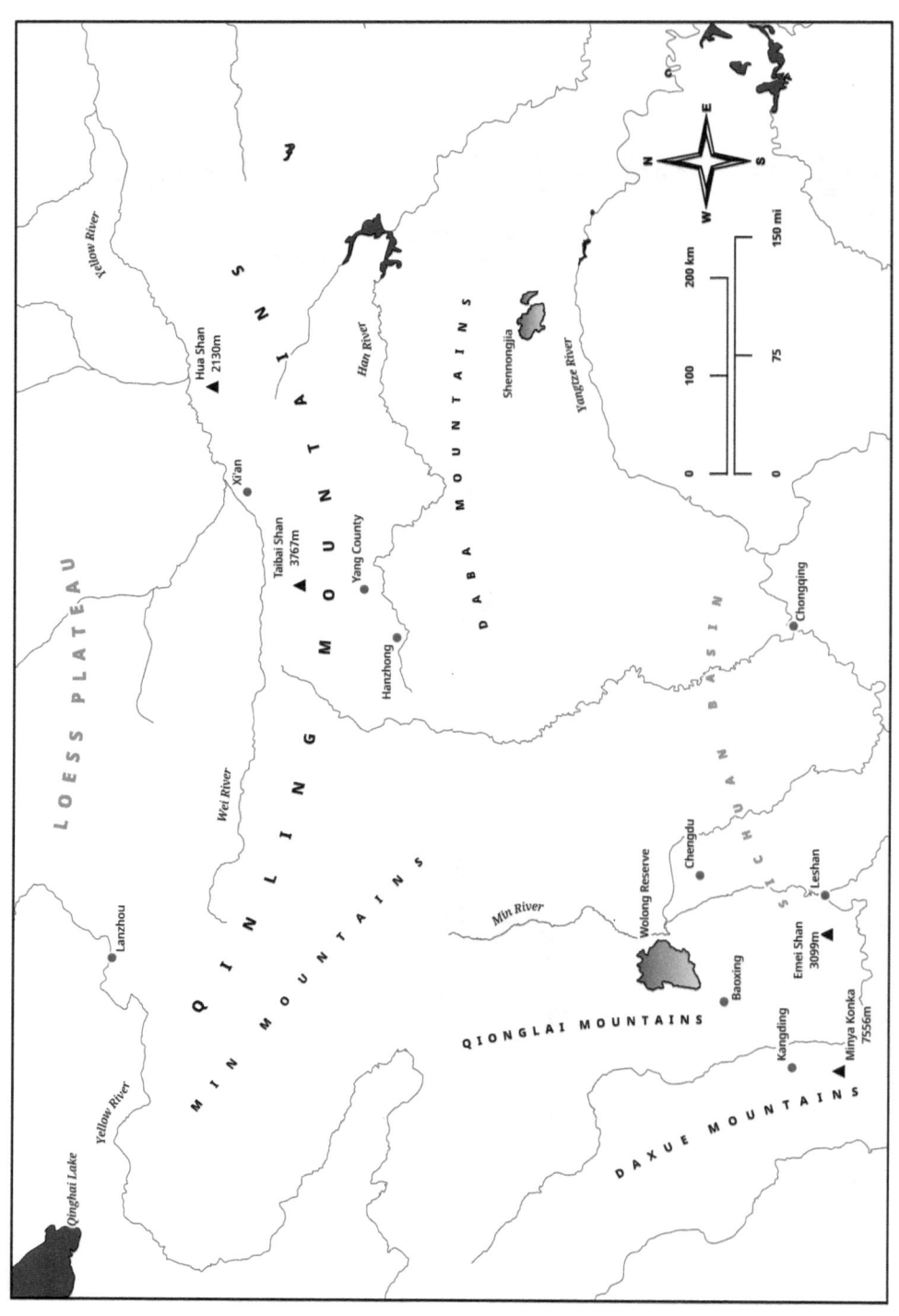

THE Qinling mountains stretch from west to east, running from Gansu across southern Shaanxi to Hebei. The range, which marks the watershed between the Yellow and Yangtze rivers, is considered a major boundary between north and south China, both geographically and culturally. There is a marked difference between the ecosystems of the range's north and south sides. The north faces the Loess Plateau, and its slopes host temperate deciduous and coniferous forests that can endure the dry, cold winters. The southern slopes border the north rim of the Sichuan Basin, and the warm moist climate allows subtropical forests to thrive. This split gives the Qinling an exceptionally rich variety of plant and animal life.

To the south of the Qinling the Han River flows southeast to Wuhan where it meets the Yangtze. South again across the river rise the Daba Mountains, which enclose the northeast rim of the Sichuan Basin. Like the southern Qinling, the warmth and moisture from the basin give the Daba Mountains a subtropical climate. The greatest patch of intact wildlife habitat in the Daba is the easternmost and highest section of the range, Shennongjia, a rugged massif in western Hubei that forms the core of the Shennongjia forestry district, recently gazetted as a national park.[1] The dense forests of Shennongjia and the wider Daba region host a wealth of plant species, including a number of relict plants such as the dove tree and dawn redwood, and is renowned for its abundance of plants used in traditional medicine.

The high, rugged terrain and dense forests of these mountains have long resisted mass settlement.[2] Han Chinese have at times settled in the Qinling and Daba mountains, but for most of history these lands were at the edge of the Han cultural sphere. The Qinling forests became a source of timber for the imperial cities of the Guanzhong Plain as early as the Qin dynasty, and over the centuries the Chinese cleared more and more of the valleys for cultivation and the mountainsides for lumber. Despite two millennia of cutting, large and healthy forests stood into the middle of the twentieth century, but from 1949, and especially from the 1960s to 1990s, much of what remained fell to industrial forestry. What little still stands is now almost all under protection, but wildlife habitat in the region is patchy and fragmented.

To the west of the Qinling, running north to south and separating southern China from the Tibetan Plateau are the Hengduan Mountains—a great complex of towering, icy peaks. The mountains cover most of western Sichuan, northwestern Yunnan, and the eastern

Map of the Hengduan Mountains

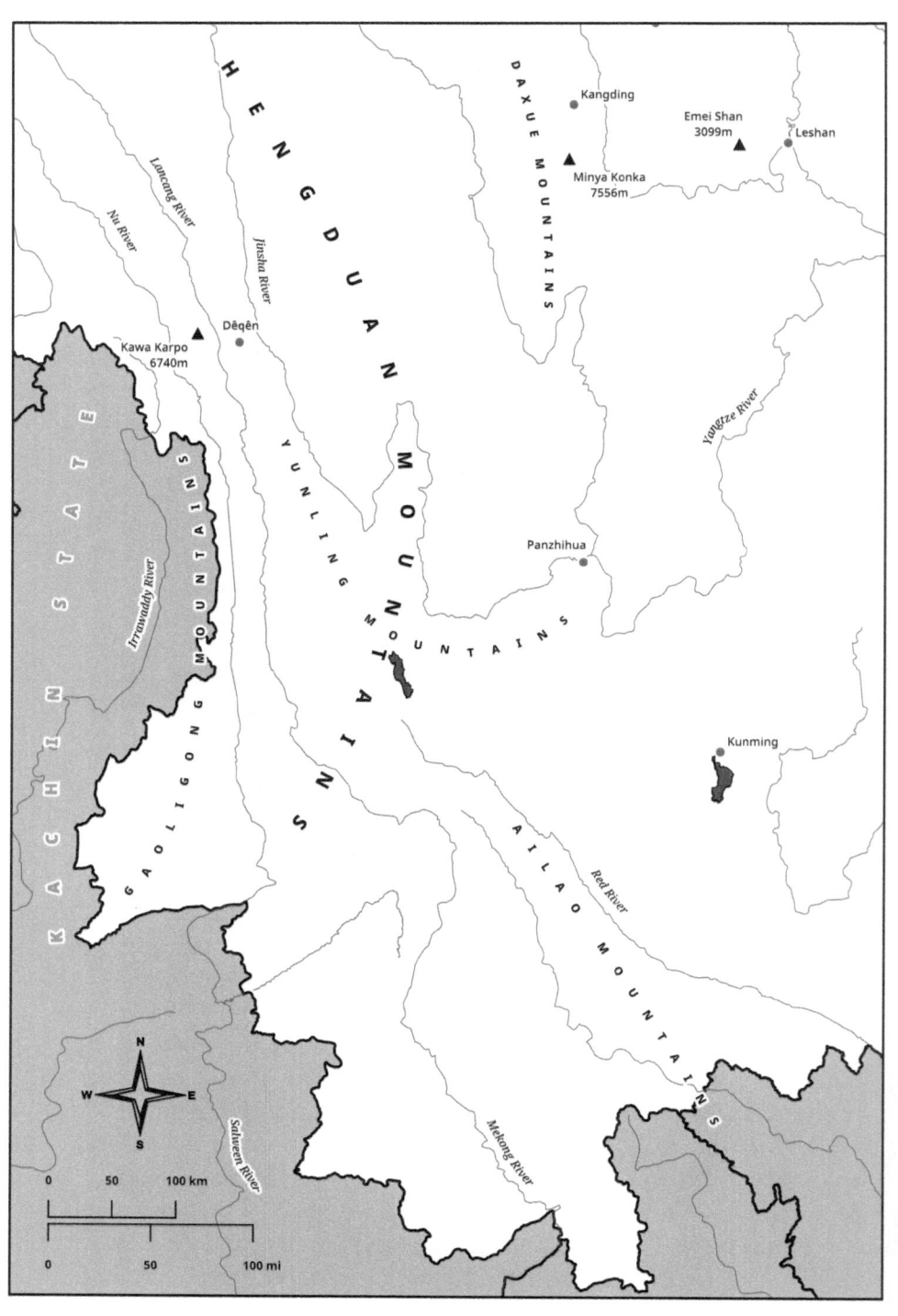

edge of Tibet.[3] The Hengduan consist of many smaller ranges, including the Min, Qionglai, and Daxue ranges in Sichuan, and the Yunling, Ailao, and Gaoligong in Yunnan. The Hengduan are much higher than the Qinling and Daba, and consequently the mix of species includes plants and animals typical of high elevation habitats.[4] Not only giant pandas and gibbons but also snow leopards and blue sheep make their homes there.

For most of history the Hengduan were at or beyond the edge of Chinese civilization. Most of the peoples who live in the region are not Han, and consequently they have generally held different views of the natural world. Tibetans and the related Qiang live in the ranges of northern and western Sichuan. To the south in western Yunnan live the Derung, Lisu, Pumi, Nakhi, Bai, and Yi. These peoples all hold different beliefs and follow different customs, and to the Han they have long been, and generally still are, viewed as exotic and primitive. They all practice agriculture or animal husbandry in some form, yet their impact has not, at least until the last several decades, been as destructive of the surrounding ecosystems and wildlife as has that of the Han. Between the formidable terrain and the less transformative practices of the local populations, the Hengduan's wildlife has managed to escape the near total devastation typically wrought on the wild flora and fauna of Han lands.

Snub-noses & Skywalkers

A MONG those species that have made these ranges their last stronghold are three members of the genus *Rhinopithecus*, the snub-nosed monkeys.[1] There are five extant species of snub-nosed monkey, four of which reside exclusively in China (the fifth, the Tonkin snub-nosed monkey *R. avunculus*, is restricted to a patch of northeastern Vietnam). Three of these species live within the Qinling and Hengduan ranges: the golden snub-nosed monkey, the black-and-white or Yunnan snub-nosed monkey, and the black or Myanmar snub-nosed monkey.[2] All are large monkey species with upturned noses, long fur, and long tails. They spend most of their time in trees, where they feed on leaves and lichens and live in large bands of up to a few hundred. The males are easy to distinguish from the females, being much larger and sporting wart-like lappets at the corners of their upper lips. All four species of *Rhinopithecus* within China share many physical and behavioral characteristics, but their ranges do not overlap, and whether they did so in the past is unknown.

The most numerous and widespread of the snub-nosed monkeys is the golden snub-nosed, *R. roxellana*.[3] As the name suggests, the golden monkeys are the most visually spectacular members of *Rhinopithecus*. The coloration of the three remaining *roxellana* populations—one in Sichuan and Gansu, one in Shaanxi, and one in Hubei—vary slightly, but all share the golden fur and blue faces that make them so arresting. Males have darker, more vibrant coats than females, as well as capes of long fur on their backs. They now live in remote forests at altitudes between 2,000–3,500 m (6,560–11,480 ft), though they would still be in the lowlands had they not been driven away by the advance of agriculture.

Fossil and historical records show that snub-nosed monkeys inhabited wide swathes of eastern, central, and southern China as recently as 2,000 years ago. Precisely which species of snub-nosed monkey lived where is unclear, but it is likely that, just as today, the golden snub-nosed was the most common and widespread of the four. Initially changes in climate forced the monkeys to shift their range northwards, but from the thirteenth century the encroachment of Han settlers moving inland from the coasts pushed *Rhinopithecus* farther and farther west.[4] Even their current and final refuge, the Qinling, was not free from this pressure.

The first great human encroachment into the Qinling came during the Warring States period. The expansionist Qin, based to the north in what is now Shaanxi, coveted the kingdoms of Shu and Ba in present-day Sichuan and Hubei, but the Qinling stood in the way. The terrain was too rugged to simply cut a road through, but Qin was undeterred. Unable to carve through so much stone, the Qin engineers bolted planks directly into the rock walls. The effort required the felling of great stands of timber along the route—not only to form the planks, but also to feed the fires to heat and shatter stone. Qin finished its road, and Shu and Ba promptly fell. The plank roads were expanded throughout the Han period, draining a steady supply of timber from the forests. All of this fragmented the monkeys' habitat, and drove them higher up the mountains.[5]

The Tang dynasty, still remembered as a golden age of power and artistic achievement, also saw the construction of immense palaces and temples, and the largest imperial capital until Ming-era Beijing. Chang'an, present-day Xi'an, was the largest city in the Tang golden age; its only rival in the world was Baghdad. Since the First Emperor subsequent dynasts had built their capitals in the area of Chang'an, and the construction of so many buildings, nearly all of wood and some of immense magnitude, exhausted most of the nearby stands of large timber. Tang Chang'an exceeded all its predecessors in size and grandeur, and in its appetite for lumber. The trees on the northern slopes of the Qinling, closest to Chang'an, fell first. Yet demand was so great and so sustained that logging moved farther and farther south as stocks were exhausted. By the end of the dynasty tens of thousands of laborers were working the southern slopes. The trees at lower elevations, easier to access and transport, were cut first, driving the monkeys further up the slopes. Eventually even trees at higher elevations were felled, further shrinking the monkeys' habitat.[6]

Habitat destruction likely had the greatest impact on *roxellana*, yet at the same time their golden coats brought the unwelcome attention of the fashion-conscious. Elite from the Tang to the Yuan prized the golden hides as status symbols, whether fashioned into cushions, quilts, or clothing.[7] Hunters, not wanting to be wasteful, were glad to sell the flesh and bones as well. The meat was believed to impart strength, and the bones were steeped in alcohol to form medicinal wine for arthritis or hearing trouble, or boiled down to a gelatinous paste for treating rheumatism. Live monkeys, too, were in demand; like gibbons and macaques they became pets for the wealthy.[8]

As China's population expanded during the Song dynasty, more and more people moved into the Qinling, settling permanently to farm. As they transformed the lower elevations into crop fields, they pushed the monkeys and nearly all the other wildlife higher up the slopes, further shrinking and fragmenting their habitat. Farther east *Rhinopithecus* had for centuries endured even more extensive destruction of its habitat, and by the start of the Ming dynasty snub-nosed monkeys had begun to retreat from the east and south of China. Despite enduring such sustained persecution for generations, there is little to indicate their populations had suffered any catastrophic reduction. They were diminished but not yet endangered. However by the late Ming, as the human population increased and moved into formerly marginal and wild lands, the impact on snub-nosed monkeys grew.[9]

During the course of the Qing dynasty *Rhinopithecus* disappeared completely from the east and south of China and from the lowlands of the west. Though the Qinling remained a haven, human refugees from south and east of the range began to flood in during the early to mid-nineteenth century. They came from regions with too many people and too little land, looking for tillable plots of their own. Neither the soil nor landscape were ideal—the terrain too rugged, the soil too rocky—which meant they had to cut down and level large patches of forest to grow enough to survive, taking away more and more from the wildlife. Populations of *roxellana* began to shrink, some to disappear. Timber factories grew during the same period, and they logged until, by the middle of the twentieth century, there were few large trees left to cut. By the beginning of the People's Republic most of the monkeys' habitat had been cleared, and only three populations survived: one straddling northern Sichuan and southern Gansu, another in Shaanxi, and the smallest in Hubei.[10]

With the founding of New China in 1949, little changed for the Qinling's wildlife until the frenzy of the Great Leap Forward. In 1958, still the early days of the movement, a people's commune in Gansu's Baishuijiang region—later a nature reserve and now part of the Giant Panda National Park—decided the golden monkeys were an untouched resource and resolved to put them to good use. Intent on forming a monkey farm, thousands of commune members encircled the forest and tightened their cordon, driving hundreds of *roxellana* into a stockade. There they were to be fruitful and multiply until, keeping to their assigned timetable, they would reach a population of 3,000 by 1967. Nothing went as planned. The monkeys had neither enough space nor food, and the cramped conditions led to outbreaks of both disease and violence. The population plummeted, and before long the monkey farm was scrapped.[11]

In neighboring Shaanxi, in the mountains just south of Xi'an, the Xi'an Zoo led three roundups to capture *roxellana* between 1958 and 1979. The first collection in December 1958 netted roughly 200 monkeys, intended not for display locally but for export. It's not clear if any were sent abroad, but it is known that within two weeks at least 180 of the monkeys were dead. The second effort was not until 1971, when sixty-five were captured. This time only twenty-eight died within two weeks. By the time of the final roundup in 1979, the zoo had refined its care regimen and of 111 captured only sixteen were dead within two weeks—the first roundup's fatality rate of ninety percent had fallen to a mere fourteen. Yet by this time *roxellana* was a legally protected species, and when word of the capture program reached higher authorities the zoo leadership was duly punished.[12]

The 1960s and 1970s saw a general assault against the golden snub-nosed monkeys' remaining populations. Crop cultivation in the Qinling expanded rapidly, leading to more and more habitat conversion. The local populations of *roxellana* suffered further fragmentation and isolation. After a forestry station was opened in Shennongjia in the early 1960s—then still so remote to be something of a mystery to the outside world—commune members discovered troops of *roxellana*, sometimes numbering in the hundreds. The monkeys soon saw their mountains deforested, and were themselves subjected to hunting for their skins and capture for zoos.[13] Into the 1980s their pelts could still be found for sale in Chengdu and other cities.[14]

As the danger from hunting and capture receded, the threat from logging surged. Logging had continued during the Maoist era, but *roxellana* had escaped the catastrophe of clearcutting. The most intensive activity had occurred in different areas. The massive construction works of the Third Front movement—Mao's scheme to move strategic industrial works far inland to keep them safe from Soviet or American attack—had stripped parts of Sichuan of its forests. Construction of the gargantuan Panzhihua steel complex in the remote mountains of southern Sichuan led to a loss of nearly a quarter of the region's forest cover after 1965.[15] Logging for the timber industry, legal and illegal, had cleared much of the rest of the region. In the Wolong Reserve, famous as the base for early studies on giant pandas, logging peaked between 1961 and 1975.

The shift away from the Maoist command economy finally reached the Qinling logging industry in the 1990s, leading to a massive jump in deforestation. State logging operations and local governments that had once relied on the central government to dictate quotas and provide set payment suddenly found themselves cut off. Left to fend for themselves they abandoned the selective cutting of only valuable trees. Now they began to raze the forests, maximizing both profit and ecological damage. The clearcutting continued unabated until 1998, when the central government imposed a logging ban throughout most of the country in response to massive flooding that had been exacerbated by erosion stemming from deforestation. Decrees from the center often hold little weight in China, especially in lands so far from the capital, but this time Beijing was serious, and soon most logging ended.

At present *roxellana* is in no imminent danger of extinction but is hardly safe. The last three populations are holding on, and although the species is thought to have declined in number by over fifty percent within the past four decades, recent surveys suggest they are rebounding. The largest population, in Sichuan and Gansu, consists of between 15,800 and 18,100 individuals, while the smaller Shaanxi and Hubei populations are much smaller, at only 5,200 to 5,700 and 1,500 to 2,100 monkeys, respectively. Their progress is uneven—while the Sichuan-Gansu population is faring quite well, those of Shaanxi and Hubei still face greater risks.[16] How those numbers compare to the distant past, no one knows. The threats to the golden snub-nosed monkeys have begun to fade and are not as severe as in recent decades.[17] Much of their habitat is now under the jurisdiction of the new national parks system, which should provide protection from further poaching and deforestation.[18]

Perhaps the greatest threat to *roxellana* is climate change. As the climate shifts the monkeys will find much of their current habitat no longer suitable. As a whole they are estimated to face a loss of between fourteen and twenty-five percent.[19] Hubei's *roxellana* face a potential loss of two-thirds of their habitat by 2050.[20] Where will the golden monkeys flee? They can only climb so high up the mountains. There are few places nearby that can act as refuge, and the journey there is often so treacherous the monkeys simply will not risk it. Much of their former habitat requires restoration if the golden snub-nosed monkeys are to thrive again.

渼

Another species nearing the highest reach of its range is the black-and-white snub-nosed monkey *Rhinopithecus bieti*.[21] The black-and-white snub-nosed makes its home in the high forests of the snowy mountains of the Hengduan range, squeezed between the Yangtze and Mekong rivers as they flow south from southern Tibet and into northwestern Yunnan.[22] Less flashy than *roxellana*, *bieti* has no gold in its coat but is instead a mix of black, gray, and white. A dark crest tops their heads, fading to light gray around their white and pink faces. Their backs, arms, legs, and tails are dark, with light bellies and bottoms. Males are much larger than females, with a disparity even greater than seen in *roxellana*. The monkeys live at high altitude, from elevations of 2,600 m to 4,600 m (8,530 ft to 15,090 ft), where they spend their time in coniferous and mixed coniferous-broadleaf forests, feeding predominantly on leaves and lichens.[23]

The black-and-white monkeys undoubtedly ranged more widely in the past than now, yet current evidence suggests they have not lived east of the Yangtze within the local peoples' cultural memory. It is entirely possible the Yangtze and Mekong have long restricted *bieti* to a limited range.[24] This helps explain why they remained all but unknown to the wider world until the late nineteenth century when French missionary-naturalists first heard of their existence. Père David heard only rumors of the monkeys in 1871, and nineteen years later fellow Frenchmen R.P. Soulie and Monseigneur Félix Biet received specimens from local hunters, confirming the existence of black-and-white snub-nosed monkeys high in the mountains.[25]

Afterwards the monkeys escaped attention until 1960, when Professor Peng Hong-Shou of the Kunming Institute of Zoology saw skins in Dêqên County, Yunnan, where he learned from the locals that the monkeys were still present and still hunted for their furs.[26] As everywhere in China, and as for all other wildlife, the Cultural Revolution was not kind to the black-and-white monkeys. Members of local communes formed teams to hunt the primates for their pelts, meat, and bones, killing them by the hundreds.[27] In one commune alone six hunters managed to kill 500 monkeys during this period.[28] Even in areas such as Baima Xueshan, where local taboos had long protected *bieti*, tradition was cast aside and the monkeys were hunted

down.[29] *Bieti* soon disappeared from portions of its range, and by the end of the 1970s the species' future looked grim.

In 1979, after the long hiatus of the Cultural Revolution, research on *bieti* began again, but in the first few years of the 1980s researchers found no live monkeys in their study areas.[30] Meanwhile the hunting continued, with state commercial agents purchasing primate parts into the mid-1980s.[31] At the same time the local human populations were rapidly growing. The implementation of the two-child policy in 1970 and the one-child policy in 1979 did little to slow population growth, as nearly everyone belonged to an ethnic minority and was thus exempt. As families grew they opened more land for cultivation and grazing, destroying and degrading the monkeys' habitat. By the end of the first thorough survey of the species, only nineteen bands numbering 2,000 monkeys were found, confined to a much smaller range than researchers had expected.[32]

The 1990s began poorly for the black-and-white monkeys. As prices for their parts increased and enforcement of new legal protections remained sparse, hunting continued unabated. Local villagers continued to chip away at *bieti*'s habitat, logging for timber to build new homes and to burn as firewood. They razed patches of forest to create grazing land for their cattle, and disturbed the monkeys while searching for matsutake.[33] But by 1995 a true catastrophe loomed. In that year wildlife photographer Xi Zhinong (奚志农, 1964–), then working for the Yunnan Forestry Department, learned that the Dêqên County government was planning to transfer large swathes of forest to commercial loggers, amounting to nearly twenty percent of *bieti*'s total remaining habitat. With the help of journalist Tang Xiyang (唐锡阳, 1930–2022) and the NGO Friends of Nature (自然之友), Xi managed to start a civic campaign to put a stop to the logging. To their own amazement, they succeeded. The State Council, the highest administrative authority in the country, ordered the Dêqên government to end logging in the monkey's habitat.[34]

Yet in China local officials often show little regard for the dictates of the central government, and the campaigners had achieved only a partial success. When they learned in 1998 that logging was continuing, they again appealed to the national leadership to intervene. This second intervention had more success, but illegal logging continued, if on a smaller scale, as villagers continued to chip away at the forests. By 2005 *bieti* was estimated to number only around 1,500 monkeys in fourteen bands.[35]

Things soon began to improve. As the government established nature reserves and tightened enforcement, pressure on some populations of the black-and-white monkeys began to weaken. By 2016 *bieti* numbered approximately 3,000 individuals, the growth due in part to the natural increase in some bands but also to the discovery of several previously unknown groups. A few bands continue to face uncertain futures and declining numbers, but now nearly ninety percent of known black-and-white snub-nosed monkeys live within protected areas, and the total population continues to grow.[36]

Perhaps the richest wildlife haven in the Hengduan is the Three Parallel Rivers region, a stretch of western Yunnan bordering Myanmar through which the Salween, Mekong, and Yangtze rivers flow north to south in parallel for over 300 km (230 mi). Steep mountains over 5,000 m (16,400 ft) tall separate each river from its neighbor. The rivers run through gorges up to 3,000 m (9,840 ft) deep, and the immense variety of ecosystems found in this landscape, from subtropical to alpine, make it one of China's most biodiverse regions. Here, straddling the Myanmar border, live two of China's recently discovered primates—the black snub-nosed monkey *Rhinopithecus strykeri*, and the Skywalker gibbon *Hoolock tianxing*.[37]

The black snub-nosed monkey resembles its *Rhinopithecus* cousins in form, its most distinguishing feature being a nearly all black coat. Except for white ear tufts, white whiskers and beard, and a pink face, *strykeri* is from head to tail-tip all but entirely black or darkest brown. As with its congeners it lives at altitude, preferring forests among steep slopes between 2,400 m and 3,300 m (7,875 ft to 10,825 ft) where it feeds on a wide buffet of plants and lichens.[38]

R. strykeri did not come to the attention of scientists until 2008, when local Lisu and Law Waw hunters in northeastern Kachin State, Myanmar mentioned their existence. Over the next two years researchers confirmed that it was a new species when they received specimens from local hunters while conducting survey work.[39] The discovery suggested that the monkeys might also live across the border in Yunnan, a fact researchers soon confirmed.[40] Locals were of course aware of *strykeri*'s presence—people had even raised them as pets—but in general they rarely caught sight of the monkeys. It remains uncertain just how widespread and numerous *strykeri* is, but there seem to be four groups in Myanmar and two in China. They inhabit rugged terrain at high altitude, move over large territories, and do their best to avoid humans. All this makes them difficult to observe and count. The latest estimate put their numbers on either side of the Sino-Myanmar border between 520 and 600, but their exact status is unclear.[41]

Strykeri has faced the same threats as so many other species, though at least one population seems to have escaped severe disturbance. In Myanmar the monkeys have been hunted for sale to Chinese buyers; bones and heads were sold to Chinese workers on construction and logging projects as well as to wildlife traders operating out of border towns.[42] Between the disruptions of first COVID-19 and then the renewal of civil war, conservation and research in Myanmar has effectively stalled, leaving the monkeys' fate uncertain.[43] In China hunting of *strykeri* was apparently common in the past, but since 2000 has fallen significantly. Having taken refuge in highlands too forbidding to attract much human attention, the snub-nosed monkeys should avoid outright extermination, but whether they atrophy into relict, isolated bands slowly withering away, or grow in number to expand back into their old haunts, remains to be seen.

The different species and subspecies of hoolock gibbon are maddeningly difficult to tell apart. Adult males are all black with prominent white eyebrows, while females have a buff coat with white fur ringing their eyes and muzzles. Such details as the thickness of and space between males' eyebrows and the completeness of females' white face rings are what serve as distinguishing traits. To human eyes they all seem perpetually perturbed. Otherwise the Skywalkers look just as a gibbon should: long legs with long feet and long hands at the ends of very long arms.

The Skywalker gibbon was only described as a new species in 2017, but in fact it has been known to science for much longer. Until researchers took a closer look at the species, the Skywalkers were considered to merely be the eastern population of the hoolock gibbon *Hoolock leuconedys*. The American Museum of Natural History's

Asiatic Zoological Expedition was the first to scientifically document the existence of the gibbons in Gaoligong Mountains in 1917, but from then little was learned about the species until studies began again in the 1980s. At that time the Skywalkers were still found across nine counties in southwestern Yunnan. The local Lisu people generally left the gibbons alone but would occasionally hunt them for their brains, which were used to treat headaches and epilepsy.[44]

As commercial logging spread into their forests and local farmers converted more and more woodland to cash crops, the gibbons began to disappear. The lowlands and foothills throughout the Skywalkers' range were long ago cleared and settled, and practically no suitable habitat remains below 2,000 m (6,560 ft). Local people continue to clear out trees for use in home construction, but a recent threat has been the expanding cultivation of the medicinal herb tsaoko.[45] Tsaoko grows in the understory, and to improve its growth cultivators clear out large trees and other vegetation to open the canopy and let in more sunlight. In this way many of the gibbon's food trees have disappeared, requiring them to travel farther and more often in search of forage. And once a tsaoko plantation is established, there is little chance of new trees replacing those that were lost. Recent research, however, suggests the Skywalkers can survive in tsaoko plantations, though they must resort to eating food they would otherwise eschew.[46]

By the early 1990s Skywalker gibbons survived in only four counties, and by 2009 they had been reduced to fewer than 200 individuals spread over three counties.[47] By 2020 there were believed to be no more than 138 Skywalkers in China, split into three clusters, with many small groups and individuals spread out and isolated from their neighbors. Poachers still hunt them, and villagers still chip away at their forests. Yet there remains hope for the gibbons as conservation efforts have strengthened in recent years. More of their habitat has come under protection, and locals are becoming increasingly aware of the Skywalkers' protected status. The species' prospects were revealed to be more optimistic than presumed after surveys across the border in Myanmar between 2021 and 2023 revealed that local populations of what were considered eastern hoolocks were in fact Skywalkers. Although their populations there are poorly protected and suspected to be declining, the Myanmar gibbons are believed to number in the tens of thousands between the Irrawaddy and Salween rivers.[48] If provided the space and peace they require, they may yet recover.

The Giant Panda

WITHOUT a doubt the most famous and beloved denizen of the Qinling and Hengduan mountains is *Ailuropoda melanoleuca*, the giant panda. There is no other animal so closely associated with China, except perhaps for the dragon, which is, alas, a creature of fantasy.[1] For an animal that is now so ubiquitous in Chinese art, there are no known artistic depictions of giant pandas from before the twentieth century.[2] Until the late nineteenth century the giant panda was all but unknown except to those who shared its mountain home. Since the outside world discovered it, the panda has become not only China's best known beast, but also one of its greatest conservation successes.

Pandas are one of the smallest bear species, by no means diminutive but not so large as to seem intimidating. Their color pattern makes them instantly recognizable: a white body with stubby tail, black legs and a black band across the chest and shoulders, with black ears and a black nose. The black patches around the eyes are perhaps pandas' signature feature. The blotches make their eyes appear much larger than they really are, which to humans makes them appear cute and harmless, but for other creatures likely has just the opposite effect. The Qinling population on rare occasion produces bears with brown in place of black fur, likely a result of their recent genetic separation from the larger populations to the south.[3]

Much of the giant panda's form stems from adaptations to its strict diet of bamboo, bamboo, and more bamboo. Most famously, the panda's paws possess thumbs, or more accurately pseudo-thumbs that are in fact enlarged wrist bones.[4] These thumbs allow the panda to better grip bamboo stalks, providing for quicker, more efficient eating, something of a necessity when each serving of bamboo provides so little energy. Likewise, the wide, round face that makes the panda appear so cuddly is a result of the large jawbones and muscles that provide it the immense biting strength required to effortlessly crush bamboo.[5]

Adorably rotund, pandas are in fact quite lean, a result of their bamboo diet, which provides barely enough calories to function and not nearly enough to plump up with a thick layer of fat in the manner of brown bears. Instead the panda's thick coat provides all the warmth it needs, providing such insulation that when a panda once barged into a research camp and stood on a burning log and coals of a fire, she completely ignored the heat, even as embers singed her fur.[6]

Bamboo has not only shaped the panda's body but also its daily routine. Though seemingly everything else about the panda has adapted beautifully to its diet, the one exception is its digestive system. The panda's ancestors were carnivores (and pandas are still happy to eat meat when given the chance, though they won't put much effort into finding any), and pandas today retain a carnivore's digestive tract. This means, unlike most herbivores, they cannot extract more than negligible amounts of nutrients from the bamboo they eat. Their solution to this conundrum is admirably simple—eat as much as possible, then eat more. The life of a panda is spent eating until no more bamboo will go down, then sleeping while they digest, after which they awaken and continue eating. This cycle continues day and night, punctuated by the occasional journey from one patch of bamboo to another.[7]

Like most endangered denizens of China, giant pandas were once far more numerous and widespread than now. Fossil records indicate they and their evolutionary ancestors once spread across much of present-day south and east China and south into Vietnam and Myanmar.[8] Changes in climate drove the pandas north and west. By historical times pandas still ranged far more widely than today. Just how widely is not at all clear; the available evidence is mainly scattered recordings in ancient texts, practically none of which can be identified with certainty as referring to giant pandas. The most expansive interpretations have pandas spread from Beijing south to Guangdong and west to the Myanmar border, with the greatest concentrations in the mountains along the middle Yangtze. It is unlikely pandas truly had such broad geographic reach. They may, however, have been denizens of lowland forests until only a few thousand years ago. Pandas' guts remain poorly adapted to their diet, and analysis of their fossils shows that they seem to have subsisted on a wider food base before switching to almost exclusively bamboo. This could be a sign that the giant panda is a refugee species, one that has retreated from its preferred home in the face of human encroachment and now ekes out an existence in far less suitable habitat.[9]

Determining just where giant pandas once existed is an almost impossible task. Pandas, perhaps better than any other species, exemplify the difficulties of determining wildlife's past. Modern genetic analysis, combined with knowledge of environmental and human history, can provide a clue to the broad patterns of past events. After sequencing the giant panda's genome, scientists determined that approximately 300,000 years ago glaciation split the panda population into two groups, one now limited to the Qinling and the other restricted to the Min and Qionglai mountains. The Qinling pandas began to decline around 4,000 years ago. Counts of ancient pollen abundance suggest the forest cover in the northern Qinling fell into steep decline then, most likely the result of advancing agriculture, sparked at least in part by the adoption of new farming technology.[10]

About 2,800 years ago the second group of pandas further split in two. The Min River Valley divides the Min Mountains from the Qionglai to the west, but this had been no impediment to the pandas for many myriad generations. The break seems to have occurred after Shu, an ancient state based in the Chengdu Plain, constructed a road through the valley.[11] Just as the Qin-Han road through the Qinling would do centuries later, this road fragmented the natural landscape. The thruway eventually fell into disuse and the pandas regained some of their lost territory, but the Min and Qionglai populations remained separated.[12]

Few physical panda specimens from before the twentieth century have been found. When the tomb of Empress Dowager Bo (薄太后, ?—155 BCE) of the Han dynasty was being excavated in 1975, archaeologists found a complete panda skull, along with skulls of other exotic and rare creatures. They speculated the bones were likely those of animals from the Empress Dowager's personal menagerie, royal pets.[13] Forty-six years later, archaeologists uncovered a complete panda skeleton while excavating the nearby mausoleum of her son, Emperor Wen of Han (漢文帝, 203–157 BCE, r. 180–157 BCE).[14] In 2001 even older panda bones were found in a tomb in Hubei, dating to approximately 4,000 years ago.[15] Aside from these three examples the remaining evidence is textual. But the written record comes with a range of uncertainties and confusions.

The most basic problem in attempting to find past records of the panda is its name. In Chinese the current word for the giant panda is *dàxióngmāo* 大熊猫 (literally, "great bearcat"), a term coined only in the twentieth century and therefore useless for historical inquiry. Before then local peoples familiar with the panda used numerous names for the bears; among the most common in Chinese were *báixióng* 白熊 "white bear," *huāxióng* 花熊 "spotted (literally 'flower') bear," and *zhúxióng* 竹熊 "bamboo bear." The first dictionary appearance of the modern term *xióngmāo* 熊猫, "bear cat," was in 1915, but originally referred to the red panda. Both *xióngmāo* and *māoxióng* 猫熊, "cat bear," were in usage until the 1940s, at which point the term *xióngmāo* became the more popular for the giant panda. In Taiwan, however, *māoxióng* 猫熊 remains in common usage.

When the panda finally began to garner widespread attention, scientists and scholars looked for references to it amongst China's extensive corpus of literature. Unable to rely on the modern names, they instead had to find other words that matched with descriptions that could conceivably fit the panda. In the *Book of Songs* (詩經), a collection of poems and songs mostly from the Western Zhou (1046–771 BCE), they found the *pí* 貔 or *píxiū* 貔貅, described as a bear-like, or perhaps a cat-like, creature (clarity is often in short supply in ancient texts).[16] It appears again in China's first known dictionary, the *Ěr Yǎ* (尔雅) from the Qin dynasty, where it is described as a white fox.[17] Although it is frequently cited as the earliest textual evidence for giant pandas, more recent scholarship has ruled out the *pí* as an early term for the bears.[18]

If the *pí* is an unlikely candidate for the panda, the *mò* 貘 shows more promise. It too appears in the *Er Ya*, though it is simply described as a white panther.[19] Later descriptions of the *mò* sketch a creature that could very well be a panda: a stocky, black-and-white creature that eats bamboo and snacks on copper and iron. The last point may seem fantastic, but pandas have in fact wandered into villages where they proceeded to lick and gnaw on cooking pots.[20] It seems that the *mò* of these early texts is likely indeed the panda. Yet having established that the ancient *mò* were pandas, it turns out they did not remain pandas. After the Tang poet Bo (or Bai) Juyi (白居易, 772–846) depicted a bizarre creature with a long trunk and gave it the name *mò*, the meaning of the word split. Some uses of the term referred to the poet's fanciful beast, while others—even into the Qing—continued to describe the panda. Scholars long debated if Bo's *mò* was a fanciful creature or perhaps referred to the Malayan tapir *Tapirus indicus*.[21] Bronze figures that some scholars have interpreted as depictions of tapirs have been found in ancient sites around China, but no physical evidence of the animals themselves was discovered until the excavations of Emperor Wen's tomb complex, where an entire skeleton was found. Dozens of other animals had been buried along with the tapir and panda, including many animals now only found far removed from the Qinling and the Guanzhong Plain. Mongolian and goitered gazelles from the steppes, yak from the highlands, and gaur and green peafowl from the tropics were buried there, along with golden snub-nosed monkey, takin, suggesting a much greater diversity of life may once have lived in the region, although without stronger evidence the likelihood remains that most or even all arrived as tribute from afar.[22]

There are plenty of other possible names for pandas besides *pí* and *mò*, far too many for any but the specialist to wade through. Undoubtedly the ancients knew of the panda; the the bones in the imperial mausoleum prove as much. Among records that scholars regard as most reliable are accounts from the Tang. Taizong, the dynasty's founding emperor, is said to have gifted panda furs to fourteen officials during a banquet.[23] In his *Miscellaneous Morsels from Youyang* (酉陽雜俎), the poet Duan Chengshi (段成式, d. 863) mentions the panda in the guise of the *mòzé* 貊澤, describing the qualities of its fat, a rarity likely used in cosmetics.[24] Many recent texts report that some years later the Tang Empress Wu Zetian (武则天, 624–705, r. 690–705) sent two live pandas along with seventy skins to the Japanese Emperor Tenmu (天武天皇, c. 631–686, r. 673–686), but this story stemmed from a misreading of the original texts and is in fact fictitious.[25] After the Tang the panda vanishes. Records of *mò* and other panda proxies continue throughout the succeeding dynasties, but the evidence to equate them with pandas is flimsy.

Remarkably for an animal that is now so beloved and so closely linked to the image of China, both for the world at large and the Chinese themselves, for centuries the panda had been largely unknown to the Chinese until a French missionary stumbled upon it in 1869. By this time, however widely spread they had once been, giant pandas were probably restricted to two separated regions—the first occupying the Qinling and some ranges of the neighboring Hengduan Mountains to the west; the second in the Daba Mountains, stretching from Shaanxi, Sichuan and Chongqing into neighboring Hubei and Hunan.[26]

Though they escaped mention in the historical records, it is certain the easternmost pandas had suffered badly in the preceding centuries. The arrival of large numbers of Han pioneers into Guizhou and eastern Sichuan (much of which is now in Chongqing) beginning around the early fifteenth century sparked off centuries of intermittent warfare.[27] Local peoples, such as the Miao, resented both the Han settlers and the imperial government's attempts to exert control.[28] The response was often violent. Campaigns of resistance and suppression were waged back and forth, on and off, until the 1870s. Both imperial armies and Miao rebels destroyed the landscape in their attempts to defeat one another. Miao cut down trees to impede the government armies; imperial forces burned forests to rob the Miao of cover. As the imperial troops advanced, Han settlers came behind, turning newly opened forest into fields. By the time it was all done the pandas had lost the eastern edge of their range.[29]

The giant panda's ascent to global icon began in March 1869 when the missionary-naturalist Père Armand David received a beautiful black-and-white skin from hunters he had employed in the Baoxing area of the Qionglai Mountains in Sichuan. Père David immediately recognized the specimen to be from a species unknown to science, and though he never did see a live panda, the specimens alone were enough to ignite a smoldering fascination in the West. The peculiar nature of the giant panda attracted immediate notice. Père David considered the panda to be a species of bear, if perhaps a highly unusual bear.[30] He sent a specimen to Alphonse Milne-Edwards in Paris, who promptly declared that Père David's *Ursus melanoleuca* was in fact no *Ursus* at all, as much as it may resemble one. No, its skeletal and dental structures placed it with the panda (which then referred only to the far smaller red panda) and the raccoons, which warranted a taxonomic change to its own unique genus, *Ailuropoda*.[31] This taxonomic battle continued for well over a century until advances in genetic analysis determined that Père David was correct—giant pandas are in fact bears.[32]

The giant panda is, to put it mildly, a difficult creature to observe in the wild. It lives in a rugged, mist-cloaked landscape and keeps to thickets of bamboo so dense and tangled as to be nearly impenetrable unless one crawls on hands and knees. Moving through such mountain jungle, much less sighting an animal that is inclined to bolt at the slightest sign of humanity, can be maddeningly difficult. Combined with the curious nature of the beast, this naturally attracted a string of European and American adventurers to try their hand at seeing, and more importantly shooting, a panda. Most failed. Finally in 1928 Kermit and Theodore Roosevelt, sons of President Theodore Roosevelt, managed to shoot and kill one.[33]

Luckily for the giant panda, within a few years it would turn from a coveted trophy for intrepid hunters to a harmless, cuddly creature in need of care and protection. This was thanks largely to Ruth Harkness (1900–1947) and Su Lin. Harkness was a recently widowed socialite who, on a whim, set off for China in 1936 after the unexpected death of her husband in Shanghai, who had been preparing an expedition to make the first capture of a live panda.[34] She hired Quentin Young, a Chinese-American explorer, to lead the effort. The result was the capture of Su Lin, a weeks-old cub that Harkness took back to Shanghai, and then onward to America. Su Lin was an immediate sensation, and sparked such affection that, after an audience with the bear, even the Roosevelt brothers were besotted.[35]

The rush for pandas, first dead then alive, that bookended Harkness and Young's success soon led to concern for the species' future. Local hunters had not traditionally bothered to hunt the bears. Pandas were considered rather benign and useless, with foul-tasting flesh, though the hides did make good rugs.[36] Unusually for an animal in China their bodies had no medicinal value.[37] The new demand for pandas came from abroad, and it induced a change in practice. Hunters now aggressively targeted the bears for capture, hoping to sell them—or, if they died in transport, at least the skins and bones—to foreign buyers. At the time of Su Lin's capture, Quentin Young judged that pandas had already been hunted out from at least two areas northwest of Chengdu. By the late 1930s, Arthur de Carle Sowerby, the preeminent naturalist in China, was sounding the alarm, and in 1946 the Chinese-language newspaper *Ta Kung Pao* warned that pandas were "on the brink of extinction."[38] The Republic of China's government had placed a partial ban on panda hunting in 1939, but it was the Communist victory in 1949 that effectively cut off foreign buyers and relieved the pressure.[39]

Come the 1950s there were no more foreigners to harass the pandas, only the Chinese themselves, and the giant panda was still by and large unknown in its native country. It wasn't until 1955, when three pandas arrived at the Beijing National Zoo, that China's general public learned to love the black-and-white bears. With no historical or political baggage, the giant panda was perfectly inoffensive, and thus a safe choice for artistic use during the Cultural Revolution, when the use of nearly anything deemed traditional was grounds for persecution. The panda quickly became ubiquitous, and soon was a symbol of China itself, so precious it was given protection from all hunting and deemed a national treasure.[40]

As the giant panda's profile rose, both within China and beyond, its prospects for survival deteriorated. A legal ban on hunting was hardly enough to stop the panda's steady decline. The growth of the human population within the panda's range had led to predictable results: expanding fields at the expense of the forests, more bamboo harvested for human use, more snares littering the landscape, more trees felled. Long ago pushed out from the valley floors, the pandas moved higher and higher up the mountains. They found themselves split into smaller and smaller patches of habitat, their populations increasingly isolated.

The 1970s proved a particularly harsh time for the bears. The rise of panda diplomacy launched a new rush into the bamboo forests in search of bears to gift. The Nationalist regime had sent pandas to the US in 1941, and the Communist government had given pandas to both the Soviet Union and North Korea, but it was gifts of panda pairs to the US and Japan in 1972 that set off a flurry of captures. From that year to 1980, ninety-two pandas were taken from the wild, far more than required to supply diplomatic needs, so the spares—seventy-six of them—went not back to the wild but to domestic zoos. The Ministry of Agriculture and Forestry attempted to stop the reckless extractions from the already dwindling wild population, but it was only able to slow them.[41]

Far more shocking to scientists and public alike was the sudden starvation of pandas. Bamboo has an unusual life cycle. Unlike most flowering plants, bamboo blooms neither often nor predictably. Depending on the species (and there are more than 1,400 of them) bamboo flowers only once every forty to 120 years. Not only do they flower rarely, but when a species blooms it is a mass event. The entire community blossoms in a synchronized release, flooding the landscape to such an extent that no matter how many animals come to feast on the bounty, they cannot possibly eat all the seeds. Having sown the earth with its descendants, the bamboo dies. When just such an event occurred in the Min Mountains in 1976, the result was starving pandas.[42]

Yet pandas had survived through countless bamboo flowerings for hundreds of thousands of years. Why was it now so devastating? The blame was not on the pandas for having wandered into an evolutionary cul-de-sac, but on humans for having deprived them of the ability to migrate to other patches of bamboo. Already pushed to the margins, between the mid-1970s and mid-1980s alone panda's lost half of their remaining habitat.[43] Giant pandas are not so inept as to limit themselves to feeding on only a single species of bamboo, though they do have their preferences. Normally a mass flowering would have prompted the bears to move to wherever a different bamboo species was growing, where they would resume their lives with a slightly more limited diet. But this time when the flowering hit there was no other source.[44] Bamboo that had once covered the lower slopes of the mountains was now gone, removed by man.

A lucky break came with the end of the Maoist period. The giant panda had enjoyed greater protection through the chaotic years of the Cultural Revolution than most other species, but it was hardly enough to prevent their rapid decline. With the advent of Reform and Opening, China began to take wildlife conservation seriously. Short of money, equipment, and trained and experienced wildlife scientists, China looked abroad for expertise and assistance. The first priority was the giant panda. Many foreign conservation organizations were eager for the chance to work in China; for decades there had been practically no news of the state of the country's wildlife. China chose the largest and richest of them all, the World Wildlife Fund (WWF), to bankroll the first intensive field studies of the giant panda at Wolong Nature Reserve in the Qionglai Mountains.[45] WWF hired George Schaller, the world's preeminent field naturalist, to lead the effort.[46]

By the time Schaller arrived at Wolong in 1980, both the pandas and Chinese wildlife science were in poor shape. Chinese scientists, foremost among them Hu Jinchu (胡锦矗, 1929–2023), had begun field research on the bears, but the turmoil of the Mao era had not been conducive to scientific achievement. Knowledge of where pandas lived had long remained incomplete—it wasn't until 1969 that researchers even discovered there were pandas in the Qinling.[47] The first attempt to census the bears began in 1974 and continued through 1977, when an estimate of 1,100 pandas was reached—in the Qinling there were only 250. Much of the basic life history of the panda remained a mystery, as did the true state of their populations.

What Schaller found was a deeply dysfunctional system. The preferred method for saving the giant panda, as it was for all species at the time, was to remove bears from the wild and attempt to breed them in captivity. For years this was an abysmal failure, and not only because no one yet understood the subtleties of panda breeding behavior. The facilities were inadequate and the staff even more so. Just as with all other work in China, reserve staff, from scientists to cooks, had not chosen their professions, but had simply accepted the work the government directed them to. The predictable result was that few of them had any interest, much less passion, in working with wild animals. To compound this, the raw memories of the Cultural Revolution left everyone unwilling to take risks, especially when a foreigner such as Schaller was involved. The tangles of bureaucracy further complicated matters, and often worked directly against the interests of conservation.

This was a mix ripe for poor decision making. When another bamboo bloom occurred in the Qionglai Mountains in 1982–1983, the initial assumption was there would be another panda famine. Indeed there were a few areas where bears could not find new food sources and starved, but by and large there were enough intact stands of bamboo species that had not flowered to support the pandas. This fact did not reach, or perhaps simply did not persuade, the officials in charge. They offered cash rewards for any kindly souls who delivered pandas, starving or not, to the breeding center. The central government requested help, and help they received, as their own citizens, schoolchildren in America, and many others around the world donated to save the pandas. When the government realized the situation was not so dire, and that the donations were not strictly necessary, they redoubled their calls for help. Perhaps the pandas weren't starving, but if saving pandas brought in money then there was no need to clarify such details. The campaign landed dozens of healthy pandas in breeding centers and zoos, a needless drain on an already dwindling wild population.[48]

The increased attention was not all a good thing. All the gains that resulted from more research and more funding came under threat from a revived interest in the panda as a trophy. Hunters had never really stopped killing pandas, but for years the bears had been worth more alive than dead, so when pandas did die at the hand of man it was rarely deliberate. Instead their deaths were inevitable accidents of the favored hunting method: snares. Snares are cheap, so cheap even dirt-poor farmers can set dozens of them, and they require little effort beyond setting and checking. But they are indiscriminate; anything large enough that passes through the loop will become trapped, and unless found and released in time, will die, whether by asphyxiation, starvation or some equally terrible fate. The snares were not intended for pandas, but they caught them all the same.

During the course of Schaller's work, one of the pandas the research team collared died in a poacher's snare. Only a few months later Schaller came across the body of another snared panda; a third bear in the study was thought to have died at poachers' hands as well, but they could never prove it. By this time not all killings of giant pandas were accidental. Poaching of wildlife increased nationwide through the 1980s—for subsistence, for sale, for fun. Most poachers were poor and simply after meat for their tables or money for their bills. Pandas are no good to eat, but a skin would sell for a small fortune; buyers in Hong Kong, Taiwan, and Japan would pay $10,000 or more for one, and a poacher might see two or three thousand of those dollars, an astounding sum in such poor places. Panda killings spiked.[49]

The extent of poaching is unclear, but for a time it was the pandas' most acute and urgent threat. Authorities took the problem seriously and gradually stamped out the trade in pelts. Hundreds of people were tried and convicted for poaching or smuggling over the course of the 1980s and 1990s, a few even sentenced to death. Cases of harming, capturing, or killing pandas are now vanishingly rare. Accidental snaring remained a problem long after, but it too has become exceptional.

Through the 1990s and into the new millennium the threats and the trends were largely the same. The human population within panda territory increased, and with it the impact on the panda's ever-shrinking habitat. Logging continued apace. By 2000 the pandas were left with only a fifth of the space they had enjoyed forty years prior.[50] Yet things

219

started to improve. The farmers whose fields encroached so steadily on the forests were paid to plant trees instead. Logging practically stopped with the nationwide ban on chopping down natural forests that took effect in 1999. Poaching continued but gradually came under control. Research expanded and knowledge of the bears improved dramatically. Attempts to breed pandas in captivity proceeded slowly yet surely, producing a ready supply of bears for zoos domestic and foreign, although returning none to the wild. Each census of the bears seemed to show a growing population. There remained no shortage of threats to guard against and problems to fix, but with decades of work conservationists had earned a sense of cautious optimism.

Things are now looking up for the panda. The fourth and most recent census came to an estimate of just over 2,000 bears. Such population counts are by no means infallible, but combined with evidence of expanding forests and recolonizing bears, panda experts are increasingly optimistic about the species' future. The efforts showered on the pandas have benefited many other species that share their habitat. The giant panda has long been considered an umbrella species, one whose conservation provides protection for other species in turn. To save the giant panda you must save its bamboo forests. In saving the bamboo forest you provide not only for the pandas but for everything else that lives within.

Except that protecting the giant panda has not done much good for one group of animals—large predators. Most classic examples of umbrella species are apex predators such as the tiger or wolf. The largest carnivores rely on large herbivores, which in turn rely on vegetation, so that to protect the predators you must protect the entire food web. Yet pandas rely on bamboo, not prey, and because of that they fall just short of this ideal. The large ungulates that feed tigers are recovering but are far from their past abundance. This is no bother to the pandas but is crucial for the predators. Pandas live and feed in small territories, not much beyond a dozen square kilometers at the most expansive. Leopards and wolves require far more land to find enough prey to feed themselves. Protecting relatively small patches filled with bamboo is enough to help pandas, but is only a first step to protecting the dhole or tiger.[51]

There are very few of the apex predators left in panda country. Tigers disappeared before the end of the Maoist era, and leopards are now few and far between, restricted to the Qinling. Snow leopards live high above the the panda's umbrella, but a scattering survive in the Qionglai, which hosts some of the last wolves and dholes in the region as well. It is mostly the smaller carnivores that remain. Small cats, and a medley of mustelids and viverrids survive where their larger brethren cannot, eager and able to sustain themselves on cramped territories and smaller prey. Even the cryptic Asian golden cat *Catopuma temminckii*, though barely researched and little understood, seems to be rare, a lingering consequence of the same habitat loss and persecution its larger feline kin faced.[52]

Although giant pandas still face many threats old and new, their prospects are much brighter now. George Schaller ended his 1993 account of his panda studies on a pessimistic note, but in the intervening years he has become optimistic.[53] Upon its latest assessment, the International Union for Conservation of Nature—the body which maintains the Red List of Threatened Species detailing the conservation status of thousands of lifeforms—saw enough evidence to move the bears from Endangered to the less dire Vulnerable.[54]

Scientists are nonetheless careful to explain that the change by no means implies pandas' future is now secure.[55] Indeed, not all pandas are faring so well. There remain small, isolated populations dotted throughout the range. To survive, these groups will need the freedom to travel and connect with others of their kind. They are running out of time as climate change threatens to soon ruin large swathes of their habitat, at least thirty percent and up to sixty-five percent before the end of this century.[56] Without the ability to migrate to new homes the pandas' prospects could quickly turn dire. The Chinese government has established dozens of panda reserves over the last several decades, littered throughout their range. It is now bringing them together in the Giant Panda National Park. The park should integrate and streamline the management of the formerly disparate reserves, and, over time and with much effort, will build the physical connections necessary for the bears to roam freely.[57]

Firefoxes & Gnu Goats

SHARING much of the same territory as the giant panda is the original, first panda—the red panda.[1] The two pandas share many peculiarities. They both have white-furred faces with dark patches that exaggerate their eyes and thereby make them irresistibly adorable. They are both carnivores who feast almost exclusively on bamboo. Like the giant panda, the red panda has an enlarged wrist bone on each forepaw that functions as a pseudo-thumb, allowing it to better grip tree limbs while climbing.[2] And they share the same habitat, with much of the red panda's easternmost range overlapping the giant panda's.[3] There are nonetheless plenty of differences. As its name unsubtly hints, the red panda has predominantly red fur, although its underside and limbs are black, and there are white patches around its muzzle and on its cheeks and ears. The red panda is the far smaller of the two, about the size of a house cat but with a bushier, black-ringed tail. That tail, unlike the giant panda's, is long, over a third of the lesser panda's entire length. The tail helps the red panda keep its balance while climbing through the forest canopy, where it spends much of its time foraging or sleeping.

The two pandas share a name, superficial resemblance, and basic diet, yet they are not closely related, separated by forty million years of evolutionary divergence.[4] Red pandas, long thought close kin to giant pandas or raccoons, are in fact the sole members of a separate taxonomic family, Ailuridae. There are now two species of red panda, *Ailurus fulgens*, the Himalayan red panda, and *A. styani*, the Chinese red panda.[5] China, which has about half the world's red panda territory and a third of its population, is home to both species—*styani* in Sichuan and northeastern Yunnan, *fulgens* in northwestern Yunnan and Tibet.

Similar to its larger namesake, the red panda seemingly escaped wide notice in China until the twentieth century. When Westerners began exploring the natural history of Sichuan and Yunnan they noticed the popularity of red panda furs. The tails were put to use as dusters or brushes, some sent as far away as Guangzhou. Furs were most commonly made into hats, an accessory popular not only among local communities in China but across the red panda's range in Bhutan, India, and Nepal. These pandaskin caps remained a relatively common sight in parts of the red panda's range up to as recently as the last decade.[6] Reports of poaching and trade in the furs are very rare, but conservationists worry this stems from anemic law enforcement, not the end of trade.[7]

By the time scientists began to pay close attention they realized the red pandas were disappearing from large areas, particularly in Sichuan. The firefoxes were hunted for their furs but also trapped for display in zoos, first within China and over a few years in the late 1980s and 1990s for export around the globe. From the 1950s onward at least 1,500 of the pandas were taken from the wild for exhibition, a seemingly sizable number, but what impact it ultimately had on the population isn't clear.[8]

What undoubtedly did drive the retreat of the red panda was the same mix of threats that has proven so crushing for hundreds of other species—habitat destruction and the fragmentation and isolation of populations that accompany it. Relentless deforestation shrank the red pandas' range within China by as much as forty percent from the 1960s. They disappeared from portions of Sichuan, Yunnan, and Tibet, and completely from Guizhou, Shaanxi, Gansu, and Qinghai.[9] The rapid slowdown of deforestation at the turn of the millennium has given the red pandas in China a chance to bounce back, and what threats remain are considered relatively minor. If their forests can be restored and their populations reconnected, the firefoxes may one day recolonize the lands they lost.

The precarious survival of the giant panda has long drawn the world's concern (and a greater share of funding than any other species could hope to match), but another resident of the Qinling for decades quietly faced far more desperate odds—the crested ibis *Nipponia nippon*.[10]

Like all ibises the crested ibis has a long, downcurved bill used for probing for prey in the mud. It feeds on a smorgasbord of small aquatic creatures—fish, frogs, snails, crabs, beetles, etc. The bill is black except for a red tip. The bare skin of its face and legs is red too. The crested ibis's plumage varies from white to gray depending on the season. For most of the year it is white, but as January turns to February the ibis changes into its nuptial plumage in preparation for mating season.

Uniquely among birds, the crested ibis forgoes molting and instead excretes a black, tar-like substance from its neck, which it spreads over its upper body, turning the feathers gray. The ibis is named for the dapper crest of long plumes that drape from the top of its head down its neck. But it only reveals its most striking feature when it spreads its wings, and the otherwise hidden peach-pink flight feathers on the wings' undersides finally come into view. It is a handsome if not particularly arresting bird, neither so stately as the crane nor as garish as the peacock. Perhaps that is why it seems to have been overlooked for so long.

The crested ibis appears in literature as early as the Spring and Autumn period, and references to it appear on rare occasion throughout the dynastic period, but it seems the ibis never attracted much attention.[11] Once Western naturalists arrived in the nineteenth century, they too made only passing note of the birds. Back then crested ibises were a common sight, widespread throughout much of the country. They were especially common across their breeding range in the northeast, and in north China, particularly along Shaanxi's Wei River Valley. Over winter the ibises migrated to warmer climes, seeming to favor the Lower Yangtze. In the 1920s the birds were noted to be "extraordinarily plentiful" in parts of north China, and in the following decade they were still found in fourteen provinces.[12] Then over the next three decades they vanished completely.

The ibises seemingly disappeared without anyone noticing. Certainly no one rushed to save the species. By the early 1960s they were seen only in a few counties in Shaanxi, and after a final bird was caught in 1964 nothing more was seen or heard of the crested ibis. It took fifteen years before any serious effort was made to find survivors.[13] And it wasn't merely in China. The ibises had once stretched north into the Russian Far East, and from there south and east to Korea, Japan, and Taiwan. Their numbers had been falling for decades, and by the middle of the twentieth century they were gone from practically everywhere.

Feather hunters had decimated the birds in Japan by the turn of the century; the plumes were prized domestically for use in feather dusters and sent abroad to adorn fashionable ladies' hats. The few survivors then succumbed to the same threats that wiped out the birds across the rest of their range.

The crested ibis requires a very particular habitat to survive. There must be shallow wetlands for feeding, and tall trees for nesting. Across China, as well as Korea and Japan, natural wetlands were drained and converted to farmland hundreds or even thousands of years ago. Luckily for the ibis many of the new fields were rice paddies, unnatural but wetland all the same, good enough to live in. For centuries the ibis had little untouched habitat left to it, but it made do living alongside rice farmers. Some observers had noted the ibis nested along and fed in rice fields, but no one seemed to realize just how dependent it was on the paddies and surrounding trees.[14] When traditional farming began to die out, the changes proved deadly for the ibis. Nesting trees were cut down; remnant wetlands were drained; rice paddies were drenched with poisonous fertilizers and pesticides, and drained in winter for new crops. Year after year there was less and less space for the ibis.

By the time someone finally went looking for ibises it seemed all but certain they were gone. But the man chosen for the job, Liu Yinzeng (刘荫增, 1936–), was determined to make a thorough search. Assigned the task in 1979, he searched for nearly three years, travelling tens of thousands of miles crisscrossing thirteen provinces. He found no ibises, but in the landscape itself he saw why they had disappeared. Finally in 1981, on his third visit to rural Yang County, Shaanxi, he found them. Here, in the village of Yaojiagou on the southern slopes of the Qinling, the last population of crested ibises had somehow managed to endure. There were seven birds. They had survived by sheer luck. The village graveyard had fifteen old oaks in which the ibises could nest. The villagers had left them untouched, unwilling to disturb the spirits.[15]

With only seven birds from which to repopulate the species, there was little room for error or misfortune. Conservation work began immediately, with measures quickly implemented to protect the ibises, their nesting sites, and food supplies. Pesticides were restricted on area farms, and the local villagers were encouraged and cajoled into helping protect the birds.[16] Inevitably a captive breeding program was established, with a number of birds whisked to Beijing Zoo in 1986, where three years later they hatched their first chicks.

Since their rediscovery in 1981, the ibises have made a remarkable recovery. Two chicks hatched and survived to the end of that first year, and the ibis population has been growing ever since. By 2002 there were 140 ibises in the wild and over 130 in captivity. Releases of captive-bred birds began in 2004, and gradually more and more captives left the breeding centers and settled into the Qinling. By the middle of 2020, there were approximately 2,600 crested ibises in the wild, with another 1,800 or so in captivity in China, and their numbers have continued to increase.[17] Crested ibises have even been sent to South Korea and Japan to reestablish populations across their former range.[18] The first wild-born chicks in Japan fledged in 2016, and in Korea the first chicks hatched in April 2021.[19]

The ibises have escaped extinction but they have not escaped the unavoidable fact that they still have few places to live. The last population's immediate surroundings have been well tended to serve the ibises' needs, but as they multiply and leave in search of new homes to settle, they discover the rest of the country remains largely inhospitable. Traditional rice farming is less common than ever, and many once flooded winter fields are now dry. Some are drained for the season and planted with wheat, others have been removed from cultivation as part of the government drive to encourage the return of marginal agricultural lands to nature. Even within protected reserves established expressly for the ibises, many fields have gone dry as farmers leave in search of better lives. Often birds that attempt to survive in these places have been found dead, their stomachs empty. Outside of the reserves the fields are still saturated with fertilizers and pesticides, and nesting trees remain a rare sight. Some fear the crested ibises are at the limits of their current home and now have no where else to go.[20]

If the ibises are to thrive and grow, conservationists must find ways to reshape the landscape over larger and larger swathes of territory. They are also looking farther afield for suitable ibis habitat, and the birds are already being reintroduced to select sites around the country. Saving the ibises will likely prove to have been the easy part. As the ibises have grown in number they have begun to settle in farmland they would once have avoided. Some paddies have been free of pesticides long enough to again be safe for the birds.[21] Restoring more land so that they can return to something of their former range and numbers will be a long-lasting challenge, but their recovery no longer seems impossible.

One of China's oddest looking mammals, the takin *Budorcas taxicolor*, grazes the pastures and forests of the Qinling and Hengduan. George Schaller gave perhaps the best description of the takin, writing that if

> "the camel resembles an animal designed by committee, then the takin looks like an animal assembled by the same committee from spare parts....they look as if they are constructed from ill-considered body parts of other animals. Assemble the bulky, humped body of a brown bear, the legs of a cow, the broad flat tail of a goat, the knobby horns of a wildebeest, and the black, bulging face of a moose with mumps and you have a takin."[22]

The result is no one's first idea of beauty, but there's a definite charm to their unconventional looks.

There is one subspecies of takin in the Qinling, the golden or Qinling takin, *B. t. bedfordi*, and another in the Hengduan, the Sichuan or Tibetan takin, *B. t. tibetana*. As its appellation implies, the golden takin has the brightest and most spectacular coat of the four takin subspecies, a nearly uniform gold that some have speculated may have inspired the legend of the Golden Fleece of the winged ram Chrysomallos.[23] The Sichuan takin's coat retains plenty of gold but is mixed with darker hairs, ranging from black to brown to gray. In spite of having what appears to be a leading candidate for nature's worst camouflage, as takins graze on the mountainsides they can blend in astoundingly well, standing fully visible at one moment only to turn out of the light and seemingly evaporate.

Like so many species hidden away in rugged mountains, the takin attracted little attention from Chinese writers of past centuries. It earned brief mention in texts as far back as the Han dynasty, but otherwise the takin was invisible until the arrival of Western naturalists and sport hunters in the late nineteenth and early twentieth centuries. Large, peculiar, and with a spectacular golden coat, the takin proved an irresistible draw for many of the men stationed in or passing through China. Some of them left behind accounts of their hunts, but none took the time to learn much more than what could be gleaned from stalking and butchering the animal. The best anyone could discern was that takin lived in the western mountains, from the Qinling south to the Hengduan in Sichuan, reaching at least as far south as Kangding, and that in the early twentieth century they seemed plenty numerous.[24]

Research on the takin began in the 1960s, although the extenuating circumstances of the time ensured slow progress.[25] Scientists undertook a first attempt to census the Qinling population in 1974. The number they arrived at—1,242 head of takin—was likely little better than a guess, but the census takers were certain that whatever the number, it was drastically lower than in the recent past. All of the Qinling's wildlife was clearly far less abundant than it had once been, takin included.[26]

The culprits behind the decline were the same as for the giant panda. Deforestation from logging and agriculture had shrunk available habitat, and hunting for their meat had further thinned their numbers. During his research at Wolong Reserve, George Schaller noted an abundance of old rusting snares but never spotted a single takin, the golden bovids long since hunted out. While visiting a reserve in late 1999, two American scientists and their Chinese counterparts even stumbled on a poacher hauling away a poached takin carcass only a few kilometers from reserve headquarters.[27] The devastation did not reach all populations. After establishing a new project in Tangjiahe Reserve to the north in the Min Mountains, Schaller found a healthy takin community, one which still thrives today.[28]

In those areas where hunting did not decimate the populations, the takin have enjoyed a freedom from fear unknown to their ancestors. Without human predation there was nothing left to stalk them. The last tiger in the Qinling was shot in 1964, and the few remaining leopards and dholes were little threat to full-grown takin. The same is true for the rest of the ungulates' range. When scouting the mountains of southern Sichuan for Third Front work in the mid-1960s, party cadres carried submachine guns for fear of the tigers, leopards, and wolves that villagers warned still prowled the forests.[29] Not long after there would be few if any predators left, and to this day they remain vanishingly rare.

Now the greatest threat to takin is the limits of their current habitat. As their numbers have risen they face the problem of increasing mouths to feed with a stagnant food supply. In summer takin climb to higher elevation and feed undisturbed until the cold drives them back down the mountain. Food is always harder to find in the lean winter months, but the greater competition now drives some brave bovids to look to humans for their sustenance. Every year the normally shy animals descend to the valleys and enter farming villages in search of feed. Walking into a village is usually an act of desperation, the last chance for an old or weak animal to find enough food to last another season. But an old, weak takin is still plenty big and strong to hurt a human, and that is inevitably what happens. Injuries and even deaths from takin incursions have become a yearly occurrence, straining villagers' tolerance for the animals.[30] As happens with so many other species that rebound from generations of decline, the takin are now struggling to find an accommodation with the people who have moved into their range.

The Hengduan and neighboring Tibetan Plateau are home to an endemic deer little known to the outside world, the white-lipped deer *Cervus albirostris*.[31] White-lipped deer are found only on the Sino-Tibetan frontier lands from southern Gansu to northern Yunnan, living in the forests, shrub lands and meadows above 3,500 m (11,480 ft), where they feed in available open pasture.[32] A large species of deer, *C. albirostris* is well adapted to life at high elevation, in winter growing a coat thicker than even that of the moose. Though primarily grayish-brown with a darker head and face, it is the stark white fur around their lips and nose which gives the species its common name.

The deer first became known to the outside world when the Russian explorer Col. Przhevalsky obtained a specimen in 1876.[33] Westerners who traveled through the deer's range in the following decades noted that the deer were heavily hunted and did not seem abundant.[34] An expedition in the 1930s found much the same situation, noting that though the deer were common in some areas, in others Tibetan soldiers with newly acquired British military rifles had drastically reduced their numbers in the several years prior.[35]

Like the sika and red deer, white-lipped deer have been valued not only for their meat and hides but especially for their antlers. The antler trade drove much of the hunting, which, though now much reduced, continues to this day.[36] As had happened to their more common cervid cousins long before, people began to farm white-lipped deer in hopes of securing a steady and self-expanding supply of antlers. The first farms were established in the initial frenzy of the Great Leap Forward in 1958—large scale hunting of the deer to supply urban centers with venison began the same year—but as with other wildlife farms they did nothing to conserve the species.[37] Farms were stocked with deer caught from the wild, and when a deer farming boom took off after Reform and Opening the transfer of so many deer to captivity was a blow to the wild populations. White-lipped deer farming quickly proved unprofitable, and by the 1980s most operations had failed, while the survivors limped on, poorly managed and unprofitable.[38]

After decades of overhunting and increasing competition with growing herds of livestock, white-lipped deer are now found only over an estimated ten percent of their historic distribution. They still survive over a broad stretch of territory, from Gansu to Yunnan, but they are fragmented into many small and isolated populations scattered across the uplands. Such fragmentation is in part a natural consequence of the terrain, but its severity is due to the effects of man and livestock.[39] Forced to compete with domestic yak, most have been pushed to the margins of usable habitat.[40] The deer are now most numerous in northwestern Sichuan, and in a few areas such as southern Qinghai they may even be increasing in number.[41] With their herds so scattered and with so many isolated from one another, it will be difficult for the deer population to return to long-term health. Much work is needed to restore the landscape and reconnect the herds.

A number of fellow ungulates share the forests and slopes with the takin, from little Reeves's muntjacs *Muntiacus reevesi* in the Qinling, to the dwarf musk deer *Moschus berezovskii* that spreads south into the Hengduan. Despite suffering a sharp decline during the last century or so, the Reeves's muntjac remains one of the most widespread and commonly sighted hoofed animals in China, and has proven exceptionally resilient to human pressures.[42] Its wild populations are little studied, but analysis has indicated that they retain much of their genetic diversity, and future changes in climate are likely to work in their favor.[43] Closest to the takin in appearance, if neither so bulbous of nostril nor so large, are the brown goral *Naemorhedus goral* and mainland serow *Capricornis sumatraensis*. They spend most of their time out of sight or reach of people, scaling sheer rock faces with ease much like their distant North American relative the mountain goat *Oreamnos americanus*. Like the muntjacs, the serow may see their suitable habitat expand over the coming decades as the climate changes.[44] As elsewhere in China, the region's wild sika deer are nearly gone, hunted out and replaced with semi-tamed descendants farmed for their antlers and meat. Wild boar thrive here as well as any animal can, and continue to prove themselves worthy adversaries in their forever war with farmers. As the youth of farming villages leave for the promise of the cities and the government resettles many of their elders outside of the reserves, the porcine foe no doubt senses fortune increasingly tipping in its favor.

Of the smaller hoofed residents the little tufted deer *Elaphodus cephalophus* may be the most endearing. Similar in size to the musk deer and muntjacs, they also sport prominent tusks, but it is the single great cowlick, hiding their minuscule antlers, that distinguishes them and gives them their name. Tufted deer live not only in the Qinling and Hengduan but clear east to China's coast. Like many other species the tufted deer suffered dramatic range contractions during past glaciations, but they thrived after the ice retreated, only to see their number begin to decline again roughly 4,400 years ago under human pressure.[45] As with nearly all medium and small mammals in China, the species is poorly studied; such basic facts as where it survives and in what numbers remain nearly total mysteries. The most that is known of present populations is that in the late 1970s and into the early 1980s upwards of 100,000 tufted deer were legally hunted each year, with many more undoubtedly poached. Most of these came from the western forests of Sichuan, Hunan, and Guizhou, and it is hard to believe such intensive killing did not send the deer into decline. Whether they have begun to recover is still unknown.[46]

The mammals and birds of the Qinling and Hengduan have won the greatest share of scientific and popular attention, but the mountains and valleys are laced with many rivers that contain a wealth of aquatic life. Among these is the Sichuan taimen *Hucho bleekeri*, a large salmonid that lives in the cold-flowing rivers that feed into the upper reaches of the Yangtze. It's likely *bleekeri* has never had a large range, perhaps not much beyond the 5,000 sq km (1,930 sq mi) of waterways it inhabited in the 1960s. The intervening years cut that expanse down to below 100 sq km (38.6 sq mi), within which a remnant of at best 2,500 taimen survived. Dams have fragmented the waterways and broken the fish into isolated groups. They have changed not only the rivers' flows but even water temperatures. Factories and communities have dumped untreated waste into the waters, poisoning and choking the life within them.[47] And fishing—legal and illegal—has devastated not only the taimen but many other species as well. These factors have wreaked devastation not only on *bleekeri* in the Yangtze's upper tributaries, but have recurred in waterways throughout China, most devastatingly along the Yangtze itself. Recent studies suggest the taimen are beginning to recover, yet they still face a difficult future.[48]

Emei Shan, a holy Buddhist mountain, rises at the western edge of the Sichuan Basin. The mountain is littered with temples and has long attracted pilgrims, although tourists now far outnumber devotees. Emei is best known for its temples and the Tibetan macaques that alternately entertain and terrorize tourists, but it is also home to a surprising diversity of plants and amphibians.[49] From a base of only 500 m Emei rises to a peak of 3,099 m (from 1,640 ft to 10,170 ft), cut through with a maze of canyons and gorges. This has resulted in a great range of landscapes with varying temperatures and rainfalls, leading to a rich variety of plant and animal communities.

Among these is the Emei moustache toad *Leptobrachium boringii*, named for the mountain but found in broadleaf forests elsewhere in Sichuan and nearby provinces.[50] Males of *boringii* and a handful of related species are peculiar among amphibians in that, not only do they grow larger than females, they also sport a row of spines on their upper lips, a weaponized mustache for dueling with rivals. The moustache toad shares the mountain with members of the genus *Scutiger*, the lazy toads. Many of this genus, as well as *Oreolalax*, are found only in small areas within the mountains of southwest China, and are particularly rich in the Hengduan. Their restricted ranges have made them exceptionally vulnerable to habitat loss and capture, whether as food or for sale as pets. Inevitably many—the Emei moustache toad included—are now endangered.[51]

In addition to mustachioed toads, China hosts an exceptionally rich array of galliform birds, many of them endemic, and the Hengduan and Qinling possess the greatest variety and concentration. They range from the spectacularly adorned golden pheasant *Chrysolophus pictus* to the modest buff-throated partridge *Tetraophasis szechenyii*. Many of the males sport stunning plumage; golden pheasant males are a gaudy mix of gold, red, blue, green, black, and cinnamon. In the nineteenth century European and American sport fishermen favored the golden's feathers for fashioning fly lures.[52] The Western millinery trade's demand for ornate feathers early the following century may have led to the disappearance of males from some areas, but the captive-bred populations in Europe proved largely sufficient to satisfy the market.[53] Its congener, the Lady Amherst's pheasant *Chrysolophus amherstiae*, has a more subdued scheme of black, white, red, blue, and dark green. Both have long tail feathers that trail behind them. But neither can match the Reeves's pheasant *Syrmaticus reevesii*, found also to the east in central China, the males of which have the longest tail feathers of any birds on Earth. The Reeves's pheasant's long plumes have proven too remarkable for their own good; the males have for centuries been hunted for their feathers, used to decorate hats for Chinese opera. Demand is estimated to be over 2,200 plumes a year, almost entirely

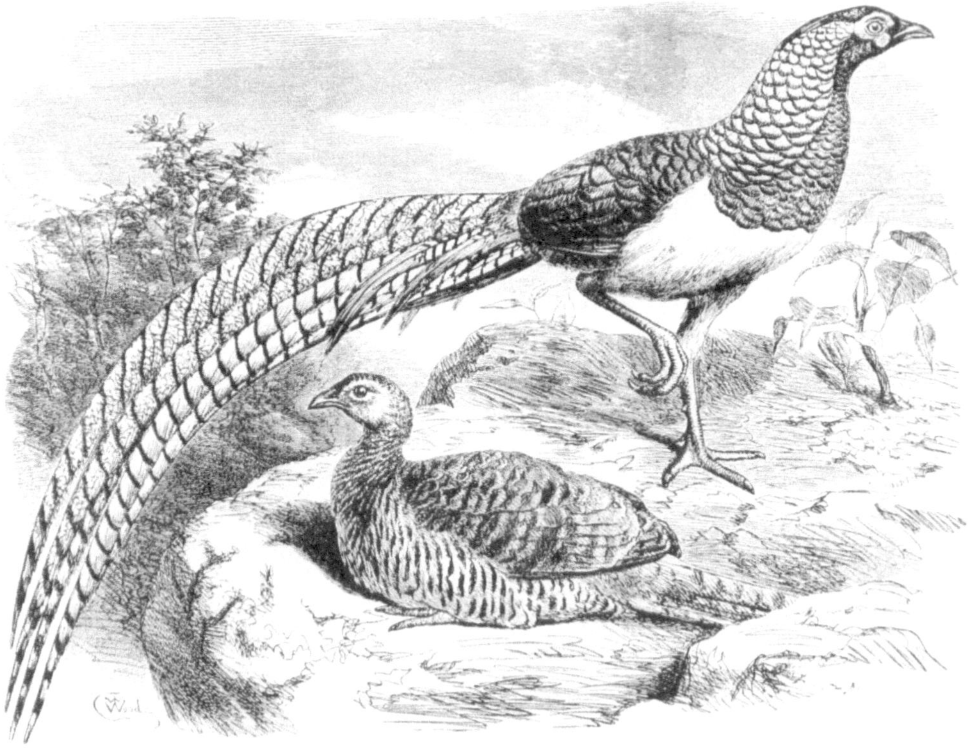

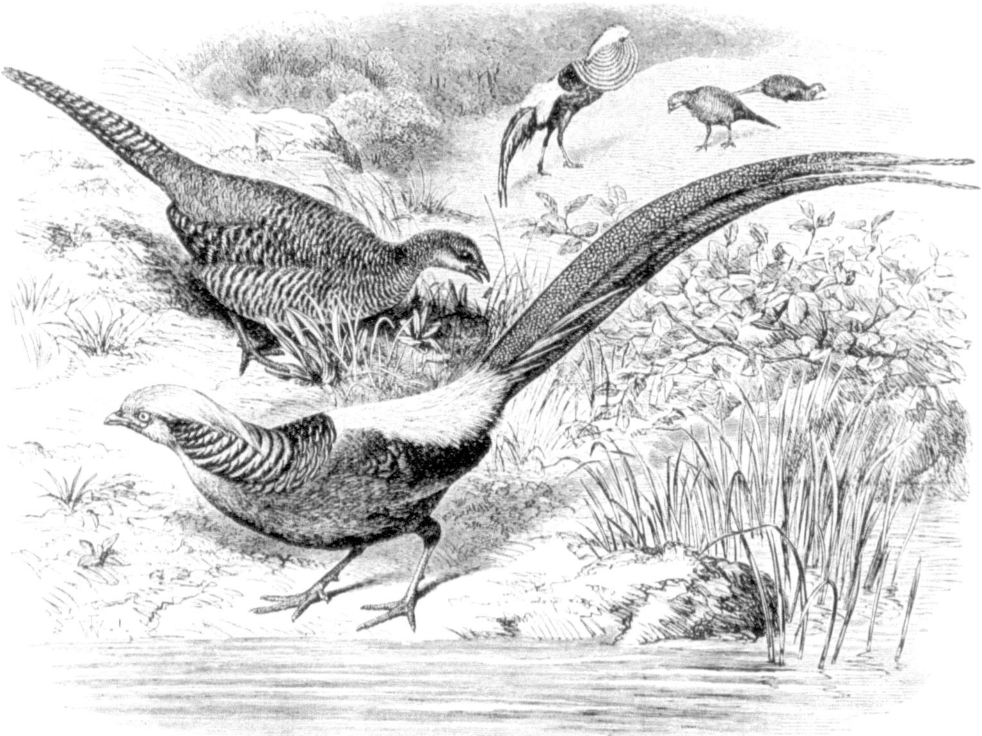

from wild pheasants, but they have suffered even more severely in recent decades from deforestation and hunting for the pot.[54]

Males of the Chinese monal *Lophophorus lhuysii* have magnificently iridescent feathers of purple, green, ruddy-gold, and blue, though its kin, the Sclater's monal *Lophophorus sclateri*, is decidedly less flashy. Chinese monals have suffered much loss and degradation of their alpine meadow habitat to encroachment from herds of yaks. People foraging for *Fritillaria* and other medicinal herbs on which the birds feed have also deprived the monals of food and disturbed their homes—their nests often destroyed under the feet of careless herb collectors.[55]

Most of these species have suffered decreases in both range and population over the course of the twentieth century, due, as with most species, to habitat loss and hunting. Few face the clear prospect of extinction, but for those that live only on the high alpine slopes, climate change could prove a fatal threat as their habitat recedes ever up the mountains until there is nowhere left to climb.

MIDDLE & LOWER YANGTZE

Map of the Middle & Lower Yangtze

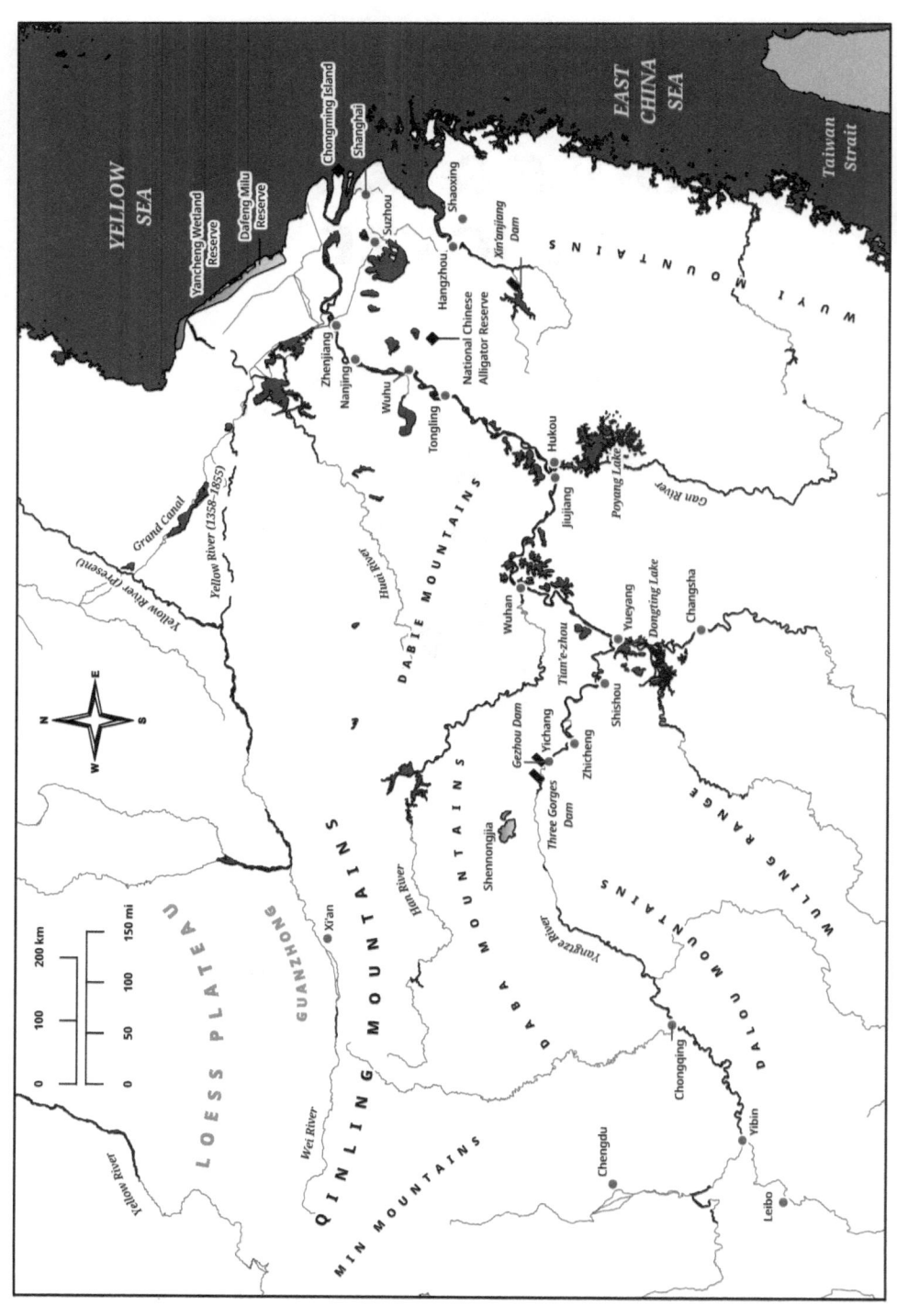

THE Yellow River may be considered the cradle of Chinese civilization, but the Yangtze River has exceeded it in importance, both cultural and economic, for over a thousand years. Called simply the Long River, *Cháng Jiāng* 长江 in Chinese, it is indeed the longest river in China and the third longest in the world.[1] It arises in the mountains of Qinghai in the eastern Tibetan Plateau and flows 6,300 km (3,900 mi) to the East China Sea at Shanghai.[2] Over 7,000 tributaries feed into the river, many of them major waterways in their own right, and the entire drainage basin covers a fifth of China. Along the banks of the Yangtze and its tributaries sit many of the largest and most vibrant cities in China, from Chongqing to Wuhan and Shanghai.

The Yangtze is traditionally split into three parts: the Upper Yangtze from its headwaters to Yichang in Hubei; the Middle Yangtze from Yichang to Hukou in Jiangxi; and the Lower Yangtze from Hukou to Shanghai. Much of the Upper Yangtze is extremely turbulent, so much so that many sections of the river host little aquatic life. The Middle and Lower Yangtze, where the river widens and slows, hosts a wealth of species, in not only the river itself but also its connected waterways and wetlands. The rivers and lakes of the Yangtze Basin host a great wealth of fish species, and the wetlands provide wintering grounds for dozens of species of migratory birds.

In addition to the thousands of tributaries that swell its waters, the Yangtze is connected to some of China's largest lakes. The two largest are Poyang and Dongting. Poyang Lake is the largest freshwater lake in China, and Dongting the second. Their surface areas fluctuate greatly with the seasons; Poyang ranges from 3,583 sq km (1,878 sq mi) to as little as 200 sq km (77 sq mi) at the most extreme. Both water bodies have shrunk and expanded over history as people have changed the hydrology of the lakes and their source rivers through such actions as deliberate empoldering, as well as unintended siltation due to the deforestation of the surrounding highlands. Massive engineering works during the Communist era have only sped and exacerbated these changes.[3]

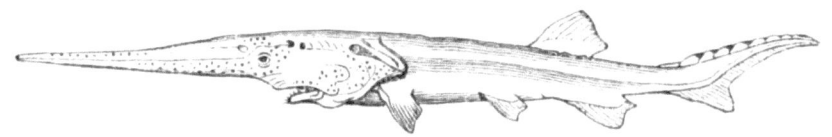

The Yangtze follows a natural rhythm, alternating between low waters in winter and high waters during summers when the monsoon brings rain inland, and glaciers on the Tibetan Plateau release their meltwater. Summer waters regularly flooded the riparian lowlands of the Middle and Lower stretches. This flood cycle was the impetus for a complete reworking of the river basin's hydrology over the course of the past two to three thousand years.[4]

The surging waters provided nutrients for the floodplains, making them extremely fertile. The lowlands thus hosted a great array of animal life. Poyang and Dongting lakes, as well as many now dried wetlands, hosted immense flocks of migratory birds in winter. The floodplains provided grazing for elaphure, water deer, and water buffalo. Higher up, elephants and rhinoceroses shared the forests with macaques, gibbons, black bears, clouded leopards, tigers, and many other species now gone from the region.[5]

Humans have lived along the Yangtze for millennia—wet rice was cultivated throughout the region by 5,000 BCE.[6] As people began to settle and farm rice permanently, summer flooding became a serious impediment to reliable harvests. To keep out the waters they built dikes to form polders, and as the population grew and both society and technology grew in sophistication, the networks of dikes grew in size and complexity. During times of turmoil the earthworks would fall into disrepair and the waters would flow back in, but over the centuries the lowlands were all but completely walled off and drained for agriculture.[7]

The dikes provided farmland, but came at a cost, one that increased as more people crowded into the lowlands and changed the hydrology ever more radically. Dikes and other water control works likely started small and expanded over time until they became so extensive they began to impact the flow of the river. Confined to a narrower passage, floodwaters rose higher and higher, forcing people to build ever larger and more elaborate defenses to redirect the waters. As the system moved further away from its natural state, it demanded ever greater amounts of money and labor to expand and maintain.[8]

After space in the lowlands ran out, people moved upwards and cleared the forested hillsides. First the trees were felled for lumber and then replanted as timber plantations. After the introduction of New World crops such as sweet potatoes and maize, the hills were settled and tilled. It took centuries longer, but the Yangtze Basin was reshaped just as radically as the North China Plain.

The greatest human impact on the Yangtze and its aquatic life has been the construction of gargantuan dams from the late twentieth century to present. The first major dam to span the Yangtze was the Gezhou Dam. Begun in 1970 and finished in 1981, it straddles the river at Yichang.[9] There has perhaps never been a single structure more devastating to more species than the Gezhou Dam. That includes the larger and more notorious Three Gorges Dam, which stands only 38 km (23.6 mi) upriver. When its structure was finished in 2006 the Three Gorges Dam created a massive reservoir stretching 600 km (370 mi) upriver and covering 1,084 sq km (419 sq mi). More dams farther upstream—some built, some unfinished, others only planned—have further scrambled the Yangtze's hydrology, with predictably devastating impacts on the river basin's aquatic life.

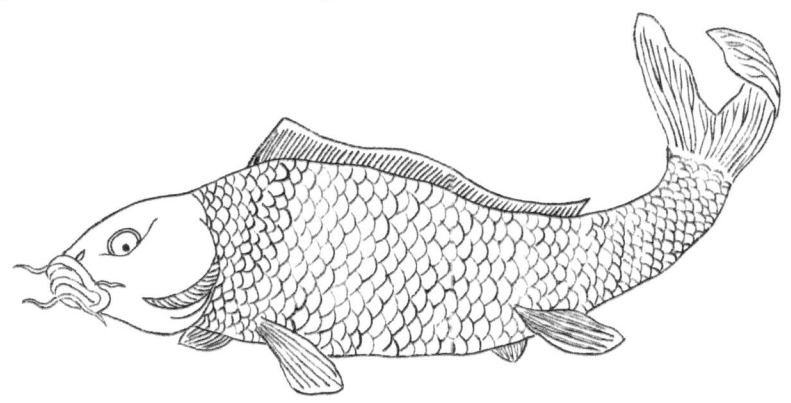

The River Goddess & The River Pig

I F there is to be a single cautionary tale for the dangers China's frenzied development have posed to its wildlife, it must be that of the Yangtze river dolphin or baiji *Lipotes vexillifer*.[1] A species unique to China, known to fishermen and scholars for centuries, revered and mythologized by some, the baiji fell prey to the relentless drive to exploit the Yangtze waters for all their worth. Hooked, netted, bombed, electrocuted, cut up, poisoned, deafened, the dolphins dwindled decade by decade until they disappeared only a few years into this millennium. Their fate holds crucial lessons for saving other Yangtze species that now barely hang on.

In form the baiji was an attractive creature, though it could seem a bit homely compared to the sleek, graceful elegance of its oceanic cousins such as the bottlenose or orca. It grew 2.3–2.5 m (7–8 ft) long, with a slightly humped back topped with a short, triangular dorsal fin. Its flippers were broad, the finger bones within splayed. Its body was predominantly gray with lighter undersides. A dark back with a light belly is a common color pattern in both aquatic animals and birds. When seen from above the darker top blends in with the riverbed or ground below; seen from below the light underside melts into the sky. As with other river dolphins of the world, such as those of South Asia and the Amazon, the baiji had a long, thin beak with rows of small, sharp, conical teeth.[2] Like the similarly snouted gharial, river dolphins are fish specialists, and they hunt using sonar, a far better method than sight for finding prey in the murky waters they swim through. Their eyes are tiny and placed at the sides of their heads, leaving them with very poor vision.

The baiji's ancestors came to the Yangtze long before the river took its current shape. Over millions of years they adapted as the waters shifted and turned from salt to sweet. The Yangtze is a murky river, especially its middle and lower reaches once it has gathered immense loads of silt from the mountains through which it and its tributaries flow. With nothing to see, the eyes of the baiji shrank until they were of almost no use. Instead the dolphins relied on their sonar and their ability to sense changes in the waters' currents and warmth. These adaptations allowed them to hunt and thrive though they were nearly blind.

There is little evidence to go on, but it is likely the baiji were restricted to the Middle and Lower Yangtze, from the delta upstream to the impassable rapids above Yichang at the end of the Three Gorges. They swam, too, in the Yangtze's many tributaries, as well as its great lakes, Dongting and Poyang. Restricted to the Yangtze system, even at their most numerous the baiji probably never totaled more than several thousand. Genomic analysis suggests the baiji population suffered a severe contraction roughly 10,000 years ago during the end of the last ice age; this was perhaps because the melting glaciers caused a rapid rise in sea levels, which led to the submergence of the Yangtze Valley under seawater, depriving the dolphins of much of their freshwater habitat. Once the valley refilled with sediment and a new freshwater network formed, the baiji made a strong recovery; their numbers grew consistently until around a thousand years ago.[3] When the first known reference to the dolphins in the *Er Ya* was written over two thousand years ago, they were numerous enough in their home waters that they were referred to as common.[4] In annotating the same text several centuries later, the Jin dynasty scholar Guo Pu (郭璞, 276–324) noted that the Yangtze was then "teeming" with baiji. Guo and the authors of the *Er Ya* accurately describe the dolphins in both form and function, relieving any doubt they may have mistaken the baiji for some other species.[5]

The baiji never achieved the favored status of gibbons or cranes in Chinese art and literature, but they made appearances in records throughout history, and even had a few poems dedicated to them. During the Tang the renowned physician Chen Cangqi (陳藏器, 681–757) noted that baiji meat tasted similar to water buffalo, and that when dried the flesh could be eaten as treatment for illnesses including malaria, miasma, poisoning, and demonic possession.[6] The Song dynasty literatus Kong Wuzhong (孔武仲, 1042–1097) made both the baiji and finless porpoise the subjects of his poem "Ode to River Dolphins (江豚詩)," which he opened by distinguishing the two by their colors.[7] Kong also mentioned that fishermen caught the cetaceans for their fat and watched their behavior for clues to impending inclement weather. Oil rendered from baiji was not renowned for its quality as a lamp oil. It gave only a dim light no good for literary pursuits. Yet peasants thought it adequate for loom work, and it could be used to give extra illumination for social occasions. It would also keep a flame against the wind, valuable for use onboard ships.

The baiji's most prominent appearance in literature is as one of the main characters in a tale in the Qing dynasty writer Pu Songling's (蒲松齡, 1640–1715) *Strange Stories from a Chinese Studio* (聊齋誌異). The story recounts the marriage of Bai Qiulian (白秋練), a baiji turned beautiful young woman, to a handsome young man. Unsurprisingly, there are more surviving references to the baiji from the Qing period than from prior times, though many of these are unquestioning recitations of earlier works, typical of traditional Chinese scholarship. There are continued notes about the capture and use of the dolphins, but not enough information to know whether these too were mere reiterations or instead reflected an increase in take. Perhaps the latter, as by the reign of the Guangxu Emperor (光緒帝, 1871–1908, r. 1875–1908) baiji had reportedly become a rare sight.[8]

Known to the Chinese for ages, the baiji finally came to the attention of Westerners in February 1914 when seventeen-year-old Charles Hoy (1897–1923), the son of American missionaries living near Dongting Lake, shot and killed one while out duck hunting. He already knew of the dolphins and porpoises that inhabited the lake's waters (indeed he had already shot several of the smaller finless porpoises but never secured a carcass), but this was his first capture. Hoy was not the first Westerner to see the baiji. In 1793 Lord George Macartney (1737–1806) had reported porpoises in the Yangtze during the return journey from his failed mission to Beijing, though he did not claim to have spotted any himself. Robert Swinhoe (1836–1877), however, had spotted them in the 1850s but, uncharacteristically, he had misidentified them, mistaking them for the Indo-Pacific humpback dolphins. Hoy thus won claim to the scientific discovery of a new species. After giving away the fat and flesh to eager locals (who, Hoy reported, used the blubber to treat coughs and colds and enjoyed the meat which he likened to "a mixture of beef and liver"), Hoy saved the skull and several vertebrae which he later sold to the Smithsonian.[9]

At the time of Charles Hoy's hunt, the dolphins were still a common sight in at least some of the Yangtze waters. Hoy reported seeing groups of up to fifteen during Dongting Lake's winter dry season, but he had only ever seen them around the mouth of the lake where it meets the Yangtze. Undoubtedly they were not so restricted, but by the 1920s there were already signs that dramatic increases in fishing could impact the baiji's numbers. When American zoologist Clifford Pope (1899–1974) visited Dongting in 1921, he noted that "there were thousands of fishermen actually straining creatures of all sizes from the rapidly vanishing lake, and it seemed that the dolphin must soon fall victim to one of their innumerable methods of separating the water from everything in it but the mud."[10]

The ensuing years of turmoil brought few records of the baiji, but they reappeared during the Great Leap Forward. As Maoist voluntarism swept over China, communities hatched an endless variety of bizarre schemes to force the country into the front ranks of the family of nations through sheer force of will. The baiji fell victim to the mania, as did every other plant and animal that someone somewhere could conceive a use for. Repeating the claims of contemporary news reports (with perhaps too much trust, given the rampant fabrication and exaggeration typical of the time), Zhou Kaiya later wrote that a leather factory was opened near Zhenjiang on the lower Yangtze where baiji skins were turned into bags and gloves. Purchasing stations were set up along the river, and fishermen were encouraged to bring in as many dolphins as they could catch. Some fishermen held to a traditional taboo against killing the baiji—plenty of others allowed no such concerns to stop them.

Whatever the truth of the leather factory (it was said to have shuttered after only a short time in operation), the 1950s saw the baiji's gradual decline turn swiftly to collapse. The decade saw an explosion of hydrological engineering that has continued unabated to the present. Hundreds and then thousands of dams, sluices, locks, and floodgates were built across the country, most small but many major projects.[11] They fragmented the waterways, changed the flows and temperatures of waters, altered silt loads, and otherwise radically remade China's inland water systems. Fish found their migration routes blocked and their spawning grounds destroyed. As for the baiji, lakes and rivers they had once been free to swim through were now cut off from the Yangtze. The dams had an immediate impact. Baiji were spotted in the Qiantang

River in the mid-1950s, but after the erection of the Xin'anjiang hydropower station at the end of the decade the dolphins were never seen there again.[12] The later Gezhou Dam on the Yangtze's main channel would prove even more devastating, not only for the baiji but many other species as well.

Into the 1960s baiji were already in decline, but they were still present over the full length of their former range, found from Yichang to Shanghai.[13] Yet the cold utilitarian demands of Maoism began to grind the dolphins down. The baiji remained a resource, which was plainly laid out in the 1962 edition of *Economic Mammalian Fauna of China*:

> "According to the residents of Dongting Lake, baiji blubber will not lose its quality for a number of years and is efficacious in treating coughs. Blubber from dolphins caught during the winter is quite thick, but in summer is thin. The meat is delicious but rather coarse."[14]

That same decade a Hubei fish farm worker enthused:

> "The economic value of the baiji is quite high. The wax from its head can be turned into a high-grade oil suitable for use as a lubricant for precision instruments. The blubber (usually consisting of approximately thirty to forty percent oil) can be used for industrial purposes, and fisherfolk use it as a lamp oil. The meat can be ground and eaten, the skin turned to leather, and the bones can be processed into meal for use as fertilizer."[15]

Enthusiasm for building a communist land of plenty was hardly the sole impetus behind fishing for baiji. The hardships of the time were motivation enough. Years later an old fisherman recalled that "in the sixties we needed to eat. I took a lot of the dolphins out, and I sold them, or took the meat for my family. It didn't matter that we had once called them goddesses. We didn't care."[16] Such targeted prosecution thinned out the baiji's numbers further, and by the late 1970s, as China's economy broke free of its Maoist bonds, the dolphins were in desperate need of protection.

No one knew just how desperate the situation was. The few scientists then studying the baiji knew there couldn't be many and that the dolphins had been dwindling in number and disappearing from parts of their distribution, but that was about all they could be sure of. For years all of their information came from talking to fishermen and occasionally inspecting a carcass. Only at the close of the 1970s were biologists finally able to mount surveys.

They found the dolphins no longer swam into either Poyang or Dongting and were no longer seen as far upriver as Yichang, only up to Zhicheng, about 60 km (37 mi) downriver. Extrapolating from the data they had, the researchers guessed there were 400 dolphins left. But it is hard to know how accurate this was. Such estimates are always difficult, even with the best information and most sophisticated methodology, neither of which were available. Even something so basic as identifying a baiji was not always a certainty. This became depressingly clear to zoologist Samuel Turvey after the failure to find a single baiji during a 2006 expedition:

> "... at dawn, Wei [Zhuo, chief ecologist of the Wuhan Institute of Hydrobiology's baiji study group] suddenly burst into my cabin, brimming with excitement. 'Dr. Sam! Dr. Sam!' He cried. 'There is a baiji beside the boat!' Wiping the sleep from my bleary morning eyes, I stumbled to the railings and looked out over the water. There right in front of me, less than ten metres away from the ship, was a pair of finless porpoises, rolling and breathing noisily in the still morning air. It was the best view I had had of the animals during the whole expedition, and it was immediately obvious that they were black, with no fin and no beak. It was absolutely impossible to mistake them for baiji. I stood for a long time watching the beautiful spectacle and saying nothing. 'Ah,' said Wei eventually. 'Maybe...they are porpoises?' I was too tired to reply. Later that day, Leigh [Barrett of the baiji.org Foundation, who had organized the survey] reminded me that this was the man who had reported over 110 official baiji sightings on previous surveys, including some of the last verified reports from the surveys in 1997 to 1999. How many of these sightings had been imaginary too?"[17]

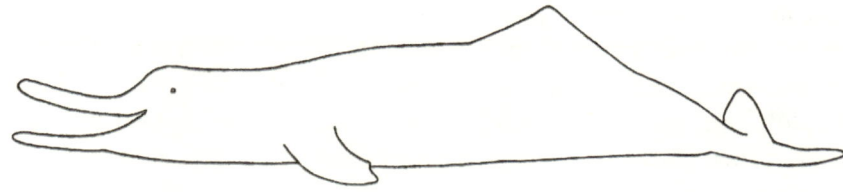

How many baiji remained was far from clear, but there was no doubt that they faced even worse conditions than before. As the government loosened its grip on society and the economy, ship traffic along the Yangtze exploded. More and bigger ships plied the river year after year until the Yangtze became clogged with by far the largest fleet of vessels and flow of goods of any river in the world. Nearly all of these ships were equipped with motors, which caused immense trouble for the baiji. The ships' propellers were deadly enough, and many dolphins were found dead or dying of deep gashes from the blades. But the engine noise was worse, for it was all but inescapable. Already nearly blind, the constant roar of ship engines rendered the dolphins practically deaf, no longer able to use their fine tuned senses to echolocate obstacles or prey. In fact it was the noise that led so many baiji into propellers. The dolphins had lived with ships for centuries and knew to dive and wait to resurface once the vessels passed, but the din of the engines disoriented them, and in their confusion they would attempt to surface too early and swim into the paths of the blades.[18] Not only the ships themselves but the locks built to ease their passage proved a danger to the baiji. When one newly installed pumping station first began operating, a strange sound soon began to emanate from it. On inspection workers found the intake pump had sucked a baiji to the bottom of the river and held it there until it drowned.[19]

Ships were only one of the threats to baiji. The Yangtze was and remains home to many factories, and until recently few took any care to prevent even the worst of their waste from spilling into the river. Added to this were the tonnes of pesticides and fertilizers from fields, the flow of sewage from cities and towns, as well as the occasional spill from leaking or wrecked freighters. Predictably it did the baiji no good to spend their lives immersed in such a toxic brew. A freighter collision in March 1984 spilled benzene into the Yangtze, killing nearby fish and one dolphin; tests of its organs showed it already had DDT in its system.[20] Another animal was found that May just as it was dying, its body bony and wasted; a necropsy found it too had been poisoned with DDT.[21]

As deadly as ship strikes and chemical pollutants were, it was probably fishing that did the most to kill off the baiji. By the end of the Maoist period the dolphins were rarely the target of fishermen, but they were caught all the same. Eager to bring in the largest hauls and with little to restrain them, Yangtze fishermen adopted devastatingly effective methods. Fine mesh nets trapped and killed many dolphins, but the worst for the baiji were the rolling hooks, long-lines of nearly 100 meters studded with hundreds of hooks. The lines floated behind boats or were fixed to the riverbed where they would drift and roll with the current. Fishermen would set them and check their catch once or twice a day. A hook would grab a baiji, and the dolphin would thrash about in an attempt to escape, only to find more and more hooks slashing and digging into its body. Fishermen would find the baiji covered in hundreds of cuts and gashes, doomed if not already dead.

For fishermen with little skill or patience there were simpler methods. When the central government broke up many of the giant state companies during the economic reforms of the 1990s, millions of men and women found themselves suddenly out of work and slipping into poverty. Many along the Yangtze turned to the river for their livelihoods, even if they had never fished a day in their lives. Dynamite was a favorite, the shock from the explosions being both an efficient and indiscriminate killer. Even more devastating was electro-fishing, in which a battery is used to jolt the water and everything in it, bringing stunned or dead creatures floating to the surface for easy collection.

Efforts to save the baiji began in earnest in the 1980s, but there was little Chinese scientists could do. The Cultural Revolution had thoroughly disrupted China's academic system, and combined with the long practice of assigning work regardless of people's interests and desires, this meant that there were few people able to do the necessary work, and among those few only a handful who cared to do so. Resources were scarce as well, not only money and scientific equipment but basic items such as telephones. Factionalism and distrust meant that calls often went unanswered or unreturned. Intense and petty rivalries are a seemingly universal feature of academia, and this proved true for those few working to protect the baiji. Two institutes worked to study and save the dolphins, the River Dolphin Research Group at the Institute of Hydrobiology in Wuhan, and a team at the Biology Department of Nanjing Normal University. Cooperation did not come easily.[22]

As is *de rigueur* in Chinese conservation, it was universally agreed early on that the best course of action would be to start a captive baiji breeding program. The catch was that no one knew how to do this. Baiji were captured all the time of course, but it was either done deliberately with the intent to kill, or accidentally, which was usually just as lethal. A few dolphins did survive long enough to end up in research facilities, but they didn't survive long. Most arrived weak and never fully recovered. Only two baiji lasted more than a year. One was Qiqi (淇淇), a yearling male found on a riverbank in January 1980 after suffering wounds from fishhooks. Local fishermen took him to a nearby fisheries institute, and from there he made his way to a pool in Wuhan at the Institute of Hydrobiology. Another stranded baiji arrived the next April but died in January 1982 after the water temperature dropped nearly to freezing. Qiqi endured, but was moved into a new, temperature-controlled dolphinarium for his safety.

One baiji couldn't repopulate the waters, so as Qiqi matured his handlers went in search of a mate for him. In March 1986 two baiji were captured and airlifted to join Qiqi. One was an old male who died within three months of arrival. The other was a young female, Zhenzhen (珍珍), and her arrival was cause for great hope and excitement. She was too young to breed, but in time she would be crucial to saving her species. Had things gone to plan. Instead she never adjusted to life in a cramped pool. Zhenzhen was constantly ill, hardier than most of the others who had expired within days or weeks, but not hardy enough. After two and a half years she died, and Qiqi was alone again.[23] He lived nearly fourteen more years, dying in July 2002 after twenty-two years in captivity. He was promptly stuffed, then given a funeral ceremony.

Qiqi never made it back into natural waters, but before his death plans were well along to establish a small enclosed reserve in a natural setting where captured baiji could live and multiply safe from the dangers of the Yangtze. Professor Zhou Kaiya (周开亚, 1932–) of the Nanjing baiji group helped establish one of these "semi-natural" reserves in Tongling, Anhui. Great efforts went into preparing the stretch of water and building necessary facilities. The local community proved extremely supportive; when Douglas Adams and Mark Carwardine arrived in 1988 for the BBC radio program *Last Chance to See*, they found that "now there was not only Baiji Beer, there was also the Baiji Hotel, Baiji shoes, Baiji Cola, Baiji computerized weighing scales, Baiji toilet paper, Baiji phosphorous fertiliser, and Baiji Bentonite."[24] It was all for nothing. No baiji ever swam in the Tongling semi-natural reserve.

Unhappy at the prospect that the Nanjing team would have the only semi-natural baiji population, the Wuhan team built their own, bigger and better, preserve. They chose an oxbow lake near Shishou, Hubei. Named Tian'e-zhou, it was 21 km (13 mi) long and held more than enough fish to feed up to perhaps eighty baiji. By the time the Wuhan Baiji Research Group began attempts to capture dolphins to move to Tian'e-zhou in the early 1990s, it wasn't clear there were even eighty baiji left. The latest surveys suggested there were at best a little over a hundred dolphins remaining. Astoundingly, in December 1995 a team managed to not only find but capture one of the last baiji, an adult female. She was rushed to Tian'e-zhou and placed in the oxbow. The Western advisers now working with their Chinese colleagues to save the species were surprised but hopeful. They had been promised that if a wild baiji was successfully brought to Tian'e-zhou then Qiqi would be transferred as well. He was now rather old, but this was the best chance yet for the start of a captive breeding population. Qiqi never arrived. The Wuhan team kept Qiqi in his dolphinarium, unwilling to part with their greatest source of prestige. The next summer the oxbow flooded and overflowed into the Yangtze. Fourteen finless porpoises that had shared Tian'e-zhou with the captured female baiji escaped back into the river, but the baiji stayed, entangled and dead in nets meant to keep in the animals during floods.[25] No more captures were attempted.

In those same years when conservationists were desperately scrambling to save the species, the baiji still appeared on lists of economically and medicinally valuable animals. In the aquatic goods volume of the *Agricultural Encyclopedia of China*, published in 1995, there is an entry on the baiji which states, "Baiji skin can be turned into leather. The meat is edible, and the subcutaneous fat makes for a high quality lubricant and is especially effective at treating scalds. The teeth can be used to make necklaces and other adornments." The following year a compendium of animal-derived medicinal ingredients listed baiji fat as a folk remedy which, administered three to six grams a dose, would "relieve coughing as well as clear heat and resolve toxins."[26] Imminent extinction was not grounds for removal from such texts.

If there hadn't been enough cause already, the next few years brought ample reason to remove the baiji from the lists of animal resources. From 1997 to 1999, surveys along the entire length of the dolphins' range discovered desperately low numbers of remaining baiji.

Seventeen were sighted in 1997, seven in 1998, and four in 1999. The low end of the estimated total was thirteen dolphins. The signs did not improve. In November 2001 a carcass washed ashore near Zhenjiang, between Nanjing and Shanghai. It was a pregnant female. The next May a live baiji was spotted and photographed, the last verified sighting of a wild dolphin. Qiqi was then the last baiji known to be alive, until he died two months later. Sightings continued but there was nothing concrete, no incontrovertible evidence to prove any Yangtze river dolphin still lived. Despite the clearly desperate situation, no one thought the baiji was already extinct. Not yet.

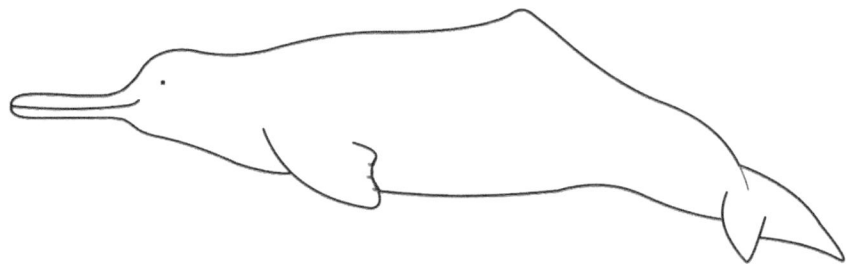

Any remaining baiji had to be found. Conservationists needed to know how many were left, and where along the river they could still survive so that all efforts to protect them could be focused for maximum effect. After several false starts, a survey expedition of the entire Middle and Lower Yangtze was cobbled together. It launched in autumn 2006 and surveyed the main channel of the Yangtze between Shanghai and Yichang, 1,669 km (1,037 mi), once upriver and again downriver.[27] It found no baiji. Instead it found ships, by rough count a minimum of 19,830 large shipping vessels. Illegal fishing was rampant as ever, and pollution of every sort choked the river for the entire length of the survey.[28]

The survey had been undertaken with the understanding that the baiji were in dire need of help, and yet there was hope that if only a few could be found and their waters protected the species might still be saved. At the close of 2006 there was little doubt the baiji were already gone. If any survivors remained they were too few, too scattered, and faced too many dangers. The Yangtze river dolphin was extinct, the first cetacean to disappear at the hands of humankind. The next year, in the *Faunal Medicinal Resources of China*, there was an entry on baiji fat.[29]

Perhaps the baiji never had a chance. The rush to industrialize and enrich the nation was never going to be kind to the Yangtze or its inhabitants. But whatever the dolphins' chances, the conservation community simply failed, leaving a record of poor decisions and missed opportunities. Conservationists immediately agonized over what was to be learned and, inevitably, who was to blame. There was plenty of disgrace to go around. The Chinese had paid little heed to protecting the baiji until it was nearly too late, and even then their efforts were not merely too little but marred by shortsighted and selfish factionalism. The Western conservation community was no more help, overly concerned with debating, for years and until the very end, the merits and demerits of whether to conserve the dolphins in their natural habitat or to place them in captivity. The uncertainty of how best to proceed paralyzed them, and when it came time to fund the work of saving the species, they proved unwilling to put forward more than a pittance. There was genuine concern and heroic effort from a few dedicated souls, but it wasn't enough, and now the baiji is gone, a sad warning for many other creatures of the Yangtze and those who would protect them.

With the disappearance of the baiji there remains only one cetacean that swims the Yangtze and its lakes, the Yangtze finless porpoise *Neophocaena asiaeorientalis asiaeorientalis*, a subspecies of the narrow-ridged finless porpoise. Not even reaching 1.8 m (6 ft) in length, the finless porpoises are quite diminutive. Their bodies are a uniform dark gray, and, true to their name, the finless porpoises lack a dorsal fin. Instead a long, narrow ridge runs down their back, topped with between one and five rows of small tubercles.[30] Typical of porpoises, the Yangtze subspecies lacks the long beak found in dolphins and instead has a blunt snout with a slightly curved mouth, giving them a faint, perpetual smile.

The porpoises were noted in literature from at least the Han dynasty, with scattered mentions throughout the centuries. They most often appeared as accent pieces to the river itself, mere evocative detail, spraying water as they surfaced and giving sailors hints at the coming weather.[31] Notable exceptions came during the Song, when the poet Wang Yucheng (王禹偁, 954–1001) composed "Song of the River

Dolphins (江豚歌)," and Kong Wuzhong later wrote his "Ode to River Dolphins." Since ancient times the porpoises were a common sight from the Yangtze's mouth up to Yibin and in the connecting lakes along the way, the same waters the baiji swam.

It is unlikely that fishermen often targeted the porpoises, as their meat was said to be unpalatable. The Three Kingdoms warlord Cao Cao (曹操, c. 155–220) explicitly advised against eating porpoise.[32] There were apparently exceptions however, as the Northern Song writer Fan Zhiming (範致明, ?–1119) noted in his account of the city of Yueyang that local fishermen were enthusiastic in catching the porpoises as sources of lamp oil and meat.[33] An additional use for the porpoises arose during the late Ming dynasty. During the Wanli Emperor's reign (萬曆帝, 1563–1620, r. 1572–1620), the war ministry ordered river communities to collect porpoise fat and bones. Like baiji oil, porpoise oil kept a flame against the wind, and so was considered a key ingredient in several specialized gunpowders.[34] How many porpoises ended up in Ming munitions is anyone's guess, but perhaps not as many as hoped, as the porpoises evidently proved cunning prey for fishermen.[35] They were not so wily as to escape the Emperor Kangxi, however, who in 1706 reminisced of shooting a porpoise between Nanjing and Zhenjiang during his first tour of the region twenty-two years prior.[36]

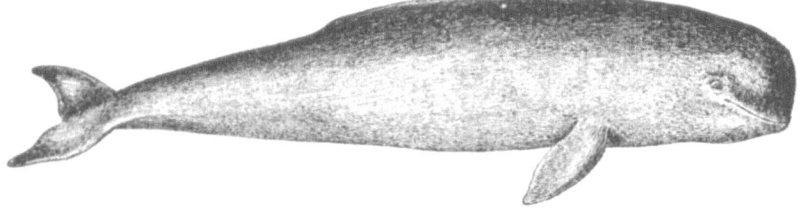

By the early twentieth century they were still a regular sight, so much so that one Western resident in Shanghai referred to them as "legion."[37] The porpoises continued to escape close attention until the 1960s when the first attempts to capture and rear them in captivity began and soon failed.[38] As scientists intensified their studies of the Yangtze's wildlife in the mid to late 1970s, they began to notice that the finless porpoises were suffering the same fate as the baiji. Of the dozens of dead porpoises that came to their attention, most were the victims of fishermen's hooks and nets. Researchers began to make small surveys across the greater Yangtze system. They noticed a steady decline in the porpoises' numbers, and by the early 1990s they estimated only around 2,700 of the little cetaceans remained. By the end of the decade the number had dropped to 2,000.[39]

The baiji drew the great bulk of attention from scientists and conservationists from the late 1970s until the realization of its extinction dawned in late 2006. The finless porpoises were acknowledged to be rapidly dwindling, and the same causes were presumed to be at fault, but no one was very sure. Come 2007 the population had already dropped further to 1,800—a collapse of over fifty percent in less than two decades—and the porpoises were no longer found in the large tributaries of the Yangtze. Their numbers seemed stable only in Dongting and Poyang lakes, but they were hardly safe there. In 2004 six porpoises were found dead in Dongting, the victims of poisoning from pesticides intended to kill off the snails that carry the parasitic blood flukes that cause schistosomiasis.[40]

Surveys continued and soon it became clear the porpoises were disappearing from stretches of the Yangtze, their population not only dropping but fragmenting. The porpoises of Poyang Lake have proven the safest and most stable, their numbers holding steady for now. In Dongting their numbers dropped rapidly between 2006 and 2012, but the decline slowed and perhaps even began to reverse thereafter. Nonetheless, there remain only around a hundred of the cetaceans in the lake. In the mainstream of the Yangtze the porpoises continue to decline, albeit more slowly than decades past; there are perhaps 500 remaining, fragmented into several new populations.[41] Even though their total numbers have hovered around 1,000 for several years now, they remain on a course frightfully similar to that of the baiji.

There are plenty of threats remaining. Despite the dizzying amount of commercial shipping traffic already moving up and down the Yangtze, construction continues to provide improved infrastructure and access for more and bigger ships. As did the baiji, the finless porpoises suffer from the intense and endless din of ships' engines, the cacophony deafening and confusing them, leaving them more likely to wander into the blades of a ship's propellers. More sections of river are being deepened, widened, and paved—channelized to ease passage for gargantuan vessels. The porpoises find it difficult to survive in such deep, fast-moving waters. More ports, roads, and bridges are being built along and across the river, and the construction both disturbs the porpoises and leaks pollutants into the waters.[42] Over a decade of sand mining to supply construction around the region has also caused severe erosion and loss of habitat in Dongting Lake.[43]

Now at least there are the resources and the people needed to save the Yangtze porpoises from extinction. The central government has placed a ten-year moratorium on commercial fishing in the river, which if successful will remove a major source of danger to the porpoises. Efforts to clean the waters by reducing pollution and soil erosion could also help over time. Local citizens along the river have taken up the cause of protecting the porpoises, and there are now organizations dedicated solely to the cetaceans.

Yet even with resources and attention the baiji never enjoyed, the efforts to save the porpoises are hardly free from conflict and controversy. In 2018 government wildlife authorities declared their intention to relocate fourteen porpoises in an attempt to improve captive breeding efforts. Protests from conservationists seemed to have succeeded in scuppering the plan, until the successful relocation of nineteen porpoises was announced in early May 2021. Having anticipated the conservation community's objections, the Ministry of Agriculture and Rural Affairs simply went ahead in secret. Reaction was swift, and all the more vehement for the fact that some of the animals—a number the Ministry did not care to divulge—had been sent to two large commercial aquariums, both favored targets of criticism from conservationists and animal welfare activists. Moving a number of porpoises into captivity for safekeeping and breeding was not the problem, instead it was that any should go to aquariums where they would stand little chance of successful breeding and even less chance of ever returning to their natural habitat.[44]

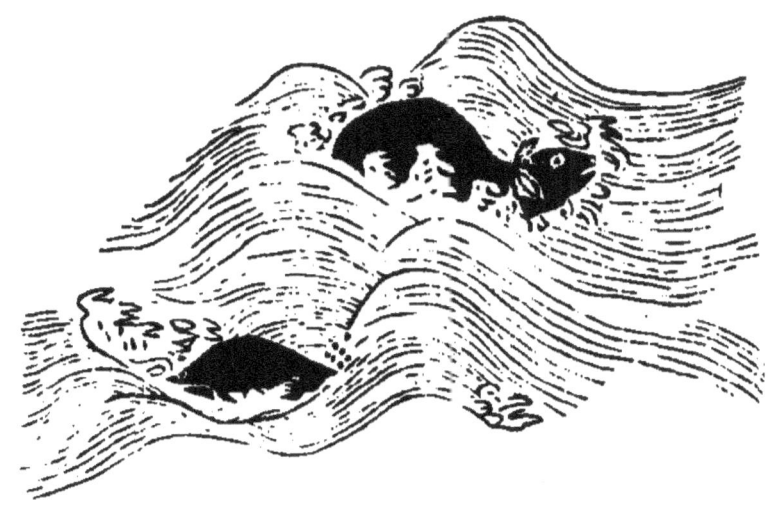

Fishing

THE baiji is not the only Yangtze native to have disappeared in the last twenty years. The Chinese paddlefish *Psephurus gladius*, a distant cousin to the sturgeons, faded away at the same time. The paddlefishes are named for their extremely long snouts, or rostrums, which are covered with electroreceptors that allow the fish to detect the weak electrical fields that betray the presence and movements of their prey.[1] Aside from their immense nasal appendages, Chinese paddlefish were remarkable for their overall size. Mature fish measuring 3 m (10 ft) and longer were commonly caught. In fact *Psephurus* was possibly the world's largest freshwater fish; a specimen caught near Nanjing was reported to measure over seven meters long.[2]

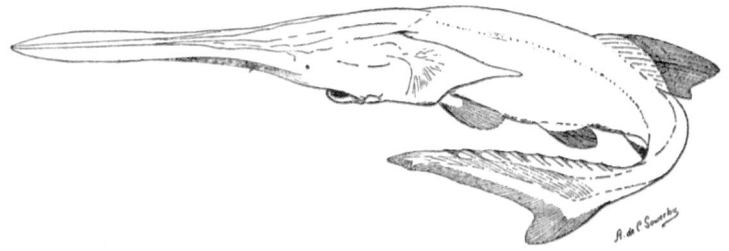

The paddlefish swam the length of the Yangtze from its estuary all the way past Yibin to Leibo on the Sichuan-Yunnan border. Their spawning grounds were mostly in the upper reaches of the river, past Chongqing, where the riverbed was sandy or muddy, suitable for their eggs and hatchlings. Although the paddlefish was found primarily in the Yangtze and its tributaries, records show the fish also swam the Yellow and Huai rivers, as well as the East China and Yellow Seas.[3] Numbers of *Psephurus* in the Yellow River seem to have declined beginning as far back as the thirteenth century, and they were last sighted in the river's waters in the 1960s.[4] Their appearance in both inland and marine waters suggest that they were an anadromous species, leaving the seas and swimming upriver to spawn, but their life history was never understood well enough to confirm this.[5]

The giant and impressively-snouted fish were noted in literature as early as the Qin dynasty, and they were a common catch for Yangtze fishermen throughout the centuries. In the mid to late nineteenth century Western travelers along the Yangtze regularly spotted the fish for sale, its unusual appearance assuring they made note of it in their writings.[6] Mature, large paddlefish were caught in the upper reaches of the Middle Yangtze, while juveniles were netted in the river's estuary, and the fish were taken in smaller numbers along the rest of the river and its tributary waters.[7]

Annual hauls of *Psephurus* in the 1970s averaged around twenty-five tonnes, a small percentage of the Yangtze's total catch.[8] The rampant overfishing of the time inevitably affected the paddlefish population, but it was the completion of the Gezhou Dam at Yichang, Hubei in 1981 that sealed their fate. The dam blocked any chance of migration and split the paddlefish into two separate populations. Their spawning grounds were likely all upriver from the dam, and though some juveniles did appear below the Gezhou Dam between 1983 and 1985, from 1986 no more young were sighted downstream. By the early 1990s even mature paddlefish were extremely rare, with only a few seen a year.[9]

Hopes for saving the species rested on a bid to artificially spawn and rear paddlefish fry for release into the Yangtze. Successful American paddlefish hatcheries had been operating since the 1960s, but similar efforts for *Psephurus* failed. There were too few fish left in the river to catch for use as broodstock, and those few that were captured did not survive the wait for a partner.[10] At the turn of the millennium hopes for the paddlefish were fading fast.

The last known Chinese paddlefish was caught on 24 January 2003 at Yibin in Sichuan. A gravid female with tens of thousands of eggs inside her, the fish was 3.35 m (11 ft) long and weighed 150.9 kg (332 lb). The previous month another paddlefish had been caught and kept at a sturgeon hatchery for twenty-nine days before dying in an unfortunate accident. Afraid to have another paddlefish die in captivity, the scientists caring for the fish patched up her wounds and attached a radio tracker before returning her to the river. Hoping to follow her to her spawning grounds and perhaps find more paddlefish there, they tracked her until losing the signal late on 29 January. Despite their best efforts, they never regained the signal, and no paddlefish were seen again.[11] Nineteen years followed with no evidence that any paddlefish still survive before experts relented and declared the species extinct.[12]

Even with the disappearance of the Chinese paddlefish there remain two Acipenseriformes in the Yangtze—the Chinese sturgeon *Acipenser sinensis*, and the Yangtze or Dabry's sturgeon *A. dabryanus*. Chinese sturgeon are among the world's largest sturgeon, with females reaching up to 4 m (13 ft) long and weighing in at up to 680 kg (1,500 lb) or more.[13] The Yangtze sturgeon is decidedly smaller, rarely growing beyond 1.3 m (4.3 ft) and 16 kg (35 lb) in the wild.[14] Like the Chinese paddlefish, the Chinese sturgeons swim to the sea after hatching only to return to their birth waters to spawn—an attribute that has earned them the moniker of "patriotic fish."[15] Although the Yangtze sturgeons migrate up and down the Yangtze, they never venture all the way downstream to saltwater.

The Chinese sturgeon once swam the waters from the Yellow Sea off the Korean Peninsula to the South China Sea, from where they would swim past Hong Kong up the Pearl River.[16] The Long River hosted its own population of Chinese sturgeon, as well as the Yangtze sturgeon, which, true to its name, was limited to the Yangtze and its connecting waters.[17] Both species were known to the Chinese and were fished for centuries, first documented at least as far back as 1104 BCE.[18] However, the two species were not formally distinguished until the introduction of Linnaean taxonomy in the mid nineteenth century, and confusion over the two continued until the 1960s.[19]

The sturgeons first clearly began to decline as a result of overfishing in the 1960–1970s. Chinese sturgeon juveniles were caught in the Yangtze estuary; adults were fished upstream in the upper and middle reaches of the river. But, just as with the Chinese paddlefish, it was the damming of the river that caused the collapse of the two sturgeons. The Gezhou Dam, with no fish ladders to give the sturgeons even a chance of passing through, cut off the fish downstream from their spawning grounds in the upper reaches of the river. Some sturgeon have managed to persist, but any that still survive represent a tiny remnant with practically no hope of surviving another generation.[20]

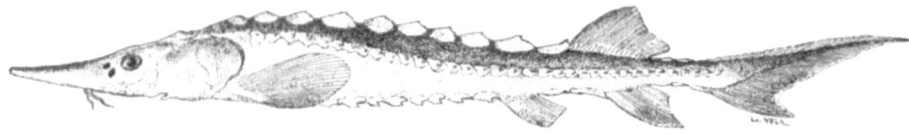

The sturgeon upstream from the Gezhou Dam suffered a further blow when the Three Gorges Dam started operating in 2003. Its massive reservoir turned once fast flowing waters into a still, deep lake ill-suited to the sturgeons. Later dams farther upstream fragmented the Yangtze sturgeon's spawning grounds, though they at least have not yet been shut out from the major tributaries of the Upper Yangtze.[21]

Both wild fish populations are in dire straits. Following the completion of the Gezhou Dam in 1981 the breeding population of Chinese sturgoen plummeted ninety percent by 1999. In 2005 it was down to 235 fish, a decade later to only fifty.[22] Now likely no more than ten females lay eggs in a given year.[23] Young of both the Chinese and Yangtze sturgeons have been released from hatcheries in an ongoing effort to boost the wild populations, but so far the results have been dismal. Of the over seven million juvenile Chinese sturgeons released between 1983 and 2013 almost none survived to maturity.[24] The Yangtze sturgeon has fared no better, which is all the more devastating as there has been no evidence of natural spawning in over a decade.[25] The only fish now found in the river seem to be those released from hatcheries, and although over 500 mature fish have been released, there remains no sign of breeding.[26] In 2022 the IUCN listed the Yangtze species as extinct in the wild, but its assessment included an optimistic note that if current conservation measures continue there is a good chance the fish will reestablish a wild population.[27]

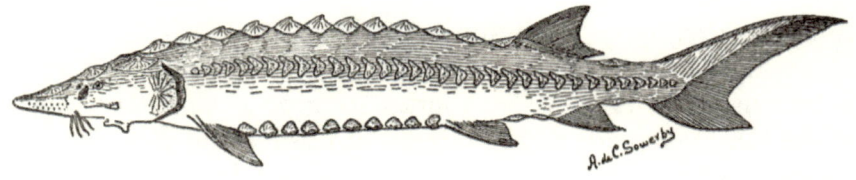

Beyond the Yangtze the only other Chinese sturgeon population known to persist is the Pearl River population, but it remains little studied and is likely already gone, replaced with the hybrid and foreign escapees of local sturgeon farms. The Yangtze's two sturgeons seem fated to perpetual captivity, extinct in their native waters. They may adapt and find new spawning grounds below the Gezhou Dam, but that is far from certain, and the cascading effects of new upstream dams and reservoirs will only bring new challenges. Climate change, too, threatens to narrow the window in which any survivors can spawn.[28]

Yet hope may remain. Wei Qiwei (危起伟, 1960–), the foremost expert on China's sturgeons, is optimistic that, as hatchery operations improve and releases increase, the sturgeons will recover. Although there is no sign that Chinese sturgeon have bred in the wild since 2017, Dr. Wei predicts if conservation efforts are sufficiently funded, greater numbers of hatchery fish will reach maturity, and if enough mature fish can be released every year, the sturgeons may be able to successfully breed in the wild as early as 2036.[29] His optimism may prove warranted; in early 2024 thirty-one pairs of Yangtze sturgeon successfully spawned in a patch of river modified to match their natural spawning habitat.[30] Not all experts are convinced, however. Some posit that the very basis of Dr. Wei's position is flawed, and that so long as the dams are in place the fish will not have the habitat they require to sustain themselves.[31] It may not be long before it becomes clear whether or not the dams truly prove fatal to the sturgeons.

The Acipenseriformes are hardly the only fish of the Yangtze to have suffered the ill effects of humanity's works. The river's population of Japanese eel *Anguilla japonica* disappeared after the Gezhou Dam was completed.[32] So, too, did the population of the Chinese high-fin banded shark (more humbly known as the Chinese sucker) *Myxocyprinus asiaticus* below the dam, and the copper fish *Coreius heterodon* above it.[33] The surviving population of *M. asiaticus* in turn dwindled to nothing after the completion of the Three Gorges Dam; attempts to revive the wild population through the release of captive bred fish have shown no clear success.[34] The concrete behemoth's reservoir robbed *Coreius guichenoti* of the fast flowing waters it required, and more dams on the Jinsha section of the Upper Yangtze and on the Yalong River blocked its migratory routes. Its population has plummeted, and it now faces extinction.[35]

Other species have declined due to overfishing. The common carp *Cyprinus carpio* and crucian carp *Carassius carassius* both survive in abundance, but the black carp *Mylopharyngodon piceus*, grass carp *Ctenopharyngodon idella*, silver carp *Hypophthalmichthys molitrix*, and bighead carp *H. nobilis* populations are all shadows of their former plenty.[36] The Reeves's or Chinese shad *Tenualosa reevesii* was long a large portion of Yangtze fishermen's takes; in the 1950s and until 1962 the average annual catch was over 500 tonnes.[37] After a record haul in the early 1970s, the population collapsed and in 1986 only reached twelve tonnes. After the Wan'an Dam went up in 1985 the shad disappeared from Jiangxi's Gan River and have not been seen in the Yangtze system since the 1990s. Far to the south the Pearl River's population has all but vanished, with only a struggling remnant still in the lower reaches.[38] The Chinese longsnout catfish *Leiocassis longirostris* was treasured for its swim bladder, and so served as a status-conferring delicacy, but it is no longer found along much of the river.[39]

Another denizen of the Yangtze and terror to many of its fish species is the now rarely seen Eurasian otter *Lutra lutra*. One of three otter species native to China, along with the Asian small-clawed otter *Aonyx cinereus* and the smooth-coated otter *Lutrogale perspicillata*, the Eurasian otter is very close in size and appearance to the North American river otter *Lontra canadensis*, but with a shorter neck and longer tail.[40] Once common across the waters of China, it is now found only in small numbers scattered around the country.

Nineteenth and early twentieth century Westerners who voyaged down the Yangtze made sure to stop at a village across the river from Yichang, which they named Otter Village on account of the tamed otters the local fishermen kept.[41] Much the same as the tame cormorants still used in South China and Japan, the otters were used to catch fish, but unlike the cormorants they did not seize hold of the fish themselves. Instead the otters were tethered to a line and released into the water to chase their quarry into the fisherman's net, and having done so they would come up in the net along with the fish.[42] The use of fishing otters was apparently not restricted to Yichang—Western travelers reported seeing them in Jiangxi and Sichuan as well.[43] The practice died out after the 1960s as modern, more efficient fishing methods took its place.[44]

The taming of otters was an ancient practice, referenced as far back as the *Huainanzi* (淮南子) written in the second century BCE, in which the reader was admonished not to ply their pet otters with alcohol.[45] Fishing with otters apparently began centuries later, and was first documented during the reign of Emperor Xianzong of Tang (唐憲宗, 778–820, r. 805–820).[46] Otters were more commonly put to use dead. Of course they ended up in medicines—their guts, meat, and bones were all held to have some therapeutic use. But it was otter pelts that found the largest market. The furs were valued for their warmth, sheen, and for being waterproof; they typically were used to line and trim clothing and were in high demand among not only the Chinese but many others as well. Tibetans were especially fond of otter furs, to the point that Tibet's own otter populations could not meet demand.[47] River otter pelts were imported from Bengal, while many sea otter pelts that came from America and Russia made their way through China to Tibet. Tibetan demand dropped off during the Maoist period but revived afterwards, only to die off again in 2006 after the Dalai Lama spoke out against the use of furs.[48] Otters were therefore widely hunted, but at the Communist takeover of China they were still commonly found throughout the country.[49]

From the start of New China in 1949 until the mid-1980s, China sustained a long campaign of fur trapping that led to the collapse of much of its otter population. The killing was unconstrained, many provinces recording intakes of thousands of pelts per year in the 1950s and 1960s. In 1955 over 14,000 otters were caught in Hubei; in neighboring Hunan the highest annual take was 25,733 pelts. Beyond the Yangtze Basin the slaughter was just as intense. Inevitably otter numbers began to plummet. In the southern coastal province of Guangdong the take of otter pelts had dropped by ninety-six percent between the 1950s and 1981.[50] Neighboring Fujian averaged between 2,000 and 3,000 pelts a year in the mid-1960s, but by 1983 only sixty-six pelts came in, a drop of ninety-eight percent. Guangxi, Anhui, Jilin and other provinces across China all recorded similarly precipitous drops of over ninety percent. By the 1990s otters were difficult to find anywhere in China.[51]

Scientists have only begun to survey for otters in recent years, and though China's population of Eurasian otters is a pathetic fraction of its former plentitude, the mustelids have managed to survive across a surprising expanse of the country. To be sure, the survivors are few in number and scattered, but their widespread persistence gives hope that they may rebound in time. The middle and lower reaches of the Yangtze's main stem have very few, if any, otters, but there are remnants in some of its tributaries that could eventually repopulate the rest of the river system.

Herptiles

The one species whose future is more precarious than any other's, along the Yangtze or anywhere else in China, is the Yangtze giant softshell turtle *Rafetus swinhoei*.[1] The Yangtze softshell has a rather flat olive shell. The skin on its long neck and head are covered in an intricate mix of yellow and dark olive spots and splotches. It has a small pig-like snout and pudgy little jowls. When combined with its two tiny yellow eyes set at the top of its head, it is easy to understand why the turtle has not become a beloved conservation symbol in the same manner as sea turtles. The Yangtze softshell is also exceptionally large—one turtle had a carapace (the back portion of the shell; the underside is the plastron) that measured over 1 m (3.3 ft), though most of course do not reach such a prodigious size. One of only two members of the *Rafetus* genus, *R. swinhoei* has the distinction of being not only among the largest freshwater turtle species in the world, but also the rarest turtle species anywhere.[2] At the time of writing, only one survives in China.

Unlike most of the animals threatened with extinction in China, the Yangtze softshell was likely already a rare species long before human impacts further fragmented and devastated its populations. All evidence suggests the turtles were separated into disparate populations millennia ago, likely the result of geologic changes.[3] Of course the turtles did not escape notice. They were hunted for their meat, and their bones and shells were used in medicines. How this contributed to their decline is unknown, but by the 1870s when Western naturalists first encountered and described the species, they were already rare.[4] Centuries of hunting and habitat change through the drainage and conversion of wetlands to rice paddies likely contributed to the gradual disappearance of *R. swinhoei*. No one knows for sure because no one paid much attention until the close of the twentieth century. Even after its first description in scientific literature in the 1870s, the Yangtze softshell was usually conflated with the more widespread and common (yet still critically endangered) Asian giant softshell turtle *Pelochelys cantorii*. In fact the taxonomy was not settled until 1988, and subsequent work to determine the turtles' actual distribution only concluded in the late 1990s.[5]

In the past turtles were found in Lake Tai close to Suzhou, in the Huangpu River near Shanghai, and farther afield along the Red River in Yunnan. By the end of the last century there were no more Yangtze softshells in the wild, not beyond the odd rumor of a sighting that never yielded a living turtle. Luckily there were a few remaining in captivity. At the beginning of the Communist period in 1949 there were turtles in several collections around the country, but by 2000 most had died.[6] One death was particularly tragic, if slightly comic. In an effort to breed the turtles a female was introduced to a male, Susu (苏苏), at Suzhou Zoo. The hoped for romance soon descended into violence, and after a vicious fight Susu killed his new companion. On inspecting the deceased, the zoo staff were dismayed to find that the dead female was in fact male, and they had lost one of the only Yangtze softshells on the globe due to sheer ignorance.[7] As if the loss of one male wasn't enough, the male at the Beijing Zoo died in 2005, and then the male at the Shanghai Zoo in 2006. The following year another male died, a resident of Suzhou's Buddhist West Garden Temple, a turtle the resident monks believed to have been over 400 years old. Another turtle at the same temple had not been seen for several years.[8]

New hope came when a female was found. Knowing that *R. swinhoei* had often been misidentified, the Wildlife Conservation Society asked zoos to reexamine their turtles to determine if any were in fact Yangtze softshells. In January 2007 the Changsha Zoo in Hunan announced that one of their turtles, purchased from a traveling circus fifty years prior, was a fertile Yangtze softshell female. Named Xiangxiang (湘湘), she was the only female of her species known to still be alive and already at least 80 years-old.[9] After initial reluctance from both the Changsha and Suzhou zoos to participate in a captive breeding attempt (wary of both the costs and the dangers of failure), Xiangxiang was sent to Suzhou to meet Susu.[10]

After Xiangxiang and Susu finally met in May 2008 they soon went through their courtship rituals and mated. The next month Xiangxiang dug a nest in the beach of her enclosure and laid forty-five eggs. Later in the year she laid sixty more eggs. None of them hatched.

The next year they went through the same routine, and this time Xiangxiang laid four clutches totaling over 200 eggs. Again none of them hatched. In 2010 and 2011 it was no different.[11] Clearly something was wrong, and on examination it came to light that the problem was with Susu. In the course of his battle with his false mate years early, Susu's penis had been badly injured. The number and motility of his sperm were so low that the only hope for success lay with artificial insemination.[12] Four attempts over the next several years all ended in failure. On April 13, 2019, after the fifth attempt, something went wrong. The attending team of veterinarians tried for twelve hours to resuscitate Xiangxiang, but their efforts failed. She died, leaving Susu, now in his twelfth decade of life, the last Yangtze softshell in China.[13]

Hope seemed lost, but in October 2020 a female was captured in Đồng Mỏ Lake, Hanoi, where another turtle, possibly a male, was also spotted.[14] The minuscule population of softshells in Vietnam had suffered the same fate as their cousins in China, hunted and deprived of their homes over the centuries. One turtle, Cụ Rùa, was known to live in Hoàn Kiếm Lake in central Hanoi, but he died in 2016 and was embalmed to be put on display at the lake's Temple of the Jade Mountain.[15] Yet hopes of any successful mating were dashed on 23 April 2023 when the Đồng Mỏ female was found dead.[16] With the only two remaining turtles both males, all hopes rest on scientists' continued search for more turtles in both China and Vietnam. Though their early findings are discouraging, there may yet be a few Yangtze softshells remaining.[17] Susu is likely to live out his life alone, but now there remains the slimmest chance that the species will survive, and that sometime in the future the giant softshell turtles will repopulate the waters of the lower Yangtze.

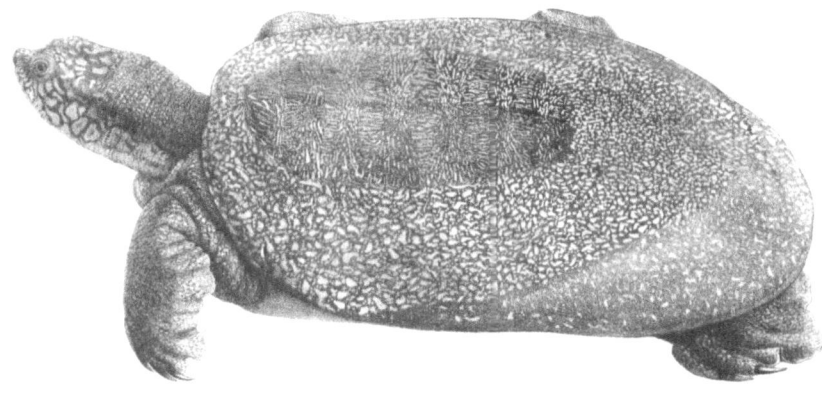

The lower Yangtze is home to one of the only two extant members of the *Alligator* genus, the Chinese alligator *Alligator sinensis* (the other is of course the American alligator *A. mississippiensis*).[18] Chinese alligators are only about half the length of their American cousins and much lighter. Captive individuals seem to grow larger than their wild relatives, but given the very few wild alligators that have been found and measured—and how few of that small sample have managed to grow to their full potential—a direct comparison is perhaps misleading. In both wild and captive populations the largest males can exceed 2 m (6 ft 7 in) from snout to tail, with the largest on record reaching 2.46 m (8 ft) and 84 kg (185 lb), only about the average size of a female American alligator.[19] *A. sinensis* also has a shorter snout and broader tail, and, unlike *A. mississippiensis*, its feet are not webbed. It bears a striking resemblance to the dwarf crocodile *Osteolaemus tetraspis* of the West and Central African tropics.

Perhaps no species in China has endured a more sustained retreat than the Chinese alligator. For over 7,000 years *A. sinensis* has endured the steady encroachment of humanity, little by little losing its forever war as its wetlands were drained and replaced with grain fields.[20] In the Neolithic period the alligator lived much farther north than today, perhaps even into the Yellow River Basin. Archaeological excavations have found alligator remains as far back as the Peiligang Culture (裴李崗文化, c.7000~5500 BCE) south of the Yellow River in modern Henan. There are even hints that there were alligator farms in the distant past. *The Commentary of Zuo* (左傳), a Zhou dynasty text covering the time between 722 and 468 BCE, and the later *Bamboo Annals* (竹書紀年) both mention the existence of two "dragon keeper" clans from the time of the mythical Xia dynasty rulers Yao and Shun.[21] Some scholars have gone so far as to speculate that the alligators—or perhaps instead their larger saltwater crocodile cousins *Crocodylus porosus* that once lived in the coastal waters of South China—were the inspiration for the mythic Chinese dragon.[22]

Whether these and similar remains indicate the past presence of native alligators or whether they were instead captured and traded from farther south is uncertain. Their initial southward retreat was as much due to cooling of the climate as manmade changes in the landscape, but the widespread presence of alligator bones and osteoderms—the bony deposits that form the scales—in ancient tombs around North China suggest people hunted them for ritual use or to use their skins as drum covers. Alligator remains become less and less common in sites from the Bronze Age (c.2000~475 BCE), replaced with an increasing number of artistic depictions in bronzes and ceramics. What is perhaps the first record of live alligators describes King Mu of the Zhou dynasty (周穆王, r. 976–922 BCE) leading his army across of the Yangtze, where they sighted thousands of the crocodilians lining the banks (in ancient texts the numbers of animals, much the same as for armies, were likely exaggerated for effect; still, hundreds of alligators spread over a wide length of riverbank is conceivable).

An elite taste for alligator-skin drums and burial companions was hardly a mortal threat to the population. Alligators were eaten and used as medicine—the great Ming-era *Compendium of Materia Medica* listed the meat as a delicacy favored for wedding banquets and the scales as a treatment for syphilis—but there is no evidence there was ever great demand for their meat or bones. Instead it was the destruction of their wetland homes and the persecution of those that stayed behind as agricultural pests. Chinese alligators feed mostly on fish and invertebrates, from crustaceans to insects and snails. When the opportunity arises they will also dine on rodents. This would seem a service to the agriculturalist, but in recent times farmers have not returned the favor with kindness, more concerned instead with the worry that alligators eat too many fish and even have the temerity to take the occasional duck. Farmers of centuries past were unlikely to have been any more generous.

The past distribution of the Chinese alligator remains largely a mystery, but what little has come to light suggests they were restricted to the Middle and Lower Yangtze Basin by the Song, and were even disappearing from parts of the region, such as Shaoxing and Dongting Lake, by 1200. They remained in strength through much of the region into the Ming, but were by then trapped and killed as destructive vermin. The problem was not their taste for fish and ducks but their burrowing. Chinese alligators dig into the banks of rivers and ponds, and there spend most of the time they do not devote to the water or sun, as well as the entirety of their winter hibernation. Over time enough burrowing could cause sections of riverbank to collapse. During the Ming dynasty, near Nanjing, this became a great nuisance for people, and they solved the problem by clearing the area of alligators. By the middle of the dynasty the dragons were a rare sight around the city.[23]

By the Qing dynasty alligators were still widely seen through the Middle and Lower Yangtze, but their numbers continued to dwindle. As the human population of the region exploded from the late Ming and throughout the Qing, all available land was dedicated to agriculture. Alligators were left with fewer and fewer wetlands, though some attempted to survive in the rice paddies and agricultural ponds. Farmers were not welcoming. Space was so precious that paddies and ponds had nothing more than thin banks of land to separate them, just wide enough for people and livestock to walk along. When alligators tried to burrow into such paltry barriers the result was often collapse. This produced a general intolerance for alligators.

Western naturalists began to take an interest in the species in the late nineteenth century, but the fact that the earth dragons were now vanishingly rare impaired their efforts. By the 1930s the alligators remained only in swampy marshlands south of the Yangtze in Anhui, Jiangsu, and Zhejiang; most of them were in three populations near Wuhu, Anhui. Their fate seemed so certain that Arthur de Carle Sowerby declared the species "doomed to extinction, its haunts slowly diminishing...while the local fishermen appear to be killing off the few specimens that remain."[24]

This last hiding place for the Chinese alligators had escaped intensive farming for centuries. Annual floods kept the plains underwater for much of the year, making it unsuitable for crops.

During the Qing farming was prohibited in the area to reserve the land as cattle pasture. These factors protected the alligators, but they were not safe for long. In New China no land was to go unused, and soon people came to change the swamp into cropland, seizing the Chinese alligators' final refuge. Today most of the few wild alligators are in ponds created during this period. At the same time collectors came to gather specimens for zoos, taking many young. More disaster struck in 1957 when severe floods drowned most of the dragons that had denned along the Yangtze tributaries, leaving only those in the ponds and lakes. They were drenched in chemicals—sodium pentachlorophenate to kill schistosome-hosting snails, insecticides for pests, pesticides for rodents, and fertilizers for crops.[25] Some died from direct exposure, others succumbed after eating the poison-filled bodies of dead rodents carelessly disposed of in the waters.

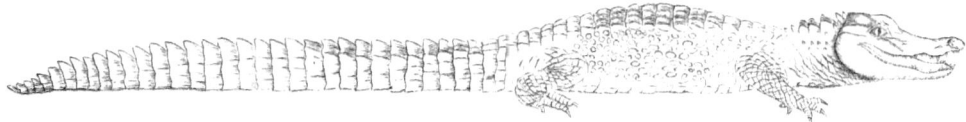

When efforts to conserve *A. sinensis* began in earnest in the late 1970s, the earth dragons were found in only a few scattered ponds in the hills of their last refuge. Construction of rice paddies during the preceding two decades had pushed them from the lowlands, and they were now at the very edge of their world. The small population left in Jiangsu disappeared by the beginning of the 1980s, and the Zhejiang alligators soon followed them, the last few taken away to zoos or a newly-founded breeding center. Anhui now had the last wild-living earth dragons, and they too were fast disappearing. They had been commonly seen in twenty-nine sites in the 1950s, but in 1976 they were gone from nine and rare in another sixteen. The alligators' situation was so desperate—and reliable information from inside China so hard to come by in the wider world—that in 1978 *National Geographic* speculated the species might already have gone extinct.

As always in China, the first choice for saving the species was captive breeding. In this case it was practically the only choice; there was almost no habitat left for the alligators. Early efforts were mixed. Without a large existing captive population, the new breeding centers in Anhui and Zhejiang required alligators and eggs collected from the wild. Out of around 1,000 alligators living wild in Anhui in the late

1970s, 212 were collected to stock the Anhui Research Center for the Chinese Alligator Reproduction (ARCCAR). Not enough care was taken to ensure smaller populations were left intact, and several groups of wild alligators disappeared, some gone to ARCCAR and those left behind too few to sustain their communities. Local farmers were paid to notify the breeding center of alligator nests, and the eggs were then taken away. Egg collecting continued for years, well after the breeding centers had self-sustaining populations. This lowered the already minuscule hopes of a revival of the wild populations; the conservationists assumed they had no chance, and having come to that conclusion they made no effort to improve the odds.

This lack of attention to the wild alligators led to their continuing decline. While the captive population exploded, even to the point where the breeding centers could handle no more alligators, the wild population struggled. Farmers continued to kill them into the 1980s, annoyed by the burrows dug into water control dikes. What little suitable habitat was left continued to disappear. Surveys through the 1990s repeatedly gave optimistic estimates of the population, and even claimed rapid growth rates. Yet when scientists took a closer look they realized the situation was dire. By the close of the decade the signs pointed to the imminent extinction of the wild dragons. In 1998, for the first time in the species' millions of years of existence, there were no wild nests. The next year a month of surveys across the National Chinese Alligator Reserve (NCAR) found no natural habitat of livable size. When researchers reached the site with the largest reported group of wild alligators, they found the only known female had died two years prior, dead from eating poisoned mice thrown heedlessly into the pond. They spotted all of four alligators. Three of the thirteen sites said to have alligators had none at all, none had more than two adult females. There were fewer than 130 alligators left in the wild. Of the few eggs that were laid each year, most were taken to the breeding centers, already overflowing with more alligators than they could handle.

In 2005 the wild population was at a low of at best 120. But things were starting to improve. Egg collection from wild nests, long unnecessary and harmful, finally ended in 2002. NCAR began to give more attention to protecting and eventually expanding the few remaining alligator ponds. Small numbers from the thousands of captive dragons were released to fend for themselves. The wild population stabilized and then began to grow.

A 2023 survey estimated the wild population had risen to nearly 1,400, and further releases of captive-bred alligators have continued; between 2019 and summer 2024, 1,818 alligators were released in Anhui.[26] The earth dragons seem to have adapted well to life outside the breeding centers. A year after the 2019 releases reserve workers had found over 300 eggs and over 200 naturally hatched babies. A small population has been established on Shanghai's Chongming Island in the mouth of the Yangtze and, though still small, has held on and even grown. There are plenty of captive alligators ready to enter the wild—28,000 in 2016 and doubtless many more now.[27] Yet the population's genetic diversity is worryingly low, which may lead to any number of ill effects.[28] There also remains almost no suitable habitat for *A. sinensis*, indeed the reintroduced alligators have so little space they have already started to leave in search of new waters.[29] But NCAR has begun to acquire and convert agricultural land into alligator habitat, and as the alligators' habitat grows so can their numbers. They will especially need the new territory as the changing climate threatens to further reduce what little remains.[30]

The clear mountain streams of the Yangtze Basin host the largest salamander—indeed the largest amphibian—in the world, the Chinese giant salamander *Andrias davidianus*.[31] The Chinese giant salamander fully deserves its name, the largest specimens reaching nearly 2 m (6 ft 7 in) in length and weighing over 50 kg (110 lb).[32] Few would describe the massive amphibians as attractive. The salamanders seem curiously flat, with squat limbs and huge rounded heads with wide mouths and topped with small black eyes. Their skin is dark and mottled, a jumble of dark brown, olive, and rust-colored splotches. To their great misfortune they do not inspire the same urge to protect as cuddlier species.

The earliest record of the giant salamander comes from a figure on a ceramic vessel vaguely dated to between 3000–4000 BCE. The vessel may have been a container for salamander oil, which is known to have been later used as lamp fuel and to make candles. Written records as far back as 1700 BCE mention hunting for the salamander, likely for its oil and meat.[33] *Andrias* made an appearance in the *Classic of Mountains and Seas*, (山海經), compiled in the early Han dynasty or even centuries earlier, as the baby-fish (娃娃鱼), due to the resemblance of the salamander's cry to a human child's. This name is faithfully repeated in seemingly every account of the species, always asserted to be a common folk name across China, but it was found in a recent survey to be one of many ("dogfish," 狗鱼, and variants thereof were the most used).[34] Just as often the baby-fish moniker refers not to the salamander's cry but to darker beliefs such as that dead babies turn into salamanders or that salamanders eat the corpses of children.[35]

The salamander's astounding size assured it received remarks from those who encountered it. The species appeared in many texts over the centuries, some describing it quite accurately while others depict a more fantastic creature, such as one that can climb trees. A commonly repeated piece of trivia was that salamander fat was used to make the candles that lit the First Emperor's tomb.[36] There is too little evidence in the literary record to know with any specificity where the salamander lived in the past, but its range was undoubtedly wide, as far to the northwest as the Tibetan Plateau, and south into South China's mountain forests.[37] It was a common sight in the Qinling and eastward all the way to Shanghai, where in the early twentieth century it was still spotted in the Huangpu River that flows through the city.[38] In some communities people hunted the salamanders for their meat or oil, and of course they could be put to medicinal use, but there is little evidence of large scale hunting until the late twentieth century.

Evidence for just when the salamander population began to decline is scanty. Recorded catches, likely only a fraction of the total, began to decline as early as the 1960s, but *Andrias* remained widespread into the next decade, from the Yellow to the Yangtze and the Pearl. Later surveys of locals across the salamanders' distribution showed that people still easily found and caught the animals until the 1980s.[39] In some regions, especially in South China, the salamanders were hunted for their meat, but in much of the rest of the country they were regarded as unclean and unlucky. The beliefs that salamanders were associated with babies—either as reincarnations or devourers of children—meant that in some areas, such as the Qinling, even touching a salamander was considered an ill omen.[40]

With the end of the Maoist period people became free to move about China to pursue their entrepreneurial urges, bringing disaster to the giant salamanders. Some people left home for new opportunities while others returned from years in exile. Migrants from South China took with them their taste for salamander, and when they came to areas with thriving populations of the amphibians they saw not only a source of meat for their own enjoyment but an abundance of tradable goods. The liberalizing economy allowed the southerners to catch and ship salamanders without restraint. Their tastes began to spread as well, even to those who had previously considered salamander meat taboo. As demand for the animals rose so did the price, enticing more and more people to hunt salamanders.[41] By the 1990s *Andrias* was becoming rare over parts of the country.

As their populations dropped, the salamanders of course became harder to find. Whereas before people had caught the salamanders by hand, line, or trap, now such methods often yielded no catch. Undeterred, hunters poisoned the waters. They dumped insecticides into the upper reaches of streams and rivers so that the poison would wash downstream and kill any salamanders hiding in the waters.[42] This went on for several years, but in most areas it began to peter out in the late 1990s once even poison yielded no quarry.[43]

By 2000 scientists were hard pressed to find salamanders to count for population surveys. They found instead hunters, some having resorted to electro-fishing.[44] Researchers estimated that populations had crashed by up to ninety percent over the prior fifty years.[45] Wild salamanders were no longer abundant, yet were still in high demand, so attention shifted to establishing salamander farms. It took little time to work out how to keep salamanders in captivity, but much longer to learn to breed them. Without their own breeding populations, salamander farmers instead sought out wild larvae. The few remaining wild *Andrias* had found sanctuary in karst caves and underground rivers where they had escaped from both hunters and poison, but now the hunters found these last holdouts, and with them the larvae that were meant to repopulate the waters.[46] Between 1998 and 2007 the market price for salamander larvae shot from ¥50 to ¥1,500 as the number of salamander farms exploded, all of them desperate for larvae to seed their stocks.[47] By the time the industry finally succeeded in breeding salamanders, much of the future wild population was already trapped in the farms.

The success of salamander aquaculture did not save the remnant wild population. The general Chinese preference for wild over captive animals meant that each new farm wanted wild salamanders to start its population. By 2013 there were over 2,600 large farms that had populated their stocks through the capture of an estimated 42,000 adult and 164,000 juvenile wild salamanders. Thousands more went into scattered smallholder operations. For such a long-lived apex predator, few of whose young survive their first year and grow slowly thereafter, such numbers proved devastating.[48] Intensified efforts to survey and protect the salamanders in the 2010s found that there simply were no wild populations in much of the country, and that the few left were still at risk from hunters.[49]

Even at this nadir things worsened. After early taxonomic disputes over the relationship of China's giant salamanders to each other and to their Japanese kin, scientists had finally agreed they were a single species, *Andrias davidianus*. Recent genetic testing has upended this consensus, finding there are at least five, and perhaps up to nine separate species of Chinese giant salamander.[50] One past claim, that the salamanders of South China represented a unique species, the South China giant salamander *A. sligoi*, was in fact correct. This means *A. sligoi*, not *A. davidianus*, now claims the crown of world's largest amphibian.[51] Although *A. sligoi* now has the dignity of its own name, and a third and fourth— *A. jiangxiensis* and *A. cheni*—have also been identified in the wild in Jiangxi and Anhui, respectively, the other species still await their own designations.[52] One native to the Tibetan Plateau and known from a single specimen collected in the 1960s, is perhaps already extinct, its clear mountain streams now clouded with silt from sand and gravel mining.[53]

Although a minor triumph of taxonomic investigation, this discovery means that the chances for successful conservation of the Chinese giant salamanders are even bleaker than first believed. With the wild populations of most of the species nearly—or perhaps already—extinct, the captive populations of the salamander farms represent the great hope for the species.[54] There are now millions of salamanders raised for food across China, and in the past two decades tens of thousands have been released in hopes of boosting the wild populations; there have been few signs of success. Even more worrisome is that the captive populations were established without any regard for keeping the different species separate, a mistake for which the salamander farmers can safely claim innocent ignorance. Now most of the captive salamanders are either *A. davidianus* or hybrids, meaning that unless large enough populations of the other *Andrias* species can be found, separated, and sustained, from either the wild or captive populations, those newly discovered species may already be doomed.

The future for the Chinese giant salamanders in the wild is bleak. Already hunted out from nearly the entirety of their range, they persist as tiny fragments of their former populations. Millions of their hybridized fellows now live in tanks, awaiting their fate as an exotic meal or an additive into medicines or cosmetics. As though the current situation was not dire enough, climate change is all but certain to render much of the salamanders' former range uninhabitable within the next fifty years, making any rebuilding of their wild numbers all the more difficult and precarious.[55] Saving the giant salamanders, however many species still remain, will require immediate action of a daunting breadth and intensity. Otherwise the only ones left will be in tanks and on dinner plates.

Lakes & Wetlands

T HE Lower Yangtze's great lakes—Poyang and Dongting—are crucial havens for numerous species, but none more so than the migratory birds that winter on their banks and waters. For the Chinese, the most cherished of these are the cranes. Although the most beloved species—the red-crowned cranes—winter along the coast, many of their congeners pass the season inland. The most beautiful and most endangered of them are the Siberians.

Scientists did not know where Siberian cranes wintered until 1980. The cranes had of course been sighted in lakes and wetlands across the Lower Yangtze, but no one had determined where the birds gathered in force. Efforts in the 1950s had failed, and the societal disruption over the next two decades prevented further investigations. In that time the western population of Siberians, subjected to intense hunting, dwindled to small remnants that wintered on the southern shore of the Caspian Sea in Iran and a second flock that wintered in Keoladeo wetland in Rajasthan, India.[1] In winter 1980 two researchers finally discovered a sedge of only ninety-one birds wintering in one of the smaller lakes connected to Poyang's main body. Over the next few years the flock grew in size until in 1984 a far larger number, around 800 birds, arrived at Poyang.[2] The next year there were 1,350. The western flocks were by then nearly gone, which meant these cranes represented almost the entirety—ninety-nine percent—of the species, not only in China but the whole world.[3]

These years were extremely precarious for the cranes. Poyang, though by now a protected nature reserve, still had a dense human population of around 17,000 in the early 1980s, many of whom looked to the cranes as a resource. Locals had long hunted the birds with guns and cannons, but when government officials became aware of the cranes' presence they confiscated the firearms. The people simply switched their methods. In the winter of 1983–1984 local villagers killed hundreds of cranes, storks, and swans for their white feathers, used to make fans. The Jiangxi Forestry Bureau then set aside the crane's habitat as a strictly protected area and tried to crack down on hunting, but they ran into new problems. In 1975 a small village had begun draining one of the cranes' two preferred lakes through a sluice gate to easily seine for fish. Forestry officials wanted the villagers to stop so as not to shrink and damage the cranes' habitat, but the villagers demanded compensation that the bureau could not afford. Upset with the bureau's interference, the villagers drained the lake and forced the cranes to find lesser habitat. It was only in 1993 that the government managed to gain control of the water.[4] When the cataclysmic floods of 1998 destroyed many of the local communities, the government seized the opportunity and relocated much of the population away from the reserve.[5]

The effects of the growing economy soon multiplied the threats to the Siberians. Locals cleared aquatic vegetation in which the cranes fed to make way for aquaculture. While more and more of the lake was drained to expand paddies and fields, dredging and sand mining altered the hydrology and damaged large sections of habitat. Pollution from industry and agriculture increased, and hunting continued. More recently tourists—especially enthusiastic but ill-disciplined birders and nature photographers intent on coming as close as possible to their subjects—have become a regular source of disturbance for the cranes, disrupting their routines and driving them from their preferred feeding grounds.[6]

The Siberians now number over 5,600 birds, an increase from the preceding decades.[7] For now the population appears stable and is perhaps even growing.[8] Yet they face looming and potentially existential threats. Their breeding habitat in the Russian arctic is expected to shrink in the coming decades, and they will have to compete with increasing numbers of sandhill cranes for what remains.[9] In China the current looming threat to the cranes is a long-proposed sluice wall between Poyang and the Yangtze. The Three Gorges Dam—along with the effects of climate change and extensive sand mining—has radically upset the already heavily altered hydrology of Poyang, keeping back so much water in its reservoir that Poyang's water levels during winter dry seasons have become dangerously low, shrinking the lake and thus the cranes' habitat, thereby increasingly pushing them to seek food on agricultural lands.[10] Floods and droughts have become more frequent, and the water quality, too, has suffered.[11] The heat wave and drought that hit southern China over 2022 and 2023 led to record low water levels in the lake, and left scarce winter feed for migratory birds.[12] The sluice wall is meant to restore winter waters to a deeper level, but opponents fear the waters will be too deep and cause even greater damage to the cranes and other migratory birds.[13] Finless porpoises are also expected to become isolated for part of the year should the sluice wall go up.[14] If the wall is built, and if conservationists' fears prove accurate, the Siberians could suffer heavy losses in the coming years.[15]

The Siberians share the lake with their kin, the white-naped cranes *Grus vipio*, hooded cranes *G. monacha*, and common cranes *G. grus*. Similarly large and imposing as the cranes, eighty percent of the world's oriental white storks *Ciconia boyciana* winter in Poyang. Counts of their numbers over the past three decades have shown great fluctuations—perhaps due to difficulties in the counting or maybe to genuine changes in their populations—but over time the storks have been steadily increasing.[16]

The Yangtze floodplain also hosts large seasonal populations of many members of the Anatidae family, the ducks, swans, and geese. Like the cranes, most of the birds breed far to the north in Russia, Mongolia, and the northern regions of China before they migrate to East China's wetlands for winter. Some congregate on the coasts, others inland, especially on the Yangtze Basin's great lakes. Their populations have declined severely since the 1950s; in total they reach perhaps only a third or even a quarter of their former numbers.[17] Pressures on their breeding grounds are partly responsible for these declines, but the birds face no shortage of difficulties in East China. Habitat loss, the usual culprit, is of course to blame. The lakes have shrunk over the past century, in part due to construction of extensive water control and diversion systems, in part due to land reclamation.

Many of the waterfowl species spread their winter populations across East Asia, from Japan southwest to Myanmar, but several species gather in their entirety in China. The whole of the world's population

of swan geese *Anser cygnoides* stops in China, as do nearly all of the falcated ducks *Mareca falcata*, and all of East Asia's lesser white-fronted geese *A. erythropus*, a species that has suffered severe declines since the 1980s but seems for now to have found a safe redoubt in Dongting Lake.[18] The swan geese have faced contracting habitat across their breeding and wintering ranges. The Yangtze floodplain is their last winter haven, but the space for them there is shrinking too. The population now must squeeze into ever fewer and smaller areas, limiting their potential for recovery.[19]

Unsurprisingly, the other major threat to the water birds has been hunting. Some birds are coveted for their meat, others for feathers, and some for eggs. Locals used to catch the birds for their own use, but more recently they sell them to distant urban markets for large profits.[20] Guns were long the preferred means of bringing down masses of birds. In the late nineteenth to mid-twentieth centuries, Westerners entertained themselves with hunting trips in which each man would gun down dozens of birds. Even the few who recognized the slaughter as a threat to the birds' long-term survival rarely let such thoughts restrain them. Local hunters, too, killed tens of thousands of birds every season, though for the market and not sport. Even into the late 1980s and early 1990s hunters still used primitive guns and matchlock cannons to slaughter great numbers of waterfowl.[21] When ducks, geese, swans and other birds would arrive for winter, hunting season would begin. Teams of hunters would take out their boats and align them abreast, camouflaged and topped with guns or cannons. Other boats would herd birds to the waiting gunners, and once their prey settled in range the guns would fire, killing dozens or hundreds—and if hunters' boasts are to be believed—even up to two thousand birds with one salvo.[22] When the state confiscated firearms in the late 1990s, poachers switched to nets, crossbows, and poisoned baits.[23] Already reeling from habitat loss in its northern breeding grounds, hunting has hit the region's Baer's pochard *Aythya baeri* especially hard. Found in their thousands into the 1990s, only 194 were spotted in the Middle and Lower Yangtze in 2011, with much of their former territory empty of the birds.[24] Broader survey work has revealed the diving ducks have seemingly shifted their range in response to climate change, but even so there is no indication they survive in great numbers.[25]

Just as in Beijing, the milu or Pére David's deer has returned to the wetlands of the Yangtze. When the last of the wild herds disappeared is a mystery. Pére David's speculation that the wild deer had died out 1,500 years prior to his discovery was far too pessimistic; records of milu continued for centuries, though the animals were clearly increasingly rare. With the shifts in climate and expansion of intensive agriculture that began over 2,000 years ago, the elaphure disappeared from North China and the Yangtze wetlands became the center of their range. The scholar Zhang Hua's (張華, 232–300) *Record of Diverse Matters* (博物誌) mentions groups of "hundreds of thousands" of milu in present-day Jiangsu, an exaggeration certainly, but a clear indication of their plenitude.[26] By the Tang dynasty, however, the deer were becoming harder to find.[27] During the following centuries of the Song, the Yangtze Valley's human population grew quickly, squeezing the remaining deer into a shrinking territory.[28] They still appeared in Ming-era *materia medica*, noted as much for their rarity as the medicinal efficacy of their antlers.[29]

It was long believed the Lower Yangtze was the wild elaphure's final holdout, where they persisted until perhaps the reign of the Qing Jiaqing Emperor (嘉慶帝, 1760–1820, r. 1796–1820).[30] A recent study of hides collected in 1868 on Hainan off the South China coast revealed that milu survived on the island at least through the mid-nineteenth and perhaps into the twentieth century, and was likely the source population for the captive herd in Beijing.[31]

After an absence of nearly two centuries, milu returned to the Lower Yangtze when a herd of thirty-nine deer were released into paddocks on the Dafeng forestry farm south of Yancheng on the Jiangsu coast. The farm was expanded and made into a reserve especially for the elaphure, and in 1998 some of the deer were finally released from their paddocks to roam freely, though they remain fenced within the confines of the reserve. The Dafeng herd of Pére David's deer is now the world's largest, with nearly 5,700 members at the end of 2021.[32] A second Yangtze population was established far inland at Shishou, Hubei in 1993 with a founding group of thirty deer.[33] Five years later during the 1998 Yangtze floods a group escaped through the reserve's fencing, and forestry officials decided to allow the escapees to establish their own wild herd. This wild population has since expanded in number and reach, with some of their number having migrated south into Hunan.[34] Shishou now hosts about 1,800 elaphure, with roughly 800 living wild outside the reserve.[35]

Like most Han Chinese lands, the Middle and Lower Yangtze are now largely bereft of large animals, with vanishingly few apex predators. Even the large herbivores are scarce, survived by smaller creatures that can live on less land and less forage, such as the water deer *Hydropotes inermis*, which shares the wetlands of the Yangtze region with the elaphure. Water deer once lived along the whole of China's eastern seaboard, from the Korean Peninsula south all the way to Guangdong, and up the Yangtze to the Three Gorges. They kept to the coastal plains, marshes and rivers, sticking to the shrub-studded lands by the water and away from the depths of the forests. With long tusks instead of antlers, *Hydropotes* closely resembles the musk deer, but unlike *Moschus* the water deer belong to the family of true deer, Cervidae.[36] The fanged deer have a golden brown coat and white belly similar to the white-tailed and mule deer of North America, but are quite small, rarely exceeding 65 cm (1 ft 10 in) at the shoulder and 14 kg (31 lb) in weight.

Although much human action in Chinese history resulted in destruction of wildlife habitat, on occasion the results were to animals' benefit. For over seven centuries the water deer of Jiangsu benefited immensely from the unintended consequences of war. In 1128 the Song army, in a desperate attempt to stop the advancing Jurchens of the Jin dynasty, breached the southern dikes of the Yellow River. The subsequent course change shifted the river south of the Shandong Peninsula, where it captured the Huai River and many of its tributaries. The immense flows of silt then settled on the northern coast of Jiangsu, gradually expanding the province into the Yellow Sea. The resulting coastal grassland was ideal habitat for water deer. This habitat continued to expand, adding over 20,000 sq km (7,700 sq mi) of land to Jiangsu, until after several years of massive floods the river shifted back north of the Shandong Peninsula in 1855.[37]

The river's northward shift marked a severe reversal of fortune for the coastal grasslands and their water deer. Without the constant addition of silt, the sea began to encroach on the low-lying coast.

Farmers cam from inland in search of tillable land. And as their habitat disappeared to cultivation, hunters slaughtered them for the market. Water deer were extremely abundant in the Yangtze Basin in the latter half of the nineteenth century, having swiftly moved into the areas humanity abandoned due to the destruction of the Taiping Rebellion (1850–1864). The deer were found in great numbers, and hunters brought so many into Shanghai in the early 1870s that the price for them crashed and many went unsold and rotted.[38] In later years they were exported. The incredible fecundity of the water deer, which two researchers recently described as "comparable to large rodents," allowed the species to withstand the years of slaughter, but slowly their numbers began to fall.[39] By the 1920s Sowerby noted that, though they were still numerous, they were not as common as they once had been.[40]

Water deer continued to lose ground to agriculturalists and die at the hand of hunters until in 1990 there were fewer than 10,000 left in the Lower Yangtze. The coastal grasslands that the Yellow River had gifted them in northern Jiangsu were now completely devoted to agriculture. Continuing development across their remaining range fragmented what habitat they had left. Many of the newly-arrived farmers saw the deer as pests, while others valued them for their meat or even for the partially digested milk in the bellies of fawns, said to cure children's indigestion; either way the result was dead deer.[41]

The water deer of North China and southern Manchuria are now gone, as are those in Fujian and the rest of the southeast.[42] The populations in the Yangtze Basin, and especially the Yangtze estuary, have held on, but mostly in protected reserves, and even there only in pockets. There have been several efforts to reestablish populations in their former territory; initial reintroductions near Shanghai proved successful, but an increase in the feral dog population during the first year of the COVID-19 pandemic led to high mortality rates for recent reintroductions.[43] In the northeast, deer from Korea are expanding north into Jilin, Heilongjiang, and the Russian Far East.[44] Water deer apparently do not adapt well to changes in their habitat, but given their impressive ability to multiply with great speed, their prospects will be bright so long as China can give them the habitat they need.

SOUTHERN FORESTS

杯森森

Map of Southern China

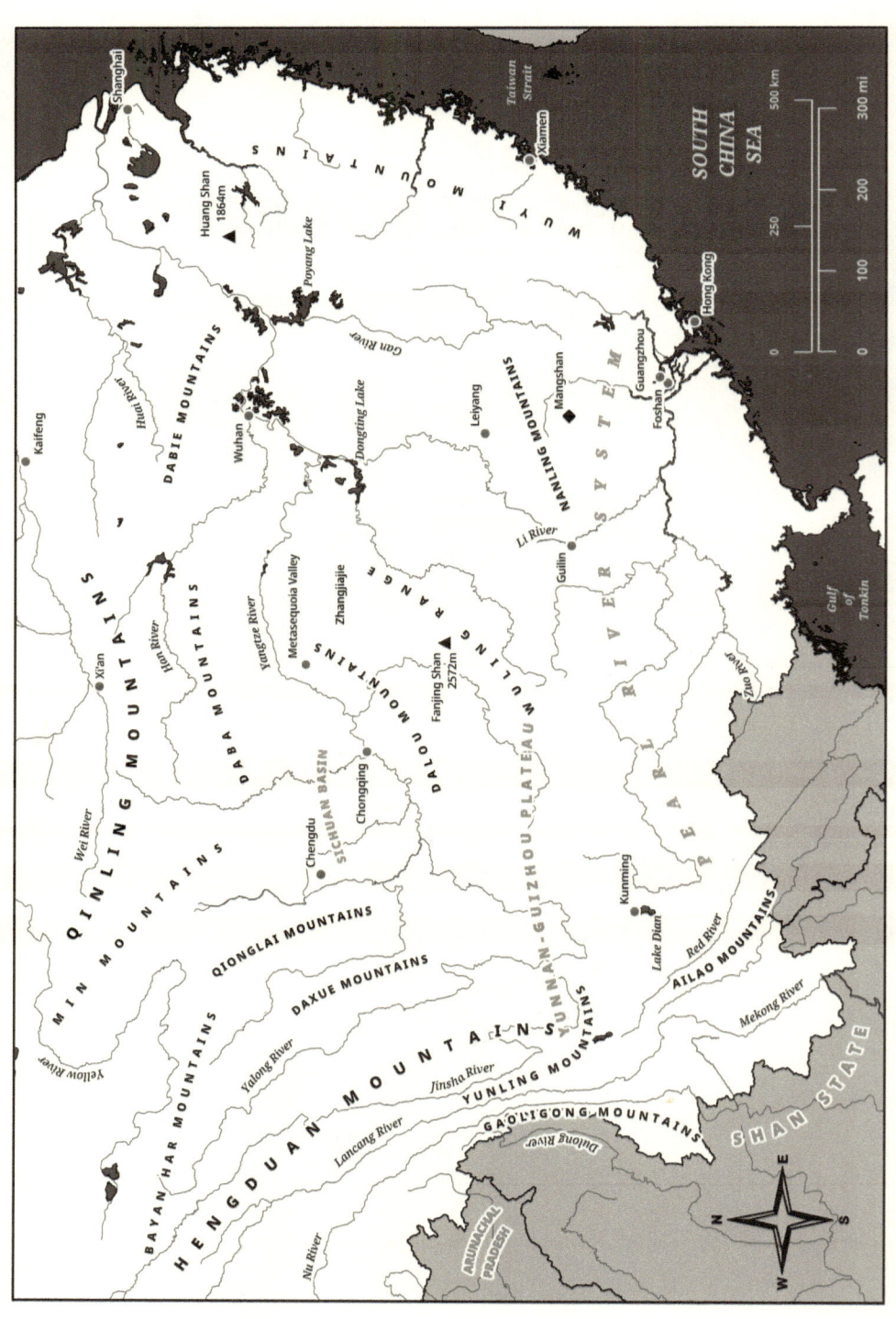

ENTRAL and South China were once lands of forested hills and low mountains. Here stands some of China's most remarkable scenery—the mountains of Huang Shan, the towering stone pillars of Zhangjiajie, the famed karst hills along the Li River. The summer monsoon waters a lush subtropical vegetation and once supported a vast patchwork of evergreen and bamboo forests, now mostly turned to paddies and fields. The Yunnan-Guizhou Plateau dominates the southwest, rising to between 1,000 and 2,000 m (3,280 to 6,560 ft) above sea level. The plateau is famed for its mild, subtropical environment, a land of perpetual spring littered with spectacular limestone formations, forested hills, and lakes.[1]

Thousands of years ago the development of agriculture, namely intensive paddy cultivation of rice, resulted in major changes in the region's forests. Many of the ancient denizens south of the Yangtze adopted rice farming, and in time the agriculturalists took over the lowlands in the river valleys. The uplands belonged to those who kept to hunting and gathering, which they supplemented with slash-and-burn agriculture.[2]

In the east, rice farming moved south from the Middle and Lower Yangtze Valley into Fujian and Guangdong around 3,000 years ago, before several hundred years later spreading into Guangxi. The same pattern played out in the west, with cultivation moving out from the Sichuan Basin into Guizhou and Yunnan. The transitions began slowly, with many false starts, but once the older farming communities along the Yangtze developed mature agricultural systems, the spread of knowledge and technology quickened.[3]

Studies on ancient charcoal and pollen levels in the southeast give an idea of what happened across much of Central and South China. Around 3,500 years ago fires became much more common in the forests, likely a result of swidden agriculture. Clearing patches of forest would have also resulted in the growth of grassland in which people could more easily hunt deer and other prey. From the late Warring States to the Han dynasty, the native tree cover declined significantly, with agricultural grasses and common secondary trees such as pine replacing them, a sure indication that settled agriculture had arrived.[4]

Most of the native peoples of the Yangtze Basin and south spoke languages unrelated to Chinese, and were culturally distinct from the Han. The rice farmers of the lowlands spoke languages related to Thai, while hunter-gatherers lived in the highlands and had a relatively light impact on the environment. The arrival of the Han forced most of the natives to choose between adopting Chinese language and customs, or migrating south or west. Many stayed put, while those that left eventually settled in present-day Guizhou and Guangxi or farther afield in Vietnam, Laos, Thailand and Myanmar.

The Han began to push south more aggressively during the Tang and Song dynasties. Many of the arrivals were soldiers sent to settle frontier farm colonies, while the common migrants were a mix of fortune seekers and peasants the state had compelled to serve in its agrarian vanguard. As agriculturalists they naturally settled in the valleys, but the farther south they pushed the more difficult they found the environment. This was less a matter of the vegetation or even unwelcoming natives than it was disease, particularly malaria. As such, in the far south the Han often initially settled in whatever uplands they could make suitable for farming, leaving the lowlands to the natives until later centuries.[5]

After the early dynasties had deforested most of North China, the southern forests became the empires' preferred source of timber. By then the forests were largely restricted to the uplands, but timber was still abundant during the late tenth century when the Song sought large trees for their temples and palaces in their capital, Kaifeng. Over time all but the most inaccessible of the great trees were logged, and monumental imperial projects had to source the largest pillars from the southwest. Despite the constant demand for wood, the forests of Central and South China survived for centuries. They did not, however, survive as natural stands, but became managed plantations that supplied an ever-hungry market. Thus, many of the region's primary forests were replaced with far less biodiverse stands of commercial species planted for timber or fuelwood. These managed and privately-held forests supported far less wildlife than their natural predecessors, but they were far less ecologically destructive than the lowland paddies and fields.[6] Timber remained a precious resource over the centuries, pushing the merchants and temples that owned the forests to replant their logged stands, ensuring the landscape would not become denuded as it had to the north. It was only in the face of overwhelming environmental degradation and resource shortages in the waning decades of the Qing dynasty that the system failed and the managed forests were cleared.[7]

The uplands of the south became far more vulnerable in the sixteenth century as cash cropping spread throughout the region. Trees, tea, tobacco, and dozens of other crops were cultivated, many for use in manufactured goods—e.g. hemp, ramie, indigo, bamboo, etc.[8] The subsequent arrival of New World crops such as sweet potatoes and corn allowed for more of the highlands to be converted to food production. These could take hold and thrive in poorer soils than rice and other traditional crops. This allowed marginal groups such as the Hakka, a Han subgroup, to turn the uplands into farmlands. The Han employed the same crops and techniques when they pushed into the hilly borderlands of Yunnan and the southwest, again following in the wake of military colonists. Although the native highlanders had farmed the hills, they had moved from plot to plot, allowing forest to regrow before cycling back after many years. Neither the Hakka nor other Han followed this practice, instead farming intensively year after year. Allowed to neither rest nor regenerate, the ground was depleted of nutrients, which compelled the settlers to destroy more forest in search of virgin soils.[9]

The southwest was the last region to come under Chinese control. The Ming dynasty pushed aggressively into Guizhou, settling soldiers in colonies as had been common imperial practice for well over a thousand years. As before, settlers were forced or enticed to follow them to open the forests and help overwhelm the native peoples. The project took centuries, but in the end it succeeded in transforming the landscape and bringing the indigenes firmly under Chinese control.[10]

During the late Qing, China's environment suffered immense damage at the hands of a desperate population. In the nineteenth century the population had grown to the point of outstripping what the land could support. Combined with the simultaneous weakening of the Qing state and economy, the result was decades of astoundingly destructive turmoil, marked by war and famine. Damage to the forests had been building since the beginning of the Qing dynasty, but it was only in the nineteenth century that shortages of timber and fuelwood became so acute and widespread that much of the land was left bare of not only trees but any woody plants. Wood theft became a common crime, and many communities were reduced to using grass and chaff to fuel their stoves and warm their homes.[11] By the early twentieth century, much of the south was totally empty of trees.[12]

Glacial Refugees

Central and South China are home to a great collection of relics of the distant past. Many of the endangered trees of the mountain forests represent the last populations of species that were far more widespread many hundreds of thousands or even millions of years ago. These ancient species arose in the Paleogene, from sixty-six to twenty-three million years ago, when the climate was warmer and wetter. As the world cooled and dried, the successive ice ages covered much of the north with glaciers, and the trees lost most of their range. They found a final refuge in the rugged mountains and valleys of China's south.[1]

One such relict, *Glyptostrobus pensilis*, known either as the Chinese water pine or Chinese swamp cypress, is a conifer that grows near or even in water, found primarily in swamps or along the banks of rivers and ponds. The last surviving member of its genus, *G. pensilis* was found across much of the northern hemisphere in the Late Cretaceous, from Europe and Siberia across Beringia to North America. The spread of Pinaceae—the pine family—over the course of the Miocene and Pliocene and the onset of the Ice Ages in the Pleistocene pushed *G. pensilis* out of North America and Europe as its habitats cooled and dried. By the time of the arrival of humans in East Asia, the species was only found from southern China to Thailand.[2]

Glyptostrobus pensilis was still widespread in South China into the Late Holocene. Pollen records from the Pearl River Delta tell a story that was likely typical of the wider region. Forests of *G. pensilis* stood in flood plains and mountainous wetlands for thousands of years, surviving intact even after the settlement of humans in the area. So long as the local communities subsisted primarily on hunting and fishing, they did little to disturb the forest and wetland habitats. Everything changed with the arrival of agriculturalists, who burned the forests and eventually replaced them with cultivated fields and paddies. In the Pearl River flood plain this process occurred rapidly (relatively speaking), and *G. pensilis* had largely disappeared from the delta around 2,000 years ago. Stands of *G. pensilis* in the mountains survived another millennium, until technological advances and a dearth of available land lower down pushed people into the highlands.[3]

Before the destruction of the great stands of *Glyptostrobus pensilis* and conversion of its habitats, the tree could be found over much of southern and eastern China, from Fujian, Jiangxi, and Hunan south through Guangdong, Guangxi, and Yunnan into Vietnam and Laos. Over the centuries humans pushed the species—once found scattered across a range of well over 1 million sq km (over 400,000 sq mi)—nearly to extinction. After the large stands of *G. pensilis* were destroyed, most of the remaining trees survived singly or in small groups of only a few, standing near villages or along rice paddies.[4] The trees were not only victims to agriculture's advance, but were also felled for their wood, which is resistant to decay and so has been valued for use in a wide range of items, such as coffins, boats, bridges, and furniture.[5] Some of the problems they face are more recent; the severe water pollution typical of much of China has made it difficult for *G. pensilis* seeds to germinate, casting doubt on the ability of new generations to replace the old.[6] Without human help, this ancient species is unlikely to be able to pull itself back from the edge of extinction.

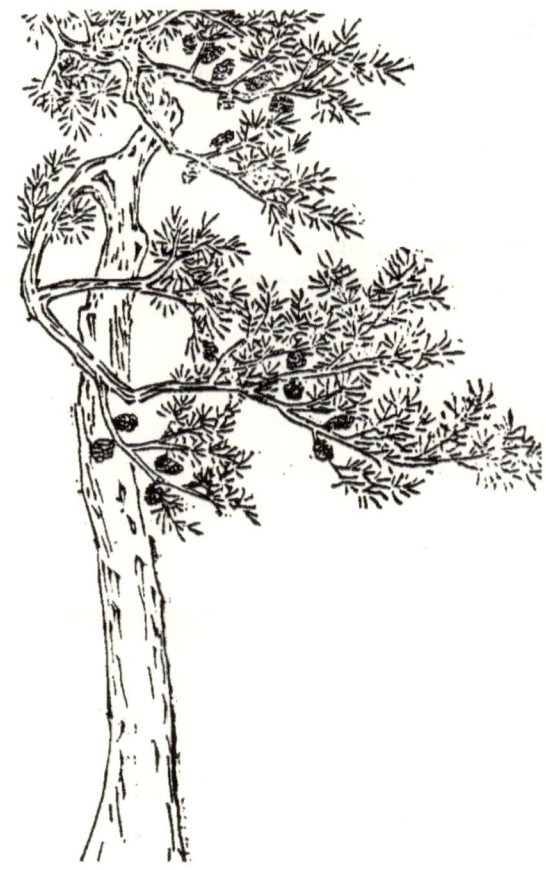

銀

In 1955 another glacial relict was found in the mountains of northeastern Guangxi.[7] Named *Cathaya argyrophylla* or the Cathay silver fir for the silvery glint that comes off its pine-like needles when light hits their undersides, the tree is a member of the pine family, Pinaceae, and the only species of its genus.[8] Since its discovery, stands of the silver fir have been found in three other regions in the provinces of Guangxi, Guizhou, Hunan, Chongqing, and Sichuan.[9] The trees survive only on the crests, crevices, and overhanging rocks of isolated mountainsides where few people dare to venture.[10] Already rare due to the effects of repeated glaciations, *C. argyrophylla* seedlings also struggle to compete with broad-leaved trees that have overtaken much of its former range.[11] Like other relicts now found in the mountains, in all likelihood some populations of silver fir remained in the lowlands until they were deforested to make way for fields and paddies.[12]

There are just over 3,000 of the trees remaining in the wild, most in the Dalou and Bamian Mountains.[13] Unlike other ancient rarities such as the ginkgo, dove tree, or *Metasequoia*, the Cathay silver fir has not yet found favor with horticulturalists, and so outside of its natural habitat it remains restricted to specialist collections and gardens.[14] The future of the species in the wild is bleak. Although their forests are now well-protected from cutting and thinning, this has in fact served *C. argyrophylla* poorly; with the forest canopies now closing and shading the understory, seedlings struggle to grow.[15] Over the last few decades this has led to a severe decline in the number of mature trees.[16] Even worse, the silver fir is especially vulnerable to the expected effects of a changing climate, and it may well lose much of what little habitat it still has.[17]

One relict tree, *Metasequoia glyptostroboides* or the dawn redwood, garnered extensive media coverage upon its discovery, and quickly became a popular fixture of parks and gardens. Related to the sequoias and redwoods of California and Oregon, the dawn redwood has a striking difference from its American kin. Like the larch or bald cypress, the dawn redwood is a deciduous conifer, and its needles turn reddish-brown and shed over winter. The species was first discovered in 1941, only two years after the *Metasequoia* genus was first identified from the fossil record. Due to the difficulties of conducting surveys during wartime, the first dedicated fieldwork did not occur until 1947. A small population of over 1,000 trees was found in a valley in southwestern Hubei, with additional, smaller populations later found in neighboring Hunan and Chongqing.[18] Hailed as living fossils, the trees were the last surviving members of the *Metasequoia* genus. During the Cretaceous the genus had been widespread over the Northern Hemisphere, but after the early Paleogene its range contracted.[19] Eventually the only remnant was *M. glyptostroboides*, confined to a few areas in the mountains of the Upper Yangtze.

Like *Glyptostrobus pensilis*, the dawn redwoods were more numerous and widespread until they were cut down to make way for agriculture and to provide timber or fuelwood.[20] The last great concentration of *Metasequoia* survived in a single valley in Hubei, one of the last to be settled in the region, likely between 300 and 400 years ago.[21] There the trees enjoyed the protection of superstition.[22] Revering the trees but having modified their habitat too greatly for seedlings to grow where they sprouted, locals took to replanting seedlings and saplings to ensure their survival.[23]

Today there are still relatively few wild *Metasequoia*, all growing in fragmented populations. Their habitats continue to degrade, and consequently seedlings do not survive.[24] Luckily the dawn redwood is a particularly attractive tree, and has become a widespread ornamental in temperate climates throughout the globe.[25] This guarantees the species' survival, but the wild trees are likely to suffer considerably under the coming changes in climate.[26]

Another relict species, the dove or handkerchief tree *Davidia involucrata*, continues to struggle in the wild but thrives as an ornamental. The medium-sized tree takes its common names from its large white bracts—two surrounding each flower head—that flutter in the wind.[27] The dove tree is native to the cool, cloudy mountain forests of much of southern China; it is split into three large populations, ranging from Yunnan and Guizhou north through Sichuan, Hunan and Hubei, and into southern Gansu and Shaanxi.[28] In the wild the tree

survives largely where it remained at the end of the Ice Ages. It first came to the attention of Westerners when Père Armand David described it in 1868, but it was not until the first years of the twentieth century that seeds arrived in Europe and North America, where the tree soon became a popular ornamental. Despite its success as a resident of parks and gardens, the widespread cultivation of the dove tree has resulted in no discernible benefit to the wild trees.[29] In the coming decades the wild populations will once again be forced to retreat to their most secure refugia, this time in response to the rapidly warming climate. By 2070 the trees may well lose over half their potential habitat. Quick migration is no easy feat for such a species, with heavy stone fruits ill-suited to dispersal.[30] Nonetheless, having survived dramatic climatic fluctuations many times before, the wild dove trees may manage to survive again.

Of China's many living fossil trees the best known is the ginkgo or maidenhair tree *Ginkgo biloba*, known in Chinese as the silver apricot *yínxìng* 银杏. The ginkgo's fossil record is extensive, extending back prior to the formation of the Atlantic Ocean and spreading over every continent.[31] Gingko was a remnant species long before humans encountered the tree. Its decline began millions of years ago, and the successive Ice Ages preceding the Holocene left the last survivors standing in valleys of southwestern China.[32] The ginkgo survived long enough to be cultivated, and people planted the trees in cities and on temple estates. The oldest surviving trees and groves are in villages or on the grounds of Buddhist temples, and it is unclear if any truly wild trees survive.[33] If there are any wild ginkgo remaining, they are likely among the trees growing in the Dalou Mountains of Guizhou and Chongqing.[34] The ginkgo is in no danger of extinction; it has been widely cultivated in China, Korea, and Japan for centuries, and is now a common ornamental in Europe and North America.

Stripes & Spots

UNTIL the late twentieth century the South China tiger *Panthera tigris amoyensis* was the most widespread of China's tigers. Among the Chinese faunal pantheon, no species sits higher than the tiger. Tigers have a special place in Chinese culture, functioning not merely as powerful and fearsome predators of the wild, but as creatures of great supernatural power. As the scholar Chris Coggins has noted,

> "[T]he tiger was seen as a representative of heaven that could bring justice to the aggrieved, aid the righteous in times of need, or impose a reign of terror on wrong-doers. Good relations between people and tigers thus depended on how well the country was being governed—on the Mandate of Heaven and on the degree of harmony in the terrestrial realm. The tiger appeared to come and go of its own accord, or by the will of heaven."[1]

Before the Han pushed out or assimilated them, the ancient tribal peoples of Central and South China had their own beliefs and practices centered on the tiger. Some tied their identities to it, claiming descent from mythical tigrine ancestors. Tiger motifs featured in the art of many cultures, and it is likely that beliefs in were-tigers and perhaps even the modern Mandarin word for tiger, *hǔ* 虎, derive from the pre-Han southerners.[2]

Until the mid-twentieth century, many Han Chinese saw the tiger as cause for fear. The cats were held to be rationally thinking creatures, capable of criminal acts, but tigers were also instruments of the will of Heaven. They inflicted the most harm and terror on humanity when the ruler of the realm and his officials were failing in their duties to the people. Conversely, their attacks could be acts of justice, striking down those who had defiled the natural world. The power of the tiger made it a favored talisman among the Chinese. Tiger symbols, depictions, and body parts were used to impart protection or power on the wearer. Among the most common were tiger-face caps placed on babies to protect them from illness.[3]

Accounts of tiger attacks are extensive in the historical records, and they give some impression of the fear the cats sowed. Even though most attacks in any given time and place were likely the work of only one or a small handful of tigers, the damage they inflicted could be paralyzing. Some areas were said to suffer hundreds of deaths and massive losses of livestock, and even in daylight people dared not leave their walled villages except with strength in numbers. Farm fields and mountain roads would be abandoned for fear of attack. Even walls and moats failed against especially determined tigers, who found their way past the barriers to snatch away victims.[4] Attacks in South China seem to have spiked in the mid-sixteenth century and continued apace late into the seventeenth. At that time more and more people were pushing out of the lowlands to clear and settle the hills. Their invasion of the tigers' habitat led to increased conflict between cats and settlers, as tigers found themselves with both less space and fewer prey.[5]

Tigers apparently disappeared first from the surroundings of major cities. The last record of a tiger attack around Guangzhou was in 1690, and most other large cities in Guangdong saw tigers fade away in the eighteenth or early nineteenth century. They held on in the hills for longer, but by the mid nineteenth century there were few tigers left in the province outside the Nanling Mountains in the province's north.[6]

Westerners, too, left many accounts of tigers and their depredations. The earliest came from Marco Polo, who reported that "lions" were numerous in parts of the country and often preyed on locals and travelers.[7] When missionaries, fortune-seekers, and adventurers arrived after China's forced opening six centuries later, many of them told similar tales. In many rural mountain communities across Central and South China, tigers were a constant presence and terror to the villagers.[8] They regularly took livestock—Western observers often blamed the farmers themselves for their losses, as they observed little effort was made to protect domestic animals from predators. For those communities that sought revenge, poison was the favored weapon.[9]

Just as killer tigers had captivated the Chinese for centuries, so, too, were Westerners eager to hear and tell of man-eaters. Most tales they recounted came from the hinterlands of the port cities along the coasts and the Yangtze, places where foreigners were most numerous. Tigers were blamed for the deaths of "no fewer than 20 people" in the Pearl River Delta in the early 1900s, and were said to still be carrying off children and killing villagers in Anhui and Zhejiang into the 1920s.[10]

The Methodist missionary Harry Caldwell (1876–1970) lived and preached in inland Fujian in the early twentieth century, and there made a name for himself as an expert tiger hunter. He noted that tigers were found throughout much of the province, even among the barren hills of the coastal strip, where they somehow managed to survive by sheltering in small patches of woodland and venturing forth to prey on livestock and humans.[11] His son John recalled that many villages surrounded themselves with high walls to ward off the combined threats of marauding tigers and roving bandits. The gates were closed at dusk, and livestock were brought into the courtyards of homes before the doors were locked each night for fear of the cats. Despite such precautions, he noted that in the worst years tigers killed over 500 people merely in the four districts where his father preached.[12]

In an age when big game hunting was a popular pastime amongst Western men, tigers were an irresistible draw for many resident and visiting foreigners. In some cases they hunted purely for the enjoyment or prestige of killing one of the world's most feared creatures.[13] Others, when their presence became known to local villagers, were asked to hunt tigers the locals had been unable to kill themselves. Caldwell and others were always sure to note how eager the local Chinese were to collect—to use or sell—every last part of a dead tiger, even mopping up any blood spilt on the ground.[14]

When the Communist Party established the People's Republic in 1949, South China tigers were gone from the most heavily populated areas, but several thousand were still scattered in the hinterlands. Yet even in the backcountry their numbers had been dwindling for many years, and they remained numerous in very few places.[15] In 1950 roughly 4,000 South China tigers remained, but their numbers soon collapsed after they became a target of Maoist anti-pest campaigns. Official numbers compiled from 1951 to 1981 tell that in those three decades about 3,000 tigers were killed.[16]

The most intense period of hunting occurred in the campaign's first decade. In those years the threat from tigers was very real in some communities, and injuries and deaths a daily risk. But in the spirit of the times, the threat also became subject to wild exaggeration. Particularly farfetched is a story of tigers besieging a village. As reported, in 1957 a man captured several tiger cubs and surreptitiously brought them back to his village. That night, a hundred tigers arrived and encircled the village, driving the cattle from the fields and frightening the dogs into silence. For three days and three nights, the villagers lived in terror, baffled as to why the tigers would not leave. Finally they discovered the stolen cubs. Hoping to assuage their besiegers, they released the cubs, only for the tigers to sack the village in revenge, slaughtering all the animals within and dragging away a mother and her two children. Such claims make it difficult to trust official statistics, such as that in Hunan from 1952 to 1962 tigers hurt or killed over 2,000 people. Then again, the figures may well be true—there is no way to know.[17]

Whatever the true extent of danger that tigers presented, neither they nor other large predators were to have a place in the coming Communist Utopia. The government launched a "Kill the Tiger Movement," and local authorities and military units formed teams to hunt and kill as many tigers as they could find. Groups were formed to exterminate tigers as early as 1952 in Hunan, where tigers were considered a great scourge to rural society. That year over 120 deaths-by-tiger were reported in Leiyang alone, along with the theft of a far greater number of livestock. In response over a thousand tiger killing teams were formed across the province. They killed 170 of the cats over the next two seasons.[18]

To the east in Fujian, one hunt shows the lengths the tiger hunters would go to kill their enemies. In 1956 an army veteran was made leader of a platoon of over thirty local men and tasked with killing wildlife deemed hazardous to the community. After a tiger killed a child and several head of livestock across two counties, the team was called to action and equipped with military arms, including machine guns and hand grenades. For three months their efforts were fruitless, but finally they found a tiger—whether it was the culprit that had sparked the hunt or not hardly mattered. After the cat was wounded, it took refuge in a stretch of tall grass. Understandably reluctant to approach the wounded predator, and without a clear line of sight, the hunters lobbed in grenades to finish off the tiger, which they discovered to have been a small female, pregnant with cubs.[19]

Over eight provinces where the South China tigers ranged, the annual number of pelts collected dropped as fewer and fewer tigers were left to kill. In the first five years from 1951, an average of over 400 pelts came in each year. From 1961 to 1965 the average dropped to 152. By then perhaps only a thousand South China tigers were left, and they continued to fall to hunters until by the 1970s most provinces only brought in one or two pelts a year.[20] Along with the effects of ongoing habitat loss and the near extermination of the tigers' prey, hunting drove the cats to near extinction by the early 1980s, when only an estimated 150 to 200 South China tigers survived in the wild.[21]

Over the 1980s and 1990s each tiger count was lower than the last.[22] By then China had shifted from exterminating its wildlife to protecting its most prized species. Tigers were given legal protection, and reserves were established to provide them refuge. But the measures were too late and ineffectual. Fearing the worst, a survey of the best remaining habitat over 2001 and 2002 was conducted to determine the state of the subspecies. The surveyors found that the landscapes that had been designated as tiger reserves were too small to support them. Within the forests they found no evidence of living tigers, heard no reports of tiger depredations on livestock in the preceding decade, and detected very few prey species. After months of work it became clear that the South China tiger was extinct, except for the small inbred population in China's zoos.[23]

The Chinese government hoped to use the captive population to reestablish the South China tigers in the wild. To date that prospect remains far off. There is still too little habitat, and the prey is still too sparse. Researchers estimated that, at best, two to nine tigers could survive in the land available, and then only with intensive management.[24] Today the South China tigers number barely over 200, all captive—with the exception of a semi-wild population on a game reserve in South Africa that is part of a quixotic program to train them for reintroduction into the wild. The remaining tigers are highly inbred, despite a closely managed breeding program.[25] It is questionable if they will ever be able to repopulate their ancestral homes. But other species—in China and around the world—have come back from similarly desperate straits. Perhaps the South China tigers will too.

The common leopard, the most ubiquitous of China's big cats, was until the twentieth century widespread across Central and South China.[26] When Westerners started to enter the interior after the Opium Wars, they found that although some areas had already been largely cleared of leopards, the cats were still numerous in many places.[27] The expanding human population of the late Qing, and the widespread environmental destruction that accompanied it, often led to direct conflict between people and leopards. Attacks on livestock were common in many far-flung communities, and officials would respond by placing bounties on the cats.[28]

Conflict between farmers and leopards continued into the Communist period.[29] But over the first decades of the People's Republic the leopards were relentlessly hunted, both as pests and for their furs. Furs from the leopards of the south and southwest—particularly Guizhou, Yunnan, and southeastern Tibet—were considered to be the highest quality. Most pelts were exported, while Tibetans provided the largest market within the country. By the early 1980s leopards were a rarity across the entire southern half of China.[30]

Today the few remaining leopards struggle against the combined effects of a depleted prey base, habitat loss and fragmentation, and ongoing conflict with humans.[31] One consequence of this is that China's populations of Indochinese and Indian leopards (*Panthera pardus delacouri* and *P. p. fusca*) are now close to extirpation, if not already gone. At last estimate there were fewer than twenty of each remaining.[32]

Scales, Musk, Antlers, & Tusks

IN recent years one animal has come to widespread attention for two of the worst possible reasons. Pangolins have won fame for the dubious distinction of being the most trafficked mammals on the planet, and for likely playing a crucial role in sparking the outbreak of the COVID-19 pandemic.

Among the most curious of creatures, pangolins look almost dinosauric with their scale-covered bodies and plodding walk. Insectivores, they use their long, sticky tongues to devour thousands upon thousands of ants and termites each day.[1] They live primarily underground—which explains their formidable claws—or in the trees; their prehensile tails allow them to more effectively climb and hang while on the hunt.[2] When threatened, pangolins are able to roll tightly into a ball and let their scales protect them from attack.[3] A quiet and shy animal, it is rarely seen, as it retreats into its burrow for the day, only to emerge at night.[4]

There are nine pangolin species, five in Asia and four in Africa.[5] The Chinese pangolin *Manis pentadactyla* is by far the most widespread of the two species found in China.[6] Like many animals, pangolins faced great population declines in the distant past. The Ice Ages were particularly harsh on the Chinese pangolins, causing their numbers to fall by over seventy percent.[7] But with the retreat of the glaciers the pangolins expanded both in number and in range, spreading across most of China south of the Yangtze, and finding their way north of the river in some regions, even up to the Qinling.[8]

As such a strange creature, the pangolin inevitably caught the attention and sparked the imaginations of the communities who lived alongside it. Two of its attributes—its scales and its underground burrows—inspired most of the names people gave the pangolin.[9] Across South China it is known variously as the "mound carp" or "dragon carp," but the standard name today is *chuānshānjiǎ* 穿山甲, literally meaning "armor piercing through mountains."[10] The Chinese found the pangolin's scales so unusual that ultimately it was categorized not with other quadrupeds but as a fish. Because of its subterranean habits, some communities considered the pangolin to have dreadful powers, and either avoided them or were careful to chant incantations for protection against their dark magic.[11]

Despite the pangolin's fantastic nature, it attracted surprisingly little attention from educated Chinese through most of history. The earliest known reference to pangolins comes from the Han dynasty, but the scaly anteaters feature little in the literary corpus except as ingredients in pharmacological texts.[12] In the surviving literature, pangolins are first listed as a medicinal ingredient in the fifth century during the turbulent Northern and Southern dynasties (420–589).[13] The author of the text, the Daoist polymath Tao Hongjing (陶弘景, 456–536), clearly knew that pangolins' scales protect them from the bites of the ants they feed on, as the scales were attributed with the power to cure ant bites in people. He also wrote that, when burnt, the scales served as a cure for nighttime hysteria.[14]

As the centuries passed the uses for pangolin scales became more varied, and the preparations more elaborate. Tang-era physicians recommended their scales be used to treat malaria, one method being to ground them into powder and brewed into a soup.[15] The scales remained in use as treatment for ant bites, first mixed with pig fat and burnt to ash. Later they came to be prescribed, as a galactagogue, to help mothers produce more milk for their babies, one of the main purposes for which they are still used today. During the Song dynasty, pangolin scales saw their first use to remove blood clots and improve circulation.[16]

Eating pangolins was likely an ancient practice, at least in some communities, but mention of its consumption appears comparatively late in literature. An early reference to pangolin meat—from a twelfth century text—lists it as a winter street food in part of Jiangxi. The Miao people of the southwest dried and smoked pangolin meat during the Qing, and had probably done so for many centuries.[17] When Westerners began to explore China in the nineteenth century, pangolins were still commonly used in Chinese medicine, but consumption of their flesh remained relatively rare. The English naturalist Arthur Adams (1820–1878) noted that pangolins were available in the markets of Guangzhou, often carried about to attract curious onlookers. Adams also related that locals believed that to capture its prey, a pangolin

> "lays a trap for insects by erecting its scales, which suddenly closing on the entrance of flies, ants, &c., these intruders are secured, and, when dead, fall out and are eaten. It is also said to feed upon fish; but both these stories appear to be myths, something similar to those told of our own familiar 'hedge-pig'

sucking the teats of cows, and impaling apples on her quills in the orchards."[18]

Over time the demand for scales grew to the point that pangolins began to disappear from many localities. The tigers of Fujian preyed on the scaly anteaters, and the caves in which they often ate and took refuge were frequently littered with large numbers of scales. Tiger lairs thus became a source of scales for villagers or itinerant buyers of medicinal animals.[19] By the 1930s, pangolins had been so heavily hunted in Fujian that they had become difficult to find throughout much of the province. This of course only drove up the price of their scales.[20]

Hunting was not the only threat. Among others, habitat loss of course had significant impact, and the introduction and widespread overuse of pesticides killed off large numbers of the pangolins' insect prey.[21] But beyond a doubt, hunting was the overwhelming driver of the pangolins' decline.

The massive exploitation of the world's pangolins began in China. Before the mid twentieth century hunting had already caused noticeable drops in many local populations. Once the Maoist demand for maximum exploitation of the nation's resources took hold, it overwhelmed any local taboos that still existed and accelerated the species' decline. Over the 1960s China was bringing in an estimated 150,000 to 160,000 pangolins from the wild every year. Despite earlier declines, enough pangolins remained that massive annual harvests continued through the 1970s, only tailing off in most provinces early the next decade.[22] In places such as Hainan where local customs had traditionally restrained hunting, large harvests lasted longer, but by the 1990s they, too, had collapsed.[23]

Just as China's wild pangolins were disappearing, they were hit with a sudden surge in demand for their flesh. The market for wild game boomed, and pangolins came into fashion among the growing number of connoisseurs. The market peaked in the early 1990s, but the scaly anteaters remained on menus for years after, with diners claiming an unknown number of pangolins.[24]

In modern Chinese medicine pangolin scales are still prescribed to improve blood circulation and increase lactating mothers' milk production. They have also been administered to treat infertility and a wide array of gynecological diseases. They have even been used to treat breast cancer.[25] Conservationists have long attempted to convince practitioners of Chinese medicine to stop using pangolin scales, and instead substitute them with herbal or alternative animal ingredients. Candidates such as hooves and horns, and various seeds and stems have been put forward, but a minority of practitioners maintain that no replacement can match the efficacy of scales.[26] This is in spite of the fact that pangolin scales are made of keratin—the same substance that forms horns, hairs, feathers, nails, claws, and hooves—and are of no clinical use whatsoever.[27]

China's appetite for pangolin scales and meat drove not only the country's own scaly anteaters to near extinction, but extended out to all the pangolin species across Asia and then Africa. Several tonnes of Sunda pangolin *Manis javanica* scales were already being imported to China in the 1920s, and after the Communist takeover scales continued to come in, at first funneled through Hong Kong. Once pangolins within China became scarce, imports of both scales and live pangolins increased. At the beginning most imports were Sunda pangolins coming from Southeast Asia, but as their populations fell, the trade shifted west. In the 2000s it reached Africa, and to this day huge numbers of pangolins continue to be killed, their scales illegally sent off to become medicine in China and other East Asian countries.[28]

Although China's pangolins have suffered terribly since the mid twentieth century, they are not yet extinct. Since 2010 research on pangolins has grown immensely, and in those years they have been sighted in eleven provinces, indicating that scattered populations still exist.[29] Compared to the past, their numbers are no doubt few, but optimistic estimates place them above 10,000.[30] With increasing protections put in place in response to pangolins' linkage to the spillover of the SARS-CoV-2 virus, Chinese authorities and conservationists may eventually succeed in both rejuvenating the pangolins within China and cracking down on the trafficking of scales from overseas that is driving the rest of the world's scaly anteaters to extinction.

Along with pangolin scales, musk is one of the most coveted medicinal goods to come from China's wildlife. Sourced from the musk pods of male musk deer, musk has been used in Chinese medicine since at least the Han dynasty. The medical traditions of China and other East Asian nations attribute a great many healing properties to musk. It is said to help revive the unconscious, to stimulate the movement of *qi* and blood, and to treat delirium, trauma, stroke, and even paralysis. Today pharmacists still use raw musk in preparing prescriptions, and it is also included in hundreds of patented medicines within China and around the world.[31]

In the West musk is better known as an aromatic, used especially as a fixative in perfumery. In China, too, it has been used for similar purposes as far back as the Tang dynasty. Eventually European demand came to dominate the export market for musk, and China became the primary source country by the late nineteenth century. In the 1930s China supplied seventy percent of the musk on global markets.[32]

Over time its value grew, and musk became one of the most precious substances in the world. In the 1850s, by weight, it stood at only a quarter the value of gold. A century later it had come to equal the precious metal, and in 1978 musk was worth three and a half times what gold demanded. Prices could range widely, based on the purity of the musk on sale and the buyer. In the 1980s and 1990s Japan became the largest market for musk, and the Japanese paid the highest prices; the highest prices in the 1990s reached over $24,150/kg ($53,242/lb).[33] Some of the musk that made its way into Japan came through the legal market, but large amounts were smuggled in, either directly through China or via Hong Kong. The amount that flooded through the British colony so saturated the local market that its price fell by twenty-five percent from 1979 to 1981.[34]

There are two sources of natural musk: wild-caught and captive-raised musk deer. In the forests of Central and South China, there are two species of *Moschus*. The more common and widespread is the dwarf musk deer *Moschus berezovskii*.[35] Their range is extensive, stretching from Shaanxi, Gansu, and southeastern Tibet in the west to Guangdong and Jiangxi in the east.[36] Until recently believed to be the same species, their close relative, the Anhui musk deer *M. anhuiensis*, is known only from the region around the Dabie Mountains in the west of Anhui province.[37]

Despite millennia of being trapped and hunted, the dwarf musk deer still seemed quite numerous in the mid twentieth century. Working backwards from the amount of musk that came into the hands of government buyers, researchers estimate that in the 1960s there were more than a million dwarf musk deer still roaming the forests and shrublands. Overhunting drove their numbers down to roughly 600,000 by the late 1970s. That decline was followed by even more intense hunting pressure, as the global price of musk took off. By 1992, between 100,000 and 200,000 of the deer were believed to survive.[38]

The Anhui musk deer fared even worse. With a far more restricted range and fewer numbers to begin with, they could withstand less than their cousins. In 1957 31 kg (68 lb) of musk were harvested, equal to roughly 6,200 deer. Hunting continued apace until *anhuiensis* became so rare that they were nearly impossible to find. By 1967 the musk output in Anhui was down to 2 kg (4.4 lb), and a decade later it was nearly zero.[39] A 1985 estimate put the total population of Anhui musk deer at between 700 and 800, and a survey a decade later noted the species was still in decline. Since then there have been no further surveys to determine their current status.[40]

One reason the musk deer suffered such precipitous declines was the indiscriminate nature of the trapping. Most musk deer were caught with snares, and hunters made little or no effort to target mature males. Females and young do not produce musk, and so are useless to the musk hunter. Traditionally many hunters therefore aimed only to catch musk-producing males, aware that to do otherwise risked wasting time and effort for little return, and also presented a danger to the musk deer population. Under Maoist maximalism, and later drawn along by the lure of stratospheric prices, hunters left behind the restraint of earlier practice. Anything and everything was snared.

There were two hopes for providing musk without harming the wild populations. Synthetic musk, created in the lab and produced industrially, saw great success in replacing the natural stuff in perfumery—today little natural musk finds its way into perfumes. In Chinese medicine, however, the synthetic stuff has been slower to take hold.[41] The other alternative source is farmed musk. Musk deer farming started in 1958, holding to the often mistaken belief that captive breeding of a coveted species would undermine the market for wild-caught animals. The dwarf and Anhui species made up the bulk of the animals used to start the farms, which by the 1980s only reached about 3,000 deer. As with many other species, musk deer proved ill-suited to captivity. Solitary, territorial, and high-strung, they fared poorly when crowded together on farms. Many of the operations folded.[42] Musk farming continues to this day, with roughly 25,000 farmed deer in 2019 producing 250 kg (550 lb) of musk a year—far short of the annual demand of 1,500 kg (3,307 lb).[43]

Like the musk deer, many of the small hoofed animals of the forests are still poorly understood. One example is the black or hairy-fronted muntjac *Muntiacus crinifrons*, a small barking deer native to the southeastern forests. The black muntjac once ranged from Zhejiang south to Guangdong. Now *crinifrons* lives only in southeastern Anhui, northern Fujian, northeastern Jiangxi, and western Zhejiang. Hunting and deforestation were the main causes of the decline, although both threats now appear greatly reduced. However, the species is so little studied that it is unknown if the muntjac has yet to begin to recover.[44] Even if that is the case, climate change could present a further danger to the black muntjac. Under the rosiest projections they are expected to suffer only minimal habitat loss of around ten percent. But in the worst case scenarios they may face a loss of over half their habitat.[45]

As elsewhere, large deer species of the south such as the sika *Cervus nippon* and sambar *Rusa unicolor* were heavily hunted for their antlers. Trade in sambar antlers was especially heavy along the Sichuan-Tibetan frontier, while the South China sika was hunted from the Yangtze Basin south to Guangdong. The sika gradually succumbed to hunting and habitat loss and fragmentation, and by the 1930s there were few left beyond Anhui or the Lower Yangtze Valley.[46] Today South China sika survive in small numbers in Jiangxi, Anhui, and Zhejiang.[47] Sambar are more widespread, found from Jiangxi and Guangdong in the east to Sichuan and Yunnan in the west.[48] Today they are most abundant in the southwest, where they share habitat with the protected panda.[49]

In South China wild boar are every bit as destructive and consequently every bit as hated as elsewhere. Boars had largely been pushed out of the heavily populated coastal and river valley regions by the mid nineteenth century, but the Taiping Rebellion wrought such devastation that many areas were depopulated of humans, and the boars and other animals quickly reclaimed what they had lost.[50] By the early twentieth century most of the large coastal cities and their hinterlands again supported only small herds, but in the most isolated and rugged country the swine remained abundant. Their depredations on farmland could often be so severe as to drive farmers to abandon their fields and paddies, allowing the forests to reclaim the land.[51] Today, just as in the north, the wild boar populations have grown so large and so bold after enjoying years of protection that they have again become a threat to some farmers' livelihoods, at times once again driving the abandonment of cultivated lands.[52] With their legal protections recently removed, the boars may again have to contend with farmers and hunters seeking to control their numbers.[53]

Monkey Business

O N a lone mountain in a stretch of the Wuling range in northeastern Guizhou lives the fourth of China's snub-nosed monkeys, the Guizhou or gray snub-nosed monkey *Rhinopithecus brelichi*.[1] Restricted to the holy mountain of Fanjing Shan, the monkeys eluded outside notice until the early twentieth century. They remain the least known of the *Rhinopithecus* species, perhaps because they are so keen to avoid humans. Instead it may simply be that they are the least flashy of the snub-noses. *Brelichi*'s fur is rather drab, mostly blackish-gray with a band of chestnut across the chest and inner arms, and another two patches on the forehead and upper back. Their faces are blue but of a subdued hue, without *roxellana*'s vibrancy.[2] It has likely been to the gray monkeys' great benefit that their coats don't stoke people's desires for luxury.

The first record of the gray snub-nosed monkeys was made in 1903 in the form of a single skin.[3] After that nothing was heard of the species until 1962 when a scientist obtained a skull.[4] It was only five years later that researchers saw their first live specimen after a lone female wandered into Jinzhanping, a village west of Fanjing Shan, in search of food; instead it found a trap. The man who captured the female then sold her to the local government, which flew her off to the Institute of Zoology in Beijing.[5]

During their short recorded history the gray monkeys have always been restricted to Fanjing Shan and its immediate surroundings. It is, however, likely that earlier they were more widely distributed throughout northeastern Guizhou. They may well have disappeared and escaped discovery altogether except for their good luck that Chinese Buddhists consider Fanjing Shan a sacred mountain. Consequently there have been temples drawing pilgrims since at least the Song dynasty, but the harm has been minimized as killing has been forbidden on the holy ground of the mountain, sparing the monkeys from human depredation.[6] Even during the Maoist era, when such traditions crumbled and China waged a people's war on nature, killings of *brelichi* remained remarkably rare. In fact, through the 1960s and 1970s all the monkeys known to have died at human hands were killed accidentally, most caught in traps intended for other game.[7]

For years after finding *brelichi*, no one knew how many there might be. Once researchers decided to find out they produced a mess of estimates, ranging from only a paltry ninety to a blindly optimistic 3,000. At the end of the first intensive survey of their range in 1993, scientists settled on an estimate of 655 to 873 monkeys. A followup survey in 2008 came to roughly the same range, citing 750 as the most reasonable guess. This agreed with the gut feelings of Fanjingshan Nature Reserve's staff, who believed the population was stable.

Brelichi seemed to face no severe threats on Fanjing Shan. There was no targeted hunting pressure, only the danger of accidental trapping. Local villagers grazed livestock in the forests, cut and burned the trees for firewood and charcoal, and collected herbs and other foods from the woods, leading to some destruction and degradation of the monkeys' habitat. Roads, a cable car, and hotels were put in for the flow of tourists visiting the mountain, further fragmenting the landscape.[8] Yet the monkeys appeared to weather it all quite well. In the 1990s scientists even thought *brelichi* had reached its limits on Fanjing Shan, with a steady trickle of males attempting to venture beyond the mountain, perhaps in search of new territory.[9]

Yet perhaps it has not all been as benign as it seemed. There had been subtle clues for some time that *brelichi* was rapidly losing space. When first found in the 1960s the monkeys were often seen at low elevations, but by the 1980s they had retreated several hundred meters up the mountain. By the 1990s they were restricted to a band between 1,400 m and 2,100 m (4,600 to 6,900 ft). Fanjing Shan's highest peak only reaches 2,570 m (8,430 ft), and the monkeys' forests stop well below that. They can go no higher. The most recent investigation into the gray monkeys and their habitat arrived at sobering conclusions. The construction of an aerial tramway in 2009 split the monkeys' habitat into two patches, one in the north and one in the south of the reserve, each isolated from the other. Recent surveys have found not a scrap of evidence of the monkeys in the southern habitat, leaving only the north. There the monkeys are left with just over 40 sq km (15.4 sq mi) of usable land, broken into three parcels with narrow, fragmented strips of habitat connecting them. *Brelichi* was found in only two of these parcels, leaving the entire population with less than 28 sq km (10.8 sq mi) in which to live. Researchers estimated there are at least 125 *brelichi* remaining, but that at most only 336 monkeys could survive in the space available.[10]

If the gray snub-nosed monkeys have indeed dwindled to so few in such a small patch of forest, then their future may be grim. Already at the highest edge of their habitat, Fanjing Shan's forests must be protected and restored if the monkeys are to survive into the next century. With nowhere else to go, the best chance for *brelichi* is to restore the species' only home.

Along with macaques and snub-nosed monkeys, China is also home to several species of another monkey genus, the langurs or leaf monkeys *Trachypithecus*. Slender and long-tailed, langurs are herbivores that feed on leaves, buds, and fruits. Over twenty species of *Trachypithecus* live across Southeast Asia, six of them in China.

In China the most widespread of the leaf monkeys is François' langur *Trachypithecus francoisi*.[11] François' langurs are born bright orange, but over the course of infancy the coat fades to a silky black. Males are longer and heavier than females, but otherwise the two sexes look very similar. The monkeys' most prominent features are the white sideburns that run from their ears across their cheeks. Residents of limestone forests, they spend much of their time on cliffs, ledges, and in caves. Highly sociable, they live in matriarchal groups of usually one to two dozen.

During the Tang dynasty and for many centuries after, poets often wrote of the calls of apes in the cliffs and gorges of the Yangtze. Based on the name used for the animals, *yuán* 猿, scholars have long assumed the writings referred to gibbons. A recent reevaluation of the evidence, however, suggests the calls instead came from François' langurs, which are far better suited to living in the rocky habitat of the cliffs. So, too, do they more closely fit with the behaviors described in ancient texts. If accurate, that would place the leaf monkeys as far north as the Yangtze in Hunan during the Tang and likely for centuries longer.[12] Eventually the destruction of their habitat would have pushed them further and further south.

By the time of more certain records in the early nineteenth century, François' langurs were still present across much of the south, from Guangdong as far west as Chongqing.[13] Over the nineteenth and through the first half of the twentieth century, the leaf monkeys saw their range contract further in the face of continuing human encroachment. Little is known about what happened to the langurs until the 1970s, but by that time they were found only in southwestern

Guangxi, neighboring counties in Guizhou, and a small area of Chongqing.[14]

In addition to the ever-tightening vice of agricultural expansion, François' langurs died in great numbers to feed demand for medicinal goods. Locals traditionally collected female langurs' menstrual blood from caves to use as a remedy for anemia and other ailments, but it was bones that were most valuable. Langur bones were used to make a medicinal wine said to cure fatigue and rheumatism, and the market for "black ape wine" extended across South China and to the ethnic Chinese communities of Southeast Asia.[15]

The monkeys' habit of sleeping as a group in caves made them easy to catch; all hunters had to do was block the cave entrance while the langurs were inside. In Guangxi, where the largest collection of langurs live, the numbers lost caused huge strain on the population. In the 1970s hunters killed over 1,400 langurs, and in the 1980s over 1,500. Given that the province only hosted an estimated 4,000 to 5,000 François' langurs in 1983, their losses to the bone trade were clearly devastating. The nationwide confiscation of privately-owned firearms in 1999 put an end to the worst of the hunting.[16]

Even as hunting receded, habitat destruction continued unchecked. An expanding local human population turned to the langurs' limestone forests for the land and fuel wood they required. Most families met their cooking and heating needs from the use of firewood, and the forest was the best source available.[17] By the mid-1990s Guangxi's population of *francoisi* had fallen to between 2,000 and 2,500, and by that time they had disappeared from many of the forests they had once occupied. The decline continued unabated, and in 2003 there were believed to be just over 300 François' langurs left in Guangxi.[18]

The Guizhou population is today much larger than Guangxi's, standing at between 900 and 1,000. Along with the few hundred in Guangxi and perhaps 200 in Chongqing, there remain fewer than 2,000 François' langurs left in China.[19] Now restricted to a triangle covering less than 200 sq km, the leaf monkeys will have to wait many years for the restoration of their limestone forests.[20] Then they may be able to begin the long process of rebuilding their numbers and recolonizing their old haunts, although the warming climate will much reduce the space available to them.[21]

Another species of leaf monkey lives in the karst hills of southwest Guangxi, south of the Zuo River. The white-headed langur *Trachypithecus leucocephalus* is *T. francoisi*'s closest kin. The two split roughly a mere 290,000 years ago, and occasionally still interbreed.[22] Until very recently, however, *T. leucocephalus* was believed to be a subspecies of Vietnam's Cat Ba langur *T. poliocephalus*, or perhaps instead a subspecies of *T. francoisi*. As the name suggests, the white-headed langur has a white-furred head, although its bare face and ears are black. The white extends to the shoulders and upper back before fading to black, which covers the rest of the body until about halfway down the tail where it turns back to white.

Sparse records of the species exist back to fifteenth century poetry, but very little can be gleaned from such references.[23] The white-headed langurs were not known to science, however, until the zoologist Tan Bangjie (谭邦杰, 1915–2003) came across them in 1952 while on a collecting expedition for the Peking Zoo.[24] Nothing was known about the monkeys at the time, and little was learned until the late 1970s. In the intervening decades the langurs were subjected to the same panoply of threats their *francoisi* kin faced across the Zuo River. The forests were cut down, the mountains blasted for roads, and the langurs themselves hunted for their bones—and for their flesh during the famine years of the Great Leap Forward.[25]

Surveys finally undertaken in 1977 estimated a population of 600 white-headed langurs, all confined to a handful of counties along the Zuo. Six years later the number had dropped by a third.[26] Once hunting was brought largely under control at the end of the 1990s, some of the langur populations were then safe from imminent extinction. They were spread over four counties, only two of which retained good habitat.[27] The felling of trees for fuel wood remained a problem for years until the government stepped in to provide local communities with gas stoves and heating.[28]

Although they now enjoy greater protection than in the past, much of the langurs' habitat are landscapes they still must share with humans, and which remain badly fragmented and degraded. Despite this, their numbers have crept upwards. The latest count estimated a total 1,300 white-headed langurs.[29] They continue to face a difficult future—thousands of people in dozens of villages remain within the langurs' range—and as they are predicted to struggle to adapt in the face of climate change, they face the real risk of extinction.[30]

China's other langurs are primarily South or Southeast Asias species, reaching into China only at the margins of their distributions. A single band of capped langurs *Trachypithecus pileatus* was sighted in southeastern Tibet in 2014.[31] Three other species are known only from Yunnan. A subspecies of Phayre's leaf monkey *T. phayrei shanicus*—recently proposed to be its own species, the Shan State langur *T. melamera*[32]—straddles the Sino-Myanmar border, with a few healthy populations in the Gaoligong Mountains.[33] Approximately 250 Shortridge's langurs *T. shortridgei* survive in the valley of the Dulong (Irrawaddy) River. Since they were first surveyed in 1972, the Shortridge's langurs have suffered badly from deforestation and hunting for their meat; their numbers have fallen by at least half. Populations that once lived on the eastern slopes of the nearby Gaoligong Mountains have disappeared.[34] The Indochinese gray langur *T. crepusculus* is more widespread, but still limited to Yunnan. The gray langurs extend into central Yunnan, and groups that live on unprotected lands still face long odds against the encroachments of agriculture.[35] However, some bands within protected reserves have begun to recover and even increase in number, and as a whole the species is likely to persist in China for the foreseeable future.[36]

China hosts numerous macaque species, most of which are found in the south. The most widespread is the rhesus macaque *Macaca mulatta*, a favorite species for scientific research worldwide. The rhesus was once found across all of South China below the Yangtze Valley.[37] They were sometimes captured to be sold as pets, but also to be killed, the entire body then used to make a medicinal "monkey paste." In some regions hunting took a severe toll. Old hunters in northwestern Fujian recalled in the early twentieth century that about forty years earlier, before they had acquired modern guns, the macaques were so numerous and aggressive that they regularly raided crops.[38]

Though reduced in numbers, macaques were still abundant in some regions in the 1950s. When Tan Bangjie was on a collecting expedition in Guangxi he saw "cartloads of live monkeys, mostly rhesus," on sale in local markets almost everyday. Their numbers soon plummeted as they became targets of anti-pest campaigns. Thousands were captured for export as research animals, while others were taken for their pelts. Guangxi's crack macaque hunters caused a population crash amongst the monkeys, and then were sent to neighboring provinces to do the same. When Tan revisited Guangxi in 1982, instead of cartloads of macaques for sale each day he found only two or three dozen monkeys.[39]

Now, after years of protection from persecution, the macaques have somewhat rebounded. In some places they have regained the audacity of their ancestors, sallying forth to raid fields during the winter and early spring lean seasons. Farmers, barred from responding with lethal force, are often at a loss to stop the monkeys, who have learned they have little to fear from firecrackers and loudspeakers.[40]

Other macaque species in China include the stump-tailed macaque *Macaca arctoides*, which lives over much of the South, but is now only common in western Yunnan; many of the populations in the eastern provinces are likely extinct.[41] The Assam macaque *M. assamensis* was common across the southwest into Guangxi, but overhunting in the 1950s and 1960s diminished their populations, and they are now largely restricted to southeastern Tibet.[42] A recently discovered species, the white-cheeked macaque *M. leucogenys*, has so far been found only in the Gaoligong Mountains, southeastern Tibet, and across the Indian border in Arunachal Pradesh. Having so recently come to the attention of scientists, little is yet known about the species.[43]

Edible & Collectible

A once common sight even in the cities of South China was civets. Civets are members of the family Viverridae—distantly related to mongooses and hyenas, and even more distantly to the cats—and several species are found across wide swathes of Asia and Africa. Civets were long most famous for producing a musk used in perfumery (typically referred to simply as "civet" and taken mostly from the African civet *Civettictis civetta*). Now they are more likely to be known as the source of kopi luwak, or civet coffee.[1]

Aside from the binturong—only found at the very southern edge of Chinese territory—the civets of China are small and unobtrusive species. They managed to survive quite well into the twentieth century, and were still common even in Shanghai and other cities into the 1910s and beyond.[2] Eventually the effects of habitat loss and hunting began to catch up with them. The small Indian civet *Viverricula indica* was known as the brush cat, as its tail fur was used to make calligraphy brushes.[3] Both it and the large Indian civet *Viverra zibetha* are also hunted for their musk and meat, as is the Asian palm civet *Paradoxurus hermaphroditus*, and all have seen their numbers and ranges reduced as a consequence. The masked palm civet *Paguma larvata* ranged not only across South China but also into the north, into Shanxi and even Beijing, where overhunting had largely wiped it out by the 1970s. It has long been a favorite delicacy for Southern Chinese, and in the 1960s some 80,000 to 100,000 masked palm civets were caught every year. Before the mainland game meat market exploded they were shipped to Hong Kong.[4] It was the masked palm civet that came to world attention in 2003 when sick civets in a Guangzhou restaurant kitchen were shown to have infected a waitress and a customer with SARS.[5]

鵐

The southern Chinese have gained a lasting notoriety for eating seemingly every creature possible. To some species the region's taste for wildlife has proven devastating. One of the most dramatic cases is that of a small songbird, the yellow-breasted bunting *Emberiza aureola*. When in its breeding plumage the male has bright yellow undersides, with a black and brown topside, black face, and a black ring around his throat. The female of course wears more subdued colors, with a lighter yellow underside and whitish face. In winter the female does not appear much changed, while the male loses his black mask but retains his rich yellow front.

Yellow-breasted buntings were once one of the most abundant songbirds to pass through China. Early twentieth century Westerners noted the enormity of the murals that passed through every year.[6] The birds were caught by the thousands to be sold as pets in the north and into the Yangtze region. Ultimately most died from the ordeal, and those that did survive were thought to be rather dull singers.[7]

Beyond such observations the yellow-breasted bunting garnered no special attention until the 1990s. It was then that people noticed the buntings were declining in number and eventually disappearing from some localities.[8] The assumed culprit was the huge Guangdong market for wild birds.[9] Buntings are trapped all along their migratory route, but by far the greatest number are taken in Guangdong. There, as well as in parts of Southeast Asia, the buntings have for centuries been netted in great numbers. Unlike in the north, the Southerners did not keep the birds as pets, but ate them.[10]

While migrating and wintering the buntings stop in grasslands and rice fields, and their habit of roosting in massive decorations make them an easy and tempting target. The ease of capturing the birds, combined with the huge demand for wild meat that arose in the 1980s, led to frightening numbers of buntings being consumed.[11] An annual festival in Foshan, Guangdong saw several hundred thousand of the birds devoured each year from 1992 to 1997. Trapping was outlawed in 1997, but the ban had little effect. One researcher estimated that in 2001 alone, one million yellow-breasted buntings were sold and eaten in Guangdong Province.[12]

What makes the trapping in Guangdong so devastating is that it hits nearly the entire migratory population. The yellow-breasted buntings have an expansive breeding range in the north, originally stretching from Finland to the Pacific. But on their way south, practically every bird stops in the Yangtze Valley to molt before funneling to the eastern seaboard of China and passing south through Guangdong. This means that a great percentage of the world's yellow-breasted buntings must travel through an area where they are eagerly trapped and sold.[13]

The huge decline in the global yellow-breasted bunting population has led to their disappearance from a large swathe of their eastern breeding range. They are now gone from Finland, Belarus, Ukraine, and much of Russia—an eastward retreat of 5,000 km (3,100 mi).[14] In numbers, the collapse was far more dramatic. Scientists estimate that between 1980 and 2013, the global yellow-breasted bunting population fell by 84.3~94.7%. This happened to many populations that passed the breeding seasons in healthy habitats, leaving the trapping in China and Southeast Asia the most likely culprits.[15]

Even as conservationists turned their attention to the plight of the yellow-breasted buntings and attempted to raise a call to action, the trapping continued at the same massive scale. Once caught the birds are sold on to commercial buyers who plump them with special fattening agents. They then sell the birds to restaurants in Guangdong and beyond. In 2021 the central government placed the buntings under the highest level of protection, and launched campaigns to publicize the birds' plunge towards extinction. Law enforcement, too, has begun to crack down on trapping and trading, and farmers have been encouraged to protect and restore the birds' habitat.[16] If such efforts pay off, the buntings may escape imminent extinction and in time return to something approaching their former abundance.

Some species are thought lost or nearly so, only for it to be discovered they have been more widespread and numerous than believed. One such species is the white-eared night heron *Gorsachius magnificus*, a nocturnal, drably-colored heron that lives in forests and along rivers.[17] First described in the 1890s, for decades there were only a few records of the birds from southern China and Vietnam. The species was long believed to be on the verge of extinction, or already extinct. But in the early 2000s previously unknown populations of the birds were discovered, lending new hope to the night herons' future.[18] Nocturnal and found primarily in thick forest, the birds have proven difficult to detect, but increased survey work has shown the herons not only range across more of China than previously known, but further afield in Vietnam, Cambodia, Bangladesh, and India.[19]

Although the night herons were now known to be more numerous and widespread than previously thought, they were by no means abundant. Along with many other birds, the herons had suffered decades of heavy trapping and hunting; Southern Chinese have long had a taste for many species of wild bird, and although the herons were likely not favorite targets, hunting was so widespread and indiscriminate that their numbers fell anyway. Perhaps even more deadly was the loss of habitat. The herons can nest in disturbed and secondary forest, but without primary forests nearby they lacked refuge from hunters. Now the remaining birds are found only in the hills and mountains; it is most likely they have retreated there from their preferred choice of flat lowlands.[20]

Today the white-eared night heron's status is still little understood. It still seems, however, that the species is faring poorly. Its populations appear fragmented, and in some places, such as Guangxi, more birds are seen for sale in markets than in the wild. Hunting is now less severe, but the herons' native forests are still fragmented. Climate change will likely deprive the species of some of its habitat, yet should the forests be restored to something like their former extent, the night herons may still bounce back.[21]

In China many species of snakes, turtles, and dozens of other animals are eaten, kept as pets or curiosities, and used in Chinese medicine. Demand is high, and many of the animals—or their parts— are imported, while others are caught in China. Across rural areas of South China in the 1980s and 1990s, local governments encouraged wildlife farming as a way both to meet rising demand and raise local standards of living. Farms for every sort of consumed creature popped up across the region. Mammals such as civets, porcupines, and bamboo rats were popular choices, as were a bewildering variety of reptiles and amphibians. Just as with deer and salamanders, much of the breeding stock came from the wild, putting further strain on already dwindling populations. The industry grew enormously over the decades, but in 2020 it suddenly fell into steep decline as the COVID-19 outbreak compelled the central government to place a ban on the farming and consumption of numerous species. Though many farmers went bust, others pulled what strings they could to keep their industry alive. Many species were quietly given special exemptions or transferred to a legal gray area, allowing farms to continue breeding and selling.[22]

Snakes and turtles are hunted and bred not only for use as meat and medicine, but also for trade as pets, and for display in zoos. Demand for the most prized reptiles and amphibians has driven a number of species around the world to near extinction. Many of these are unusual and visually striking animals, and often are found only in a restricted range with a naturally small population.

The Mangshan pit viper *Protobothrops mangshanensis* is one such species, a large venomous snake of bright green blotched with brown, known only from the Nanling Mountains straddling southern Hunan and northern Guangdong. Scientists first found the snake in 1989, by which time its home forests and streams had suffered several decades of degradation and destruction. The viper's discovery received wide coverage on account of the serpent's beauty, and very quickly fanciers and zoos began to seek snakes for their collections. The demand—mostly from the US, Europe, Middle East, and Japan—created a lucrative black market for the Mangshan viper; a snake that had sold for only $30 in 1990 cost $7,000 in 1997.

The serpents live primarily within two nature reserves, but continued poaching for the live trade, combined with an array of lesser dangers, means the species remains endangered. The last survey, completed in 2010, estimated only 462 snakes survived in the wild. Conservationists worry, too, about the changing climate, which may bring more fatal cold snaps.[23] With such a small and isolated native range, the vipers are especially vulnerable to impending climate change, which in the worst-case scenarios could even rob them of all their best habitat.[24]

The Mangshan pit viper has not been China's only victim of reptile fanciers. The Chinese crocodile lizard *Shinisaurus crocodilurus* is one of South China's many Pleistocene remnants and the last surviving member of a group that evolved in the Early Cretaceous. First described in 1928, it is found only near slow streams and pools in the hill forests of Guangdong, Guangxi, and northern Vietnam.[25] The first survey of the species in China estimated that 6,000 lizards survived, but in the decades since their numbers have declined. The degradation of their native forests has removed large swathes of habitat and fragmented much that remains.[26] With changes in the forest structure have come changes in the hydrology, and many streams which once ran year-round are now seasonal, leaving the lizards unable to survive in many areas where forest still stands.[27]

     Even more than loss of habitat, the lizards have suffered from hunting and collection for sale as meat, medicine and live specimens. Traditionally considered a cure for insomnia, demand for the crocodile lizards jumped in the 1980s with the arrival of international collectors.[28] The high prices offered for the lizards prompted widespread hunting. Locals could earn up to two months' wage selling a single lizard, and by 2004, even though new populations had been discovered, wild lizards were difficult to find, with only 950 estimated to survive in China.[29] Climate change may prove especially devastating over the next century, with recent models showing habitat loss of 93% or more under even the most optimistic scenarios.[30] If those predictions prove accurate, the crocodile lizards may not survive much longer as a wild species. By 2012 another population of around 300 had been found in Guangdong, bringing the total estimate up to 1,200, with several sites no longer showing much sign of the lizards. Since then surveys have shown no great changes to the population. Nonetheless, the release of captive-bred crocodile lizards in 2019–2020 and their success surviving and breeding gives reason for optimism that the lizards may beat the odds.[31]

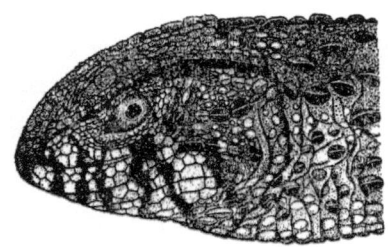

Small & Forgotten

I N China and around the globe, the small and unglamorous creatures tend to receive the least attention, even when they are in the greatest peril. One such example was the Yunnan lake newt *Cynops wolterstorffi*, which perished with little notice. A small black and red mottled amphibian found only in Lake Dian near Kunming, the capital of Yunnan, the newts were seemingly abundant when first surveyed in the late 1950s. They were still easily found several years later, but the onset of massive land reclamation works on the lake in 1969 signaled the beginning of the end. The lake's ecosystem—the newts' sole habitat— was so thoroughly degraded that by the time scientists returned to resurvey in 1976–1977, the newts were gone. After a few last individuals were sighted in 1979, no more sign of the amphibians was ever found.[1]

Bugs—insects, arachnids, all the creepy crawly creatures—tend to attract little attention or sympathy even when endangered. Across much of the Earth insect populations are crashing. The conversion of huge tracts of land to commercial monocrop agriculture has deprived many species of the plant communities on which they relied. And the extensive use of pesticides to protect those crops has compounded the damage. Bees are no exception. China is home to a great number of bee species, and the Tibetan Plateau—especially within Sichuan and Gansu—hosts the world's richest mix of bumblebee species. Though some species, such as the wild black honeybees of Manchuria, do enjoy formal protection, most receive little recognition, much less help, from humanity. In some regions, notably within Sichuan, pollinators have been absent since the mid-1980s, and people must be hired to pollinate crops by hand.[2] Many species of bees and other insects will no doubt survive and even thrive long into the future, but between the effects of modern agriculture and climate change, China's insect diversity will be greatly reduced.

The Lampyridae, better known as fireflies or lightning bugs, have become noticeably rarer around the world. Aside from the habitat loss and pesticide use that has proven devastating to so many insects, fireflies also struggle against the massive surge in artificial light that has flooded the planet. Light pollution makes it difficult for the insects to signal to potential mates with their own bioluminescent beacons, and may even disrupt the ability of larvae to disperse. Worldwide, firefly populations have collapsed, and they are now absent from many places where not long ago they illuminated the night.[3]

Lampyridae in China have recently faced a new threat. Entrepreneurs at some point realized that gathering thousands of fireflies into a single space would draw paying sightseers. Firefly parks began to open, attracting tourists to gawk and snap photos.[4] Soon after, the insects themselves appeared for sale online so that people could light up their weddings and other events with a multitude of tiny, flying, blinking lamps. Sales of live lightning bugs grew rapidly, reaching over 17 million in 2016. If the vendors were to be believed, perhaps there would not have been great reason to worry. They insisted their fireflies were bred in captivity, and that their operations were no threat to wild populations.[5] Conservationists knew differently, as even the most experienced experts could not break even breeding the insects.[6] The fireflies were wild-caught, an immense and growing drain on already falling populations. After several years the largest online platforms banned the sale of live fireflies, and since then the glowworms have fallen out of the news. But they still face all the same threats, and without widespread efforts to provide them with safe havens, future generations will only rarely have the chance to see thousands of flashing lights flitter about in the fading evening light.

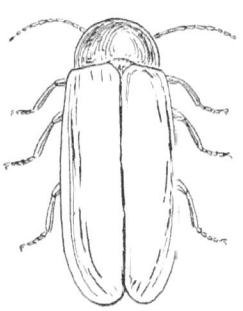

More recently, earthworms have suffered from a sudden surge in market demand. Used as a medicinal ingredient since at least the Han dynasty, worms have come under threat due to rising demand both as a therapeutic and as fishing bait.[7] Harvesting worms was traditionally a laborious affair, but the arrival of cheap machines that send electrical charges into wet soil has sparked a rush for easy worm money. The greater numbers of worms caught, as well as the damage to the soils, have caused worm populations to fall, causing a vicious cycle as prices rise, attracting more worm catchers.[8] Demand is now being exported—Chinese buyers have already spread the trade into Vietnam.[9]

Like bees and fireflies, for years the scientific community in China largely neglected the only flying mammals—bats. Now, with greater knowledge of their importance in pollinating plants, controlling insect populations, and their role as repositories for a myriad of unknown diseases that may spillover into humans, bats are beginning to receive some of the attention they are due.

China hosts among the largest number of bat species of any country, with 147 currently catalogued and more likely to be identified.[10] Of those, very few are known to be in acute danger of extinction.[11] Yet on the whole, bats in China have had a difficult last few decades. From the late 1970s and early 1980s when the earliest reliable research figures were recorded, bat populations have shown clear signs of decline.

Just why this is the case is not entirely clear. Several factors are likely to blame. For one, bats do end up in soups and on skewers, which may have damaged some populations. Perhaps more damaging is the extensive and heavy use of pesticides, which has likely led to many populations accumulating large amounts of toxic chemicals in their bodies, lowering their health and fecundity. This has been made worse by many farmers' view of bats as pests. Once farmers kill off enough insectivorous bats, the local insect population increases, requiring more pesticide to be applied to achieve the same yields, further harming the bats. Roosting sites have been demolished, particularly old buildings that have been torn down to make way for new infrastructure. And of course, deforestation has deprived many tree-roosting species of habitat.[12]

Tourism, too, has become a threat, as increasing numbers of adventure seekers enter into the caves where bats roost. In fact, disturbance of bat habitat is a nearly universal problem across China. Nearly all of the roosting sites scientists have surveyed showed signs that humans had intruded, usually in pursuit of some form of recreation. Caves that once attracted tourists but had fallen into disuse tended to host the most species, indicating that simply being left in peace is a major boost for the bats' health.[13] Lights installed for sightseers can disrupt the bats' activity cycles, and the constant flow of breathing bodies can cause carbon dioxide to accumulate in the enclosed spaces, changing the local atmosphere and temperature. Even gates erected at cave entrances can become serious obstacles for bats to navigate.[14]

Bat research in China is now facing great difficulties. Much of the current science is focused on sampling bat populations for diseases in hopes of guarding against future spillovers of zoonotic diseases. After initially encouraging and supporting such work after the outbreak of COVID-19, the Chinese government has since reversed course. With the official narrative now declaring that the pandemic could not have started within China, honest efforts to discover the truth of the virus's origins have been shut down. This has made bat research far more difficult, and could possibly have broader detrimental effects for the understanding of China's bats.[15]

TROPICS

Journey

Map of the Tropics of China

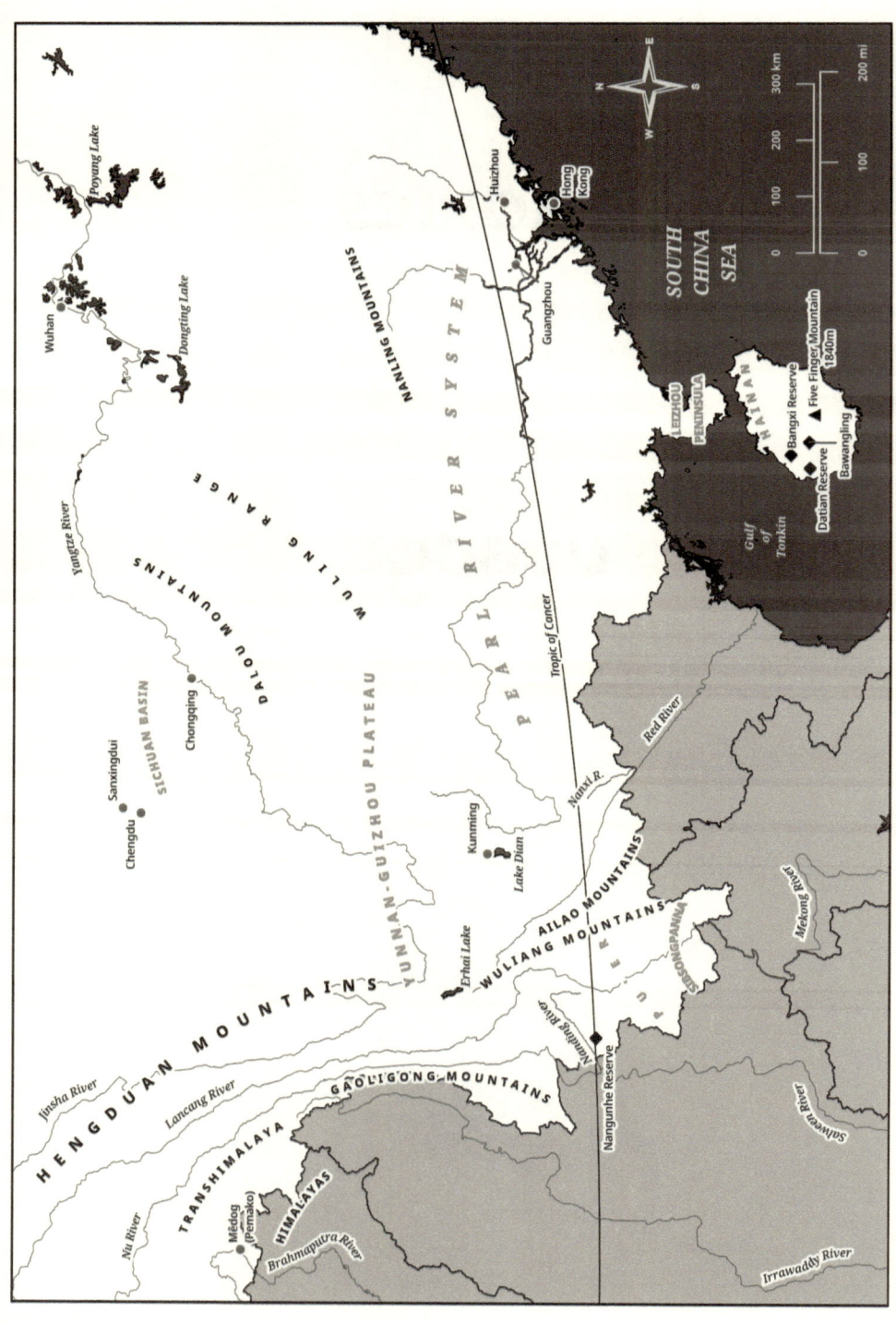

Poyang Lake

Wuhan

Dongting Lake

Yangtze River

NANLING MOUNTAINS

Huizhou

Hong Kong

SOUTH CHINA SEA

Guangzhou

300 km

200 mi

200

100

100

0

0

WULING RANGE

DALOU MOUNTAINS

SICHUAN BASIN

Sanxingdui

Chengdu

Chongqing

YUNNAN-GUIZHOU PLATEAU

PEARL RIVER SYSTEM

Tropic of Cancer

Red River

LEIZHOU PENINSULA

HAINAN

Bangxi Reserve

Five Finger Mountain 1840m

Bawangling

Datian Reserve

Gulf of Tonkin

Kunming

Lake Dian

Nanxi R.

AILAO MOUNTAINS

WULIANG MOUNTAINS

Erhai Lake

XISHUANGBANNA

Mekong River

HENGDUAN MOUNTAINS

GAOLIGONG MOUNTAINS

Nanding River

Nangunhe Reserve

Jinsha River

Lancang River

TRANSHIMALAYA

HIMALAYAS

Nu River

Mêdog (Pemako)

Brahmaputra River

Salween River

Irrawaddy River

COVERING only a few small areas at the southern edges of the country, China's tropics host an outsize fraction of its biodiversity. There is no consensus on precisely which areas should be considered tropical, but tropical monsoon forests and rainforests reach approximately up to a latitude of 22°30'N. That line lies near the very south of China, with only small amounts of Guangdong, Guangxi, and Yunnan, as well as all of Hainan, lying below it. Flora typical of the tropical ecosystems of Southeast Asia predominate south of that line, including familiar crops such as coffee and pineapple.[1] Here, too, are found many tropical animals at their northern limits. The notable exception to this demarcation is the southern edge of Mêdog, the southeast of Tibet, where the South Asian monsoon brings up moisture and warm air abundant enough to make it one of the most northerly tropical ecosystems in the world.[2]

As with the forested lands of Central and South China, dramatic human modification of China's tropical landscape began millennia in the past. Over 4,000 years ago the land was heavily forested. Although humans certainly lived within the forests, as hunters and fisherfolk they had a very light impact on the vegetation. The arrival of early rice farming led to the fragmentation of some lowland forests beginning about 4,000 years ago, but it was only around 2,000 years later, after the arrival of intensive paddy rice cultivation, that forest clearance became widespread. The river deltas and coastal plains were the first to see widespread deforestation, while the highlands were left comparatively untouched. By 1000 CE, after successive waves of migrants had arrived—often in response to wars in the north—even the mountains had suffered significant tree loss.[3]

Compared to farther north, Han Chinese settlement of the tropics was slow to succeed, largely due to the formidable deterrence of tropical diseases, malaria foremost among them. Having settled the coastal strip running south and west through Guangdong relatively early in China's dynastic history, it took until the Ming and Qing before the tropical regions of Guangxi and Yunnan were finally subdued.[4] These two provinces are still home to a large fraction of China's ethnic minorities, most of whose beliefs and practices towards the natural world were vastly different than the Han's. Those differences have been partly stamped out over the course of decades of Communist rule, but many rural communities maintain significantly different cultural practices than the Han majority.

The worst damage to China's tropics came in the twentieth century. One of the primary causes for the clearance of the forests was the country's desire to build its own rubber industry. The Nationalist government had made a failed attempt in 1947 to grow rubber in Sibsongpanna,[5] Yunnan's southernmost prefecture, and the Communists were quick to take up the challenge. With limited trade options, Maoist China was eager to become self-sufficient in producing strategic materials such as rubber. Its ally the Soviet Union was also keen for a friendly supplier, but after Sino-Soviet relations soured, China's rubber plantations became crucial for national defense.[6]

Similar to other inhospitable frontier regions, many of the first settlers assigned to the plantations were Red Army veterans and party cadres. Small plantations were set up in Sibsongpanna in 1953, but the first real impetus for expansion came with the escalation of the Vietnam War, with huge flows of matériel flowing from China to North Vietnam. Only a few years later masses of students arrived. After wreaking havoc in the cities in the first years of the Cultural Revolution, Chairman Mao decided the Red Guards had become too troublesome even for his use, and sent them to the countryside, nominally to learn from the peasants. The educated city kids were put to work clearing forests and planting rubber trees. In the spirit of the times, expert scientific advice was brushed aside, and rubber trees were planted at higher latitudes and altitudes than suitable. Many of these trees subsequently died over the cold winter of 1974–1975.[7]

The students' efforts caused immense damage to the forests, and consequently to the wildlife. Not only was a great amount of habitat destroyed or fragmented, but the students and locals hunted many of the native species and harvested many plants such as rattan.[8] In not only Yunnan but Hainan, too, forest was also logged for timber, or cleared to plant *Eucalyptus*, tea, and sugarcane.[9] The end of the Maoist period saw China reopen to world markets, but this only spurred the domestic rubber industry, as China's manufacturing expanded and required ever greater inputs. Opening to the market also led to more forest clearance for tea and other commercial crops, so forest cover continued to decline until only recently, with predictable consequences for the resident wildlife.[10]

Megafaunal Retreat

From the Yangtze Valley south to Guangdong and west to Sichuan, elephants once roamed much of the land that is now China. Over 3,000 years ago they were still widespread in the Yangtze Valley, and the artists of the Shang dynasty were familiar enough with elephants to depict them with great accuracy in their bronzes.[1] But over the succeeding millennia China's elephants moved southward, casualties of humanity's drive to turn forests to fields.

The exact northern limits of elephants in China is still a mystery. The few remains that have been found in the Yellow River Valley are tens of thousands of years old, but elephants still cropped up in the writings and artwork of the early dynasties. The absence of more recent elephant remains from the region strongly suggests they did not live north of the Huai River Basin.[2] Their presence in artworks from the north was instead likely a result of their remarkable size and nature. The Shang and their successors the Zhou were familiar with the lands to the south, and in all probability welcomed the occasional elephant brought north as a curiosity or tribute.[3]

The retreat of the elephants had begun by the end of the Warring States period, at which time the statesman Han Fei (韓非, c. 280–233 BCE) remarked: "People rarely see living elephants, but if they obtain the bones of a dead elephant, they can imagine a living elephant based on their form. Because of this, everything people use to form an idea or mental image is called 'elephant.'"[4] Yet in the Huai River Basin, covering much of the land between the Yellow and Yangtze Rivers, elephants lived for many centuries, through the unification of China (221 BCE) and the Han dynasty into the golden age of the Tang. As the climate warmed again in the early years of the Song, elephants even seemingly began to push north. But their attempts at recolonization of long-lost ancestral lands failed; the new human residents did not welcome them.[5]

China's population had gradually increased from the time of the Shang, and, as the population grew, more land came under cultivation. Farmland was created from wilderness, and the clearance of woodlands deprived the elephants of their habitat. Peasants had opened land from before the Zhou, but it was not until centuries later that humans overtook climate as the dominant restraint on elephants' range. Agricultural expansion in the Huai Basin pushed elephants south of the

river by the end of the Tang, and, once the climate turned favorable, elephants venturing north discovered the landscape—and the people on it—could no longer accommodate them.

As a general rule, elephants and agriculturalists do not get along. Both prefer lowlands but disagree on how to use them. Elephants require tree cover; farmers want trees cleared. Even a mixture of cleared and forested land will not bring peace. Elephants, as sensible beings, prefer an easy life. If it is easiest to eat crops growing within easy reach and in convenient abundance, they will eat crops. If it is quickest to cut through a farmer's field on the way to their destination they will trample whatever is in their way. Understandably, farmers who lose the fruits of their labor to the caprice of a parade of pachyderms will do their best to become a nuisance to the elephants in turn. Thus, in time the elephants learn to avoid humans, but as their habitat continues to dwindle, and with it the wild-growing foods they prefer, eventually they turn to the crops they had long avoided.

The maharajas of Indian kingdoms carefully protected their forests and the elephant herds within so that they could maintain corps of war elephants. In China, however, pachyderms were not used as beasts of battle or burden.[6] Only one Chinese kingdom—the Southern Han (917–971), which covered most of modern Guangdong and Guangxi—is known to have maintained a herd of war elephants, but it was defeated in a hail of crossbow bolts while defending against an invading Song army.[7] For China's rulers, grain was far more valuable than forests or elephants. With imperial blessings and encouragement, the Chinese spread south and west over the centuries, clearing the land as they went. Forests fell, crops sprouted, elephants retreated.

Slowly the Chinese were winning their long war against the proboscideans. After their failed push north in the early Song, elephants fell back past the Huai and to the Yangtze, then still southward until they were no longer seen north of Fujian. They held out longer farther west in the mountains of Central China, but there, too, humanity's advance shrank the elephants' range. Once found across Central China, over the course of the Song dynasty they were squeezed into the rugged provinces of Jiangxi and Hunan. But the pace wasn't fast enough for the tillers. By the middle of the twelfth century the Song dynasty's need for arable land was too urgent to continue the slow advance. The loss of the north to the Jurchens' Jin dynasty had resulted in a massive influx of refugees who needed settling, and elephants were an obstacle to be brushed aside.[8]

For millennia the Chinese had sought elephants alive and dead. Alive, they were prized as grand display pieces for the sovereign. Dead, they were valued for their tusks, hides, and meat. Shang oracle bone inscriptions record that elephants were featured as sacrifices to the royal ancestors, and their meat was prized as some of the finest available.[9] Ivory, however, was far more coveted. In ancient China the only materials more precious than ivory were jade and gold.[10] Ivory has been found in many tombs from the Shang and Zhou, and far to the southwest, just north of Chengdu in Sichuan. Excavations at the Bronze Age site of Sanxingdui have revealed not only dozens of ivory carvings and artifacts but piles of whole elephant tusks.[11] Elephants lived in Sichuan at least through the Han, when the local chieftains of the region sent them to Chang'an as tribute.[12] There is some evidence that they may have held on in the south of the Sichuan Basin through the Tang.[13] Demand for tusks and trunks, the most delicious cut of the elephant, grew with each succeeding dynasty.[14] Some people believed that, when hunted, elephants knew they were being pursued for their tusks, and before their death would break them against rocks to spite the hunter.[15]

As the Song sought more tillable land, officials in Fujian and Guangdong put bounties on elephants to speed the killings. These were to provide the courage to hunt such formidable creatures. Elephants were not generally feared; when confronted they were more likely to leave in annoyance than to attack. The exceptions were marauding males expelled from their groups, and of course elephants facing death at the hands of humans. Death underfoot an enraged pachyderm was all too possible a fate, as records from the time make clear. One account tells of the arrival of an elephant outside the walls of Huizhou in 1113. When the elephant rebuffed efforts to scare it away, hundreds of armed townsfolk sallied forth and surrounded the creature. Only one reckless man, Meng Shunguo the imperial customs collector, attacked. He fired dozens of arrows into the elephant only to be swatted down and trampled, "dying with his head smashed, ribs snapped, chest crushed, and guts spilling out."[16] Killing elephants was a dangerous business.

Having reached the southern edge of China, the elephants now retreated west, Chinese settlers pushing them all the way. Warfare has occasionally been kind to North China's wildlife. For centuries from the Han dynasty forward, the raids and invasions of horsemen from the steppes of Inner Asia drove masses of settled Chinese from their lands. In the times when the nomadic invaders stayed and founded their own dynasties, many of the emptied fields reverted to the wild. After the grasses, shrubs, and trees reclaimed abandoned farms, animals arrived in turn, until eventually farmers returned to again clear and sow the land. The elephants to the south rarely enjoyed such luck. Instead they found themselves deprived of more and more territory as the refugees from the north fled south. In their new home the new arrivals cleared land for farming, and predictably came into conflict with the resident wildlife.

The Song dynasty dissolved with the arrival of the Mongol Yuan dynasty. As Kublai Khan's armies advanced they left much of Guangdong's Pearl River Basin depopulated in their wake. In the following years settlers began to trickle back in, but the chaos of the fall of the Yuan and the rise of the Ming dynasty reversed the flow of humanity, and the forests and the elephants received a reprieve of several generations. But peace brought people, and soon the Chinese did as they always had and forced the elephants west. Some fell to professional elephant hunters, who sought their ivory and trunks.[17] Others died at the hands of farmers furious at the loss of their crops, and, despite the dangers of confronting elephants, well coordinated bands of villagers could succeed in killing an entire herd.[18]

Elephants had survived in the southern lands for centuries alongside the native communities—many of them of the Kra-Dai ethnic groups—who eventually fled southwest, and with the ancestors of the Zhuang, Miao, and others farther west who are now minorities within China. Like the Chinese they were agriculturalists, but their practices did not lead to the permanent destruction of the forests. Though they hunted and even tamed elephants as draught animals and war mounts, but not to the point of extinction.[19]

As the Chinese moved south and west, they not only expelled the elephants, they also drove out—or more often conquered and attempted to assimilate—the local peoples. This was often a slow and violent process. The southwest was thus for several centuries a large frontier, and the Ming and later the Qing kept large troop concentrations there to maintain the imperial claim. Soldiers were put to use not only subduing rebellious natives, but also capturing or killing elephants. Sometimes they confronted the natives and elephants together, such as in 1388 when the Ming defeated the Tai kingdom of

Möng Mao and its elephant corps. Elephants taken alive at the end of the battle were sent to Nanjing to join the emperor's herd of ceremonial performing pachyderms.[20]

Over the course of the Ming and Qing dynasties and through the Republican era, elephants retreated out of Guangxi, then Guizhou, and farther and farther south through Yunnan. By the time the People's Republic was established in 1949, they remained only at the far southwest of China, squeezed against the border with Laos and Myanmar. The first team of scientists sent to survey Sibsongpanna in 1956 was doubtful there even were elephants still in Chinese territory, but to their surprise they found that some survived. Research on the pachyderms suffered a severe blow the next year when many scientists were persecuted as part of the Anti-Rightist Campaign that swept the country to purge the Communist Party's enemies, real and imagined.[21]

Research carried on to some degree, with surveys discovering more herds spread across the region.[22] Until the Cultural Revolution ended, however, little work was done to study or protect the elephants. The rubber boom instead claimed much of the forest that had supported them, and even the nature reserves that had been set aside suffered serious damage. Rubber was such a high priority, and elephants such a low one, that apparently no one spoke up in defense of the pachyderms. Guns were prevalent amongst the region's villagers, and men were free to shoot at elephants that encroached on their fields.[23]

The first full survey of China's elephants, conducted in 1976, estimated only 150 remained.[24] By then the populations that had been detected in the 1960s were already starting to fracture and disappear.[25] Herds that had once been free to move across China's border found themselves separated from populations on the other side.[26] And the populations within China were increasingly cut off from one another.

By the 1980s the government had come around to protecting the elephants, and sought to put an end to hunting and retaliatory killings. Farmers began to receive compensation for crop damage, but there was little success in ending their conflicts with the elephants.[27] The elephants largely kept to a few remaining reserves, but farms and fields were littered within the boundaries, and the degraded forests did not provide enough wild forage.[28] Conflict was a regular event, especially when grains ripened late in the year, and deaths became a startlingly common occurrence. Occasionally elephants are the victims, but more often it is people. The reported number of elephant-caused deaths may not always be accurate, but what numbers are available suggest that—at least in the recent past—China's elephants were among the world's most deadly.[29]

Warding off elephants from crops became far more difficult once they came under strict legal protection. Shooting at elephants carried the danger not only of provoking a furious pachyderm, but the fury of the state. People fought back anyway, often under the cover of night. Then in the late 1990s the authorities confiscated guns, and suddenly the elephants had nothing to fear.[30] Many households were eventually relocated out of the reserves, but it was not enough to end the elephants' crop raiding. In 2009 and 2010 local authorities developed special insurance schemes to help villagers receive compensation.[31]

In the past decade, as the growth of rubber has slowed, tea has taken its place as the new cash crop.[32] Deforestation and the construction of dams and highways have cut up the landscape and isolated elephants to shrinking patches of habitat.[33] Recent improvements in conservation have allowed the largest population, in Sibsongpanna Prefecture, to grow from only 100 elephants in 1976 to nearly 300 today.[34] But the increase was not simply from new births; populations from other parts of Yunnan abandoned their homes and migrated to Sibsongpanna. Others came from neighboring Laos, where for a time poaching was so severe that some elephants fled to China.[35] For decades, a small population in Nangunhe Reserve has been completely isolated from other elephants not only in China but also in neighboring Myanmar. The group is now restricted to a reserve with under 30 sq km (11.6 sq mi) of suitable habitat, far below the minimum wild elephants should have. With so little space, the Nangunhe elephants have not grown in number for over forty years.[36]

In March 2020 a herd of elephants left their home within the Xishuangbanna Nature Reserve and headed north.[37] For months they continued on, trampling through farmers' fields, through villages and cities, frequently feeding off the food and water people had set aside for themselves or their livestock. As they made their way through a thoroughly human landscape, the authorities pulled out all the stops to both smooth and shape their path. Roadblocks were erected to divert them, piles of fruits and forage were dumped to feed them, watering holes dug and filled to slake their thirst and give them relief from the heat. The efforts succeeded in protecting both people and elephants from one another and gained brief worldwide attention. After reaching the outer districts of Yunnan's capital Kunming, the herd finally turned around, and in December 2021—after a roundtrip of 1,000 km (620 mi)—they arrived back at the reserve.[38]

The herd's failed migration highlighted both the successes and shortcomings of China's efforts at elephant conservation. The years of strict protection have given the elephants the safety required to grow their numbers, but a still badly degraded landscape has left them without the room to do so unless they spill out of their reserves. Even as their population has grown, their patches of forest have continued to shrink. In the spots where forests have been protected, the result has been a denser canopy that shades out the elephants' food plants.[39] Successive droughts in 2019 and 2020 likely triggered the elephants' departure, but with sufficient and healthy habitat such a drastic reaction would not have been necessary.[40]

There is in fact substantial unused habitat into which the elephants could expand, but they are currently cut off from most of those forests. Providing the elephants with corridors and the forests with protection will be crucial to their survival.[41] Without intensive, coordinated conservation work throughout southern Yunnan, China's elephants may not last to the end of this century. Climate change threatens what little habitat remains. Recent projections predict over half the current elephant habitat in China will no longer be suitable in 2050. This will make it impossible for the elephants to survive on their own. There will be too little habitat broken into too many pieces, and the remaining elephants will increasingly come to rely on food they take from people.[42]

Earlier mentioned as denizens of the ancient north, rhinoceroses at one time roamed throughout much of China only to face a fate similar to the elephants. All three Asian species of rhinoceros at some point lived within the lands that now make up the People's Republic, but the Sumatran rhinoceros *Dicerorhinus sumatrensis* was by far the most widespread. There are very few records of the other two species, and it is likely they never lived in more than small slivers of Chinese territory. The last record of the Indian rhinoceros *Rhinoceros unicornis* in China was made in 1920, and of the Javan rhinoceros *R. sondaicus* in 1922.[43]

Although the Sumatran rhinoceros was rare or already extirpated from North China by the middle of the Han dynasty, rhinos survived in the south for centuries longer. Based off literary evidence, scholars believe the great horned creatures still lived in Hunan, Hubei, Guizhou, and Sichuan during the Tang. The imperial court demanded rhino horns as tribute from their southern subjects, as the horns were believed to possess great powers, particularly as a medicinal.[44] It was perhaps most renowned for its supposed ability to detect and treat poisons, which made rhinoceros horn cups *de rigueur* for emperors and others who feared assassins. But that was hardly its only power. In various writings the horns were said to be able to "part water, providing safe passage across rivers...to scare chickens when employed as a vessel for their feed...[and] aid in keeping courtyards free of moisture."[45] China's demand for horn—for both medicinal and decorative use— extended well beyond its borders, reaching throughout South and Southeast Asia as well as to Africa. Imports from Africa had begun at least by the first century CE.[46]

The exact reasons for the rhinos' retreat is not clear. A cooling climate may have played some part, but there is no doubt that overhunting and deforestation for agriculture were major causes. Records of rhinos in the eastern provinces of the Yangtze Valley and west into the Sichuan Basin continued to be made into the Song and Liao dynasties of the early tenth century. Once the Yangtze's rhinos were gone, tribute horn continued to flow from farther south.[47] After the Ming dynasty expanded its reach into the southwest, the local Tusi tribal leaders were required to send horns as tribute, a practice which in southern Yunnan lasted until the rhinos finally disappeared in the early nineteenth century.[48]

The last confirmed record of the Sumatran rhinoceros in China was made in 1916, but locals in the Yunnan borderlands recalled seeing the animals as late as the 1930s.[49] Today the species is critically endangered, believed to number fewer than 250 mature individuals. With little habitat for them in China, with so few survivors, and with the closest of them far off on Sumatra, there is little hope of seeing the rhinoceroses return anytime soon.[50]

At the Frontier

CHINA's tropical lands sit at the northern limits of where tropic ecosystems can reach. This means that many of the species found within them are at the extremes of their own ranges, and in historical times were never widespread within the bounds of China. Disparate species such as the sun bear and binturong are rarely sighted today, and only ever just inside the Chinese border. This is likely a consequence of natural limitations, and there is no indication they were ever far-ranging or common within China, although the historical evidence is admittedly sparse.

Sun bears *Helarctos malayanus* were only confirmed within China in 1972, and the only recent evidence of the species' presence is of a single bear spotted in 2016 just inside Yunnan, less than a kilometer from the Myanmar border. It is unlikely there are any bears resident in China, and certainly no self-sustaining population.[1] The binturong or bearcat *Arctictis binturong*, the largest member of the civet family, has only been verified within China on a few occasions. One was seen in Guangxi in 1926, but by the 1980s the species was a rare sight, limited to Sibsongpanna.[2] No binturong was scientifically confirmed in China from the early 1990s until 2014, when a sole specimen was confiscated from a hunter on the Myanmar border.[3] In the years since, camera traps have captured a scattering of images of live binturongs.[4] But the species' future within China remains in doubt, as local hunters eagerly seek the bearcat, whose meat, they say, tastes like sticky rice.[5]

Another animal that finds the far north of its range in China is the gaur *Bos gaurus*, a species of wild cattle and the largest living bovid; males average 188 cm (6 ft 2 in) at the shoulder and 1,500 kg (3,300 lb) in weight, larger even than the American wood bison *Bison bison athabascae* or the giant eland *Taurotragus derbianus* of Africa. Once found throughout much of South and continental Southeast Asia, the gaur also lived in the forests of southeastern Tibet, the Gaoligong Mountains, and the far southwest of Yunnan in Sibsongpanna and Pu'er. Remains found at the mausoleum of Emperor Wen of Han from over 2,000 years ago may indicate that gaur once lived as far north as the Qinling, though more likely the bones belonged to animals brought north as tribute.[6] Poaching and the fragmentation and loss of their forest habitat to rubber plantations have devastated their numbers in modern times. Gaur are now gone from the Gaoligong range, and in the rest of Yunnan their population has dropped from roughly 1,000 in the late 1950s to only around 200.[7]

豚

A species whose range in China was even more marginal than that of the gaur was the hog deer *Axis porcinus*, a small cervid that has seen its populations crash across Southeast Asia since the 1990s. Within China the hog deer was only known from the Nanding River watershed in southwestern Yunnan, where in 1962 just over ten deer were sighted.

The last record of the species in China came only three years later. Hog deer live in floodplain grasslands and are averse to forests and cultivated land. Local hunters said that in the 1960s the deer were common in the area and were regularly hunted. After the grasslands were converted into agrarian land in the late 1960s and into the 1970s, the deer began to disappear, finally succumbing to the plow and rifle by the early 1980s. There is now no sign of the species in China, and it is unlikely to return without radical improvements to its former habitat.[8]

The South China tiger was not the only tiger subspecies that ranged across China's southern reaches. Small numbers of both the Bengal tiger *Panthera tigris tigris* and Indochinese tiger *P. t. corbetti* lived along the southern border. The Bengal was first noted in 1963 when the cats were found to live in broadleaf forests of southeastern Tibet on the southern slopes of the Himalayas near Assam. They were later found in western Yunnan as well. Not long after scientists learned of their presence, reports arrived of the tigers attacking domestic livestock in Tibet, but after the river valley lowlands were settled in the 1970s they were seen less and less often.[9]

Tiger activity spiked in the 1990s as human encroachment on both their land and their prey took its toll. With an ever-dwindling wild prey base, they turned again to livestock. In one community alone they killed ten percent of the livestock over sixteen months.[10] Tigers were killed in retaliation, or merely by accident when caught in snares, but due to their traditional beliefs many of the local peoples were reluctant to confront the cats. A common belief among Tibetans was that the tigers were manifestations of local deities, and they noted that although the cats may have killed livestock, they did not kill humans.[11]

But the restraint some Tibetans showed was not enough. Surveys from 2013 to 2018 made no sightings of the tigers, and what evidence there was suggested a mere one to three tigers who passed through during the dry season, spending the rest of their time in India. The population was likely never very large, and the deaths suffered in the 1990s proved too much for it to withstand. Nonetheless, two camera traps in Mêdog took three photographs of tigers between October 2018 and the following May, and more cameras spotted tigers from 2020 to 2022. The cats likely split their time between Mêdog and Arunachal Pradesh in India.[12] For now, with the habitat and prey base still badly degraded, there is little chance of the Bengals rebounding in Tibet.[13]

The Indochinese tiger was only discovered to live in Chinese territory when animal collectors went searching for zoo specimens in Sibsongpanna in the 1950s. More of the cats were later found in nearby regions of southern and western Yunnan.[14] In 1995 an estimated thirty to forty tigers remained in Yunnan, but by the next estimate in 2009 only fourteen to twenty were believed to still survive, all of them likely crossing back and forth between China and Myanmar or Laos.[15]

Pushing Towards Extinction

ASIDE from the tiger, leopard, and snow leopard, China is also home to the smallest of the Pantherinae, the clouded leopard *Neofelis nebulosa*. The clouded leopard is primarily arboreal, passing most of its life in the trees. Its short coat is a gray-brown with large "cloud" splotches of solid or mottled black. Even more elusive than the tiger or leopard, the status of clouded leopards in China remains poorly understood. Early Western naturalists reported the cats were found in the south, and Chinese scientists later noticed the leopards were far more widespread, found not only in the southernmost provinces but well north into Central China and even into the west. They were also reported north of the Yangtze, but most—perhaps all—of these were misidentified Asian golden cats, not clouded leopards. Into the 1980s knowledge of their distribution was gleaned almost entirely from the trade in pelts, and little was understood beyond the numbers that hunters brought into trade stations.[1]

Clouded leopards were until recently believed to be more common than any of the larger cats, but their numbers had clearly dropped over the preceding decades. In Jiangxi, where they were believed to be comparatively abundant, the annual number of pelts brought to government agents dropped from an average of 300 in the mid-1950s to only 119 in 1980–1981.[2] Fujian, Hubei, and Hunan each recorded annual takes of about 100 into the 1970s, while Sichuan, Guangdong and other provinces only brought in a few dozen. Guizhou seems to have been the last stronghold for the leopards, maintaining a take of roughly 100 pelts into the 1990s.[3]

Aside from hunting for their pelts the clouded leopards died as targets of the nationwide anti-pest campaigns. Like so many other species, the effects of habitat destruction and fragmentation, and the loss of their prey base further contributed to their decline. Today there is faint hope for the cats. The last record from East China was made in Anhui in 2006, and the last in the west a year later in Sichuan.[4] Elsewhere, between 2007 and 2019, over 900 camera traps spread over ten provinces detected clouded leopards in a total of three places: in two locations in Yunnan along the Laos and Myanmar borders, and one in southeastern Tibet. In 2023 a leopard was sighted in western Yunnan for the first time in eighteen years.[5] The species has seen a terrible drop in numbers across its mainland Asian range, and it appears that now the clouded leopard is all but gone from China.[6] More cats may be found, but for now it seems the clouded leopard has disappeared from China without anyone realizing until it was too late.

There is a sliver of hope, however. Recent efforts to protect forest habitat have begun to bear some fruit, and there is now a growing area that may in due time again be suitable for the leopards. If the prey populations are restored, and the existing stands of forests connected, future decades may see clouded leopards able to return.[7]

犺

Just as happened throughout the rest of China, the disappearance of dholes in the south was largely unnoticed. Some naturalists in the first half of the twentieth century noted the wild dogs were dwindling, and that by the 1920s they were nearly absent from much of Guangdong.[8] The causes of their final disappearance from most of the region were the same as elsewhere—poisoning, snaring, habitat loss, and a depleted prey base.[9] Like clouded leopards, the only places in the south that dholes are still found are in southeastern Tibet and the borderlands of Yunnan.[10]

There are few birds more recognizable than the Indian or blue peafowl *Pavo cristatus*, better known as the peacock.[11] Celebrated in myth, folktale, and philosophy, it is one of the most recognizable birds on the planet, and because of its beauty—the male's beauty, to be exact—people have carried it to nearly every corner of the Earth. There is one other member of the genus *Pavo*, far less renowned but no less beautiful. The green peafowl *Pavo muticus* bears close resemblance to its cousin, but in place of the Indian peafowl's blue the green peafowl is covered in iridescent green feathers. Even the females wear the shimmering green, unlike the rather drab Indian peahens. For much of the year male and female are difficult to tell apart, but in breeding season the male grows the same long, eyespotted train for which the Indian peacock is famed.

In the past the green peafowl lived throughout much of Southeast Asia, from northeastern India to Java. Within China archaeological evidence has placed the green peafowl in Henan up to 5,000 to 6,000 years ago. It is possible that birds native to Henan left behind the bones, or instead that they arrived via prehistoric trade routes. More bones dating between 1046–1 BCE have been unearthed in Shaanxi and Hubei. If green peafowl did in fact once live in those regions, too little is known to say when or why they disappeared. The few dozen available records suggest that by 1000 CE the peafowl were restricted to south and southwest China, and by the Qing dynasty they were found only in Guangdong, Guangxi, and Yunnan. The green peafowl remained widespread throughout the Qing, but towards the end of the dynasty the growing human population—from both births and internal immigration—began to constrict the birds' range.[12]

Little research was done on China's green peafowl until the 1990s, by which time they had been reduced to scattered populations in Yunnan.[13] The spread of smallholder and commercial agriculture caused habitat loss and fragmentation, which contributed to the birds' decline. So, too, did the deliberate killing of the peafowl. In the 1960s and 1970s when agrarian expansion was one of the country's primary goals, farmers were encouraged to lay out poisoned seed to kill entire flocks of green peafowl and other avian pests, a practice that lingered on for many decades. The peafowl were also targeted for their flesh and feathers, and their eggs, too, were collected for food.[14] Just as with the Indian peafowl, males' long train feathers were widely sought as decorative items. Within China the feathers mostly stayed inside Yunnan or were sent to Beijing. They were also traded internationally, finding their way onto the Southeast Asian market.[15]

In the late 1990s the remaining, scattered populations numbered fewer than 100 birds, with one exception that may have passed 200.[16] Pressure did not let up over the next three decades, and today China's green peafowl— now likely under a total of 300 birds— are severely fragmented and reduced to flocks averaging only three to five members.[17] Most are now in central Yunnan, where the bulk of the suitable habitat remains.[18] An artificial breeding program has begun in hopes of building a captive population that can one day augment the wild flocks, but to date the effort still has some hurdles to overcome.[19]

In the last few years the birds' plight has risen in prominence with the filing of China's first preventative civil suit to protect an endangered species. The NGO Friends of Nature filed the case in 2017 to stop the construction of a dam on the upper reaches of the Red River in central Yunnan.[20] If completed, the dam threatens to inundate some of the last remaining green peafowl habitat, which could deal a fatal blow to the population. The case has won the peafowl at least a few more years; construction began in 2016, but was ordered to stop two years later. In 2020 a court ordered that the dam-builder must cease work until it completed an environmental impact assessment, and a higher court upheld the ruling the following year. Unfortunately for the birds, the same court dismissed Friends of Nature's request to completely cancel construction of the dam.[21] Judges have decided the fate of species before, but in China, the green peafowl is the first to be offered salvation or doom by court order.

猱

Gibbons are now rare in China, with small populations of a few species found only in a handful of patches in the far south. Yet once they were spread far to the north and east, until over the centuries they lost their homes as the forests were felled. The fossil record indicates that gibbons once lived across southern China and as far north as the Yangtze Delta. Modern analysis suggests that other regions of China possessed suitable gibbon habitat as well, notably Shandong, Shanxi, and Shaanxi in the north.[22] The discovery of the remains of *Junzi imperialis* in a third century BCE Shaanxi tomb suggests those northern habitats may in fact have hosted gibbon populations for some stretch of the past two millennia.[23]

In Chinese art and literature, the gibbon stood in opposition to the ill-mannered and earthy macaque. Gibbons, aloof in the high canopy, became a symbol for the detached and mystical side of existence, and thus were a favorite subject of poets and philosophers.[24] Gibbons are consequently a common sight in Chinese paintings from the Song dynasty onwards. As the animals themselves became rarer, inaccuracies increasingly crept into their depictions. The apes also became a common trope in poetry, their calls depicting the mournful longing for a faraway home, or happier times since lost.[25]

Like other primates, gibbons were sometimes kept as pets. The *Huainanzi* states that King Zhuang of the state of Chu (楚莊王, r. 613–591 BCE) was so fond of his pet that when it was lost he ordered an entire forest razed so that it might be found.[26] Since they kept to the high forest canopy and could not easily be trapped, capturing gibbons alive was a difficult task. The preferred method was to find a mother gibbon with young, and then to shoot her with an arrow or dart. Once she fell dead from the tree—her young still clinging to her body—the hunter would take the baby.[27]

One caveat should be kept in mind concerning gibbons' historical distribution in China. A recent paper has reexamined past scholarship and concluded that many of the historical records believed to refer to gibbons are most likely instead references to François' langurs.[28] If their analysis is correct, the current consensus on gibbons' past distribution will need to be reexamined. This does not mean that the general course of events will prove to have been a fiction, but more likely that the minutiae of the history will require revision.

Although the recently discovered gibbon species *Junzi imperialis* has been extinct at least for a few hundred years, China is still home to several more gibbon species, all confined to the far south. As is true of the snub-nosed monkeys and langurs, the gibbons have all been reduced to small remnant populations confined to extremely restricted and fragmented ranges. In all cases the primary culprits are the usual suspects of habitat loss and hunting.

Gibbons have been an object of some fascination in Chinese culture for over a millennium, yet the status of their populations was poorly known until quite recently. Scientists were not even aware that one species, the lar gibbon *Hylobates lar*, lived in China until the 1970s, when several groups were found near the Myanmar border.[29] When scientists returned in later years, they could no longer find the gibbons. The last sighting was made in 1988, though for years afterwards few truly believed the gibbons were gone.[30] No gibbons were spotted during a survey in 1992, but their calls were detected, confirming that at least a few remained. The available habitat had shrunk dramatically, however, and when subjected to the further pressure of hunting the lar gibbons could no longer survive. Villagers recalled that they heard gibbon calls every morning in the 1960s. Four decades later a final survey found no trace of the lar gibbons, and in 2009 they were declared to be extinct within China.[31]

Sadly, the lar gibbon is likely not the only species to have been extirpated from China in recent years. The calls of another species, the northern white-cheeked gibbon *Nomascus leucogenys*, were heard every morning in many rural villages in southern Yunnan between the Mekong and Red Rivers. Over a thousand of the gibbons still lived in the forests in the 1960s, but over the next two decades their home was replaced with rubber plantations, driving their numbers down to perhaps only a hundred, all found in a single county.[32] Men of the local Aini people hunted the gibbons, especially the females, as a successful kill of a gibbon female was considered proof of one's status as a good husband. The government unwittingly exacerbated the threat of hunting when officials handed out guns so that locals could act as militia during the brief 1979 war with Vietnam. In the time it took for the guns to be reclaimed over the next several years, the area's wildlife saw a huge decline at the hands of the newly armed locals.[33] By the end of the 1980s only thirty-six white-cheeked gibbons were believed to survive in China. After conducting extensive surveys and finding no evidence of their presence, scientists concluded by 2013 that China's *N. leucogenys* were extinct.[34]

Today the most numerous and widespread gibbon species in China is the black crested gibbon *Nomascus concolor*. Males are entirely black, while females are a golden buff with a black crest atop their heads. *N. concolor* is native to much of Yunnan, but now few survive outside of the Wuliang and Ailao Mountains near the center of the province.[35] The Ailao Mountains host about 270 gibbons divided into dozens of groups spread over a large area.[36] In the Wuliang Mountains there were 104 groups—likely close to 1,000 individuals—indicating that the population is probably growing.[37] However, limited habitat availability and competition with macaques and langurs over food and space likely constrain their growth.[38] In southern Yunnan the situation is dire; at last count there were likely fewer than twenty-five black crested gibbons left.[39]

The black crested gibbons in the Wuliang Mountains are by far the best studied population. For a time practically every hunter in the area targeted the primates. Hunting seems to have peaked in the 1960s and 1970s before petering out over the following decade. Logging was also a major threat and wiped out large areas of gibbon habitat. The combined effects led to the disappearance of gibbons from several areas of the mountains, while the surviving groups became separated from one another.[40] Groups became so isolated that young gibbons could not leave to find new homes, and were forced to stay with their birth families, leading to inbreeding.[41] With better protection of the forests, most of the groups have reconnected, although there remain a small number of divisions.[42] For now, at least in the Wuliang Mountains, threats to the gibbons seem manageable, and they are likely past the worst danger.

Far less widespread and numerous than the black crested gibbon is the cao vit gibbon *Nomascus nasutus*. Both the cao vit gibbon and Hainan gibbon were originally thought to be subspecies of *N. concolor*, but both have since been deemed their own species.[43] *N. nasutus* was once found in much of the southeast, but its population declined so radically that by the 1950s it was believed extinct in China. In neighboring Vietnam, it survived into the 1960s before records stopped when war intervened. Scientists did not know the fate of the species until 2002 when a small remnant population was rediscovered in Vietnam.[44]

Just four years later, in 2006, scientists heard that gibbons still lived in a limestone forest in remote southwest Guangxi on the Vietnamese border. When the area was first surveyed it was clearly in need of immediate protection. The forest was almost devoid of timber trees, while lower value trees of any size were cut down for charcoal. Luckily some of the plants on which gibbons feed were of no value to locals and so were left untouched.[45] Follow up work estimated that only three groups totaling nineteen cao vit gibbons lived in Chinese territory.[46]

Since their rediscovery, the cao vit gibbons of both Vietnam and China have received extensive attention from scientists of both countries and beyond. Although their range remains tightly constrained due to a lack of habitat, their numbers grew steadily over the last two decades.[47] Estimates of their numbers in both countries consistently hovered around twenty groups of 120 gibbons.[48] However, a new and more accurate method of counting the population has revealed the gibbons to be far fewer in number than presumed. The latest survey estimated only eleven groups of seventy-four gibbons, with perhaps a few additional dispersing individuals.[49] Although they are now well protected, continued human disturbance and forest fragmentation limit their further growth.[50] With a much smaller, albeit growing population than believed only several years ago, there is a renewed urgency to study and preserve the survivors.

Hainan

JUST 20 km (12 mi) off the Leizhou Peninsula that juts from western Guangdong is Hainan, China's only island province. Once covered in lush tropical forest, it is now a tourist mecca with only a few remaining patches of its original vegetation. Just over 35,000 sq km (13,500 sq mi), Hainan is large enough to support one of the most biologically diverse communities in China.[1] However it is much too small for its biodiversity to compare to the great rainforests of Southeast Asia, Central Africa, or South America.

The first known people to settle Hainan were the Hlai, known in Chinese as the Li. The Hlai—whose descendants are the largest ethnic minority on the island—traditionally lived by hunting, gathering, and practicing shifting agriculture. Hainan was initially brought into the Chinese realm during the first century BCE, but was soon abandoned. Until only recently the island held a grim reputation as a malarial wasteland beyond the edge of civilization, populated with savage natives and teeming with deadly creatures and maladies. Han settlers and administrators eventually returned, but largely kept to the island's northeastern plains, then over the centuries they took over the coastal strip and pushed into the interior's lowlands. The Chinese cleared the jungle just as they did on the mainland, which forced the Hlai—reliant on the forests—to retreat into the highlands.[2]

The Hlai managed to seize the island away from the Han in the chaotic final years of the Yuan dynasty, but the Ming wrested back control, and over the course of the dynasty Han settlements expanded substantially, especially in the mid-sixteenth century. By then the Chinese were pushing deep into the interior, and settlers burned large tracts of forest, turning much of the land they left uncultivated into savanna or grassland. This expansion largely stopped in the chaos of the Ming collapse, but after more mainland settlers arrived during the late Qing, the destruction began anew and at an accelerated pace. Han and assimilated Hlai had settled nearly all of the island by the end of the eighteenth century.[3]

Hainan became a largely lawless place after the fall of the Qing. The Japanese occupied part of the island from 1939 to 1945, and during that time logged large stretches of forest to supply their war effort. After the Communist regime took over, the forests continued to shrink, logged for timber and replaced with plantations of rubber and

Eucalyptus. Although the remnant natural forests came under legal protection in 1994, they have nonetheless continued to disappear as plantations expand. Today there is vanishingly little of the original ecosystem intact, and the forests' wildlife now struggles to survive in the small patches of habitat that still stand.[4]

猿

As precarious as things are for the cao vit gibbons, the Hainan gibbons *Nomascus hainanus* are even closer to extinction. As their name suggests, Hainan gibbons are found only on Hainan. Almost identical in appearance to the black-crested and cao vit gibbons, the Hainan gibbons hold the dubious distinction of being the rarest primate species in China, and perhaps the entire world. The few survivors have spent the last several decades teetering on the edge of extinction, and their future is still far from assured.

Although Han Chinese have been on Hainan for two millennia, and many educated men were banished to the island during the dynastic era, few writers left behind any observations about the island's wildlife.[5] The oldest extant reference to gibbons in Hainan is from an eleventh century poem. The author was one of China's great literary figures, Su Shi (蘇軾, also known by his pen name Su Dongpo 蘇東坡, 1037–1101), who was exiled to Hainan—at that time the Song dynasty's most dreaded backwater. In his poem "Baijiadu" he mentions the sound of gibbon song, by then a well-established trope in Chinese poetry, but in his case likely an accurate description of the music of many mornings:[6]

> In Baijiadu the western sun longs to set;
> From summit to valley, the verdant mountains
> sing with the music of gibbons and birds. [7]

The gibbons entered modern scientific literature when Robert Swinhoe toured Hainan in 1870. He was aware of the local "Black Ape" and attempted to secure specimens—dead or alive—before returning to the mainland. Many of the people he encountered knew of or and had even seen the gibbons, but his search proved fruitless except for a portion of a skull and a pair of ulnae, the long forearms bones, which a local official had intended to use as chopsticks.[8]

Records from local gazetteers suggest gibbons once lived across most of Hainan.[9] They had likely begun to disappear from the most heavily settled areas by the end of the nineteenth century. Despite their decline, genetic assessment of specimens from the time suggest the island-wide population stood around 10,000.[10] By 1900 the gibbons were found primarily in the island's interior, and they lost more and more habitat as more people moved to the island. The first investigation of the gibbons' status in 1964 concluded there had been roughly 2,000 of the apes still alive around 1950.[11] From that point their situation rapidly deteriorated, and they plunged towards extinction.

Up to the 1950s the gibbons had primarily faced the usual dual threat of hunting and habitat loss to farmland. But it was the arrival of China's rubber industry that sent the gibbon population into free-fall. Maoist China's need for a domestic rubber supply sparked the destruction of immense stretches of Hainan's remaining natural vegetation. Entire forests were clear cut and replaced with rubber. Gibbons cannot survive in such plantations, and where native vegetation was allowed to grow back, the resulting mix of pine and fir were equally unsuited to their needs. The result was that gibbons and many other species disappeared from most of the island, left only in shrinking patches of primary forest. When the market economy returned in the 1980s, the destruction only accelerated as more money and people came to the island. By 1999, rubber, other crops, and expanding infrastructure and industry had destroyed over ninety-five percent of Hainan's natural vegetation.[12]

On top of the near total loss of their habitat, the gibbons faced constant danger from hunters. Between the 1960s and 1980s local hunters and employees of state logging companies killed hundreds of gibbons. Many were sold, their bones made into a medicinal paste used to treat arthritis.[13] The combined effect was catastrophic. From an estimated 2,000 at mid-century, the gibbons fell to between 450 and 500 by 1978, to forty or fifty in 1983, and as low as thirty by 1995. By 2003 only thirteen Hainan gibbons were alive, confined to a single spot on the island at the core of the Bawangling Nature Reserve, a mere 66 sq km (25.5 sq mi).[14]

Luckily for the species, the gibbons at Bawangling finally received the protection they needed. With increasing attention from scientists, better protection from rangers and law enforcement, and growing efforts to protect and restore habitat, the gibbons began the slow process of rebuilding their numbers. By 2008 the thirteen gibbons had grown to seventeen or twenty.[15] Three years later they reached twenty-five.[16] As their numbers expanded the gibbons began to form new groups, growing from two to four by 2015.[17]

In 2021 the Bawangling reserve was subsumed into the newly established Hainan Tropical Rainforest National Park, enshrining the Hainan gibbons as one of the country's foremost conservation priorities. The gibbons now seem on the path to recovery, but they are hardly in the clear. A fifth group formed in 2019, and the latest count in 2024 found forty-two gibbons, most among the aforementioned groups, but with a handful of males and females living solitary lives.[18] Conservationists are now worried that the gibbons' growth has not reached what scientists believe to be its full potential. The reasons for this are not clear, but, with more research, perhaps eventually the gibbons can be helped to multiply more quickly.[19] They need any boost they can get.

The Hainan gibbon is hardly the only critically endangered animal on the island. Eld's deer *Rucervus eldii*, otherwise known as the brow-antlered deer or thamin, is an elegant, medium-sized deer now endangered across its entire range.[20] There are four subspecies of *eldii*, one native to Manipur in Northeast India, one to the central plains of Myanmar, and a third to the lowlands of Thailand, Laos, Cambodia, and Vietnam.[21] The Hainan eld's deer is considered to be its own subspecies, *R. e. hainanus*; it is smaller than its mainland counterparts, and the shape of it antlers less elaborate.[22]

Eld's deer are believed to have once populated southern China, and crossed to Hainan by a land bridge in the distant past. Eventually the mainland population perished, but the island deer survived. Records from the early sixteenth to the early twentieth century show the deer were widespread across the lowlands of Hainan, and were most numerous on the western plains.[23] However, by the 1920s they were already disappearing from parts of the island,[24] and by the 1950s, they were gone from all but six counties, restricted to less than 300 sq km (116 sq mi) of territory.[25]

The Hainan population of *eldii* saw a precipitous decline starting in the 1950s. No thorough counts were made until the following decade, and the disruption of the Cultural Revolution turned the work into a nearly decade-long affair. Finally scientists came to an estimate of about 100 deer remaining on the island. Yet by 1976 they could be found at only two locations. In Bangxi district there remained twenty deer; in Datian district another twenty-six. Realizing the severity of the situation, the government established two nature reserves, one for each population. The Datian Nature Reserve covered over 20 sq km (7.7 sq mi) at its establishment, but soon agricultural land encroached on it, and by 1990 it stood at only 13.14 sq km (5 sq mi). Bangxi Nature Reserve had been significantly smaller, and by 1982 it was defunct—all the deer within had been poached.[26]

Habitat loss was of course a major cause of *eldii*'s decline. The deer disappeared from Hainan's east over the course of the Qing, and were largely gone by 1700 in the face of waves of settlers arriving from the mainland.[27] The process repeated itself in the west after the People's Republic was established. From the 1950s to the 1980s the available natural habitat collapsed by roughly eighty-five percent, dropping another ten over the next two decades.[28] Their habitat had been converted to farmland or turned over to commodity production for sugarcane, sesame, rubber, and more.[29]

Hunting of the deer was primarily for subsistence until the 1950s. At that time they came into great demand for their purported medicinal properties, fetching prices ten times that of farmed sika or sambar.[30] Eating *eldii* venison was said to protect against disease; it could prevent one feeling cold while swimming; it would help cure a woman's infertility; and the benefits of consuming deer meat would pass down to future generations. A deer's velvet, bones, heart, blood, skin, tail, sinews, as well as deer fetuses and penises all had their own uses. Since the demand for deer parts made them a market commodity, their rarity only made them more valuable, drawing more hunters to seek them out.[31]

Hunting continued unabated even after the deer were given legal protection. Organized hunting parties undertook much of the poaching. After wiping out the Bangxi population of deer by 1982, they turned to the last available population at Datian. Poaching continued into the 2000s, but the deer at Datian enjoyed enough protection to withstand it.[32] Fences went up to keep the poachers out, but with inadequate funding only 1 sq km (0.4 sq mi) was enclosed to begin with. Over the years the fences were pushed out to include more and more of the reserve, until in 1995 it covered the whole of the reserve region. By 1993 the deer had increased in number to 375, becoming too densely packed for the reserve's resources to support.[33]

With careful management the Datian deer population ballooned to over 1,050 in 2003–2004. To relieve the pressure, 484 deer were released to three sites over the next four years. A founding group of eighteen was even sent to revive the failed Bangxi Reserve, where now over 250 deer crowd into only 3.6 sq km (1.4 sq mi). Three herds were released to live wild, though only one—at Mihouling, adjacent to Datian—has survived. The other two herds found the local humans to be too unwelcoming.[34]

Hainan's Eld's deer are now numerous enough and well enough protected within their reserves that they no longer face imminent extinction. They remain intensively managed, however, and there is little prospect in the near future that more than a small number will be able to return to living truly wild. The surrounding human population is still present, and so the habitat available to the deer remains extremely restricted. Even within the reserves their numbers—combined with the arrival of invasive plants—has caused significant degradation of the native vegetation. For now they remain safe from extinction, but they are no longer wild.

Hainan hosts a handful of endemic species, many if not most of them endangered. Among them are two galliform birds, the Hainan peacock-pheasant *Polyplectron katsumatae* and the Hainan partridge *Arborophila ardens*. The peacock-pheasant, a large gray bird with a short crest and ruff, was once found across most of the island, but it now remains only in the mountainous tropical forests of the center and southwest.[35] Massive habitat loss since the 1950s, combined with unrestrained hunting has left the peacock-pheasant perilously close to extinction. In 1990 there were only an estimated 2,700 of the birds remaining, having since fallen to an estimated 1,865.[36] Even though hunters considered the bird too scrawny to target, and it commanded a low price on the market, accidental catches were still more than enough to impact the population.[37] Today the peacock-pheasants are still endangered, but just how rare they are is far from clear. Locals still see the birds, if rarely, but camera traps have caught them often enough to suggest they may be more numerous than previously believed. As cryptic birds that keep to dense forest and avoid humans, they and others like them are exceptionally difficult to monitor.[38]

The Hainan partridge suffered from the same plight as the peacock-pheasant. Found in the evergreen forests, it, too, lost most of its habitat.[39] The partridge seems to be more numerous than the peacock-pheasant, however, with a population last estimated between 3,900 and 5,200 birds. Such numbers, though hardly disastrous, still leave the species vulnerable, especially with the looming threat of climate change.[40]

Trade Species

Rosewood furniture has represented the epitome of Chinese material culture for hundreds of years. Rosewood, *hóngmù* 红木 in Chinese, is an umbrella term for over thirty species of tropical hardwood, many now endangered. Rosewood furniture was made in China as early as the Tang, but only became a coveted symbol of rank and sophistication during the Ming.[1] For much of the Ming it was legally restricted to the highest strata of nobility and literati, but as social divisions crumbled the growing merchant class displayed its wealth by accumulating the material symbols of their social superiors.[2] China's stands of tropical hardwoods had already begun to decline by the fourteenth century, and were so thinned out that during a brief window during the early Ming when the dynasty was open to foreign trade, supplies of rosewood from Southeast Asia were imported to help ease the pressure on trees within China. Once the country closed itself off, pressure on domestic stands grew until several species were nearly wiped out from Chinese territory.[3]

Demand continued unabated throughout the Qing. An imperial monopoly on domestic stands did nothing to protect the trees, merely reserving them for the emperor's projects. Imported rosewood increasingly replaced domestic supplies in the popular market. After being condemned and targeted as a sign of bourgeois excess during the Maoist period, rosewood regained its stature as a symbol of wealth and refined taste.[4] Today, because domestic species of rosewood within China are few and far between, Chinese demand drives an extensive and often illegal trade that has devastated stands across much of the world.

By far the largest snake in China is the Burmese python *Python bivittatus*, among the largest snake species in the world. Snakes have long been both feared and valued in China, in both Han and other cultures. Stories from well over a thousand years ago tell of massive pythons that terrorized the people of the Yunnan's Erhai Lake region, consuming both humans and their livestock. There, winning control of the land for farming meant first exterminating the snakes.[5] To the north, in Tang-era Chang'an, pythons from the south were a source of not fear but medicine. The snakes' gall bladders were reputed to cure bleeding, and large numbers were imported from Nanyue, which encompassed much of China's far south and present-day northern and central Vietnam. The people of Nanyue had their own uses for the serpents, using their bile to protect against malarial miasmas. Some enterprising men had even taken to farming the snakes.[6]

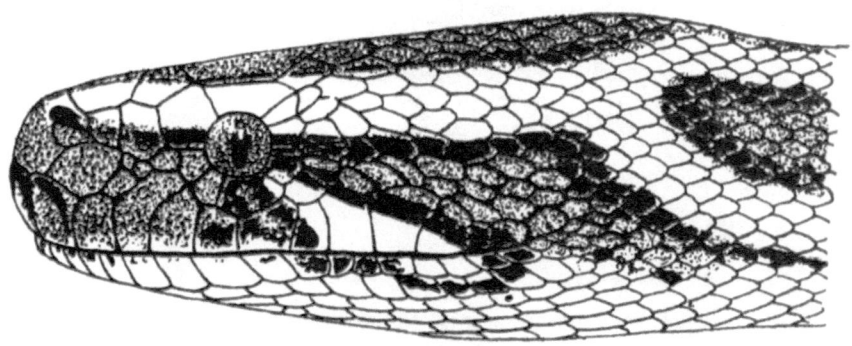

Pythons have remained a valued commodity to the present. Hunting them, however, was a dangerous affair. As time passed and the snakes were found only at increasing distance from market towns, hunters had to capture the serpents alive if they hoped to sell them fresh and unspoiled. This gave the snakes the opportunity to fight back, and some took full advantage. On a tiger hunt in rural Guangdong in 1934, an American adventurer and his party of coolies stumbled across a snake hunter who had grown tired and let down his guard. They found him in a python's embrace, immobile and with his eyes glazed over. They managed to free the man, but the locals said such incidents were an all-too-common occurrence.[7] The pythons were hunted not merely for their medicinal value and meat, but also for their skins, which were turned into leather or used as the preferred covering on musical instruments, particularly the sound box of the *erhu*, a traditional two-stringed, bowed instrument.[8]

At the turn of the twentieth century pythons were found from Fujian south to Guangdong and Hainan, and west into southern and western Yunnan.[9] Hunting led to a dramatic decline in their population. The stocking of snake farms with wild-caught serpents caused further damage, but farming operations now no longer seem reliant on bringing in wild snakes.[10] The shift to farmed and imported snakes and skins has afforded the wild populations enough safety that the Burmese python's level of protection was downgraded in 2020.

Far less formidable reptiles than the pythons are now used in great numbers in Chinese medicine, perhaps none more profusely than the geckos, including the Tokay geckos *Gekko gecko* and *G. reevesii*. Many gecko species are used in traditional medicines around the world, and in China they have had special uses since at least the Tang. At that time geckos were put to a very peculiar end; fed cinnabar until they turned red, the lizards were then ground into a paste and used to paint spots on the bodies of the emperor's concubines. The spots were believed to disappear only when a woman engaged in intercourse, allowing the emperor to determine whether any infidelities were afoot.[11]

In more recent times the geckos have been used for more mundane purposes. They are popular as pets, but their primary use in China is as a medicinal ingredient, used to treat coughs and asthma.

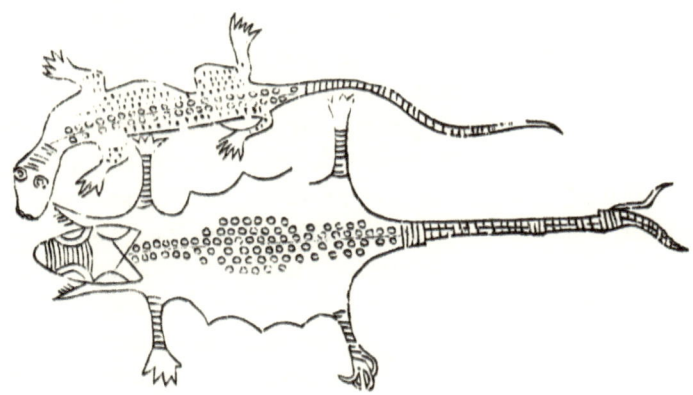

Though caught and farmed within China, demand is so high that millions of the lizards are imported every year.[12] Farmed geckos were originally carefully husbanded, with only their tails—which the lizards can grow back—removed for harvest. However, during the Maoist period, pressure to maximize the utilization of all resources led to the consumption of the entire animal.[13] Hunting was extensive, and harvest numbers peaked by 1965, then quickly collapsed after 1978. The Tokay gecko *G. gecko* was once found across the southernmost provinces of China, but it is now rare within the country. Luckily it is widespread in other parts of Asia, and therefore not in danger of extinction.[14] Reeve's Tokay gecko *G. reevesii* is not so fortunate. The great majority of its range is within China, and it is now found only in a few karst forests. Still in high demand, its long-term survival is uncertain.[15]

Also popular in the pet trade are the Bengal and pygmy slow lorises *Nycticebus bengalensis* and *N. pygmaeus*.[16] Small, fuzzy, and cute, the minuscule primates are eagerly sought as companions, even though as nocturnal and venomous wild animals they are utterly unsuited to the role.[17] But before they came into demand as pets, lorises suffered from the standard threats of habitat destruction and hunting. As late as the 1960s Bengal slow lorises were widespread throughout much of Yunnan and southwestern Guangxi.[18] By the 1980s they were practically wiped out from Guangxi, and only a few hundred were thought to survive in southwestern Yunnan.[19]

Recent surveys in Guangxi suggest that vanishingly few or perhaps no Bengal slow lorises remain. In Yunnan they have disappeared from the northernmost stretch of their range, but they still survive in the southern and western borderlands.[20] Encroachment on loris habitat has driven some populations to survive as best they can in banana plantations, urban greenspaces, or in the highlands. However, the primary threats to the species have been hunting and capture for the pet trade and use in traditional medicine; loris medicinals are believed to cure rheumatism and epilepsy. Small and easily smuggled, policing the illegal loris trade presents a difficult challenge.[21]

Pygmy slow lorises were first recorded in China only in 1986 near the Vietnamese border.[22] Surveys undertaken from 2022 to 2023 along the Nanxi River in southwestern Yunnan found small populations of the pygmies, estimated at a total of under a hundred. They live mostly within and at the edges of nature reserves, and enjoy little in the way of formal protection. The surveyors are hopeful that active management and community engagement may give the pygmy lorises the prospect of a long future within China.[23]

COASTS & MARINE WATERS

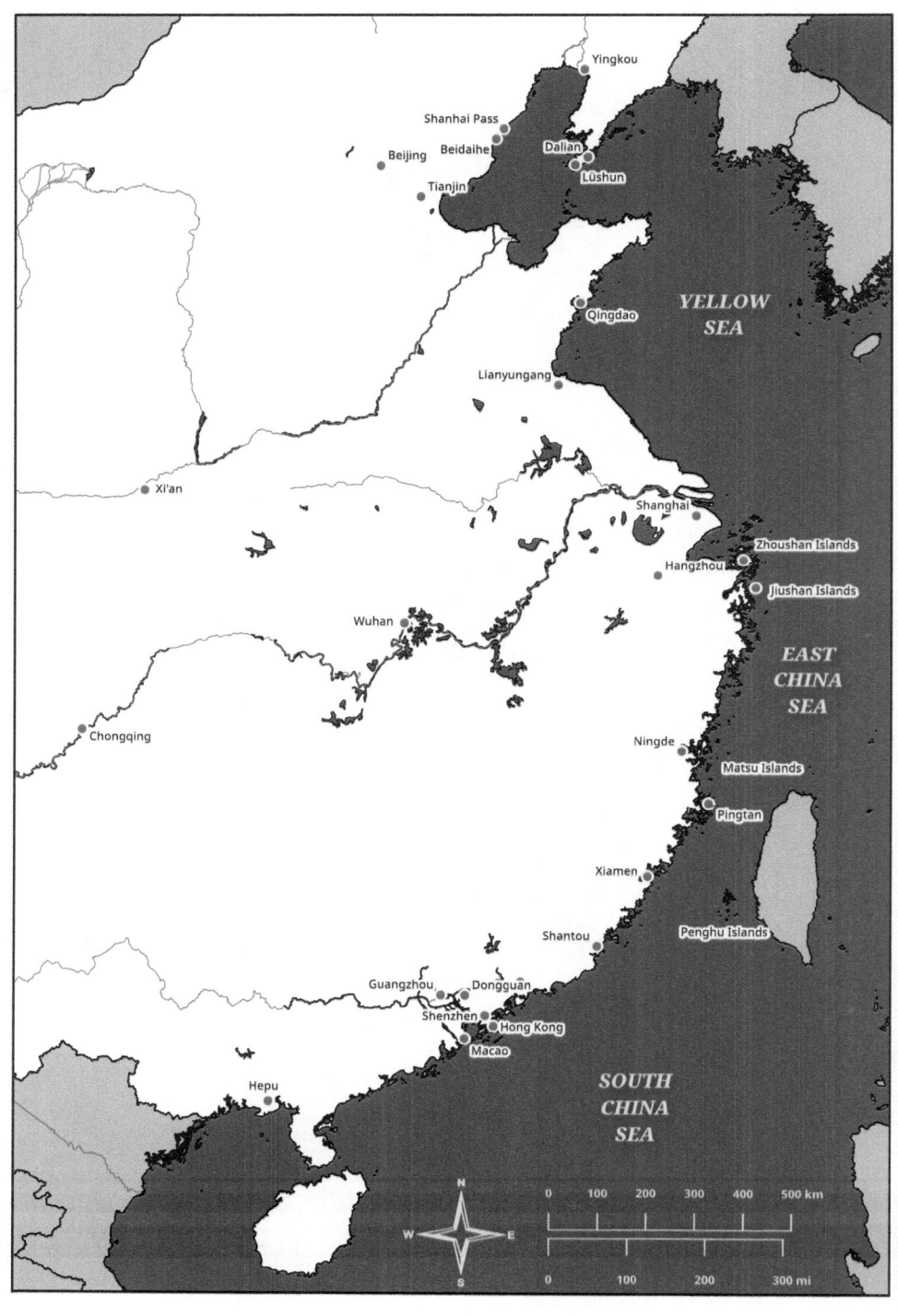

Map of the Coasts & Marine Waters of China

CHINA'S coastline is divided into three parts. In the north the coast lies along the Bo Hai and the Yellow Sea.[1] The Bo Hai is a northwestern extension of the Yellow Sea, a shallow gulf enclosed by the Liaodong and Shandong Peninsulas. In winter its waters freeze into large ice floes, but in recent decades less and less ice has formed as the climate warms. Sections of the coastline are rocky, but most of the Yellow Sea coast is flat due to the huge sediment loads that flow from the Yellow River. The sediment arrives in such immense volumes that—viewed from space—massive plumes of yellow silt can be seen expanding out into the waters. The many wetlands along the coast have long served as important stopover sites for migratory birds that travel the East Asian–Australasian flyway.

Farther south lies the East China Sea, into which the Yangtze River flows. South of Hangzhou Bay, the coasts of Zhejiang and Fujian are predominantly rocky, and in times past were favored haunts of smugglers and pirates. Piracy has waxed and waned across China's history, but the most famous period was that of the *wokou*, from the fourteenth to sixteenth century.[2] *Wokou* were largely based out of Japan, although—especially in the sixteenth century—many of the pirates themselves were Chinese. Raids along the southern coast of the East China Sea were especially prevalent and audacious during the reign of the Ming Jiajing Emperor (嘉靖帝, 1507–1567, r. 1521–1567), but were largely stamped out in the 1550s.

From Guangdong west to the Vietnamese border, China's coast lies on the South China Sea. It is here that the former colonies of Hong Kong and Macao sit, now firmly back in the embrace of the motherland. West of the Leizhou Peninsula and Hainan is the Gulf of Tonkin.[3] A tropical body of water, the South China Sea is host to China's greatest mix of marine biodiversity. Here live China's mangroves, coral reefs, and in times past its populations of such tropical species as dugongs.[4]

China's claims on the South China Sea extend not merely to the nearshore waters but to almost the entirety of the sea. Based on aspirations to control the entire expanse of the South China Sea, and justified with a mix of false readings of history and blatant force, China's claims overlap with those of nearly every other nation that lies along the sea's edge. This has led to minor but sometimes deadly conflict over the small islands and atolls within the confines of China's claim. The South China Sea remains a sore point between China and its neighbors, as well as with the US and other maritime powers that insist the sea is not a Chinese lake but international waters.[5]

Just as was the case inland, non-Han peoples originally inhabited the coastal regions south of the Yangtze. Many of these were speakers of Austronesian languages who fished and hunted for their sustenance, and perhaps supplemented their catches with slash-and-burn farming. As elsewhere, once the Han Chinese moved in, the native peoples were compelled to submit and assimilate.[6]

Although premodern technology limited the damage humans could inflict on most species, they proved capable of driving some populations to collapse. One example were the pearl oysters off Guangzhou's Leizhou Peninsula. Sent north since the Han dynasty, pearl harvests during the Tang became so heavy that the oyster populations repeatedly collapsed. To restore the pearl supply, officials imposed harvesting limits until production was able to resume.[7]

In the seventeenth century, the Manchu conquerors of China gave the southern coastline an extraordinary period of relative freedom from human activity. The Manchu declared the Qing dynasty in 1636, but it was only in 1644 that they passed through the Great Wall and seized Beijing, declaring an end to the Ming. Many Ming loyalists, however, refused to submit, and it took until 1662 for the Manchu and their allies to fully vanquish the rump Southern Ming dynasty.

In the 1650s a major faction of the anti-Qing forces was under the command of the half-Japanese general Koxinga (1624–1662).[8] With a large army and strong naval forces, he controlled much of the Zhejiang and Fujian coasts. Koxinga's position on the mainland became untenable after his forces suffered a severe defeat when attempting to take Nanjing in 1659, and two years later he retreated to Taiwan—then known as Formosa. There he defeated and expelled the Dutch—at that time the primary power on the island—and established the Kingdom of Tungning (東寧國 1661–1683). From Formosa and a few holdfasts in Fujian, Koxinga and his descendants harassed the Qing up and down the coast.

Unable to defeat Tungning at sea or on Taiwan, the Qing decided to undermine its power by cutting off support from the sympathetic coastal population. Their means to accomplish this was simple: along with a ban on coastal trade, the entire populace—from Zhejiang to the Vietnam border—was ordered to move inland 50 *li*, approximately 27 km (17 mi).[9] Although it is uncertain how thoroughly the order was implemented, it is clear that much of the coastal strip was left depopulated except for military units that enforced the expulsion and guarded against Ming loyalist and pirate incursions.

The high costs that stemmed from the mass expulsion eventually led to its lifting. Farmers were allowed to begin returning to their fields and the coast in 1669, and trade was reopened in 1683. But in those years of absence the flora and fauna along the coastal strip had been allowed free rein to recolonize the land. How much the various habitats and species were able to recover is unknown, but the separation proved short-lived. Once the Qing allowed the repopulation of the coast, most of the abandoned agrarian land quickly came back under cultivation. As quickly as the respite had been granted, just as quickly it was taken away.[10]

For most of the past century China's waters and coasts have suffered tremendous damage.[11] Few species of commercial fish or other sea life have escaped serious overharvesting, and many have seen their numbers collapse. The waters themselves have been badly polluted, with industrial and agricultural effluent creating myriad dead zones and damaging the health of countless plants and animals. Coastal and marine habitats have been damaged and destroyed, with many wetlands lost to land reclamation.[12] The very geography of the coasts and seas has changed as China's massive reworking of its inland waterways has led to an enormous drop in the flows of waters and sediments to the seas. With less water flowing through, fewer nutrients and higher concentrations of pollutants are deposited in estuaries, making it harder for life to thrive.[13] Most of the country's mangroves and seagrass beds— crucial habitat for many species and natural protection against the worst effects of erosion and typhoons— have been degraded or destroyed.[14]

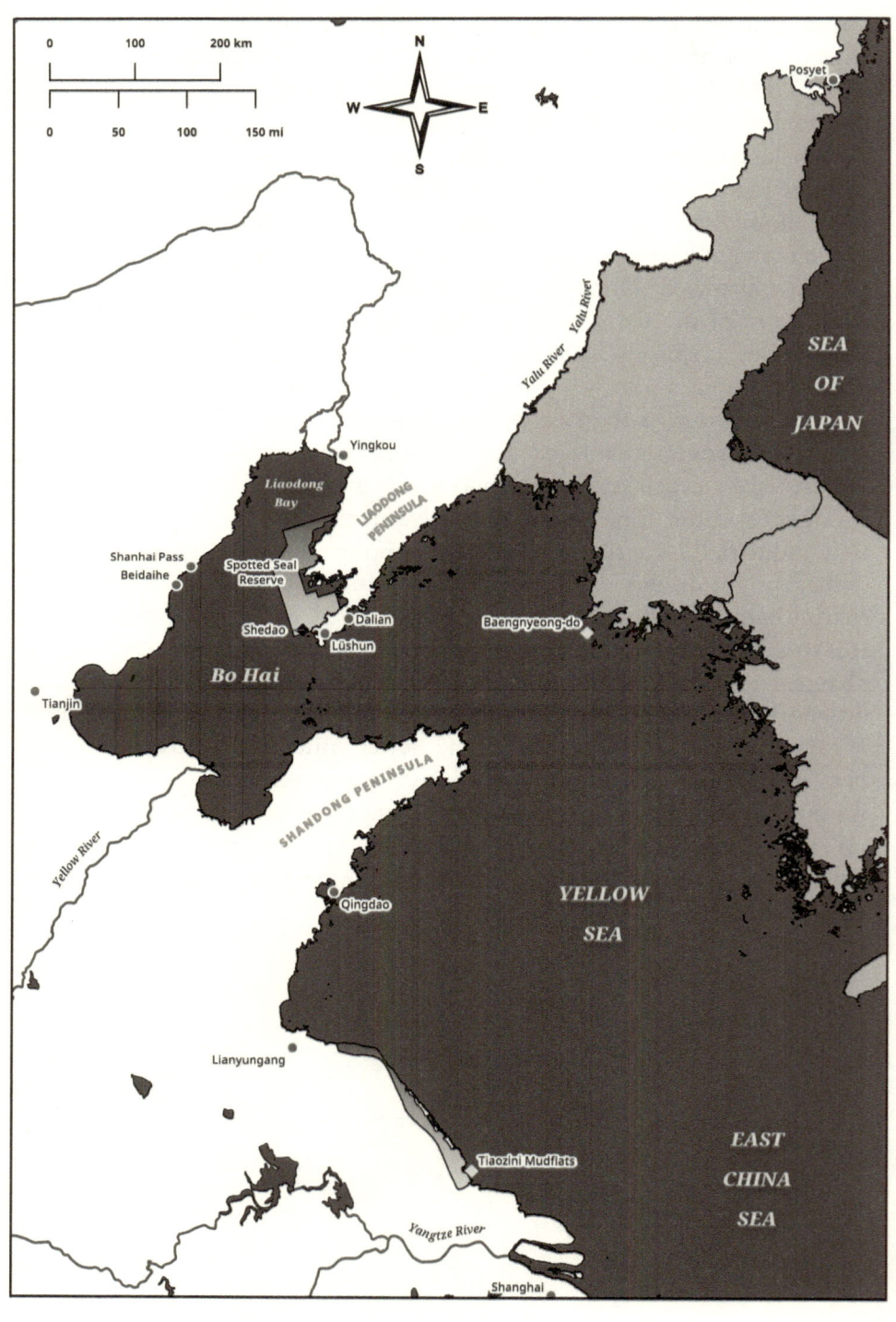

Map of the Yellow Sea

Yellow Sea

C HINA's first marine reserve was established to protect, of all things, a snake. Not a sea snake, fully committed to an aquatic life, but a pit viper, found only on a single dry, rocky island. The Shedao pit viper *Gloydius shedaoensis* is restricted to Shedao (蛇岛 literally "snake island") near the strategic port of Lüshun, formerly known as Port Arthur, at the tip of the Liaodong Peninsula. Some 60,000 years ago, there was a far larger population of the vipers, and their range likely extended onto the mainland before changes in climate and sea level eventually trapped a single group on its current island home. With the entire species restricted to an island of only 0.73 sq km (0.28 sq mi), the Shedao vipers face strict limits on their population.[1]

Despite this, the island can support a great number of the snakes. Early surveys from the 1930s suggested there were approximately 100,000 serpents. Such a high density is due to the snakes' cold-blooded nature, which allows them to remain largely dormant throughout much of the year. This is necessary, as there is little food or water available on the island.[2] The sole exception is twice a year in spring and autumn, when great flocks of migratory birds land to rest for a few days. For those few weeks the snakes hunt most of the food they will consume until the next wave of migrants arrives.[3]

Though inhospitable for human habitation, people still came to the island to hunt the pit vipers. The snakes were used to make medicinal wine and powder, or simply turned into pig feed. The Japanese shipped 7,000 snakes to Taiwan in 1937 to make snake wine, and for long afterwards local Chinese captured thousands of snakes each year for their perceived tonic qualities. Shedao's proximity to Lüshun also exposed them to the dangers of the port's military residents. In 1946 Soviet forces based at Lüshun sent a team to Shedao, where they killed many snakes while building a firing range. During an exercise in 1958 the Chinese air force mistakenly bombed the island, which started a fire that killed over 2,000 snakes.[4] Combined with the damage an invasive vine wrought on the native vegetation, such accidents and overhunting drove down the viper population to around 50,000 in the 1950s and to only 9,000 in 1982. Luckily, since being protected, the viper population has steadily grown.[5] Today it stands at approximately 20,000 snakes.[6]

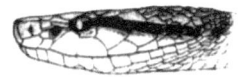

Not far from Shedao, a small population of seals come to breed every winter. Despite its vast coastline, China sees very few pinnipeds in its waters. A number of species of seals, sea lions, and fur seals do occasionally swim to its shores, but they are considered vagrants, animals off course and beyond the bounds of their usual range. The only species native to Chinese waters is the spotted seal *Phoca largha*.[7] A true seal with no external ears and a sleek yet rotund body, the spotted seal is named for the irregular spots and splotches of dark fur that pepper its silvery-gray coat. It closely resembles its closest relative, the far more widespread harbor or common seal *P. vitulina*.

The seals winter in China after spending spring through autumn at Baengnyeong-do, an island off the Korean Peninsula.[8] They arrive in Liaodong Bay every November, and in early December settle at their winter home near Lüshun, now a district of Dalian, the Northeast's largest port city. The seals breed on the ice floes, where pups are born from January to mid-February. They remain on the ice to molt, and then return to their Korean home.[9] Small numbers will sometimes instead wander south as far as the Yangtze estuary or even the Fujian coast.[10]

The first known record of spotted seals along the Chinese coast reaches back to 1116.[11] In the mid eighteenth century the scholar Zhao Xuemin (趙學敏, 1719–1805) recorded accounts of fishermen who hunted sea dogs (*hǎigǒu* 海狗) during the coldest months off northern Shandong. The seals—especially their blubber—were so valuable on the medicinal market that there were always men willing to hunt them, even though many drowned while working on the sea ice.[12] Sparse writings from the late nineteenth century suggest the seals were numerous and largely left alone.[13] By the 1920s, however, Japanese sealers were capturing the seals from the ice floes.[14] Despite this, naturalists of the time still thought the pinnipeds fairly abundant.[15] Reliable hunting records began to be taken in the 1930s, and in the early 1940s an estimated 8,000 seals were present in Liaodong Bay, even though annual harvests reached a thousand or more.[16] Such hunting pressure was still high in the 1950s, but in the following two decades the numbers dropped to between 400 and 500 a year.[17] Between 1930 and 1990, official records came to a total of 30,395 seals harvested. Counts of their population had dropped to a low of 2,269 in 1979, but with the implementation of protections in the 1980s the seals roughly doubled by 1990.[18]

Once the seal fishery closed, sealers became poachers. The seals' fur, meat, and oil all found eager buyers, so did seal penises, predictably used to brew up medicinal concoctions.[19] But hunting was hardly the only pressure on the seals. Coastal development led to the blockage of rivers, drying up the estuaries and depriving the seals of haul outs.[20] The most unrelenting threat has been the slow disappearance of the ice. Temperatures in the Bo Hai have been rising since the 1950s, and by the 1970s the thickness and extent of the ice had reached its lowest levels since records began in the 1880s. By the 1990s the decline had become clearly noticeable, and today it continues with no reversal in sight. Winters in the sea are predicted to become ice-free by the end of this century, leaving the seals without their traditional breeding and molting habitat. Some of them have already made the move to passing the winter onshore, but it remains to be seen if all of the seals can adapt, and if there is enough space to accommodate them all.[21]

Poaching has been much reduced since the 1990s, but still the seals have dwindled in number. During the 1970s and 1980s a small number were captured for placement in zoos and aquaria, but demand dropped away afterwards.[22] In the past decade China has seen an explosion in the number of aquaria and marine parks built around the country. Many are less than scrupulous in how they acquire animals, and the spotted seals have drawn their attention. In February 2019 police raided a facility in which poachers were keeping 100 captured seal pups. Had they not been seized from their captors, whichever pups survived their ordeal would likely have ended up on display for the enjoyment of the general public.[23]

The seals face many other threats. Pollution has left not only the waters but also the fish the seals eat loaded with toxic chemicals. The fish themselves have fallen in numbers, making it harder for the seals to find sufficient food. Algal blooms have become frighteningly frequent, killing off large masses of fish and other sea creatures.[24] In 2010 Dalian was the site of the largest oil spill in China's history, which caused great damage to the area's marine life.[25] Just a year later a series of spills occurred across the Bo Hai, off the Shandong Peninsula; the spills were covered up and only reported a month afterwards.[26] With pipelines and other facilities still active near the seals' habitat, oil spills will remain a potential threat for many years. To add to their troubles, a new airport—expected to be the largest offshore airport in the world upon completion in 2026—is under construction on an artificial island about 10 km (6.2 mi) from the seals' favored gathering place. Although researchers predict that there should be little disturbance to the seals or their prey once construction is finished, the accuracy of that assessment will only come to light in time.[27]

The seals' numbers have been dropping for years. Over the winter of 2006–2007 researchers counted between 600 and 800 seals, which yielded an estimated total of around 1,500. When the China Biodiversity Conservation and Green Development Foundation (CBCGDF), a Chinese NGO, conducted its own survey in 2020, only 338 seals were sighted, giving an estimate of no more than 500 total remaining in the population.[28] Now reduced to such a small size, the population faces the many dangers that come from having so few members with already low genetic diversity.[29] It seems that no matter how well protected they are, the seals have a difficult future ahead.

Whaling in China never became the immensely lucrative and destructive enterprise it did for the great European and American fleets. Records of whaling go back to the Tang, but there is no indication it was more than a few localities' strictly limited specialty. The imperial court was a major customer of whatever whale oil was harvested, valuing it for giving off little smoke or scent.[30]

In the modern era, foreign ships undertook the majority of whaling in Chinese waters. The Scottish missionary Reverend Alexander Williamson (1829–1890) noted that sperm whales and other whale species were abundant in the waters off Posyet, now on the Russian coast near the convergence of Russia, China, and North Korea, but which only several years prior to his visit was still a part of the Manchu empire.[31]

It was the Japanese who soon arrived for the whales. After defeating the Qing in the First Sino-Japanese War, Japan took control of Taiwan, where it built whaling stations. Then, after prevailing over Russia in the Russo-Japanese War (1904–1905), they began establishing stations on the Yellow Sea coast. One was built in Dalian (then called Dairen) in 1914, with more constructed on the Korean and Shandong coasts.[32] In its first season the Dalian whaling fleet caught forty-eight fin whales, and from 1915 to 1921 it brought in 710 large-bodied whales, mostly fins but also humpbacks and sperm whales. Having exhausted the waters around the Liaodong Peninsula, operations then concentrated closer to Korean shores. By 1934 there were too few large whales remaining, and whaling activity in the Yellow Sea dropped off. Whalers shifted their attention to smaller species, especially the minke. The Japanese fleet only ended its hunts with the collapse of the Japanese Empire in 1945, having caused grave damage to the whales of the Yellow Sea. The fleet around Taiwan and the Penghu Islands concentrated on humpbacks as well as blue, fin, sei, and sperm whales. It too ceased operating with the end of the war.[33]

After the Communist victory in 1949, the People's Republic established its own near-shore whaling fleets. One operated from Guangzhou sailing mostly small vessels, and from 1953 to 1960 it only managed to catch forty-eight whales, ninety percent of them humpbacks. After 1961 very few whales were caught, and the fleet ceased operations in 1970. Another fleet began sailing from Dalian in 1953, and added a large, modern vessel for offshore whaling in 1959, with a second in 1963. The whalers were disappointed however, as the waters of the Yellow Sea had few whales left. The two large ships caught a small number, but from 1973 there were practically no fin whales or other sizable cetaceans present in the region. Having had little success, the fleet folded in 1980, ending China's whaling industry.[34]

Whales are little studied in Chinese waters. Like other cetacean populations around the globe, many of those that swim along China's coasts have yet to really recover from the effects of whaling. Sperm whales are still found, but not in numbers comparable to the past.[35] The most endangered whale seen in Chinese waters is the western gray whale *Eschrichtius robustus*, which was already widely believed extinct in the 1930s.[36] Nonetheless they were still sighted in the Yellow Sea and more often off Guangdong in the 1950s.[37] In the last several decades sightings in China have been extremely rare, and the most recent was a female accidentally entangled off the Fujian coast in 2011; so far that remains China's only gray whale sighting of the twenty-first century.[38] Although their numbers seem to be growing, a recent 2016 estimate concluded that fewer than 250 mature western gray whales remained.[39]

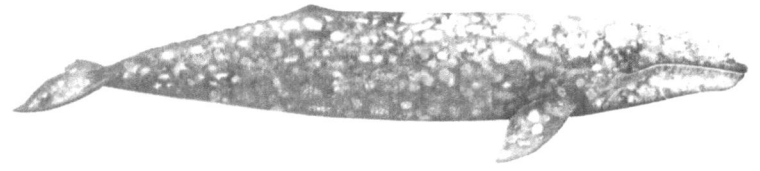

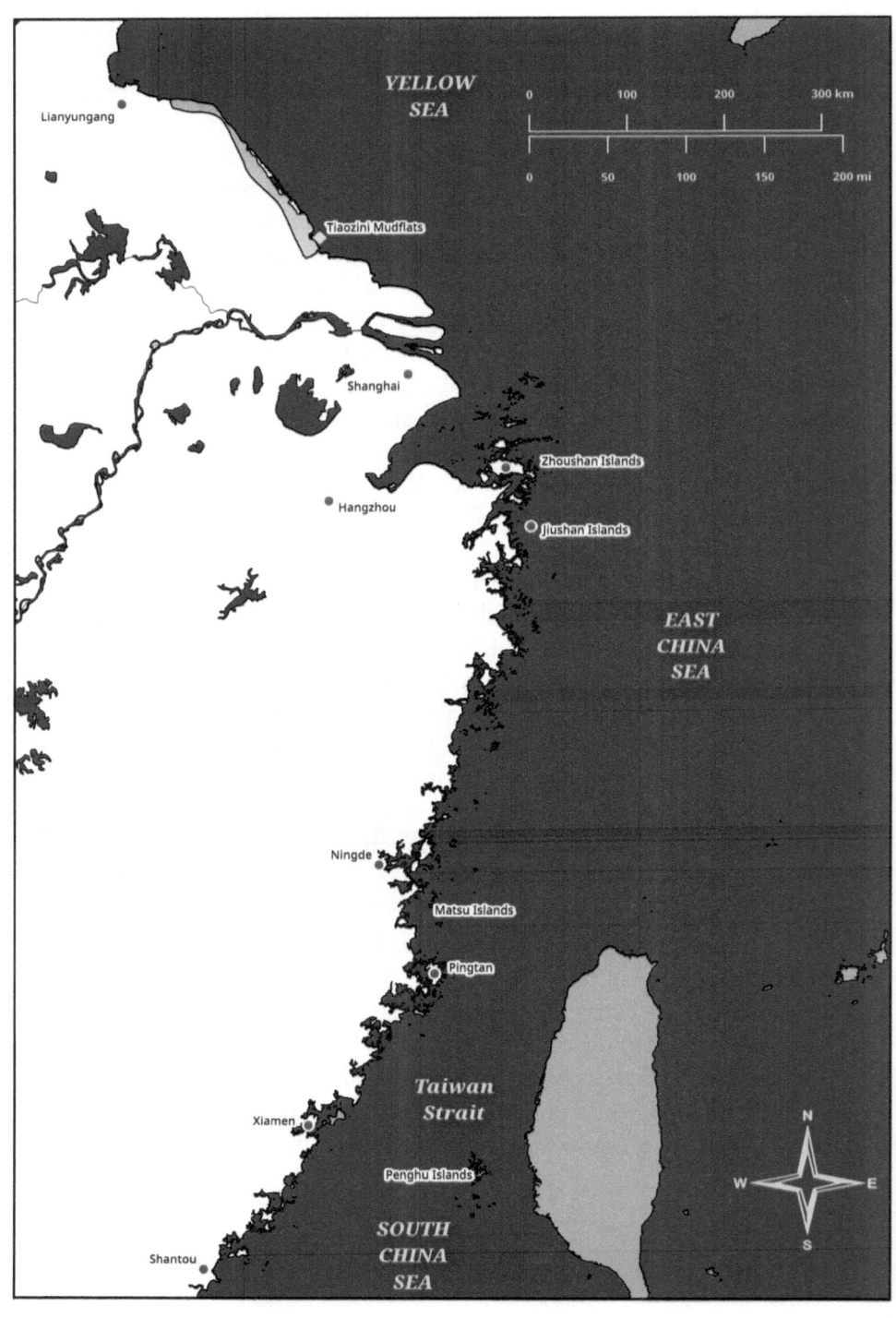

Map of the East China Sea

YELLOW
SEA

Lianyungang

Tiaozini Mudflats

Shanghai

Zhoushan Islands

Hangzhou

Jiushan Islands

EAST
CHINA
SEA

Ningde

Matsu Islands

Pingtan

Taiwan
Strait

Xiamen

Penghu Islands

SOUTH
CHINA
SEA

Shantou

0   100   200   300 km

0   50   100   150   200 mi

N
W   E
S

East China Sea

T HEIR relatives in the Yangtze may receive far more attention, yet off China's eastern shores there are populations of another subspecies of East Asian finless porpoise, *Neophocaena asiaeorientalis sunameri*.[1] The marine porpoises live in the shallow waters of the Yellow Sea, south through the East China Sea and Taiwan Strait, and east into the waters of Korea and Japan. Another species is found from the southern half of the East China Sea to the Gulf of Tonkin and South China Sea.[2]

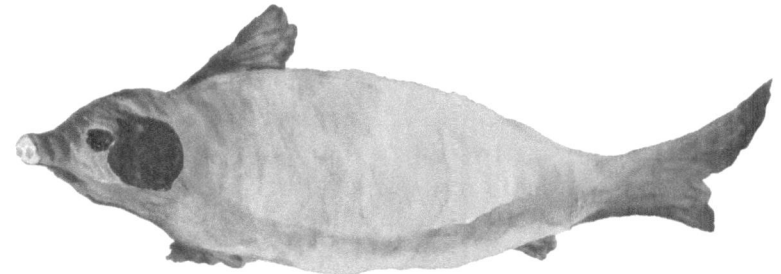

Just like their riverine kin, the marine finless porpoises have faced a litany of threats. At least dozens and more likely hundreds are caught accidentally each year.[3] The Chinese marine mammalogist Wang Peilie (王丕烈, 1927–2021) reported that likely over a thousand porpoises are caught every year, particularly the inexperienced young.[4] Whatever the true numbers, incidental catch—combined with the effects of habitat degradation, pollution, and dangers from heavy ship traffic—has caused a clear drop in finless porpoise numbers.

There has so far been very little research on the porpoises.[5] Surveys of the northern *sunameri* population in the Bo Hai in 2015 and 2016 counted only 137 porpoises.[5] Following studies have been more encouraging, estimating around 4,000 porpoises in the coastal waters of Shandong.[7] Much research is still required, however, to paint a clear picture of the porpoises' status.

The related Indo-Pacific finless porpoise *N. phocaenoides* is found in the Taiwan Strait and in the shallow coastal waters of the South China coast and the Gulf of Tonkin.[8] However, aside from some preliminary studies in and around Hong Kong, little is known of China's population of this species.[9]

The offshore islands of the East China Sea host large colonies of seabirds. Among them is the Chinese crested tern *Thalasseus bernsteini*, a rare bird that for many years was believed extinct. *T. bernsteini*'s common name refers to the black crest atop its head.[10] The entire top half of its head is black, with a line running just below the eyes where the feathers suddenly change to white. The tern's underside is white, and the back a pale gray. The bill is yellow with a black tip, and a white point at the very end.

There is little to say about the Chinese crested tern prior to its rediscovery. Genomic analysis shows that the tern population was steadily growing before the onset of the last ice age, but suffered a severe and continual decline afterwards, for reasons not entirely clear.[11] In the first half of the twentieth century a handful of records were made in Fujian, Guangdong, and Shandong. The birds were also spotted in a number of places across Southeast Asia in those years. A few were seen at Beidaihe in 1978, and another three at the mouth of the Yellow River in 1991. But practically nothing was known about the terns other than they were exceedingly scarce.[12]

After years without any sightings, the crested terns were considered likely to be extinct. But in June 2000, a Taiwanese film crew collected footage of nesting greater crested terns *Thalasseus bergii* on islets in the Matsu Islands off the Fujian coast.[13] They noticed nothing special at the time, but while editing the footage they spotted an unfamiliar species. A team went back to the nesting colony at the end of June and discovered there were twelve Chinese crested terns among the other birds—four breeding pairs and four chicks.[14]

In 2004 the terns were found off the Taiwan coast, and another small population was found off Zhejiang on the Jiushan Islands, but no terns were found along the Shandong coast where they had been seen decades before. A total of no more than twenty-nine birds were counted between Matsu and Jiushan in 2004, which fell to twenty-three in 2007. The terns faced acute danger from fishermen poaching their eggs. Seabird eggs were eagerly harvested because they were believed to be more nutritious than eggs from farmed birds. Egg poaching sabotaged the terns' breeding seasons in 2001, 2003, and 2005, preventing an already minuscule population from growing.[15]

Egg collecting was particularly damaging to the terns because they were already at the mercy of typhoons. If a first clutch of eggs was lost or damaged, the terns could lay again, a simple but effective defense against the likelihood of losing eggs to the weather. But a clutch's chances of hatching plummet when faced with both egg thieves and typhoons. This happened to the terns on the Jiushan Islands in 2004, when their first clutch disappeared in the hands of poachers, and their second washed away over the course of successive typhoons. It was a problem that not only the Chinese crested terns faced, but many other seabirds in the region as well, and the increase in tourism along the coast only strengthened demand for eggs.[16] Over ten breeding seasons, the combined damage of egg collecting and typhoons caused over half of the tern's nesting attempts to fail. It is likely that these two threats were the primary causes of the birds' initial decline decades earlier.[17]

In 2008 the Jiushan terns packed up and moved to the Zhoushan Islands at the mouth of Hangzhou Bay.[18] In 2013 the Zhoushan terns still numbered only twenty birds, fourteen adults and two nestlings. The year prior there were only four adult terns and no nestlings in the Matsu colony.[19] Though the situation was dire, a six-year restoration project, begun in 2013, aimed to provide the terns with safe habitat. The benefits came within a few years. The restoration work brought terns, likely from undiscovered colonies, to Zhoushan and even back to Jiushan.[20] Others were later found in South Korea and Japan.[21] 2018 was the first year the total global population of Chinese crested terns was confirmed to exceed 100 birds.[22] By late 2023 their estimated numbers had climbed to 221.[23] Although still very few in number, the terns are currently on the right trajectory. For now, with the continuing hard work of conservationists, they seem likely to weather the storm and pass safely through the threat of extinction.

Over the last two decades a once little-noticed wading bird, the spoon-billed sandpiper *Calidris pygmaea*, has sparked a conservation effort spanning the entire Pacific coast of Asia. As their name suggests, the diminutive sandpipers have spatulate bills, and their bodies have white undersides with brown and gray backs. When in breeding plumage their heads and backs gain an auburn hue. Every June and July the spoon-billed sandpipers breed on Russia's Bering Sea coastline, from the Chukchi Peninsula south to the isthmus of Kamchatka. From there they fly south along the coasts of the Asian mainland and Japan, finally reaching Southeast and South Asia to pass the winter.[24]

In 2000, while surveying the sandpipers' breeding grounds along the Russian coast, researchers discovered that there were far fewer birds than anticipated. There were so few that areas where the birds normally gathered were empty, even though the habitat was still perfectly suitable. Fewer than 1,000 breeding pairs were estimated to be alive. Finding no clear dangers to the birds at the breeding grounds, scientists turned their attention south to the sandpipers' migration routes and winter homes.[25] But it took time. Even ten years later little was known about what threats the sandpipers faced other than a general notion that habitat loss and hunting were likely to blame. By then their numbers had fallen to no more than 220 pairs.[26]

Eventually what came to light was not far off from what had been expected. The sandpipers had lost much of the habitat along their migration routes and in their wintering grounds. Land reclamation and coastal development were partly to blame, but so were invasive plants such as smooth cord-grass, used to stabilize mudflats. Hunting, too—in China, Vietnam, Myanmar, and Bangladesh—killed off some of the birds.[27]

During migration the sandpipers stop primarily on the Yellow Sea coast. They have few other suitable sites at which to rest and molt, so these sites are crucial to their survival.[28] Their Yellow Sea habitat has been severely reduced, lost to land reclamation. While flying south in the autumn they stop at the Tiaozini mudflats on the Jiangsu coast, where they sometimes fly into fishing nets staked into the mud that remain exposed to the air except during high tides.[29] Fishermen think of any birds they catch as nuisances and leave them to die and rot, wary of damaging their nets while attempting to free them.[30]

The spoon-billed sandpipers are still at the precipice. Their decline may not now be as precipitous as only a few years ago, but their numbers continue to drop. Winter counts in 2021 gave an estimated global total of only 330~340 sandpipers, and as of early 2024 the number was only a little improved, at about 400 birds.[31] Climate change, too, will be a danger, with up to 57% of their breeding habitat predicted to be lost by 2070.[32] Luckily for the little sandpipers, they have a dedicated international network of conservationists working to save them. They will need all the help they can get.

In the late nineteenth century a craze for elaborate ladies' hats swept through the Western world. The millinery trade developed an insatiable demand for feathers and even entire birds, the more spectacular the better. The immense damage this caused to wild bird populations sparked some of the earliest wildlife conservation movements, leading to the establishment of such organizations as the Audubon Society in America. In China the Chinese egret *Egretta eulophotes*—an elegant, all-white egret that breeds in northeastern China, Korea, and Russia, and winters in Southeast Asia—was hunted so heavily for its plumes that it was nearly wiped out. But the egret held on and survived to the present day. The greatest threat now is no longer hunting for the feather trade, but the destruction of its coastal habitats. Tidal flats, estuaries, and offshore islands have been destroyed or degraded, leaving the egrets shrinking space to survive.[33]

395

The egrets have lost large swathes of habitat to land reclamation for industry and agriculture, and much that is still available to them is polluted with heavy metals and agricultural runoff.[34] Migratory birds, they also suffer from threats to their breeding and wintering grounds outside China. Nonetheless the current Chinese egret population does not seem to be in obvious decline. New colonies have even been discovered off the coast of South China, though it is unclear if these were overlooked in the past or represent an expansion in the species' range.[35] The egrets seem a hardy species, and if China's professed desire to clean and restore its coastline comes to pass, the birds are likely to take full advantage.

鵜

The Dalmatian pelican *Pelecanus crispus* is another of China's rare coastal birds. The largest pelican species and largest waterbird in East Asia, the Dalmatian is thought to number perhaps no more than 14,000 birds worldwide. Most of the pelicans live in either southeastern Europe or in Central and South Asia. But there is also an East Asian population that is by far the smallest. The birds are known to have declined precipitously over the past 150 years, due primarily to habitat loss and hunting. The East Asian population of Dalmatian Pelicans breeds in Mongolia and in former times also in Xinjiang. For winter they fly to South China, or stop in the Lower Yangtze and along the East China coast.[36]

Until both steady wildlife monitoring and recreational birdwatching took off in mainland China in recent years, for decades the only reliable observations of the East Asian Dalmatian pelicans came from Hong Kong. There the pelicans wintered in the Deep Bay area between Hong Kong and Shenzhen, and birdwatchers kept records of them from the 1960s.

In that time the pelicans' numbers declined from over seventy birds to between twenty and thirty in the 1990s. There was a particularly steep drop in the late 1980s to early 1990s, believed to be due to fishermen from the mainland illegally crossing into Hong Kong waters and disturbing the birds. In the early 2000s the number of pelicans wintering in Hong Kong declined further, eventually to zero over the winter of 2006–2007.[37] A final pelican was seen in Deep Bay over the winter of 2009–2010, and they have since been absent.[38] As observations on the mainland increased from the 1980s onwards, it became clear the pelicans were abandoning their northern wintering sites. The numbers observed in the Lower Yangtze and Yangtze Delta began to dwindle. For a time they were spotted wintering solely along the coasts of Zhejiang, Fujian, and Guangdong.[39] Most recently they have also been seen in Jiangsu, with small numbers seen in Shanghai, Anhui, Shaanxi, Henan, Guizhou, and Sichuan.[40]

The pelicans' decline is only in part due to circumstances in China. They have lost much of the wetland and coastal habitat they once used, and have no doubt suffered a fair share of hunting.[41] Additionally, many of the oases in which they stopped during migration have dried out, adding strain to an already arduous journey. But the pelicans' breeding grounds in Mongolia have also seen severe degradation in the past several decades. The intrusion of horses and cattle into their wetlands, and damage caused by invasive muskrats has deprived them of large expanses of habitat. To make things worse, their food supply has been heavily overfished, and they have been hunted for their bills, which are used as horse grooming tools.[42]

The most recent winter count from 2024 recorded 161 birds, but allowing for multiple counts of individuals, the East Asian population of Dalmatian pelicans is estimated to be under 130 birds.[43] Conservationists from around the globe are working to protect the birds across the whole of their range. The pelicans of Mongolia and China no doubt present the most urgent and difficult challenge.

In October, when they leave their Manchurian breeding grounds, red-crowned cranes head south to the coast of East China to pass the winter, returning north the following March. Over time these wintering grounds have shifted northward, in part due to natural changes in the landscape, but also due to the impact of humankind. From at least the Three Kingdoms period (220–280) through to the Song dynasty the cranes wintered south of the Yangtze Delta. Then in the early eleventh century, as the coastline grew out into the sea, the cranes moved eastwards with it. By the middle of the fourteenth century the cranes had shifted north of the Yangtze Delta where they have since remained, following the coastline as it crept farther and farther east.[44]

Some populations eschewed the coasts and favored wintering at the great lakes and waterways of the Lower Yangtze, and even north into Henan. Over the course of the Ming and Qing dynasties more and more land was converted to agriculture or salt works, and the encroachment pushed out the cranes. By the late Qing the cranes had left the inland waters and become rare even along the coasts.[45] They found refuge in lands with soil unsuited for crops, the only place humans had not claimed.[46]

What little space was available to the cranes continued to shrink after the Qing. The smaller flocks that had wintered scattered over inland lakes were all but gone by the early 1990s.[47] Those that preferred the Yellow River Delta numbered no more than seventy-five by the 2000s. The largest number remained on the East China coast. In the 1980s they were spread over the Jiangsu coast, from north of Shanghai to just shy of Lianyungang. But the 1980s brought a rush of development, and the coast was soon transformed. Soon little of the natural tidal wetlands remained.[48] The cranes had no choice but to congregate in the few surviving wetlands, only six or seven of which remained by 2008.[49]

The cranes have not only lost the great majority of their wintering habitat, but their stopovers have dwindled as well. Erosion and rising sea levels have in fact expanded the area of tidal water bodies in some areas. But those gains have been matched or exceeded by the ever-expanding area devoted to human use. With most sites no longer welcoming, nature reserves in the Liao River estuary and Yellow River Delta are now the birds' most important resting sites.[50]

    Most of China's wintering red-crowned cranes now concentrate at one site, the Yancheng Nature Reserve. Year by year the cranes have dwindled in the face of immense pressures across their range—on their breeding, stopover, and wintering grounds. Over the winter of 1999–2000 1,163 cranes were counted wintering in China; by 2014–2015 they had fallen to 737 birds, in 2019–2020 there were only 353.[51] Releases of captive birds caused their numbers to shoot back up to 711 over 2021–2022 and even higher the following winter, but they dipped slightly over 2023–2024.[52] Larger populations pass their winters in Japan and Korea, ensuring the species will not perish anytime soon.[53] But without a dramatic turnaround, the cranes' days in China may be numbered.

Map of the South China Sea

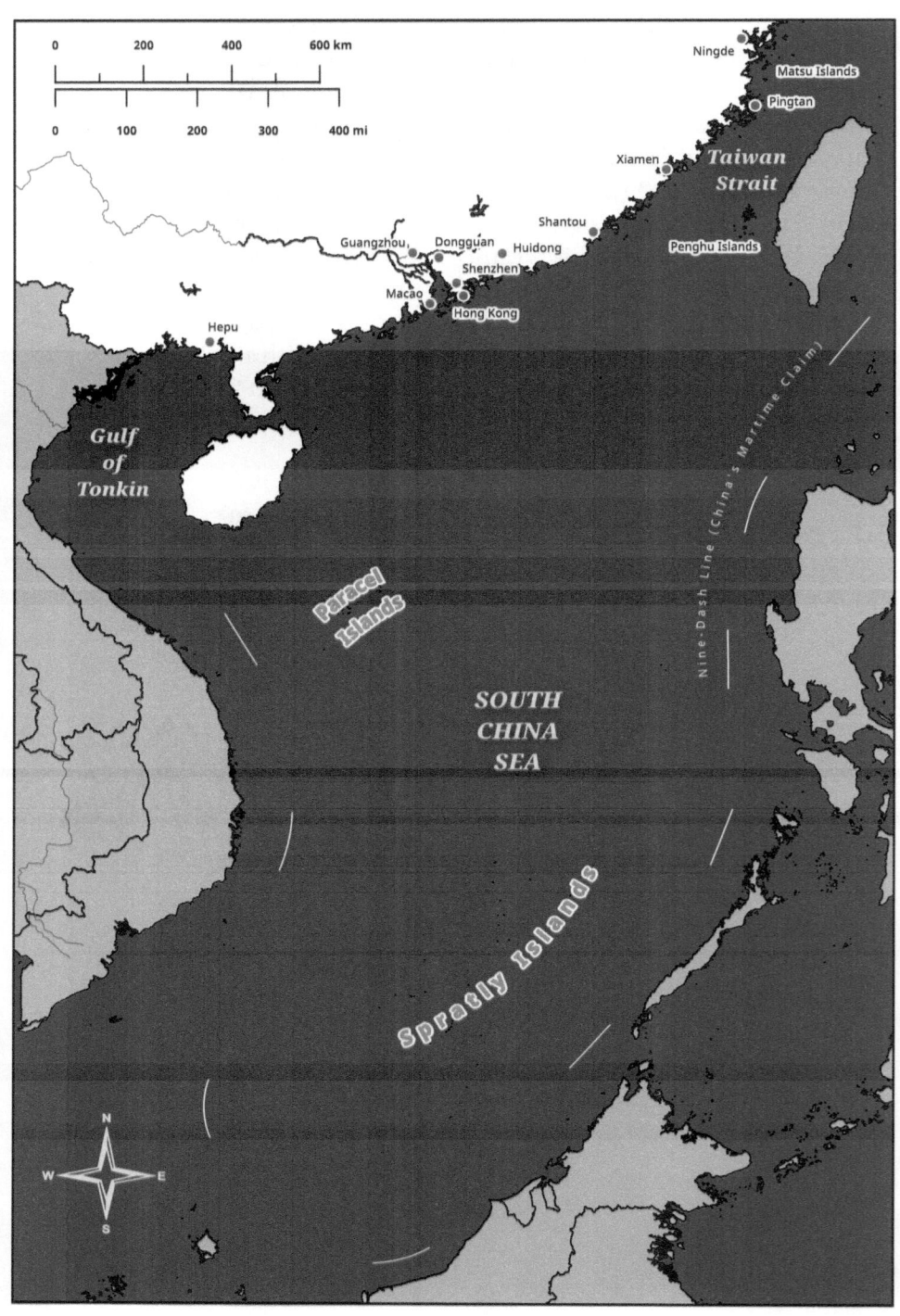

South China Sea

Today the only crocodilian in China is the Chinese alligator, restricted to a tiny remnant of its range. Far to the south the much larger and fiercer saltwater crocodile *Crocodylus porosus* once struck terror into the local populace. Descriptions of crocodilians in the coastal south go back to at least the Han dynasty, and records place the great reptiles in the estuaries and lower reaches of most of the region's large river systems, from Fujian to Guangxi, as well as on Hainan and the Penghu Islands. Tang-era records spoke of the great numbers of crocodiles in the waters and their depredations on people and livestock. The damage they inflicted inspired one poet and official, Han Yu (韓愈, 768–824), to issue a proclamation addressed to the reptiles, commanding they depart or face death. In spite of ongoing persecution, crocodiles remained numerous into the Song dynasty, by the end of which the region's expanding human population began to drive down their numbers. Populations persisted in more remote stretches of river into the late nineteenth century, but they, too, eventually died out.[1]

Along with the saltwater crocodile, another crocodilian once lived in the waterways of coastal South China. Now extinct, the species was discovered from skeletal remains dating to the Shang and Zhou dynasties. Named the Chinese gharial *Hanyusuchus sinensis*, it was a large crocodilian with a long, narrow snout evolved for catching fish. Reconstructing the species' range and history from archaeological records and historical writings, researchers have determined the Chinese gharial lived along the rivers and coasts of Fujian, Guangdong, Guangxi, and Hainan. Feared as dangerous to both livestock and humans, the gharials were killed along with the more fearsome saltwater crocs. The great expansion of the region's human population in the second millennium CE also deprived the gharials of habitat. Just when the species went extinct is a mystery, and now, other than a few bones, there is little remaining to show the Chinese gharial ever existed.[2]

Five of the world's seven species of sea turtle are known to swim China's waters. Green sea turtles *Chelonia mydas* are the most commonly found, swimming all the seas south of the Shandong Peninsula. The loggerhead *Caretta caretta*, olive ridley *Lepidochelys olivacea*, and the leatherback *Dermochelys coriacea*—the largest of the sea turtles—are far less commonly sighted.[3] With their beautifully patterned shells, hawksbill turtles *Eretmochelys imbricata* have always been the most valued. During the Tang their shells were sent to Chang'an and other centers of wealth, where they were crafted into hair ornaments, inlay for wood, or adornment for musical instruments. Hawksbill shell was also believed to be a powerful defense against poison, and was deemed most powerful when removed from a live turtle.[4]

Sea turtles are little studied along China's coasts. Records and interviews tell that turtles once nested on South China's coastline and offshore islands, from Fujian to Guangxi and Hainan. Nesting sites began to disappear after the 1940s, as coastal development and land reclamation took their toll. Nests and turtles were also directly attacked, due to the insatiable demand for turtle meat and eggs. At one nesting beach in Huidong, Guangdong, around 400 turtles were believed to nest annually before the 1950s. Over the next several decades between sixty and eighty nesting turtles were killed each year, and nearly all the eggs were harvested. In 1985 scientists found only fourteen nesting sites in Fujian, Guangdong, and Hainan, but only the site at Huidong was still undoubtedly in use.[5] Even the Huidong beach is now rarely used— a lone turtle who nested there in June 2023 was the first in six years.[6]

Now the few active nesting sites remaining within Chinese jurisdiction are on the disputed islands of the South China Sea, a vast body of water cut into many—often overlapping—claims from six different claimants.[7] China has declared nearly the entirety of the South China Sea as its territorial waters, though its claims are contested and its control incomplete. It is here that the great majority of the sea turtles counted as living within Chinese waters reside. The Spratly and Paracel island groups in particular are believed to host significant foraging grounds, while the Paracels host the largest remaining nesting grounds within China's control.[8]

Sea turtles were not only targeted on the beaches but in the waters. Official figures from 1959 to 1988 show that an average of over a thousand sea turtles were reported caught every year. As time wore on the numbers of turtles dropped, as did their size. By the end of the 1980s very few remained. Though now legally protected from fishermen, illegal fishing continues, and many turtles are still caught on hooks and in nets meant for other prey.[9] Recently, demand for live turtles in China's growing number of aquaria and marine parks has emerged as an additional strain. Local governments that are charged with protecting the turtles often collude with aquaria to instead secure them for display, as they prioritize economic growth over the conservation of wildlife.[10]

Dugongs, *Dugong dugon*, once grazed in beds of seagrass off the southwestern coasts. Along with the three species of manatees, which they closely resemble, dugongs are the last extant members of the Sirenia, or sea cows.[11] Large, gentle herbivores, dugongs live in warm coastal waters from the Red Sea and East African coast all the way past Australia to New Caledonia and Vanuatu. They feed primarily on seagrass, and are thus reliant on intact seagrass habitat.

Ancient mentions of mermaids were likely references to dugongs, but the first clear records of the sirenians in Chinese waters come from Dutch sailors traveling to Guangzhou in the mid seventeenth century. The Dutchmen reported that the Chinese valued stones found in the dugongs' heads—likely their tympanic bones—for their medicinal properties.[12] The records then fell silent until the twentieth century, when the sea cows were once again noted in the Gulf of Tonkin in 1935, and were also found to the east off the coasts of western Guangdong and southern Taiwan. Traditionally, fishermen of the South China coast saw the dugongs as auspicious creatures and avoided harming them.[13] With the onset of the Great Leap Forward, such attitudes were swept aside, and the sirenians became another resource to be exploited.[14] Netted, trapped, speared, harpooned, and dynamited, dugongs became a source of meat, medicine, leather, and fuel oil.[15]

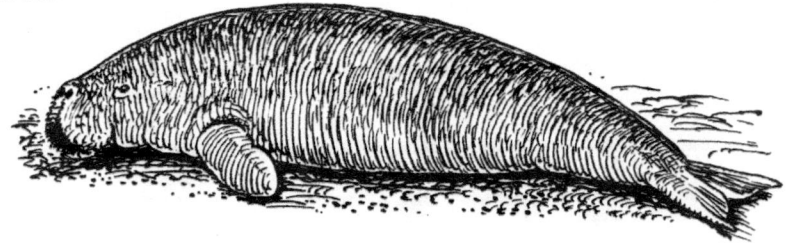

China's dugongs suffered terribly from the years of Maoist frenzy. Dugongs were abundant off northern Hainan before the hunting began, but the last individual there was seen—and caught—in 1972. The sea cows that had grazed off western Hainan were wiped out by the 1980s. Off Guangxi dugongs survived into the 1990s, and by that time the threat from hunting had been superseded by accidental capture in fishing nets, pollution of their waters, and destruction of the seagrass beds on which they fed. In 1992 a reserve was established for the remaining sirenians in Hepu, on the Guangxi coast, but it was too little too late—the largest groups spotted had only a meager five individuals.[16] No dugongs have been spotted along the coast for over a decade, and now the species is believed extinct in Chinese waters.[17] Conservationists hope to restore enough seagrass habitat along the coasts to allow dugongs to return one day, but it will be a slow process. The seagrass at the country's only dugong reserve is too sparse to feed a single dugong, and the dugongs of surrounding countries are now so few and distant that it is unlikely any will naturally migrate to Chinese waters. It may be decades before China hosts a new population of the sea cows.[18]

Indo-Pacific humpback dolphins *Sousa chinensis*, one of the four species of the *Sousa* genus, inhabit shallow coastal and estuarine waters from eastern India to southeast China.[19] *S. chinensis* calves begin life with dark skin which lightens to white with age except for dark spots on the body and dorsal fin.[20] Some among the Pearl River estuary population—including the dolphins of Hong Kong—take on a pink hue when active.[21]

Historically, the dolphins likely lived in a more-or-less continuous band along the Chinese coast.[22] In the Pearl River estuary human impact on the dolphins' waters may stretch back to the Qin and Han dynasties, when the arrival of Han migrants began a millennia-long expansion of the land as deforestation led to increasing sediment flow into the waters. The Han initially settled the hills to avoid the lowland diseases, but the after the lowlands were transformed into rice paddies during the Song, the rate of sedimentation increased markedly. By the early twentieth century, humanity had unwittingly deprived the dolphins of much of their estuarine habitat.[23]

The present status of China's white dolphins is murky. There are believed to be eight separate populations, ranging from Ningde on the northern Fujian coast south and west to the coasts of Guangxi and southwestern Hainan in the Gulf of Tonkin. The dolphins' home ranges are disconnected, and the groups very rarely mix, which has left most of the populations with low levels of genetic diversity.[24] The largest group is the Pearl River estuary population, with around 2,000 members. Several hundred of these spend some of their time in Hong Kong waters, with roughly forty present at any one time.[25]

Barely anything was written about the white dolphins of China's coasts before the second half of the twentieth century. Even earlier Western observers had little to say about the cetaceans; when the Swedish naturalist Pehr Osbeck (1723–1805) visited Canton in 1751 he merely remarked that "Snow-white Dolphins (*Delphinus Chinenſis*) tumbled about the ſhip; but at a diſtance they ſeemed in nothing different from the common ſpecies, except in the white colour."[26]

Though undoubtedly frequent accidental victims of fishermen, the humpbacks do not seem to have been deliberately targeted except for thirty-six dolphins that were caught in Xiamen Harbor between 1960 and 1962 in an attempt to prevent them from eating fish the local fishery wanted.[27] It's unclear how severe an impact the losses were to the Xiamen pods, but whether great or small, after the 1970s they were rarely seen anymore.[28] Their population today is below 100, and with a wide panoply of threats still present, they are considered at real risk of extirpation.[29] The same is true of the dolphins off Shantou to the south; a common sight in the 1980s, in 2022 they were estimated to number only twelve.[30] Land reclamation—coupled with dwindling prey abundance—seems to be the primary cause for their decline.[31]

Study of the white dolphins only began in earnest in Hong Kong in the mid 1990s when two small islands just north of Lantau were flattened, and the rock and soil were used to reclaim land from adjacent waters to construct Hong Kong International Airport. Research on the dolphins in mainland waters started about a decade later.[32] Three decades of research have made clear that the dolphins are in decline across their Chinese range. They seem to have suffered most severely due to the effects of land reclamation and disturbance from coastal and marine construction projects such as the Hong Kong airport and the Hong Kong–Zhuhai–Macau (HZM) Bridge, a 55 km (34 mi) string of bridges, tunnels, and artificial islands that spans the mouth of the Pearl River estuary.[33] The noise from underwater blasting, pile driving, and other activities can be so loud as to disorient and drive away dolphins and other marine life from large areas of coast where they might otherwise feed and rest.[34] Even the noise and vibration from traffic using the HZM Bridge appears to deter dolphins from swimming in the surrounding waters.[35]

The dolphins' numbers continue to dwindle. Researchers and conservationists are raising the alarm about the possible disappearance of China's humpback dolphins, but it is hard to see an end to the reclamations and other threats coming soon enough to save them.

China's seas have been heavily overfished for decades. Catches of most commercial fisheries showed dramatic drops after reaching unsustainable heights in the 1960s. The most badly hit were those at the top of the food web, predators such as tuna, mackerel, jacks, and sharks.[36] As the more valuable fish dwindled, fishermen shifted to species lower down the trophic chain. By the 2000s even fisheries for small fry such as shrimp and anchovy were grossly overfished or had even collapsed. To make up for the increasing difficulty in catching large quantities, fishermen used increasingly effective—and increasingly damaging—methods such as bottom trawling using nets with illegally small mesh.[37] The government is now attempting to reign in the fleets and end their most destructive practices, but it is likely to take years or decades for fisheries to recover.

Among the myriad medicinal goods derived from animals in Chinese medicine, one item that commands extraordinary prices is fish maw or swim bladder, a gas-filled organ that helps certain bony fish species control their buoyancy. Deemed a delicacy and general health tonic, it is also considered an excellent source of collagen, coveted by people seeking to improve their skin. The source of the most valued fish maw is the Chinese bahaba *Bahaba taipingensis*, also known as giant yellow croaker. A large fish that reaches up to 2 m (6 ft 6 in) in length and can weigh over 100 kg (220 lb), it is prized not for its flesh but exclusively for its swim bladder. The Chinese bahaba ranged from the Yangtze south to Hong Kong, and young fish stayed in estuarine and coastal water before swimming out to deeper waters once mature, only returning to the estuaries to spawn.[38]

A bahaba fishery existed well before the fish was first scientifically described in the early 1930s, but little was said about it in Chinese writings. When first described, the market value of a bahaba swim bladder was only several US dollars, but the fishery nonetheless grew in size, driving down the numbers of surviving bahaba. By the 1960s landings in Hong Kong were clearly falling, and the sizes of the fish themselves grew smaller; by the 1990s, fish larger than 50 kg (110 lb) were so rare they could make the local news. Landings among mainland fisheries followed a similar pattern. The primary measure of the fish's abundance—the numbers landed—showed astounding declines. The Dongguan fishery showed a total collapse of over ninety-nine percent from the mid-twentieth century to the turn of the millennium. Overall, between the 1930s and the early 2000s catches of Chinese bahaba fell by over ninety percent.[39]

Overfishing only caused the price of bahaba swim bladders to rise, and by 2000–2001, a single swim bladder could sell for between 20,000 and 64,000 US dollars, seven times the price of gold. That of course encouraged fishermen all the more.[40] So far there is little good news for the bahaba. On top of the toll overfishing has taken, habitat degradation in the river estuaries has made it more difficult for survivors to spawn. And fishing for the croaker continues. Hong Kong has yet to offer the species any protections, while the mainland's efforts have failed to deter fishermen. The last hope—that the species can be artificially bred and reintroduced—is still in its earliest stages, its chances unclear.[41]

The demand for swim bladders has led to tragedy not only for the Chinese bahaba, but also for two species on the far side of the Pacific. In the Gulf of California lives the totoaba *Totoaba macdonaldi*, a fish similar in size to the Chinese bahaba and with an equally coveted swim bladder. After bahaba numbers collapsed, and prices for their maw skyrocketed, traders turned to the totoaba. Before long the species suffered the same fate, and it is considered vulnerable to extinction.[42] To add to the tragedy, a small porpoise unique to the northern Gulf of California, the vaquita *Phocoena sinus*, has been an unintended victim of totoaba fishing. So many vaquita have been caught in nets meant for totoaba that the species now faces imminent extinction.[43] At the time of writing, fewer than ten vaquita are thought to survive.[44] With the bahaba and totoaba unable to meet demand, pressure is now shifting onto other species of croaker, as well as species with valuable maws, such as perch, pufferfish, catfish, and pike congers.[45]

Chinese medicine has earned a reputation as a devastating source of demand for wild animal parts. But demand from scientific medicine can be just as damaging. One animal that has had the misfortune of being uniquely valuable to the modern pharmaceutical industry is the horseshoe crab. Living fossils whose ancestors lived at least 480 million years into the past, horseshoe crabs are not true crabs, but related arthropods that appear to have changed startlingly little over the last 200 million years.

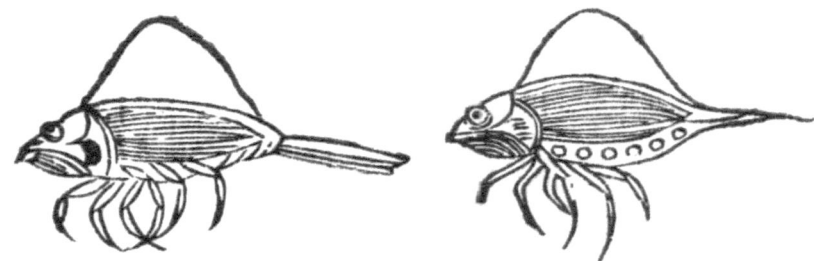

There are four living species of horseshoe crab, one of which resides in the Atlantic, while the other three live in Asian waters. China sits firmly within the range of two species, the tri-spine horseshoe crab *Tachypleus tridentatus* and the mangrove horseshoe crab *Carcinoscorpius rotundicauda*. Along the South China coast the crabs were traditionally eaten, used medicinally, and their shells sometimes used as scoops or decorations.[46] But the off-take was not great, and their populations remained healthy until the start of an industrial fishery in the 1950s. The horseshoe crabs provided not only food, but the chitin from their carapaces went to a wide range of industrial and agricultural uses. One Fujian fishery for *T. tridentatus* provides a telling example. From its beginnings in the 1950s, the Pingtan fishery fell by over eighty percent over the next two decades. Once fishermen moved away, the horseshoe crabs began to recover, only for their population to crash again after the boats returned. By 2002, only an estimated 1,000 mating pairs survived, due not only to overfishing, but to extensive water pollution and the loss of habitat.[47] The population off Guangxi saw a similar decline between the 1990s and 2010s.[48]

Such population collapses occurred along the entirety of the horseshoe crabs' range, both in China and throughout Southeast Asia. Having already lost most of their suitable habitat and been fished to near collapse, a new threat appeared. In 1977 the U.S. Food and Drug Administration approved *Limulus* amebocyte lysate (LAL) to be used to test for bacterial contamination in pharmaceuticals or devices that come in contact with blood or cerebrospinal fluid. This ensures that the drugs and their delivery systems are safe for use, and the LAL test has become a mainstay of the modern medical industry. LAL itself is an extract from the blood of the Atlantic horseshoe crab *Limulus polyphemus*.[49] The horseshoe crabs are captured alive, bled, and released. Nonetheless, many die from the ordeal, and biomedical demand for *L. polyphemus* blood—primarily in the United States—is a continuing threat to the species.[50]

Limulus is not the only species that can be used to produce the tests. *Tachypleus tridentatus* can be bled just the same to provide *Tachypleus* amebocyte lysate (TAL). China's native horseshoe crab populations are now so low they cannot possibly meet the country's demand for TAL, and so China imports large numbers from Southeast Asia, exacerbating the danger those populations already face.[51] To make matters worse, although companies that harvest horseshoe crab blood are required to release the animals after bleeding them, few comply. Many instead are sold for the meat and chitin.[52] Among those that are released, some are soon recaptured and bled again before they have recovered.[53] With the global rush to produce billions of vaccines for COVID-19 in 2020, demand for TAL only increased.[54] As there is still no way to artificially breed horseshoe crabs, and with synthetic alternatives to LAL and TAL yet to gain widespread adoption in China, the demand for the crabs' blue blood will remain a heavy weight on their populations.

Today there are vanishingly few horseshoe crabs in Chinese waters. Their numbers along the coast are believed to have dropped by roughly ninety percent from the 1950s to 2004. They dwindled to so few that between 2011 and 2016 almost no crabs were spotted,[55] and researchers cannot catch enough to make statistically valid predictions of their populations.[56] In 2021 they were finally given a measure of legal protection, and there are efforts underway to protect and restore populations. Hopefully it will not prove to be too little too late.

礁

Coral reefs are found from the southern Fujian shore down the coasts of Guangdong and Guangxi, as well as off the island of Hainan. Except for those off Hainan, these reefs do not host especially large varieties of marine species. The waters China claims in the South China Sea contain far more reefs with much greater biodiversity.[57] China's reefs have been in decline for decades, many of them now with much smaller areas of living coral than in the past. Today none of them are in good health, and all face an uncertain future as the waters warm over the coming years.[58]

Along China's coasts, the reefs have suffered for decades from pollution and the use of bottom trawls, dynamite, cyanide, and electricity for fishing. Many reefs were mined for their limestone, which was used to make quicklime.[59] Hainan's lime kilns were only shut down after the province finally banned coral harvesting in 1999, but locals continued to remove coral to sell as trinkets to Hainan's burgeoning number of tourists.[60] In Hainan especially, the surge in tourism from the 1990s led to more damage from divers and anchors dropped from sightseeing boats. The expansion of aquaculture,—of pearls, prawns, abalone, and seaweed—was even more destructive.[61]

In the South China Sea, China's aggressive expansion of military facilities and encouragement of its fishing fleet has compounded the dangers the region's corals already face from the warming waters. China—along with the other claimant nations—has had airstrips and other military facilities spread throughout its possessions in the sea for decades. Recently, however, it has rapidly expanded these and constructed entirely new islands atop existing atolls and shoals. The work is extremely destructive, and many reefs have been left severely damaged.[62]

As damaging as humans can be, sometimes the worst devastation can come from the broader climate or the animal world. As sea temperatures rise in response to greater concentrations of carbon

dioxide, mass bleaching of corals has become a terribly common event around the world. Bleaching occurs when external stressors compel coral polyps to expel the symbiotic algae which live inside them and provide sustenance through photosynthesis. The loss of the algae also leads to a loss of color, and the corals' white calcium carbonate skeletons then become visible. Bleaching does not kill corals so long as they are not separated from their algal companions for too long, but prolonged or repeated bleaching will eventually cause mass coral die offs. Such events are nothing new, and have occurred many times in the past.[63] But, as across the rest of the world, China's corals now face increasingly frequent and severe bleachings, and are likely to see many more in the future.[64]

Natural predators can also devastate entire reefs. Found across the Indo-Pacific waters, the crown-of-thorns starfish *Acanthaster planci* is an aggressive predator of many corals, and periodic explosions in their numbers can lead to the near total destruction of entire reefs. Whether such outbreaks are directly the result of human actions is unclear—warmer waters are a factor, though likely only one of many—but repeated outbreaks over the last two decades have seen some South China Sea reefs left with practically no living coral.[65]

CONCLUSION

THE history of wildlife in China is grim, but not uniquely so. Humanity's impact on Earth's biodiversity stretches back to even before the appearance of *Homo sapiens*, reaching an early crescendo in the megafaunal extinctions after the last ice age. Afterwards the widespread transformation of landscapes into croplands led to centuries of displacement for myriad species, with some—but not most—dying out entirely. The onset of the Industrial Age led to an even more intense level of destruction, spurred by rapid growth in human populations and in demand for natural resources.[1] China's wildlife history closely follows this basic course, varying only in the timing and extent of the changes. Land clearance and the dwindling of wildlife populations happened as early in China as anywhere else, and continued largely unabated until Western nations outstripped it, primarily because they industrialized first.[2]

Within China the process of biodiversity loss varied region to region. The country today is the result of many centuries of imperial expansion, punctuated with many periods of division and dissolution. Geographically, most of China consists of mountains, deserts, and steppes that once were the realms of separate states, many only fully incorporated after 1949. The lands where Han Chinese dominated typically experienced the earliest and most severe changes to the land and its flora and fauna. In those regions many species were killed off or reduced to scattered remnants centuries ago. Regions with little arable land hosted smaller, primarily non-Han populations that relied on animal husbandry or less intense forms of agriculture. These regions saw comparatively little loss of wildlife, and only suffered severe losses more recently.

Compared with other regions with long histories of intensive agriculture, China's record of ecological damage is neither appreciably better nor worse. India is today another large, super-populous state with rich biodiversity. The human and ecological histories of India and China, however, have myriad differences. Unlike China with its long periods of unification, for most of its history, what is today India was a shifting patchwork of states, from empires to petty kingdoms. As in China, the rulers of these states often conducted massive hunts and encroached on forests to exert their control over the resources within or to convert the land to fields. Yet they also often valued intact and healthy forests in a way their Chinese counterparts did not, even if only as sources of war elephants or as hunting preserves.[3] Although never quite reaching as low of an ecological nadir as China, as a rapidly developing nation India today struggles with many of the same pressures on its biodiversity.[4]

Once European settlers arrived in North America in force, they wrought widespread and lasting destruction on the native flora and fauna. Many species and ecosystems suffered more rapid and dramatic collapses than had occurred for similar species over the course of many centuries in China. Conservation efforts in America, however, began earlier than in China, and a number of species have made strong recoveries since the early twentieth century.[5] Europe, too, has seen a significant and ongoing wildlife recovery since the Second World War, with many species recolonizing lands from which they had been pushed out centuries earlier.[6]

Looking north, China's environmental record in the second half of the twentieth century in many ways resembled that of its friend and foe the Soviet Union. Neither regime's rejection of capitalism prevented decades of ecological pollution and destruction. Their efforts to industrialize and grow rich and powerful led to many of the same results seen in other industrialized nations. Environmentally, the major difference between the communist giants and their western rivals was not the damage they did, but that the corruption and inefficiencies of their regimes resulted in immense waste and little accountability, allowing problems to fester for years and even decades.[7] China and Russia's embrace of the market late in the century brought mixed results. Market demands initially brought accelerated ecological destruction, but in time the resulting wealth and efficiency allowed for more resources to be devoted to environmental protection.

As a large, continental area, China's biodiversity experienced less damage—and far fewer extinctions—than that of comparatively fragile island ecosystems. The islands of the Caribbean, the Hawaiian Islands and others of the Pacific, Mauritius, Madagascar, New Zealand, and even Australia are all well documented cases of islands that developed unique, largely isolated biotic communities. These proved especially vulnerable in the face of the suite of changes that came with humans, especially during the time of European colonization.[8]

The details of extinctions—local or total—are rarely discernible. Even today the monitoring of species is a tricky and often uncertain affair. Prior to the development of modern techniques few people paid much heed to the disappearance of species, much less attempted to keep running records of their populations. Determining the causes is also an imperfect exercise, not least for the paucity of information typically available. Besides such knowledge gaps, the timing of a species' extinction does not always neatly align with the primary causes. Many species can linger for generations—even centuries—despite no longer having any prospect of long-term survival in a phenomenon known as extinction debt.

The history of wildlife conservation is littered with failures, the most tragic—such as in the cases of the baiji or Chinese paddlefish—ending in extinction. Yet there are dozens of species around the world still alive today only thanks to the intervention of conservationists.[9] The survival and recovery of the giant panda, crested ibis, Chinese alligator, and others are all testament to the good that can come from timely and dedicated action. Problems of course persist. Illegal hunting continues, with not only individuals but also large criminal rings poaching animals for the market.[10] On the whole, however, the trend over recent decades has been positive. More researchers with better educations have more funding and more sophisticated equipment and techniques to employ. Public awareness, sympathy, and participation increase year by year.

Some trends, however, are worrisome. In many countries environmental non-governmental organizations (NGOs)—whether domestic or international—play an integral role in research and conservation. Such groups were nonexistent in China until the mid-1980s, but have since proliferated and now do invaluable work.[11] Yet official mistrust of independent organizations never dissipated, and has grown stronger in recent years. Coupled with rising suspicion of foreign influence, international NGOs have found China much less welcoming than it once was.[12] Fear and mistrust of presumed enemies has led to restrictions on access to official archives, online databases, and other valuable sources of information for researchers.[13]

A renewed focus on ideological adherence has shown signs of seeping into some of China's science. Official sources often paint a questionably rosy picture. Skim through nature articles and blurbs from any state news source and the impression is that practically everything is improving. Independent blogs, journals, and scientific works provide more accurate appraisals, but there are hints that ideological enforcement has begun to creep back into those sources as well—the long abandoned habitat of acknowledging the crucial contributions of Mao Zedong Thought in any publication is returning as extraneous praise for Xi Jinping Thought. Even though there is no serious prospect of a return to the ideological extremes or rigidity of the Maoist years, the implications of the current trends are still worrisome.

The preservation of biodiversity is ultimately a task with no set end. Bringing a species back from the brink of extinction is merely the first response to an emergency; without continued care, such action may be required again. So long as humans dominate the Earth, the other living things on the planet will be subject to our whims. That alone is enough reason to doubt the long-term survival of many of the species covered in this book, although there are many others, climate change first and foremost among them.

Nonetheless, China has made great strides in the protection of its biodiversity over the last decades. Even with the loss of several species, many others have seen their numbers restored to some semblance of health, with the same true of the environment more broadly. More people with better methods and tools, and more money and resources are now working to understand and protect not only the species covered here but many more, from the most obscure and smallest creatures to the largest and most complex ecosystems. Having decided to live alongside tigers, elephants, and the myriad other birds and beasts, China now has decades of work ahead undoing the damage of the past.

APPENDIX

SPECIES MENTIONED IN TEXT

Latin	English	Chinese (Simplified)	Chinese (Traditional)	Chinese (Pinyin)
Plantae	**Plants**	植物	植物	*zhíwù*
Cathaya argyrophylla	Cathay silver fir	银杉	銀杉	*yínshān*
Davidia involucrata	dove tree	珙桐	珙桐	*gǒngtóng*
Fritillaria cirrhosa	yellow Himalayan fritillary	川贝	川貝	*Chuān bèi*
Fritillaria delavayi		梭砂贝母	梭砂貝母	*suōshā bèimǔ*
Ginkgo biloba	ginkgo	银杏	銀杏	*shuǐsōng*

Latin	English	Chinese (Simplified)	Chinese (Traditional)	Chinese (Pinyin)
Glyptostrobus pensilis	Chinese water pine; Chinese swamp cypress	水松	水松	*yǐnxíng*
Metasequoia glyptostroboides	dawn redwood	水杉	水杉	*shuǐshān*
Panax ginseng	Asian ginseng	人参	人參	*rénshēn*
Fungi	**Fungi**	**真菌**	**真菌**	**zhēnjùn**
Ganoderma lingzhi	lingzhi; reishi	灵芝	靈芝	*língzhī*
Leucocalocybe mongolica Imai	steppe mushroom	蒙古口蘑	蒙古口蘑	*Ménggǔ kǒumó*
Ophiocordyceps sinensis	*yartsa gunbu*; Chinese caterpillar fungus	虫草；冬虫夏草	蟲草；冬蟲夏草	*chóngcǎo; dōngchóng xiàcǎo*
Tricholoma matsutake	matsutake	松口蘑	鬆口蘑	*sōng kǒumó*
Invertebrata	**Invertebrates**	**无脊椎动物**	**無脊椎動物**	**wú jǐchuí dòngwù**
Apidae	bees	蜜蜂科	蜜蜂科	*mìfēng kē*

Latin	English	Chinese (Simplified)	Chinese (Traditional)	Chinese (Pinyin)
Lampyridae	fireflies ; lightning bugs	萤科 ; 萤火虫	螢科 ; 螢火蟲	*yíng kē ; yínghuǒchóng*
Margaritiferidae	freshwater pearl mussels	河蚌 ; 珍珠蚌	河蚌 ; 珍珠蚌	*hébàng ; zhēnzhūbàng*
Carcinoscorpius rotundicauda	mangrove horseshoe crab	圆尾蝎鲎	圓尾蠍鱟	*yuánwěi xiēhòu*
Tachypleus tridentatus	tri-spine horseshoe crab	中国鲎 ; 中华鲎 ; 三棘鲎	中國鱟 ; 中華鱟 ; 三棘鱟	*Zhōngguó hòu ; Zhōnghuá hòu ; sānjí hòu*
Amphibia	**Amphibians**	**两栖动物**	**兩棲動物**	**liǎngqī dòngwù**
Leptobrachium boringii	Emei moustache toad ; Taosze spiny toad	峨眉髭蟾	峨眉髭蟾	*Éméi zīchán*
Oreolalax spp.	toothed toads	齿蟾属	齒蟾屬	*chǐchán shǔ*
Scutiger spp.	lazy toads	齿突蟾属	齒突蟾屬	*chǐtūchán shǔ*
Andrias cheni	Qimen giant salamander	祁门大鲵	祁門大鯢	*Qímén dàní*
Andrias davidianus	Chinese giant salamander	中国大鲵 ; 大鲵	中國大鯢 ; 大鯢	*Zhōngguó dàní ; dàní*

423

Latin	English	Chinese (Simplified)	Chinese (Traditional)	Chinese (Pinyin)
Andrias jiangxiensis	Jiangxi giant salamander	江西大鲵	江西大鯢	*Jiāngxi dàni*
Andrias sligoi	South China giant salamander	华南大鲵	華南大鯢	*Huánán dàni*
Cynops wolterstorffi	Yunnan lake newt	滇池蝾螈	滇池蠑螈	*Diān Chí róngyuán*
Reptilia	**Reptiles**	**爬行动物**	**爬行動物**	***páxíng dòngwù***
Alligator sinensis	Chinese alligator; Yangtze alligator	扬子鳄；鼍	揚子鱷；鼉	*Yángzǐ è; tuó*
Crocodylus porosus	saltwater crocodile	湾鳄	灣鱷	*wān è*
Hanyusuchus sinensis	Chinese gharial	中华韩愈鳄	中華韓愈鱷	*Zhōnghuá Hán Yù è*
Gekko gecko	tokay gecko	大壁虎	大壁虎	*dàbìhǔ*
Gekko reevesii	Reeves's tokay gecko	黑疣大壁虎	黑疣大壁虎	*bēiyóu dàbìhǔ*
Shinisaurus crocodilurus	Chinese crocodile lizard	鳄蜥	鱷蜥	*è xī*

Latin	English	Chinese (Simplified)	Chinese (Traditional)	Chinese (Pinyin)
Gloydius shedaoensis	Shedao pit viper	蛇岛蝮	蛇島蝮	*Shé Dǎo fù*
Protobothrops mangshanensis	Mangshan pit viper	莽山烙铁头蛇	莽山烙鐵頭蛇	*Mǎng Shān làotiětou shé*
Python bivittatus	Burmese python	蟒蛇；蟒；缅甸蟒	蟒蛇；蟒；緬甸蟒	*mǎngshé; mǎng; Miǎndiàn mǎng*
Pelochelys cantorii	Asian giant softshell turtle	鼋	鼋	*yuán*
Rafetus swinhoei	Yangtze giant softshell turtle	斑鳖	斑鱉	*bānbiē*
Caretta caretta	loggerhead sea turtle	红海龟	紅海龜	*hóng hǎiguī*
Chelonia mydas	green sea turtle	绿海龟	綠海龜	*lǜ hǎiguī*
Dermochelys coriacea	leatherback sea turtle	棱皮龟	棱皮龜	*léngpí guī*
Eretmochelys imbricata	hawksbill turtle	玳瑁	玳瑁	*dàimào*
Lepidochelys olivacea	olive ridley turtle	太平洋丽龟	太平洋麗龜	*Tàipíngyáng lìguī*

Latin	English	Chinese (Simplified)	Chinese (Traditional)	Chinese (Pinyin)
Piscis	**Fish**	**鱼类**	**魚類**	*yúlèi*
Psephurus gladius	Chinese paddlefish	白鲟	白鱘	*báixún*
Acipenser dabryanus	Yangtze sturgeon; Dabry's sturgeon	长江鲟	長江鱘	*Cháng Jiāng xún*
Acipenser schrenckii	Amur sturgeon	施氏鲟	施氏鱘	*Shìshì xún*
Acipenser sinensis	Chinese sturgeon	中华鲟	中華鱘	*Zhōnghuá xún*
Huso dauricus	kaluga	鳇	鰉	*Huáng*
Hucho bleekeri	Sichuan taimen	川陕哲罗鲑	川陝哲羅鮭	*Chuān Shǎn zhéluóguī*
Leiocassis longirostris	Chinese longsnout catfish	长吻鮠	長吻鮠	*chǎngwěnwéi*
Aspiorhynchus laticeps	Big-head schizothoracin	扁吻鱼；新疆大头鱼	扁吻魚；新疆大頭魚	*biǎnwěnyú; Xīnjiāng dàtóuyú*
Schizothorax biddulphi	Tarim schizothoracin	塔里木裂腹鱼；塔里木弓鱼	塔里木裂腹魚；塔里木弓魚	*Tǎlìmù lièfùyú; Tǎlìmù gōngyú*

Latin	English	Chinese (Simplified)	Chinese (Traditional)	Chinese (Pinyin)
Carassius carassius	crucian carp	黑鲫	黑鯽	*hēijì*
Coreius guichenoti	largemouth bronze gudgeon	圆口铜鱼	圓口銅魚	*yuánkǒu tóngyú*
Coreius heterodon	bronze gudgeon	铜鱼	銅魚	*tóngyú*
Ctenopharyngodon idella	grass carp	草鱼	草魚	*cǎoyú*
Cyprinus carpio	Eurasian carp; common carp	鲤；欧亚鲤；欧洲鲤	鯉；歐亞鯉；歐洲鯉	*lǐ, Ōuyà lǐ, Ōuzhōu lǐ*
Hypophthalmichthys molitrix	silver carp	鲢鱼	鰱魚	*liányú*
Hypophthalmichthys nobilis	bighead carp	鳙鱼	鱅魚	*yōngyú*
Mylopharyngodon piceus	black carp; Chinese black roach	青鱼	青魚	*qīngyú*
Myxocyprinus asiaticus	Chinese high-fin banded shark; Chinese sucker	胭脂鱼	胭脂魚	*yānzhīyú*
Tenualosa reevesii	Reeves's shad; Chinese shad	鲥；鲥鱼	鰣；鰣魚	*shí, shíyú*

Latin	English	Chinese (Simplified)	Chinese (Traditional)	Chinese (Pinyin)
Anguilla japonica	Japanese eel	日本鳗鲡	日本鰻鱺	*Rìběn mánlí*
Bababa taipingensis	Chinese bahaba; giant yellow croaker	黄唇鱼	黃唇魚	*huángchúnyú*
Aves	**Birds**	**鸟类**	**鳥類**	***niǎolèi***
Aquila chrysaetos	golden eagle	金雕	金雕	*jīndiāo*
Falco cherrug	saker falcon	猎隼	獵隼	*lièsǔn*
Gypaetus barbatus	lammergeier; bearded vulture	胡兀鹫	胡兀鷲	*hú wùjiù*
Gyps himalayensis	Himalayan vulture; Himalayan griffon	高山兀鹫	高山兀鷲	*gāoshān wùjiù*
Ciconia boyciana	Oriental stork; Oriental white stork	东方白鹳	東方白鸛	*dōngfāng báiguàn*
Antigone canadensis	sandhill crane	沙丘鹤	沙丘鶴	*shāqiūhè*
Grus grus	common crane	灰鹤	灰鶴	*huīhè*

Latin	English	Chinese (Simplified)	Chinese (Traditional)	Chinese (Pinyin)
Grus japonensis	red-crowned crane	丹顶鹤	丹頂鶴	*dāndǐnghè*
Grus monacha	hooded crane	白头鹤	白頭鶴	*báitóuhè*
Grus nigricollis	black-necked crane	黑颈鹤	黑頸鶴	*hēijǐnghè*
Grus vipio	white-naped crane	白枕鹤	白枕鶴	*báizhěnhè*
Grus virgo	demoiselle crane	蓑羽鹤	蓑羽鶴	*suōyǔhè*
Leucogeranus leucogeranus	Siberian crane	白鹤	白鶴	*báihè*
Chlamydotis macqueenii	Asian houbara bustard ; Macqueen's bustard	波斑鸨	波斑鴇	*bōbānbǎo*
Otis tarda	great bustard	大鸨	大鴇	*dàbǎo*
Tetrax tetrax	little bustard	小鸨	小鴇	*xiǎobǎo*
Arborophila ardens	Hainan partridge	海南山鹧鸪	海南山鷓鴣	*Hǎinán shānzhègū*

Latin	English	Chinese (Simplified)	Chinese (Traditional)	Chinese (Pinyin)
Chrysolophus amherstiae	Lady Amherst's pheasant	白腹锦鸡	白腹錦雞	*báifù jǐnjī*
Chrysolophus pictus	golden pheasant	红腹锦鸡	紅腹錦雞	*hóngfù jǐnjī*
Crossoptilon mantchuricum	brown eared pheasant	褐马鸡	褐馬雞	*hèmǎjī*
Lophophorus lhuysii	Chinese monal	绿尾虹雉	綠尾虹雉	*lùwěi hóngzhì*
Lophophorus sclateri	Sclater's monal	白尾梢虹雉	白尾梢虹雉	*báiwěi Shāo hóngzhì*
Pavo muticus	green peafowl	绿孔雀	綠孔雀	*lùkǒngquè*
Polyplectron katsumatae	Hainan peacock-pheasant	海南孔雀雉	海南孔雀雉	*Hǎinán kǒngquèzhì*
Syrmaticus reevesii	Reeves's pheasant	白冠长尾雉	白冠長尾雉	*báiguān chángwěizhì*
Tetraophasis szechenyii	buff-throated partridge	黄喉雉鹑	黃喉雉鶉	*huánghóu zhìchún*
Emberiza aureola	yellow-breasted bunting	黄胸鹀	黃胸鵐	*huángxiōngwú*

Latin	English	Chinese (Simplified)	Chinese (Traditional)	Chinese (Pinyin)
Passer montanus	Eurasian tree sparrow	麻雀	麻雀	*máquè*
Podoces biddulphi	Xinjiang ground jay	白尾地鸦	白尾地鴉	*báiwěi dìyā*
Pseudopodoces humilis	ground tit; Tibetan ground jay	地山雀	地山雀	*dìshānquè*
Egretta eulophotes	Chinese egret	黄嘴白鹭	黃嘴白鷺	*huángzuǐ báilù*
Gorsachius magnificus; *Oroanassa magnifica*	white-eared night heron	海南鳽	海南鳽	*Hǎinán yán*
Nipponia nippon	crested ibis	朱鹮	朱鷺	*zhūhuán*
Pelecanus crispus	Dalmatian pelican	卷羽鹈鹕	卷羽鵜鶘	*juǎnyǔ tíhú*
Anser cygnoides	swan goose	鸿雁	鴻雁	*hóngyàn*
Anser erythropus	lesser white-fronted goose	小白额雁	小白額雁	*xiǎobái'éyàn*
Anser indicus	bar-headed goose	斑头雁	斑頭雁	*bāntóuyàn*

Latin	English	Chinese (Simplified)	Chinese (Traditional)	Chinese (Pinyin)
Mareca falcata	falcated duck; falcated teal	罗纹鸭	羅紋鴨	*luówényā*
Calidris pygmaea	spoon-billed sandpiper	勺嘴鹬	勺嘴鷸	*sháozuǐyù*
Thalasseus bergii	greater crested tern	大凤头燕鸥	大鳳頭燕鷗	*dàfēngtóu yàn'ōu*
Thalasseus bernsteini	Chinese crested tern	中华凤头燕鸥	中華鳳頭燕鷗	*Zhōnghuá fēngtóu yàn'ōu*
Mammalia	**Mammals**	**哺乳动物**	**哺乳動物**	**bǔrǔ dòngwù**
Chiroptera	bats	蝙蝠	蝙蝠	*biānfú*
Castor fiber birulai	Sino-Mongolian beaver	河狸; 欧亚河狸	河狸, ; 歐亞河狸	*belí; Ōuyà belí*
Marmota sibirica	Mongolian marmot	西伯利亚旱獭; 蒙古旱獭	西伯利亞旱獺; 蒙古旱獺	*Xibólìyà hàntǎ; Měnggǔ hàntǎ*
Eospalax fontanierii	Chinese zokor; plateau zokor	中华鼢鼠	中華鼢鼠	*Zhōnghuá fénshǔ*
Ochotona argentata	Silver Pika; Helan Shan Pika	宁夏鼠兔; 贺兰山鼠兔	寧夏鼠兔; 賀蘭山鼠兔	*Níngxià shǔtù; Hélán Shān shǔtù*

Latin	English	Chinese (Simplified)	Chinese (Traditional)	Chinese (Pinyin)
Ochotona cansus	Gansu Pika ; Gray Pika	间颅鼠兔	間顱鼠兔	*jiānlú shǔtù*
Ochotona curzoniae	plateau pika ; black-lipped pika	高原鼠兔	高原鼠兔	*gāoyuán shǔtù*
Ochotona dauurica	Daurian pika	达乌尔鼠兔	達烏爾鼠兔	*Dáwūěr shǔtù*
Ochotona koslowi	Kozlov's pika	柯氏鼠兔	柯氏鼠兔	*Kēshì shǔtù*
Elephas maximus	Asian elephant ; Indian elephant	亚洲象	亞洲象	*Yàzhōu xiàng*
Dugong dugon	dugong	儒艮	儒艮	*rúgěn*
Balaenoptera acutorostrata	common minke whale	小须鲸； 小鰮鲸	小鬚鯨；小鰮鯨	*xiǎoxūjīng ; xiǎowēnjīng*
Balaenoptera borealis	sei whale	塞鲸	塞鯨	*sāijīng*
Balaenoptera musculus	blue whale	蓝鲸	藍鯨	*lánjīng*
Balaenoptera physalus	fin whale	长须鲸	長鬚鯨	*chángxūjīng*

Latin	English	Chinese (Simplified)	Chinese (Traditional)	Chinese (Pinyin)
Megaptera novaeangliae	humpback whale	大翅鲸；座头鲸	大翅鯨；座頭鯨	*dàchìjīng; zuòtóujīng*
Eschrichtius robustus	western gray whale	灰鲸 (西北太平洋种群)	灰鯨 (西北太平洋種群)	*huījīng (Xīběi Tàipíng Yáng zhǒngqún)*
Physeter macrocephalus	sperm whale	抹香鲸	抹香鯨	*mǒxiāngjīng*
Sousa chinensis	Indo-Pacific humpback dolphin	中华白海豚	中華白海豚	*Zhōnghuá báihǎitún*
Neophocaena asiaeorientalis sunameri	East Asian finless porpoise	东亚江豚	東亞江豚	*Dōng Ya jiāngtún*
Neophocaena a. asiaeorientalis	Yangtze finless porpoise	长江江豚；江豚	長江江豚；江豚	*Cháng Jiāng jiāngtún; jiāngtún*
Neophocaena phocaenoides	Indo-Pacific finless porpoise	印太江豚	印太江豚	*Yin Tai jiāngtún*
Lipotes vexillifer	baiji; Yangtze river dolphin	白鳖豚；白鳖	白鱀豚；白鱀	*báijìtún, báijì*
Phoca largha	spotted seal	斑海豹	斑海豹	*Bānhǎibào*
Canis lupus	wolf	狼	狼	*láng*

Latin	English	Chinese (Simplified)	Chinese (Traditional)	Chinese (Pinyin)
Canis lupus himalayensis ; Canis himalayensis	Himalayan wolf	喜马拉雅狼	喜馬拉雅狼	*Xǐmǎlāyǎ láng*
Cuon alpinus	dhole ; Asiatic wild dog ; red dog	豺	豺	*chái*
Nyctereutes procyonoides	raccoon dog ; tanuki	貉	貉	*háo*
Vulpes corsac	corsac fox	沙狐	沙狐	*shāhú*
Vulpes ferrilata	Tibetan fox ; Tibetan sand fox	藏狐	藏狐	*Zàng hú*
Vulpes vulpes	red fox	赤狐	赤狐	*chìhú*
Helarctos malayanus	sun bear	马来熊	馬來熊	*Mǎlái xióng*
Ursus arctos	brown bear	棕熊	棕熊	*zōngxióng*
Ursus arctos gobiensis	Gobi bear	戈壁熊	戈壁熊	*Gēbì xióng*
Ursus arctos pruinosus	Tibetan bear ; Tibetan blue bear	西藏棕熊 ; 马熊 ; 蓝熊	西藏棕熊 ; 馬熊 ; 藍熊	*Xīzàng zōngxióng ; mǎxióng ; lánxióng*

Latin	English	Chinese (Simplified)	Chinese (Traditional)	Chinese (Pinyin)
Ursus thibetanus	Asiatic black bear; Asian black bear; moon bear	黑熊；亚洲黑熊	黑熊；亞洲黑熊	*hēixióng; Yàzhōu hēixióng*
Ailuropoda melanoleuca	giant panda	大熊猫；大猫熊	大熊貓；大貓熊	*dàxióngmāo; dàmāoxióng*
Ailurus fulgens	red panda	小熊猫；小猫熊	小熊貓；小貓熊	*xiǎoxióngmāo; xiǎomāoxióng*
Aonyx cinereus	Asian small-clawed otter	小爪水獭；亚洲小爪水獭	小爪水獺；亞洲小爪水獺	*xiǎozhǎo shuǐtǎ; Yàzhōu xiǎozhǎo shuǐtǎ*
Lutra lutra	Eurasian otter	水獭；欧亚水獭	水獺；歐亞水獺	*shuǐtǎ; Ōuyà shuǐtǎ*
Lutrogale perspicillata	smooth-coated otter	江獭	江獺	*jiāngtǎ*
Gulo gulo	wolverine	貂熊	貂熊	*diāoxióng*
Martes flavigula	yellow-throated marten	黄喉貂	黃喉貂	*huánghóudiāo; migǒu*
Martes zibellina	sable	紫貂；黑貂	紫貂；黑貂	*zǐdiāo; hēidiāo*
Meles leucurus	Asian badger	亚洲狗獾	亞洲狗獾	*Yàzhōu gǒuhuān*

Latin	English	Chinese (Simplified)	Chinese (Traditional)	Chinese (Pinyin)
Mustela eversmanii	steppe polecat	艾鼬	艾鼬	*àiyòu*
Mustela sibirica	Siberian weasel	黄鼬	黃鼬	*huángyòu*
Arctictis binturong	binturong ; bearcat	熊狸	熊狸	*xióngli*
Paguma larvata	masked palm civet ; gem-faced civet	果子狸 ; 白鼻心 ; 花面狸	果子貍 ; 白鼻心 ; 花面貍	*guŏzili ; báibíxīn ; huāmiànli*
Paradoxurus hermaphroditus	Asian palm civet ; toddy cat	椰子猫、 椰子狸	椰子貓 ; 椰子貍	*yēzimāo ; yēzili*
Viverra zibetba	large Indian civet	大灵猫	大靈貓	*dàlíngmāo*
Viverricula indica	small Indian civet	小灵猫	小靈貓	*xiăolíngmāo*
Catopuma temminckii ; Pardofelis temminckii	Asian golden cat ; Asiatic golden cat	金猫 ; 亚洲金猫 ; 彪	金貓 ; 亞洲金貓 ; 彪	*jīnmāo ; Yàzhōu jīnmāo ; biāo*
Felis bieti ; Felis silvestris bieti	Chinese mountain cat	荒漠猫	荒漠貓	*huāngmòmāo*
Lynx lynx	Eurasain lynx	猞猁	猞猁	*shēli*

Latin	English	Chinese (Simplified)	Chinese (Traditional)	Chinese (Pinyin)
Octocolobus manul	manul; Pallas's cat	兔狲	兔猻	tùsūn
Prionailurus bengalensis	leopard cat	豹猫	豹貓	bàomāo
Neofelis nebulosa	clouded leopard	云豹	雲豹	yúnbào
Panthera pardus	leopard; common leopard	豹；金钱豹；花豹	豹；金錢豹；花豹	bào; jīnqiánbào; huā bào
Panthera pardus delacouri	Indochinese leopard	印度支那豹；华南豹	印度支那豹；華南豹	Yìndù Zhīnà bào; Huánán bào
Panthera pardus fusca	Indian leopard	印度豹；孟加拉豹	印度豹；孟加拉豹	Yìndù bào; Mèngjiālā bào
Panthera pardus japonensis	North China leopard	华北豹	華北豹	Huáběi bào
Panthera pardus orientalis	Amur leopard	远东豹；东北豹	遠東豹；東北豹	Yuǎndōng bào; Dōngběi bào
Panthera tigris	tiger	虎；老虎	虎；老虎	hǔ; lǎohǔ
Panthera tigris altaica	Amur tiger; Siberian tiger	东北虎；西伯利亚虎	東北虎；西伯利亞虎	Dōngběi hǔ; Xībólìyà hǔ

Latin	English	Chinese (Simplified)	Chinese (Traditional)	Chinese (Pinyin)
Panthera tigris amoyensis	South China tiger	华南虎	華南虎	*Huánán hǔ*
Panthera tigris corbetti	Indochinese tiger	印度支那虎	印度支那虎	*Yìndù Zhīnà hǔ*
Panthera tigris tigris	Bengal tiger	孟加拉虎	孟加拉虎	*Mèngjiālā hǔ*
Panthera tigris virgata	Caspian tiger	里海虎	里海虎	*Lǐhǎi hǔ*
Panthera uncia	snow leopard	雪豹	雪豹	*xuěbào*
Manis pentadactyla	Chinese pangolin	穿山甲；中华穿山甲	穿山甲；中華穿山甲	*chuānshānjiǎ; Zhōnghuá chuānshānjiǎ*
Sus scrofa	wild boar	野猪	野豬	*yězhū*
Dicerorhinus sumatrensis	Sumatran rhinoceros	苏门答腊犀；苏门犀	蘇門答臘犀；蘇門犀	*Sūméndálà xī ; Sūmén xī*
Rhinoceros sondaicus	Javan rhinoceros	爪哇犀	爪哇犀	*Zhǎowā xī*
Rhinoceros unicornis	greater one-horned rhino;印度犀；独角犀 Indian rhinoceros	印度犀；独角犀	印度犀；獨角犀	*Yìndù xī ; dújiǎo xī*

Latin	English	Chinese (Simplified)	Chinese (Traditional)	Chinese (Pinyin)
Equus ferus przewalskii	Przewalski's horse	普氏野马	普氏野馬	*Pǔshì yěmǎ*
Equus hemionus hemionus	khulan ; kulan ; Mongolian wild ass	蒙古野驴	蒙古野驢	*Ménggǔ yělǘ*
Equus kiang	kiang ; Tibetan wild ass	藏野驴	藏野驢	*Zàng yělǘ*
Camelus ferus	wild camel ; wild Bactrian camel	野骆驼	野駱駝	*yěluòtuó*
Moschus anhuiensis	Anhui musk deer	安徽麝	安徽麝	*Ānhuī shè*
Moschus berezovskii	dwarf musk deer ; forest musk deer	林麝	林麝	*línshè*
Moschus moschiferus	Siberian musk deer	原麝	原麝	*yuánshè*
Alces alces	moose ; elk	驼鹿	駝鹿	*tuólù*
Axis porcinus	hog deer	豚鹿	豚鹿	*túnlù*
Capreolus pygargus	Siberian roe deer	狍子	狍子	*páozi*

Latin	English	Chinese (Simplified)	Chinese (Traditional)	Chinese (Pinyin)
Cervus albirostris; Przewalskium albirostris	white-lipped deer; Thorold's deer	白唇鹿	白唇鹿	*báichúnlù*
Cervus canadensis xanthopygus	red deer; wapiti	马鹿；东北马鹿	馬鹿；東北馬鹿	*mǎlù, Dōngběi mǎlù*
Cervus hanglu (or elaphus) yarkandensis	Tarim red deer	塔里木马鹿	塔里木馬鹿	*Tǎlǐmù mǎlù*
Cervus nippon	sika deer	梅花鹿	梅花鹿	*méihuālù*
Elaphodus cephalophus	tufted deer	毛冠鹿	毛冠鹿	*máoguānlù*
Elaphurus davidianus	elaphure; milu; Père David's deer	麋鹿	麋鹿	*mílù*
Hydropotes inermis	water deer	獐	獐	*zhāng*
Muntiacus crinifrons	black muntjac; hairy-fronted muntjac	黑麂	黑麂	*bēijǐ*
Muntiacus reevesi	Reeves's muntjac	山羌	山羌	*shānqiāng*
Rangifer tarandus	reindeer; caribou	驯鹿	馴鹿	*xùnlù*

Latin	English	Chinese (Simplified)	Chinese (Traditional)	Chinese (Pinyin)
Rucervus eldii; Panolia siamensis	Eld's deer; thamin; brow-antlered deer	坡鹿	坡鹿	*pōlù*
Rusa unicolor; Cervus equinus	sambar; sambar deer	水鹿	水鹿	*shuǐlù*
Bos gaurus	gaur	野牛；印度野牛	野牛；印度野牛	*yěniú; Yìndù yěniú*
Bos mutus	wild yak	野牦牛	野犛牛	*yěmáoniú*
Bubalus mephistopheles	short-horned water buffalo	圣水牛	聖水牛	*shèngshuǐniú*
Budorcas taxicolor bedfordi; B. bedfordi	golden takin; Qinling takin	秦岭羚牛	秦嶺羚牛	*Qínlíng língniú*
Budorcas taxicolor taxicolor; B. taxicolor	Mishmi takin	贡山羚牛；高黎贡山羚牛	貢山羚牛；高黎貢山羚牛	*Gòng Shān língniú; Gāolígòng língniú*
Budorcas taxicolor tibetana; B. tibetanus	Sichuan takin; Tibetan takin	四川羚牛	四川羚牛	*Sìchuān língniú*
Budorcas taxicolor whitei; B. whitei	Bhutan takin	不丹羚牛	不丹羚牛	*Bùdān língniú*
Capra sibirica	Siberian ibex	北山羊	北山羊	*běi shānyáng*

Latin	English	Chinese (Simplified)	Chinese (Traditional)	Chinese (Pinyin)
Hemitragus jemlahicus	Himalayan tahr	塔尔羊；喜马拉雅塔尔羊	塔爾羊；喜馬拉雅塔爾羊	*tǎ'ěryáng; Xǐmǎlāyǎ tǎ'ěryáng*
Ovis ammon	argali	盘羊	盤羊	*pányáng*
Ovis ammon hodgsoni; O. hodgsoni	Tibetan argali	西藏盘羊	西藏盤羊	*Xīzàng pányáng*
Pseudois nayaur	bharal ; blue sheep	岩羊；青羊	岩羊；青羊	*yányáng ; qīngyáng*
Capricornis sumatraensis	Himalayan serow	喜马拉雅鬣羚	喜馬拉雅鬣羚	*Xǐmǎlāyǎ lièlíng*
Capricornis sumatraensis thar; C. thar	mainland serow	鬣羚；中华鬣羚	鬣羚；中華鬣羚	*lièlíng, Zhōnghuá lièlíng*
Naemorhedus baileyi	red goral	赤斑羚	赤斑羚	*chì bānlíng*
Naemorhedus caudatus	Amur goral	长尾斑羚	長尾斑羚	*chángwěi bānlíng*
Naemorhedus goral	brown goral ; Himalayan goral ; Chinese goral	华南山羚；喜马拉雅斑羚	華南山羚；喜馬拉雅斑羚	*Huánán shānlíng ; Xǐmǎlāyǎ bānlíng*
Pantholops hodgsonii	chiru ; Tibetan antelope	藏羚；藏羚羊	藏羚；藏羚羊	*Zàng líng, Zàng língyáng*

Latin	English	Chinese (Simplified)	Chinese (Traditional)	Chinese (Pinyin)
Gazella subgutturosa	goitered gazelle	鹅喉羚	鵝喉羚	ébóulíng
Procapra gutturosa	Mongolian gazelle	蒙原羚；黄羊	蒙原羚；黃羊	Méng yuánlíng; huángyáng
Procapra picticaudata	goa; Tibetan gazelle	藏原羚	藏原羚	Zàng yuánlíng
Procapra przewalskii	Przewalski's gazelle	普氏原羚	普氏原羚	Pǔshì yuánlíng
Saiga tatarica	saiga; saiga antelope	高鼻羚羊；赛加羚羊	高鼻羚羊；賽加羚羊	gāobí língyáng; sàijiā língyáng
Nycticebus bengalensis	Bengal slow loris	蜂猴	蜂猴	fēnghóu
Nycticebus pygmaeus	pygmy slow loris	倭蜂猴	倭蜂猴	wō fēnghóu
Macaca arctoides	stump-tailed macaque; bear macaque	短尾猴；红脸猴；红面猴	短尾猴；紅臉猴；紅面猴	duǎnwěi hóu; hóngliǎn hóu; hóngmiàn hóu
Macaca assamensis	Assam macaque; Assamese macaque	熊猴	熊猴	xiónghóu
Macaca leucogenys	white-cheeked macaque	白颊猕猴	白頰獼猴	báijiá míhóu

Latin	English	Chinese (Simplified)	Chinese (Traditional)	Chinese (Pinyin)
Macaca mulatta	rhesus macaque; rhesus monkey	猕猴；普通猕猴	獼猴；普通獼猴	*míhóu; pǔtōng míhóu*
Rhinopithecus bieti	black-and-white snub-nosed monkey	滇金丝猴	滇金絲猴	*Diān jīnsīhóu*
Rhinopithecus brelichi	gray snub-nosed monkey	黔金丝猴	黔金絲猴	*Qián jīnsīhóu*
Rhinopithecus roxellana	golden snub-nosed monkey	金丝猴；川金丝猴	金絲猴；川金絲猴	*jīnsīhóu; Chuān jīnsīhóu*
Rhinopithecus strykeri	black snub-nosed monkey	怒江金丝猴；缅甸金丝猴	怒江金絲猴；緬甸金絲猴	*Nùjiāng jīnsīhóu; Miǎndiàn jīnsīhóu*
Trachypithecus crepusculus	Indochinese gray langur	印支灰叶猴	印支灰葉猴	*Yìnzhī huī yèhóu*
Trachypithecus francoisi	François' langur; François' leaf monkey	黑叶猴	黑葉猴	*hēi yèhóu*
Trachypithecus leucocephalus	white-headed langur	白头叶猴	白頭葉猴	*báitóu yèhóu*
Trachypithecus phayrei shanicus; T. melamera	Phayre's langur; Shan State langur	菲氏叶猴	菲氏葉猴	*Fēishì yèhóu*
Trachypithecus pileatus	capped langur; capped leaf monkey	戴帽叶猴	戴帽葉猴	*dàimào yèhóu*

Latin	English	Chinese (Simplified)	Chinese (Traditional)	Chinese (Pinyin)
Trachypithecus shortridgei	Shortridge's langur	肖氏乌叶猴	肖氏烏葉猴	*Xiàoshì wū yèhóu*
Hoolock tianxing	Skywalker gibbon	高黎贡白眉长臂猿；天行长臂猿	高黎貢白眉長臂猿；天行長臂猿	*Gāolígòng báiméi chángbìyuán ; tiānxíng chángbìyuán*
Hylobates lar	lar gibbon ; white-handed gibbon	白掌长臂猿	白掌長臂猿	*báizhǎng chángbìyuán*
Junzi imperialis	imperial gibbon	帝国君子长臂猿	帝國君子長臂猿	*dìguó jūnzǐ chángbìyuán*
Nomascus concolor	black crested gibbon	西黑冠长臂猿	西黑冠長臂猿	*xī bēiguān chángbìyuán*
Nomascus hainanus	Hainan gibbon	海南长臂猿	海南長臂猿	*Hǎinán chángbìyuán*
Nomascus leucogenys	northern white-cheeked gibbon	北白颊长臂猿	北白頰長臂猿	*bēi báijiá chángbìyuán*
Nomascus nasutus	cao vit gibbon ; Eastern black crested gibbon	东黑冠长臂猿	東黑冠長臂猿	*dōng bēiguān chángbìyuán*

GLOSSARY

Manchu   *Manju gisun*   滿文

When the Jurchens became the Manchu, their language also changed names. A new writing system, adapted from traditional Mongolian script, was also adopted. The language is now nearly extinct, but the existence of historical records in the language has lead to renewed schoarly interest in studying Manchu texts. Manchu script is alphabetical, and written vertically fro right to left. Today it is mainly seen at historical sites on bilingual Chinese-Manchu inscriptions dating from the Qing dynasty.

1   2   3   4   5   6   7

1.	Manchuria	*Dergi Ilan Golo*	東三省
2.	to be in the wilderness	*bigarambi*	野遊
3.	marten	*harsa*	蜜鼠
4.	badger	*dorgon*	狗獾
5.	wolverine	*ongnika*	貂熊
6.	sable	*seke*	貂
7.	pearl from east Manchuria	*tana*	東珠

8	9	10	11	12	13	14

8.	pearl	*nicuhe*	珍珠
9.	ginseng	*orhoda*	人參
10.	sika deer	*suwa*	梅花鹿
11.	wapiti	*ayan*	馬鹿
12.	roe deer	*sirga*	獐子
13.	roe deer	*gio*	狍子
14.	moose	*kandahan*	駝鹿

15	16	17	18	19	20	21

15.	reindeer (domesticated)	*oron*	馴鹿
16.	reindeer (wild)	*iren*	野角鹿
17.	musk deer	*miyahū*	麝父
18.	goral	*imahū*	青羊
19.	wild boar	*ulgiyan*	野豬
20.	wild boar	*hamgiyari*	野豬
21.	tiger	*tasha*	虎

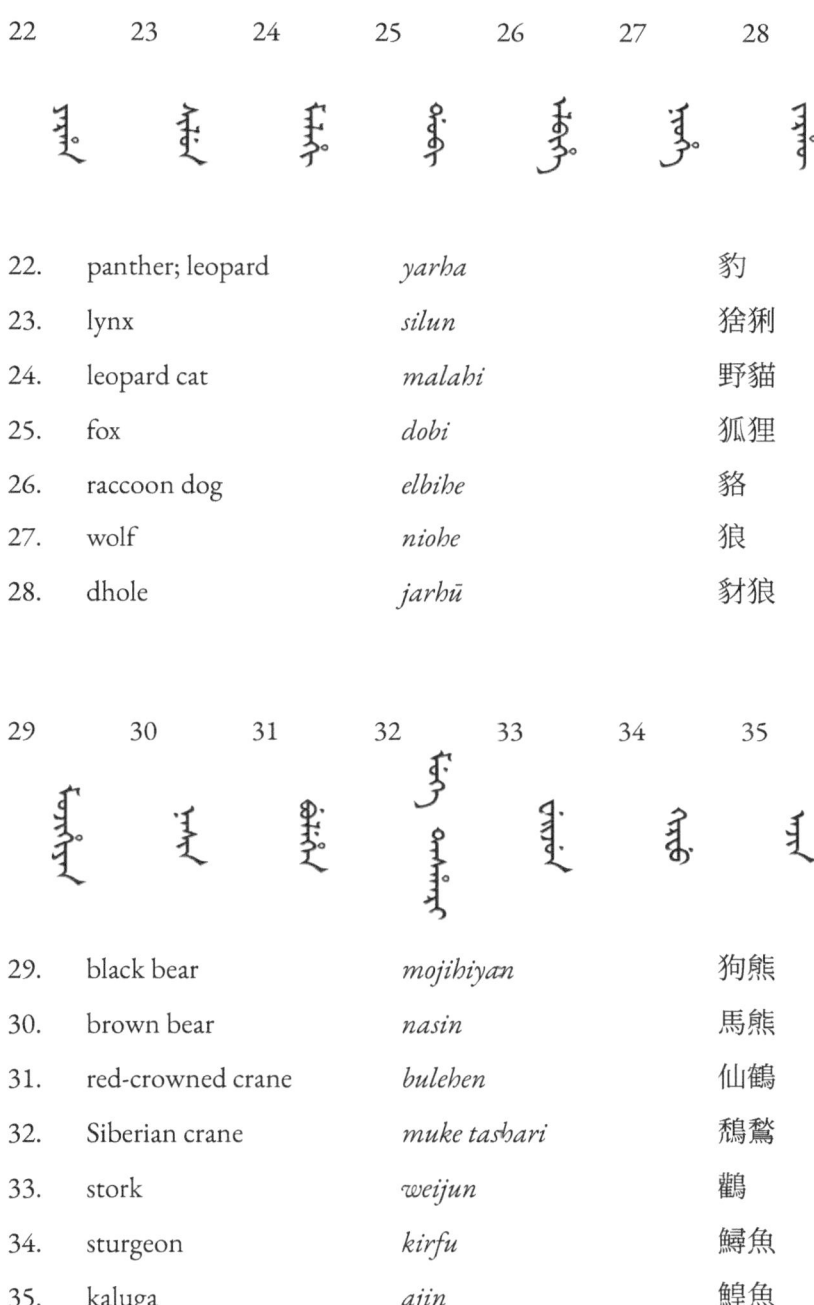

22	23	24	25	26	27	28

22. panther; leopard   *yarha*   豹
23. lynx   *silun*   猞猁
24. leopard cat   *malahi*   野貓
25. fox   *dobi*   狐狸
26. raccoon dog   *elbihe*   貉
27. wolf   *niohe*   狼
28. dhole   *jarhū*   豺狼

29	30	31	32	33	34	35

29. black bear   *mojihiyan*   狗熊
30. brown bear   *nasin*   馬熊
31. red-crowned crane   *bulehen*   仙鶴
32. Siberian crane   *muke tashari*   鶄鶩
33. stork   *weijun*   鸛
34. sturgeon   *kirfu*   鱘魚
35. kaluga   *ajin*   鰉魚

击乩使　Jurchen　女真文

Created by the Jurchen minister Gushen (穀神) between 1120 and 1145, the Jurchen script was based off of Chinese and the Khitan large script of the Jurchens' former masters, the Khitans of the Liao dynasty. After the fall of the Jurchens' Jin dynasty, they continued to use their native script into the 16th century, eventually replacing it with traditional Mongolian script, which was later modified and became the Manchu alphabet.

夾	tiger	*tasha*	虎
宋	panther; leopard	*yarha*	豹
重	fox	*dorbi*	狐狸

两刂 夭ㄨ　Khitan　契丹字

The Khitan created two separate writing systems after establishing the Liao dynasty. One, known as Khitan large script, was based on Chinese. The other, Khitan small script, was said to have been based on the Old Uyghur alphabet. The scripts fell out of use after the Khitan language went extinct following the Mongol conquest of the Liao's successor state in Central Asia, the Qara Khitai.

| 馬 | horse | *muri* | 馬 |

级祸　Tangut　西夏文

Tangut script was devised in the eleventh century, based on Khitan and Chinese scripts. It was used to write the language of the Tangut Empire's ruling people. The Tangut Empire's destruction at the hand of the Mongols began the slow extinction of the Tangut language. The script is astoundingly difficult; like Chinese, there are thousands of separate characters to learn, but Tangut characters tend to be even more complex in structure and opaque in meaning and sound than Chinese.

Tangut phonolgy is uncertain, and the pronunciations provided are inferred reconstructions.

tiger	牪	*dzji*	辬	*le*	牪	*rjir*
river	觉	*śjwa*	毃	*mja*	尿	*tśhjwā*
Mongolian gazelle	祝	*lju*	觮	*phjo*	滂	*phə*
wolf	診	*śjwi*	翅	*lji*		

Mongolian　　Монгол хэл　　*Mongol khel*

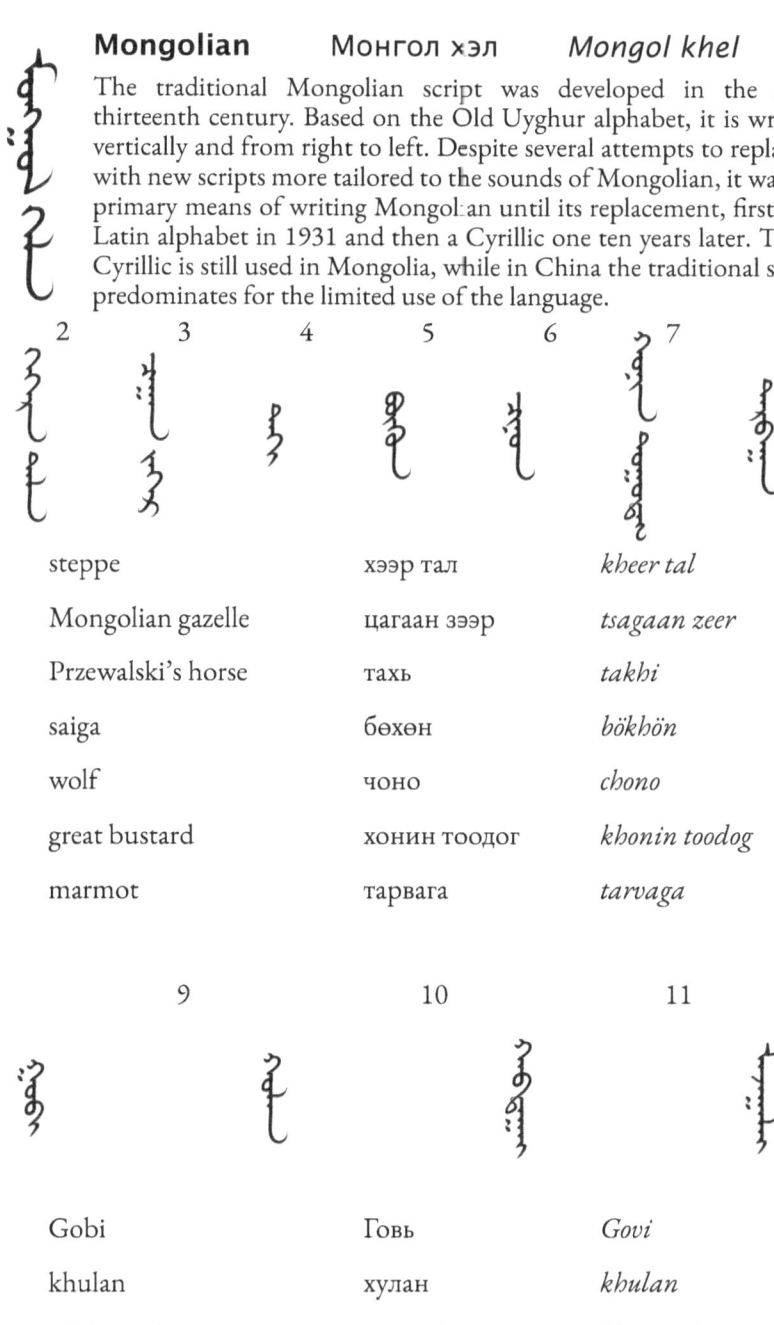

The traditional Mongolian script was developed in the early thirteenth century. Based on the Old Uyghur alphabet, it is written vertically and from right to left. Despite several attempts to replace it with new scripts more tailored to the sounds of Mongolian, it was the primary means of writing Mongolian until its replacement, first by a Latin alphabet in 1931 and then a Cyrillic one ten years later. Today Cyrillic is still used in Mongolia, while in China the traditional script predominates for the limited use of the language.

1.	steppe	хээр тал	*kheer tal*
2.	Mongolian gazelle	цагаан зээр	*tsagaan zeer*
3.	Przewalski's horse	тахь	*takhi*
4.	saiga	бөхөн	*bökhön*
5.	wolf	чоно	*chono*
6.	great bustard	хонин тоодог	*khonin toodog*
7.	marmot	тарвага	*tarvaga*

8.	Gobi	Говь	*Govi*
9.	khulan	хулан	*khulan*
10.	wild camel	хавтгай	*khavtgai*
11.	Gobi bear	мазаалай	*mazaalai*

LIST of ILLUSTRATIONS

All images are in the public domain unless otherwise indicated in the image credits. Images modified and used under Creative Commons Share Alike licenses have been uploaded to Wikimedia Commons in fulfillment of the license terms.

The Chinese seal script included in the cover design is in Chong Xi Small Seal font (崇義篆體) from Academia Sinica (中央研究院). (CC BY-ND 4.0) https://xiaoxue. iis.sinica.edu.tw/chongxi/copyright.htm.

453

455

91 "*Huso dauricus*" in Берг (Berg), *Рыбы пресныхъ водъ Российской Имперіи* (*Freshwater Fish of Russia*) (1916): 9, fig. 17, originally from *Біологія осетровыхъ Амура* (*Biology of Sturgeons of the Amur*) by V.K. Soldatov (В. К. Солдатова)

92 "Head of male Saiga in its winter dress. (P. Z. S. 1870, p. 495.)" in Sclater and Thomas, *The Book of Antelopes, Vol. III* (1897–1898): 40, fig. 51.

93 "野馬 [Wild horse]" in 1456 edition of *Proper and Essential Things for the Emperor's Food and Drink* (*Yǐnshàn zhèngyào* 飲膳正要).

96 Detail from "Различные позы байбака [Various bobak poses], Marmota bobac schaganensis Bashanov," in Огнёв [Ognev], *Звери СССР и Прилежащих Стран, Том V* [*The Mammals of USSR and Adjacent Countries, Vol. V*] (1947): facing 244, pl. 9.

98 "The Mongolian Gazelle Gazella gutturosa" by Joseph Wolf in Sclater and Thomas, *The Book of Antelopes, Vol. III* (1897–1898): Pl. LIV.

101 Detail from "Ice Age spotted hyena clan hunting Przewalski horse" in by G. "Rinaldino" Teichmann in Diedrich, "Palaeopopulations of Late Pleistocene Top Predators in Europe: Ice Age Spotted Hyenas and Steppe Lions in Battle and Competition about Prey," *Paleontology Journal* (2014): 13, fig. 9e. https://doi.org/10.1155/2014/106203. (CC BY 4.0)

102 "Сайга [Saiga]" by В. А. Ватагина (V.A. Vatagina) in *Большой советской энциклопедии, Том 3* (*Great Soviet Encyclopedia, Vol. 3*) (1926): Антилопы (Antilopes), fig. 7.

103 Mongolian gazelles with mountains in the distance on back cover of *Sport and Science on the Sino-Mongolian Frontier* (1918).

104 "狼圖 [Wolf Illustration]" in 古今圖書集成 (*Complete Classics Collection of Ancient China*) (1726).

107 "Großer Trappe. O. tarda L." in Reichenbach, *Deutschlands Fauna, oder, Praktisch-gemeinnützige Naturgeschichte der Thiere des Inlandes, Zweiter Theil, Die Vögel* (1839): pl. XLIV, fig. 412–415.

110 "塔剌不花 [Marmot]" in *Compendium of Materia Medica* (*Běncǎo Gāngmù* 本草綱目).

111 "靈芝 [Lingzhi]" in 新評繡像紅樓夢全傳 (1832).

112 Deer illustration from the Tangut site of Khara-Khoto (in Tangut 𗁮𘜶) (12th–14th century).

113 "獵駝圖 [Illustration of a Camel Hunt]" rubbing detail of a Eastern Han period relief from present-day Suide, Shaanxi.

115 "Part of Sadak-köl in 1896, showing a regular bajir-depression filled with water. The dead forest shows, that there was an early wet period followed by a dry period, which killed the toghraks. At the present time the depression is once more filled." by Sven Hedin in Hedin, *Scientific Results of a Journey in Central Asia, 1899-1902: Vol.II Lop-Nor* (1904): 346, fig. 169.

116 “Antilopen [Antilopes (goitered gazelles)]” in Müller-Simonis, *Vom Kaukasus zum Persischen Meerbusen: durch Armenien, Kurdistan und Mesopotamien* (1897): 317.

117 “*Equus onager*” by T. W. Wood in Sterndale, *Natural History of the Mammalia of India and Ceylon* (1884): 400.

119 “Kulan (Equus hemionus)” in *Brehms Tierleben : Allgemeine Kunde des Tierreichs, Bd. 3 Die Säugetiere* (1891): 60.

120 “Gazella subguturosa, *var.* yarkandensis. ♂ & ♀. [Goitered gazelles]” by Joseph Smit in Blanford, *Scientific Results of the Second Yarkand Mission; Based Upon the Collections and Notes of the Late Ferdinand Stoliczka, Mammalia* (1879): Pl.XV.

122 “Beaver” in *Collier's New Encyclopedia, Vol. 1* (1921): 461.

124 “The first wild camels we came across” by Sven Hedin in *My Life as an Explorer* (1925): 194.

126 Sketch of a wounded wild camel by Sven Hedin, version of illustration “Abdu Rehims villa kamel” found in Hedin, *Asien: tusen mil på okända vägar. D. 1.* Stockholm: Bonnier, 1903, 421.

128 “རྔ་མོང [Camel]” in *An Illustrated Tibeto-Mongolian Materia Medica of Ayurveda of 'Jam-dpal-rdo-rje of Mongolia*.

129 “Grizzly bear” from Pearson Scott Foresman.

130 “Podoces biddulphi, *Hume*” by J. Gould and W. Hart in Gould, *The Birds of Asia, Vol. V* (1850–1883): Pl. 60.

131 “Ptycobarbus longiceps [an early synonym for *Aspiorhynchus laticeps*]” by C.L. Griesbach in Day, *Scientific Results of the Second Yarkand Mission: Ichthyology* (1878): PL. IV, fig. 2.

132 “A herd of wild pigs” by Sven Hedin in *My Life as an Explorer* (1925): 258.

133 “Kashmir Stag or Barasingh (Cervus cashmirianus)” in Ward, *Records of Big Game, 2nd ed.* (1896): 38.

134 “Der Turan- oder Araltiger im Zoologischen Garten zu Berlin [The Turan or Aral tiger in the Berlin Zoological Garden]” by Don W. Kuhnert in *Illustrirte Zeitung* 109 (1897): 160.

135 Caspian tiger (*Panthera tigris virgata*) from the Caucasus in the Berlin Zoo (first published 1899).

136 Detail from “Животная жизнь въ сѣв. Тибетѣ (долина р. Шугà) [Animal life in northern Tibet].” in *Из Зайсана через Хами в Тибет и на верховья Желтой рѣки* [*From Zaisan Through Hami to Tibet and the Headwaters of the Yellow River*] (1883).

137 “གཡག་རྒོད 兕 [wild yak]” in *An Illustrated Tibeto-Mongolian Materia Medica of Ayurveda of 'Jam-dpal-rdo-rje of Mongolia*.

250   "[T]racing from another photograph [of *Lipotes vexillifer*] by Mr. Hoy " in Miller, "A New River-Dolphin from China," *Smithsonian Miscellaneous Collections* 68 (1918): Pl. 1.

255   Baiji, modified from an illustration by Wikimedia Commons user Bosphore9. https://commons.wikimedia.org/wiki/File:Baiji_Size_(V2).jpg. (CC BY-SA 4.0)
Modification available at https://commons.wikimedia.org/wiki/File:Figure_of_baiji_from_Baiji_Size_(V2).png.

257   "*Phocæna phocænoides*. (From a drawing by R. A. Sterndale.)" in *The Fauna of British India, including Ceylon and Burma, Mammalia* (1888–1891): 575, fig. 187.

259   "江豚 [river porpoise]" in 三才圖會 (1609).

260   "趕網 [Net fishing]" in 古今圖書集成 (*Complete Classics Collection of Ancient China*) (1726).

261   "The Yangtze Beaked Sturgeon (*Psephurus gladius*)" by Arthur de Carle Sowerby in *A Naturalist's Note-Book in China* (1925): 92.

262   "鱘魚 [Chinese paddlefish]" in a 1655 edition of *Compendium of Materia Medica* (*Běncǎo Gāngmù* 本草綱目).

263   "*Acipenser dabryanus*, 318 mm. standard length" by Louise Nash in Nichols, "Chinese fresh-water fishes in the American Museum of Natural History's Collections: A Provisional Check-list of the Fresh-water Fishes of China," *Bulletin of The American Museum of Natural History* 58 (1928): 2, fig.1.

264   "The Chinese Sturgeon (*Acipenser sinensis*)" by Arthur de Carle Sowerby in *A Naturalist's Note-Book in China* (1925): 92.

265   "*Myxocyprinus asiaticus fukiensis*, type" by Louise Nash in Nichols, "Chinese fresh-water fishes in the American Museum of Natural History's Collections: A Provisional Check-list of the Fresh-water Fishes of China," *Bulletin of The American Museum of Natural History* 58 (1928): 10, fig.2.

267   "Wydra [Otter]" in Dyakowski, *Z naszej przyrody: obrazy z życia zwierząt i roślin krajowych* (1915): 549, ryc. 236.

268   Fisherman with a tame fishing otter (historical photograph).

269   "Yuen maculatus [*Rafetus swinhoei*]" by C. Rahtouis in Heude, "Mémoire sur les Trionyx." *Mémoires concernant l'histoire naturelle de l'Empire chinois* (1880): PL. I.

271   "Oscaria swinhoei [*Rafetus swinhoei*]" in *The Annals and Magazine of Natural History: Zoology, Botany, and Geology* 12, ser. 4 (1838): Pl. V.

272   "Chinefifcher Alligator. Alligator sinensis" in *Die Verbreitung der Tierwelt gemässigte Zone* (1902): 258, fig.73.

275   "Alligator sinensis" in Fauvel, *Alligators in China: Their History, Description & Identification* (1879).

276 "Autogr. De la Mission Cathol. De Zi-ka-wei (Tou-sè-wè), 1878" in Fauvel, *Alligators in China: Their History, Description & Identification* (1879).

277 "Figure of the t'o [*tuo*] found on a stone tablet in Silver Island, Chinkiang [Zhenjiang 鎮江]" in Fauvel, *Alligators in China: Their History, Description & Identification* (1879): plate between 24–25.

278 "Salamandra maxima" the Japanese giant salamander, closely related and visually similar to the Chinese giant salamanders, in Temminck and Schlegel, *Fauna Japonica* (1838): 315, Tab. VII.

282 "鯑魚 [Salamander]" in a 1655 edition of *Compendium of Materia Medica* (*Běncǎo Gāngmù* 本草綱目).

284 "Grus leucogeranus" in Blyth, *The Natural History of the Cranes* (1881): Pl. I, fig. 2.

286 Above: "Duck Punt and Gingal" in Kum Ayean, "Some Chinese Methods of Shooting and Trapping Game" in Wade, *With Boat and Gun in the Yangtze Valley, 2nd ed.* (1910): 140.
Below: "Cangue used in Duck Catching" in Kum, "Some Chinese Methods" (1910): 139.

287 "弋鳧與雁 [To shoot wild ducks and geese]" by 橘国雄 in 1785 edition of *Máoshī Míngwù Túshuō* 毛詩名物圖說.

290 "Water Deer. *Hydropotes inermis.*" in *The Cambridge Natural History, Volume X—Mammalia* (1902): 297, fig. 155.

291 "River-deer (*Hydropotes inermis*)" by Arthur de Carle Sowerby in *A Sportsman's Miscellany* (1917): 43.

292 Detail from "Davidia involucrata" in *Les Missions catholiques: bulletin hebdomadaire de l'Oeuvre de la propagation de la foi, Tome 20* (1888): 260.

293 Detail from "鯪鯉甲 [pangolin scales]" in 新編類要圖注本草.

298 "水杉 Metasequoia glyptostroboides Hu et Cheng 果枝" in 安徽經济植物志 (1960): 114, fig. 55.

300 "水松 [Chinese water pine]" in 吳其濬 (Wu Qijun), 植物名實圖考 (*Illustrated Catalogue of Plants*) (1848).

303 "Davidia involucrata" by E. Goldring in *Bean, Trees and Shrubs, Hardy in the British Isles, Vol. 1* (1914): 476.

304 "虎圖 [Tiger Illustration]" in 古今圖書集成 (*Complete Classics Collection of Ancient China*) (1726).

309 Detail of tiger from "虎豹圖 [Tiger and Leopard Illustration]" in 古今圖書集成 (*Complete Classics Collection of Ancient China*) (1726).

310 Detail of leopard from "虎豹圖 [Tiger and Leopard Illustration]" in 古今圖書集成 (*Complete Classics Collection of Ancient China*) (1726).

314 "川山甲 [Pangolin]" in 李中立, 本草原始 (1628–1644).

316 "Musk (deer)" in *Cassell's Natural History, Vol. III* (1893): 43.

325　"毋教猱升木 [Do not teach a monkey to climb trees]" Macaque illustration by 橘国雄 1785 edition of *Máoshī Míngwù Túshuō* 毛詩名物圖說.

326　"The Drag-net," depicting two men using a dragnet to catch birds in a grassy field, in Kum, "Some Chinese Methods" (1910): 138.

327　"*Paradoxurus hermaphroditus* [Asian palm civet]. (From a drawing by Colonel Tickell)" in *The Fauna of British India, including Ceylon and Burma, Mammalia* (1888–1891): 109, fig. 27.

332　"鱷蜥 鱷蜥科 [Crocodile Lizard Shinisauridae] *Shinisaurus crocodilurus* Ahl" in 中国动物图谱—爬行动物 (1962): 21.

333　"Molge wolterstorffi [Yunnan lake newt]" female above and male below, by J. Green in *Proceedings of the Zoological Society of London* (1905): Pl. XVII.

334　"蜜蜂 [Honey bees]" in a 1655 edition of *Compendium of Materia Medica* (*Běncǎo Gāngmù* 本草綱目).

335　"Firefly" from Pearson Scott Foresman.

337　"伏翼 [Bat]" in 新編類要圖注本草.

338　"Burmese peacock" in Lydekker, *Wild Life of the World : A Descriptive Survey of the Geographical Distribution of Animals, Vol. II* (1916): 197.

339　"H. leueozenys [Northern white-cheeked gibbon]" in *Большой советской энциклопедии, Том 16* (*Great Soviet Encyclopedia, Vol. 16*) (1929): Гиббоны (Gibbons), fig. 2.

344　"*Asiatic Elephant* (Elephas Indicus)" in *Popular Science Monthly* 2 (1873): 144, fig. 8.

351　"Side view of head of *R. lasiostis* [Sumatran rhino]," in *Proceedings of the Scientific Meetings of the Zoological Society of London* (1872): 792, fig. 3.

352　"Hairy-eared Rhinoceros. (From the *Proceedings of the Zoological Society*.)" in *Cassell's Natural History, Vol. II* (1878): 333.

353　"The Binturong" in *Cassell's Natural History, Vol. II* (1878): 95.

354　"Bull Gaur" in Lydekker, *The New Natural History, Vol. II* (1901): 176.

355　"Hog Deer (Cervus porcinus)" in Ward, *Records of Big Game, 2nd ed.* (1896): 10.

356　"虎別錄中品 [Tiger]" in 李中立, 本草原始 (1628–1644).

358　"The Clouded Tiger (*Felis macrocelis*)" in Mivart, *The Cat: An Introduction to the Study of Backboned Animals, Especially Mammals* (1881): 398, fig. 168.

360　"孔雀 [Peafowl]" in a 1637 edition of *Compendium of Materia Medica* (*Běncǎo Gāngmù* 本草綱目).

369　"Thamin [Eld's deer]" in Lydekker, *The Great and Small Game of India, Burma, and Tibet* (1900): Pl. VI, fig. 8.

371　"Polyplectron thibetanum" by Joseph Wolf and Joseph Smit in *A Monograph of the Phasianidae: or, Family of the Pheasants, Vol. I* (1872): Pl. 1.

401 "Life restoration of *Hanyusuchus sinensis*, gen. et sp. nov. from the Bronze Age of southern China" by Hikaru Amemiya in Iijimia et al, "An intermediate crocodylian linking two extant gharials from the Bronze Age of China and its human-induced extinction," *Proceedings of the Royal Society B* (2022), fig. S27 (p. 39 of supplementary material at https://doi.org/10.6084/m9.figshare.c.5870758.v1). (CC BY 4.0)

402 "Green Turtle" (right) and "Hawksbill" (left) in Verrill, *The Bermuda Islands* (1902): 281, figs. 47–48.

403 "瑇瑁 [Hawksbill sea turtle]" in 紹興校定経史証類備急本草 (1933).

404 "Dugong" from Pearson Scott Foresman.

406 "Dolphin Mark" by Wikipedia user 春卷柯南.

409 "鱟 [Horseshoe crabs]" in a 1655 edition of *Compendium of Materia Medica* (*Běncǎo Gāngmù* 本草綱目).

410 "The Chinese King Crab (*Xiphosura longispina*) from Fukien [Fujian]" by Arthur de Carle Sowerby in *A Naturalist's Note-Book in China* (1925): 183.

412 "九罭之魚鱒魴 [The nine enclosures of the net; The rud and bream keep tight]" A trout or bream illustration 橘国雄 1785 edition of *Máoshī Míngwù Túshuō* 毛詩名物圖說.

413 "珊瑚 [Coral]" in a 1655 edition of *Compendium of Materia Medica* (*Běncǎo Gāngmù* 本草綱目).

414 "鹽井 [Salt Wells]," rubbing detail of an Eastern Han period brick relief from present-day Qionglai, Sichuan, now in the Sichuan Museum.

414 "Кабаны на солнопеке. [Wild boars in the sunshine.]" by N. A. Baikov in Байков [Baikov], *В дебрях Маньчжурии* [*In the Wilds of Manchuria*] (1934): facing 12.

419 "Musk Deer. *Moschus moschiferus.* ×1/6. (From *Nature*.)" by Joseph Wolf in Beddard, *The Cambridge Natural History, Vol. X: Mammalia* (1902): 300, fig. 158.

420 "Ailuropus Melanoleucus" in *Hunting in Many Lands: The Book of the Boone and Crockett Club*, ed. Theodore Roosevelt and George Bird Grinnell (1895): facing 263.

452 "Горал — обитатель скалистых вершин. [Goral — an inhabitant of rocky peaks.]" by N. A. Baikov in Байков [Baikov], *В дебрях Маньчжурии* [*In the Wilds of Manchuria*] (1934): facing 14.

467 "鷺圖 [Heron Illustration]" in 古今圖書集成 (*Complete Classics Collection of Ancient China*) (1726).

468 Deer, titled "玄麈," in 1588 edition of *Fāng Shì Mò Pǔ* 方氏墨譜.

474 "Ribbed faced deer, barking deer, *Cervulus muntjac.* 20 to 22 in. high" in Whitney, *Jungle Trails and Jungle People: Travel, Adventure and Observation in the Far East* (1905): facing 94, "The Far Eastern Deer," fig. 3.

LIST of SECTION BREAKS

4   𣦸 Seal script of 滅 *miè*, meaning "destroy," "exterminate," or "extinguish."

5   農 Seal script of 農 *nóng*, meaning "farming."

6   氣 Seal script of 氣 *qì*, meaning "air."

     文 Seal script of 文 *wén*, meaning "script" or "writing."

7   冊 Seal script of 冊 *cè*, meaning "book."

23   耕 Seal script of 耕 *gēng*, meaning "to plough" or "to cultivate."

28   君 Seal script of 君 *jūn*, meaning "sovereign" or "gentleman."

29   Oracle bone script for 虎 *hǔ*, meaning "tiger."

32   Oracle bone script for 麋 *mí*, meaning "elaphure."

35   "*Bos mephistopheles*, front view of type-specimen." in Hopwood, "A new species of buffalo from the Pleistocene of China" (1925).

37   豬 Seal script of 豬 *zhū*, meaning "pig."

38   狼 Seal script of 狼 *láng*, meaning "wolf."

39   "Leopard" pictogram by YuguDesign from the Noun Project. https://thenounproject.com/icon/leopard-246357/

42   Oracle bone script for 鹿 *lù*, meaning "deer."

44   Archaic form of 羚, *líng* meaning "antelope."

     鵤 Seal script of 鶡 *hé*, an archaic name for the brown eared pheasant.

46   狐 Seal script of 狐 *hú*, meaning "fox."

47   鼬 Seal script of 鼬 *yòu*, meaning "weasel."

56   Wolverine pictogram made from detail of Distinctive Unit Insignia of the 94 Engineer Battalion.

57   Sable pictogram made from detail of coat of arms of Sobolevo rayon.

61   珠 Seal script of 珠 *zhū*, meaning "pearl."

62   參 Seal script of 參 *shēn*, part of the word 人參 *rén shēn*, meaning "ginseng."

67 "Deer" pictogram by Michael Bundscherer from the Noun Project. https://thenounproject.com/icon/deer-1149/

68 "Moose" pictogram by Road Signs from the Noun Project. https://thenounproject.com/icon/moose-145927/

"reindeer" pictogram by Road Signs from the Noun Project. https://thenounproject.com/icon/reindeer-145926/

69 麝 Seal script of 麝 *shè*, meaning "musk deer."

71 "boar" pictogram by Ealancheliyan s from the Noun Project. https://thenounproject.com/icon/boar-37057/

77 豹 Seal script of 豹 *bào*, meaning "panther" or "leopard."

78 Lynx pictogram from from detail of coat of arms of Jēkabpils, Latvia.

79 Seal script of 貓 *māo*, meaning "cat."

虫 Jurchen character *dorbi*, meaning "fox."

狼 *láng*, meaning "wolf" written in "Phags-Pa script.

81 Illustration of an Asiatic black bear by Arthur de Carle Sowerby, from p.30 of *A Sportsman's Miscellany* (1917).

89 鶴 Seal script of 鶴 *hè*, meaning "crane."

鸛 Seal script of 鸛 *guàn*, meaning "stork."

90 Illustration of an Amur sturgeon from plate 1 of 庄 (Shō), 滿洲重要淡水魚類圖說 (*Illustrated Catalogue of Important Freshwater Fish of Manchuria*, 1940).

99 馬 Khitan large script character muri, meaning "horse."

102 Saiga pictogram made from detail of 2013 stamp from Kazakhstan.

106 鴇 Seal script of 鴇 *bǎo*, meaning "bustard."

108 Asian houbara bustard pictogram modified from illustration "Szammarowsi's chlamydotis macqueeni" by Wikimedia Commons user The Great Mule of Eupatoria. https://commons.wikimedia.org/wiki/File:Szammarowsi's_chlamydotis_macqueeni.png CC BY-SA 4.0
Modification available at https://commons.wikimedia.org/wiki/File:Houbara_bustard_1_-_Szammarowsi%E2%80%99s_chlamydotis_macqueeni_black_copy.png

109 "marmot standing" pictogram by Philipp Lehmann from the Noun Project. https://thenounproject.com/icon/marmot-standing-2140234/

111 "Mushrooms" pictogram by Graphic Nehar from the Noun Project. https://thenounproject.com/icon/mushrooms-3525586/

120 Goitered gazelle pictogram made from illustration from Большая советская энциклопедия (*Great Soviet Encyclopedia*, 1926) by В. А. Ватагина (V. A. Vatagina).

121 "Beaver" pictogram by parkjisun from the Noun Project. https://thenounproject.com/icon/beaver-930992/

129   夫 轡 Seal script of 戈壁 *Gēbì*, meaning "Gobi."

130   Xinjiang ground jay pictogram made from illustration by J.G. Keulemans on Plate IV of *Scientific Results of the Second Yarkand Mission; Based Upon the Collections and Notes of the Late Ferdinand Stoliczka, Aves* by R. Bowdler Sharpe (1891).

132   蒤 Tangut character *mja*, meaning "river"

133   "elk" pictogram by Ho Ching from the Noun Project. https://thenounproject.com/icon/elk-714220/

135   䏻 Tangut character *rjir*, meaning "tiger."

145   དྲེད་མོང་ *dred mong*, a Tibetan name for the Tibetan blue bear.

147   སྦྲེ *sbre*, a Tibetan name for the Tibetan fox.

149   འཕར་བ་ *'phar ba*, a Tibetan name for the dhole.

150   སྤྱང་ཀི *spyang ki*, a Tibetan name for the wolf.

151   ཁྲི་ལེ་ *khri le*, a Tibetan name for the manul of Pallas's cat.

152   རྩྭ་གཡི *rtswa g.yi*, a Tibetan name for the Chinese mountain cat.

153   ཁྲུང་ཁྲུང་སྐེ་ནག *khrung khrung ske nag*, a Tibetan name for the black-necked crane.

159   རྒོ་སྐྱ *rgo skya*, a Tibetan name for the goa or Tibetan gazelle.

161   འབྲོང་ *'brong*, a Tibetan name for a type of wild yak.

165   བོང་རྐྱང་ *bong rkyang*, a Tibetan name for the kiang or Tibetan wild ass.

170   གཉན་ *gnyan*, a Tibetan name for the argali.

171   "Ibex" pictogram by Sophia Lee from the Noun Project. https://thenounproject.com/icon/ibex-58418/

172   གནའ་བ་ *gna' ba*, a Tibetan name for the bharal or blue sheep.

173   གསའ་ *gsa'*, a Tibetan name for the snow leopard.

179   ཨའུ་རྩི་སྨུག་ཁྲ *a'u rtsi smug khra*, a Tibetan name for *Fritillaria*.

180   Matsutake pictogram made from an illustration by 服部雪齋 (Hattori Sessai) in 有用植物圖說 (*Yūyō shokubutsu zusetsu*) (1891).

181   དབྱར་རྩྭ་དགུན་འབུ་ *dbyar rtswa dgun 'bu*, Tibetan for *yartsa gunbu* or Chinese caterpillar fungus.

185   གཙོད་ *gtsod*, a Tibetan name for the chiru or Tibetan antelope.

203   𤴡 Seal script of 滇 *Diān*, a character used as an abbreviation for Yunnan Province, in reference to the ancient Dian Kingdom centered on the Dian Lake plateau.

206   怒 Seal script of 怒 *nù*, meaning "anger" or "fury" and part of the name of the Salween River in Chinese (*Nù Jiāng* 怒江).

207   Symbol based on the emblem of the Jedi Order from Star Wars, from Font Awesome Free 5.4.1 by @fontawesome https://fontawesome.com/icons/jedi?f=classic&s=solid.

214 "Giant panda drawing" by Wikimedia Commons user Max Ronnersjö. https://commons.wikimedia.org/wiki/File:Giant_panda_drawing.png

219 Giant pandas by Sun Chuanzhe (孙传哲) from a postal stamp of the People's Republic of China (1963).

224 Crested ibis pictogram made from detail of 1960 stamp from Japan.

228 Takin pictogram made from an illustration by Arthur de Carle Sowerby on p.195 of *A Sportsman's Miscellany* (1917).

231 鷹 Dongba pictograph for "white-lipped deer."

Sichuan taimen pictogram made from illustration by 任仲年 on p.13 of 秦岭鱼类志 (1987).

234 𦊆 Dongba pictograph for "frog."

235 𦘣 Dongba pictograph for "pheasant."

256 Finless porpoise pictogram modified from illustration "Finless porpoise size" by Wikimedia Commons user Chris_huh. https://commons.wikimedia.org/wiki/File:Finless_porpoise_size.svg. CC BY-SA 3.0
Modification available at https://commons.wikimedia.org/wiki/File:Finless_porpoise_size_pictogram_copy.png.

263 Yangtze sturgeon illustration from Plate 22 in *Nouvelles archives du Muséum d'histoire naturelle* 4 (1868).

265 Bronze script for 魚 *yú*, meaning "fish."

獺 Seal script of 獺 *tǎ*, meaning "otter."

272 鼉 Seal script of 鼉 *tuó*, an archaic name for the Chinese alligator.

279 鯢 Seal script of 鯢 *ní*, meaning "salamander."

285 "Swan" pictogram by bmijnlieff from the Noun Project. https://thenounproject.com/icon/swan-95057/

288 Elaphure pictogram made from illustration on Plate V of *The Great and Small Game of Europe, Western & Northern Asia, and America* by Richard Lydekker (1901).

289 Seal script for 獐 *zhāng*, meaning "water deer."

301 銀 Seal script of 銀 *yín*, meaning "silver."

杉 *shān*, meaning "fir."

302 桐 Seal script of 桐 *tóng*, a character included in the names for trees such as the paulownia, tung tree and others.

303 "Ginkgo" pictogram by Olivier Guin from the Noun Project. https://thenounproject.com/icon/gingko-1183/

310 豹 Sui script *peu*, meaning "leopard."

315 徽 Seal script of 徽 *Huī*, a character used as an abbreviation for Anhui Province.

317 麂 Dongba pictograph for "black muntjac."

318 Sambar pictograph made from illustration in *Archives du Muséum d'Histoire Naturelle, Tome VI* (1852): Pl. XXIX.

    Dongba pictograph for "wild boar."

321 Seal script of 黑 *hēi*, meaning "black."

323 Seal script of 白 *bái*, meaning "white."

324 Seal script of 葉 *yè*, meaning "leaf."

    Sui script *mon*, meaning "monkey."

328 鵐 *wú*, meaning "bunting."

329 Seal script of 鳽 *yán*, a character used in the names of bitterns and other types of herons.

330 Dongba pictograph for "bamboo rat."

331 Seal script of 蝮 *fù*, meaning "pit viper."

332 Seal script of 蜥 *xī*, meaning "lizard."

334 Dongba pictograph for "bees' nest."

335 螢 *yíng*, meaning "firefly."

336 "蚯蚓 [Earthworms]" in a 1655 edition of *Compendium of Materia Medica* (*Běncǎo Gāngmù* 本草綱目).

    Dongba pictograph for "bat."

350 Seal script of 犀 *xī*, meaning "rhinoceros."

354 Dongba pictograph for "gaur."

355 豚 *tún*, meaning "pig."

    Dongba pictograph for "tiger."

358 Seal script of 豺 *chái*, meaning "dhole."

359 Dongba pictograph for "peafowl."

361 猱 *náo*, an archaic character for a type of primate.

366 猿 *yuán*, meaning "gibbon."

368 Seal script of 鹿 *lù*, meaning "deer."

371 鷓 *zhè*, part of the word 鷓鴣 *zhègū* meaning "partridge."

374 蟒 *mǎng*, meaning "python."

375 Tokay gecko illustration from Pearson Scott Foresman.

376 Illustration from a copy of the *Compendium of Materia Medica* (*Běncǎo Gāngmù* 本草綱目) of a *fēnglí* 風狸, an animal recorded in Chinese texts that in some cases likely referred to slow lorises.

386 Illustration of a seal from *The Cambridge Natural History, Volume X—Mammalia* (1902): 452, fig. 230.

388 鯨 *jīng*, meaning "whale."

392 Seal script of 鷗 *ōu*, meaning "gull."

393   鷸 Seal script of 鷸 *yù*, meaning "sandpiper."

395   鷺 Seal script of 鷺 *lù*, meaning "egret" or "heron."

396   鵜 *tí*, part of the word 鵜鶘 *tíhú*, meaning "pelican."

398   丹 Seal script of 丹 *dān*, meaning "cinnabar" or "red."

402   龜 Seal script of 龜 *guī*, meaning "turtle."

404   Illustration of a dugong from p.106 of Cabrera, *Manual de Mastozoología* (1922).

405   Indo-Pacific humpback dolphin pictogram modified from illustration "Humpback dolphins size" by Wikimedia Commons user Chris huh. https://commons.wikimedia.org/wiki/File:Humpback_dolphins_size.svg CC BY-SA 3.0
Modification available at https://commons.wikimedia.org/wiki/File: Humpback_dolphin_pictogram.png.

407   魚 *yú*, meaning "fish."

       鰾 *biào*, meaning "swim bladder."

409   鱟 *hòu*, meaning "horseshoe crab."

411   礁 *jiāo*, meaning "reef."

417   保 Seal script of 保 *bǎo*, meaning "to protect," or "to preserve."

NOTES & CITATIONS

Introduction

[1] The People's Republic of China (PRC) corresponds closely to the territory of the Qing Empire— the last imperial dynasty of China's history—at the time of its collapse. The most glaring difference is that Mongolia is now independent. Taiwan— which was part of the Qing Empire from 1683 until ceded to Japan in 1895—is claimed by the PRC, but has been *de facto* independent since the Nationalist defeat in the Chinese Civil War in 1949. Despite this, no Taiwanese government has declared independence since that time, and so the island officially remains part of China—though the two sides differ on what precisely that means.

[2] "China's Biodiversity Conservation Strategy and Action Plan (2023-2030)." *Ministry of Ecology and Environment of the People's Republic of China*. January 2024.

[3] Erle C. Ellis. "Land Use and Ecological Change: A 12,000-Year History." *Annual Review of Environment and Resources* 46 (2021): 9.

J. A. J. Gowlett. "The discovery of fire by humans: a long and convoluted process." *Philosophical Transactions of the Royal Society B* 371, 20150164 (2016).

[4] Jens-Christian Svenning et al. "The late-Quaternary megafauna extinctions: Patterns, causes, ecological consequences and implications for ecosystem management in the Anthropocene." *Cambridge Prisms: Extinction* 2, e5 (2024): 10–12.

[5] Felisa A. Smith et al. "After the mammoths: The ecological legacy of late Pleistocene megafauna extinctions." *Cambridge Prisms: Extinction* 1, e9 (2023).

[6] Yinon M. Bar-On, Rob Phillips and Ron Milo. "The biomass distribution on Earth." *Proceedings of the National Academy of Sciences* 115 (2018): 6508.

The most recent best guess is that the total biomass of wild land mammals has dropped more than seven-fold since roughly 50,000 years ago, and that marine mammal biomass has fallen approximately five-fold. Humans and their domesticated livestock and poultry now massively outnumber and outweigh wild mammals and birds.

[7] Ella Tsahar et al. "Distribution and Extinction of Ungulates during the Holocene of the Southern Levant." *PLoS ONE* 4, e5316 (2009).

Peter Pfälzner. "The Elephant Hunters of Bronze Age Syria," in *Cultures in Contact. From Mesopotamia to the Mediterranean in the Second Millennium B.C.*, ed. Joan Aruz, Sarah B. Graff and Yelena Rakic (New York: Metropolitan Museum of Art, 2013) 112–131.

Canan Çakırlar and Salina Ikram. "'When elephants battle, the grass suffers.' Power, ivory and the Syrian elephant." *Levant* 48 (2016): 167–183.

Elephants also have lived in the Levant, Mesopotamia, and Anatolia into historic times, but the status of the Syrian elephant, *Elephas maximus asurus*, as a native as opposed to imported species remains disputed. Whatever their origins, they seem to have been extirpated by 700 BCE.

[8] N. Roberts et al. "Europe's lost forests: a pollen-based synthesis for the last 11,000 years." *Scientific Reports* 8, 716 (2018).

Jed O. Kaplan, Kristen M. Krumhardt and Niklaus Zimmermann. "The prehistoric and preindustrial deforestation of Europe." *Quaternary Science Reviews* 28 (2009): 3016–3034.

[9] Jennifer J. Crees et al. "Millennial-scale faunal record reveals differential resilience of European large mammals to human impacts across the Holocene." *Proceedings of the Royal Society B* 283, 20152152 (2016).

[10] Maureen Alden. "Lions in Paradise: Lion Similes in the Iliad and the Lion Cubs of IL. 18.318-22." *The Classical Quarterly* 55 (2005): 335–342.

Nancy R. Thomas. "A Lion's Eye View of the Greek Bronze Age." *Aegaeum* 37 (2014): 375–379.

[11] J. Donald Hughes. *Pan's Travail: Environmental Problems of the Ancient Greeks and Romans*. Baltimore: John Hopkins University Press, 1994, 106.

[12] Ka-wai Fan. "Climate change and Chinese history: a review of trends, topics, and methods." *WIREs Climate Change* 6 (2015): 225–238.

Xiuqi Fang et al. "Social Impacts of Climate Change in Historical China," in *Socio-Environmental Dynamics along the Historical Silk Road*, edited by Jiang Emlyn Yang, Hans-Rudolf Bork, Xiuqi Fang and Stefan Mischke, 231–245. Cham: Springer Open, 2019.

[13] The end of the Ming dynasty is perhaps the best example of this pattern. The late Ming already suffered from a myriad of ills when a sudden and extended period of

dramatically cooler conditions pushed the Ming economy to collapse. During the same period, the Manchu heartland to the northeast enjoyed a period of relative warmth and moisture, leading to increased agricultural yields and the in-migration of Han Chinese and nomadic Mongolians seeking refuge. This allowed the Manchu to increase their strength at just the period when the Ming were losing theirs. Conditions within the Ming realm eventually grew so dire that rebel groups seized the capital, at which point the Manchu marched south and conquered China.

Jianxin Cui et al. "Climatic change and the rise of the Manchu from Northeast China during AD 1600–1650." *Climate Change* 156 (2019): 405–423.

[14] Zooarchaeology in China has contributed some important and fascinating knowledge in recent years, but remains a barely tapped resource. Most archaeology in China has traditionally been and remains focused on verifying and supplementing the claims of classical texts. As a result, most information regarding wildlife comes from excavations of sites from the Shang or earlier. Investigations of later periods mostly center on cities and tombs, and provide far fewer insights.

North China

[1] Although most of North China hosts little in the way of natural habitat, and wildlife populations are often low, the overall diversity of species is nonetheless quite high, especially for small creatures such as insects, reptiles, and birds.

[2] Cultural and economic influence gradually shifted from the Yellow River Basin south to the Yangtze River Basin until the Southern Song (1127–1279), by which time the south was paramount. Political power, however, remained centered in the north, where most dynasties continued to base their capitals.

[3] In Chinese the Great Bend of the Yellow River, or Ordos Loop, is known as the *Hé Tào* 河套, or "river loop."

[4] In English, the Bo Hai (*Bó Hǎi* 渤海) or Bo Sea, is more typically named the Bohai Sea.

[5] According to traditional historiography, the first dynasty was not the Shang 商 but the Xia 夏. There remains no consensus on whether the Xia in fact existed, or were merely a mythic or semi-mythic concoction of later times. Despite this, a 1996 PRC-sponsored project officially dated the Xia from 2070 to 1600 BCE.

The dating of the Shang to 1600 BCE is also controversial, and many experts favor later dates. The PRC's Xia-Shang-Zhou Chronology Project settled on 1600 BCE as a broadly acceptable compromise. It should not be viewed as highly accurate, but as a least-objectionable rough guess.

[6] North China's water scarcity continues to be a problem. The region's available freshwater per capita—at around 300 m³ for the region and down to 100 m³ for Beijing—is far below the international standard for water scarcity of 1,000 m³. Aside from a mix of standard water conservation measures, the central government has also been pursuing the largest water diversion project in history, the South–North Water Transfer Project (南水北调工程). The mega project aims to construct three separate canal systems to divert water from the Yangtze River to North China. The idea stretches back to Mao Zedong, and consists of Eastern, Central, and Western routes. The Eastern Route is an upgrade to the Grand Canal system. The Central Route, consisting of a canal from Danjiangkou Reservoir on the Hubei-Henan border north to Beijing, was completed in 2014. The Western Route is by far the most ambitious, and is meant to divert flow across the Tibetan Plateau. It remains controversial and construction work has yet to begin. According to present plans, it is meant to transfer 17 billion m³ of water annually. This may prove to be wishful thinking. Both the Eastern and Central routes have fallen far short of their planned capacities. Meant to divert 14.8 billion m³ and 13 billion m³ of water, respectively, each year, they have averaged only 1 billion m³ and 6 billion m³.

Wildlife in Chinese Thought

[1] Both Daoism and Buddhism exist, broadly speaking, in two forms: philosophical and religious. The forms are more clearly distinguished in Chinese than English. The philosophical school of Daoism, exemplified in the works of Laozi and Zhuangzi, is known as *Dàojiā* 道家, whereas *Dàojiào* 道教 refers to the later collection of folk religious beliefs and practices that—though borrowing many symbols and concepts from philosophical Daoism—bears little resemblance to it in principle or practice. Similarly, the philosophical form of Buddhism, traced back directly to the teachings of Gautama Buddha, is referred to as *Fóxué* 佛学; religious Buddhism, closer to the folk traditions of religious Daoism than the scholarly practice of the philosophical form, is known as *Fójiào* 佛教. In English these distinctions are rarely made, leading to considerable confusion about the teachings and practices of the different systems. Here, unless otherwise specified, the use of the phrases "Daoism" or "Buddhism" refers to the philosophical forms.

[2] Some of this impression is down to problems of translation. For those unfamiliar with the classical texts, Chinese concepts such as *zìrán* 自然—often translated into English as "nature"—seem to equate to Western concepts of a natural world at least in part separate from man. This is far from the case, and the use of the word "nature" in translations of such texts as the *Dao De Jing* has done much to give the false impression of a greater reverence for flora and fauna than is actually expressed.

[3] Accessible explanations of past Chinese views of nature can be found in Mark Elvin's *The Retreat of the Elephants: An Environmental History of China* (2004), Robert B.

Marks' *China: Its Environment and History* (2012), and Roel Sterckx's *Ways of Heaven: An Introduction to Chinese Thought* (2019).

⁴ *Qū hǔ bào xī xiàng ér yuǎn zhī, tiānxià dà yuè.* 驅虎豹犀象而遠之，天下大悅。 *Mencius*, Book 3B 《孟子·滕文公下》

⁵ Brian Lander and Katherine Brunson. "The Sumatran rhinoceros was extirpated from mainland East Asia by hunting and habitat loss." *Current Biology* 28 (2018): R252–R253.

⁶ Nei Xuan-hua. "The Distribution and Transition of Rhinoceros Sinensis in the Perspective of Environmental History." *Journal of Wenshan University* 28 (2015): 70.

⁷ Before Present is the dating system typically used when measuring time based on radiocarbon dating. Specifically, the "present" in Before Present is 1950—meaning that although the term is no longer accurate in the strictest sense, the time scale is consistent, since all dates are measured from a fixed point.

⁸ The presence of elephants in the Yellow River Valley and as far north as Beijing was made famous (at least among the small cadre interested in China's environmental history) with the publication of Mark Elvin's seminal work *The Retreat of the Elephants* in 2004 (though the narrative had appeared in English as early as Berthold Laufer's 1925 leaflet *Ivory in China*). Elvin's analysis relied on the work of Wen Huanran 文焕然, a pioneering historical biogeographer whose exhaustive cataloguing of historical, zooarchaeological, and paleontological evidence on the past distributions of China's wildlife forms the basis of much succeeding analysis. Wen's conclusion—which Elvin accepted—was that elephants had lived along the Yellow River into the Shang and perhaps Zhou periods, and moved south primarily in response to a cooling climate. More recent scholarship has cast this in doubt. Recent testing has pushed back the date of crucial physical evidence, and other remains from Anyang, Hebei are suspect, as they likely came from elephants brought northward and held captive at the Shang court. Moreover, new research on North China's ancient climate suggests the cooling was less dramatic than earlier presumed, and would have had little impact on the distribution of mammals, elephants included. The most likely scenario is that the southern border of the Yellow River Valley was elephants' northern limit.

Brian Lander and Katherine Brunson. "Wild Mammals of Ancient North China." *Journal of Chinese History* 2 (2018): 301–302.

⁹ Roel Sterckx. "Attitudes Towards Wildlife and the Hunt in Pre-Buddhist China," in *Wildlife in Asia: Cultural Perspectives*, ed. John Knight. London: RoutledgeCurzon, 2004, 15–35.

[10] Charles Sanft. "Environment and Law in Early Imperial China (Third Century BCE–First Century CE): Qin and Han Statutes Concerning Natural Resources." *Environmental History* 15 (2010): 701–721.

[11] Edward H. Schafer. "The Conservation of Nature under the T'ang Dynasty." *Journal of the Economic and Social History of the Orient* 5 (1962): 301.

[12] For a thorough discussion of the wilderness ideal in American thought, see Roderick Nash's classic work *Wilderness in the American Mind* (1967); for a history of the evolution of American thought and action towards wildlife see Thomas R. Dunlap's *Saving America's Wildlife: Ecology and the American Mind, 1850-1990* (1988).

[13] One way the Chinese graded different southern barbarian peoples was as either *shēng* 生 (raw or uncooked) or *shú* 熟 (cooked). The raw barbarians were the more savage, while the cooked barbarians were closer to a civilized existence. The measure of their status was their willingness to submit to Chinese authority. Compliant barbarians were cooked, resistant ones raw.

Magnus Fiskesjö. "On the 'Raw' and the 'Cooked' Barbarians of Imperial China." *Inner Asia* 1 (1999): 139–164.

[14] This is, in the interest of brevity, a gross simplification of a complex topic. Though broadly accurate, there was of course a wide range of views on nature and wilderness throughout the long course of Chinese intellectual history. As Mark Elvin pointed out in *The Retreat of the Elephants*, "There was no one view of nature that can be called the 'Chinese' view. There was not even a spectrum. Rather a kaleidoscope of fragments most of which reflected something of most of the other fragments."

[15] Richard B. Harris. *Wildlife Conservation in China: Preserving the Habitat of China's Wild West*. Armonk, NY: M.E. Sharpe, 2008, 59.

Robert B. Marks. *China: Its Environment and History*. Lanham: Rowman & Littlefield. 2012, 222.

[16] Fa-ti Fan explores the early decades of British natural history exploration in China in *British Naturalists in Qing China: Science, Empire, and Cultural Encounter*, Cambridge: Harvard University Press, 2004.

[17] Michael Kiefer. *Chasing the Panda: How an Unlikely Pair of Adventurers Won the Race to Capture the Mythical White Bear*. New York: Da Capo Press, 2002, 28.

[18] For example, Harry Caldwell, a Methodist missionary from Tennessee, used his skills as a hunter to convince entire villages in rural Fujian to convert to Christianity en masse. Caldwell became famous in the region as a tiger hunter, and when called to rid a community of tigers, he would first preach to the village leaders and elicit an assurance that should he succeed when their traditional beliefs held he would fail, in return the village would reject their old ways and turn to Christianity. Caldwell recounted his hunting and preaching experiences in his book *Blue Tiger* (1924), and

his son John C. Caldwell later added some of his own recollections in *China Coast Family* (1953).

[19] American and European influences had dominated the trends of China's intellectual ferment since the late nineteenth century, but the newly established Communist regime favored Soviet thought to the near exclusion of all others. This applied across all sciences, and led to the adoption of disastrously misguided ideas such as Lysenkoism, an ideologically-based theory of genetics that rejected natural selection and Mendelian genetics; it contributed in part to the catastrophic famine that marked the Great Leap Forward.

[20] An in-depth exploration of the Mao-era campaigns to subjugate nature to the needs of the revolution can be found in Judith Shapiro's seminal work *Mao's War Against Nature: Politics and the Environment in Revolutionary China* (2001).

[21] Judith Shapiro. *Mao's War Against Nature: Politics and the Environment in Revolutionary China*. Cambridge: Cambridge University Press, 2001, 86–89.

The rodents and insects were targeted as carriers of disease, while the sparrows were disliked for eating grain seed and fruit. The sparrows were targeted in mass efforts across the country, in which communities frightened the birds into flight, then continued their efforts until the sparrows exhausted themselves and dropped from the skies. Nests, eggs, and chicks were also found and destroyed. The "smash the sparrows campaign" (*dǎ máquè yùndòng* 打麻雀运动) was seemingly a great success—the birds were driven nearly to extinction in China by 1960, when ornithologist Tso-hsin Cheng managed to impress upon the national leadership that sparrows were in fact beneficial to crop yields because they acted as a check on crop-depredating insects. The campaign ended—bedbugs replaced sparrows on the pest list—and China then imported 250,000 sparrows from the Soviet Union to reestablish local populations. Echoes of the campaign live on, as the four pests campaign's slogan, "Wipe out the four pests" (*Chú sì hài* 除四害), is still in use today, though cockroaches have replaced bedbugs as the fourth pest.

[22] "New China" (*Xīnhuá* 新华) is a moniker denoting China since the Communist takeover, and is most commonly encountered as the name of the state press agency, the Xinhua (or New China) News Agency.

[23] Lu Houji. "Habitat Availability and Prospects for Tigers in China," in *Tigers of the World: The Biology, Biopolitics, Management, and Conservation of an Endangered Species*, ed. Ronald L. Tilson and Ulysses S. Seal. Park Ridge: Noyes Publications, 1987, 71.

[24] E. Elena Songster. *Panda Nation: The Construction and Conservation of China's Modern Icon*. New York: Oxford University Press, 2018, 41.

[25] Vaclav Smil. *The Bad Earth: Environmental Degradation in China*. New York: M.E. Sharpe, 1984, 131.

[26] What I refer to as "Chinese medicine" is most often referred to in English as Traditional Chinese Medicine or TCM. I eschew the use of "traditional" on the grounds that much of Chinese medicine as it now exists is not in the least bit traditional, having been developed in the last century. Similarly, Chinese medicine is typically contrasted to "Western medicine," a term I also consider inaccurate and misleading. Though it is true that modern scientific medicine first developed in Europe and the Americas, its defining feature is not its geographic or cultural origins but the use of the scientific method to test and confirm or refute hypotheses, thereby advancing theory and practice. Chinese medicine, in contrast, because of its foundational tenets is inherently unscientific. As such, I venture a more accurate term than "Western medicine" would be "scientific medicine."

[27] Animals remain an integral part of the modern medical industry, though in a qualitatively different manner. No more slathering fox fat into your eyes or wearing a whole donkey skin for two weeks to cure what ails you.

[28] Liz P. Y. Chee's *Mao's Bestiary: Medicinal Animals and Modern China* (2021) is an excellent in-depth study of the expanded use of animal parts—wild and domestic—in Chinese medicine during the Communist-era.

[29] The 2013 figure of 2,341 includes both species and subspecies.

[30] China's medicinal demand for animals is not exclusive to wildlife, and has led to catastrophic declines in Africa's donkey population in order to manufacture *ē jiāo* 阿胶, a gelatin made from donkey hide used to treat such problems as bleeding, dizziness, insomnia and dry cough. For more information on the donkey skin trade refer to The Donkey Sanctuary's reports at https://www.thedonkeysanctuary.org.uk/.

[31] Harris, *Wildlife Conservation in China*, 58–68.

[32] China's legal regime, however, continues to categorize and treat animals, wild and domestic, as resources for present—or if so rare as to currently require protection, future—use.

Deborah Cao. *Animals in China: Law and Society*. Basingstoke: Palgrave Macmillan, 2015.

[33] As in the rest of the world, popular concern for endangered species is limited by and large to charismatic megafauna, those animals people tend to find attractive. Other species, whether deemed somehow unattractive or simply uninteresting, are equally in need of and deserving of attention and protection. Unfortunately they remain obscure to all but specialists.

[34] Although many of China's wildlife professionals are as well-trained and dedicated to preserving their country's wildlife heritage as their peers abroad, the government agency tasked with administering China's terrestrial wildlife, the National Forestry and Grassland Administration, by wide account remains a bastion of the old

utilitarian view of wildlife as natural resource. Long-standing ties to a variety of industries and business ventures that rely on the exploitation of wildlife—often farmed—no doubt goes a long way to explain this reluctance to abandon old notions and habits.

A World Made for Farming

[1] The question of when and where agriculture first arose in China is wracked with uncertainty, claims, and counterclaims. Given that experts in the field cannot seem to agree on the geography or chronology, I have opted to take a conservative approach and use the places and dates that—in my untrained judgement—have the strongest evidential base.

C. Leipe et al. "Discontinuous spread of millet agriculture in eastern Asia and prehistoric population dynamics." *Science Advances* 5, eaax6225 (2019).

[2] E.N. Anderson. *Food and Environment in Early and Medieval China*. Philadelphia: University of Pennsylvania Press, 2014.

[3] Recent historiography largely rejects the notion that a monolithic Chinese culture arose in the Yellow River Valley and was exported across the continent as neighboring peoples were conquered or drawn voluntarily by the irresistible cultural superiority of the Han. Current thinking emphasizes that there were other, contemporary peoples whose cultures— though they did not survive as fully separate—nonetheless left notable and lasting influence on the dominant culture. Early examples of these contributing cultures were the southern state of Chu 楚 (c. 1030–223 BCE) that encompassed much of present-day Central and South China, including the Middle and Lower Yangtze Valley; as well as the southwestern state of Shu 蜀 (?–c. 316 BCE) centered in present-day Sichuan, which recent and on-going archaeological work is only beginning to elucidate.

[4] Brian Lander. "Birds and beasts were many: the ecology and climate of the Guanzhong basin in the pre-imperial period." *Early China* 43 (2020): 234–236.

[5] Nicholas K. Menzies. "Forestry," in *Science and Civilisation in China: Vol. 6, Part III, Biology and Biological Technology, Agro-Industries and Forestry*, ed. Joseph Needham. Cambridge: Cambridge University Press, 1996, 555–558.

[6] Lander and Brunson, "Wild Mammals of Ancient North China," 291–312.

The exact mix of wild equids on the ancient grasslands of North Asia is still uncertain. Remains found in North China, Manchuria, and Mongolia have generally been identified as either ancestors of domestic horses *Equus caballus* or as wild takhi (Przewalski's horse) *E. ferus przewalskii*. However, bones from multiple Neolithic sites have recently been discovered to instead belong to *E. ovodovi. E. ovodovi*, or the Ovodov horse, is an extinct equid first identified as a species only in 2011, one year after its subgenus *Sussemionus* was named. Remains of *E. ovodovi* from North China and Manchuria indicate the horses survived until at least about 3,500 years ago. Having already suffered a long and drastic population drop over the course of the ice ages, the arrival of modern humans —and the subsequent spread of their domesticated horses—may well have spelled the end of *E. ovodovi*. Too little research has yet been done, however, to confidently determine the exact timing or cause of its extinction, or the full extent of its range.

Dawei Cai et al. "Radiocarbon and genomic evidence for the survival of *Equus Sussemionus* until the late Holocene." *eLife* 11, e73346 (2022). https://doi.org/ 10.7554/eLife.73346.

[7] China's deforestation was paralleled in Japan from the end of the seventh century, where the emulation of the Tang in the form of architectural style and the construction and maintenance of multiple capitals led to the clearance of forests in the Kinai region (the vicinity of modern Nara, Kyoto, and Osaka). The process began in 690 under the Empress Jitō (*Jitō-tennō* 持統天皇, 645–703, r. 686–697), who constructed a new capital, Fujiwara-kyō, in present-day Kashihara. The new capital proved short lived, and in 710 the court moved to a new capital in Nara until a final move to Kyoto in 794 CE. It was not merely the raising of three capitals in quick succession that required vast amounts of lumber, but the Tang architectural style demanded the use of much more wood than prior Japanese styles. The use of clay tile roofing was especially demanding. Making the tiles required large amounts of firewood to fuel the kilns, and the great weight of the tiles on top of the structure required heavy and strong support structures composed of large pillars and beams. The ultimate result was widespread deforestation of the Kinai capital region, with a myriad of connected environmental degradations.

Conrad Totman. *Japan: An Environmental History*. London: I.B. Taurus. 2014, 76–92.

[8] Marks, *China: Its Environment and History*, 100.

[9] Peter Lorge. "The Great Ditch of China and the Song-Liao Border," in *Battlefronts Real and Imagined: War, Border, and Identity in the Chinese Middle Period*, ed. Don J. Wyatt. New York: Palgrave Macmillan, 2008, 59–62.

[10] Yuan Julian Chen. "Frontier, Fortification, and Forestation: Defensive Woodland on the Song–Liao Border in the Long Eleventh Century." *Journal of Chinese History* 2, sp. 2 (2018): 313–334.

[11] Ling Zhang. "Ponds, Paddies and Frontier Defence: Environmental and Economic Changes in Northern Hebei in Northern Song China (960–1127)." *The Medieval History Journal* 14 (2011): 41.

[12] Schafer, "The Conservation of Nature under the T'ang Dynasty," 299–300.

[13] Marks, *China: Its Environment and History*, 236.

[14] Lander and Brunson. "Wild Mammals of Ancient North China," 291.

[15] The First Emperor reigned as King of Qin from 247 until 221 BCE, at which time he became the emperor of the Qin dynasty until his death in 210 BCE.

[16] Samuel T. Turvey et al. "New genus of extinct Holocene gibbon associated with humans in Imperial China." *Science* 360 (2018) 1346–1349.

[17] Brian Lander. "Deforestation in Early China: How People Adapted to Wood Scarcity," in *The Cultivated Forest: People and Woodlands in Asian History*, ed. Ian M. Miller, Bradley Camp Davis, Brian Lander and John S. Lee. Seattle: University of Washington Press, 2022, 1–19.

[18] Aili Kang et al. "Historic distribution and recent loss of tigers in China." *Integrative Zoology* 5 (2010): 335.

[19] Marks, *China: Its Environment and History*, 150.

[20] Armand David. *Natural History of North China with Notices of that of the South, West and North-east, and of Mongolia & Thibet, compiled chiefly from the travels of Père Armand David*. Shanghai: Da Costa & Co., 1873, 10.

N. Prejevalsky. *Mongolia, the Tangut Country, and the Solitudes of Northern Tibet: Being a Narrative of Three Years' Travel in Eastern High Asia, Vol. I*. London: Sampson Low, Marston, Searle, & Rivington, 1876, 103.

[21] Arthur de Carle Sowerby. "The Tiger in China." *The China Journal* 18 (1933): 97–99.

Controlling the Waters

[1] For an idea of the scale of China's water management, at the start of 2012 China had over 98,000 reservoirs, and has since only constructed more dams and assorted water projects, among them the largest and most ambitious in human history, such as the partially finished South–North Water Transfer Project. Other massive works are planned, including a dam on the Yarlung Tsangpo in Tibet that would dwarf the Three Gorges dam and all but certainly cause immense ecological damage to the rich biodiversity of the region, as well as potential hydrological havoc downstream in India and Bangladesh where the river is more famously known as the Brahmaputra.

Ministry of Water Resources, *Dam Construction and Management in China*, 2016. https://web.archive.org/web/20210811134736/http://www.mwr.gov.cn/english/mainsubjects/201604/P020160406515342504682.pdf.

[2] The historicity of both Yu the Great and the Xia dynasty are disputed. The earliest written records come from the later Shang dynasty, and currently the archeological evidence is inconclusive on the existence of the Xia. As for the sage-king Yu, there is

currently no supporting archeological evidence dating to the supposed time of his life, and the earliest extant records of him date only from the Western Zhou, nearly a millennia after he is said to have died.

[3] China hosts not only great river systems such as the Yellow, Yangtze, and Pearl, but also the world's greatest canal system, the Grand Canal. The Grand Canal's earliest sections were constructed at the end of the Spring and Autumn period (770–476 BCE), but the full system only took shape during the Sui dynasty (581–618) when a number of preexisting canals were connected and extended into one great network. Indeed the Grand Canal is not a single course but a complex network of linked waterways. The canal connects the southern entrepôt of Hangzhou with the great rivers and cities to the north, including the Yangtze, Huai, Yellow and Wei rivers. Most importantly the canal served as a highway for grain shipped from the rich agricultural lands of the Yangtze region north to the imperial capitals, first Xi'an and Luoyang, then later Kaifeng and finally Beijing. The great cities of the north were unable to supply themselves from their hinterlands and thus relied on massive grain transfers from the south.

The construction and maintenance of the Grand Canal required a major reworking of the North China Plain's hydrology. Streams and rivers were redirected to feed the canal, and the inflows from the Yellow River and its tributaries brought massive loads of silt. This in turn required regular dredging to maintain the water's depth, just one of the forms of maintenance needed. The canal was so dependent on continued human engineering that in times of upheaval when the state could not maintain the necessary support, the hydraulic system would break down, leading to devastating floods.

[4] The sediment load of the lower course of the Yellow River has in fact dramatically declined since the 1950s, by an estimated 90%. This primarily has been due to the reworking of the Loess Plateau through massive revegetation and terracing, which has reduced erosion, as well as the construction of check dams and reservoirs to trap sediment before reaching the river.

Wang Shuai et al. "Reduced sediment transport in the Yellow River due to anthropogenic changes." *Nature Geoscience* 9 (2016): 38–41.

[5] There have been three especially dramatic course changes in recorded history. The first was in 1128, when the Song dynasty deliberately broke the dikes to hold off the Jurchens. This caused the Yellow River to shift fully south of the Shandong Peninsula and empty into the Yellow Sea. Massive flooding between 1851 and 1855 shifted the river back north of Shandong. The most recent and infamous course change came in 1938, when the Nationalist military breached the dikes at Huayuankou, Henan to slow the Imperial Japanese Army's advance on the crucial rail junction at Zhengzhou. The river shifted south, capturing the Huai River, and the resulting flood killed perhaps 500,000 people and turned another three million into refugees. The breach was repaired after the war in 1946–1947, returning the river to its northern course.

[6] The Yellow River (*Huáng Hé* 黄河) was in fact called the Great River (*Dà Hé* 大河) for much of history. The name changed only once massive erosion of loess noticeably changed the river's hue. The first document to use the name "Yellow River" in its title only appeared in 798 CE, and the term became common over the following decades.

[7] Ruth Mostern. *The Yellow River: A Natural and Unnatural History*. New Haven: Yale University Press, 2021.

[8] Marks, *China: Its Environment and History*, 242.

[9] Or the nose of a cow, antlers of a deer, body of a donkey, and tail of a horse; or hooves of a cow, head of a horse, antlers of a deer, and tail of a donkey. Or however you prefer.

[10] This may be the same reason for domestic cattle's wide, splayed hooves. Though cattle (unlike the domesticated water buffalo) are not generally thought of as wetland creatures, their wild progenitor, the aurochs *Bos primigenius*, is believed to have inhabited marshes and other wetlands—however at present there is no consensus on their exact habitat preference.

[11] 马连义, 杨国美. 大丰麋鹿. 南京: 江苏人民出版社, 2016, 36–42.

[12] Z. Jiang and R.B. Harris. "*Elaphurus davidianus.*" *The IUCN Red List of Threatened Species* (2016): e.T7121A22159785.

[13] 马, 杨, 大丰麋鹿, 61–64.

[14] Zheng Xinxian. "Animals as Wonders: Writing Commentaries on Monthly Ordinances in Qing China," in *Animals through Chinese History: Earliest Times to 1911*, ed. Roel Sterckx, Martina Siebert and Dagmar Schäfer. Cambridge: Cambridge University Press, 2019, 219.

[15] Herman Reichenbach. "Zoological Gardens of China," in *Zoo and Aquarium History: Ancient Animal Collections to Conservation Centers, 2nd Edition*, ed. Vernon N. Kisling, Jr. Boca Raton: CRC Press, 2022, 301–302.

[16] Reichenbach, "Zoological Gardens of China," 301–302.

[17] Glover M. Allen. *The Mammals of China and Mongolia, Part 2*. New York: The American Museum of Natural History, 1940, 1179–1184.

[18] Samuel Turvey. *Witness to Extinction: How We Failed to Save the Yangtze River Dolphin*. New York: Oxford University Press, 2008, 20–21.

[19] Today you can find Père David's deer in zoos in North America, Europe, and Asia. If so inclined, you can even hunt them on private ranches in the US and Argentina. This in spite of the fact that the species is not merely endangered, but remains officially categorized as extinct in the wild.

[20] Jiang and Harris, *"Elaphurus davidianus."*

[21] Lander and Brunson. "Wild Mammals of Ancient North China," 299.

The Difficulties of Coexistence

[1] Arthur de Carle Sowerby. *Fur and Feather in North China*. Tientsin: Tientsin Press, 1914, 2–3.

[2] Harry R. Caldwell. *Blue Tiger*. New York: Abingdon Press, 1924, 137.

[3] Sowerby, *Fur and Feather*, 2.

[4] For general studies on the relation between humans and large predators, see David Quammen's *Monster of God: The Man-Eating Predator in the Jungles of History and the Mind* (2003) and William Stolzenburg's *Where the Wild Things Were: Life, Death, and Ecological Wreckage in a Land of Vanishing Predators* (2008).

[5] For the story of Japan's now extinct wolves, see Brett L. Walker's *The Lost Wolves of Japan* (2005), and John Knight's *Waiting for Wolves in Japan: An Anthropological Study of People-Wildlife Relations* (2006).

[6] Arthur de Carle Sowerby. *The Naturalist in Manchuria, Vols. II & III*. Tientsin: Tientsin Press, 1923, 42–43.

[7] Rev. Alexander Williamson. *Journeys in North China, Manchuria, and Eastern Mongolia; With Some Account of Corea, Vol. I*. London: Smith, Elder & Co., 1870, 98.

T. R. Jernigan. *Shooting in China*. Shanghai: Methodist Publishing House, 1908, 136.

George Lanning. *Wild Life in China or Chats on Chinese Birds and Beasts*. Shanghai: "The National Review" Office, 1911, 214 & 241.

Harold Frank Wallace. *The Big Game of Central and Western China: Being an Account of a Journey from Shanghai to London Overland Across the Gobi Desert*. London: John Murray, 1913, 88–89.

[8] Arthur de Carle Sowerby. *A Sportsman's Miscellany*. Tientsin: Tientsin Press, 1917, 223–224.

[9] Taxonomy is perhaps the single most contested subfield of zoology, and leopards have stirred their fair share of argument. Most recently, the IUCN's Cat Specialist Group formed a Cat Classification Task Force to revise the taxonomy of the cat family Felidae. Among their conclusions were that the North China leopard (*Panthera pardus japonensis*) was the same subspecies as the Amur leopard (*P. p. orientalis*). Predictably the folding of *P. p. japonensis* into *P. p. orientalis* has not been universally

accepted, due to what is deemed insufficiently strong molecular evidence for the change. For now most published work continues to keep the two leopards separate, as does official state policy.

Awkwardly, the subspecific name of the North China leopard's trinomen, *japonensis*, places the cat in Japan, where they have not lived for over 10,000 years. This mistake arose because the subspecies was designated based on a skin sent to the British Museum from a furrier who had received the pelt in Japan. John Edward Gray, the zoologist who inspected the skin and named the subspecies, no doubt assumed that, as the pelt had been obtained in Japan, it must have come from a leopard native to that country.

John Edward Gray. "Descriptions of some New Species of Mammalia." *Proceedings of the Zoological Society of London* (1862): 262.

[10] The most well-known example of this is the community of leopards that lives in Mumbai's Sanjay Gandhi National Park where they enthusiastically prey on the feral—and sometimes pet—dog population.

[11] Yixin Diao et al. "Predicting current and future species distribution of the raccoon dog (*Nyctereutes procyonoides*) in Shanghai, China." *Landscape and Urban Planning* 228, 104581 (2022).

Shanghai's raccoon dog population has grown rapidly in recent years, and the canines are now found on the grounds of hundreds of apartment complexes. A research team from Fudan University estimated there were 3,000 to 5,000 raccoon dogs in Shanghai in 2023.

Ding Rui, "City Slickers: How Shanghai Is Outfoxing Its Raccoon Dog Problem," *Sixth Tone*, November 30, 2023. https://www.sixthtone.com/news/1014179.

[12] J. Wong-Quincey. *Chinese Hunter*. New York: John Day, 1939, 125.

[13] Wong-Quincey, *Chinese Hunter*, 368.

[14] Tan Bangjie. "The Status of Felids in China." *Proceedings from the Cat Specialist Group meeting in Kanha National Park.* (1984): 37–38.

[15] K. Vitekere et al. "Insights on the North China leopard (*Panthera pardus japonensis* Gray, 1862): challenges in distribution, population status, threats, and implications for conservation." *The Journal of Animal & Plant Sciences* 31 (2021): 6.

5,947 kg would equate to somewhere around 743 leopards, given a rough average of 8 kg of bone per animal, as according to the Wildlife Protection Society of India.

Cattle bones are a favorite choice when making fake tiger bones. Dyed and stretched dog pelts are the standard choice for counterfeit tiger or leopard skins.

[16] The recent international trade in leopard bone arose largely as a consequence of China's 1993 ban on the use of tiger bone. According to a 2006 regulation, only leopard bone—in Chinese the term is *bàogǔ* 豹骨, which can include not only common leopards but also clouded leopards and snow leopards—from existing stockpiles could be used. However, details of those stockpiles have never been made public, and the continuing use of large quantities of leopard bone three decades later strongly suggests that pharmaceutical companies are making use of imported—perhaps illegally imported—bones. The byzantine and opaque labeling and approval system that regulates the use of wildlife parts in China's medical industry easily allows for fraud, not only regarding leopard bone but many other animal parts.

EIA. *A Bitter Pill to Swallow: China's flagrant trade in leopard bone products.* (2020). https://eia-international.org/report/bitter-pill-to-swallow-chinas-flagrant-trade-in-leopard-bone-products/.

[17] Wang Yan, "A spotty revival amid decline for China's endemic leopards," *Mongabay,* July 7, 2017. https://news.mongabay.com/2017/07/a-spotty-revival-amid-decline-for-chinas-endemic-leopards/.

[18] Alice Laguardia, Jan F. Kamler, Sheng Li, Chengcheng Zhang et al. "The current distribution and status of leopards *Panthera pardus* in China." *Oryx* 51 (2015): 155.

The flagship program of China's premier cat conservation organization, the Chinese Felid Conservation Alliance (CFCA—in Chinese *Zhōngguó Māokēdòngwù Bǎohù Liánméng* 中国猫科动物保护联盟, generally shortened to *Māo Méng* 猫盟, Felid Alliance), is focused on North China's leopards. Called "Bring Leopards Home" (*Dài Bào Huíjiā* 带豹回家) it is a campaign to protect the existing North China leopards in Shanxi and build habitat corridors for them to use to migrate eastwards and repopulate the mountains around Beijing, including those within the municipality. The programs's website (in Chinese) can be found at https://homingleopards.org.

Putting Animals to Use

[1] Linyao Du et al. "How Did Human Activity and Climate Change Influence Animal Exploitation During 7500–2000 BP in the Yellow River Valley, China?" *Frontiers in Ecology and Evolution* 8 (2020).

[2] Edward H. Schafer. "Hunting Parks and Animal Enclosures in Ancient China." *Journal of the Economic and Social History of the Orient* 11 (1968), 318–343.

[3] The Tang's ruling Li family and many noble houses were of at least partial Xianbei or Turkic blood, and Central Asian fashions were widely popular, from clothing and music to sport and beyond.

[4] As evidenced from contemporary paintings, the Mongols carried on a Persianate tradition the Tang had also adopted: hunting with cats. The preferred cats were

cheetahs, or hunting leopards, *lièbào* 猎豹 in Chinese (the English "cheetah" comes from the Hindustani *cītā* چیتا चीता, and only gained favor over "hunting leopard" in the twentieth century). Cheetahs were an esteemed hunting companion in Persianate realms, reaching their peak of popularity in Mughal India where the Emperor Akbar the Great (1556–1605) was said to have kept a thousand of the cats. The practice even reached medieval Europe, and was especially fashionable in Italy, where a number of frescoes and paintings from the time depict princes and nobles with their tame hunting leopards (the cheetahs' handlers typically arrived from the east with the cats, and were referred to as "leopardieri" or "pardieri"—leopard handlers. Some of their descendants still bear the surname Pardieri). In India the practice continued into the early twentieth century, until shortly before the extirpation of India's cheetah population. The Asiatic cheetah is now nearly extinct, and fewer than fifty survive in the deserts of central Iran.

Cheetahs were never native to Chinese territory, but were brought in from the west, most often as tribute to the imperial court. Tang and later hunters also used another cat as a hunting companion, but just which species is uncertain. The few extant depictions show a smaller cat with tufted ears, reminiscent of a lynx. The most likely candidate is the "hunting lynx" or caracal, which was used from India to the Middle East. Some researchers, however, believe the cat was the Eurasian lynx. Although there is no known evidence the lynx was used for hunting in Central Asia, lynx were captured and tamed in some areas, a fact witnessed firsthand by American adventurer Leonard Clark during his 1949 expedition to Amne Machin in Qinghai. While Clark was riding with Muslim Hui companions, the group spotted a lynx and gave chase. They cornered the cat in a gulch, at which point one man dismounted and threw himself at the lynx, wrestling it barehanded until he subdued and collared the animal, which thereafter followed along beside his horse. What became of the lynx, and whether taming the cats for hunting was a local practice, Clark did not say.

[5] David M. Robinson. *Martial Spectacles of the Ming Court*. Cambridge: Harvard University Asia Center, 2013.

[6] Thomas T. Allsen. *The Royal Hunt in Eurasian History*. Philadelphia: University of Pennsylvania Press, 2006.

[7] Roel Sterckx. *Ways of Heaven: An Introduction to Chinese Thought*. New York: Basic Books, 2019, 376–381.

[8] The name "sika" comes from the Japanese "*shika* 鹿," meaning "deer." In Chinese the sika is known as the "plum blossom deer," *méi huā lù* 梅花鹿. Despite the suggestion implicit in its binomial, *C. nippon* is native not only to Japan but mainland Asia from the Russian Far East to northern Vietnam. Populations have also been introduced over wide areas of Europe and North America. The deer are most famous, however, as the spoiled denizens of Nara, the ancient capital of Japan, where they peruse the parks and souvenir shops in search of tourists handing out specially made deer snacks.

[9] Dale R. McCullough, Zhi-Guang Jiang and Chun-Wang Li. "Sika Deer in Mainland China," in *Sika Deer: Biology and Management of Native and Introduced Populations*, ed. Dale R. McCullough, Seiki Takatsuki and Koichi Kaji. Tokyo: Springer, 2009, 525.

[10] Katherine Brunson and Brian Lander. "Deer and Humans in the Early Farming Communities of the Yellow River Valley: A Symbiotic Relationship." *Human Ecology* 51 (2023): 609–625.

[11] Brunson and Lander, "Deer and Humans in the Early Farming Communities of the Yellow River Valley."

[12] McCullough, Jiang and Li. "Sika Deer in Mainland China," 526.

[13] Allen, *The Mammals of China and Mongolia*, 1186–1188.

[14] The Chinese goral was once considered a separate species, *Naemorhedus griseus*. It is now considered the same species as the brown goral (*N. goral*), as are the Himalayan goral (*N. bedfordi*) and Burmese goral (*N. evansi*).

Emiliano Mori, Luca Nerva and Sandro Lovari. "Reclassification of the serows and gorals: the end of a neverending story?" *Mammal Review* 40 (2019): 256–262.

[15] Jing Yang et al. "Non-invasive genetic analysis indicates low population connectivity in vulnerable Chinese gorals: concerns for segregated population management." *Zoological Research* 40 (2019): 439-448.

[16] In the early twentieth century these included most of the white boar bristles used to manufacture toothbrushes in the West (though from domesticated and not wild pigs), and the intestine linings of wild sheep which were sent to the US for use as sausage casings and gut strings for tennis rackets.

[17] Timothy H. Barret and Mark Strange. "Walking by Itself: The Singular History of the Chinese Cat," in *Animals through Chinese History: Earliest Times to 1911*, ed. Roel Sterckx, Martina Siebert and Dagmar Schäfer. Cambridge: Cambridge University Press, 2019, 89.

[18] Yilin Li et al. "Determining the distribution loss of brown eared-pheasant (*Crossoptilon mantchuricum*) using historical data and potential distribution estimates." *PeerJ* 4:e2556 (2016).

[19] David, *Natural History of North China*, 10.

[20] Wong-Quincey, *Chinese Hunter*, 141–142.

[21] Williamson, *Journeys in North China*, 99.

[22] For the uninitiated there is inevitably some confusion regarding the size of Beijing and China's three other municipalities: Tianjin, Shanghai, and Chongqing. These

three cities are directly administered from the center, and are not part of larger provinces (though typically translated into English as simply "municipality," the Chinese term for them is *zhíxiáshì* 直辖市, which more accurately translates to "directly controlled city"). This simply means that, unlike most cities in China where provincial leadership appoints the municipal powers, in the four directly administered municipalities it is the central leadership who appoints the mayor and party secretary (China runs on a parallel power structure in which each government position has a Communist Party counterpart; the Party position is invariably the more powerful and important). These four municipalities are much larger than the word "city" suggests. Beijing, for instance, sprawls over 16,000 sq. km. (6,300 sq. mi.), but the urban core covers only 4,100 sq. km. (1,600 sq. mi.). If Washington D.C. was expanded to include Virginia north of Fredericksburg, it would be roughly analogous in area to Beijing. Chongqing is the most extreme. Often labelled the largest city in the world, the urban core of Chongqing in fact only consists of a—still gargantuan—5,470 sq. km. (2,100 sq. mi.) and 22 million people. The entire municipality, however, covers 82,400 sq. km. (31,800 sq. mi.), with a population of over 32 million. For comparison, that is roughly the area of Austria or the UAE, or the state of South Carolina. An American analogy would be if St. Louis was directly administered by the US federal government and expanded to include half of Missouri.

[23] Terry Townshend, "Leopard Cat in Beijing 北京豹猫," *Birding Beijing*, January 2024 update. https://wildbeijing.org/leopard-cat-in-beijing-豹猫在北京/.

Sicheng Han et al. "Distribution of leopard cats in the nearest mountains to urban Beijing and its affecting environmental factors." *Biodiversity Science* 32, 24138 (2024).

[24] 姜雅风. 我的野生动物邻居. 上海: 上海科学技术出版社, 2020, 64–68.

Manchuria

[1] The use of the toponym Manchuria is controversial. During the period of Manchu rule, the region was known as the Three Eastern Provinces (*Dōng Sān Shěng* 東三省), referring to the divisions of Mukden (*Shèngjīng* 盛京), Girin Ula (*Jílín* 吉林), and Sahaliyan Ula (*Hēilóngjiāng* 黑龍江). The first use of the name Manchuria occurred in the late eighteenth century on Japanese maps, which turned the Chinese name for the Manchu people (*Mǎnzhōu* 滿洲, *Manju* in Manchu, and *Manshū* 満洲 in Japanese), into a place name for their homeland. From these maps the name spread to Europe, and eventually to China, where the word came into limited use in the late nineteenth century. The term became the standard name for the region in non-Chinese languages, and remained in regular if uncommon use in Chinese until the Japanese takeover of 1931. With the establishment of the Manchukuo puppet state, the use of "Manchuria" became unacceptable within China. In Chinese the region is now referred to as the Three Northeastern Provinces (*Dōngběi Sān Shěng* 东北三省), or more commonly as The Northeast (*Dōngběi*

东北). In English the use of Manchuria has also fallen somewhat out of favor, but as it does not have the same taint of colonialism and separatism as in Chinese, and more accurately encompasses the broader geographic scope covered in this chapter, I have chosen it as the preferred term.

[2] These lands encompass the most commonly understood definition of Manchuria. However, some scholars differentiate between Inner Manchuria, the portion currently within the People's Republic of China, and Outer Manchuria, which includes the lands to the north and east that once belonged to the Qing Empire but were ceded to Russia in the mid-nineteenth century. Although including Outer Manchuria better reflects the ecological boundaries of the region, the text focuses primarily on Inner Manchuria, as information concerning the territory currently under Russian control is scarce prior to the handover and the focus of the book is on the wildlife populations within the PRC.

[3] The Changbai Range, and the highest peak in particular, are known in Korean as Baekdusan (백두산 白頭山, also spelled Paektusan), the White-Headed Mountain. The mountain is sacred to Korean and Manchu cultures, and notoriously is the mythic birthplace of the late North Korean dictator Kim Jong-il (who was in fact born Yuri Irsenovich Kim in the Soviet Far East while his father was training with the Red Army). In a caldera near its peak lies a crater lake, and the Sino-Korean border runs through the middle of its waters. Because access from the North Korean side is off limits to South Koreans, they must visit the lake from the Chinese side.

[4] The province of Heilongjiang is named after the Amur, known in Chinese as the Black Dragon River, *Hēi Lóng Jiāng* 黑龙江. That name derives from the Manchu name for the river, *Sahaliyan Ula*. In English, though both Heilongjiang and Black Dragon River are sometimes seen, Amur is the most commonly used. Though the Manchu name is no longer used for the river, it still survives with slight modification as the name for the large island off Russia's Pacific coast, Sakhalin. The name for Jilin Province also derives from Manchu. The province was called *Girin Ula*, meaning "along the river", which was transliterated into Chinese as *Jílín Wūla* 吉林烏拉, in turn shortened to *Girin* in Manchu and *Jílín* 吉林 in Chinese. Until the Cold War, Western sources hewed closer to the Manchu form, using the name Kirin.

[5] From the establishment of the Qing dynasty Manchu control stretched past the Amur and Ussuri, north to the Stanovoy Range and east to the Pacific Ocean, even for a time imposing tribute on the Ainu of Sakhalin. The Russian Empire acknowledged the extent of Manchu power in the Treaty of Nerchinsk in 1689, but by the mid-nineteenth century the Qing had weakened and Manchu control in the far north had faded. In 1858, while the Qing were fighting several rebellions and a separate war against Britain and France, Russia seized its chance. Seeking control of the Amur, Russia pressed the Qing to cede them its territories north of the river. Knowing they were indefensible, the Qing signed over the lands in the Treaty of Aigun, only for the Russians to press for the lands east of the Ussuri two years later during the Convention of Peking.

[6] After Japan's victory in the Russo-Japanese War (1904–1905), the southern branch of the Chinese Eastern Railway (Китайско-Зосточная железная дорога) from Changchun to Port Arthur (Lüshun) was transferred to Japan and became known as the South Manchuria Railway (南満州鉄道).

[7] Patrick J. Caffrey. "Transforming the Forests of a Counterfeit Nation: Japan's 'Manchu Nation' in Northeast China." *Environmental History* 18 (2013): 309–332.

Juliane Schlag. "Living in decline – the dynamics of anthropogenic disturbances in the recent landcover history of Manchuria and its consequences for Northeast Asia." *Asian Geographer* 38 (2021): 179–196.

[8] Dupao Yu et al. "Forest Management in Northeast China: History, Problems, and Challenges." *Environmental Management* 48 (2011): 1122–1135.

[9] The Black Dragon Fire connected with concurrent fires across the Amur in Soviet Russia, where an astounding 130,000 sq km (50,200 sq mi) of forest burned.

Wenru Xu et al. "Estimating burn severity and carbon emissions from a historic megafire in boreal forests of China." *Science of the Total Environment* 716, 136534 (2020).

[10] Zige Lan et al. "Are Climate Factors Driving the Contemporary Wildfire Occurrence in China?" *Forests* 12, 392 (2021): 13.

Northeastern Treasures

[1] 朴正吉. 密林寻踪 野生动物观察笔记. 北京: 人民邮电出版社, 2021, 10–11.

[2] David A. Bello. *Across Forest, Steppe, and Mountain: Environment, Identity, and Empire in Qing China's Borderlands.* Cambridge: Cambridge University Press, 2015, 105.

[3] Jonathan Schlesinger. *A World Trimmed with Fur: Wild Things, Pristine Places, and the Natural Fringes of Qing Rule.* Stanford: Stanford University Press, 2017, 17–25.

[4] Tan Bangjie. "Conservation and economic importance of the mustelids and viverrids in China." *Mustelid & Viverrid Conservation* 1 (1989): 5.

[5] Arthur de Carle Sowerby. *The Naturalist in Manchuria, Vols. II & III.* Tientsin: Tientsin Press, 1923, 72.

[6] 任林举. 虎啸——野生东北虎追踪与探秘. 北京: 北京十月文艺出版社, 2021, 141.

[7] 朴仁珠, 张明海. 貂熊. 哈尔滨: 东北林业大学出版社, 2000, 80–82.

[8] Sowerby, *The Naturalist in Manchuria, Vols. II & III*, 71.

[9] 朴, 张, 貂熊, 82–84.

[10] Zhu Shibing, Shifang Zhang and Minghai Zhang. "Update on the status of wolverines in China." *Journal of Forestry Research* 28 (2017): 425–429.

[11] Liu Xu et al. "A preliminary study of wolverine in Altay, Xinjiang." *Acta Theriologica Sinica* 38 (2018): 522–523.

[12] David A. Bello. "Rival Empires on the Hunt for Sable and People in Seventeenth-Century Manchuria," in *Empire and Environment in the Making of Manchuria*, ed. Norman Smith. Vancouver: UBC Press, 2017, 59.

[13] Seonmin Kim. *Ginseng and Borderland: Territorial Boundaries and Political Relations between Qing China and Chosŏn Korea, 1636–1912.* Oakland: University of California Press, 2017, 26–27.

[14] The sable tribute was called *sekei alban* in Manchu and *diāo gòng* 貂貢 in Chinese.

[15] Chia Ning. "The Solon Sable Tribute, Hunters of Inner Asia and Dynastic Elites at the Imperial Centre." *Inner Asia* 20 (2018): 26–63.

[16] A northern parallel to the Great Silk Road, the sable trade to the west has been called the Great Sable Road.

[17] The Russian pioneers were exceptionally brutal in their quest for furs. They did little hunting or trapping themselves, instead forcing the native peoples to do the work for them. To make sure they received what they wanted, the Cossacks would regularly kidnap tribal members, often respected leaders, and ransom them for furs and supplies. Massacres of native communities were common, and the relentless search for furs took a terrible toll on the local wildlife populations, pushing the Russians further and further east. Sable are today found throughout much of Siberia and the Russian Far East, but the current populations do not descend from local lineages, but are the result of repopulation efforts undertaken from the 1940s.

[18] Philip D. Curtin. *Cross-Cultural Trade in World History*. Cambridge: Cambridge University Press, 1984, 211.

[19] Chia, "The Solon Sable Tribute," 44–45.

[20] Like the wolverine, an additional, small population of sable in China still lives far to the west in the small section of the southern Altai Mountains that run into far northern Xinjiang.

[21] Sowerby, *The Naturalist in Manchuria, Vols. II & III*, 63–65.

[22] Rui Zhang et al. "Geographic characteristics of sable (*Martes zibellina*) distribution over time in Northeast China." *Ecology and Evolution* 7 (2017): 4019.

[23] 朴正吉, 密林寻踪, 39–43.

[24] Steven W. Buskirk, Ma Yiqing and Xu Li. "Sables (*Martes zibellina*) in managed forest of northern China." *Small Carnivore Conservation* 10 (1994): 12.

[25] Rui Zhang et al., "Geographic characteristics of sable (*Martes zibellina*) distribution," 4022.

[26] Piao Zhengji 朴正吉 points out that growing popular interest in wildlife and natural scenery has not been entirely beneficial to the sable and other species. Reminiscent of scenes at Yellowstone National Park until the 1960s, visitors to Changbaishan Nature Reserve and other popular sites often feed wildlife, both for entertainment and to obtain better photo opportunities. Garbage is also often improperly disposed of and left unsecured, so that sable and other wildlife spend less and less time hunting or foraging and instead come to rely on human foods for their sustenance.

[27] It is impossible to know from which species the pearls were harvested during the Qing. There are at least fourteen species of mussels in the Amur River Basin that produce pearls. Schlesinger determines that the most likely species is the freshwater pearl mussel *Margaritifera dahurica*.

[28] Schlesinger, *A World Trimmed with Fur*, 55–74.

[29] There is not enough evidence to definitively determine the cause of the drop in the mussel population. It is possible natural causes were partly to blame, or perhaps human impacts aside from direct harvesting. Despite the ultimate uncertainty, far and away the most likely reason was excessive harvesting of mussels for pearls.

[30] The region's freshwater mussels are poorly studied, but a likely major reason for the continued endangered status of the mussels is the reduction in fish populations. Mussel larvae first develop within the gills of host fish, and as fish numbers have dropped fewer and fewer mussel larvae are able to survive to maturity. Available historical evidence suggests fish in the Amur Basin were abundant until at least the late nineteenth century, so the earlier collapse in mussel numbers is very unlikely to have been related to drops in fish populations.

[31] Schlesinger, *A World Trimmed with Fur*, 80.

[32] Kim, *Ginseng and Borderland*, 33–43.

[33] Robert H. G. Lee. *The Manchurian Frontier in Ch'ing History*. Cambridge: Harvard University Press, 1970, 88.

[34] The Qing court was so set on maintaining complete control of the ginseng trade that even cultivation of the plant was prohibited, to the point that patrols were dispatched to destroy any ginseng farms they could find. While it is conceivable legal ginseng cultivation would have reduced the harvesting of the wild plant, more likely it would

have at best only delayed the disappearance of wild ginseng. Indeed, despite the state prohibition, ginseng cultivation became widespread and by the early nineteenth century was the source of the majority of ginseng sent to the court from Shengjing, the region including and surrounding the secondary Qing capital of Mukden (present-day Shenyang).

[35] Kim, *Ginseng and Borderland*, 82.

[36] Kim, *Ginseng and Borderland*, 131–135.

[37] Schlesinger, *A World Trimmed with Fur*, 86–87.

[38] H. E. M. James. *The Long White Mountain or A Journey in Manchuria: With Some Account of the History People, Administration and Religion of that Country*. London: Longmans, Green, and Co., 1888, 272.

[39] Yuri N Zhuravlev et al. "*Panax ginseng* natural populations: their past, current state and perspectives." *Acta Pharmacologica Sinica* 29 (2008): 1127–1128.

Antlers & Tusks

[1] Musk deer, members of the family Moschidae, are not true deer of the family Cervidae. They in fact are more closely related to the family Bovidae, the family to which cattle, antelopes, sheep, and goats belong.

[2] The velvet antler trade surged in the early nineteenth century, and antlers became so valuable that the Qing authorities began to regulate it closely, requiring paperwork for all exchanges. Schlesinger cites the trade from Khüree, modern Ulaanbaatar in Mongolia, where velvet antlers became the most valuable commodity on the market. In 1841, a large pair of antlers commanded 180 bricks of tea, enough to fill thirty-five oxcarts. Unsurprisingly, as the price surged so did poaching.

[3] Dale R. McCullough, Zhi-Guang Jiang, and Chun-Wang Li. "Sika Deer in Mainland China," in *Sika Deer: Biology and Management of Native and Introduced Populations*, ed. Dale R. McCullough, Seiki Takatsuki and Koichi Kaji. Tokyo: Springer, 2009, 526–529.

[4] Sowerby, *The Naturalist in Manchuria, Vols. II & III*, 107.

[5] Liz P.Y. Chee. *Mao's Bestiary: Medicinal Animals and Modern China*. Durham: Duke University Press, 2021, 83.

[6] Nicolas Baikov, a Russian soldier assigned to the Chinese Eastern Railway from 1901 to 1914, frequently hunted throughout the region and in his memoirs described several fatal encounters with thieves who attempted to steal velvet-antlered deer he had killed, as well as the gruesome end of a band of Russian pelt thieves at the hands

of aggrieved Chinese trappers. He also described the rough frontier justice of the taiga, where the condemned were usually buried alive in summer, but in winter when the ground was frozen were instead tied to a tree to await execution by tiger. The justice system has since improved.

[7] Chee, *Mao's Bestiary*, 67.

[8] Chee, *Mao's Bestiary*, 81–86.

[9] McCullough, Jiang and Li, "Sika Deer in Mainland China," 527–529.

[10] The IUCN lists the red deer of Northeast Asia as *Cervus canadensis xanthopygus*, but many publications continue to classify the Manchurian wapiti and its relatives as *Cervus elaphus*, the red deer of North Africa, Europe, and West Asia.

[11] Sowerby, *The Naturalist in Manchuria, Vols. II & III*, 103–105.

[12] Wen Wu et al. "Suitable winter habitat for *Cervus elaphus* on the southern slope of the Lesser Xing'an Mountains." *Biodiversity Science* 24 (2016): 22–26.

[13] Yu Si-Yu et al. "The Status of Red Deer Population in the Southern Part of the Greater Khingan Mountains in Inner Mongolia." *Chinese Journal of Zoology* 57 (2022): 759–765.

[14] Li Yuehui et al. "Estimating Abundance of Siberian Roe Deer Using Fecal-DNA Capture-Mark-Recapture in Northeast China." *Animals* 10, 1135 (2020).

[15] Glover M. Allen. *The Mammals of China and Mongolia, Part 2*. New York: The American Museum of Natural History, 1940, 1207.

Sowerby, *The Naturalist in Manchuria, Vols. II & III*, 111.

[16] Hongliang Dou et al. "Climate change impacts population dynamics and distribution shift of moose (*Alces alces*) in Heilongjiang Province of China." *Ecological Research* 28 (2013): 626–627.

[17] 马合木提·哈里克 等. "新疆阿尔泰山驼鹿的初步考察." 兽类学报 15 (1995): 159.

蒋志刚 等. "分布在新疆阿尔泰山的欧亚驼鹿." 动物学杂志 49 (2014): 303–304.

Shaopeng Cui et al. "Camera-trapping survey on mammals and birds in the Kanas River Valley of Altai Mountains, Xinjiang, China." *Biodiversity Science* 28 (2020): 435–441.

[18] Zhang Wei et al. "Effects of climate change on the potential habitat of *Alces alces cameloides*, an endangered species in Northeastern China." *Acta Ecologica Sinica* 36 (2016): 1818–1820.

[19] Meng Xiuxiang et al. "Population trends, distribution and conservation status of semi-domesticated reindeer (*Rangifer tarandus*) in China." *Journal for Nature Conservation* 22 (2014): 539–546.

[20] Hang Lin. "Reindeer, Taiga, Ethnic Culture: State-Forced Resettlement and the Changing Human-Animal Interactions in the Aoluguya Ewenki Community," in *Human-Animal Interactions in Anthropocene Asia*, ed. Victor Teo. London: Routledge, 2023, 98.

[21] Lin, "Reindeer, Taiga, Ethnic Culture," 99.

[22] Meng et al. "Population trends, distribution and conservation status," 539–546.

[23] Meng et al. "Population trends, distribution and conservation status," 539–546.

[24] Yan Ju et al. "Genetic diversity and population genetic structure of the only population of Aoluguya Reindeer (*Rangifer tarandus*) in China." *Mitochondrial DNA Part A* (2018).

[25] Yuanyuan Xie. *Ecological Migrants: The Relocation of China's Ewenki Reindeer Herders*. New York: Berghahn, 2015, 178–179.

[26] B. Nyambayar, H. Mix and K. Tsytsulina. "*Moschus moschiferus*." *The IUCN Red List of Threatened Species* (2015): e.T13897A61977573.

[27] N. Baikov. *Big Game Hunting in Manchuria*. London: Hutchinson & Co, 1936, 196.

[28] Sowerby, *The Naturalist in Manchuria, Vols. II & III*, 109.

[29] Qisen Yang et al. "Conservation status and causes of decline of musk deer (*Moschus* spp.) in China." *Biological Conservation* 109 (2003): 336.

[30] 吴家炎, 王伟 等编著. 中国麝类. 北京: 中国林业出版社, 2006, 373–379.

[31] 朴正吉, 密林寻踪, 114–116.

[32] 吴, 王 等, 中国麝类, 373–379.

[33] Chao Zhang et al. "Identification of Conservation Priority Areas and a Protection Network for the Siberian Musk Deer (*Moschus moschiferus* L.) in Northeast China." *Animals* 12, 260 (2022).

[34] Sowerby, *The Naturalist in Manchuria, Vols. II & III*, 118–120.

[35] E. Bragina et al. "*Naemorhedus caudatus*." *The IUCN Red List of Threatened Species* (2020): e.T14295A22150540.

[36] 朴正吉, 密林寻踪, 123.

[37] Sowerby, *The Naturalist in Manchuria, Vols. II & III*, 131.

[38] Baikov, *Big Game Hunting in Manchuria*, 80.

[39] Yongchao Jin et al. "Multi-Scale Spatial Prediction of Wild Boar Damage Risk in Hunchun: A Key Tiger Range in China." *Animals* 11, 1012 (2021): 2.

[40] Chen Jiu-Yi et al. "Amur Tiger and Prey in Jilin Hunchun National Nature Reserve, China." *Chinese Journal of Zoology* 46 (2011): 51.

Puren Ambani

[1] The Amur tiger is still popularly known as the Siberian tiger, and was once also referred to as the Manchurian or Ussurian tiger. Though "Siberian" is still in common use, "Amur" is now the prevailing name used in scientific and conservation circles. The scientific trinomial, however, places the subspecies far to the west in the Altai mountains. This came from Coenraad Jacob Temminck's suggestion in Philipp Franz von Siebold's *Fauna Japonica* that tiger skins found in Japan originated from the Altai chain. Any tigers found in the Altai would have instead belonged to the now extinct Caspian subspecies, *Panthera tigris virgata*.

The native Nanai (known in Chinese as the Hezhe 赫哲族, and formerly in English as the Goldi) regard the tiger as a dangerous spirit, and use the euphemism *puren ambani*, "dangerous spirit of the taiga," when speaking of it. The Udege people across the border in Russia use the related word *amba*. The other common euphemism used to speak of the tiger is "grandfather."

[2] The Amur tiger is frequently mentioned as the largest of the tiger subspecies, but this is not necessarily true. The oldest claims of size are unreliable and include many exaggerations and outright falsifications, but confirmed historical measurements show that the physical size of Amur tigers has in fact shrunk over time, likely due to difficulties in finding sufficient prey and to human hunters' preference for killing the largest animals, removing them from the gene pool and thereby selecting for smaller tigers. This phenomenon is seen with many species around the world, in numerous cases extending back thousands of years to the hunting patterns of prehistoric humans. Perhaps due to this unnatural selection, Bengal tigers are now on average the largest tiger subspecies.

[3] The current name Shenyang traces back to the Yuan dynasty, but after the Manchu conquered the city it was renamed *Shèngjīng* 盛京, "Prosperous Capital." The city was also often known as *Fèngtiān* 奉天, "Mandated by Heaven," the name of the city's encompassing prefecture. For many years in the West and Japan, Shengjing was better known by its Manchu name, Mukden, 'Prosperity." Since 1914 the Yuan-Ming period name Shenyang has been used, except for a change to Fengtian during the Manchukuo era. The name Mukden, however, still appeared on CIA maps into the late 1960s.

[4] 孙海义. 东北虎. 哈尔滨: 东北林业大学出版社, 2011, 41 & 67.

Qianlong would have been the longest-reigning emperor in Chinese history, except that in 1796—in a fit of ostentatious filial piety—he abdicated after over sixty years on the throne so as not to exceed the reign of his grandfather the Kangxi Emperor who ruled for a record sixty-one years. Qianlong did not relinquish power, however, and continued as Emperor Emeritus (*Tàishàng Huáng* 太上皇) to remain the *de facto* ruler until his death three years later in 1799.

[5] David Bello. "The Cultured Nature of Imperial Foraging in Manchuria." *Late Imperial China*, 31 (2010): 10.

[6] 孙海义, 东北虎, 41.

[7] Alexander Hosie. *Manchuria: Its People, Resources and Recent History*. London: Methuen & Co., 1901, 209.

[8] N. A. Baikov. "The Manchurian Tiger." *Manchuria Monitor* (1925). Translated by Alex Shevlakov.

[9] Rev. Alexander Williamson. *Journeys in North China, Manchuria, and Eastern Mongolia; With Some Account of Corea, Vol. I*. London: Smith, Elder & Co., 1870, 68.

[10] Charles McDougal. "The Man-Eating Tiger in Geographical and Historical Perspective," in *Tigers of the World: The Biology, Biopolitics, Management, and Conservation of an Endangered Species*, ed. Ronald L. Tilson and Ulysses S. Seal. Park Ridge: Noyes Publications, 1987, 438.

[11] 孙海义, 东北虎, 42.

[12] Baikov, "The Manchurian Tiger."

[13] 孙海义, 东北虎, 42–46.

[14] Jiang Guangshan et al. *Population and Habitat Dynamics of Amur Tigers and Their Targeted Management Strategies in China*. Beijing: Science Press, 2020, 171.

[15] McDougal, "The Man-Eating Tiger," 438.

[16] 孙海义, 东北虎, 47–48.

[17] Luo Shu-jin. "The status of the tiger in China. *Cat News* sp. 5 (2010): 11.

[18] The Korean Peninsula's Amur tigers were killed off over the course of the twentieth century. Increasingly aggressive hunting and deforestation devastated the tigers from the last years of the Joseon dynasty through the decades of Japanese colonial rule. After independence and the division of Korea in 1945, sparse sightings and reports of tigers continued only into the 1950s in South Korea. In the North, what little

evidence is available to outsiders suggests that some tigers survived in the Paektu (Changbai) Mountains, but no solid evidence of their presence has been found since 1987.

[19] Dmitry G. Pikunov. "Population and Habitat of the Amur Tiger in the Russian Far East." *Achievements in the Life Sciences* 8 (2014) 146.

[20] Dale G. Miquelle et al. "Science-based Conservation of Amur Tigers in the Russian Far East and Northeast China," in *Tigers of the World: The Science, Politics, and Conservation of Panthera tigris, 2nd Ed*, ed. Ronald L. Tilson and Philip J. Nyhus. Amsterdam: Academic Press, 2010, 408–409.

[21] Jinzhe Qi et al. "Integrated assessments call for establishing a sustainable meta-population of Amur tigers in northeast Asia." *Biological Conservation* 261, 109250 (2021).

[22] Jiang Guangshun et al. *Population and Habitat of Amur Leopard in China*. Beijing: Science Press, 2016, 84.

[23] Schlesinger, *A World Trimmed with Fur*, 22.
Bello, "The Cultured Nature of Imperial Foraging," 10.

[24] Sowerby, *The Naturalist in Manchuria, Vols. II & III*, 35–36.

[25] Li Yang et al. "Reconstructing the historical distribution of the Amur Leopard (*Panthera pardus orientalis*) in Northeast China based on historical records." *ZooKeys* 592 (2016): 147.

[26] Chee, *Mao's Bestiary*, 144.

[27] Eva Jutzeler et al. "Leopard." *Cat News* sp. 5 (2010): 31–32.

[28] Russia's Amur leopards had fared better than China's, but barely so. Over the twentieth century their range shrank until they remained only in the southwest of Primorsky Krai, the southernmost division of the Russian Far East. Their population reached a low at the turn of the millennium at around 20–30 cats, some of which may have crossed back and forth to China. Since then assiduous conservation work has helped the leopards expand to a present number of over 100. They have a national park, Land of the Leopard, dedicated to their protection, which borders China's own newly gazetted Northeast China Tiger and Leopard National Park.

[29] The now standard Chinese name for the lynx, *shēlì* 猞猁, is of undetermined origin, but is most likely a borrowing from the Mongolian *silügüsün*, which became *shèlìsūn* 猞猁孙 in Chinese. This was among, or itself begat, a number of variations, and *shēlì* became the widespread standard only in the 1980s.

[30] Bao Weidong. "Eurasian lynx in China - present status and conservation challenges." *Cat News* sp. 5 (2010): 22.

Liu Ke, Liu Yanlin and Li Sheng. "The current distribution and prediction of suitable habitat of Eurasian lynx (*Lynx lynx*) in China." *Acta Theriologica Sinica* 43 (2023): 653.

[31] Schlesinger, *A World Trimmed with Fur*, 28.

[32] 文榕生. 中国珍稀野生动物分布变迁 (续:) 中. 济南: 山东科学技术出版社, 2018, 1482.

[33] 朴正吉, 密林寻踪, 56–64.

[34] Li Yang et al. "Historical Distribution of Lynx (*Lynx lynx*) in Northeast China on the Basis of Historical Records." *Russian Journal of Ecology* 48 (2017): 572–573.

[35] Sowerby, *The Naturalist in Manchuria, Vols. II & III*, 38.

[36] 朴正吉, 密林寻踪, 83.

[37] Williamson, *Journeys in North China, Manchuria, and Eastern Mongolia*, 99.

[38] China is the largest producer of both fox and raccoon dog pelts in the world. Between 2010 and 2018 annual pelt production averaged over ten million for each species. In spite of the efforts to close the industry in the wake of the COVID-19 pandemic, foxes, raccoon dogs, and the American mink all remain approved for wildlife farming within China.

[39] Francis Harper. *Extinct and Vanishing Mammals of the Old World*. New York: American Committee for International Wild Life Protection (1945): 216–217.

[40] 朴正吉, 密林寻踪, 105–108.

[41] Sowerby, *The Naturalist in Manchuria, Vols. II & III*, 42.

[42] Dale G. Miquelle et al. "Tigers and Wolves in the Russian Far East: Competitive Exclusion, Functional Redundancy, and Conservation Implications," in *Large Carnivores and the Conservation of Biodiversity*, ed. Justina C. Ray et al. Washington DC: Island Press, 2005, 187–189.

[43] 朴正吉, 密林寻踪, 107–108.

[44] English translators have long done great disservice to the dhole. Whether due to their own ignorance or a fear of their audience's ignorance, translators have almost always used "jackal"— more familiar to Western minds—for the Chinese character for dhole, *chái* 豺. Though the golden jackal now expanding into Europe does range across the south of the Eurasian continent to Myanmar and Thailand, it is not native to China. The golden jackal was first confirmed within the borders of the PRC in 2018, when a single jackal was photographed in southern Tibet near the Nepalese border.

45 Edward H. Schafer. "Brief Note: The Chinese Dhole." *Asia Major* 4 (1991): 1–3.

46 Sowerby, *The Naturalist in Manchuria, Vols. II & III*, 45.

Groups of dholes are called clans instead of packs because the social structure differs from that of wolves and other pack-forming canines. Whereas a pack is marked by a strict social hierarchy and typically only contains a single breeding pair, dhole clans show little dominance hierarchy and can contain several breeding females. They are also not territorial, and will typically welcome young members of other clans into their group.

47 朴正吉, 密林寻踪, 107.

48 "这次，豺可不可以拥有一级动物的牌面，" 山水自然保护中心, June 21, 2020. https://mp.weixin.qq.com/s/7ecuIfug01ya5YMsxmeslA.

49 宋大昭. "今天说说中国的豺，消逝和归来，" // 来！聆听大自然的呼唤. 宋大昭, 黄巧雯 主编. 上海: 上海科技教育出版社, 2020, 64–69.

50 Sowerby, *The Naturalist in Manchuria, Vols. II & III*, 53.

51 Jien Gong and Richard B. Harris. "The Status of Bears in China," in *Understanding Asian Bears to Secure Their Future*, ed. Japan Bear Network. Ibaraki: Japan Bear Network, 2006, 97.

52 Piao Zheng-Ji et al. "Population Size Variation of Black Bear (*Ursus thibetanus*) and Brown Bear (*U. arctos*) between 1986 to 2010 in the Changbai Mountain Nature Reserve, China." *Chinese Journal of Zoology* 47 (2012): 67.

53 J. A. Mills. *Blood of the Tiger: A Story of Conspiracy, Greed, and the Battle to Save a Magnificent Species*. Boston: Beacon Press, 2015, 31–33.

54 D. Garshelis and R. Steinmetz. "*Ursus thibetanus* (amended version of 2016 assessment)." *The IUCN Red List of Threatened Species* (2020): e.T22824A166528664.

55 Gong and Harris, "The Status of Bears in China," 99.

56 Among a long list of medicinal items, Mills lists bear bile shampoo and toothpaste as the most egregious examples of the shameless expansion of bear bile's uses.

57 Piao Zheng-Ji et al. "Population Size Variation," 67–71.

58 尹峰, 梦梦 主编. 药用濒危物种可持续利用与保护. 北京: 中国农业出版社, 2013, 97.

59 Sowerby, *The Naturalist in Manchuria, Vols. II & III*, 53–58.

[60] Tigers and brown bears have been documented to kill one another. Russian scientists have documented numerous cases of tigers hunting brown bears, the cats usually ambushing their ursine prey from above. More rarely bears sometimes kill tigers, often in confrontation over prey. Which species triumphs largely depends on the size of the individuals involved. Full grown male bears are typically able to overpower tigresses and juveniles, but any bear's success against an adult male tiger is far less certain.

[61] Harper, *Extinct and Vanishing Mammals of the Old World*, 228.

[62] Gong and Harris, "The Status of Bears in China," 97.

[63] Piao Zheng-Ji et al. "Population Size Variation," 67–71.

Fowl & Fin

[1] Zongming Wang et al. "Loss and Fragmentation of Marshes in the Sanjiang Plain, Northeast China, 1954–2005." *Wetlands* 31 (2011): 949.

[2] Hao Chen et al. "Climate Change and Anthropogenic Impacts on Wetland and Agriculture in the Songnen and Sanjiang Plain, Northeast China." *Remote Sensing* 10, 356 (2018): 9.

[3] *Grus japonensis* is also commonly called the Manchurian crane or Japanese crane. "Red-crowned" is now the preferred name, as it does not falsely suggest the birds are restricted to one locality. This is doubly true within China, as any variation of the word "Manchuria" is considered objectionable and therefore stringently avoided.

[4] Although often translated as "phoenix," the *fènghuáng* 鳳凰 in fact has no relation to the phoenix of ancient Mediterranean myth. The Chinese bird began as separate male and female counterparts, *fèng* 鳳 and *huáng* 凰 respectively, only later combining into a single, female bird. In Chinese myth and cosmology, the *fènghuáng* stands as the greatest of birds and the feminine counterpart to the masculine dragon. Whereas emperors of China were associated with the dragon, empresses were connected to the *fènghuáng*. The *fènghuáng* is sometimes associated or depicted with fire, yet unlike the phoenix there is no tradition of the *fènghuáng* arising reborn from the ashes of its former self.

[5] Hongfei Zou and Dongyu Hu. "The status and conservation of the Red-crowned Crane in the breeding site in China," in *The Current Status and Issues of the Red-crowned Crane*, ed. Kimiya Koga, Dongyu Hu and Kunikazu Momose. Kushiro: Tancho Protection Group, 2008, 49.

[6] 文榕生. 中国珍稀野生动物分布变迁 (续:) 上. 济南: 山东科学技术出版社, 2018, 650–657.

[7] Zhijun Ma, Zijian Wang and Hongxiao Tang. "History of Red-crowned Crane *Grus japonensis* and its habitats in China." *Bird Conservation International* 8 (1998): 13.

[8] Sun Xiaoping. "'War against the Earth': Military Farming in Communist Manchuria, 1949–75," in *Empire and Environment in the Making of Manchuria*, ed. Norman Smith. Vancouver: UBC Press, 2017, 249–268.

[9] 马逸清 等. 中国丹顶鹤. 哈尔滨: 东北林业大学出版社, 2019, 194.

[10] Ma, Wang and Tang, "History of Red-crowned Crane," 12.

[11] Peter Matthiessen. *The Birds of Heaven: Travels with Cranes.* New York: North Point Press, 2001, 26.

[12] A second, eastern population of red-crowned cranes is native to Japan, residing on the country's northernmost main island of Hokkaido. Unlike the western population which breeds in China, Russia and Mongolia, the Hokkaido cranes are thriving, growing from only 213 birds in the winter of 1973–1974 to 1,900 in 2020–2021.

[13] BirdLife International. "*Grus japonensis.*" *The IUCN Red List of Threatened Species* (2021): e.T22692167A175614850.

[14] Yulia S. Momose and Kunikazi Momose. "Species Review: Red-crowned Crane (*Grus japonensis*)," in *Crane Conservation Strategy*, ed. Claire M. Mirande and James T. Harris. Baraboo: International Crane Foundation, 2019, 249.

[15] BirdLife International, "*Grus japonensis.*"

[16] Gong Minghao et al. "The Path Forward: Conservation of Climate Change-Affected Breeding Habitat of Red-crowned Cranes near Zhalong Reserve, China." *Pakistan Journal of Zoology* 53 (2021): 733–742.

[17] Matthiessen, *The Birds of Heaven*, 7–8.

[18] James Harris and Claire Mirande. "A global overview of cranes: status, threats and conservation priorities." *Chinese Birds* 4 (2013): 196.

[19] Claire M. Mirande, Nyambayar Batbayar, and James T. Harris. "Species Review: White-naped Crane (*Grus vipio*)," in *Crane Conservation Strategy*, ed. Claire M. Mirande and James T. Harris. Baraboo: International Crane Foundation, 2019, 275–282.

[20] Claire M. Mirande and Elena I. Ilyashenko. "Species Review: Hooded Crane (*Grus monacha*)," in *Crane Conservation Strategy*, ed. Claire M. Mirande and James T. Harris. Baraboo: International Crane Foundation, 2019, 315–317.

[21] 田秀华, 王进军 等. 东方白鹳. 哈尔滨: 东北林业大学出版社, 2011: 40–44.

[22] Bello, "The Cultured Nature of Imperial Foraging," 22.

With little evidence aside from quota shortfalls to inform out judgement, it is impossible to know if hunting was the primary cause of the seeming drop in stork numbers. The failure to meet quotas may well have been seasonal instead of long-term. Other factors such as weather could have contributed, or the numbers may have been deliberately misreported to conceal poaching. The same is true for other species for which little alternative evidence is available.

[23] Xu Xu et al. "Exploring conservation strategies for oriental white stork fledglings (*Ciconia boyciana*) across the breeding wetland landscape: Hints from tracking movement patterns." *Global Ecology and Conservation* 26, e01531 (2021).

[24] BirdLife International. "*Ciconia boyciana*." *The IUCN Red List of Threatened Species* (2018): e.T22697695A131942061.

[25] Lei Cheng et al. "Flexible nest site selection of the endangered Oriental Storks (*Ciconia boyciana*): Trade-off from adaptive strategies." *Avian Research* 14, 100088 (2023), 2.

[26] Yuan Ye, "With Nowhere to Go, Rare Birds Face Off With Irate Fish Farmers," *Sixth Tone*, December 16, 2021. https://www.sixthtone.com/news/1009167.

[27] Ruth Rogaski. *Knowing Manchuria: Environments, the Senses, and Natural Knowledge on an Asian Borderland*. Chicago: University of Chicago Press, 2022: 96–97.

[28] Mikhail L. Krykhtin and Victor G. Svirskii. "Endemic sturgeons of the Amur River: kaluga, *Huso dauricus*, and Amur sturgeon, *Acipenser schrenckii*." *Environmental Biology of Fishes* 48 (1997): 231–232.

Despite the ban on commercial fishing, several dozen tonnes of the sturgeons were caught annually to monitor the populations and to stock hatcheries.

[29] Wang Yamin and Jianbo Chang. "Status and conservation of sturgeons in Amur River, China: A review based on surveys since the year 2000." *Journal of Applied Ichthyology* 22, s1 (2006): 45.

[30] V. N. Koshelev, G. Ruban and A. Shmigirilov. "Spawning migrations and reproductive parameters of the kaluga sturgeon, *Huso dauricus* (Georgi, 1775), and Amur sturgeon, *Acipenser schrenckii* (Brandt, 1869)." *Journal of Applied Ichthyology* 30 (2014): 1129–1130.

[31] V. Koshelev, A. Shmigirilov and G. Ruban. "Current status of feeding stocks of the kaluga sturgeon *Huso dauricus* Georgi, 1775, and Amur sturgeon *Acipenser schrenckii* Brandt, 1889, in Russian waters." *Journal of Applied Ichthyology* 30 (2014): 1310–1315.

[32] V. N. Koshelev, O. Yu. Vilkova and D. V. Kotsyuk. "Modern Data on the Distribution, Abundance and Qualitative Structure of the Populations of the Kaluga *Huso dauricus* and the Amur Sturgeon *Acipenser schrenckii* (Acipenseridae) in the Amur River and the Amur Estuary." *Journal of Ichthyology* 62 (2022): 1394–1403.

Steppes

[1] Emperor Wu of Han was the great expansionist emperor of the early Han dynasty, and reversed years of military failure to defeat the Xiongnu by adopting the nomads' own style of mobile, cavalry warfare. Emperor Taizong of Tang was of partial Xianbei—a nomadic steppe people—ancestry, and relied heavily on the services of Turkic troops when waging steppe warfare. Later Han Chinese dynasties had little success against the nomadic horselords, while conquest dynasties large and small repeatedly brought the steppe and plains together under unified rule. These included the Khitan and Jurchen dynasties, and later the Mongol and Manchu empires.

[2] Megan Kram et al. *Protecting China's Biodiversity: A Guide to Land Use, Land Tenure, and Land Protection Tools*. Beijing: The Nature Conservancy, 2012, 7–11.

[3] National Research Council. *Grasslands and Grassland Sciences in Northern China*. Washington DC: National Academy Press, 1992.

[4] For the history of the Qing conquest of Xinjiang and the destruction of the Dzungar people, see Peter C. Perdue's *China Marches West: The Qing Conquest of Central Eurasia*, Cambridge: Belknap Press, 2005.

[5] Adeeb Khalid. *Central Asia: A New History from the Imperial Conquests to the Present*. Princeton: Princeton University Press, 2021.

Grassland Herbivores

[1] The name dzeren—different forms of which were common in English-language accounts before the late twentieth century—stems from a Russian misinterpretation of the Mongolian name for *Procapra gutturosa*, Зээр *zeer* .

[2] The word *yáng* 羊 is a general term for both goats and sheep. The two domestic species are commonly differentiated by the addition of a second character. For goats the character for "mountain" is added (*shān yáng* 山羊); for sheep it is the character for "cotton" (*mián yáng* 绵羊).

[3] Père Gerbillon, along with his Portuguese colleague Tomás Pereira (1645–1708), was traveling with a party of Manchu ambassadors to Nerchinsk, located on a tributary of the Amur River. There they negotiated the Treaty of Nerchinsk (1689) with representatives of joint Tsars Peter I (Peter the Great, 1672–1725) and Ivan V

(1666–1696), Peter's half brother (at the time their elder sister Sophia Alekseyevna [1657–1704] was in fact directing policy as regent). The treaty demarcated the border between the Manchu and Russian empires. The Jesuits were needed because the language of negotiation and the final, authoritative version of the treaty was Latin, with translations made into Manchu and Russian.

[4] Jean-Baptiste Du Halde. *The General History of China: Containing a Geographical, Historical, Chronological, Political and Physical Description of the Empire of China, Chinese-Tartary, Corea and Thibet, Vol. 4, 2nd ed*. London: John Watts, 1739, 239 & 299–301.

Père Gerbillon's remarks were printed in Jean-Baptiste Du Halde's (1674–1743) seminal work, *The General History of China* (1738). Père Du Halde himself never traveled to China, but instead used the knowledge collected in the reports of his Jesuit brethren who had visited or lived there to write his works. His *General History* had a great impact on Europe's intellectual firmament. Many major enlightenment figures, most famously Voltaire, were greatly impressed with the work and its portrayal of Chinese culture.

[5] N. Prejevalsky. *Mongolia, the Tangut Country, and the Solitudes of Northern Tibet: Being a Narrative of Three Years' Travel in Eastern High Asia, Vol. I*. London: Sampson Low, Marston, Searle, & Rivington, 1876, 28–31.

There are several English-language spellings for "Przhevalsky." Confusingly, though, when referring to *Equus ferus* it is generally spelled "Przewalski," while in contemporary translations of Przhevalsky's works, his name was spelled "Prejevalsky." These three are not an exhaustive list.

[6] Prejevalsky. *Mongolia, the Tangut Country*, 31

[7] Glover M. Allen. *The Mammals of China and Mongolia, Part 2*. New York: The American Museum of Natural History, 1940, 1212–1214.

[8] Roy Chapman Andrews. *Across Mongolian Plains*. New York: D. Appleton & Company, 1921, 15–16.

[9] Arthur de Carle Sowerby. *The Naturalist in Manchuria, Vols. II & III*. Tientsin: Tientsin Press, 1923, 123.

[10] Roy Chapman Andrews et al. *The New Conquest of Central Asia: A Narrative of the Explorations of the Central Asiatic Expeditions in Mongolia and China, 1921–1930*. New York: American Museum of Natural History, 1932, 32.

[11] E.J. Milner-Gulland and Badamjavin Lhagvasuren. "Population dynamics of the Mongolian gazelle *Procapra gutturosa*: an historical analysis." *Journal of Applied Ecology* 35 (1998): 241–242.

[12] 谭邦杰. "野生动物的灭种和保种." 自然杂志 2 (1979): 427.

[13] Xiaoming Wang et al. "Recent history and status of the Mongolian gazelle in Inner Mongolia, China." *Oryx* 31 (1997): 120–122.

[14] Zhenhua Luo et al. "Influences of Human and Livestock Density on Winter Habitat Selection of Mongolian Gazelle (*Procapra gutturosa*)." *Zoological Science* 31 (2014): 21.

[15] Lupeng Shi, Xiufeng Yang, Muha Cha et al. "Genetic diversity and structure of mongolian [*sic*] gazelle (*Procapra gutturosa*) populations in fragmented habitats." *BMC Genomics* 24, 507 (2023): 2.

Exact figures are difficult to ascertain, and to complicate matters the Mongolian gazelle is prone to large fluctuations in population as their numbers periodically crash due to natural events such as disease and the effects of severe winters, the latter often called a *dzud*, the Mongolian word for disastrous livestock die-offs.

[16] 韩永刚, 王艳清, "17年的坚守, 为了一群野生黄羊," 中国网 February 2, 2021. http://grassland.china.com.cn/2021-02/12/content_41469592.html.

[17] As with so many species, the taxonomy of *Equus ferus przewalskii* has a long and ongoing history of dispute. Consensus over whether it is an independent species (*E. przewalskii*), a subspecies of the wild horse (*E. f. przewalskii*), or merely a subpopulation of the domestic horse remains elusive. To further complicate matters, there is not even consensus on whether the domestic horse is a subspecies of wild horse (*E. f. caballus*) or a separate species altogether (*E. caballus*).

[18] The distinction between truly wild horses (i.e. the tarpan and Przewalski's horse) and feral horses (i.e. the American mustang and Australian brumby) is that feral populations are descendants of domestic horses, whereas the ancestors of wild horses never passed through a process of domestication.

[19] Carolyn Willekes. *The Horse in the Ancient World: From Bucephalus to the Hippodrome*. London: I.B. Taurus, 2016, 74–83.

[20] Inge Bouman and Jan Bouman. "The History of Przewalski's Horse," in *Przewalski's Horse: The History and Biology of an Endangered Species*, ed. Lee Boyd and Katherine A. Houpt. Albany: State University of New York Press, 1994, 7–8.

The Tangut Empire (in written Tangut 祚 尾 骰 羅 隃) is commonly known by its Chinese name of *Xī Xià* 西夏, or Western Xia. It stretched from eastern Qinghai and northeastern Xinjiang, over Gansu, Ningxia and northern Shaanxi, and into southwest Inner Mongolia and southern Mongolia. Its capital was at modern-day Yinchuan, Ningxia. The Tangut people dominated the empire, but it included populations of Tibetans, Uyghurs, and Han, among others. Despite the death of Chinggis Khan during the campaign, the Mongols subjugated the Tangut Empire in 1227 and effectively destroyed the Tanguts as a people.

[21] Bouman and Bouman, "The History of Przewalski's Horse," 12.

22 Bouman and Bouman, "The History of Przewalski's Horse," 13.

23 Inge Bouman, Jan Bouman, and Lee Boyd. "Reintroduction," in *Przewalski's Horse: The History and Biology of an Endangered Species*, ed. Lee Boyd and Katherine A. Houpt. Albany: State University of New York Press, 1994, 255.

24 Canjun Xia et al. "Reintroduction of Przewalski's horse (*Equus ferus przewalskii*) in Xinjiang, China: The status and experience." *Biological Conservation* 177 (2014): 142–147.

25 Pei Pengzu et al. "Re-introduced Przewalski's horses's breeding success and population viability analysis in Anxi National Nature Reserve." *Acta Theriologica Sinica* 38 (2018): 128–129.

26 Shengnan Ji et al. "The road home for Przewalski's horse in China." *Oryx* 56 (2022): 652.

27 Joel Berger. *Extreme Conservation: Life at the Edges of the World*. Chicago: University of Chicago Press, 2018, 187.

28 The saiga's taxonomy is subject to dispute. There is agreement that there are two distinct forms of saiga, a Mongolian form in the east and another in the west. It is not definitively decided, however, whether these represent two species—*Saiga tatarica* and *S. borealis*—or two subspecies—*S. tatarica mongolica* and *S. t. tatarica*. The division into subspecies is more widely accepted. China likely hosted both forms.

29 Shaopeng Cui et al. "Historical range, extirpation and prospects for reintroduction of saigas in China." *Scientific Reports* 7, 44200 (2017): 1.

The Classic of Herbal Medicine is believed to be a compilation of oral traditions compiled between 200 and 250 CE. The original work is long lost, but much of its contents exist as quotations in later texts. There is no definitive English title for *The Classic of Herbal Medicine* (*Shénnóng Běncǎo Jīng* 神農本草經). Among the many choices are *Shennong's Materia Medica*, *The Divine Farmer's Materia Medica*, *The Divine Farmer's Classic of Materia Medica*, and *The Divine Husbandman's Canon of Materia Medica*.

30 E.J. Milner-Gulland et al. *The Sustainable Use of Saiga Antelopes: Perspectives and Prospects*. Saiga Conservation Alliance Report to the Bundesamt für Naturschutz and the UN Convention on Migratory Species. 2021, 21.

31 William J. Morden. *Across Asia's Snows and Deserts*. New York: G. P. Putnam's Sons, 1927, 258.

Cui et al. "Historical range," 4.

32 Cui et al. "Historical range," 2–4.

33 Cui et al. "Historical range," 1–2.

[34] Zhigang Jiang et al. "A Case of Reintroducing Saiga Highlights the Conservation Needs of Migratory Species." *Preprints* 2020020375 (2020).

[35] Cui et al. "Historical range," 2–6.

Fang, Feather, & Fur

[1] Today Alxa Banner (*Ālāshàn Qí* 阿拉善旗) is in Inner Mongolia, but at the time it was a part of neighboring Ningxia. A banner is an administrative division in Inner Mongolia that corresponds to a county elsewhere in China. The term derives from the Manchu banner system of administrative and military organization.

Sheep and goats are lumped together because the Chinese refers only to *yáng* 羊, a term that encompasses both animals.

[2] 张久卿, "档案揭秘——宁夏打狼往事," 宁夏档案信息网, October 10, 2015. https://web.archive.org/web/20220813121911/http://www.zgdazxw.com.cn/culture/2015-10/10/content_118547.htm.

[3] Strictly speaking, Ningxia is not a province but an autonomous region, along with Inner Mongolia, Xinjiang, Tibet, and Guangxi. Autonomous regions in China are by-and-large legally equivalent to provinces, except they have greater legislative rights allowing more self-rule for the resident ethnic minority peoples. To what degree those legal rights can actually be exercised is another matter.

[4] In the aggressively anti-American spirit of the time—this was during the long stalemate period of the Korean War when China and the US hammered away at each other across both the battlefield and the negotiating table—one woman on a wolf-smashing team, after helping kill six wolves, declared: "Only this way can we wipe out our enemy, the American wolf (只有这样才能消灭我们的仇敌美国狼)."

[5] Richard B. Harris. *Wildlife Conservation in China: Preserving the Habitat of China's Wild West*. Armonk, NY: M.E. Sharpe, 2008, 160.

[6] A 2015 study of Tibetan families in Sichuan's Jiuzhaigou County found that they were no more well-disposed towards wolves than their Han counterparts, a surprise to the researchers, who had expected the Tibetans' Buddhist beliefs to have made them more accepting of the canines.

Yu Xu, Biao Yang and Liang Dou. "Local villagers' perceptions of wolves in Jiuzhaigou County, western China." *PeerJ* 3:e932 (2015). https://doi.org/10.7717/peerj.982.

[7] George B. Schaller. *Tibet's Hidden Wilderness: Wildlife and Nomads of the Chang Tang Reserve*. New York: Harry N. Abrams, 1997, 31.

[8] Wolves return to north China's pasture after decades," *People's Daily Online*, June 26, 2010. https://web.archive.org/web/20210410215757/http://en.people.cn/90001/90776/90882/7041785.html.

[9] Li You, "The Biggest Winners From China's Protected Species List? Wolves," *Sixth Tone*, February 19, 2021. https://www.sixthtone.com/news/1006865.

[10] The specific name *tarda*, meaning "slow" or "deliberate," comes from the Latin name as reported by Pliny the Elder, *aves tardas*. Though not further explained, this was likely in reference to the bustard's walking gait, but many of the English-language authors writing about the bird in China in the early twentieth century took it as a reference to the bustard's flight speed. Arthur de Carle Sowerby once made an informal test of the great bustard's speed while riding along the Peking-Kalgan [Beijing to Zhangjiakou] railway. Having spotted a flock of bustards flying parallel to the train, he compared their progress with the train's—they were slowly but surely pulling ahead of it—and judged the birds were flying at approximately forty miles an hour (64 km/h), a very respectable pace.

[11] The Kori bustard *Ardeotis kori* of Africa rivals the great bustard for size, and both species are cited as the largest flying birds. The largest confirmed specimen on record, however, was a male great bustard who weighed 21 kg (46 lb).

[12] BirdLife International. "*Otis tarda*." *The IUCN Red List of Threatened Species* (2023): e.T22691900A226280431.

[13] Liu Gang et al. "Genetic structure and population history of wintering Asian Great Bustard (*Otis tarda dybowskii*) in China: implications for conservation." *Journal of Ornithology* 158 (2017): 770.

[14] In *Fur and Feather in North China* (1914) Sowerby noted the country west of the Taihang Mountains in Shanxi had a particular abundance of bustards, and in his other writings gave no indication that he thought the bustard populations were falling. However, in *Chinese Hunter* (1939), J. Wong-Quincey judged that bustards were "not common" in North China and were restricted to empty fields where they subsisted "on the surplus of grain dropped from the last harvesting." There is not enough information to judge whether this was merely a difference in opinion on what constituted "common," or in fact reflected a genuine diminution of the bustard population.

[15] Western writers from the first decades of the twentieth century repeatedly note what difficulties and scant success foreign hunters in China had shooting bustards, while commenting with some consternation on the great number of birds native hunters supplied to markets every winter. Unlike the foreigners who attempted to sneak close to the birds across open ground, local hunters hid—day after day if need be—in specially dug pits with decoys made from stuffed bustard skins set nearby to draw in their prey. The decoys were so lifelike that on one occasion when Sowerby was out with a hunting party, the men spotted three bustards, dismounted their ponies and

carefully trudged over muddy ground until they were in range. One hunter fired at a bird, only for nothing to happen until a local villager appeared from hiding and informed them they were stalking decoys.

[16] The resident English-speaking community in the nineteenth and early twentieth centuries commonly referred to the great bustard as "wild turkey."

[17] Chunrong Mi, Huettmann Falk and Yumin Guo. "Climate envelope predictions indicate an enlarged suitable wintering distribution for Great Bustards (*Otis tarda dybowskii*) in China for the 21st century." *PeerJ* 4, e1630 (2016): 2–3.

[18] Mi, Falk and Guo "Climate envelope predictions," 8–9.

[19] Muyang Wang et al. "The Probable Strong Decline of the Great Bustard *Otis tarda tarda* Population in North-Western China." *Ardeola* 65 (2018): 291–297.

[20] Muyang Wang and Weikang Yang. "The diminishing status of the Great Bustard *Otis tarda tarda* in Xinjiang province, north-west China." *Sandgrouse* 44 (2022): 96–100.

[21] The Asian houbara *Chlamydotis macqueenii* is otherwise known as MacQueen's bustard to better distinguish it from the African houbara *Chlamydotis undulata*.

[22] N. J. Collar et al. "Averting the extinction of bustards in Asia." *Forktail* 33 (2017): 5.

[23] XingYi Gao et al. "Distribution and migration of houbara bustard (*Chlamydotis undulata*) in China." *Journal of Arid Land* 1 (2009): 74–79.

[24] Tris Allinson. "Review of the global conservation status of the Asian Houbara Bustard *Chlamydotis macqueenii*." BirdLife International: Report to the Convention on Migratory Species Office – Abu Dhabi (2014): 35.

[25] Gao et al. "Distribution and migration of houbara bustard," 75–77.

[26] Christophe Tourenq et al. "Alarming houbara bustard population trends in Asia." *Biological Conservation* 121 (2005): 5–7.

[27] Collar et al., "Averting the extinction of bustards," 2.

[28] Tarbagan is the Russian name for *Marmota sibirica*, and derives from the Mongolian *tarbaga* (plural: *tarbagad*). In Chinese marmots in general are called *hàntǎ* 旱獭, or land-otter, but other words such as *tǔbōshǔ* 土拨鼠 and *tuóbá* 鼧䶟 are also used. *M. sibirica* is now referred to as either the Mongolian or Siberian marmot, *Měnggǔ hàntǎ* 蒙古旱獭 or *Xībólìyà hàntǎ* 西伯利亚旱獭, respectively.

[29] William C. Summers. *The Great Manchurian Plague of 1910–1911: The Geopolitics of an Epidemic Disease*. New Haven: Yale University Press, 2012, 117–118.

[30] A. S. Loukashkin. "The Tarbagan or the Transbaikalian Marmot and its Economic Value." in *Extrait des comptes rendus du XIIe Congrès International de Zoologie, Lisbonne 1935*, 2233–2293. Lisboa: Casa Portuguesa, 1937, 2240–2244.

[31] Shen Yubin. "Pneumonic Plagues, Environmental Changes, and the International Fur Trade: The Retreat of Tarbagan Marmots from Northwest Manchuria, 1900s–30s." *Frontiers of History in China* 14 (2019): 298.

Mongols also made medicinal use of marmots, applying marmot fat as "a remedy for pains in the abdomen, cough and lung diseases."

[32] Shen, "Pneumonic Plagues," 299–300.

[33] Shen, "Pneumonic Plagues," 298–299.

[34] Shen, "Pneumonic Plagues," 310–312.

[35] Other factors were involved in the destruction of China's populations of tarbagans. The construction and operation of the railroad—and the accompanying railroad towns—through the steppe damaged their habitat. In the same period an influx of settlers attempting to cultivate the grasslands arrived. The planters saw the rodents as a threat to their efforts, and accordingly killed any marmots found nearby. Ultimately, however, it was the fur trade that caused their destruction.

[36] Loukashkin, "The Tarbagan," 2266–2267.

Marmot furs continued to pass through Manchuria on the way to world markets, but came from the steppes of neighboring Mongolia and Soviet Russia. The marmot populations there sustained similar damage, and today *Marmota sibirica* is classified on the IUCN Red List as endangered.

[37] Based on contemporary investigations, Dr. Wu Lien Teh, the head of the plague response effort, concluded there was only circumstantial evidence linking the marmots to the plague outbreak in the human population. The connection has yet to be definitively proven, but marmots remain the most likely source of the epidemic.

The Manchurian epidemic was not bubonic plague, famously transmitted by fleas jumping from rats to humans, but pneumonic plague, transmitted through the air and with a far higher fatality rate nearing 100%.

[38] Summers, *The Great Manchurian Plague*, 51–79.

[39] Shen, "Pneumonic Plagues," 292–293.

Dou Huashan et al. "Wolf Predation on Livestock around the Dalai Lake National Nature Reserve, Inner Mongolia," in *Proceedings of the International Conference for the 20th anniversary of the DIPA*, 21–25. Ulaanbaatar: Wildlife Conservation Society Mongolia, 2014, 21.

[40] Yulong Chen et al. "Genetic characterization of four wild species of Chinese marmots using microsatellite markers." *Biologia* 67 (2012): 1013.

[41] In English *língzhī* 靈芝 mushroom is also known by its Japanese name *reishi*.

[42] *Leucocalocybe mongolica* was formerly and is still often known as *Tricholoma mongolicum*. In Chinese *L. mongolica* is one the mushroom species known as *kǒumó* 口蘑, the name indicating in times past that they were found at Zhangjiakou 张家口 (better known to Westerners until recent decades as Kalgan, from the city's Mongolian name), a city on the Great Wall that functioned as the principal frontier post between Beijing and the steppe.

[43] Jonathan Schlesinger. *A World Trimmed with Fur: Wild Things, Pristine Places, and the Natural Fringes of Qing Rule*. Stanford: Stanford University Press, 2017, 93–110.

[44] Tie Lu, Haiying Bao and Tolgor Bau. "Genetic diversity and population structure of endemic mushroom *Leucocalocybe mongolica* in Mongolian Plateau uncovered by EST-SSR markers." *Biotechnology & Biotechnological Equipment* 32 (2018): 1196.

Deserts

[1] Y. Chen and H. Tang. "Desertification in north China: background, anthropogenic impacts and failures in combating it." *Land Degradation & Development* 16 (2005): 367–376.

[2] The Badain Jaran Desert has the world's tallest stationary sand dunes. The highest rises to 500 meters (1,600 ft).

[3] The Gobi Desert takes its name from a Mongolian word that denotes not so much a place as a type of landscape, so that in its native usage there is less a single Gobi Desert than there are many gobi regions. Further, some geographers consider many of China's deserts, including the Badain Jaran, to be regions within the larger Gobi Desert, which can lead to some confusion.

[4] The name Lop Nur (Лоб Нуур, alternatively spelled Lop Nor) is Mongolian and means "Lop Lake." In Mandarin it is called *Luóbù Pō* 罗布泊 or less commonly *Luóbù Nào'ér* 罗布淖尔.

[5] Zhao Ji et al. *The Natural History of China*. London: Collins, 1990, 173–175.

[6] Steffen Mischke, Chenglin Liu and Jiafu Zhang. "Lop Nur in NW China: Its Natural State, and a Long History of Human Impact," in *Large Asian Lakes in a Changing World: Natural State and Human Impact*, ed. Steffen Mischke. Cham: Springer Nature, 2020, 207–233.

Loulan was likely abandoned when the Tarim River changed course and Lop Nur dried as a result. The exact cause and timing of the drying of Lop Nur, as well as the course change of the Tarim, are uncertain. Many historians suspect human actions were the primary cause for the change, similar to the desiccation of the Aral Sea straddling Kazakhstan and Uzbekistan during the Soviet period.

[7] For a general history of Xinjiang, including discussion of the ongoing campaign against the Uyghur people, see James A. Millward's *Eurasian Crossroads: A History of Xinjiang, Revised and Updated*, New York: Columbia University Press, 2022.

Black Tails & Paddle Tails

[1] 郑生武, 高行宜. "中国野驴的现状、分布区的历史变迁原因探讨." 生物多样性 8 (2000): 86.

[2] 郑 & 高, "中国野驴的现状," 86.

[3] Armand David. *Natural History of North China with Notices of that of the South, West and North-east, and of Mongolia & Thibet, compiled chiefly from the travels of Père Armand David*. Shanghai: Da Costa & Co., 1873, 10.

[4] 天上的龍肉，地下的驢肉 (*Tiānshàng de lóng ròu, dìxià de lǘ ròu*)

[5] Petra Kaczensky et al. *A Conservation Strategy for Khulan in Mongolia: Background and Key Considerations*. NINA Report 1889. Trondheim: Norwegian Institute for Nature Research, 2020, 15.

[6] 毕俊怀 等 著. 中国蒙古野驴研究. 北京: 中国林业出版社, 2015, 15–16.

[7] Xu et al gave an estimate of 3,246 ± 575 khulan within the Kalamaili Reserve, along with several hundred more elsewhere in Xinjiang and up to 100 in Gansu. Their estimated total population in China is around 4,000.

Wenxuan Xu et al. "Current status and future challenges for khulan (*Equus hemionus*) conservation in China." *Global Ecology and Conservation* 37, e02156 (2022), 6.

[8] Yingying Zhuo et al. "The effect of mining and road development on habitat fragmentation and connectivity of khulan (*Equus hemionus*) in Northwestern China." *Biological Conservation* 275, 109770 (2022).

[9] Gao Shuaishuai et al. "Vulnerability assessment of suitable habitats for *Equus hemionus* in the Kalamaili National Park under climate change." *Acta Theriologica Sinica* 44 (2024): 287–296.

[10] P. Kaczensky et al. "*Equus hemionus* (amended version of 2015 assessment)." *The IUCN Red List of Threatened Species* (2020): e.T7951A166520460.

[11] 毕俊怀, 中国蒙古野驴研究, 2015, 30–31.

[12] Xu et al, "Current status and future challenges for khulan," 7.

[13] Xu et al, "Current status and future challenges for khulan," 115–118.

[14] N. Prejevalsky. *Mongolia, the Tangut Country and the Solitudes of Northern Tibet: Being a Narrative of Three Years' Travel in Eastern High Asia, Vol. I.* London: Sampson Low, Marston, Searle, & Rivington, 1876, 207–210.

[15] Percy W. Church. *Chinese Turkestan with Caravan and Rifle.* London: Rivingtons, 1901, 42 & 204.

Harold Frank Wallace. *The Big Game of Central and Western China: Being an Account of a Journey from Shanghai to London Overland Across the Gobi Desert.* London: John Murray, 1913, 253.

Allen (1940) pointed out that Wallace misidentified the goitered gazelle as *Gazella gutturosa*, the Mongolian gazelle.

[16] Prejevalsky, *Mongolia, the Tangut Country*, 210.

On a similar note, Theodore Roosevelt Jr. and his brother Kermit, President Theodore Roosevelt's sons, encountered two pet goitered gazelles on their journey through Xinjiang in the 1920s. The first was an ill-tempered buck who charged at one of their party members who attempted to photograph him. The second, encountered at a different town, was docile and friendly.

Theodore Roosevelt and Kermit Roosevelt. *East of the Sun and West of the Moon.* New York: Charles Scribner's Sons, 1926, 77 & 80.

[17] Wenxuan Xu et al. "Diet of *Gazella subgutturosa* (Güldenstaedt, 1780) and food overlap with domestic sheep in Xinjiang, China." *Folia Zoologica* 61 (2012): 54–60.

[18] Shamshidin Abduriyim, Azizjan Nabi and Mahmut Halik. "Low Genetic Diversity in the Goitered Gazelle *Gazella subgutturosa* (Güldenstädt, 1780) (Artiodactyla: Bovidae) in North-western China as Revealed by the Mitochondrial Cytochrome *b* Gene." *Acta Zoologica Bulgarica* 70 (2018): 211–218.

[19] The Dzungar Basin is, strictly speaking, considered a semi-desert, or semi-arid climate, not a full desert.

Russia introduced both species of beaver, the Eurasian beaver *Castor fiber* and the North American beaver *Castor canadensis*, into the Amur River in the far east, but neither species is known to have established itself on the Chinese side.

[20] Duncan J. Halley, Alexander P. Saveljev and Frank Rosell. "Population and distribution of beavers *Castor fiber* and *Castor canadensis* in Eurasia." *Mammal Review* 51 (2021): 1

21 初雯雯. "天寒地冻，你贴得一身好膘，我却酸了，" // 走！守护动物及其家园, 宋大昭, 黄巧雯 主编. 上海: 上海科技教育出版社, 2020, 149–156.

In hopes of boosting its struggling beaver population, Mongolia has a beaver breeding program and is bringing in beavers from Germany and Russia.
Anudari M., "Relocated beavers from Germany and Russia restore river habitat," MONTSAME, August 13, 2018. https://montsame.mn/en/read/136320.

22 Du Cong-cong, Zhao Jing, Chu Hong-jun, Liu Yuan-chao et al. "Research on genetic diversities of Asiatic beaver (*Castor fiber birulai*) on mtDNA D-loop HV-I in Xinjiang, China." *Journal of Shandong University (Natural Science)* 51 (2016): 19–28.

23 初, "天寒地冻," 153.

24 Hongjun Chu and Zhigang Jiang. "Distribution and conservation of the Sino-Mongolian beaver *Castor fiber birulai* in China." *Oryx* 43 (2009): 199.

25 初, "天寒地冻," 154–156.

26 Su Canxia et al. "Potential distribution changes of *Castor fiber birulai* under climate changes in the upper reaches of the Ulungur River, Xinjiang." *Arid Zone Research* 41 (2024): 509–520.

In the Deep Desert

1 Yadong Xue et al. "Assessing the vulnerability and adaptation strategies of wild camel to climate change in the Kumtag Desert of China." *Global Ecology and Conservation* 29, e01725 (2021).

The wild progenitors of both the domesticated Bactrian *Camelus bactrianus* and the single-humped dromedary *C. dromedarius* are believed to have been extinct for around 2,000 years. There are, however, feral camel populations, most notably in Australia, where the camels (mostly dromedaries but also a smaller number of Bactrians) have become too successful for the health of the local ecosystems, leading to an ongoing culling program begun in 2009.

2 Camels' humps are large stores of fat that provide energy when food is sparse, not portable water towers as commonly believed.

3 Yuguang Zhang et al. "RAD-Seq data advance captive-based conservation of wild bactrian camels (*Camelus ferus*)." *Conservation Genetics* 20 (2019): 817.

4 R. Tulgat & George B. Schaller. "Status and distribution of wild Bactrian camels *Camelus bactrianus ferus*." *Biological Conservation* 62 (1992): 11.

[5] Richard B. Harris. *Wildlife Conservation in China: Preserving the Habitat of China's Wild West*. Armonk, NY: M.E. Sharpe, 2008, 156–157.

Harris bases his determination of the wild camel's past range on the work of Wen Huanran. His son Wen Rongsheng 文榕生 has continued his work, producing the monumental four-volume series *The Distributions and Changes of Rare Wild Animals in China* (2009 & 2019). This later work extends the range of *Camelus ferus* east into Manchuria up through the Qing dynasty. I have ignored this as I believe the records on which Wen relied refer not to wild camels but to domesticated Bactrians, which for centuries were a common sight in much of North China, widely used as pack animals. If there were ever wild-living camels in North China or Manchuria, they were all but certainly feral Bactrians and not true wild camels.

[6] N. Prejevalsky. *From Kulja, Across the Tian Shan to Lob-Nor: Including Notices of the Lakes of Central Asia*. London: Sampson Low, Marston, Searle, & Rivington, 1879, 88–97.

[7] George R. Littledale. "A Journey across Central Asia." *The Geographical Journal* 3 (1894): 456.

[8] Sven Hedin. *Through Asia*. London: Methuen, 1898, 828–31.

[9] Sven Hedin. *Central Asia and Tibet: Towards the Holy City of Lassa, Volume I*. London: Hurst and Blackett, 1903, 357–358 & 373;

Hedin. *Scientific Results of a Journey in Central Asia 1899-1902, Vol. I The Tarim River*. Stockholm: Lithographic Institute of the General Staff of the Swedish Army, 1904, 144, 227–228, 400 & 466–467;
Hedin. *Scientific Results of a Journey in Central Asia 1899-1902, Vol. II Lop-Nor*. Stockholm: Lithographic Institute of the General Staff of the Swedish Army, 1905, 185;
Hedin. *Scientific Results of a Journey in Central Asia 1899-1902, Vol. III North and East Tibet*. Stockholm: Lithographic Institute of the General Staff of the Swedish Army, 1905, 22 & 300–301.

[10] George B. Schaller. *Into Wild Mongolia*. New Haven: Yale University Press, 2020, 46.

[11] John Hare. "The wild Bactrian camel *Camelus bactrianus ferus* in China: the need for urgent action." *Oryx* 31 (1997): 45–48.

[12] John Hare. *Mysteries of the Gobi: Searching for Wild Camels and Lost Cities in the Heart of Asia*. London: I.B. Taurus, 2009, 57.

[13] John Hare. "*Camelus ferus*." *The IUCN Red List of Threatened Species* (2008): e.T63543A12689285.

[14] During the course of their survey work in 1995–1996, the team heard of a gun battle between two groups over gold-mining rights that had occurred only two days before their arrival in the area.

[15] Hare, *Mysteries of the Gobi*, 135.

[16] Landmines were perhaps not the best idea, as the survey team met a miner that had lost an arm and a leg to one of his own explosives.

[17] Hare, "The wild Bactrian camel," 47.

[18] John Hare. *The Lost Camels of Tartary: A Quest into Forbidden China*. London: Little, Brown, 1998, 105 & 169.

[19] Hare, *Mysteries of the Gobi*, 32.

[20] Xue et al, "Assessing the vulnerability and adaptation strategies."

[21] Yadong Xue, Jia Li, and Diqiang Li. "The wild camel (*Camelus ferus*) in China: Current status and conservation implications." *Journal for Nature Conservation* 60, 125979 (2021).

[22] "China's wild camel population increases steadily," *CGTN*, November 29, 2021. https://news.cgtn.com/news/2021-11-29/China-s-wild-camel-population-increases-steadily-15zSVWJ4Zm8/index.html.

[23] These climate projections were made according to Representative Concentration Pathway (RCP) 4.5, the greenhouse gas (GHG) concentration trajectory in which GHG emissions peak around 2040–2050. This is considered the Intergovernmental Panel on Climate Change's (IPCC) intermediate scenario, in which global average temperatures rise between 2 and 3 degrees Celsius by 2100.

[24] Xue et al, "Assessing the vulnerability and adaptation strategies."

[25] Douglas Chadwick. *Tracking Gobi Grizzlies: Surviving Beyond the Back of Beyond.* Ventura: Patagonia, 2017, 282–283.

[26] Aili Qin et al. "Predicting the current and future suitable habitats of the main dietary plants of the Gobi Bear using MaxEnt modeling." *Global Ecology and Conservation* 22, e01032 (2020): 8.

[27] Tiziano Londei. "About the geographic distribution of the Xinjiang Ground Jay (*Podoces biddulphi*)." *Chinese Birds* 4 (2013):184–186.

[28] Ming Ma. "Status of the Xinjiang Ground Jay: population, breeding ecology and conservation." *Chinese Birds* 2 (2011): 59–62.

Oases

[1] Yaning Chen, Zhaoxia Ye and Yanjun Shen. "Desiccation of the Tarim River, Xinjiang, China, and mitigation strategy." *Quaternary International* 244 (2011): 264–271.

[2] Mark B. Bain. "The conservation status of large migratory cyprinids including *Aspiorhynchus laticeps* of Xinjiang China." *Journal of Applied Ichthyology* 27, suppl. 3 (2011): 80–85.

[3] Lei Cheng, Dan Song, Xiaoli Yu, Xue Du and Tangbin Huo. "Endangered Schizothoracin Fish in the Tarim River Basin Are Threatened by Introgressive Hybridization." *Biology* 11, 981 (2022).

The authors identify the hybrid fish as *Schizothorax esocinus*, the Chirruh snowtrout found in mountain streams and rivers of the Himalayas and Inner Asia. This seems to be a misidentification, and—assuming their analysis is otherwise correct—the hybrid species is therefore due its own taxonomic designation.

[4] Prejevalsky, *From Kulja*, 104, 117 & 122.

[5] Sven Hedin. *Central Asia and Tibet: Towards the Holy City of Lassa, Volume I.* London: Hurst and Blackett, 1903, 245.

[6] Red deer taxonomy, and ungulate taxonomy more generally, has long been a particularly active taxonomic battlefield. For example, in the 2016 assessment for the IUCN Red List, the Tarim red deer is listed as a subspecies of *Cervus hanglu* as *C. h. yarkandensis*. So far most subsequent literature has continued to use the *C. elaphus* classification, as I do here, but undoubtedly the future holds more taxonomic drama for the Tarim red deer.

[7] At present the Konchi Darya is most commonly known by its Mandarin name *Kǒngquè Hé* 孔雀河, which translates to the Peacock River. The Qarqan River is also known by its Mandarin names, the Qiemo River (*Qiěmò Hé* 且末河) or Cherchen River (*Chē'ěrchén Hé* 车尔臣河).

[8] Church. *Chinese Turkestan*, 42 & 153.

Prejevalsky, *From Kulja*, 166.

[9] Halik Mahmut et al. "The present status of the Tarim red deer in Xinjiang, China." *Biosphere Conservation* 4 (2002): 79–86.

S.M. Brook et al. "*Cervus hanglu* (amended version of 2017 assessment)." *The IUCN Red List of Threatened Species* (2017): e.T4261A120733024.

[10] 刘少英, 吴毅 主编. 中国兽类图鉴. 福州: 海峡书局, 2019, 285.

[11] Prejevalsky, *From Kulja*, 166.

[12] Sven Hedin. *Through Asia*. London: Methuen, 1898, 460.

Hedin, *Central Asia and Tibet*, 1903, 126 & 186.

Hedin, *Scientific Results, Vol. I*, 18.

Sven Hedin related a local belief as to why tigers had disappeared from a particular locale, Kara-koschun. The local villagers believed that mother tigers always avoided areas with ants, as the ants would swarm in their thousands over her cubs and kill them. They saw proof of this in the fact that the ants of the area had been more numerous the preceding two years than normal, and no tigers had been seen in that period.

Hedin, *Scientific Results, Vol. II*, 138–139.

[13] Hedin, *Central Asia and Tibet*, 1903, 186 & 327.

Sven Hedin. *Adventures in Tibet*. London: Hurst and Blackett, 1904, 71.

Douglas Carruthers. *Unknown Mongolia: A Record of Travel and Exploration in North-West Mongolia and Dzungaria, Vol. II*. London: Hutchinson & Co., 1914, 609.

[14] Ablimit Abdukadir and Urs Breitenmoser. "The Last Tigers of Xinjiang." *Cat News* 47 (2007): 26.

[15] Tan Bangjie. "The Status of Felids in China." *Proceedings from the Cat Specialist Group meeting in Kanha National Park*. (1984): 36.

[16] Igor E. Chestin et al. "Tiger re-establishment potential to former Caspian tiger (*Panthera tigris virgata*) range in Central Asia." *Biological Conservation* 205 (2017): 42.

[17] Aidana Yergaliyeva, "Kazakhstan Finalizes Plan to Restore Native Turanian Tigers In Ile-Balkhash Region," *The Astana Times*, November 6, 2020. https://astanatimes.com/2020/11/kazakhstan-finalizes-plan-to-restore-native-turanian-tigers-in-ile-balkhash-region/.

Aliya Haidar, "Tigers to Return to Kazakhstan," *The Times of Central Asia*, July 17, 2024. https://timesca.com/return-of-tigers-to-kazakhstan/.

Western Highlands

[1] The Tibetan name for Mount Everest is written in several ways, the most common two being either *Chomolungma* or *Qomolangma*, the latter of which is written in Tibetan pinyin, the official romanization used within China. In Nepali, the mountain is named *Sagarmāthā* सगरमाथा.

[2] Zhao Ji et al. *The Natural History of China*. London: Collins, 1990, 36–40 & 137–142.

[3] Fahu Chen et al. "Climate change, vegetation history, and landscape responses on the Tibetan Plateau during the Holocene: A comprehensive review." *Quaternary Science Reviews* 243, 106444 (2020).

[4] Juan Li et al. "Role of Tibetan Buddhist Monasteries in Snow Leopard Conservation." *Conservation Biology* 28 (2014): 87–94.

The Buddhist compassion for all life is not always beneficial to wildlife, however. A brief mania in China for the large and fierce Tibetan mastiff led to a massive increase in the number of breeding operations from the 1990s to mid-2010s. When the bubble finally burst, many breeders were forced out of business. Unwilling to kill their dogs because of their religious beliefs, they instead set them loose. Consequently, feral Tibetan mastiffs are now the region's most numerous large predator, attacking wildlife, livestock, and even humans. Despite the danger the mastiffs often present to animals seeking refuge near monasteries, monks extend their compassion to the dogs and refuse to kill them in order to protect the wildlife.

Elaine Yau, "Tibetan mastiff dogs ravaging wildlife, mauling people, and spreading disease in China after collapse of pet market," *South China Morning Post*, December 17, 2020. https://www.scmp.com/lifestyle/family-relationships/article/3114112/tibetan-mastiff-dogs-ravaging-wildlife-mauling.

[5] Toni Huber. "The chase and the Dharma: the legal protection of wild animals in premodern Tibet," in *Wildlife in Asia: Cultural Perspectives*, ed. John Knight. London: RoutledgeCurzon, 2004, 36–55.

[6] Richard B. Harris. *Wildlife Conservation in China: Preserving the Habitat of China's Wild West*. Armonk, NY: M.E. Sharpe, 2008, 72–75.

[7] Huber. "The chase and the Dharma," 47.

[8] Harris, *Wildlife Conservation in China*, 73–74.

[9] Fan Yang, Quanqin Shao and Zhigang Jiang. "A Population Census of Large Herbivores Based on UAV and Its Effects on Grazing Pressure in the Yellow-River-Source National Park, China." *International Journal of Environmental Research and Public Health* 16, 4402 (2019).

[10] Galen Rowell. *Mountains of the Middle Kingdom: Exploring the High Peaks of China and Tibet*. San Francisco: Sierra Club Books, 1983, 157–159.

[11] R.B. Harris. "Rangeland degradation on the Qinghai-Tibetan plateau: A review of the evidence of its magnitude and causes." *Journal of Arid Environments* 74 (2010): 1–12.

[12] Richard B. Harris et al. "Rangeland responses to pastoralists' grazing management on a Tibetan steppe grassland, Qinghai Province, China." *The Rangeland Journal* 38 (2016): 1–15.

Emily T. Yeh et al. "Pastoralist Decision-Making on the Tibetan Plateau." *Human Ecology* 45 (2017): 333–343.

[13] John D. Farrington and Juan Li. "Climate Change Impacts on Snow Leopard Range," in *Snow Leopards: Biodiversity of the World: Conservation from Genes to Landscapes*, ed. Thomas McCarthy and David Mallon. Boston: Academic Press, 2016, 85–89.

Alpine Steppe

[1] Joseph P. Lambert et al. "The pikas of China: a review of current research priorities and challenges for conservation." *Integrative Zoology* 18 (2023): 110–128.

[2] The Chinese name for pika—*shǔtù* 鼠兔, which combines the words *shǔ* 鼠 meaning "mouse" or "rat," and *tù* 兔 meaning "rabbit"—captures well their resemblance to rodents. Richard Harris notes that when speaking Chinese, locals of all ethnicities tend to use the common word for rats or mice, *lǎoshǔ* 老鼠, instead of *shǔtù*.

[3] Andrew T. Smith and J. Marc Foggin. "The plateau pika (*Ochotona curzoniae*) is a keystone species for biodiversity on the Tibetan plateau." *Animal Conservation* 2 (1999): 236.

[4] Smith and Foggin, "The plateau pika (*Ochotona curzoniae*) is a keystone species," 236.

[5] Smith and Foggin, "The plateau pika (*Ochotona curzoniae*) is a keystone species," 237–239.

[6] Harris, *Wildlife Conservation in China*, 145.

[7] A.T. Smith and C.H. Johnston. "*Eospalax fontanierii*." *The IUCN Red List of Threatened Species* (2016): e.T14118A115120816.

Andrew T. Smith and Yan Xie, ed. *A Guide to the Mammals of China*. Princeton: Princeton University Press, 2008, 209–212.

[8] Plateau zokor require so much energy that on average they consume 4.1 times as much energy per unit of body mass as a typical Tibetan domestic sheep.

[9] Yanming Zhang. "The Biology and Ecology of Plateau Zokors (*Eospalax fontanierii*)," in *Subterranean Rodents: News from Underground*, ed. Sabine Begall, Hynek Burda and Cristian E. Schleich. Berlin: Springer, 2007, 237–249.

[10] Robert B. Ekvall. *Fields on the Hoof: Nexus of Tibetan Nomadic Pastoralism*. New York: Holt, Rinehart and Winston, 1968, 6.

[11] Smith and Foggin, "The plateau pika," 237.

The area poisoned at the peak of the pika-zokor extermination campaign—130,000 sq km (50,190 sq mi)—is larger than the US state of Mississippi and just smaller than the country of Nicaragua. The area reached by 2006–357,060 sq km (137,861 sq mi)—is almost the exact size of Germany.

[12] Badingqiuying et al. "Plateau pika *Ochotona curzoniae* poisoning campaign reduces carnivore abundance in southern Qinghai, China." *Mammal Study* 41 (2016): 1–6.

[13] Andrew T. Smith et al. "Functional-trait ecology of the plateau pika *Ochotona curzoniae* in the Qinghai–Tibetan Plateau ecosystem." *Integrative Zoology* 14 (2019): 95–96.

[14] Harris, *Wildlife Conservation in China*, 147.

[15] Smith et al., "Functional-trait ecology of the plateau pika," 90.

[16] Chien Hsun Lai and Andrew T. Smith. "Keystone status of plateau pikas (*Ochotona curzoniae*): effect of control on biodiversity of native birds." *Biodiversity and Conservation* 12 (2003): 1901–1912.

Smith et al., "Functional-trait ecology of the plateau pika," 90–92.

[17] Wu Lan and Hao Wang. "Poisoning the pika: must protection of grasslands be at the expense of biodiversity?" *Science China Life Sciences* 60 (2017): 545–547.

Smith and Foggin (1999) were adamant that pika control measures were of no good use, stating that "Control is a lose–lose situation; costs are high and there are no demonstrable benefits."

[18] Harris, *Wildlife Conservation in China*, 148–150.

[19] Wu and Wang, "Poisoning the pika," 545–547.

Yujie Jiu et al. "Plant diversity is closely related to the density of zokor mounds in three alpine rangelands on the Tibetan Plateau." *Peerj* 7, e6921 (2019).

[20] The Tibetan blue bear (along with other bears such as the Himalayan brown bear *Ursus arctos isabellinus*) is a prime candidate for the true identity of the Yeti—the Abominable Snowman— of Himalayan folklore.

[21] Tibetan blue bears can have extremely large ranges. One male bear fitted with a GPS collar ranged over an area greater than 7,000 sq km (2,700 sq mi).

[22] Glover M. Allen. *The Mammals of China and Mongolia, Part 1*. New York: The American Museum of Natural History, 1938, 328.

[23] George B. Schaller. *Tibet Wild: A Naturalist's Journey on the Roof of the World*. Washington, DC: Island Press, 2012, 312.

[24] Fiona R. Worthy and J. Marc Foggin. "Conflicts between local villagers and Tibetan brown bears threaten conservation of bears in a remote region of the Tibetan Plateau." *Human–Wildlife Conflicts* 2 (2008): 200–204.

[25] Xu Ai-Chun et al. "Food habits and hunting patterns of Tibetan brown bear during warm seasons in Kekexili region on Qinghai-Tibetan Plateau." *Zoological Research* 31 (2010): 670–674.

[26] Yunchuan Dai et al. "The human-bear conflicts and herder attitudes and knowledge in the Yangtze River Zone of Sanjiangyuan National Park." *Acta Ecologica Sinica* 39 (2019): 8245–8253.

Bears rarely attack livestock but do occasionally kill herders' animals. However, damage to homes is far more common and more costly to people's livelihoods.

[27] Su Kaiwen et al. "Balancing human–bear coexistence with biodiversity conservation." *Human Dimensions of Wildlife* (2021): 9.

[28] Su et al. "Balancing human–bear coexistence," 8.

[29] Yunchuan Dai et al. "Mitigation Strategies for Human–Tibetan Brown Bear (*Ursus arctos pruinosus*) Conflicts in the Hinterland of the Qinghai-Tibetan Plateau." *Animals* 12, 1422 (2022).

[30] Yunchuan Dai et al. "Identifying climate refugia and its potential impact on Tibetan brown bear (*Ursus arctos pruinosus*) in Sanjiangyuan National Park, China." *Ecology and Evolution* 9 (2019): 13283–13287.

[31] The Tibetan fox's impassive, narrow-eyed countenance has made it a minor star of the Mainland Chinese internet in recent years, where it has been featured in a number of popular memes.

[32] 王正寰 叶晓青. "第三极"的原住民: 藏狐. 上海: 上海科技教育出版社, 2015, 71.

[33] Richard B. Harris et al. "Notes on the biology of the Tibetan fox." *Canid News* 11 (2008): 1–4.

[34] Richard B. Harris et al. "Evidence that the Tibetan fox is an obligate predator of the plateau pika: conservation implications." *Journal of Mammalogy* 95 (2014): 1215–1217.

[35] B. H. Hodgson. "Notice of the Mammals of Tibet, with Descriptions and Plates of some new Species." *Journal of the Asiatic Society of Bengal* 11 (1842): 277.

Alexander Kinloch. *Large Game Shooting in Thibet, the Himalayas, and Northern India*. Calcutta: Thacker, Spink and Co., 1885, 41.

Ernest Henry Wilson. *A Naturalist in Western China: With Vasculum, Camera, and Gun: Being Some Account of Eleven Year's Travel, Exploration, and Observation in the More Remote Parts of the Flowery Kingdom, Vol. II*. London: Methuen & Co., 1913, 189.

[36] Dholes have disappeared from over 75% of their historic worldwide range. As of the latest IUCN Red List assessment in 2015, there had been no confirmed sightings of the wild dogs for over 30 years in Russia, Mongolia, Kazakhstan, Afghanistan, Tajikistan, or Uzbekistan. Genetic sampling of scat found in 2019 is the first confirmation in decades that dholes remain in or have returned to Kyrgyzstan's Pamir Mountains.

[37] Harris, *Wildlife Conservation in China*, 161–162.

[38] Yadong Xue et al. "Records of the dhole (*Cuon alpinus*) in an arid region of the Altun Mountains in western China." *European Journal of Wildlife Research* 61 (2015): 905–906.

Philip Riordan et al. "New evidence of dhole *Cuon alpinus* populations in north-west China." *Oryx* 49 (2015): 203–204.

[39] J.F. Kamler et al. "*Cuon alpinus*." *The IUCN Red List of Threatened Species* (2015): e.T5953A72477893.

[40] baboon & 赵翔, "这次，豺可不可以拥有一级动物的牌面，" 山水自然保护中心, June 21, 2020. https://mp.weixin.qq.com/s/7ecuIfug01ya5YMsxmeslA.

[41] The Himalayan wolf—*Canis lupus himalayensis* if determined to be a subspecies of the grey wolf, or *C. himalayensis* if deemed to be a species—is often lumped taxonomically with *C. l. chanco* the Mongolian wolf. The wolves of the Tibetan Plateau, separate from those further south in the Himalayas of India, Nepal, and Bhutan, are sometimes categorized as their own subspecies, *C. l. laniger*, known as the Tibetan wolf or Tibetan grey wolf.

[42] Geraldine Werhahn et al. "The unique genetic adaptation of the Himalayan wolf to high-altitudes and consequences for conservation." *Global Ecology and Conservation* 16, e00455 (2018): 9–10.

[43] Geraldine Werhahn et al. "Phylogenetic evidence for the ancient Himalayan wolf: towards a clarification of its taxonomic status based on genetic sampling from western Nepal." *Royal Society Open Science* 4 (2017): 9–11.

[44] Geraldine Werhahn et al. "Himalayan wolf foraging ecology and the importance of wild prey." *Global Ecology and Conservation* 20, e00780 (2019): 6.

[45] Harris, *Wildlife Conservation in China*, 58–59.

46 The case of an old and malnourished wolf that grew considerably heavier after numerous passing motorists threw food to it along a highway running through Qinghai's Hoh Xil reserve is a clear sign of how far perceptions of wolves have changed within China.

Ding Rui, "'Lying Flat' Wolf Fed Well by Tourists, But Concerns Raised," *Sixth Tone*, November 14, 2023. https://www.sixthtone.com/news/1014078.

47 Peter Simon Pallas (1741–1811), for whom the Pallas's cat and many other species are named, was a Prussian naturalist who spent most of his working life in Russia under the patronage of Empress Catherine the Great (1729–1796, r. 1762–1796). Pallas led two expeditions into the eastern lands of the Russian Empire to document its natural history. Over a dozen species now bear his name, including Pallas's fish eagle *Haliaeetus leucoryphus* and the now extinct Pallas's or spectacled cormorant *Urile perspicillatus*.

48 Eva Jutzeler, Xie Yan and Kristina Vogt. "The smaller felids of China: Pallas's cat *Otocolobus manul*." *Cat News* sp. 5 (2010): 37–39.

49 David Barclay et al. "Legal status, utilisation, management and conservation of manul." *Cat News* sp. 13 (2019): 37.

50 Tan, "The Status of Felids in China," 42.

51 Steven Ross. "Providing an ecological basis for the conservation of the Pallas's cat (*Otocolobus manul*)." Doctoral thesis, University of Bristol. 2009.

52 Tashi Dhendup et al. "Distribution and status of the manul in the Himalayas and China." *Cat News* sp. 13 (2019): 31–34.

53 Steven Ross et al. "Past, present and future threats and conservation needs of Pallas's cats." *Cat News* sp. 13 (2019): 46.

54 More accurate alternatives to Chinese mountain cat have been suggested—namely Chinese steppe cat or Chinese alpine steppe cat—but have yet to catch on. The Chinese name for *Felis bieti*, *huāngmò māo* 荒漠猫, translates to wilderness cat and suggests a creature found in broad desert expanses.

55 S.-J. Luo et al. "*Felis bieti*." *The IUCN Red List of Threatened Species* (2022): e.T8539A213200674.

56 Blue eyes are of course a typical eye color in various breeds of the domestic cat, but this attribute is one sustained through selective breeding at the hand of humanity, and not the result of natural selection as is the case with the Chinese mountain cat.

57 宋大昭，"中国特有野生猫，不许再说不认识！"猫盟*CFCA*, January 6, 2021. https://mp.weixin.qq.com/s/66SDy0qpuf64NNmXPIdCCQ.

[58] Yin Yufeng et al. "First Photographs in Nature of the Chinese Mountain Cat." *Cat News* 47 (2007): 6–7.

[59] Jim Sanderson, Yin Yufeng and Drubgyal Naktsang. "Of the only endemic cat species in China. The Chinese mountain cat — *Felis bieti*." *Cat News* sp. 5 (2010): 18–20.

[60] Chunyue Wei et al. "By their foes and by their kins — endemic Chinese mountain cats are threatened by domestic dogs and cats." *Authorea* Preprint (2023).

[61] 宋大昭，"中国特有野生猫."

[62] He Yu et al. "Genomic evidence for the Chinese mountain cat as a wildcat conspecific (*Felis silvestris bieti*) and its introgression to domestic cats." *Science Advances* 7, eabg0221 (2021): 9–10.

[63] David Grimm, "China's most mysterious wildcat may not be its own species," *Science*, June 23, 2021. https://www.science.org/content/article/china-s-most-mysterious-wildcat-may-not-be-its-own-species

[64] Nancy C. Dwyer et al. "Black-necked cranes nesting in Tibet Autonomous Region, China," in *Proceedings of the Sixth North American Crane Workshop, Oct. 3-5, 1991, Regina, Sask.*, ed. D. W. Stahlecker. Grand Island, NE.: North American Crane Working Group, 1992, 79.

[65] Paul A. Johnsgard. *Cranes of the World*. Bloomington: Indiana University Press, 1983, 219–223.

[66] "Cao Hai is a Treasure," *International Crane Foundation*, October 18, 2011. https://savingcranes.org/cao-hai-is-a-treasure/ [dead link].

[67] Yang Jun, "Cao Hai Lake; Crown jewel of Guizhou," *China Daily*, February 24, 2022. https://www.chinadaily.com.cn/a/202202/24/WS621735c2a310cdd39bc88b6a.html.

[68] Peter Matthiessen. *The Birds of Heaven: Travels with Cranes*. New York: North Point Press, 2001, 127–130.

[69] Fengshan Li. "Species Review: Black-necked Crane (*Grus nigricollis*)," in *Crane Conservation Strategy*, ed. Claire M. Mirande and James T. Harris. Baraboo: International Crane Foundation, 2019, 304.

[70] Mardan Aghabey Turghan, Paul Jason Buzzard and Roller Maming. "Current Status of Black-Necked Crane Grus Nigricollis in Southern Xinjiang China: Conservation Implications." *Wetlands* (Preprint under consideration 2021).

[71] Li, "Species Review: Black-necked Crane (*Grus nigricollis*)," 303–304.

[72] Chen Jiajia et al. "Global distribution and number of overwintering black-necked crane (*Grus nigricollis*)." *Biodiversity Science* 31, 22400 (2023).

[73] James Harris and Claire Mirande. "A global overview of cranes: status, threats and conservation priorities." *Chinese Birds* 4 (2013): 193–194.

[74] Li, "Species Review: Black-necked Crane (*Grus nigricollis*)," 305.

Upland Ungulates

[1] Unlike many species, *Procapra przewalskii* has only one name in English: Przewalski's gazelle. The gazelle's name in Chinese, *Pǔshì yuánlíng* 普氏原羚, has the same meaning. However, one man, photographer Ge Yuxiu 葛玉修, is on a campaign to change the species' Chinese name to *Zhōnghuá duìjiǎo líng* 中华对角羚, which translates awkwardly to "Chinese diagonal gazelle," "diagonal" referring to the angle at which males' horns veer off. He has suggested this new appellation in spite of the fact that locals of the gazelle's habitat already have alternative names for the animals: *tān huángyáng* 滩黄羊 and *tān yuánlíng* 滩原羚, both meaning "sandbar" or "beach" gazelle, presumably in reference to its habitat. Ge's choice accomplishes two things—highlighting that the species is endemic to the People's Republic, and removing what could be seen as the commemoration of a foreigner who spied on the Qing Empire, looted cultural artifacts, and killed a large number of Tibetans. The new name has yet to catch on, with most uses limited to Ge's own writings or those that mention him and his quixotic quest. This may change as an increasingly prickly nationalism grows stronger across much of Mainland Chinese society, prompting a widening Sinification of names in an effort to wash away linguistic traces of past foreign domination or influence. For now at least, Ge graciously limits his national pride to the Chinese language, allowing that non-Chinese speakers may go on using the old, imperialist moniker. Indeed, China's English-language media, including state-run outfits, continue to use "Przewalski's gazelle."

[2] 吴梦婷, "2023年青海湖水位较近十年平均上升1.3米," 西海都市报, August 8, 2024. https://epaper.tibet3.com/xhdsb/html/202408/08/content_187855.html.

[3] Harris, *Wildlife Conservation in China*, 127–128.

[4] Harris, *Wildlife Conservation in China*, 129–131.

[5] 李玉坤, "青海普氏原羚数量14年增加近9倍，一度比大熊猫还稀少," 新京报, June 6, 2021. https://news.sina.com.cn/c/2021-06-06/doc-ikqcfnaz9267059.shtml.

[6] David M. Leslie, Jr., Colin P. Groves and Alexei V. Abramov. "*Procapra przewalskii* (Artiodactyla: Bovidae)." *Mammalian Species* 42, 860 (2010): 128.

[7] Lu Zhang et al. "Influence of Fencing on Przewalski's Gazelle, Qinghai Province, China." Report. 2010, 5.

[8] Zhang et al. "Influence of Fencing," 17–22.

[9] Lu Zhang et al. "Fencing for conservation? —The impacts of fencing on grasslands and the endangered Przewalski's gazelle on the Tibetan Plateau." *Science China Life Sciences* 61 (2016): 1594–1595.

[10] He Yu et al. "Effects of the Qinghai-Tibet Railway on the Landscape Genetics of the Endangered Przewalski's Gazelle (*Procapra przewalskii*)." *Scientific Reports* 7, 17983 (2017): 1–9.

[11] Junhua Hu, Zhigang Jiang and David P. Mallon. "Metapopulation viability of a globally endangered gazelle on the Northeast Qinghai–Tibetan Plateau." *Biological Conservation* 166 (2013): 28.

[12] Lu Zhang et al. "Distribution and population status of Przewalski's gazelle, *Procapra przewalskii* (Cetartiodactyla, Bovidae) " *Mammalia* 77 (2013): 31–37.

Xiaoge Ping et al. "The distribution, population and conservation status of Przewalski's gazelle, *Procapra przewalskii*." *Biodiversity Science* 26 (2018): 179.

[13] Zhenyuan Cai et al. "Protecting Przewalski's gazelle." *Oryx* 56 (2022): 652.

Tian Liu et al. "Changes in habitat suitability and population size of the endangered Przewalski's gazelle. *Global Ecology and Conservation* 43, e02465 (2023).

[14] Junhua Hu and Zhigang Jiang. "Climate Change Hastens the Conservation Urgency of an Endangered Ungulate." *PLoS ONE* 6, e22873 (2011): 6.

[15] David M. Leslie, Jr. "*Procapra picticaudata* (Artiodactyla: Bovidae)." *Mammalian Species* 42, 861 (2010): 140–146.

[16] Prejevalsky, *Mongolia, the Tangut Country, Vol. II*, 208–209.

Rawling, *The Great Plateau*, 232.

[17] IUCN SSC Antelope Specialist Group. "*Procapra picticaudata*." *The IUCN Red List of Threatened Species* (2016): e.T18231A115142581.

[18] Schaller, *Wildlife of the Tibetan Steppe*, 109–116.

[19] Rawling, *The Great Plateau*, 232.

[20] Harris, *Wildlife Conservation in China*, 164–165.

[21] Jingjie Zhang et al. "The four antelope species on the Qinghai-Tibet plateau face habitat loss and redistribution to higher latitudes under climate change." *Ecological Indicators* 123, 107337 (2021).

The study's projections indicated that the best case scenario would see a loss of only 2.2% of goa habitat, with the worst case scenario resulting in a loss of 36.3%.

[22] Jianlin Han. "Wild yak (*Bos mutus* Przewalski, 1883)," in *Ecology, Evolution and Behaviour of Wild Cattle: Implications for Conservation*, ed. M. Melletti and J. Burton. Cambridge: Cambridge University Press, 2014, 201.

[23] David M. Leslie, Jr. and George B. Schaller. "*Bos grunniens* and *Bos mutus* (Artiodactyla: Bovidae)." *Mammalian Species* 836 (2009): 4.

[24] P. Buzzard and J. Berger. "*Bos mutus*." *The IUCN Red List of Threatened Species* (2016): e.T2892A101293528.

Abhaya Raj Joshi, "Nepal's wild yaks 'need more conservation than research': Q&A with Naresh Kusi," *Mongabay*, November 15, 2022. https://news.mongabay.com/2022/11/nepals-wild-yaks-need-more-conservation-than-research-qa-with-naresh-kusi/.

Wild yak were once present in Bhutan as well, but are now believed extirpated from the kingdom.

[25] M. Huc. *Travels in Tartary, Thibet and China During the Years 1844–5–6, Vol. II.* Chicago: Open Court, 1900, 124.

N. Prejevalsky. *Mongolia, the Tangut Country, and the Solitudes of Northern Tibet: Being a Narrative of Three Years' Travel in Eastern High Asia, Vol. II.* London: Sampson Low, Marston, Searle, & Rivington, 1876, 190.

Cecil Godfrey Rawling. *The Great Plateau: Being an Account of Exploration in Central Tibet, 1903, and of the Gartok Expedition, 1904–1905.* London: Edward Arnold, 1905, 309.

[26] Prejevalsky, *Mongolia, the Tangut Country, Vol. II*, 189.

[27] Sven Hedin. *Through Asia*. London: Methuen, 1898, 1037–1038.

[28] George B. Schaller. *Wildlife of the Tibetan Steppe*. Chicago: Chicago University Press, 1998, 129.

[29] Prejevalsky, *Mongolia, the Tangut Country, Vol. II*, 195–200.

[30] Frank Bagnall Bessac and Susanne Leppmann Bessac, with Joan Orielle Bessac Steelquist. *Death on the Chang Tang; 1950: The Education of an Anthropologist.* Missoula: University of Montana Printing and Graphic Services, 2006, 87.

[31] Prejevalsky, *Mongolia, the Tangut Country, Vol. II*, 201.

[32] M. S. Wellby. *Through Unknown Tibet*. London: T. Fisher Unwin, 1898, 181.

[33] George B. Schaller and Liu Wulin. "Distribution, Status, and Conservation of Wild Yak *Bos grunniens*." *Biological Conservation* 76 (1996): 4.

Ernst Schäfer (1910–1992) accompanied the American naturalist Brooke Dolan II and his party working for the Philadelphia Academy of Sciences on two expeditions to western China and eastern Tibet in the 1930s. Schäfer led a third, German expedition in 1938–1939, as a member of the SS, whose leader Heinrich Himmler sponsored the trip.

[34] Leonard Clark. *The Marching Wind*. London: Hutchinson & Co., 1954, 253–254.

[35] Harris, *Wildlife Conservation in China*, 155.

[36] Daniel J. Miller, Richard B. Harris and Gu-Quan Cai. "Wild yaks and their conservation on the Tibetan Plateau," in *Proceedings of the 1st International Congress on Yak*, ed. R. Zhang, J. Han and J. Wu. Lanzhou: Gansu Agricultural University, 1994, 29.

[37] Schaller and Li, "Distribution, Status, and Conservation of Wild Yak," 4–5.

[38] Paul J. Buzzard et al. "A globally important wild yak *Bos mutus* population in the Arjinshan Nature Reserve, Xinjiang, China." *Oryx* 44 (2010): 577–579.

[39] Schaller and Li, "Distribution, Status, and Conservation of Wild Yak," 7.

[40] Joel Berger. *Extreme Conservation: Life at the Edges of the World*. Chicago: University of Chicago Press, 2018, 157.

[41] Ramacandra Wong, "Community-based wild yak conservation in Tibet," *WCS*, July 22, 2013. https://china.wcs.org/News/Latest-News/articleType/ArticleView/articleId/1088/Community-based_wild_yak_conservation_in_Tibet.aspx.

[42] Harris, *Wildlife Conservation in China*, 155.

For those who worry about the genetic dilution of wild yak from hybridizing with domestic yak, even more horrific is the fact that many domestic yak are themselves hybridized with domestic cattle, representing a further dilution of the wild species' gene pool. In spite of these concerns, what little genetic testing that has been done on the wild yak has shown the species maintains very rich levels of genetic diversity.

[43] Berger, *Extreme Conservation*, 154–156.

[44] P. Buzzard and J. Berger. "*Bos mutus*." *The IUCN Red List of Threatened Species* (2016): e.T2892A101293528.

"Population of protected wild yak sees stable growth in China," *CGTN*, December 4, 2023. https://news.cgtn.com/news/2023-12-04/Population-of-protected-wild-yak-sees-stable-growth-in-China-1pgAqho6b0A/p.html.

[45] Schaller, *Wildlife of the Tibetan Steppe*, 142.

[46] Berger, *Extreme Conservation*, 177.

[47] For a long time the taxonomic distinction between kiang and khulan was unsettled, with the kiang for many years more commonly considered a subspecies of *Equus hemionus*. Molecular research has recently shown the kiang is distinct enough to qualify as a species.

[48] Antoine St-Louis and Steeve D. Côté. "*Equus kiang* (Perissodactyla: Equidae)." *Mammalian Species* 835 (2008): 2–4.

[49] Prejevalsky, *Mongolia, the Tangut Country, Vol. II*, 146–148.

[50] Sven Hedin. *Trans-Himalaya: Discoveries and Adventures in Tibet, Vol. III*. London: Macmillan and Co., 1913, 11.

[51] Melvyn C. Goldstein and Cynthia M. Beall. *Nomads of Western Tibet: The Survival of a Way of Life*. Berkeley: University of California Press, 1990, 114.

[52] Clark, *The Marching Wind*, 94.

[53] 郑生武，高行宜. "中国野驴的现状、分布区的历史变迁原因探讨." 生物多样性 8 (2000): 86.

[54] Huc, *Travels in Tartary, Thibet and China*, 125.

[55] Prejevalsky, *Mongolia, the Tangut Country, Vol. II*, 146–148.

[56] George R. Littledale. "A Journey across Central Asia." *The Geographical Journal* 3 (1894): 463

Sven Hedin. *Trans-Himalaya: Discoveries and Adventures in Tibet, Vol. II*. London: Macmillan and Co., 1910, 285.

[57] Leonard Clark—who was rumored to be on a CIA mission to support anti-Communist resistance—did succeed in reaching and taking measurements of Amne Machin. His traveling companion and translator, Prince Tsedan Dorje, a Mongolian polymath, surveyed the mountain, but his measurements were wildly inaccurate, calculating the peak rose 9,041 m (29,662 ft) above sea level. Amne Machin, though a high mountain, in fact rises only to 6,282 m (20,610 ft), substantially lower than Mt. Everest at 8,848 m (29,031 ft). At least one WWII pilot later admitted that he and others had radioed in claims of mountains higher than Everest in remote Tibet as a shared joke, and were surprised the claims were taken seriously.

[58] Clark, *The Marching Wind*, 129.

[59] Thomas Laird. *Into Tibet: The CIA's First Atomic Spy and His Secret Expedition to Lhasa*. New York: Grove Press, 2002, 163.

[60] N. Shah, A. St. Louis and Q. Qureshi. "*Equus kiang*." *The IUCN Red List of Threatened Species* (2015): e.T7953A45171635.

61 Schaller, *Wildlife of the Tibetan Steppe*, 167.

62 郑生武, 高行宜, "中国野驴的现状," 86.
谭邦杰. "野生动物的灭种和保种." 自然杂志 2 (1979) 427.
Because these figures for kiang killed in Qinghai from 1959 to 1961 come from the time of the Great Leap Forward, they should be taken with a grain of salt. Whatever the accuracy of the numbers, it is certain that the region's kiang suffered massive losses at the hands of hunters during this period.

63 Schaller, *Wildlife of the Tibetan Steppe*, 167.

64 George B. Schaller, *Tibet's Hidden Wilderness: Wildlife and Nomads of the Chang Tang Reserve*. New York: Harry N. Abrams, 1997, 62 & 128.

George Schaller describes a meeting in 1991 with the local party secretary of Shuanghu (双湖县), a remote county in the eastern Changtang, where he was told that hunting parties traveled north every autumn to hunt yak. During the meeting the official handed out rifles and ammunition to his staff members to go hunt kiang to supply meat for a Han Chinese construction crew working within his jurisdiction. At that time both the yak and kiang were already legally protected species. Two years later the Tibetan provincial government awarded the same man recognition as a National Wildlife Protection Model for his contributions to conservation.

65 Schaller, *Wildlife of the Tibetan Steppe*, 169.

66 Robert L. Fleming, Jr, Dorje Tsering and Liu Wulin. *Across the Tibetan Plateau: Ecosystems, Wildlife, and Conservation*. New York: W. W. Norton & Co., 2007, 81.

67 St-Louis and Côté, "*Equus kiang*," 4.

68 Harris, *Wildlife Conservation in China*, 167.

69 St-Louis and Côté, "*Equus kiang*," 8.

On Cliffs & Crags

1 S. Nijhawan. "*Naemorhedus baileyi*". The *IUCN Red List of Threatened Species* (2020): e.T14294A179947455.

2 The taxonomy of the takin is in dispute, with some scientists advocating for the currently recognized four subspecies to be split into four species. In that case, the Mishmi takin would become *Budorcas taxicolor* and the Bhutan takin *B. whitei*.

3 Y.-L. Song, A.T. Smith and J. MacKinnon. "*Budorcas taxicolor*." The *IUCN Red List of Threatened Species* (2008): e.T3160A9643719.

[4] Ian Baker. *The Heart of the World: A Journey to the Last Secret Place*. New York: Penguin Press, 2004, 139–140.

[5] Argali were the foremost draw for big-spending foreign hunters during China's brief foray into international trophy hunting. They commanded the highest prices, and the proceeds went to funding the overseeing government agencies. Reserves designated for argali hunting consequently drew a disproportionate amount of personnel and focus within the region's nature reserve system. The argali themselves, however, were poorly managed and conserved. Had trophy hunting and its target species been better managed, it could potentially have contributed significantly to local and regional conservation efforts. As it was, the central government suspended the practice in 2006, and there are no signs it will be allowed to resume.

[6] Schaller, *Wildlife of the Tibetan Steppe*, 80–93.

[7] Harris, *Wildlife Conservation in China*, 133–141.

[8] Alexander K. Fedosenko and David A. Blank. "*Capra sibirica*." *Mammalian Species* 675 (2001): 4.

[9] 宋延龄 主编. 动物与人. 南京: 江苏凤凰科学技术出版社, 2014, 340.

[10] Outside of their native range, Himalayan tahr have been introduced to New Zealand's South Island and South Africa's Western Cape, while in New Mexico and Argentina some have also escaped from game ranches to establish feral populations.

[11] J.W. Duckworth and J. MacKinnon. "*Naemorhedus goral*". *The IUCN Red List of Threatened Species* (2008): e.T14296A4430073.

T.D. Phan et al. "*Capricornis sumatraensis*." *The IUCN Red List of Threatened Species* (2020): e.T162916735A162916910.

The Himalayan goral and Himalayan serow were until recently considered individual species. The Himalayan serow was named *Capricornis thar*, but now is a subspecies of the mainland serow *C. sumatraensis*. Similarly, *Naemorhedus goral* now includes not only the Himalayan gorals, but also those previously classified as *N. griseus, N. bedfordi*, and *N. evansi*.

[12] The name "blue sheep," though still common, has somewhat fallen out of favor, as *Pseudois nayaur* is not a member of the sheep genus *Ovis*, and so the Hindi "bharal" is also commonly used. In Tibetan the species is called *na* གནའ་བ|, while in Mandarin its common name is *yán yáng* 岩羊, meaning "cliff sheep" or "cliff goat." Other names are used across its range. In Qinghai *shí yáng* 石羊 "rock sheep" is used, while in Gansu *qīng yáng* 青羊 "blue sheep" is preferred (although to be pedantic, *qīng* 青 is not merely blue, but covers a range of blue and green hues).

[13] Wang Sung, ed. *China Red Data Book of Endangered Animals: Mammalia*. Beijing: Science Press, 1998, 256.

The source for the export destinations for bharal meat is a Chinese-English bilingual document, but only the Chinese language entry lists an individual destination country. It lists Germany (*Déguó* 德国) as the primary importing country, but does not differentiate whether it was East Germany, West Germany, or both. Considering that the PRC and West Germany did not establish diplomatic relations until 1972, "Germany" all but certainly refers to East Germany.

[14] Schaller, *Wildlife of the Tibetan Steppe*, 107–108.

[15] Harris, *Wildlife Conservation in China*, 168–169.

[16] B. Huffman and R. Harris. "*Pseudois nayaur ssp. schaeferi.*" *The IUCN Red List of Threatened Species* (2014): e.T18535A64313668.

[17] Shengwang Bao and Fan Yang. "Influences of Climate Change and Land Use Change on the Habitat Suitability of Bharal in the Sanjiangyuan District, China." *International Journal of Environmental Research and Public Health* 19, 17082 (2022).

[18] The snow leopard's taxonomy has changed over the years, as is common. For a time it was placed in its own genus, *Uncia*, but genetic testing has shown it is better placed in the genus *Panthera*. Despite its name and large rosettes, the snow leopard is most closely related not to the common leopard or two clouded leopard species, but to the tiger. There is also ongoing investigation into whether the species should be divided into two subspecies, but no major organization such as the IUCN has yet decided on the matter.

T. McCarthy et al. "*Panthera uncia.*" *The IUCN Red List of Threatened Species* (2017): e.T22732A50664030.

[19] The term "big cats" does not hue to a strict taxonomic definition, but typically refers to the cats of the *Panthera* genus (tiger, lion, leopard, snow leopard, jaguar), as well as the cheetah and mountain lion. The clouded leopards are occasionally thrown in as well.

[20] The effectiveness of snow leopards' camouflage can surprise even experienced observers. In *Tibet Wild*, George Schaller describes investigating a cliff base near a monastery for snow leopard sign with two Chinese colleagues, Li Juan and Lu Zhi. They found a cave with a carcass just inside, and Li Juan entered to take a closer look. When Schaller and Lu Zhi approached the cave mouth to see for themselves, a snow leopard bounded off a ledge that Li Juan had passed only moments earlier, and ran away for fear of the three scientists, none of whom had until that moment spotted the cat while it sat and watched them from only meters away.

[21] Ingo Rieger. "Tail Functions in Ounces, *Uncia uncia.*" *International Pedigree Book of Snow Leopards,* Panthera uncia 4 (1984): 85–97.

[22] The snow leopard's ancient predecessors lived over a much broader range, with the remains—over half a million years old—of an ancestral subspecies recently found in the Pyrenees Mountains of southern France.

[23] Kun Shi et al. "Snow leopard status and conservation in China," in *Snow Leopards: Biodiversity of the World: Conservation from Genes to Landscapes, 2nd ed.*, ed. David Mallon and Tom McCarthy. London: Academic Press, 2023, 587–592.

[24] In Sikkim, India, there has even been proof from camera traps showing a snow leopard using the same territory as a Bengal tiger. Both tigers and common leopards are creatures of woodlands and wooded grasslands, while snow leopards only spend small amounts of time in forests at the edges of their range. Therefore the overlap and any resultant competition between snow leopards and the other two species is minimal.

[25] 马鸣 等. 新疆雪豹. 北京: 科学出版社, 2013, 1.

[26] 马 等, 新疆雪豹, 5–18.

[27] Arthur de Carle Sowerby. *Fur and Feather in North China*. Tientsin: Tientsin Press, 1914, 46.

[28] Armand David. *Natural History of North China with Notices of that of the South, West and North-east, and of Mongolia & Thibet, compiled chiefly from the travels of Père Armand David*. Shanghai: Da Costa & Co., 1873, 10.

There is no solid evidence to support Père David's assertion that snow leopards could be found near Beijing. However, recent analysis has suggested that Shanxi does host suitable snow leopard habitat, so there is a remote possibility that the cats did at one time occur there.

[29] 文榕生. 中国珍稀野生动物分布变迁 (续:) 下. 济南: 山东科学技术出版社, 2018, 1750–1783.

For records prior to the twentieth century, Wen wisely resists the urge to differentiate between species of *bào* 豹 or "panthers," which at minimum can refer to common leopards, snow leopards, and clouded leopards. However, for twentieth century records he boldly—and, I would judge, unwisely—attempts to assign each record to one of the three above-mentioned species. The results are often questionable, especially for the snow leopard. Wen even includes a record from Shanxi in the 1950s that he considers could possibly have been a snow leopard, as well as numerous records from Manchuria. All of these are far more likely refer to common leopards, despite the use of terms Chinese scholars more commonly associate with snow leopards. (Admittedly, the possibility cannot be entirely dismissed, as the appearance of a single snow leopard in Dorbod Banner, Inner Mongolia—as far east as Shanxi—in September 2021 shows. Without more evidence to support past populations so far east, the most likely explanation is the young male was dispersing in search of territory and had unwittingly wandered far from the nearest fellow snow leopard.)

[30] Helmut Hemmer. "*Uncia uncia.*" *Mammalian Species* 20 (1972): 1.

There were even rare reports of snow leopards present on Sakhalin, off the Eurasian mainland and very far east of any other confirmed records of the species.

[31] Ernest Henry Wilson. *A Naturalist in Western China: With Vasculum, Camera, and Gun: Being Some Account of Eleven Year's Travel, Exploration, and Observation in the More Remote Parts of the Flowery Kingdom, Vol. II.* London: Methuen & Co., 1913, 180.

[32] William J. Morden. *Across Asia's Snows and Deserts.* New York: G. P. Putnam's Sons, 1927, 187.

[33] Tan Bangjie. "The Status of Felids in China." *Proceedings from the Cat Specialist Group meeting in Kanha National Park.* (1984): 39.

[34] George B. Schaller, Ren Junrang and Qui Mingjiang. "Status of the Snow Leopard *Panthera uncia* in Qinghai and Gansu Provinces, China." *Biological Conservation* 45 (1988): 185–193.

George B. Schaller et al. "The snow leopard in Xinjiang, China." *Oryx* 22 (1988): 202–203.

[35] Rodney, Jackson et al. "Snow Leopards in the Comolangma Nature Preserve of the Tibet Autonomous Region," in *Proceedings of the Seventh International Snow Leopard Symposium* ed. J. Fox and J. Du. Seattle: International Snow Leopard Trust, 1994, 87.

[36] Liao Yanfa. "Snow leopard distribution, purchase locations and conservation in Qinghai Province, China," in *Proceedings of the Seventh International Snow Leopard Symposium* ed. J. Fox and J. Du. Seattle: International Snow Leopard Trust, 1994, 68.

[37] D.J. Miller and Rodney Jackson. "Livestock and Snow Leopards: making room for competing users on the Tibetan plateau," in *Proceedings of the Seventh International Snow Leopard Symposium* ed. J. Fox and J. Du. Seattle: International Snow Leopard Trust, 1994, 317.

[38] Tibetans prefer common leopard and tiger skins for their clothing. Snow leopard fur is considered to shed too easily, and the more distinct rosettes of the common leopard are thought more aesthetically pleasing than the larger and less defined rosettes of the snow leopard.

[39] 马鸣, 新疆雪豹, 362.

[40] Juan Li et al. "Human-snow leopard conflicts in the Sanjiangyuan Region of the Tibetan Plateau." *Biological Conservation* 166 (2013): 120–121.

[41] Juan Li and Zhi Lu. "Snow leopard poaching and trade in China 2000–2013." *Biological Conservation* 176 (2014): 207–211.

[42] Kristin Nowell et al. *An Ounce of Prevention: Snow Leopard Crime Revisited.* Cambridge: TRAFFIC, 2016.

[43] Yanlin Liu et al. "China: The Tibetan Plateau, Sanjiangyuan Region," in *Snow Leopards: Biodiversity of the World: Conservation from Genes to Landscapes*, ed. Thomas McCarthy and David Mallon. Boston: Academic Press, 2016, 518.

[44] Kun Shi et al., "Snow leopard status and conservation in China," 587–592

Despite the great advances in snow leopard research within China, as of 2018 only 1.69% of estimated snow leopard range within the country had been surveyed.

[45] T. McCarthy et al. "*Panthera uncia.*" *The IUCN Red List of Threatened Species* (2017): e.T22732A50664030.

[46] Juan Li, Lingyun Xiao and Zhi Lu. "Challenges of snow leopard conservation in China." *Science China Life Sciences* 59 (2016): 637–639.

[47] 李娟, "雪豹带我看到的世界," filmed February 25, 2023 in Hangzhou, China, *YiXi*, 35:18. https://yixi.tv/#/speech/detail?id=1155.

[48] Juan Li et al. "Human-snow leopard conflicts," 120.

[49] Schaller, *Tibet Wild*, 333.

[50] Charudutt Mishra, Stephen R. Redpath and Kulbhushansingh R. Suryawanshi. "Livestock Predation by Snow Leopards: Conflicts and the Search for Solutions," in *Snow Leopards: Biodiversity of the World: Conservation from Genes to Landscapes*, ed. Thomas McCarthy and David Mallon. Boston: Academic Press, 2016, 62.

[51] Farrington and Li. "Climate Change Impacts on Snow Leopard Range," 85–89.

[52] Juan Li et al. "Climate refugia of snow leopards in High Asia." *Biological Conservation* 203 (2016): 191–192.

Natural Riches

[1] Dongdong Wang et al. "Plant Resource Availability of Medicinal *Fritillaria* Species in Traditional Producing Regions in Qinghai-Tibet Plateau." *Frontiers in Pharmacology* 8, 502 (2017): 2.

[2] A.B. Cunningham et al. "High altitude species, high profits: can the trade in wild harvested *Fritillaria cirrhosa* (Liliaceae) be sustained?" *Journal of Ethnopharmacology* 223 (2018): 142–151.

[3] Wang et al, "Plant Resource Availability," 5–8.

[4] Yang Niu, Martin Stevens and Hang Sun. "Commercial Harvesting Has Driven the Evolution of Camouflage in an Alpine Plant." *Current Biology* 31 (2021): 446–447.

[5] Daniel Winkler. "Forest use and implications of the 1998 logging ban in the Tibetan Prefectures of Sichuan: Case study on forestry, reforestation and NTFP in Litang County, Ganzi Tap, China." *Informatore Botanico Italiano* 35, Suppl. 1 (2003): 121–123.

[6] There are fifteen or so species of matsutake worldwide, with five found in China. *Tricholoma matsutake* is the most valuable and therefore by a wide margin the most heavily harvested of these species.

[7] J. He. "Globalised forest-products: commodification of the matsutake mushroom in Tibetan villages, Yunnan, Southwest China." *International Forestry Review* 12 (2010): 28.

[8] Michael J. Hathaway. *What a Mushroom Lives For: Matsutake and the Worlds They Make*. Princeton: Princeton University Press, 2022, 107–114 & 168–169.

[9] Hathaway. *What a Mushroom Lives For*, 128–129.

[10] Michael Hathaway writes that Chinese matsutake dealers could not fathom the willingness of Japanese to pay such high prices for a mushroom most Chinese considered unpalatable. They therefore suspected the Japanese had ulterior motives and must instead be secretly using matsutake medicinally. Their baseless suspicions spurred the Chinese to begin researching potential therapeutic uses for matsutake.

[11] David Arora. "The Houses That Matsutake Built." *Economic Botany* 62 (2008): 287.

[12] Hathaway. *What a Mushroom Lives For*, 120.

[13] Xuefei Yang et al. "Matsutake Trade in Yunnan Province, China: An Overview." *Economic Botany* 62 (2008): 269–270.

[14] Winkler, "Forest use and implications of the 1998 logging ban," 122. Arora, "The Houses That Matsutake Built," 278–284.

[15] Hathaway. *What a Mushroom Lives For*, 136–139.

[16] Li Ruijun, "Can China's 'All-Natural' Mushrooms Make the Grade?" *Sixth Tone*, January 18, 2023. https://www.sixthtone.com/news/1012133.

[17] Guo Yanlong et al. "Prediction of the potential geographic distribution of the ectomycorrhizal mushroom *Tricholoma matsutake* under multiple climate change scenarios." *Scientific Reports* 7, 46221 (2017): 2.

[18] Lyric Li, "Climate change in China hikes price of rare mushroom, a delicacy in Asia." *The Washington Post*, August 23, 2022. https://www.washingtonpost.com/world/2022/08/23/china-matsutake-mushroom-prices-climate-change/.

[19] *Ophiocordyceps sinensis* was for many years categorized as *Cordyceps sinensis*, and often is still cited by that name.

[20] Daniel Winkler. "*Yartsa Gunbu* (*Cordyceps sinensis*) and the Fungal Commodification of Tibet's Rural Economy." *Economic Botany* 62 (2008): 294–295.

[21] Winkler, "*Yartsa Gunbu*," 291–293.

[22] 胡献国 等 编著. 东方珍宝: 冬虫夏草. 北京: 人民军医出版社, 2008, 8–11.

Carla Nappi. *The Monkey and the Inkpot: Natural History and Its Transformations in Early Modern China*. Cambridge: Harvard University Press, 2009: 142–146.

[23] Jean-Baptiste Du Halde. *The General History of China: Containing a Geographical, Historical, Chronological, Political and Physical Description of the Empire of China, Chinese-Tartary, Corea and Thibet*, Vol. 4, 2nd ed. London: John Watts, 1739: 41–42.

Jean-Baptiste Du Halde and his Jesuit informants believed the "*Hia Tſao Tong Tchong*" to be a plant that simply bore a remarkable resemblance to a caterpillar. To quote Du Halde: "nothing can be a ſtronger Repreſentation of a long Worm, with nine Streaks, and of a yellowiſh Colour; you ſee the directt Form of the Head, Eyes, Feet, Belly, and Back....We have not been able to get an account either of the Shape of its Leaves, the colour of its Flowers, or the height of its Stalk." In contrast, early Chinese authors believed it was an insect that transformed into a plant during the summer before turning back into an insect in winter.

[24] Yanda Xu et al. "Quantitative assessment of the ecological impact of Chinese cordyceps collection in the typical production areas." *Écoscience* 22 (2015): 168.

[25] Jun He. "Harvest and trade of caterpillar mushroom (*Ophiocordyceps sinensis*) and the implications for sustainable use in the Tibet Region of Southwest China." *Journal of Ethnopharmacology* 221 (2018): 87.

Hopping, Chignell and Lambin (2018) report that top-grade pieces of *yartsa gunbu* reached prices of over 140,000 USD per kg in Beijing in 2017, a price over three times that of gold at the time.

[26] Winkler, "*Yartsa Gunbu*," 298–299.

Destruction of monasteries and temples in Tibetan regions began in earnest during the Anti-Rightist Campaign of 1957–1959. Tibetan Buddhist compounds in other regions—primarily Inner Mongolia and Xinjiang—met the same fate during the Cultural Revolution (1966–1976).

[27] Daniel Winkler. "Steps towards Sustainable Harvest of Yartsa Gunbu (Caterpillar Fungus, *Ophiocordyceps sinensis*)." *Proceedings of the 7th International Medicinal Mushroom Conference, Beijing, August 26-29* (2013): 638–641.

[28] Daniel Winkler. "Caterpillar Fungus (*Ophiocordyceps sinensis*) Production and Sustainability on the Tibetan Plateau and in the Himalayas." *Asian Medicine* 5 (2009): 300–307.

[29] Kelly A. Hopping, Stephen M. Chignell and Eric F. Lambin. "The demise of caterpillar fungus in the Himalayan region due to climate change and overharvesting." *Proceedings of the National Academy of Sciences* 115 (2018): 11490–11491.

[30] Xiao Li et al. ""A breakthrough in the artificial cultivation of Chinese cordyceps on a large-scale and its impact on science, the economy, and industry." *Critical Reviews in Biotechnology* 39 (2019): 181–191.

[31] Daniel Winkler, unpublished manuscript.

[32] Daniel Winkler, unpublished manuscript.

[33] Yanqiang Wei et al. "Chinese caterpillar fungus (*Ophiocordyceps sinensis*) in China: Current distribution, trading, and futures under climate change and overexploitation." *Science of the Total Environment* 755, 142548 (2021): 7–12.

[34] Part of ensuring the long-term survival of *yartsa gunbu* will entail educating harvesters of the natural history of the caterpillar and fungus. In the course of interviewing many *yartsa gunbu* pickers, Daniel Winkler (2013) discovered that most had no knowledge of how the fungus reproduces. Instead they believed *yartsa gunbu* to be autogenic, miraculously self-manifesting. They therefore had no notion that harvest practice or intensity could potentially impact the abundance of the species.

[35] Although the chiru is also widely referred to as the Tibetan antelope, and indeed was long believed to be a member of the antelope group, it is in fact a member of the subfamily Caprinae, along with sheep, bharal, takin, ibex, serow, goral, and others. In Tibetan, besides "chiru," there are many terms for the species, most of which distinguish the sex and age of a given animal. In Przhevalsky's writings, he uses the Mongolian term "orongo" when referring to chiru.

[36] The chiru has been cited as an inspiration for the mythical unicorn. When seen in profile the chiru's horns can align so that there appears to be only one sprouting from its head. Przhevalsky noted that residents of Gansu and Koko Nor (Qinghai) who knew of but had no direct experience with chiru believed that individuals with a single centrally placed horn existed, but were rare. The Mongols of the Qaidam Basin, who knew of chiru first-hand, found such notions ridiculous; they did not, however, discount the possibility of unicorn chiru far to the south where they themselves had never ventured.

[37] Outside of the People's Republic, chiru are found only in Ladakh, India, and there only in small numbers. The species once ranged into western Nepal, but has not been seen there for many years.

[38] Yu-Rong Du et al. "Demographic history of the Tibetan antelope *Pantholops hodgsoni* (chiru)." *Journal of Systematics and Evolution* 48 (2010): 495.

[39] Hodgson, "Notice of the Mammals of Tibet," 282.

[40] H. H. P. Deasy. *In Tibet and Chinese Turkestan: Being the Record of Three Years' Exploration*. London: T. Fisher Unwin, 1901, 26–31.

[41] Rawling, *The Great Plateau*, 85.

[42] N. Prejevalsky, *Mongolia, the Tangut Country, Vol. II*, 206–207.

[43] Belinda Wright and Ashok Kumar. *Fashioned for Extinction: An Exposé of the Shahtoosh Trade, Second Edition*. New Delhi: Wildlife Protection Society of India, 1998.

[44] Goldstein and Beall, *Nomads of Western Tibet*, 124.

[45] Rawling, *The Great Plateau*, 313.
Deasy, *In Tibet and Chinese Turkestan*, 71.

[46] Bessac and Bessac, *Death on the Chang Tang*, 83.

[47] David M. Leslie, Jr. and George B. Schaller. "*Pantholops hodgsonii* (Artiodactyla: Bovidae)." *Mammalian Species* 817 (2008): 10.

[48] William Moorcroft and George Trebeck. *Travels in the Himalayan Provinces of Hindustan and the Punjab; in Ladakh and Kashmir; in Peshawar, Kabul, Kunduz, and Bokhara from 1819 to 1825, Vol. I*. London: John Murray, 1841, 348–350.

Alexander Cunningham. *Ladák, Physical, Statistical, and Historical; With Notices of the Surrounding Countries*. London: Wm. H. Allen and Co., 1854, 200–201.

[49] Schaller, *Tibet Wild*, 69–71.

The Siberian goose is not, in fact, a real animal, but instead a creature conjured for misleading marketing efforts to promote the supposedly exceptional warmth of whatever down product is being sold.

[50] Ravindran Gopinath et al. *Beyond the Ban: A Census of Shahtoosh Workers in Jammu & Kashmir*. New Delhi: Wildlife Trust of India & Internaional Fund for Animal Welfare, 2003, 18–25.

Shahtoosh workers' assertion of innocent ignorance about the origins of the wool are at least plausible, as the raw wool is separated from the chiru hides prior to being traded onwards to Kashmir. Spinners, weavers, and other workers therefore do not have any direct contact with the dead animals except for the hairs that arrive in their workshops.

[51] Schaller, *Tibet Wild*, 76.

[52] Wright and Kumar. *Fashioned for Extinction.*

[53] Schaller, *Wildlife of the Tibetan Steppe*, 47.

[54] Wright and Kumar, *Fashioned for Extinction.*

[55] Schaller, *Tibet Wild*, 78.

[56] Schaller, *Tibet Wild*, 82–83.

[57] Elizabeth C. Economy. *The River Runs Black: The Environmental Challenge to China's Future.* Ithaca: Cornell University Press, 2004, 153–155.

[58] Schaller, *Tibet Wild*, 92.

[59] Lin Xia et al. "The effect of the Qinghai-Tibet railway on the migration of Tibetan antelope *Pantholops hodgsonii* in Hoh-xil National Nature Reserve, China." *Oryx* 41 (2007): 356.

Wenjing Xu et al. "Railway underpass location affects migration distance in Tibetan antelope (*Pantholops hodgsonii*)." *PLoS ONE* 14, e0211798 (2019): 8–9.

[60] Tong Wu et al. "Adaptation of migratory Tibetan antelope to infrastructure development." *Ecosystem Health and Sustainability* 7, 1910077 (2021): 3.

[61] Paul J. Buzzard, How Man Wong and Huibin Zhang. "Population increase at a calving ground of the Endangered Tibetan antelope *Pantholops hodgsonii* in Xinjiang, China. *Oryx* 46 (2012): 266–268.

[62] "2020年西藏自治区生态环境状况公报," 西藏自治区生态环境厅, June 3, 2021. http://ee.xizang.gov.cn/hjzl/hjgb/202106/t20210603_259800.html.

[63] Harris, *Wildlife Conservation in China*, 144.

[64] Schaller, *Tibet Wild*, 92.

Adam Popescu, "It takes up to 5 of these endangered antelopes to make one $20,000 shawl," *Washington Post*, May 30, 2024. https://www.washingtonpost.com/style/of-interest/2024/05/30/shahtoosh-luxury-scarf-endangered-chiru/.

Qinling & Hengduan Mountains

[1] The name *Shénnóngjià* 神农架, meaning Shennong's Ladder, refers to *Shénnóng* 神农, the Divine Farmer or Husbandman, a mythological ruler turned deity said to have bestowed the earliest practices and implements of agriculture on Chinese civilization. Shennong was also the originator of traditional herbal medicine, and appropriately Shennongjia is famed for the great array of medicinal plants that grow within it.

Shennongjia is also home to China's most famous counterpart to North America's Bigfoot or Sasquatch. Tales of the *Yě Rén* 野人, literally "wild man," of Shennongjia bear remarkable resemblance to the Yeti and Bigfoot, and like those cryptids the wild men of Shennongjia almost certainly stem predominantly from misidentified bears and bear sign.

[2] The highest peak in the Qinling is Taibai Shan 太白山 at 3,750 m (12,300 ft).

[3] Texts from the first half of the twentieth century often refer to western Sichuan as Sikang or Hsikang. Most of this part of Sichuan was part of Xikang 西康 province from 1939 until 1955. Xikang consisted of most of Kham (ཁམས, *Kāng* 康), one of the three traditional divisions of the Tibetan lands, which included not only the western half of present-day Sichuan but also Chamdo (ཆབ་མདོ, *Chāngdū* 昌都), now the easternmost part of the Tibet Autonomous Region. The Communist government dissolved the province in 1955.

[4] The Hengduan's highest peak is Minya Konka (མི་ཉག་གངས་དཀར་རི་བོ, *Gònggá Shān* 贡嘎山) in the Daxue range, at 7,556 m (24,790 ft).

Snub-noses & Skywalkers

[1] The Chinese for *Rhinopithecus, yǎngbíhóu* 仰鼻猴, is roughly equivalent to the English "snub-nosed monkey." *Rhinopithecus* comes from the Greek ῥίς (*rhís*) "nose" and πίθηκος (*píthēkos*) "monkey;" *yǎngbíhóu* 仰鼻猴 consists of *yǎng* 仰 "raised," *bí* 鼻 "nose," and *hóu* 猴 "monkey."

[2] The Chinese common names for these species are somewhat confusing. Sensibly enough the golden snub-nosed is *jīnsīhóu* 金丝猴, golden-haired (more literally, "golden-silk" or "golden-thread") monkey, or more specifically *Chuān jīnsīhóu* 川金丝猴, meaning the Sichuan golden-haired monkey. The other three species are also named according to their distributions: the Yunnan golden-haired monkey (*Diān jīnsīhóu* 滇金丝猴), the Guizhou golden-haired monkey (*Qián jīnsīhóu* 黔金丝猴), and the Myanmar or Nujiang golden-haired monkey (*Miǎndiàn jīnsīhóu* 缅甸金丝猴 or *Nùjiāng jīnsīhóu* 怒江金丝猴). All well and good, except none of these three species have golden hair.

[3] Alphonse Milne-Edwards, the nineteenth century French mammalogist who first scientifically described the golden snub-nosed monkey, gave it the specific epithet *roxellana* after Hürrem Sultan, chief consort of the sixteenth century Ottoman Sultan Suleiman the Magnificent. The name Roxellana means "the Ruthenian" and alludes to her origins in Ruthenia (in modern day Ukraine). She was enslaved and taken into Suleiman's harem before rising to become his chief consort and a major power within the Ottoman court. In *The Last Panda*, George Schaller states that Milne-Edwards chose "*roxellana*" in reference to Hürrem Sultan's upturned nose, but this is doubtful. Though it may be that none of the extant portraits of Hürrem Sultan were painted from life, none of them depict her with a snub nose. In his original description of the species Milne-Edwards gave no explanation for his choice of "Roxellana," but there is one shared trait between Hürrem Sultan and the golden monkey that he likely had in mind: brilliant gold-red hair.

[4] Xumao Zhao et al. "Impacts of human activity and climate change on the distribution of snub-nosed monkeys in China during the past 2000 years." *Diversity and Distributions* 24 (2018): 93–99.

[5] Chengliang Wang et al. "Influence of Human Activities on the Historical and Current Distribution of Sichuan Snub-Nosed Monkeys in the Qinling Mountains, China." *Folia Primatologica* 85 (2014): 350.

[6] Wang et al. "Influence of Human Activities," 351–352.

[7] Zhao et al. "Impacts of human activity," 99.

[8] Frank E. Poirier. "The Golden Monkey in the People's Republic of China." *Primate Conservation* 3 (1983): 31.

[9] Ruling Pan et al. "A New Conservation Strategy for China—A Model Starting With Primates." *American Journal of Primatology* 78 (2016): 1140.

[10] Zong Fei Chang et al. "Human influence on the population decline and loss of genetic diversity in a small and isolated population of Sichuan snub-nosed monkeys (*Rhinopithecus roxellana*)." *Genetica* 140 (2012): 106.

[11] Tan Bangjie. "The Status of Primates in China." *Primate Conservation* 5, (1985): 68.

[12] Tan, "The Status of Primates in China," 68.

[13] Tan, "The Status of Primates in China," 68.

[14] George B. Schaller. *The Last Panda*. Chicago: University of Chicago Press, 1993, 27.

[15] For information on the environmental damage from the Panzhihua complex see Judith Shapiro's *Mao's War Against Nature: Politics and the Environment in Revolutionary China* (2001). For a broader overview of the Third Front see Covell F. Meyskens' *Mao's Third Front: The Militarization of Cold War China* (2020).

[16] Yang Yu et al. "Climate change challenge, extinction risk, and successful conservation experiences for a threatened primate species in China: Golden snub-nosed monkey (*Rhinopithecus roxellana*)." *Zoological Research* 43 (2022): 941.

[17] Old threats such as poaching do still occur, however. In February 2022 Sichuan law enforcement broke up a poaching ring that had been capturing golden snub-nosed monkeys and red pandas. The animals that survived capture were placed in private zoos where they could be passed off as captive-bred and then sold onwards. Whether similar operations still occur is unknown, but if so their impact currently seems too small to present a major conservation threat.

[18] Y. Long and M. Richardson. "*Rhinopithecus roxellana*." *The IUCN Red List of Threatened Species* (2020): e.T19596A17943886.

[19] Yu et al. "Climate change challenge, extinction risk, and successful conservation experiences," 943.

[20] Zhang Yu et al. "Identifying refugia and corridors under climate change conditions for the Sichuan snub-nosed monkey (*Rhinopithecus roxellana*) in Hubei Province, China." *Ecology and Evolution* 9 (2019): 1685.

[21] Which common name to use for *Rhinopithecus bieti* in English has recently become rather complicated. Originally it was referred to as either the Yunnan snub-nosed monkey or the black snub-nosed monkey. The first option made sense as its range was believed to be constrained to Yunnan, but now that it is known to occur in Tibet as well, the name is restrictive. As for the second choice, the recently discovered *R. strykeri* has an all black body, and so some have transferred the name to it, preferring the hyphen-rich black-and-white snub-nosed monkey for *R. bieti*. As that option seems to be increasingly preferred, I have chosen to use it here.

[22] Through southern Tibet and northwestern Yunnan, the Yangtze is known as the Jinsha River (*Jīnshā Jiāng* 金沙江) and the Mekong as the Lancang River (*Láncāng Jiāng* 澜沧江).

[23] For comparison, the highest mountain in the contiguous United States, Mount Whitney, is 4,421 m (14,505 ft). The highest peak in Western Europe, Mont Blanc, reaches 4,808 m (15,774 ft).

[24] Lee E. Harding and Lian-Xian Han. "*Rhinopithecus bieti* (Primates: Cercopithecidae)." *Mammalian Species* 50 (2018): 150.

[25] Yuan-Ye Ma. "Yunnan snub-nosed monkey research of the Kunming Institute of Zoology, Chinese Academy of Sciences." *Zoological Research* 37 (2016): 189.

[26] Ma, "Yunnan snub-nosed monkey research," 189.

[27] Xumao Zhao et al. "Effects of habitat fragmentation and human disturbance on the population dynamics of the Yunnan snub-nosed monkey from 1994 to 2016." *PeerJ* 7, e6633 (2019): 7.

[28] Qikun Zhao. "Status of the Yunnan Snub-nosed Monkey." *Primate Conservation* 9 (1988): 132.

[29] Tan, "The Status of Primates in China," 68.

[30] Ma, "Yunnan snub-nosed monkey research," 139.

[31] Zhao, "Status of the Yunnan Snub-nosed Monkey," 133.

[32] Yongcheng Long et al. "Report on the Distribution, Population, and Ecology of the Yunnan Snub-nosed Monkey (*Rhinopithecus bieti*)." *Primates* 35 (1994): 249–250.

[33] T. Zhong et al. "A Brief Report on Yunnan Snub-Nosed Monkeys, *Rhinopithecus (R.) bieti*, at Bamei in Northern Yunnan Province, China." *Primate Conservation* 18 (1998): 79.

[34] Olivia Boyd, "The birth of Chinese environmentalism: key campaigns," in *China and the Environment: The Green Revolution*, ed. Sam Geall. New York: Zed Books, 2013, 46–49.

[35] Zuo-Fu Xiang et al. "Distribution, status and conservation of the black-and-white snub-nosed monkey *Rhinopithecus bieti* in Tibet." *Oryx* 41 (2007): 530.

[36] Zhao, "Effects of habitat fragmentation," 6.

Bao-Guo Li et al. "Achievements and challenges of primate conservation in China." *Zoological Research: Diversity and Conservation* 1 (2024): 68–70.

[37] The Skywalker gibbon's English names derives from its Chinese moniker, *tiānxíng* 天行, meaning "heavenly movement," a reference to brachiation, the swinging from arm to arm that gibbons use to move among the branches. *Tiānxíng* can also be translated as "skywalker," a happy coincidence the scientists who named the gibbon were happy to seize.

[38] Dirk Meyer et al. *Conservation status of the Myanmar or black snub-nosed monkey Rhinopithecus strykeri*. Yangon: Fauna & Flora International, 2017, 21–28.

[39] Thomas Geissmann et al. "A New Species of Snub-Nosed Monkey, Genus *Rhinopithecus* Milne-Edwards, 1872 (Primates, Colobinae), From Northern Kachin State, Northeastern Myanmar." *American Journal of Primatology* 73 (2011): 96–107.

[40] Yongcheng Long, et al. "*Rhinopithecus strykeri* found in China!" *American Journal of Primatology* 74 (2012): 871–873.

[41] Yin Yang et al. "The 10th anniversary of the scientific description of the black snub-nosed monkey (*Rhinopithecus strykeri*): It is time to initiate a set of new management strategies to save this critically endangered primate from extinction." *American Journal of Primatology* 84, e23372 (2022), 6.

[42] T. Geissmann, F. Momberg and T. Whitten. "*Rhinopithecus strykeri*." *The IUCN Red List of Threatened Species* (2012): e.T13508501A13508504.

[43] Yang et al., "The 10th anniversary," 9.

[44] Jian-Huan Yang et al. "Filling a longstanding knowledge gap: Population size and conservation status of the Endangered Gaoligong hoolock Gibbon (*Hoolock tianxing*) in Houqiao Town, Yunnan." *Global Ecology and Conservation* 24, e01347 (2020): 6.

[45] *Fructus tsaoko* or *Lanxangia tsaoko*, is sometimes known as Chinese black cardamom and is a member of the Zingiberaceae family, along with ginger, turmeric, and cardamom. The name tsaoko comes directly from the Chinese *cǎo guǒ* 草果.

[46] Ahebota Hazitai et al. "Cardamom (*Amomum tsaoko*) agroforest is important habitat for skywalker hoolock gibbon (*Hoolock tianxing*) in Mt. Gaoligong, Yunnan, China." *Global Ecology and Conservation* 54, e03129 (2024).

[47] Peng-Fei Fan and Huai-Sen Ai. "Conservation status of the eastern hoolock gibbon (*Hoolock leuconedys*) in China." *Gibbon Journal* 6 (2011): 22.

[48] Pyae Phyo Aung et al. "Confirmation of Skywalker Hoolock Gibbon (*Hoolock tianxing*) in Myanmar Extends Known Geographic Range of an Endangered Primate." *International Journal of Primatology* (2024).

The Giant Panda

[1] There are many forms of dragon in Chinese myth and legend, but they are in general benign, auspicious creatures closely associated with water.

[2] Susan Lumpkin & John Seidensticker. *Smithsonian Book of Giant Pandas*. Smithsonian Institution Press, 2002, 16.

[3] The Qinling pandas' genetic distinctiveness, along with slight variations in coat color compared to the Min and Qionglai populations, has led some scientists (see Wan et al. 2005) to propose the Qinling panda be named a separate subspecies, *Ailuropoda melanoleuca qinlingensis*. This has not gained wide acceptance.

Aside from the brown coated Qinling pandas, to date, only one albino panda has ever been sighted in the wild.

[4] The panda's enlarged wrist bones are, to be more precise, radial sesamoid bones.

[5] Cuddly as giant pandas may appear, cuddly they are not. A number of drunk or clumsy zoo patrons have discovered, no doubt to their great surprise, that pandas are not huggers.

Zhang et al. "Three cases giant panda attack on human at Beijing Zoo." *International Journal of Clinical and Experimental Medicine* 7 (2014): 4515–4518. https://www.ijcem.com/files/ijcem0002333.pdf.

[6] Schaller, *The Last Panda*, 158.

[7] George B. Schaller et al. *The Giant Pandas of Wolong*. Chicago: University of Chicago Press, 1985, 127–154.

[8] In *Panda Nation* (2018), Elena Songster notes that the giant panda's prehistoric presence outside of China was rarely admitted in Chinese-authored studies before the 1990s, presumably in an effort to claim the panda, past and present, as solely Chinese.

[9] Graham I. H. Kerley et al. "The Protected Area Paradox and refugee species: The giant panda and baselines shifted towards conserving species in marginal habitats." *Conservation Science and Practice* 2, e203 (2020).

[10] Shancen Zhao et al. "Whole-genome sequencing of giant pandas provides insights into demographic history and local adaptation." *Nature Genetics* 45 (2013): 69–70.

[11] Shu (蜀) was both geographically and culturally separate from the ancient Chinese states, but after the Qin conquest of 316 BCE it gradually integrated into the Han sphere, losing much of its cultural distinctiveness.

[12] Zhao et al, "Whole-genome sequencing," 69–70.

[13] Schaller et al, *The Giant Pandas of Wolong*, 7.

[14] 胡松梅, 曹龙, 张婉婉, "令人叹为观止的西汉皇家苑囿——霸陵与南陵出土珍禽异兽及," 中国社会科学报, August 4. 2023. https://www.cssn.cn/skgz/bwyc/202308/t20230804_5677049.shtml.

[15] "Giant panda skeleton found in ancient tomb," *China Daily*, February 24, 2005. http://www.chinadaily.com.cn/english/doc/2005-02/24/content_418861.htm

[16] *Xiàn qí pí pí, chì bào huáng pí.* 獻其貔皮、赤豹黃羆。

[17] *Pí, báihú. Qí zi, bó.* 貔,白狐。其子,豰。

[18] Donald Harper (personal communication).
郭郛, 李约瑟, 成庆泰. 中国古代动物学史. 北京: 科学出版社, 1999, 102.

[19] The original texts provide very little information about just what animals the *pí* and *mò* might be (*Mò, bái bào.* 貘，白豹。). Later commentaries add greater detail, but nothing definitive.

[20] Schaller et al, *The Giant Pandas of Wolong*, 6.

[21] Donald Harper. "The Cultural History of the Giant Panda (*Ailuropoda melanoleuca*) in Early China." *Early China* 35 (2013): 185–224.

Harper describes how the misidentification of *mò* with the tapir came about, after the French sinologist Jean-Pierre Abel-Rémusat (1788–1832) equated descriptions and illustrations of *mò* based on Bo Juyi's poetic creation with the Malayan tapir of Southeast Asia. This equivalence later entered Chinese scholarship from Western and Japanese sources with the arrival of modern zoology. The confusion has persisted even to the present, with the *mò* still regularly equated with *Tapirus indicus*. Although the recent discovery of a tapir skeleton in Emperor Wen of Han's tomb complex shows that the tapir was known to the ancient Chinese, there remains no evidence to suggest a link between *mò* and tapirs. Harper also stresses that scholarly association between ancient bronze figures and tapirs are impressionistic, not evidential.

[22] 胡, 曹, 张, "令人叹为观止的西汉皇家苑囿."

Where exactly all the animals buried in the mausoleum came from is as yet undetermined. Researchers plan to test the remains for any available evidence of their provenance, so that within a few years it may become clearer whether many of the species no longer found in or around the Qinling were in fact residents just over two millennia ago.

[23] Taizong 太宗, meaning "Great Ancestor," is the temple name of Tang founder Li Shimin 李世民. The names commonly used to refer to Chinese emperors are the source of much confusion. Emperors from the Tang to Yuan are usually referred to by their temple name (庙号 廟號), a posthumous title reserved for sovereigns. In contrast, emperors of the Han are known by their posthumous names (谥号 謚號). Ming and Qing emperors are instead known by their era names (年号 年號). Using the era name for earlier emperors would be terribly impractical, as many emperors used multiple era names throughout their reign. During the Ming and Qing, however, each emperor used only one era name, drastically simplifying matters. The first emperor to unify China, Qin Shi Huang 秦始皇, had no use for any such niceties, and simply opted to title himself Shi Huang 始皇, "First Emperor."

[24] Harper, "The Cultural History of the Giant Panda," 205–206.

[25] E. Elena Songster. *Panda Nation: The Construction and Conservation of China's Modern Icon*. New York: Oxford University Press, 2018, 86–87.

Wu Zetian was the only reigning empress in China's history, founding her own short-lived Zhou dynasty (武周, 690–705) before her son, Emperor Zhongzong of Tang (唐中宗, 656–710, r. 684 & 705–710) seized power and ended the interregnum.

[26] Donald G. Reid and Jien Gong. "Giant Panda Conservation Action Plan," in *Bears: Status Survey and Conservation Action Plan*, ed. Christopher Servheen, Stephen Herrero and Bernard Peyton. Gland: IUCN, 1999, 244.

[27] The territory that now makes up Chongqing Municipality was long administered as part of Sichuan until split off on March 14, 1997. It is also known in English by its former romanization, Chungking, by which it gained fame as the wartime capital of Nationalist China from 1938 to 1945 (though it was only formally made the wartime capital in 1940).

[28] The Miao (苗族) are not a cohesive ethnic group, but a collection of linguistically related peoples. Miao is a Chinese designation, and was used as a convenient umbrella term for the native peoples the Han encountered in the southwestern mountains.

[29] Mark Elvin. *The Retreat of the Elephants: An Environmental History of China*. New Haven: Yale University Press, 2004, 216–220.

[30] Armand David. "Extrait d'une lettre de même, datée de la principauté Thibétaine (indépendante), de Mou-pin, le 21 mars 1869." *Nouvelles archives du Muséum d'histoire naturelle de Paris, Bulletin* 5 (1869): 11–13.

[31] Alphonse Milne-Edwards. "Note sue quelques mammifères du Thibet Oriental." *Annales des sciences naturelles*, 13 (1870).

The origin of the word "panda" is unknown. In English "parti-coloured bear" was initially the favored name, with some referring to it as the "coon bear." The adoption of "panda" came after the presumed taxonomic connection with the red panda was accepted. "Panda" is simply a borrowing from French, but how it came into use in that tongue is a mystery. The most likely explanation is that it derives from a local language in Nepal and Sikkim.

[32] Johannes Krause et al. "Mitochondrial genomes reveal an explosive radiation of extinct and extant bears near the Miocene-Pliocene boundary." *BMC Evolutionary Biology*. 8 (2008).

[33] Theodore Roosevelt and Kermit Roosevelt. *Trailing the Giant Panda*. New York: Charles Scribner's Sons, 1929: 225–226.

According to the Roosevelt brothers' account of the trip, they fired simultaneously at the panda, and thus claimed equal share in the glory.

[34] Little did Ruth Harkness or her husband know Emperor Wen and Empress Dowager Bo had beat them to capturing a live panda by two millennia.

[35] Ruth Harkness. *The Lady and the Panda: An Adventure*. New York: Carrick & Evans, 1938.

Harkness treated Su Lin like her own daughter, but eventually left her with the Brookfield Zoo of Chicago in exchange for a tidy sum. Su Lin unfortunately died of a sudden illness in 1939, upon which it was discovered after necropsy that she was, in fact, male.

[36] Michael Kiefer. *Chasing the Panda: How an Unlikely Pair of Adventurers Won the Race to Capture the Mythical White Bear*. New York: Da Capo Press, 2002, 4.

[37] More precisely, giant pandas do not have much medicinal use in Chinese tradition. In *The Last Panda* George Schaller recounts asking panda researcher Hu Jinchu if the local people used the pandas in traditional medicine. Hu said the only thing was panda urine, used to dissolve a swallowed needle.

[38] Vicki Constantine Croke. *The Lady and the Panda: The True Adventures of the First American Explorer to Bring Back China's Most Exotic Animal*. New York: Random House, 2005, 266.

Schaller et al, *The Giant Pandas of Wolong*, 8.

[39] "China Bans Panda Hunting To Save Dwindling Species," *The New York Times*, April 25, 1939. https://www.nytimes.com/1939/04/25/archives/china-bans-panda-hunting-to-save-dwindling-species.html.

[40] Songster, *Panda Nation*, 95.

Hunting of giant pandas (and many other species) was officially banned in 1959, but little attention was paid to enforcement until some years later.

[41] Songster, *Panda Nation*, 95–101.

[42] Donald G. Reid et al. "Giant Panda *Ailuropoda melanoleuca* behaviour and carrying capacity following a bamboo die-off." *Biological Conservation* 49 (1989): 86.

[43] Lumpkin and Seidensticker, *Smithsonian Book of Giant Pandas*, 6.

[44] Aside from people removing large stretches of bamboo forest, another factor in the severity of the 1976 bamboo bloom was that, very unusually, three separate species flowered at the same time, depriving the pandas of alternative food sources they would normally be able to fall back on.

[45] The World Wildlife Fund is now known as the World Wide Fund for Nature, but still uses the WWF abbreviation.

[46] By the time Dr. Schaller began his giant panda research, he had already conducted the first intensive field studies of mountain gorillas, African lions, Bengal tigers, and several species of ungulates in the mountains of Central Asia. His account of his time at Wolong, *The Last Panda*, is a necessary read for anyone who wishes to understand the challenges of wildlife conservation in China during the early post-Mao era.

[47] Lü Zhi and George B. Schaller. *Giant Pandas in the Wild*. New York; Aperture, 2002, 54.

[48] Songster, *Panda Nation*, 112–125.

[49] Schaller, *The Last Panda*, 224–227.

[50] Jianjun Peng, Zhigang Jiang and Jinchu Hu. "Status and conservation of giant panda (*Ailuropoda melanoleuca*): a review." *Folia Zoologica* 50 (2001): 82.

[51] Sheng Li et al. "Retreat of large carnivores across the giant panda distribution range." *Nature Ecology & Evolution* 4 (2020): 1327–1331.

[52] Liu Jianyu et al. "Research Progress and Threat Analysis on Asiatic Golden Cat (*Catopuma temminckii* Vigors and Horsfield)." *Journal of Sichuan Forestry Science and Technology* 41 (2020): 137–146.

Fei Duan et al. "Distribution of the Asiatic golden cat (*Catopuma temminckii*) and variations in its coat morphology in China." *Ecology and Evolution* 14, e10900 (2024).

[53] Kyle Obermann, "China declares pandas no longer endangered—but threats persist," *National Geographic*, September 1, 2021. https://www.nationalgeographic.com/animals/article/pandas-are-off-chinas-endangered-list-but-threats-persist.

[54] R. Swaisgood, D. Wang and F. Wei. "*Ailuropoda melanoleuca* (errata version published in 2017)." *The IUCN Red List of Threatened Species* (2016): e.T712A121745669.

Though perhaps the most famous endangered species in the world, the giant panda has in fact never been placed in the IUCN's most dire category of Critically Endangered.

[55] Dongwei Kang and Junqing Li. "Giant panda protection: challenges and hopes." *Environmental Science and Pollution Research* 26 (2019): 18001–18002.

[56] Fang Wang et al. "Incorporating biotic interactions reveals potential climate tolerance of giant pandas." *Conservation Letters* 11, e12592 (2018).

[57] The Giant Panda National Park does not in fact constitute a single unbroken landscape. The park consists of three large but separate sections, with a smaller fourth section at the southern end. There are four administrative units: one covering the Qinling, a second in Gansu's Baishuijiang region, the third covering the Sichuan section of the Min Mountains, and the fourth administering the Qionglai and Xiangling mountains. All together the entire park is three times the size of Yellowstone National Park in the US.

Firefoxes & Gnu Goats

[1] For those familiar with the conventions of naming animals in Chinese, but unfamiliar with the red panda itself, its name may initially cause some confusion. In English the red panda is sometimes, albeit rarely, referred to as the lesser panda, in reference to its small size relative to the giant panda. Chinese follows this same convention—the giant panda is *dàxióngmāo* 大熊猫, or "great bearcat," while the red panda is *xiǎoxióngmāo* 小熊猫, or "little bearcat." But in Chinese affixing *xiǎo* 小 "little," before an animal's name generally signifies a baby or juvenile; thus *xiǎoxióngmāo* 小熊猫 could easily be mistaken to mean "giant panda cub." A giant panda cub is in fact called *xiǎo dàxióngmāo* 小大熊猫 "little big bearcat." The red panda's alternative name *hóngxióngmāo* 红熊猫 "red bearcat" is rarely used. Like the giant panda, the name can also be reversed to *xiǎomāoxióng* 小貓熊, again most often in Taiwan.

[2] Unlike the giant panda's, the red panda's thumb did not evolve as an adaptation to its bamboo-centered diet. The fossil record shows that the thumb appeared before specialized, bamboo-adapted dentition. The radial sesamoid arose most likely as a way to help the red panda's evolutionary ancestors climb trees, perhaps to better flee large predators.

[3] Yisi Hu et al. "Conservation Genomics and Metagenomics of Giant and Red Pandas in the Wild." *Annual Review of Animal Biosciences* 12 (2024): 70–71.

[4] Forty million years is about the same time our ancestors split from those of the New World monkeys, placing us at about the same distance in evolutionary time from marmosets and sakis as red pandas are to giant pandas.

[5] Yibo Hu et al. "Genomic evidence for two phylogenetic species and long-term population bottlenecks in red pandas." *Science Advances* 6, eaax5751 (2020).

The determination that there are two species of red panda is recent enough that many publications continue to use the prior categorization of two red panda subspecies, *Ailurus fulgens fulgens* and *A. f. styani*. Acceptance of the revised taxonomy is likely to widen over time.

[6] Glover M. Allen. *The Mammals of China and Mongolia, Part 1*. New York: The American Museum of Natural History, 1938, 316.

If pandaskin caps bring to mind Davy Crockett and his coonskin cap, you're not far off.

[7] Kati Loeffler. "Management, Husbandry and Veterinary Medicine of Red Pandas Living ex situ in China," in *Red Panda: Biology and Conservation of the First Panda*, ed. Angel R. Glatston. Boston: Academic Press, 2011, 325.

Arjun Thapa, Yibo Hu, and Fuwen Wei. "The Endangered Red Panda (*Ailurus fulgens*): Ecology and Conservation Approaches Across the Entire Range." *Biological Conservation* 220, (2018): 112–121.

8 Angela R. Glatston. "Red Pandas in Zoos Today; The History of the Current Captive Population," in *Red Panda: Biology and Conservation of the First Panda,* ed. Angel R. Glatston. Boston: Academic Press, 2011, 304

Fuwen Wei and Zejun Zhang. "Red Pandas in the Wild in China," in *Red Panda: Biology and Conservation of the First Panda,* ed. Angel R. Glatston. Boston: Academic Press, 2011, 385.

9 Wei and Zhang, "Red Pandas in the Wild in China," 389.

10 The crested ibis's scientific name, *Nipponia nippon,* very conspicuously ties it to Japan (*Nippon* is one of two readings for 日本, the Japanese kanji for "Japan;" the other is *Nihon*). This is because the first person to provide an account of the bird for scientific description was Philipp Franz von Siebold, a German physician and botanist who lived in Japan from 1823 to 1829 as a resident member of the Dutch trading community on the island of Dejima at Nagasaki. While in Japan he undertook the first scientific studies of the country's flora and fauna, including the crested ibis. As Siebold had never seen nor heard of the bird elsewhere, it predictably ended up with the name *Ibis nippon* when described in his landmark *Fauna Japonica.*

11 文榕生. 中国珍稀野生动物分布变迁 (续:) 上. 济南: 山东科学技术出版社, 2018, 334–335.

12 Arthur de Carle Sowerby. *The Naturalist in Manchuria, Volumes II & III: The Mammals and Birds of Manchuria.* Tientsin: Tientsin Press, 1923, 204–205.

13 Unfortunately for the crested ibis, determining whether a bird had been extirpated from the country was apparently not deemed sufficiently revolutionary behavior during the Cultural Revolution.

14 Robert Sterling Clark and Arthur de Carle Sowerby. *Through Shên-Kan: The Account of the Clark Expedition in North China, 1908–09.* London: T. Fisher Unwin, 1912, 107.

15 Tang Xiyang. *Living Treasures: An Odyssey Through China's Extraordinary Nature Reserves.* New York: Bantam, 1987, 39–56.

16 Although some of the conservation measures for the crested ibis have no doubt caused extra hardship for villagers, there has been remarkably little trouble in response. That said, not everyone has jumped to save the birds. Between 1981 and 2007 six people faced prosecution for killing crested ibises. A case in 1990 led the Yangxian government to confiscate all rifles in the county.

17 魏丹, 李弋戈, "《陕西省朱鹮保护成果报告》发布, 陕西境内朱鹮种群数量达4100只," 汉中日报, June 24, 2020. http://epaper.hanzhongnews.cn/hzrb/20200624/mhtml/page_05_content_000.htm [dead link].

Li Hongyang, "Big increase: Crested ibis population exceeds 10,000 globally after 42 years of protection," *China Daily*, November 5, 2023. https://www.chinadaily.com.cn/a/202311/05/WS6547567aa31090682a5ec79c.html.

[18] Sara Hussein, "Modern phoenix: The bird brought back from extinction in Japan," *Phys.org*, June 21, 2022. https://phys.org/news/2022-06-modern-phoenix-bird-brought-extinction.html.

[19] Chick born to wild crested ibis pair on Sado Island marks 40-year first," *The Japan Times*, April 22, 2016. https://web.archive.org/web/20160425153104/https://www.japantimes.co.jp/news/2016/04/22/national/chick-born-wild-crested-ibis-pair-sado-marks-40-year-first/#.Vx44RS_P1qY.

"Crested ibis chicks born in the wild 42 years after extinction in Korea," *Yonhap News Agency*, April 29, 2021. https://en.yna.co.kr/view/AEN20210429007500315.

[20] Yiwen Sun, et al. "Decline of traditional rice farming constrains the recovery of the endangered Asian crested ibis (*Nipponia nippon*)." *Ambio* 44 (2015): 803–814.

[21] Liming Ma. Changes in the Habitat Preference of Crested Ibis (*Nipponia nippon*) during a Period of Rapid Population Increase." *Animals* 11, 2626 (2021).

[22] George B. Schaller. *A Naturalist and Other Beasts: Tales from a Life in the Field*. San Francisco: Sierra Club Books, 2007, 171.

Schaller, *The Last Panda*, 171.

[23] The notion that the golden takin may have inspired the mythic stories of the golden fleece is fanciful, with nothing beyond coincidence to support it.

[24] H. Frank Wallace. "The Chinese Takin and Its Pursuit." *The Badminton Magazine of Sports and Pastimes* 36 (1913): 90–97.

Glover M. Allen. *The Mammals of China and Mongolia, Part 2*. New York: The American Museum of Natural History, 1940, 1254.

In English texts written prior to the 1950s Kangding 康定 is referred to as Tachienlu or Tatsienlu (打箭炉). This is derived from the Tibetan name of the town, Dartsedo དར་རྩེ་མདོ།.

[25] Zhi-Gao Zeng, et al. "Group size, composition and stability of golden takin in Shaanxi Foping Nature Reserve, China." *Folia Zoologica*. 51 (2002): 289.

[26] 叶晓青, 杨帆. 密林隐士: 金毛羚牛. 上海: 上海科技教育出版社, 2016, 67.

[27] Lumpkin and Seidensticker, *Smithsonian Book of Giant Pandas*, 112.

[28] Schaller, *The Last Panda*, 175.

[29] Covell F. Meyskens. *Mao's Third Front: The Militarization of Cold War China*. Cambridge: Cambridge University Press, 2020, 170–171.

[30] 曾治高, 宋延龄. "秦岭羚牛的生态与保护对策." 生物学通报 43 (2008): 1–3.

叶, 密林隐士, 64–65.

[31] In English the white-lipped deer is also called Thorold's deer, after Dr. G. W. Thorold, a surgeon in the Indian Medical Service who killed and sent the species' type specimen to the British Natural History Museum in the early 1890s. The name "white-lipped deer" is likely a direct borrowing of the Chinese *bái chún lù* 白唇鹿. Though the species is now classified under the genus *Cervus*, it was for a time classified under the monotypic genus *Przewalskium*.

[32] Schaller, *Wildlife of the Tibetan Steppe*, 144–148.

[33] Glover M. Allen. *The Mammals of China and Mongolia, Part 2*. New York: The American Museum of Natural History, 1940, 1192–1193.

[34] Hamilton Bower. *Diary of a Journey Across Tibet*. London: Rivington, Percival and Co., 1894, 290–291.

V. I. Roborovsky. "The central Asian expedition of Captain Roborovsky and Lieut. Kozloff." *The Geographical Journal* 8 (1896): 168.

[35] Glover M. Allen. "Zoological results of the second Dolan expedition to western China and eastern Tibet, 1934-1936. Part III: mammals." *Proceedings of the Academy of Natural Sciences of Philadelphia* 90 (1938): 281–282.

[36] R.B. Harris. "*Cervus albirostris*." *The IUCN Red List of Threatened Species* (2015): e.T4256A61976756.

[37] 黄乘明 主编. 濒危动物. 南京: 江苏凤凰科学技术出版社, 2014, 83.

[38] 吴家炎 王伟 编著. 中国白唇鹿. 北京: 中国林业出版社, 1999, 124–125 & 152.

[39] David M. Leslie, Jr. "*Przewalskium albirostre* (Artiodactyla: Cervidae)." *Mammalian Species* 42, 849 (2010): 8–15.

[40] Joelene Hughes et al. "Confirmation of threatened white-lipped deer (*Przewalskium albirostris*) in Gansu and Sichuan, China, and their overlap with livestock." *Mammalia* 79 (2015): 243.

[41] Leslie, "*Przewalskium albirostre*," 8–15.

[42] J Timmins and B. Chan. "*Muntiacus reevesi*." *The IUCN Red List of Threatened Species* (2016): e.T42191A22166608.

Reeves's muntjacs are likely familiar to British readers. Just like the elaphure, muntjacs were brought to the Duke of Bedford's estate at Woburn Abbey over the turn of the twentieth century. Some of their descendants were released into the wild and have since colonized much of England.

[43] Zhonglou Sun et al. "How rivers and historical climate oscillations impact on genetic structure in Chinese Muntjac (*Muntiacus reevesi*)?" *Diversity and Distributions* 25 (2019): 116–128.

Zhonglou Sun et al. "Spatial dynamics of Chinese Muntjac related to past and future climate fluctuations." *Current Zoology* 67 (2021): 361–370.

[44] Jiale Zhao et al. "Potential impact of climate change on the distribution of *Capricornis milneedwardsii*, a vulnerable mammal in China." *Ecology and Evolution* 14, e11582 (2024).

[45] Zhonglou Sun et al. "Yangtze River, an insignificant genetic boundary in tufted deer (*Elaphodus cephalophus*): the evidence from a first population genetics study." *PeerJ* 4, e2654 (2016).

[46] David M. Leslie, Jr., Dana N. Lee, and Richard W. Dolman. "*Elaphodus cephalophus* (Artiodactyla: Cervidae)." *Mammalian Species* 45 (2013): 83.

[47] Yongquan Zhang et al. "Estimating the inbreeding level and genetic relatedness in an isolated population of critically endangered Sichuan taimen (*Hucho Bleekeri*) using genome-wide SNP markers." *Ecology and Evolution* 10 (2020): 1391.

[48] 杜浩, 李罗新, 危起伟, 张书环, 王成友, 孙庆亮, 杨晓鸽, 李雷. "濒危物种川陕哲罗鲑在汉江上游太白河再发现." 动物学杂志 49 (2014): 414

Xiaoqian Leng et al. "Successful Ultrasonography-Assisted Artificial Reproduction of Critically Endangered Sichuan taimen (*Hucho bleekeri*)." *Fishes* 8, 152 (2023).

[49] More famous than Emei Shan is the nearby Le Shan Giant Buddha, a 71 m (233 ft) tall seated Maitreya Buddha carved into the red sandstone cliffs at the confluence of the Min and Dadu Rivers. It was the tallest statue in the world from its completion in 803 until modern times.

[50] The Emei Moustache Toad is also known by the less colorful common name Taosze (大峨寺) Spiny Toad, as well as the scientific binomial *Vibrissaphora boringii*.

[51] IUCN SSC Amphibian Specialist Group. "*Leptobrachium boringii*." *The IUCN Red List of Threatened Species* (2020): e.T57625A63865231.

[52] William Jardine. *The Naturalist's Library, Vol. XIV, Ornithology, Gallinaceous Birds*. Edinburgh: W. H. Lizars, 1845, 210.

[53] Samuel Pollard. *In Unknown China: A Record of the Observations, Adventures and Experiences of a Pioneer Missionary During a Prolonged Sojourn Amongst the Wild*

and *Unknown Nose Tribe of Western China*. London: Seeley, Service & Co., 1921, 206.

William Beebe. *A Monograph of the Pheasants, Vol. IV*. London: H. F. & G. Witherby, 1922, 5–12.

[54] Xinming Li et al. "Conflict between cultural development and wildlife conservation: A potential threat to Reeves's pheasant (*Syrmaticus reevesii*)." *Conservation Letters* 17, e12995 (2024).

Chunfa Zhou, Jiliang Xu and Zhengwang Zhang. "Dramatic decline of the Vulnerable Reeves's pheasant *Syrmaticus reevesii*, endemic to central China." *Oryx* 49 (2015): 532.

[55] BirdLife International. "*Lophophorus lhuysii*." *The IUCN Red List of Threatened Species* (2022): e.T22679192A219003994.

Middle & Lower Yangtze

[1] Confusingly, each section of the Yangtze has its own local or regional name, some used more commonly than others. For instance the 2,308 km (1,434 mi) stretch rapidly flowing south and then east from Yǜxü 玉树, Qinghai to Yibin 宜宾, Sichuan is known as the *Jīnshā Jiāng* 金沙江, "Golden Sands River." The English name of the river, Yangtze, comes from the section of the Lower Yangtze farthest downstream, which runs from Yangzhou 扬州 to the sea at Shanghai. The local name for this stretch of the river is *Yángzǐ Jiāng* 扬子江, "Yangzi River," which Westerners who first arrived then applied to its entire length.

The Yangtze is the world's third longest river after the Nile and the Amazon. Measured from the source most distant from the sea, the Nile is 6,650 km (4,130 mi). The Amazon is only 100 km longer than the Yangtze at 6,400 km (3,976 mi), and the Mississippi only 25 km shorter at 6,275 km (3,902 mi). Many of these curiously neat figures are in fact still in dispute amongst geographers, a group apparently almost as combative as taxonomists.

[2] The source of the Yangtze is officially located in the Tanggula Mountains at 5,342 m (17,526 ft), but the source farthest from the sea is in fact along a separate tributary stream located only 5,170 m (16,960 ft) above sea level.

[3] Just one example of changes in the Yangtze lakes: Dongting Lake covered 4,955 sq km (1,913 sq mi) in the 1930s, but had shrunk to approximately 2,500 sq km (965 sq mi) in the late 1990s.

[4] Brian Lander. "From Wetland to Farmland: How Humans Transformed the Central Yangzi Basin." *Asia Major* 35 (2022): 4–5.

[5] Lander, "From Wetland to Farmland," 9–11.

[6] Robert B. Marks. *China: An Environmental History, 2nd ed*. Lanham: Rowman & Littlefield, 2017, 26.

[7] Lander, "From Wetland to Farmland," 5–7.

[8] Lander, "From Wetland to Farmland," 15–30.

[9] The word *bà* 坝 in *Gézhōubà* 葛洲坝 means "dam," but in English the dam is often referred to redundantly as the Gezhouba Dam.

The River Goddess & The River Pig

[1] The genus name Lipotes derives from the Greek λίπος (lipos), meaning "fat." The specific name *vexillifer*, meaning "flag bearer," derives from a misunderstanding of the Chinese name for the dolphin, *báijì* 白鱀, meaning "white porpoise." Some scholars have speculated that due to the peculiarities of the local dialect, Hoy mistook *jì* 鱀 for *qí* 旗, meaning "flag." Hoy himself wrote that he was told the name was *báiqí* 白旗, white flag, in reference to the dolphin's dorsal fin resembling a white banner. Perhaps instead the local fishermen were using the phrase "white-finned," *báiqí* 白鳍 in Mandarin (the name *báiqítún* 白鳍豚, "white finned dolphin" in fact later entered common parlance).

[2] There are two subspecies of South Asian river dolphin (*Platanista gangetica*), the Ganges river dolphin (*P. g. gangetica*) and the Indus river dolphin (*P. g. minor*). In addition to the Amazon river dolphin (*Inia geoffrensis*) a third member of the river dolphin group, the La Plata dolphin (*Pontoporia blainvillei*), also lives in South America, but uniquely among the group it lives in oceanic waters and coastal saltwater estuaries instead of freshwater rivers.

[3] Xuming Zhou, Fengming Sun, Shixia Xu et al. "Baiji genomes reveal low genetic variability and new insights into secondary aquatic adaptations." *Nature Communications* 4, 2708 (2013): 4–5.

[4] Samuel Turvey. *Witness to Extinction: How We Failed to Save the Yangtze River Dolphin*. New York: Oxford University Press, 2008, 5–6.

[5] Zhou Kaiya and Zhang Xingduan. *Baiji: The Yangtze River Dolphin and Other Endangered Animals of China*. Washington, D.C.: Stone Wall Press, 1991, 9.

[6] Turvey, *Witness to Extinction*, 22.

[7] 黑者江豚，白者白鱀。狀異名殊，同宅大水。

[8] 于江. 悲情国宝：白鱀 豚生死全记录. 北京：华龄出版社，2012, 33.

[9] Charles M. Hoy. "The 'White-Flag' Dolphin of the Tung Ting Lake." *The China Journal of Science & Arts* 1 (1923): 155.

[10] Clifford H. Pope. *China's Animal Frontier*. New York: Viking Press, 1940, 178.

[11] Hundreds of the dams built during the Maoist period, especially those from the Great Leap Forward years, subsequently failed, some catastrophically so. The worst was the Banqiao Dam collapse in August 1975, when the Banqiao Dam (板桥水库大坝) in Henan failed under heavy typhoon rains. As a consequence, sixty-one other dams broke or were breached or bombed (to direct floodwaters away from other dams downstream) over the following days. Tens or maybe hundreds of thousands of people died, and the disaster was covered up for over a decade.

[12] Zhou, *Baiji*, 20.

[13] Zhou, *Baiji*, 34.

Zhou Kaiya, Stephen Leatherwood, and Thomas A. Jefferson. "Records of Small Cetaceans in Chinese Waters: A Review." *Asian Marine Biology* 12 (1995): 133.

[14] 寿振黄　主编. 中国经济动物誌——兽类 [*Economic Mammalian Fauna of China*]. 北京: 科学出版社, 1962: 293.

In fairness to the compilers of the text, after describing the uses of the baiji, they conclude the entry with a cautionary note describing the dolphins as an endemic species of great scientific value that should be protected and not overhunted. (仅产于我国境内，是我国所特有的种类，在学术上有很大意义。应予保护，不宜滥捕。)

[15] 于, 悲情国宝, 447.

[16] Simon Winchester. *The River at the Center of the World: A Journey Up the Yangtze & Back in Chinese Time*. New York: Picador, 1996, 97–99.

[17] Turvey, *Witness to Extinction*, 175–176.

[18] Douglas Adams and Mark Carwardine. *Last Chance to See*. New York: Harmony Books, 1991, 165.

[19] Zhou, *Baiji*, 34.

[20] DDT is short for dichlorodiphenyltrichloroethane. Hence why everyone shortens it to DDT.

[21] Zhou, *Baiji*, 38.

[22] Even between cooperating parties communication often proved difficult. When Douglas Adams and Mark Carwardine traveled to try to see a wild baiji in 1988 they first met with Zhou Kaiya of Nanjing Normal University before heading to

Tongling, Anhui to see the planned baiji reserve there. Prof. Zhou had led the establishment of the Tongling project and promised to call ahead, but he warned he had been trying himself to get hold of the Tongling staff for weeks without success.

[23] Poor Qiqi never again had the prospects of mating, but scientists at the institute were determined to be ready for any eventualities and so set about collecting and cryogenically storing his sperm. According to Samuel Turvey, he was told this resulted in "endless rounds of dolphin electro-ejaculation" that led Qiqi to "swim over excitedly, roll over, and show his penis to any visitors coming into his enclosure—an unfortunate kind of 'Pavlov's baiji' response." In the end the scientists never managed to successfully preserve any sperm.

[24] Adams, *Last Chance to See*, 174.

[25] Turvey, *Witness to Extinction*, 76.

[26] 于, 悲情国宝, 448.

[27] The expedition in fact began in Wuhan, steamed upriver to Yichang, went downriver to Shanghai, then turned upstream and returned to Wuhan. The expedition also checked two stretches of water between Poyang Lake and the main Yangtze channel, known in years prior to be a baiji "hotspot."

[28] Turvey, *Witness to Extinction*, 164–177.

[29] 于, 悲情国宝, 448.

[30] Thomas A. Jefferson and John Y. Wang. "Revision of the taxonomy of finless porpoises (genus *Neophocaena*): The existence of two species." *Journal of Marine Animals and Their Ecology* 4 (2011): 9–10.

[31] A large collection of imperial-era poetry focusing on or mentioning the Yangtze finless porpoises is gathered—along with explanations in modern vernacular Chinese—in 朱方. 历代诗文里的长江江豚. 南京: 江苏凤凰教育出版社, 2021.

[32] 鱏魚，黑色，大如百斤豬，黃肥，不可食。數枚相隨，一浮一沉。一名敷，常見首，出淮及五湖。《四時食制》曹操

Although considered a brilliant statesman, military leader, and an accomplished poet, Cao Cao is best remembered from a heavily fictionalized portrayal in the fourteenth century novel *Romance of the Three Kingdoms* (三國演義). Cao Cao's villainous reputation—stemming from the *Romance* and other works—eventually grew so great that the Chinese equivalent to "Speak of the Devil, and he shall appear" is "Speak of Cao Cao, and Cao Cao appears" (說曹操，曹操就到).

[33] 江上漁人取江豚，冬深水落，視其絕沒處佈網，圍而取之，無不獲；或用鉤釣，若鉤中喉吻，雖巨綸亦掣斷；或桂牙齒間，則隨上下，惟人所

製，曝不頓斃。然至腥臭，不可近，惟取脂油以供點照，土人間有能食者。《岳陽風土記》範致明

[34] Several late Ming-era military texts, including *On Warfare* (兵錄, 1606) and the *Encyclopedia of Military Preparedness* (武備志, 1621) include numerous gunpowder recipes. Many other odd ingredients, such as wolf dung (狼糞), are included in the texts.

In *Witness to Extinction* Samuel Turvey—using Giorgio Pilleri's 1979 article "The Chinese river dolphin (*Lipotes vexillifer*) in poetry, literature and legend," as a reference—cites both Fan Zhiming's work and the use of porpoise oil in Ming-era gunpowder as examples of early usage of the baiji, not the finless porpoise. The original texts, however, use the word "*jiāngtún* 江豚," which was most often—although not always—used to refer to the finless porpoise, while the baiji was referred to with a variety of other terms. It is, however, entirely possible both species were targeted without discrimination, but the extant texts do not provide enough clarity to make a definitive judgement.

[35] 萬曆間，兵部檄取其脂，以為火攻具，而點甚，竟不可餌而得也。《京口三山志》

江豚生江中，狀如豚。其脂能逆風延熾。明 萬曆間，兵部檄取以為火攻具，而點甚，竟不可餌也。《丹徒縣志》

[36] 上曰：「朕甲子年南巡，由江寧登舟，趣金山寺，至黃天蕩，風大作，時衆皆懼而下篷，朕獨令滿掛船篷，截風而行，佇立船頭射江豚，豦不經意。

中國第一歷史檔案館. 康熙起居注 [*The Kangxi Era Imperial Diaries*]. 北京: 中華書局, 1984: 2023.

[37] George Lanning. *Wild Life in China or Chats on Chinese Birds and Beasts.* Shanghai: "The National Review" Office, 1911, 216.

[38] Wang Ding. "Population Status, Threats and Conservation of the Yangtze Finless Porpoise." *Chinese Science Bulletin* 54 (2009): 3479.

[39] Xiujiang Zhao, et al. "Abundance and Conservation Status of the Yangtze Finless Porpoise in the Yangtze River, China." *Biological Conservation* 141 (2008): 3007.

[40] Wang, "Population Status," 48.

[41] Jie Huang, et al. "Population survey showing hope for population recovery of the critically endangered Yangtze finless porpoise." *Biological Conservation* 241, 108315 (2020).

[42] Justin Jin, "If China's finless porpoise is doomed, so is the mighty Yangtze River on which it depends," *South China Morning Post*, May 10, 2020. https://www.scmp.com/magazines/post-magazine/long-reads/article/3083297/if-chinas-finless-porpoise-doomed-so-mighty.

[43] Yi Han et al. "Ecological impacts of unsustainable sand mining: urgent lessons learned from a critically endangered freshwater cetacean." *Proceedings of the Royal Society B* 290, 20221786 (2023).

[44] Ye Ruolin, "Experts Pan Plan That Sent Endangered Porpoises to Aquariums," *Sixth Tone*, May 11, 2021. https://www.sixthtone.com/news/1007431.

Fishing

[1] There is only one other member of the paddlefish family Polyodontidae, the American paddlefish *Polyodon spathula*, native to the Mississippi River Basin. The American paddlefish is now listed as Vulnerable under the IUCN Red List due to overfishing and destruction of their habitat, primarily as a result of dam building and channelization of rivers. One of the largest freshwater fishes in North America, it is nonetheless substantially smaller than the Chinese paddlefish, growing to not even half its size.

[2] As with many size records, the veracity of the claim of the seven-meter-long paddlefish is uncertain and may have been an exaggeration.

[3] Gao Yong et al. "A Review on Conservation Issue in Chinese Paddlefish, Psephurus Glasius." *Advances in Water Resources and Hydraulic Engineering* (2009): 2280.

Strictly speaking, Chinese paddlefish were an amphidromous species. Amphidromous fish migrate to the sea from the freshwater of their birth (or vice-versa), grow into juveniles in their new saltwater habitat, and then return to their original waters where they spend the remainder of their lives.

[4] 李思忠. 黄河鱼类志. 青岛: 中国海洋大学出版社, 2017, 62–63.

[5] Qiwei Wei et al. "Biology, fisheries, and conservation of sturgeons and paddlefish in China." *Environmental Biology of Fishes* 48 (1997): 246.

[6] Thomas W. Blakiston. *Five Months on the Yang-Tsze; with a Narrative of the Exploration of its Upper Waters, and Notices of the Present Rebellions in China.* London: John Murray, 1862, 76–77.

William Spencer Percival. *The Land of the Dragon: My Boating and Shooting Excursions to the Gorges of the Upper Yangtze.* London: Hurst and Blackett, 1889, 126–127.

[7] Gao, "A Review," 2280.

8 Hui Zhang et al. "Extinction of one of the world's largest freshwater fishes: Lessons for conserving the endangered Yangtze fauna." *Science of the Total Environment* 710, 136242 (2020).

9 Gao, "A Review" 2281.

10 Wei et al., "Biology, fisheries, and conservation," 247.

11 陈诗欢, "长江最后一条白鲟，我们追丢了," 澎湃新闻 GQ报道, August 8, 2022. https://www.thepaper.cn/newsDetail_forward_19524740.

In Samuel Turvey's *Witness to Extinction* he lists the last sighted Chinese paddlefish as one fished illegally from the Yangtze in Hubei in January 2007. This is incorrect, as the English-language article used for reference mistranslated the species (中华鲟). The original Chinese-language article clearly states that the fish was a Chinese sturgeon. Although there is an accompanying photo in the English-language article, the fish is shown in a net, and its body is too obscure to identify the species. https://news.sina.com.cn/o/2007-01-11/172510977411s.shtml.

12 Zhang, "Extinction of one of the world's largest freshwater fishes."

Qiwei Wei. "*Psephurus gladius.*" *The IUCN Red List of Threatened Species* (2022): e.T18428A146104283.

13 危起伟 等. 中华鲟保护生物学. 北京: 科学出版社, 2019, 6.

14 P. Zhuang et al. "Biology and life history of Dabry's sturgeon, *Acipenser dabryanus*, in the Yangtze River." *Environmental Biology of Fishes* 48 (1997): 257.

15 Turvey, *Witness to Extinction*, 203.

16 Y. Qiao et al. "Chinese Sturgeon (*Acipenser sinensis*) in the Yangtze River: a hydroacoustic assessment of fish location and abundance on the last spawning ground." *Journal of Applied Ichthyology* 22, s1 (2006): 140.

17 Zhuang, "Biology and life history," 259.

18 Wei et al., "Biology, fisheries, and conservation," 242.

19 Zhuang, "Biology and life history," 257.

20 U.S. Fish and Wildlife Service. "Endangered and Threatened Wildlife and Plants; Listing the Yangtze Sturgeon as an Endangered Species." *Federal Register* 86 (April 26, 2021).

21 USFWS, "Listing the Yangtze Sturgeon."

22 危, 中华鲟, 96.

[23] Li You, "Can Shanghai's New Law Save the Endangered Chinese Sturgeon?" *Sixth Tone*, June 5, 2020. https://www.sixthtone.com/news/1005766.

[24] 危, 中华鲟, 214.

The difficulty of determining survival rates means the exact number of released fish to survive their journey downstream is impossible to know. Researchers re-caught fish released at two months old at an abysmal rate of 0.017%. Fish released aged fourteen months did markedly better; 3.25% were recaptured.

[25] J. M. Wu et al. "Initial evaluation of the release programme for Dabry's sturgeon (*Acipenser dabryanus* Duméril, 1868) in the upper Yangtze River." *Journal of Applied Ichthyology* 30 (2014): 1423–1426.

[26] Junyi Li et al. "Foundation and Prospects of Wild Population Reconstruction of *Acipenser dabryanus*." *Fishes* 6, 55 (2021), 2.

[27] Wei Qiwei. "*Acipenser dabryanus*." *The IUCN Red List of Threatened Species* (2022): e.T231A61462199.

[28] Adrienne Lohe. *Adriatic Sturgeon (Acipenser naccarii), European sturgeon (Acipenser sturio), Chinese sturgeon (Acipenser sinensis), Sakhalin sturgeon (Acipenser mikadoi), Kaluga sturgeon (Huso dauricus) 5-Year Review: Summary and Evaluation*. NOAA, 2021.

[29] 吴采倩, "鲟鱼专家危起伟：中华鲟自然繁殖已中断7年，预计2036年恢复," 新京报, January 31, 2024. https://www.bjnews.com.cn/detail/1706696421168691.html.

[30] Xuan Ban et al. "The silver lining in rewilding the vanished sturgeon in the Yangtze River." *The Innovation Life* 2, 100070 (2024).

[31] Zhenli Huang and Haiying Li. "Dams trigger exponential population declines of migratory fish." *Science Advances* 10, eadi6580 (2024).

Xiaoying You, "China's Yangtze fish-rescue plan is a failure, study says," *Nature*, May 20, 2024. https://doi.org/10.1038/d41586-024-01444-3.

[32] Huang Liangliang and Jianhua Li. "Status of Freshwater Fish Biodiversity in the Yangtze River Basin, China," in *Aquatic Biodiversity Conservation and Ecosystem Services*, ed. Shin-ichi Nakano, Tetsukazu Yahara and Tohru Nakashizuka. Singapore: Springer, 2016, 18.

[33] D. Chen et al. "Status and Management of Fishery Resources of the Yangtze River," in *Proceedings of the Second International Symposium on the Management of Large Rivers for Fisheries, Volume 1*, ed. Robin L. Welcomme and T. Petr. Bangkok: FAO-RAP, 2004, 177.

[34] Dongqi Liu et al. "Low genetic diversity in broodstocks of endangered Chinese sucker, *Myxocyprinus asiaticus*: implications for artificial propagation and conservation." *ZooKeys* 792 (2018): 117.

Haile Yang et al. "Status of aquatic organisms resources and their environments in Yangtze River system (2017–2021)." *Aquaculture and Fisheries* 9 (2024): 833–850: 845.

Yang et al. note that 413 individuals of *M. asiaticus* were found in 2017–2021 surveys of the Yangtze Basin, including a number of mature fish. However it was unclear whether any natural reproduction continues.

[35] Kang Ning, "Ten-year Yangtze fishing ban not enough to save migratory species," *China Dialogue*, November 4, 2020. https://dialogue.earth/en/nature/ten-year-yangtze-fishing-ban-not-enough-to-save-migratory-species/.

Huang and Li (2024) estimate that *Coreius guicoenoti* will be extinct in the wild by 2030.

[36] Chen, "Status and Management," 177.

[37] During the Qing dynasty, the Reeves's shad was one of the numerous prized foods from around the Manchu empire on which the imperial court claimed first catch or pick. The first shad of the season were sent from the Yangtze north to the imperial seat at Beijing by way of a specially maintained system of relay stations.

Zhang Min. "A Brief Discussion of the Banquets of the Qing Court." *Proceedings of the Denver Museum of Natural History* 3 (1998) 67–71.

[38] F. Di Dario. "*Tenualosa reevesii* (errata version published in 2019)." *The IUCN Red List of Threatened Species* (2018): e.T166910A143829403.

[39] Zhongwei Wang et al. "Genetic structure and low-genetic diversity suggesting the necessity for conservation of the Chinese longsnout catfish, *Leiocassis longirostris* (Pisces: Bagriidae)." *Environmental Biology of Fishes* 75 (2006): 455–463.

[40] The sea otter may have once lived on the coasts of Manchuria or farther north in the Strait of Tartary between Sakhalin and what is now the Russian Far East, but which was part of the Qing dynasty until ceded to the Russian Empire as part of the 1858 Treaty of Aigun and 1860 Treaty of Peking.

[41] A. E. Pratt. *To the Snows of Tibet Through China*. London: Longmans, Green, and Co., 1892, 24.

[42] Archibald J. Little. *Through the Yang-tse Gorges or Trade and Travel in Western China*, 3rd ed. London: Sampson Low, Marston & Company. 1898, 39.

Percival, *The Land of the Dragon*, 125–126.

[43] Armand David. *Natural History of North China with Notices of that of the South, West and North-east, and of Mongolia & Thibet, compiled chiefly from the travels of Père Armand David*. Shanghai: Da Costa & Co., 1873, 36.

E. G. Kemp. *The Face of China: Travels in East, North, Central and Western China*. New York: Duffield & Company, 1909, 179–180.

[44] The 2008 Yangtze Fisheries Management Regulations (长江渔业资源管理规定) outlawed the use of otters for fishing (along with fish hawks, dynamite, poison, and electro-fishing). The practice had likely died out by this time. However, if the internet is to be trusted, at least one old fishermen in Jiangyou 江油, Sichuan was still using an otter for fishing as late as 2015. There are still fishermen in Bangladesh who used tamed otters for fishing in a similar manner.

[45] *Ài xióng ér shí zhī yán, ài tǎ ér yǐn zhī jiǔ, suī yù yǎng zhī, fēi qí dào.* 愛熊而食之鹽，愛獺而飲之酒，雖欲養之，非其道。

[46] 嘉楠．"海獭：水中灵鼬，亦盗亦友."博物 180 (2018): 38–43, 40.

[47] B. H. Hodgson. ""Notice of the Mammals of Tibet, with Descriptions and Plates of some new Species." *Journal of the Asiatic Society of Bengal* 11 (1842): 282.

[48] Lobsang Yongdan. "Precious Skin: The Rise and Fall of the Otter Fur Trade in Tibet." *Inner Asia* 20 (2018): 177–198.

[49] 中国水獭调查与保护报告编辑组．2019中国水獭调查与保护报告 (2019), 13–14.

[50] Zhang Lu and Fan Pengfei. "Conservation status of otters in China and a discussion on restoring otter populations in the Pearl River Delta." *Acta Theriologica Sinica* 40 (2020): 72.

[51] 中国水獭报告编辑组, 2019中国水獭报告, 15–16.

Herptiles

[1] Understandably, in Vietnam, where *Rafetus swinhoei* also occurs, the English name Swinhoe's giant softshell turtle is preferred.

[2] *Rafetus swinhoei*'s closest relative is the Euphrates softshell turtle, *Rafetus euphraticus*—over 6,500 km (> 4,000 mi) away, across some of the world's highest mountains and most forbidding deserts.

[3] Minh Duc Le and P. Pritchard. "Genetic variability of the critically endangered softshell turtle Rafetus swinhoei: A preliminary report." *Proceedings of the First Vietnamese National Symposium on Reptiles and Amphibians* (2009): 85.

[4] Le and Pritchard. "Genetic variability," 85.

[5] IUCN SSC-ASAP (Asian Species Action Partnership) and IUCN SSC Tortoise and Freshwater Turtle Specialist Group (TFTSG). "Conservation of *Rafetus swinhoei*." Workshop Report (2014): 1.

[6] Matthew P. Bettelheim. "Swinhoe's Softshell Turtle (*Rafetus swinhoei*): The Legendary Sword Lake Turtle of Hoan Kiem Lake." *Bibliotheca Herpetologica* 10 (2012): 5.

[7] In defense of the conservation team, the sexing of *Rafetus swinhoei* was at that time something of a guessing game, as no one had yet studied the turtles' anatomy closely enough to confidently make such a determination. This was remedied before any future introductions were attempted.

[8] Bettelheim, "Swinhoe's Softshell Turtle," 5.

The ancient, 400-year-turtle was named Fangfang 方方, and the younger turtle Yuanyuan 圆圆. Bronze statues commemorating the turtles are now at the temple garden.

[9] *Xiāng* 湘 is the standard abbreviation for Hunan 湖南 province, in reference to the Xiang River or *Xiāng Jiāng* 湘江. Similarly, *Sū* 苏 is the abbreviation for both Jiangsu 江苏 province and the city of Suzhou 苏州 within it (and in decades past the single character abbreviation for the Soviet Union, more commonly shortened to *Sū Lián* 苏联 in Chinese). In some writings Xiangxiang is referred to by the English name she was given, China Girl.

[10] Bettelheim, "Swinhoe's Softshell Turtle," 16.

[11] Bettelheim, "Swinhoe's Softshell Turtle," 17.

[12] IUCN SSC-ASAP, "Conservation of *Rafetus swinhoei*," 2.

[13] John R. Platt, "The Last Known Female Yangtze Giant Turtle Has Died — What Happens Next?" *The Revelator*, April 16, 2019. https://therevelator.org/last-female-yangtze-turtle-died/.

[14] Damian Carrington, "Hopes for most endangered turtle after discovery of female in Vietnam lake," *The Guardian*, January 1, 2021. https://www.theguardian.com/environment/2021/jan/01/hopes-for-most-endangered-turtle-after-discovery-of-female-in-vietnam-lake.

[15] Mike Ives, "Vietnam Embalms a Sacred Turtle, Lenin-Style," *The New York Times*, March 20, 2019. https://www.nytimes.com/2019/03/20/world/asia/vietnam-turtle-embalmed.html.

[16] Anh Kiet, "Hoan Kiem giant turtle in Dong Mo Lake dies," *Hanoi Times*, April 24, 2023, https://hanoitimes.vn/hanois-giant-turtle-in-dong-mo-lake-dies-323539.html.

[17] Rachel Nuwer, "The World's Rarest Turtle Has a Shot at Escaping Extinction," *The New York Times*, January 25, 2021. https://www.nytimes.com/2021/01/25/science/giant-softshell-turtle-vietnam.html.

Thong Van Pham et al. "Female wanted for the world's rarest turtle: prioritizing areas where *Rafetus swinhoei* may persist in the wild." *Oryx* 56 (2022): 397–398.

[18] *Alligator sinensis* is less commonly known as the Yangtze Alligator, which is in fact its modern name in Chinese, *Yángzǐ'è* 扬子鳄. Its more ancient name is *tuó* 鼍, and colloquially it has long been known as the earth dragon, *tǔlóng* 土龙.

[19] John Thorbjarnarson and Xiaoming Wang. *The Chinese Alligator: Ecology, Behavior, Conservation, and Culture*. Baltimore: Johns Hopkins University Press, 2010, 92–95.

For comparison, the largest American alligator verified on record measured 4.8 m (15 ft 9 in) long and weighed 458.8 kg (1,011.5 lb)—nearly twice as long and over five times as heavy as the largest known Chinese alligator. The largest reported but unverified American alligator was said to be 5.94 m long (19 ft 6 in) and was not weighed because it was too large to take to a scale.

[20] Thorbjarnarson and Wang, *The Chinese Alligator*, xiii.

The majority of information in this section on the Chinese alligator comes from Thorbjarnarson's and Wang's *The Chinese Alligator*, far and away the best source on the species.

[21] Xiaotong Wu et al. "Strontium isotope analysis of Yangtze alligator remains from Late Neolithic North China." *Archaeological and Anthropological Sciences* 11 (2019) 1049–1056.

The two "dragon keeper" clans were named Huanlong 豢龍 and Yulong 御龍. *Huàn* 豢 is an archaic term meaning to rear or raise animals; *yù* 御 means to mange, control, or govern. *Lóng* 龍 is the character for dragon; it in fact has three forms, the simplified 龙, the traditional 龍, and the ancient variant 竜, which though vanishingly rare in Chinese use has been the standard variant used in Japanese since the promulgation of *shinjitai* 新字体—simplified forms of several hundred commonly used *kanji*—in 1946.

[22] It is of course impossible to know with certainty if any one animal or event gave rise to a myth, especially one, such as the Chinese dragon, that takes so many forms. Aside from the notion that the Chinese alligator inspired belief in the Chinese dragon, other candidates include snakes (especially the large pythons), thunder and lightning, and more general nature worship. Currently the earliest archaeological evidence for dragon worship comes from the area between present-day Liaoning and Inner

Mongolia, suggesting that the Chinese dragon did not originate with the Chinese alligator, although later beliefs incorporated attributes, real and imagined, of the alligator.

[23] He Bian (2020) notes that in a late-Ming dynasty scroll which depicts a physician's shop, a reptile can be seen affixed to the ceiling. It is likely a depiction of a Chinese alligator, the skin of which was said to be useful for keeping away moths and worms and hence suitable for protecting the herbs and other *materia medica*.

[24] Arthur de Carle Sowerby. "Pangolin and alligators in Shanghai." *The China Journal* 25 (1936): 110–111. Quoted in Thorbjarnarson, *The Chinese Alligator*, 138.

[25] The campaign to eliminate schistosomiasis began in earnest in the 1950s, and the use of industrially produced molluscicides was adopted after more labor intensive methods failed. Among these were such ingenious efforts as wrangling ducks and geese to eat the snails, recruiting masses of villagers to pluck the snails from riverbanks with chopsticks (which was not only extremely inefficient but led to some participants contracting the disease after losing patience and grabbing snails with their hands), and dumping or spraying boiling water on the land to scald the mollusks. Molluscicides proved far more effective, but frequently poisoned nearby vegetation, wildlife, and domesticated animals. Local fish stocks suffered, and many farmers lost their precious oxen or water buffalo. Humans occasionally died from molluscicide exposure as well. Despite decades of effort, schistosomiasis remains endemic to much of the Yangtze region, as well as parts of Sichuan and Yunnan, but on the whole is far less prevalent than in the past.

Miriam Gross. *Farewell to the God of Plague: Chairman Mao's Campaign to Deworm China*. Oakland, University of California Press, 2016, 130–131.

[26] 祁海群, 陈瑶, 刘端群, "扬子鳄种群复壮 人鳄和谐共生——安徽省扬子鳄保护进入全新阶段," 中国绿色时报, July 31, 2024. http://www.forestry.gov.cn/search/579428.

[27] Charlie Manolis, et al. "CSG Visit to China, August 2016." IUCN-SSC Crocodile Specialist Group (2016): 8.

[28] Shangchen Yang et al. "Genomic investigation of the Chinese alligator reveals wild-extinct genetic diversity and genomic consequences of their continuous decline." *Molecular Ecology Resources* 23 (2023): 305–307.

[29] Shunqing Lu, Xiaotong Du, and Steven G. Platt. "Continued reintroduction of captive-bred Chinese alligators in Anhui National Chinese Alligator Reserve, Anhui Province, China." *Crocodile Specialist Group Newsletter* 40 (2021): 23–25.

[30] Liuyang Yang et al. "Identification of suitable habitats and priority conservation areas under climate change scenarios for the Chinese alligator (*Alligator sinensis*)." *Ecology and Evolution* 14, e11477 (2024).

[31] *Andrias davidianus* is named for the first Westerner to obtain a specimen, the ubiquitous Père Armand David.

[32] The Chinese salamander's Japanese kin, the Japanese giant salamander *Andrias japonicus*, is also gargantuan, but only grows to about 1.5 m (5 ft) and 25 kg (55 lb). The remaining member of the Cryptobranchidae, the giant salamander family, is the hellbender *Cryptobranchus alleganiensis* of the eastern United States. Though by far the largest salamander in its part of the world, the hellbender is comparatively dainty, growing up to only 74 cm (2 ft 5 in) and 2.5 kg (5.5 lb).

[33] Robert Browne et al. "The Sustainable Management of Giant Salamanders (Cryptobranchoidea)." Review (2020): 12–14.

[34] Confusingly, *gǒuyú* 狗鱼 is not only a colloquial term for the giant salamander, but also the standard name for pike.

[35] Samuel T. Turvey et al. "From dirty to delicacy? Changing exploitation in China threatens the world's largest amphibians." *People and Nature* 3 (2021): 452.

[36] 文榕生. 中国珍稀野生动物分布变迁 (续:) 上. 济南: 山东科学技术出版社, 2018, 35–37.

[37] Todd W. Pierson et al. "A survey for the Chinese giant salamander (*Andrias davidianus*; Blanchard, 1871) in the Qinghai Province." *Amphibian & Reptile Conservation* 8 (2014): 1–6.

[38] Arthur de Carle Sowerby. "The giant salamander of China." *The China Journal of Science & Arts* 1 (1925): 253–256.

[39] Xiao-ming Wang et al. "The decline of the Chinese giant salamander *Andrias davidianus* and implications for its conservation." *Oryx* 38 (2004): 197–202.

[40] Andrew A. Cunningham et al. "Development of the Chinese giant salamander *Andrias davidianus* farming industry in Shaanxi Province, China: conservation threats and opportunities." *Oryx* 50 (2016): 267.

[41] Turvey et al., "From dirty to delicacy?", 452–453.

[42] Dai Qiang, Wang Yuezhao, and Liang Gang. "Conservation Status of Chinese Giant Salamander (*Andrias davidianus*)." Report, Chinese Academy of Sciences, Chengdu (2009): 9.

[43] Cunningham, "Development of," 269.

[44] Wang et al., "The decline of the Chinese giant salamander," 197–202.

[45] Dai, Wang and Liang "Conservation Status," 4.

[46] Browne et al., "The Sustainable Management," 19.

[47] Dai, Wang and Liang, "Conservation Status," 10.

[48] Turvey et al., "From dirty to delicacy?" 453.

[49] Benjamin Tapley et al. "Range-wide decline of Chinese giant salamanders Andrias spp. from suitable habitat." *Oryx* 55 (2021): 375–379.

[50] Fang Yan et al. "The Chinese giant salamander exemplifies the hidden extinction of cryptic species." *Current Biology* 28 (2018): R592.

Melissa M. Marr et al. "What's in a name? Using species delimitation to inform conservation practice for Chinese giant salamanders (*Andrias* spp.)." *Evolutionary Journal of the Linnean Society* kzae007 (2024).

[51] Samuel T. Turvey et al. "Historical museum collections clarify the evolutionary history of cryptic species radiation in the world's largest amphibians." *Ecology and Evolution* 9 (2019): 10070.

[52] Jing Chai et al. "Discovery of a wild, genetically pure Chinese giant salamander creates new conservation opportunities." *Zoological Research* 43 (2022): 469–480.

Murong Yi et al. "Population status and habitat of critically endangered Jiangxi giant salamander (*Andrias jiangxiensis*)." *Biodiversity Science* 32, 24145 (2024).

Yan-An Gong et al. "A New Species of the Giant Salamander of the Genus *Andrias* from Qimeng, Anhui, China (Amphibia: Cryptorchiidae)." *Chinese Journal of Zoology* 58 (2023): 651–657.

[53] Pierson et al., "A survey for," 3.

[54] At the time of writing no live specimens of *Andrias sligoi* have yet been confirmed in China, but two males were discovered in separate aquariums in Japan. After the native Japanese giant salamander, *A. japonicus*, was given legal protection in 1952, Chinese salamanders were imported to meet continued demand for salamanders as food and medicine. Some were ultimately released or escaped into the wild, leading to hybridization problems similar to those within China.

Kanto Nishikawa et al. "Discovery of ex situ individuals of *Andrias sligoi*, an extremely endangered species and one of the largest amphibians worldwide." *Scientific Reports* 14, 2575 (2024).

[55] Zhixin Zhang et al. "Future climate change will severely reduce habitat suitability of the Critically Endangered Chinese giant salamander." *Freshwater Biology* 65 (2020): 1–10.

Lakes & Wetlands

[1] The western population of Siberian cranes has since fallen to a lone male, named Omid امید (meaning "Hope" in Persian). Omid winters in Iran's Fereydunkenar marsh, and he was alone after 2009 when his mate Arezoo ارزو ("Wish"), the last wild western Siberian female, died. In early 2023 a captive female, Roya رویا ("Dream"), was brought to Iran from a breeding program in Belgium and released at Fereydunkenar. In early March they departed together to begin the migration to Siberia, but Roya returned to Iran five days later, dashing hopes of a successful pairing. Omid did not return to Iran as usual in late 2023, and his fate is unknown.

[2] Tang Xiyang. *Living Treasures: An Odyssey Through China's Extraordinary Nature Reserves*. New York: Bantam, 1987, 74.

[3] Peter Matthiessen. *The Birds of Heaven: Travels with Cranes*. New York: North Point Press, 2001, 144.

[4] Matthiessen, *The Birds of Heaven*, 153.

[5] James Harris. *Safe Flyways for the Siberian Crane*. 2009, 37.

[6] Craig Simons. *The Devouring Dragon: How China's Rise Threatens Our Natural World*. New York: St. Martin's Press, 2013, 222.

[7] Wen Lijia et al. "Using unmanned aerial vehicle for a population and wintering distribution survey of Siberian crane (*leucogeranus* [sic] *leucogeranus*)." *Acta Ecologica Sinica* 43 (2024): 7693–7700.

[8] Claire M. Mirande and Elena I. Ilyashenko. "Species Review: Siberian Crane (*Leucogeranus leucogeranus*)," in *Crane Conservation Strategy*, ed. Claire M. Mirande and James T. Harris. Baraboo: International Crane Foundation, 2019, 209–222.

[9] Linqiang Gao and Chunrong Mi. "Double jeopardy: global change and interspecies competition threaten Siberian cranes." *PeerJ* 12, e17029 (2024).

[10] Qiyue Li, Geying Lai and Adam Thomas Devlin. "A review on the driving forces of water decline and its impacts on the environment in Poyang Lake, China." *Journal of Water and Climate Change* 12 (2021):, 1377–1378.

By 2001 over 9,600 dams had already been raised on the five rivers that feed into Poyang, with more built since.

[11] Luo Meihan, "Yet Again, Poyang Lake's Water Level Falls to Record Lows," *Sixth Tone*, February 2, 2023. https://www.sixthtone.com/news/1012210.

Mingqin Shao et al. "Response of Siberian Cranes (*Grus leucogeranus*) to Hydrological Changes and the Availability of Foraging Habitat at Various Water Levels in Poyang Lake." *Animals* 14, 234 (2024).

[12] Jiang Yifan, "How the Poyang Lake drought is affecting migratory birds," *China Dialogue*, December 22, 2022. https://dialogue.earth/en/water/how-the-poyang-lake-drought-is-affecting-migratory-birds/.

[13] Liu Yiman, "Poyang lake: Caught between a dam and a sluice wall," *China Dialogue*, May 11, 2021. https://dialogue.earth/en/nature/poyang-lake-caught-between-a-dam-and-a-sluice-wall/.

[14] Qiyue Li et al. "Assessing the impact of the proposed Poyang lake hydraulic project on the Yangtze finless porpoise and its calves." *Ecological Indicators* 129, 107873 (2021).

[15] BirdLife International. "*Leucogeranus leucogeranus.*" *The IUCN Red List of Threatened Species* (2018): e.T22692053A134180990.

[16] Zhen-Hua Wei et al. "Patterns of change in the population and spatial distribution of oriental white storks (*Ciconia boyciana*) wintering in Poyang Lake." *Zoological Research* 37 (2016): 338–346.

[17] Lei Cao, Mark Barter and Gang Lei. "New Anatidae population estimates for eastern China: Implications for current flyway estimates." *Biological Conservation* 141 (2008): 2307.

[18] Xin Wang et al. "Changes in the distribution and abundance of wintering Lesser White-fronted Geese *Anser erythropus* in eastern China." *Bird Conservation International* 22 (2012): 128–134.

[19] BirdLife International. "*Anser cygnoid.*" *The IUCN Red List of Threatened Species* (2023): e.T22679869A228564177.

[20] Yang Xiaohong, "Swan song at Poyang Lake," *China Dialogue*, March 16, 2012. https://dialogue.earth/en/nature/4811-swan-song-at-poyang-lake/.

[21] Wong How Man. *Exploring the Yangtze: China's Longest River*. San Francisco: China Books & Periodicals, 1989, 23–25.

In his recounting of watching hunters use cannons on Hong Lake, Wong noted that some of the cannons fell from the boats after firing, and that the hunters would have to retrieve the heavy weapons from the lake bed and let them dry before resetting and using them again. The whole process took half a day.

[22] The practice of hunting waterfowl with primitive cannons was almost identical to how Americans of the nineteenth century often hunted birds, using massive scatter guns—essentially shotgun-shaped cannons—called punt guns to blast entire rafts of resting birds.

[23] Xu Liu and Roller Ma Ming. "Swans killed by poison in China." *Swan News,* 13 (2017): 26–31.

[24] Xin Wang et al. "Serious contractions in wintering distribution and decline in abundance of Baer's Pochard *Aythya baeri*." *Bird Conservation International* 22 (2012): 121–127.

[25] Lan Wu et al. "Shifted to the South, Shifted to the North, but No Expansion: Potential Suitable Habitat Distribution Shift and Conservation Gap of the Critically Endangered Baer's Pochard (*Aythya baeri*)." *Remote Sensing* 14, 2171 (2022).

[26] 马连义, 杨国美. 大丰麋鹿. 南京: 江苏人民出版社, 2016, 46–47.

[27] 马, 杨, 大丰麋鹿, 70–71.

[28] 曹克清, 陈彬. "关于野生麋鹿绝灭原因的再探讨." 四川动物 1 (1990): 41–42.

[29] 文榕生. 中国珍稀野生动物分布变迁 (续:) 下. 济南: 山东科学技术出版社, 2018, 2308–2309.

[30] 曹克清, 陈彬. "关于野生麋鹿," 41.

[31] Turvey et al. "Imperial trophy or island relict? A new extinction paradigm for Père David's deer: a Chinese conservation icon." *Royal Society Open Science* 4, 171096 (2017).

[32] Xue Dayuan et al. "Père David's Deer (*Elaphurus davidianus*) in China: Population Dynamics and Challenges." *Journal of Resources and Ecology* 13 (2022): 41–50.

[33] The Shishou reserve borders on Tian'e Zhou, the oxbow lake intended as a semi-captive breeding haven for the baiji.

[34] Bai et al. "The 35th anniversary of the reintroduction of Milu deer to China: History, population status, achievements and challenges." *Biodiversity Science* 29 (2021): 163.

[35] Xue et al., "Père David's Deer (*Elaphurus davidianus*) in China," 46.

[36] The musk deer family, Moschidae, is a closer relative of the Bovidae (bison, sheep, gazelles, wildebeest, takin, and many more), than the Cervidae. The true deer diverged from the musk deer and their bovid cousins between 27 and 28 million years ago.

[37] Xu Hongfa, Zheng Xiangzhong and Lu Houji. "Impact of human activities and habitat changes on distribution of Chinese water deer along the coast area in northern Jiangsu." *Acta Theriologica Sinica* 13 (1998): 161–167.

[38] Robert Swinhoe. "On Chinese Deer, with the Description of an apparently new Species." *Proceedings of the Zoological Society of London* (1873): 572–576.

[39] Gérard Dubost et al. "The Chinese water deer, *Hydropotes inermis* —A fast-growing and productive ruminant." *Mammalian Biology* 76 (2011): 190.

[40] Cited in Glover M. Allen. *The Mammals of China and Mongolia, Part 2.* New York: The American Museum of Natural History, 1940, 1140–1141.

[41] R.B. Harris and J.W. Duckworth. *"Hydropotes inermis." The IUCN Red List of Threatened Species* (2015): e.T10329A22163569.

[42] The Korean populations of water deer have fared better than their Manchurian kin, and without any remaining natural predators they are now considered a nuisance animal. Some have even wandered into downtown Seoul in recent years. Introduced populations of water deer also roam parts of France, the UK, the USA, and Argentina.

[43] Chen et al. "Chinese Water Deer (*Hydropotes inermis*) Reintroduction in Nanhui, Shanghai, China." *Pakistan Journal of Zoology* 47 (2015): 1499–1501.

Haiming Tang, Qiuting Chen and Min Chen. "Free-ranging dogs threaten reintroduced Chinese water deer." *Deer Specialist Group News* 35 (2024): 3–11.

[44] Ying Li al. "Northward Range Expansion of Water Deer in Northeast Asia: Direct Evidence and Management Implications." *Animals* 12, 1392 (2022).

Southern Forests

[1] Zhao Ji et al. *The Natural History of China.* London: Collins, 1990, 45–47.

[2] Robert B. Marks. *China: Its Environment and History.* Lanham: Rowman & Littlefield. 2012, 123–124.

[3] Zhang Chi and Hsiao-chun Hung. "The emergence of agriculture in southern China." *Antiquity* 84 (2010): 19–22.

[4] Ting Ma et al. "Holocene fire and forest histories in relation to climate change and agriculture development in southeastern China." *Quaternary International* 488 (2018): 30–40.

[5] Marks, *China: Its Environment and History*, 126.

[6] Ian Matthew Miller. "Roots and Branches: Woodland Institutions in South China, 800–1600." Doctoral dissertation, Harvard University. 2015, 238–246.

[7] Ian M. Miller. *Fir and Empire: The Transformation of Forests in Early Modern China*. Seattle: University of Washington Press, 2020, 11–17.

[8] Ian Matthew Miller. "The Yangzi River and the Environmental History of South China." *Oxford Research Encyclopedia of Asian History* (2021).

[9] Marks, *China: Its Environment and History*, 205–216.

[10] Marks, *China: Its Environment and History*, 180–183.

[11] Elvin, *The Retreat of the Elephants*, 85.

[12] Robert B. Marks. *Tigers, Rice, Silk, and Silt: Environment and Economy in Late Imperial South China*. Cambridge: Cambridge University Press, 1998, 35.

Glacial Refugees

[1] Jordi López-Pujol and Ming-Xun Ren. "China: A Hot Spot of Relict Plant Taxa," in *Biodiversity Hotspots*, ed. Vittore Rescigno and Savario Maletta. New York: Nova Science Publishers, 2010, 124–130.

[2] Fagen Li and Nianhe Xia. "Population structure and genetic diversity of an endangered species, *Glyptostrobus pensilis* (Cupressaceae)." *Botanical Bulletin of Academia Sinica* 46 (2005): 155–162.

[3] Zhuo Zheng et al. "Anthropogenic impacts on Late Holocene land-cover change and floristic biodiversity loss in tropical southeastern Asia." *Proceedings of the National Academy of Sciences* 118, e2022210118 (2021).

Yaze Zhang et al. "Human Impacts on Holocene Vegetation and Wetland Degradation in the Lower Pearl River, Southern China." *Land* 13, 530 (2024).

[4] Jinlong Zhang and Gunter A. Fischer. "Reconsideration of the native range of the Chinese Swamp Cypress (*Glyptostrobus pensilis*) based on new insights from historic, remnant and planted populations." *Global Ecology and Conservation* 32, e01927 (2021).

[5] Cindy Q. Tang et al. "Forest characteristics and population structure of *Glyptostrobus pensilis*, a globally endangered relict species of southeastern China." *Plant Diversity* 41 (2019): 237–249.

[6] Li and Xia, "Population structure and genetic diversity," 155–162.

[7] A specimen of *Cathaya argyrophylla* had in fact already been collected from Jinfo Shan (金佛山) in present-day Chongqing in 1938. The unidentified specimen was eventually placed in the newly founded Institute of Botany in Beijing after its establishment in 1949, where it was not identified until the rediscovery and naming of the species.

Chris Callaghan. "*Cathaya argyrophylla*, some little known facts." *International Dendrology Society Yearbook* (2011): 95.

[8] Tang Xiyang. *Living Treasures: An Odyssey Through China's Extraordinary Nature Reserves*. New York: Bantam, 1987, 83–94.

[9] Maarten J. M. Christenhusz and Christine Battle. "1051. *Cathaya argyrophylla* Chun & Kuang." *Curtis's Botanical Magazine* 40 (2023): 11.

[10] According to Tang Xiyang, despite the clear rarity of the Cathay silver fir upon its discovery, the utilitarian mindset of the time led researchers to determine that the species had the potential to provide "high-grade timber for construction, shipbuilding, railroad ties, and furniture. Its bark, leaves, and cones possess medicinal properties, and its seeds contain a fairly high percentage of oil."

[11] G. P. Chapman and Y. Z. Wang. *The Plant Life of China*. Berlin: Springer, 2002, 50–51.

[12] Hua-Feng Wang et al. "Conservation of the Cathay Silver Fir, *Cathaya argyrophylla*: a Chinese evergreen 'living fossil'," in *Evergreens: Types, Ecology and Conservation* ed. Adriano D. Bezerra and Tadeu S. Ferreira. New York: Nova Science Publishers, 2012, 125.

[13] Shenhua Qian et al. "Effective conservation measures are needed for wild *Cathaya argyrophylla* populations in China: Insights from the population structure and regeneration characteristics." *Forest Ecology and Management* 361 (2016): 359.

[14] Christopher B. Callaghan. "The Cathay Silver Fir: Its Discovery and Journey Out of China." *Arnoldia* 66 (2009): 15–19.

For decades the PRC government was especially protective of *Cathaya argyrophylla*, refusing permission to any foreigners to either visit the wild stands or export any seeds or live specimens. No specimens are known to have left China until the Royal Botanic Gardens in Sydney, Australia obtained one in 1993. Commercial export of seeds did not begin until 1998. Because of this, there remain no mature Cathay silver firs growing outside of China. The restrictions, along with difficulties in propagating and growing the tree, have made it a relative rarity in foreign botanical collections.

[15] Qian et al. "Effective conservation measures," 364–365.

[16] Wang et al. "Conservation of the Cathay Silver Fir, *Cathaya argyrophylla*," 128.

[17] Jianguo Wu. "Risk and Uncertainty of Losing Suitable Habitat Areas Under Climate Change Scenarios: A Case Study for 109 Gymnosperm Species in China." *Environmental Management* 65 (2020): 517–533.

[18] E. D. Merrill. "Metasequoia, another 'living fossil'." *Arnoldia* 8 (1948): 1–4.

[19] Yukun Fan et al. "Spring drought as a possible cause for disappearance of native *Metasequoia* in Yunnan Province, China: Evidence from seed germination and seedling growth." *Global Ecology and Conservation* 22, e00912 (2020).

[20] Susan Sand. "The Dawn Redwood: East and west cooperated to save this living fossil from extinction." *American Horticulturist* 71 (1992): 40–44.

Cindy Q. Tang et al. "Population structure of relict *Metasequoia glyptostroboides* and its habitat fragmentation and degradation in south-central China." *Biological Conservation* 144 (2011): 279–289.

[21] Sand, "The Dawn Redwood," 43.

[22] H. H. Hu and Cheng Hsueh Chi-ju. "Reminiscences of Collecting the Type Specimens of *Metasequoia glyptostroboides.*" *Arnoldia* 45 (1985): 17.

[23] Kwei-ling Chu and William S. Cooper. "An Ecological Reconnaissance in the Native Home of *Metasequoia glyptostroboides.*" *Ecology* 31 (1950): 265.

[24] Tang et al. "Population structure of relict *Metasequoia glyptostroboides,*" 288.

[25] A. Farjon. "*Metasequoia glyptostroboides.*" *The IUCN Red List of Threatened Species* (2013): e.T32317A2814244.

[26] Wu, "Risk and Uncertainty," 523 & 529.

[27] Bracts are specialized leaves, generally at the base of a flower or inflorescence. The large white "petals" of dogwood blooms, and the colorful leaves surrounding bougainvillea flowers are also bracts.

[28] He Jinsheng, Lin Jie and Chen Weilie. "The current status of endemic and endangered species *Davidia involucrata* and the preserving strategies." *Chinese Biodiversity* 3 (1995): 213–221.

[29] Shenhua Qian et al. "Conservation and development in conflict: regeneration of wild *Davidia involucrata* (Nyssaceae) communities weakened by bamboo management in south-central China." *Oryx* 52 (2018): 443–445.

[30] Cindy Q. Tang et al. "Potential effects of climate change on geographic distribution of the Tertiary relict tree species *Davidia involucrata* in China." *Science Reports* 7, 43822 (2017).

Junfeng Tang and Xuzhe Zhao. "Forecasting the combined effects of future climate and land use change on the suitable habitat of *Davidia involucrata* Baill." *Ecology and Evolution* 12, e9023 (2022).

Tianxiang Wang et al. ""Predicting the Potential Habitat Distribution of Relict Plant *Davidia involucrata* in China Based on the MaxEnt Model." *Forests* 15, 272 (2024).

[31] Peter Crane. *Ginkgo: The Tree That Time Forgot.* New Haven: Yale University Press, 2013, 4–5.

[32] L Shen et al. "Genetic variation of *Ginkgo biloba* L. (Ginkgoaceae) based on cpDNA PCR-RFLPs: inference of glacial refugia." *Heredity* 94 (2005): 396–401.

[33] Jie Liu, Ruo-Yan Jiang and Guang-Fu Zhang. "Number and distribution of large old ginkgos in east China: Implications for regional conservation." *Nature Conservation* 42 (2020): 71–87.

[34] Cindy Q. Tang et al. "Evidence for the persistence of wild *Ginkgo biloba* (Ginkgoaceae) population in the Dalou Mountains, southwestern China." *American Journal of Botany* 99 (2012): 1412–1413.

Stripes & Spots

[1] Chris Coggins. *The Tiger and the Pangolin: Nature, Culture, and Conservation in China*. Honolulu: University of Hawai'i Press, 2003, 2.

[2] Coggins, *The Tiger and the Pangolin*, 53–54.

[3] Coggins, *The Tiger and the Pangolin*, 67–68.

[4] Coggins, *The Tiger and the Pangolin*, 64.

[5] Chris Coggins. "King of the Hundred Beasts: A Long View of Tigers in Southern China," in *Tigers of the World: The Science, Politics, and Conservation of Panthera tigris, 2nd Ed*, ed. Ronald L. Tilson and Philip J. Nyhus. Amsterdam: Academic Press, 2010, 433.

[6] Marks, *Tigers, Rice, Silk, and Silt*, 324–331.

[7] Marco Polo. *The Book of Ser Marco Polo, the Venetian, Concerning the Kingdoms and Marvels of the East, Third Ed., Vol. II*. London: John Murray, 1903, 126 & 225.

[8] Mao Zedong's father, Mao Yichang (毛贻昌, 1870–1920), once encountered a tiger not far from his village outside Shaoshan, Hunan. He avoided an attack, as both he and the tiger fled in fear.

Alexander V. Pantsov with Steven I. Levine. *Mao: The Real Story*. New York: Simon & Schuster, 2012: 14.

[9] A. E. Pratt. *To the Snows of Tibet Through China*. London: Longmans, Green, and Co., 1892, 44–47.

[10] George Lanning. *Wild Life in China or Chats on Chinese Birds and Beasts*. Shanghai: "The National Review" Office, 1911, 198.

Glover M. Allen. *The Mammals of China and Mongolia, Part 1*. New York: The American Museum of Natural History, 1938, 483.

[11] Harry R. Caldwell. *Blue Tiger*. New York: Abingdon Press, 1924, 51.

[12] John C. Caldwell. *China Coast Family*. Chicago: Henry Regnery Company, 1953, 28.

[13] William Lord Smith. "The Cave Tiger of Amoy: The Story of a Hunt for a Man-eating Tiger that Lived in a Rocky Den Back of Amoy." *Natural History* 28 (1928): 430–438.

Leonard Clark. *A Wanderer Till I Die*. New York: Funk & Wagnalls, 1937, 24–36.

[14] Caldwell, *Blue Tiger*, 60–63.

[15] Caldwell, *Blue Tiger*, 48.

Allen, *The Mammals of China and Mongolia, Part 1*, 483.

[16] Ronald Tilson, Kathy Traylor-Holzer and Qiu Ming Jiang. "The decline and impending extinction of the South China tiger." *Oryx* 31 (1997): 243–252.

[17] 任林举. 虎啸——野生东北虎追踪与探秘. 北京：北京十月文艺出版社，2021, 234–235.

[18] "上世纪五六十年代全国曾掀起打虎高潮," 看历史, 2010-10-13. green.sina.com.cn/2010-10-13/162321268397.shtml.

[19] Coggins, "King of the Hundred Beasts," 423.

[20] Coggins, *The Tiger and the Pangolin*, 78.

[21] Tilson, Traylor-Holzer and Jiang, "The decline and impending extinction," 243.

[22] Ronald Tilson, Philip J. Nyhus, and Jeff R. Muntifering. "Yin and Yang of Tiger Conservation in China," in *Tigers of the World: The Science, Politics, and Conservation of Panthera tigris, 2nd Ed*, ed. Ronald L. Tilson and Philip J. Nyhus. Amsterdam: Academic Press, 2010, 442.

[23] Ronald Tilson et al. "Dramatic decline of wild South China tigers *Panthera tigris amoyensis*: field survey of priority tiger reserves." *Oryx* 38 (2004): 40–47.

[24] Yiyuan Qin et al. "An assessment of South China tiger reintroduction potential in Hupingshan and Houhe National Nature Reserves, China." *Biological Conservation* 182 (2015): 81–84.

[25] Le Zhang et al. "Chromosome-scale genomes reveal genomic consequences of inbreeding in the South China tiger: A comparative study with the Amur tiger." *Molecular Ecology Resources* 23 (2023): 330–347.

[26] George Lanning. *Wild Life in China or Chats on Chinese Birds and Beasts*. Shanghai: "The National Review" Office, 1911, 205.

[27] William Spencer Percival. *The Land of the Dragon: My Boating and Shooting Excursions to the Gorges of the Upper Yangtze.* London: Hurst and Blackett, 1889, 131–133.

[28] T. R. Jernigan. *Shooting in China.* Shanghai: Methodist Publishing House, 1908, 129–130.

[29] During the Second Sino-Japanese War (1937–1945) even the Imperial Japanese Army would sometimes help local communities exterminate predators. In Japan one case is remembered to this day. Soldiers stationed in Hubei burned a hillside to drive out or kill a local leopard. Afterwards they found two cubs and kept the one survivor. They named the cub Hachi ハチ ("bee") and made her the unit's mascot. As the war progressed Hachi was sent to the Ueno Zoo in Tokyo on the presumption she would be safer there. She was renamed Hakkō 八紘 (from the wartime slogan *Hakkō icchu* 八紘一宇, a reference to Japan's Greater East Asian Co-Prosperity Sphere, the benign face of their imperial project), and quickly became a favorite attraction. But in 1943, Hachi and the zoo's other animals were deliberately killed in a mad and misguided display of resolve in the face of wartime deprivation. Hachi has since become the subject of several children's books, and her stuffed remains are on display in the Kōchi Mirai Science Center.

Ian Jared Miller. *The Nature of the Beasts: Empire and Exhibition at the Tokyo Imperial Zoo.* Berkely: University of California Press, 2013, 85–86.

[30] Tan Bangjie. "The Status of Felids in China." *Proceedings from the Cat Specialist Group meeting in Kanha National Park.* (1984): 37.

[31] Eva Jutzeler et al. "Leopard." *Cat News* sp. 5 (2010): 30–33.

[32] Alice Laguardia et al. "The current distribution and status of leopards *Panthera pardus* in China." *Oryx* 51 (2015): 153–159.
宋大昭. "曾经广布中国的豹, 如今散落在哪里?" // 来! 聆听大自然的呼唤. 宋大昭, 黄巧雯 主编. 上海: 上海科技教育出版社, 2020, 12–18.

Scales, Musk, Antlers, & Tusks

[1] Surprisingly, pangolins—which belong in their own taxonomic order of Pholidota—are most closely related to the carnivores—dogs, cats, bears, and so forth—and not the more morphologically or behaviorally similar armadillos or anteaters.

[2] The two species of African ground pangolins—the ground pangolin *Smutsia temmincki* and giant pangolin *S. gigantea*—do not have prehensile tails.

[3] The specific term for defensively rolling into a ball is "volvation," should you ever feel inclined to use it.

[4] The black-bellied or long-tailed pangolin, *Phataginus tetradactyla*, is an exception, being diurnal and almost strictly arboreal.

[5] The ninth pangolin species, *Manis mysteria*, was only discovered in 2023. The fifth Asian pangolin species, *mysteria* was found during genomic analysis of pangolin scales that had been confiscated from traffickers between 2012 and 2019. Beyond the mere fact of its existence, nothing is known of *M. mysteria* except that its home is likely in Southeast Asia, and it must bear a close resemblance to the two pangolins species of that region.

Tong-Tong Gu, Hong Wu, Feng Yang et al. "Genomic analysis reveals a cryptic pangolin species." *Proceedings of the National Academy of Sciences* 120, e2304096120 (2023).

[6] The Sunda pangolin *Manis javanica* lives in a small section of southern Yunnan, specifically in Pu'er and Sibsongpanna on the Myanmar border.

Peng Cen, Jiankun Sun, Qiaoyan Wang et al. "Only Sunda and Chinese pangolin (Pholidota) are naturally distributed in China." *Integrative Zoology* 18 (2023): 704–709.

[7] Jing-Yang Hu et al. "Genomic consequences of population decline in critically endangered pangolins and their demographic histories." *National Science Review* 7 (2020): 804.

[8] Fuhua Zhang, Shibao Wu and Peng Cen. "The past, present and future of the pangolin in Mainland China." *Global Ecology and Conservation* 33, e01995 (2022): 2.

[9] As opposed to the Chinese names which reference its scales and burrowing, "pangolin" derives for the Malay word "*peng-goling*," which means "one that rolls up."

[10] Coggins, *The Tiger and the Pangolin*, 2 & 311–312.

Li Shizhen. *Ben Cao Gang Mu, Volume VIII: Clothes, Utensils, Worms, Insects, Amphibians, Animals with Scales, Animals with Shells*. Oakland: University of California Press, 2021, 543–551.

[11] Coggins, *The Tiger and the Pangolin*, 238–247.

Coggins tells of an incident from his research in rural Fujian in which a villager recounted the story of a neighbor who he believed had succumbed to the pangolin's vengeful spirit. The man had caught and eaten a pangolin. Over the next two months his hair fell out, and then he died.

[12] 冯祚建, 王祖望. "中国古代对穿山甲的认识、利用及其种群现状与保护的研究," // 中國古代動物學研究. 王祖望 主編, 冯祚建, 黄复生 副主编. 北京: 科学出版社, 2019, 124–125.

[13] Yifu Wang, Samuel T. Turvey and Nigel Leader-Williams. "Knowledge and attitudes about the use of pangolin scale products in Traditional Chinese Medicine (TCM) within China." *People and Nature* 2 (2020): 904.

The original text in which the pangolins were listed, the *Bencao Jing Jizhu* 本草經集注, no longer survives, but is known from quotations in later compendia.

[14] Shuang Xing et al. "Meat and medicine: historic and contemporary use in Asia," in *Pangolins: Science, Society and Conservation*, ed. Daniel W.S. Challender, Helen C. Nash and Carly Waterman. London: Academic Press, 2020, 233.

[15] Edward H. Schafer. *The Vermilion Bird: T'ang Images of the South*. Berkeley: University of California Press, 1967, 230.

Schafer cites the *Compendium of Materia Medica*, where the relevant passage reads: 燒灰傅 惡瘡。又治山嵐瘴瘧。甄權。

Shuang Xing et al., "Meat and medicine," 233.

Xing et al. cite *Essential Prescriptions for Every Emergency Worth a Thousand Gold* (*Bèi Jí Qiān Jīn Yào Fāng* 備急千金要方) by Sun Simao (孫思邈, 581?–682) for the pangolin scale soup. The entry reads: 鯪鯉湯：治乍寒乍熱，乍有乍無，山瘴瘧方。鯪鯉甲（十四枚）鱉甲　烏賊骨（各一兩）恆山（三兩）附子（一枚）上五味㕮咀，以酒三升漬一夕，發前稍稍啜飲勿絕吐之，兼以塗身，斷食，過時乃食飲。《備急千金要方·卷十·傷寒方下·溫瘧第十五》

[16] Xing et al, "Meat and medicine," 233.

[17] Xing et al, "Meat and medicine," 232.

Pangolin meat was eaten in winter because, according to Chinese medical theory, it is a "hot" food and would help dispel "chill."

[18] Arthur Adams. *Travels of a Naturalist in Japan and Manchuria*. London: Hurst and Blackett, 1870, 79–83.

Adams also noted that locals of Guangzhou did not eat the pangolin, although he tried it himself and found it to be "very excellent food when roasted."

[19] Caldwell, *Blue Tiger*, 98.

[20] Clifford Pope. *China's Animal Frontier*. New York: Viking Press, 1940, 176.

Pope noted that the only place he found pangolins to be abundant was in a remote section of Hainan, where the animals took refuge on the sacred ground of cemeteries, which the locals were afraid to disturb.

21 Shibao Wu et al. "Chinese pangolin *Manis pentadactyla* (Linnaeus, 1758)," in *Pangolins: Science, Society and Conservation*, ed. Daniel W.S. Challender, Helen C. Nash and Carly Waterman. London: Academic Press, 2020, 65.

22 Wu Shi-Bao et al. "The status and conservation strategy of pangolin resource in China." *Journal of Natural Resources* 17 (2002): 176.

23 Yifu Wang, Nigel Leader-Williams and Samuel T. Turvey." Exploitation Histories of Pangolins and Endemic Pheasants on Hainan Island, China: Baselines and Shifting Social Norms." *Frontiers in Ecology and Evolution* 9, 608057 (2021), 7–8.

24 Wu Shibao and Ma Guangzhi. "The Status and Conservation of Pangolins in China." *TRAFFIC East Asia Newsletter* 4 (2005): 2.

25 Xing et al, "Meat and medicine," 233–235.
Pangolin scales have even been used in veterinary medicine to improve milk production in cows.

26 Wang, Turvey and Leader-Williams, "Knowledge and attitudes," 903–912.

27 Xinyao Jin et al. "Evidence for the medicinal value of Squama Manitis (pangolin scale): A systematic review." *Integrative Medicine Research* 10, 100486 (2021).

28 Daniel W.S. Challender et al. "International trade and trafficking in pangolins, 1900–2019," in *Pangolins: Science, Society and Conservation*, ed. Daniel W.S. Challender, Helen C. Nash and Carly Waterman. London: Academic Press, 2020, 260–265.

29 Zhi-Cheng Liu et al. "Chinese pangolins (*Manis pentadactyla*) are not functionally extinct in Chinese Mainland." *Zoological Research: Diversity and Conservation* 1 (2024): 79–81.

30 Zhang, Wu and Cen, "The past, present and future of the pangolin in Mainland China," 5–7.

31 Rob Parry-Jones and Joyce Y. Wu. *Musk Deer Farming as a Conservation Tool in China*. Hong Kong: TRAFFIC East Asia, 2001: iv.

32 Parry-Jones and Wu, *Musk Deer Farming*, 8.

33 According to Parry-Jones and Wu, prices for musk in the 1990s could be as low as $2,604 /kg, but that the average wholesale price was around $11,000/kg, while retail prices were around $21,000/kg.

34 Parry-Jones and Wu, *Musk Deer Farming*, iv & 8.

35 Chinese authors often use the name "forest musk deer" for *Moschus berezovskii*, a direct translation of the Chinese name for the species, *lín shè* 林麝.

36 Y. Wang and R. Harris. "*Moschus berezovskii.*" *The IUCN Red List of Threatened Species* (2015): e.T13894A103431781.

37 Y. Wang and R.B. Harris. "*Moschus anhuiensis.*" *The IUCN Red List of Threatened Species* (2015): e.T136643A61979276.

38 Yijun Zhou et al. "Review of the distribution, status and conservation of musk deer in China." *Folia Zoologica* 53 (2004): 133.

39 Qisen Yang et al. "Conservation status and causes of decline of musk deer (*Moschus* spp.) in China." *Biological Conservation* 109 (2003): 338.

40 Wang and Harris, "*Moschus anhuiensis.*"

41 Supply of artificial musk in China is also tightly controlled. The formulation and manufacture of artificial musk remain state secrets there.

42 Yang et al, "Conservation status and causes of decline of musk deer," 336.

43 Hui Feng et al. "Forest musk deer (*Moschus berezovskii*) in China: research and protection." *Journal of Vertebrate Biology* 72, 22067 (2023): 5–6.

44 R. Timmins and B. Chan. "*Muntiacus crinifrons.*" *The IUCN Red List of Threatened Species* (2016): e.T13924A22160753.

45 Juncheng Lei et al. "Potential effects of future climate change on suitable habitat of *Muntiacus crinifrons*, an endangered and endemic species in China." *Biodiversity Science* 24 (2016): 1390–1399.

46 Glover M. Allen. *The Mammals of China and Mongolia, Part 2*. New York: The American Museum of Natural History, 1940, 1171–1172 & 1189–1190.

47 Dale R. McCullough, Zhi-Guang Jiang, and Chun-Wang Li. "Sika Deer in Mainland China," in *Sika Deer: Biology and Management of Native and Introduced Populations*, ed. Dale R. McCullough, Seiki Takatsuki and Koichi Kaji. Tokyo: Springer, 2009, 527 & 530.

48 He Xingcheng et al. "Population structure and activity rhythm of sambar deer (*Rusa unicolor*)." *Acta Theriologica Sinica* 39 (2019): 134–141.

49 Pan Wang et al. "Assessment of habitat suitability and connectivity across the potential distribution landscape of the sambar (*Rusa unicolor*) in Southwest China." *Frontiers in Conservation Science* 3, 909072 (2023).

50 Allen, *The Mammals of China and Mongolia, Part 2*, 1126.

51 Caldwell, *Blue Tiger*, 140–141.

[52] Ye Ruolin, "China's Farmers Have a Feral Hog Problem. What Now?" *Sixth Tone*, September 4, 2020. https://www.sixthtone.com/news/1006125.

[53] Niu Yuhan, "Wild boar loses protections," *China Dialogue*, July 6, 2023. https://dialogue.earth/en/digest/wild-boar-loses-protections/.

Guangmei Yang et al. "Habitat suitability and crop damage risk caused by wild boar in Guizhou Plateau, China." *Journal of Wildlife Management* 88, e22542 (2024).

Monkey Business

[1] *Rhinopithecus brelichi* is named for Henry Brelich, a British mining engineer who worked as a general manager of Anglo-French mercury concessions in Guizhou, who obtained the skin first used to describe the species.

[2] *Rhinopithecus brelichi* is in fact descended from hybrids of *R. roxellana* and the common ancestor of both *R. bieti* and *R. strykeri*.

Hong Wu et al. "Hybrid origin of a primate, the gray snub-nosed monkey." *Science* 380, eabl4997 (2023).

[3] Oldfield Thomas. "Exhibition of a skin and description of a new species of monkey. *Rhinopithecus brelichi*." *Proceedings of the Zoological Society of London* (1903): 224–225.

[4] Zuo-Fu Xiang et al. "Current status and conservation of the gray snub-nosed monkey *Rhinopithecus brelichi* (Colobinae) in Guizhou, China." *Biological Conservation* 142 (2009): 470.

[5] Tang, *Living Treasures*, 116.

[6] Tan Bangjie. "The Status of Primates in China," *Primate Conservation* 5 (1985): 68–69.

[7] Tang, *Living Treasures*, 120.

[8] W. Bleisch, L. Yongcheng and M. Richardson. "*Rhinopithecus brelichi*." *The IUCN Red List of Threatened Species* (2008): e.T19595A8985249.

[9] Sun Dun Yuan et al, editors. *CBSG Guizhou Snub-nosed Monkey Conservation and PHVA Workshop Report*. Apple Valley, MN: CBSG, 1999, 30.

[10] Guo Yanqing et al. "Habitat estimates reveal that there are fewer than 400 Guizhou snub-nosed monkeys, *Rhinopithecus brelichi*, remaining in the wild." *Global Ecology and Conservation* 24, e01181 (2020).

[11] François' langurs are named for Auguste François (1857–1935), who served as French consul in southern China from 1896 to 1904. Aside from providing the first

specimen of *Trachypithecus francoisi* for Western scientists to describe, François was also an avid photographer and may have been the first person to record motion pictures of China. His collection of photographs and motion pictures are among the most extensive of any from the late Qing dynasty.

[12] Niu Kefeng et al. "Is Yuan in China's Three Gorges a Gibbon or a Langur?" *International Journal of Primatology* (2022).

[13] 黄乘明, 周岐海, 李友邦. 黑叶猴的行为生态与保护生物学. 上海: 上海科学技术出版社, 2018, 11–12.

[14] Tan, "The Status of Primates in China," 66.

[15] Tan, "The Status of Primates in China," 66.

[16] Youbang Li et al. "Dramatic decline of François' langur *Trachypithecus francoisi* in Guangxi Province, China." *Oryx* 41 (2007): 40–41.

[17] Gang Hu et al. "Evidence for a decline of François' langur *Trachypithecus francoisi* in Fusui Nature Reserve, south-west Guangxi, China." *Oryx* 38 (2004): 52.

[18] Li et al. "Dramatic decline of François' langur," 38–41.

[19] T. Nadler. "*Trachypithecus francoisi.*" *The IUCN Red List of Threatened Species* (2020): e.T39853A17958817.

[20] Zhou Qihai and Huang Chengming. "Advances in ecological research on the limestone langurs in China." *Acta Theriologica Sinica* 41 (2021): 60.

[21] Yaqiong Wan et al. "Predicting the potential distribution change of the endangered Francois' langur (*Trachypithecus francoisi*) across its entire range in China under climate change." *Ecology and Evolution* 14, e11684 (2024).

Xiulin Ye at al. "Climate and anthropogenic activities threaten two langur species irrespective of their range size." *Diversity and Distributions* 30, e13841 (2024).

[22] Xinrui Li et al. "Climate change and human activities promoted speciation of two endangered langurs (François' langur and white-headed langur)." *Global Ecology and Conservation* 38, e02185 (2022).

[23] 潘文石 等. 白头叶猴自然史. 北京: 北京大学出版社, 2016, 88.

[24] Tan, "The Status of Primates in China," 64–65

[25] 潘文石, 白头叶猴自然史, 58.

[26] Tan, "The Status of Primates in China," 65.

27 Chengming Huang et al. "Current status and conservation of white-headed langur (*Trachypithecus leucocephalus*) in China." *Biological Conservation* 104 (2002): 223–224.

28 Chengming Huang et al. "Karst Habitat Fragmentation and the Conservation of the White-headed Langur (*Trachypithecus leucocephalus*) in China." *Primate Conservation* 23 (2008): 137.

29 罗兰，"广西崇左：修复生态环境　护好石山精灵白头叶猴，" 央广网，August 24, 2022. http://gx.cnr.cn/cnrgx/yaowen/20220824/t20220824_525984627.shtml.

30 Ye at al., "Climate and anthropogenic activities threaten two langur species."

31 Yi-Ming Hu et al. "A new record of the capped langur (*Trachypithecus pileatus*) in China." *Zoological Research* 38 (2017): 203–205.

32 Christian Roos et al. "Mitogenomic phylogeny of the Asian colobine genus *Trachypithecus* with special focus on *Trachypithecus phayrei* (Blyth, 1847) and description of a new species." *Zoological Research* 41 (2020): 656–669.

33 B. Bleisch et al. "*Trachypithecus phayrei*." *The IUCN Red List of Threatened Species* (2020): e.T22040A17960739.

34 Liang-Wei Cui et al. "Distribution and conservation status of Shortridge's capped langurs *Trachypithecus shortridgei* in China." *Oryx* 50 (2016): 732–741.

35 Chi Ma et al. "Population and Conservation Status of Indochinese Gray Langurs (*Trachypithecus crepusculus*) in the Wuliang Mountains, Jingdong, Yunnan, China." *International Journal of Primatology* 36 (2015): 749–763.

36 Yuan Chen et al. "Asymmetric competition between sympatric endangered primates affects their population recovery." *Biological Conservation* 248, 108558 (2020).

37 The northernmost population of rhesus macaques lives north of the Yellow River in the Taihang Mountains, straddling the Henan-Shanxi border. Another, smaller group lived north of Beijing in Xinglong County, Hebei until dying out in the 1980s.
Lu Jiqi. *The Society of Taihangshan Macaques*. Zhengzhou: Henan Science and Technology Press, 2019. (Chinese with English chapter summaries)

38 Glover M. Allen. *The Mammals of China and Mongolia, Part 1*. New York: The American Museum of Natural History, 1938, 287–288.

39 Tan, "The Status of Primates in China," 63–81.

[40] Wenxiu Li and Erica von Essen. "Guarding crops from monkey troops: farmer-monkey interaction near a nature reserve in Guangxi, China." *Environmental Sociology* 7 (2021): 18–19.

[41] D. Chetry et al. "*Macaca arctoides.*" *The IUCN Red List of Threatened Species* (2020): e.T12548A185202632.

[42] R. Boonratana et al. "*Macaca assamensis.*" *The IUCN Red List of Threatened Species* (2020): e.T12549A17950189.

[43] Cheng Li, Chao Zhao and Peng-Fei Fan. "White-Cheeked Macaque (*Macaca leucogenys*): A New Macaque Species From Modog, Southeastern Tibet." *American Journal of Primatology* 77 (2015): 753–766.

Wenqiang Hu et al. "New records of the white-cheeked macaque provide range extension for the endangered primate in Gaoligong Mountains." *Primates* 65 (2024): 15–19.

The PRC claims Arunachal Pradesh as part of Tibet, but aside from a brief occupation of part of the state during the 1962 Sino-Indian War, China has not held or administered the territory.

Edible & Collectible

[1] In Chinese kopi luwak has an earthier name: catshit coffee (*māoshǐ kāfēi* 猫屎咖啡). The Asian palm civet *Paradoxurus hermaphroditus* is believed to eat only the choicest coffee cherries, and once the beans pass through the civet's gut and out the other end, they are still good for roasting (once thoroughly washed of course) and produce a less bitter brew. Kopi luwak can sell for exorbitant prices, but most civet coffee is produced from force-feeding caged animals, both causing great suffering to the civets and largely defeating the purpose as they then cannot choose the best beans.

Neil D'Cruze et al. "What is the true cost of the world's most expensive coffee?" *Oryx* 48 (2014): 170–171.

[2] Lanning, *Wild Life in China*, 213.

[3] Allen, *The Mammals of China and Mongolia, Part 1*, 423–429.

[4] Tan Bangjie. "Conservation and economic importance of the mustelids and viverrids in China." *Mustelid & Viverrid Conservation* 1 (1989): 5–6.

[5] Ming Wang et al. "SARS-CoV Infection in a Restaurant from Palm Civet." *Emerging Infectious Diseases* 11 (2005): 1860–1865.

[6] Arthur de Carle Sowerby. *The Naturalist in Manchuria, Vols. II & III*. Tientsin: Tientsin Press, 1923, 129–130.

[7] Lacy I. Moffett. *Common Birds of the Yangtze Delta*. Shanghai, 1912, 8.

[8] Johannes Kamp et al. "Global population collapse in a superabundant migratory bird and illegal trapping in China." *Conservation Biology* 29 (2015): 1685.

[9] Among the other threats to the yellow-breasted buntings is trapping in Thailand, Cambodia, and other Buddhist countries in Southeast Asia. There the birds are trapped and sold to Buddhist adherents who release animals back into the wild to make merit for their next life. Trappers and sellers are happy to take advantage of devotees, and the faithful are happy not to look into the consequences of their actions. Most of the released birds are already in poor health, and many end up re-caught and recycled to the next naif. This practice is hardly limited to yellow-breasted buntings, but happens with many species.

[10] Kamp et al., "Global population collapse in a superabundant migratory bird," 1689.

[11] Demand for wild birds grew so high that entire villages began to specialize in bird trapping.

[12] Kamp et al., "Global population collapse in a superabundant migratory bird," 1686.

[13] Kamp et al., "Global population collapse in a superabundant migratory bird," 1691.

[14] Between 2014 and 2018, the yellow-breasted buntings were seen again at sites in European Russia where they had not been sighted since 2000 or earlier. It is not yet clear if they have recolonized former territory, or whether instead the sightings were due to increased effort from observers.

[15] BirdLife International. "*Emberiza aureola*." *The IUCN Red List of Threatened Species* (2017): e.T22720966A119335690.

[16] Wieland Heim et al. "East Asian buntings: Ongoing illegal trade and encouraging conservation responses." *Conservation Science and Practice* 3, e405 (2021): 1–3.

[17] BirdLife International and the IUCN now list the white eared night-heron as *Oroanassa magnifica* based on the findings in Zhou et al., "Complete mitochondrial genomes render the Night Heron genus *Gorsachius* non-monophyletic," *Journal of Ornithology* 157 (2016): 505–513. At the time of writing, however, all published studies focused on the species have continued to use *Gorsachius magnificus*.

[18] John R. Fellowes et al. "Status update on White-eared Night Heron *Gorsachius magnificus* in South China." *Bird Conservation International* 11 (2001): 101–102.

[19] Wang Chao et al. "A New Bird Distribution and Breeding Record in Shaanxi Province—White-eared Night Heron (*Gorsachius magnificus*)." *Terrestrial Ecosystem and Conservation* 2 (2022): 87–89.

John D. Pilgrim et al. "The Endangered White-eared Night Heron *Gorsachius magnificus* in Vietnam: status, distribution, ecology and threats." *Forktail* 25 (2009): 142–146.

Shariq Shafi et al. "Extraordinary discovery in Bihar, India: an apparent White-eared Night Heron *Gorsachius magnificus* in Valmiki Tiger Reserve." *BirdingASIA* 29 (2018): 9–10.

Thomas N. E. Gray, Romica Grosu and Chum Sokkheng. "Unexpected discovery in the Cardamom Rainforest Landscape, Cambodia: a White-eared Night Heron *Gorsachius magnificus* in Botum Sakor National Park." *BirdingASIA* 32 (2019): 12–14.

Saeed H. Sadi et al. "White-eared Night Heron *Gorsachius magnificus* records in the Bangladesh Sundarbans: A new species for the country." *Indian BIRDS* 19 (2023): 50–52.

[20] Fellowes et al. "Status update on White-eared Night Heron," 109.

[21] Junhua Hu and Yang Liu. "Unveiling the Conservation Biogeography of a Data-Deficient Endangered Bird Species under Climate Change." *PLoS ONE* 9, e84529 (2014).

BirdLife International. "*Gorsachius magnificus.*" *The IUCN Red List of Threatened Species* (2017): e.T22697232A117359084.

[22] Jiang Yifan and Aron White, "Second draft revision of China's Wildlife Protection Law 'a big step backwards,'" *China Dialogue*, October 13, 2022. https://dialogue.earth/en/nature/second-draft-revision-of-chinas-wildlife-protection-law-a-big-step-backwards/.

Cui Qiwen, "Wildlife protection law: Controversy over captive breeding rumbles on," *China Dialogue*, July 5, 2023. https://dialogue.earth/en/nature/wildlife-protection-law-controversy-over-captive-breeding-rumbles-on/.

[23] Shi-Ping Gong et al. "Population status, distribution and conservation needs of the Endangered Mangshan pit viper *Protobothrops mangshanensis* of China." *Oryx* 47 (2013): 122–127.

[24] Zeshuai Deng et al. "Predicting the Spatial Distribution of the Mangshan Pit Viper (*Protobothrops mangshanensis*) under Climate Change Scenarios Using MaxEnt Modeling." *Forests* 15, 723 (2024).

[25] C. M. Huang et al. "Population and conservation strategies for the Chinese crocodile lizard (*Shinisaurus crocodilurus*) in China." *Animal Biodiversity and Conservation* 31 (2008): 63–70.

[26] T.Q. Nguyen, P. Hamilton and T. Ziegler. "*Shinisaurus crocodilurus*." *The IUCN Red List of Threatened Species* (2014): e.T57287221A57287235.

[27] Huang et al, "Population and conservation strategies for the Chinese crocodile lizard," 67.

[28] 黄乘明 主编. 濒危动物. 南京: 江苏凤凰科学技术出版社, 2014, 148–149.

[29] Huang et al, "Population and conservation strategies for the Chinese crocodile lizard," 66–67.

[30] Xiao-Li Zhang et al. "Climate Change and Dispersal Ability Jointly Affects the Future Distribution of Crocodile Lizards." *Animals* 12, 2731 (2022).

[31] 罗树毅, 徐芳英. "鳄蜥 '守株待兔' 的捕猎者." 森林与人类 381 (2022): 83–84.

Small & Forgotten

[1] 何晓瑞. "我国特有种滇螈的绝灭及其原因分析." 四川动物 (1998): 58–60.

[2] Jonathan L. Teichroew et al. "Is China's unparalleled and understudied bee diversity at risk?" *Biological Conservation* 210, Part B (2017): 19–28.

[3] "Hope for the Fireflies in Anlong Village," *WWF-China*, November 5, 2011. https://en.wwfchina.org/?3987/Hope-for-the-Fireflies-in-Anlong-Village.

[4] Huang Shaojie, "Conservationists in China Seek to Get Firefly Parks Closed," *The New York Times*, July 9, 2015. https://sinosphere.blogs.nytimes.com/2015/07/09/conservationists-in-china-seek-to-have-firefly-parks-closed/.

[5] Sara Lewis and Avalon C.S. Owens, "China's Endangered Fireflies," *Scientific American*, September 11, 2017. https://blogs.scientificamerican.com/observations/chinas-endangered-fireflies/.

[6] Liu Kun and Hou Liqiang, "Firefly enthusiast works to save delightful insects," *China Daily*, September 20, 2016. www.chinadaily.com.cn/china/2016-09/20/content_26836944.htm.

[7] Yu Shen. "Earthworms in Traditional Chinese Medicine: (Oligochaeta: Lumbricidae, Megascolecidae)." *Zoology in the Middle East* 51 (2010): 171–173.

[8] Alice Yan, "China faces earthworm wipeout as rampant growth in electro-harvesting threatens ecosystem," *South China Morning Post*, June 11, 2022. https://www.scmp.com/news/people-culture/environment/article/3181245/china-faces-earthworm-wipeout-rampant-growth.

Chen Nengchang, "Earthworms wiggle their way into China's policy protection," *China Dialogue*, October 12, 2023. https://dialogue.earth/en/nature/earthworms-wiggle-their-way-into-chinas-policy-protection/.

[9] Le Nguyen, "Chinese Medicinal Demand Fuels Earthworm Rush in Vietnam," *Voice of America*, August 21, 2023. https://www.voanews.com/a/chinese-medicinal-demand-fuels-earthworm-rush-in-vietnam-/7234382.html.

[10] Anderson Feijó et al. "Research trends on bats in China: A twenty-first century review." *Mammalian Biology* 98 (2019): 163–172.

[11] Jinhong Luo et al. "Bat conservation in China: should protection of subterranean habitats be a priority?" *Oryx* 47 (2013): 526.

One major reason few of China's bat species are known to be endangered is that for dozens of the species there is no information to tell whether their populations are declining. The situation for some could be dire, but then again perhaps none of them are doing too poorly. Of the populations surveyed, 62 were considered threatened within China as of 2013. In time more research will elucidate the status of the others.

[12] Libiao Zhang et al. "Conservation of bats in China: problems and recommendations." *Oryx* 43 (2009): 179–180.

[13] Luo et al. "Bat conservation in China," 526.

[14] Zhang et al. "Conservation of bats in China," 179–180.

[15] John Cohen. "Anywhere but here." *Science* 377 (2022): 805–809.

Tropics

[1] Hua Zhu. "The Tropical Forests of Southern China and Conservation of Biodiversity." *The Botanical Review* 83 (2017): 88–89.

[2] Peter Ashton and Hua Zhu. "The tropical-subtropical evergreen forest transition in East Asia: An exploration." *Plant Diversity* 42 (2020): 258–259.

Mêdog, formerly known as Pemakö, was one of the last places in the PRC to be fully explored and mapped. The region has recently seen a great increase in infrastructure construction and subsequent increase in human population and activity, but remains essentially forbidden for foreigners.

[3] Zhuo Zheng et al. "Anthropogenic impacts on Late Holocene land-cover change and floristic biodiversity loss in tropical southeastern Asia." *Proceedings of the National Academy of Sciences* 118, e2022210118 (2021): 2.

[4] Robert B. Marks. *China: Its Environment and History*. Lanham: Rowman & Littlefield. 2012, 127.

[6] Judith Shapiro. *Mao's War Against Nature: Politics and the Environment in Revolutionary China*. Cambridge: Cambridge University Press, 2001, 171–172.

[7] Shapiro, *Mao's War Against Nature*, 171–178.

[8] Shapiro, *Mao's War Against Nature*, 181–183.

[9] Hongmei Li et al. "Demand for rubber is causing the loss of high diversity rain forest in SW China." *Biodiversity and Conservation* 16 (2007): 1742.

[10] Li et al, "Demand for rubber," 1733–1743.

Megafaunal Retreat

[1] 张洁. "中国境内亚洲象分布及变迁的社会因素研究." 博士学位论文, 陕西师范大学, 2014, 18.

[2] The conclusion that elephants were not resident north of the Huai River Valley during the Bronze Age goes against the current scholarly consensus. Basing their conclusions on written records, depictions in bronzes and other artwork, and the presence of elephant bones at sites in North China, most biogeographic historians agree elephants were present in the region during the Shang dynasty and perhaps into the early period of the Zhou. Lander and Brunson (2018) strongly argue against this, pointing out that the only elephant remains found from that period in the region are likely to have been trade items or from captive elephants brought from the south. Testing has revealed that the other remains that have been offered as proof of elephant habitation are far older than initially presumed, and come from animals that lived c. 50,000 years ago. Thus, there is no clear, direct physical evidence for the presence of wild elephants in the Yellow River Valley or elsewhere north of the Huai. That conclusion, of course, is not definitive, but seems the stronger case.

[3] Brian Lander and Katherine Brunson. "Wild Mammals of Ancient North China." *Journal of Chinese History* 2, special no. 2 (2018): 302.

[4] Lander and Brunson, "Wild Mammals of Ancient North China," 302.

Han Fei was offering an explanation as to why the Chinese character for "image" 像 contained the character for "elephant" 象.

[5] 张洁, "中国境内亚洲象分布及变迁的社会因素研究," 21–25.

[6] Thomas R. Trautman. *Elephants and Kings: An Environmental History*. Chicago: University of Chicago Press 2015, 299–305.

[7] Edward H. Schafer. "War Elephants in Ancient and Medieval China." *Oriens* 10 (1957): 290–291.

[8] 张洁，"中国境内亚洲象分布及变迁的社会因素研究，" 23–35.

[9] Elvin, *The Retreat of the Elephants*, 9.

[10] Berthold Laufer. *Ivory in China*. Chicago: Field Museum of Natural History, 1925, 7.

[11] Rowan Flad. "Bronze, Jade, Gold, and Ivory: Valuable Objects in Ancient Sichuan," in *The Construction of Value in the Ancient World*, ed. John K. Papadopoulos and Gary Urton. Los Angeles: Cotsen Institute of Archaeology Press, 2012, 328–329.

[12] Laufer, *Ivory in China*, 10–13.

[13] 张洁，"中国境内亚洲象分布及变迁的社会因素研究，" 31–32.

[14] Elvin, *The Retreat of the Elephants*, 15.

[15] Fan Chengda. *Treatise of the Supervisor and Guardian of the Cinnamon Sea*. Translated by James M. Hargett. Seattle: University of Washington Press, 2010, 69–72.

[16] Nie Chuanping. "The distribution and retreat of wild elephants in Ling Nan area during the Tang and Song dynasties." *Journal of Chinese Historical Geography* 33 (2018): 74.

[17] Robert B. Marks. *Tigers, Rice, Silk, and Silt: Environment and Economy in Late Imperial South China*. Cambridge: Cambridge University Press, 1998, 45.

[18] Elvin, *The Retreat of the Elephants*, 13.

[19] Laufer, *Ivory in China*, 13–14.

[20] Trautman, *Elephants and Kings*, 303–304.

[21] Michael J. Hathaway. *Environmental Winds: Making the Global in Southwest China*. Berkeley: University of California Press, 2013, 158–159.

[22] 张立. 中国亚洲象保护研究. 北京: 科学出版社, 2018, 8.

[23] Hathaway, *Environmental Winds*, 159.

[24] Li Zhang, Lichao Ma and Limin Feng. "New challenges facing traditional nature reserves: Asian elephant (*Elephas maximus*) conservation in China." *Integrative Zoology* 1 (2006): 180.

[25] Peng Liu et al. "Conflict between conservation and development: cash forest encroachment in Asian elephant distributions." *Scientific Reports* 7, 6404 (2017): 2.

Zhang, Ma and Feng, "New challenges facing traditional nature reserves," 180.

[26] Zhang, Ma and Feng, "New challenges facing traditional nature reserves," 181.

[27] Tang Xiyang. *Living Treasures: An Odyssey Through China's Extraordinary Nature Reserves*. New York: Bantam, 1987, 57.

[28] Charles Santiapillai et al. "Distribution of Elephant in Xishuangbanna Dai Autonomous Prefecture, China." *Gajah* 12 (1994): 41.

[29] Hathaway, *Environmental Winds*, 180.

[30] Hathaway, *Environmental Winds*, 172–178.

In the 1980s throwing a stick of dynamite had become a reliable means of scaring off elephants, but the supply ran dry in the 1990s.

[31] Li Zhang. "Current Status of Asian Elephants in China." *Gajah* 35 (2011): 44–45.

[32] Liu et al. "Conflict between conservation and development," 2–4.

[33] Li Zhang et al. "Asian Elephants in China: Estimating Population Size and Evaluating Habitat Suitability." *PLoS ONE* 10, e0124834 (2015): 10.

[34] Ahimsa Campos-Arceiz et al. "The return of the elephants: How two groups of dispersing elephants attracted the attention of billions and what can we learn from their behavior." *Conservation Letters* 14, e12836 (2021).

[35] Clem Tisdell and Zhu Xiang. "Protected Areas, Agricultural Pests and Economic Damage: Conflicts with Elephants and Pests in Yunnan." *Environmentalist* 18 (1998): 106.

[36] Lauren J. Hale et al. "Social structure and demography of a remnant Asian elephant *Elephas maximus* population and the implications for survival." *Oryx* 55 (2021): 475.

[37] Zhigang Jiang, Chunwang Li and Chenchen Ding. "The roaming wild Asian elephants of Yunnan, China, pose a challenge to conservation." *Oryx* 55 (2021): 650.

[38] Yang Jinghao, "Reporter's diary: A look back on China's migrating elephants," *CGTN*, January 1, 2022. https://news.cgtn.com/news/2021-12-31/Reporter-s-diary-A-look-back-on-China-s-migrating-elephants-16rlnu07LwY/index.html.

[39] Campos-Arceiz et al. "The return of the elephants."

[40] Haijun Wang et al. "What triggered the Asian elephant's northward migration across southwestern Yunnan?" *The Innovation* 2, 100142 (2021).

[41] Ying Chen et al. "Is there scope for growth? Mapping habitat suitability for Asian elephant (*Elephas maximus*) across its range in China." *Global Ecology and Conservation* 47, e02665 (2023).

[42] Wenwen Li et al. "Identifying climate refugia and its potential impact on small population of Asian elephant (*Elephas maximus*) in China." *Global Ecology and Conservation* 19, e00664 (2019).

[43] 聂选华. "环境史视野下中国犀牛的分布与变迁." 文山学院学报 28 (2015): 68.

[44] Jan Chapman. *The Art of Rhinoceros Horn Carving in China*. London: Christie's Books, 1999: 16–17.

[45] Natasha Heller. "Why Has the Rhinoceros Come from the West? An Excursus into the Religious, Literary, and Environmental History of the Tang Dynasty." *Journal of the American Oriental Society* 131 (2011).

[46] Chapman, "*The Art of Rhinoceros Horn Carving in China*," 37–39.

After the Communist victory in 1949, lack of foreign exchange holdings made it difficult to import new rhino horn for pharmaceutical use. The solution was to turn to antiques, such as carved cups. These items, many of them outstanding works of art and literal museum pieces, were ground into powder for incorporation into medicines.
Esmond Bradley Martin. "Medicines from Chinese Treasures." *Pachyderm* 13 (1990): 12–15.

[47] Brian Lander and Katherine Brunson. "The Sumatran rhinoceros was extirpated from mainland East Asia by hunting and habitat loss." *Current Biology* 28 (2018): R252–R253.

[48] 聂选华, "环境史视野下中国犀牛的分布与变迁," 70–71.

[49] 聂选华, "环境史视野下中国犀牛的分布与变迁," 68–70.

[50] S. Ellis and B. Talukdar. "*Dicerorhinus sumatrensis*." *The IUCN Red List of Threatened Species* (2020): e.T6553A18493355.

At the Frontier

[1] Fei Li et al. "Rediscovery of the sun bear (*Helarctos malayanus*) in Yingjiang County, Yunnan Province, China." *Zoological Research* 38 (2017): 206–207.

[2] Tan Bangjie. "Conservation and economic importance of the mustelids and viverrids in China." *Mustelid & Viverrid Conservation* 1 (1989): 5–6.

[3] Huang Cheng, Li Xueyou and Jiang Xuelong. "Confirmation of the continued occurrence of Binturong *Arctictis binturong* in China." *Small Carnivore Conservation* 55 (2015): 59–63.

[4] 白德凤 等. "西双版纳尚勇自然保护区哺乳动物物种多样性." 生物多样性 26 (2018): 75–78.

[5] G. Huang et al. "Combining camera-trap surveys and hunter interviews to determine the status of mammals in protected rainforests and rubber plantations of Menglun, Xishuangbanna, SW China." *Animal Conservation* 23 (2020): 689–699.

[6] 胡松梅, 曹龙, 张婉婉, "令人叹为观止的西汉皇家苑囿——霸陵与南陵出土珍禽异兽及," 中国社会科学报, August 4, 2023. https://www.cssn.cn/skgz/bwyc/202308/t20230804_5677049.shtml.

[7] Chenchen Ding et al. "Distribution and habitat suitability assessment of the gaur *Bos gaurus* in China." *Biodiversity Science* 26 (2018): 951–961.

The status of the gaur population in southeastern Tibet is uncertain. There seems to be adequate habitat to support a population of survivors, though they would likely be in decline due to the degradation of their forests.

[8] Chenchen Ding et al. "Probable extirpation of the hog deer from China: implications for conservation." *Oryx* 56 (2022): 360–366.

[9] Qiu Mingjiang, Zhang Ming and Liu Wulin. "A preliminary study on the Bengal tiger (*Panthera tigris tigris*) in Namcha Barwa, Southeastern Tibet." *Acta Theriologica Sinica* 17 (1997): 1–7.

[10] Qiu Mingjiang. "Preserving Tigers in Southeast Tibet." Research proposal. 1996.

[11] Baker, Ian. *The Heart of the World: A Journey to the Last Secret Place*. New York: Penguin Press, 2004, 223.

In his book, Ian Baker includes a 2001 article from Chinese state media reporting on a scheme to save Tibet's Bengal tiger population by driving them away from villages, further into the hills. Since the tigers would have too little prey to sustain them there, pig farms would be built nearby, and the pigs would be used as tiger food, thus saving local herders' yaks. There is no indication the idea was ever implemented, a stroke of good luck for all concerned.

[12] Xueyou Li et al. "Camera-trap surveys reveal high diversity of mammals and pheasants in Medog, Tibet." *Oryx* 55 (2021): 177–178.

Xue-You Li et al. "Tiger reappearance in Medog highlights the conservation values of the region for this apex predator." *Zoological Research* 44 (2023): 747–749.

[13] Wang Yuan et al. "Investigation on the population of wild Bengal tiger (*Panthera tigris tigris*) in Medog, Tibet." *Acta Theriologica Sinica* 39 (2019): 504–513.

[14] Tan Bangjie. "Status and Problems of Captive Tigers in China," in *Tigers of the World: The Biology, Biopolitics, Management, and Conservation of an Endangered Species*, ed. Ronald L. Tilson and Ulysses S. Seal. Park Ridge: Noyes Publications, 1987, 144.

[15] Luo Shu-jin. "The status of the tiger in China. *Cat News* sp. 5 (2010): 12.

Pushing Towards Extinction

[1] 孙戈. "最迷人的猫，却有最恐怖的层脸杀，" // 来！聆听大自然的呼唤. 宋大昭, 黄巧雯 主编. 上海: 上海科技教育出版社, 2020, 114.

[2] Tan Bangjie. "The Status of Felids in China." *Proceedings from the Cat Specialist Group meeting in Kanha National Park*. (1984): 39–40.

[3] 宋大昭. "它们挺过640多万年，成了中国最濒危的大猫，" // 来！聆听大自然的呼唤. 宋大昭, 黄巧雯 主编. 上海: 上海科技教育出版社, 2020, 21.

[4] Zhiyu Ma et al. "An update on the current distribution and key habitats of the clouded leopard (*Neofelis nebulosa*) populations in China." *Biodiversity Science* 30, 22349 (2022): 6.

[5] 紫鹬, "又到国际云豹日，新一年里，云豹在中国的境况如何？" 猫盟 CFCA, August 4, 2023. https://mp.weixin.qq.com/s/B3ReBpgXgWrSA9ZNZ4xVJg.

[6] T. Gray et al. "*Neofelis nebulosa*." *The IUCN Red List of Threatened Species* (2021): e.T14519A198843258..

[7] David W. Macdonald et al. "Multi-scale habitat modelling identifies spatial conservation priorities for mainland clouded leopards (*Neofelis nebulosa*)." *Diversity and Distributions* 25 (2019): 1651.

[8] Allen, *The Mammals of China and Mongolia, Part 1*, 359–360.

[9] J.F. Kamler et al. "*Cuon alpinus*." *The IUCN Red List of Threatened Species* (2015): e.T5953A72477893.

[10] 宋大昭. "今天说说中国的豺，消逝和归来，" // 来！聆听大自然的呼唤. 宋大昭, 黄巧雯 主编. 上海: 上海科技教育出版社, 2020, 66.

[11] To be pedantic, the term "peacock" refers to the male peafowl, while the term for the female is "peahen."

[12] Mingxiao Yan et al. "The Range Contraction and Future Conservation of Green Peafowl (*Pavo muticus*) in China." *Sustainability* 13, 11723 (2021): 4–8.

13 The green peafowl has seen its range contract not only in China, but over most of South and Southeast Asia. It is now gone from Peninsular Malaysia, Bangladesh and India, and has suffered severe declines in Vietnam, Cambodia, Laos, Myanmar, and Indonesia. The species seems to be faring best in Thailand, where some populations are stable and perhaps even growing.

14 Dejun Kong et al. "Status and distribution changes of the endangered Green Peafowl (*Pavo muticus*) in China over the past three decades (1990s–2017)." *Avian Research* 9 (2018): 7.

15 P. J. K. McGowan et al. "A review of the status of the Green Peafowl *Pavo muticus* and recommendations for future action." *Bird Conservation International* 8 (1998): 343.

16 McGowan et al., "A review of the status of the Green Peafowl," 339 & 343.

17 Yan et al. (2021) give the latest estimate of 240 to 280 wild green peafowl still living in China.

18 Yan et al. "The Range Contraction and Future Conservation of Green Peafowl," 2–8.

19 Yang Wanli and Li Yingqing, "Warning signals flash for endangered birds," *China Daily Global*, August 11, 2021. https://www.chinadaily.com.cn/a/202108/11/WS611308a6a310efa1bd667fce.html.

20 Li You, "Yunnan Court's Ruling May Not Stop Damaging Dam, Activists Warn," *Sixth Tone*, March 26, 2020. https://www.sixthtone.com/news/1005387.

21 Laura Zhou, "Court reprieve for China's rare green peafowl but it's not out of the woods yet," *South China Morning Post*, January 3, 2021. https://www.scmp.com/news/china/politics/article/3116193/court-reprieve-chinas-rare-green-peafowl-its-not-out-woods-yet.

Juan Chu. "Protecting the Habitats of Endangered Species Through Environmental Public Interest Litigation in China: Lessons Learned from Peafowl Versus the Dam." *Journal of Environmental Law* 35 (2023): 455–466.

22 H.J. Chatterjee, J.S.Y. Tse and S.T. Turvey. "Using Ecological Niche Modelling to Predict Spatial and Temporal Distribution Patterns in Chinese Gibbons: Lessons from the Present and the Past." *Folia Primatologica* 83 (2012): 90–91.

23 Samuel T. Turvey et al. "New genus of extinct Holocene gibbon associated with humans in Imperial China." *Science* 360 (2018): 1346–1349.

24 R. H. van Gulik. *The Gibbon in China: An Essay in Chinese Animal Lore*. Leiden: E. J. Brill, 1967, 37.

25 As discussed in the section on François' langurs, the apes mentioned in Chinese poetry may in fact be the langurs and not gibbons. Whether misattributed or not, today in the popular consciousness the apes mournfully calling in the poems are gibbons.

26 van Gulik, *The Gibbon in China*, 40.

27 van Gulik, *The Gibbon in China*, 48.

van Gulik noted that killing a mother gibbon to capture her young remained the preferred method of hunters in much of Southeast Asia at the time he was writing.

28 Kefeng Niu et al. "Is Yuan in China's Three Gorges a Gibbon or a Langur?" *International Journal of Primatology* (2022).

29 Tan Bangjie. "The Status of Primates in China." *Primate Conservation* 5 (1985): 77.

30 W. Brockelman and T. Geissmann. "*Hylobates lar.*" *The IUCN Red List of Threatened Species* (2008): e.T10548A3199623.

31 Cyril C. Grueter et al. "Are *Hylobates lar* Extirpated from China?" *International Journal of Primatology* 30 (2009): 553–567.

32 Peng-Fei Fan, Han-Lan Fei and Ai-Dong Luo. "Ecological extinction of the Critically Endangered northern white-cheeked gibbon *Nomascus leucogenys* in China." *Oryx* 48 (2013): 52–55.

33 Fan Peng-Fei and Huo Sheng. "The northern white-cheeked gibbon (*Nomascus leucogenys*) is on the edge of extinction in China." *Gibbon Journal* 5 (2009): 48.

34 Fan, Fei and Luo, "Ecological extinction," 54.

35 Pengfei F. et al. "*Nomascus concolor.*" *The IUCN Red List of Threatened Species* (2020): e.T39775A17968556.

36 Li Genhui et al. "Population size and distribution of western black crested gibbon (*Nomascus concolor*) in Ailao Mountain, Chuxiong Prefecture, Yunnan Province." *Acta Theriologica Sinica* 43 (2023): 513–522.

37 Peng-Fei Fan et al. "Population recovery of the critically endangered western black crested gibbon (Nomascus concolor) in Mt. Wuliang, Yunnan, China." *Zoological Research* 43 (2022): 180–183.

38 Yuan Chen et al. "Asymmetric competition between sympatric endangered primates affects their population recovery." *Biological Conservation* 248, 108558 (2020).

[39] Ni Qing-yong and Ma Shi-lai. "Population and Distribution of the Black Crested Gibbons in Southern and Southeastern Yunnan." *Zoological Research* 27 (2006): 34–40.

[40] Xuelong Jiang et al. "Status and distribution pattern of black crested gibbon (*Nomascus concolor jingdongensis*) in Wuliang Mountains, Yunnan, China: implication for conservation." *Primates* 47 (2006): 264–271.

[41] Lori K. Sheeran and Frank E. Poirier. "The Black-crested Gibbon of China." *Primate Conservation* 11 (1990): 20–22.

[42] Fan et al., "Population recovery," 180–183.

[43] When they were considered the same species, *Nomascus concolor* was called the western black crested gibbon and *N. nasutus* the eastern black crested gibbon. Some sources still refer to them by those names.

[44] T. Geissmann et al. "Rarest ape species rediscovered in Vietnam." *Asian Primates* 8 (2003): 8–9.

[45] Chan Bosco Pui Lok, Tan Xue-feng and Tan Wu-jing. "Rediscovery of the critically endangered eastern black-crested gibbon *Nomascus nasutus* (Hylobatidae) in China, with preliminary notes on population size, ecology and conservation status." *Asian Primates Journal* 1 (2008): 17–25.

[46] Russell A. Mittermeier et al. "Primates in Peril: The World's 25 Most Endangered Primates 2008–2010." *Primate Conservation* 24 (2009): 26.

[47] Chang-yong Ma et al. "Transboundary conservation of the last remaining population of the cao vit gibbon *Nomascus nasutus*." *Oryx* 54 (2020): 776–783.

[48] O.R. Wearn et al. *Conservation Action Plan for the Cao Vit Gibbon (Nomascus nasutus) 2021 – 2030 with a Vision to 2050*. Fauna & Flora International – Vietnam Programme, Hanoi and IUCN SSC Conservation Planning Specialist Group, 2022, 8–9.

[49] Oliver R. Wearn et al. "Vocal fingerprinting reveals a substantially smaller global population of the Critically Endangered cao vit gibbon (*Nomascus nasutus*) than previously thought." *Scientific Reports* 14, 416 (2024).

[50] Wearn et al., *Conservation Action Plan for the Cao Vit Gibbon*, 19–22.

Hainan

[1] For comparison, Hainan is roughly the size of the US state of Maryland, or the country of Belgium. Compared to other islands, it is roughly the same size as Vancouver Island, slightly smaller than Taiwan, and about half the size of Tasmania or Sri Lanka.

[2] Marks, *China: Its Environment and History*, 194–196.

Marks notes the complexity of ethnic relations, and that the received narrative of a Han Chinese cultural juggernaut destroying and assimilating all in its path was not so simple. Many early Chinese migrants to Hainan in fact took on Hlai (黎族) customs, and eventually assimilated into Hlai communities, not vice versa. This was true of not only Hainan, but many frontier regions throughout Chinese history.

[3] Marks, *China: Its Environment and History*, 196–199.

[4] Mingxia Zhang and Jianguo Zhu. "Natural Forest Change in Hainan, China, 1991–2008 and Conservation Suggestions," in *Tropical Forests*, ed. Padmini Sudarshana. London: Intech, 2012, 297–301.

[5] Edward H. Schafer. *Shore of Pearls*. Berkeley: University of California Press, 1970, 48.

[6] Jessica V. Bryant. "Developing a conservation evidence-base for the Critically Endangered Hainan gibbon (*Nomascus hainanus*)." Doctoral thesis, University College London. 2014, 32–33.

[7] Translated by Tim Jeffree from the original Chinese, in Bryant (2014):
柏家渡西日欲落，青山上下猿鳥樂。
Bǎijiādù xī rì yù luò, qīngshān shàngxià yuán niǎo lè.
欲因新月望吳雲，遙看北斗掛南嶽。
Yù yīn xīn yuè wàng wú yún, yáo kàn běidǒu guà nányuè.
一夢愔愔四十秋，古人不死終未休。
Yī mèng yīn yīn sìshí qiū, gǔrén bùsǐ zhōng wèi xiū.
草舍蕭條誰與語，香風欲過白蘋州。
Cǎo shě xiāotiáo shuí yǔ yǔ, xiāng fēng yùguò bái píng zhōu.

[8] Robert Swinhoe. "On the Mammals of Hainan.' *Proceedings of the Zoological Society of London* (1870): 224–225.

[9] 文榕生. 中国珍稀野生动物分布变迁 (续:) 中. 济南: 山东科学技术出版社, 2018, 909–912.

[10] Bryant, "Developing a conservation evidence-base," 128.

[11] Jiang Zhou et al. "Hainan Black-crested Gibbon Is Headed For Extinction." *International Journal of Primatology* 26 (2005): 455.

[12] Zhou et al., "Hainan Black-crested Gibbon," 458–461.

[13] Zhou et al., "Hainan Black-crested Gibbon," 462.

[14] Zhou et al., "Hainan Black-crested Gibbon," 456.

[15] John R. Fellowes et al. "Current status of the Hainan gibbon (*Nomascus hainanus*): progress of population monitoring and other priory actions." *Asian Primates Journal* 1 (2008).

[16] Bryant, "Developing a conservation evidence-base," 48–53.

[17] T. Geissmann and W. Bleisch. "*Nomascus hainanus*." *The IUCN Red List of Threatened Species* (2020): e.T41643A17969392.

[18] "海南长臂猿种群数量稳定增长至7群42只," 新华网, June 21, 2024. http://www.xinhuanet.com/local/20240621/f0845a3c45ae432c8d16a851a4f4350c/c.html.

[19] Guioqi Liu et al. "The Critically Endangered Hainan Gibbon (*Nomascus hainanus*) Population Increases but not at the Maximum Possible Rate." *International Journal of Primatology* (2022): 9–11.

[20] The taxonomy of Eld's deer is a work in progress. Formerly placed in the genus *Cervus*, it has more recently been moved to *Rucervus*. That placement is now being reconsidered, with the latest research suggesting it is closely related to the elaphure *Elaphurus davidianus* and should be placed in the genus *Panolia*. Once done we can hope that settles the matter, but don't hold your breath.

[21] T.N.E. Gray et al. "*Rucervus eldii*." *The IUCN Red List of Threatened Species* (2015): e.T4265A22166803.

[22] Chenqing Zheng et al. "Whole-Genome Analyses Reveal the Distinct Taxonomic Status of the Hainan Population of Endangered *Rucervus eldii* and Its Conservation Implications." *Evolutionary Applications* 17, e70010 (2024).

[23] Michelle H.G. Wong, Yanni Mo and Bosco Pui Lok Chan. "Past, present and future of the globally endangered Eld's deer (*Rucervus eldii*) on Hainan Island, China." *Global Ecology and Conservation* 26, e01505 (2021): 7.

[24] Allen, *The Mammals of China and Mongolia, Part 2*, 1175.

[25] Zhi-Gao Zeng et al. "Distribution, status and conservation of Hainan Eld's deer (*Cervus eldi hainanus*) in China." *Folia Zoologica* 54 (2005): 251.

[26] Zeng et al., "Distribution, status and conservation of Hainan Eld's deer," 251.

[27] Zeng et al., "Distribution, status and conservation of Hainan Eld's deer," 255.

[28] Wong, Mo and Chan, "Past, present and future," 10.

[29] Zeng et al., "Distribution, status and conservation of Hainan Eld's deer," 255.

[30] Zeng et al., "Distribution, status and conservation of Hainan Eld's deer," 255.

[31] Tang Xiyang. *Living Treasures: An Odyssey Through China's Extraordinary Nature Reserves*. New York: Bantam, 1987, 145–146.

[32] Wong, Mo and Chan, "Past, present and future," 10.

[33] Zeng et al., "Distribution, status and conservation of Hainan Eld's deer," 252.

[34] Wong, Mo and Chan, "Past, present and future," 7.

[35] Wei Liang and Zhengwang Zhang. "Hainan Peacock Pheasant (*Polyplectron katsumatae*): an endangered and rare tropical forest bird." *Chinese Birds* 2 (2011): 111–116.

[36] BirdLife International. "*Polyplectron katsumatae*." *The IUCN Red List of Threatened Species* (2022): e.T22734897A207341783.
The study authors give an estimated population range of 700–2,000 mature individuals.

[37] Yifu Wang, Nigel Leader-Williams and Samuel T. Turvey. "Exploitation Histories of Pangolins and Endemic Pheasants on Hainan Island, China: Baselines and Shifting Social Norms." *Frontiers in Ecology and Evolution* 9, 608057 (2021): 7–8.

[38] Samuel T. Turvey et al. "Local ecological knowledge and regional sighting histories of Hainan Peacock-pheasant *Polyplectron katsumatae*: pessimism or optimism for a threatened island endemic?" *Bird Conservation International* 33, e25 (2023).

[39] Liang Wei et al. "Surveys of the Hainan partridge *Arborophila ardens* on Hainan Island, China." *International Galliformes Symposium 2004*. 174–178.

[40] BirdLife International. "*Arborophila ardens*." *The IUCN Red List of Threatened Species* (2016): e.T22679063A92802107.

Trade Species

[1] 管开云，郭忠仁 主编. 中国濒危动植物寻踪——植物卷. 北京：北京出版社, 2019, 229.

[2] Zhu, Annah Lake. *Rosewood: Endangered Species Conservation and the Rise of Global China*. Cambridge: Harvard University Press, 2022, 43–45.

[3] Zhu, *Rosewood*, 18.

[4] Zhu, *Rosewood*, 18–20.

[5] Elvin, *The Retreat of the Elephants*, 17–18.

[6] Edward H. Schafer. *The Vermilion Bird: T'ang Images of the South.* Berkeley: University of California Press, 1967, 216–217.

[7] Leonard Clark. *A Wanderer Till I Die.* New York: Funk & Wagnalls, 1937.

[8] B. Stuart et al. "*Python bivittatus* (errata version published in 2019)." *The IUCN Red List of Threatened Species* (2012): e.T193451A151341916.

[9] David G. Barker and Tracy M. Barker. "The Distribution of the Burmese Python, *Python molurus bivittatus.*" *Bulletin of the Chicago Herpetological Society* 43 (2008): 33–35.

David G. Barker and Tracy M. Barker. "The Distribution of the Burmese Python, *Python bivittatus*, in China." *Bulletin of the Chicago Herpetological Society* 45 (2010): 86–88.

[10] Stuart et al, "*Python bivittatus.*"

[11] Edward H. Schafer. *The Golden Peaches of Samarkand: A Study of T'ang Exotics.* Berkeley: University of California Press, 1963, 198.

Schafer notes that, because the geckos were used as a way to guard against sexual disloyalty to the emperor, they were called "palace warders," *shǒugōng* 守宮, while the paste into which they were made was called *shǒugōng shā* 守宮砂.

The oldest existing testament to this use is from the Western Jin scholar Zhang Hua (張華, 232–300). The original passage from his *Records of Diverse Matters* (博物志) reads: 蜥蜴或名蝘蜓，以器養之，食以朱砂，體盡赤。所食滿七斤，治擣萬杵，點女人肢體，終身不滅，唯房室事則。

[12] A.B. Cunningham and Xingchao Long. "Linking resource supplies and price drivers: Lessons from Traditional Chinese Medicine (TCM) price volatility and change, 2002–2017." *Journal of Ethnopharmacology* 229 (2019): 206–213.

[13] Liz P.Y. Chee. *Mao's Bestiary: Medicinal Animals and Modern China.* Durham: Duke University Press, 2021, 90.

[14] K. Lwin et al. "*Gekko gecko.*" *The IUCN Red List of Threatened Species* (2019): e.T195309A2378260.

[15] T.Q. Nguyen, B. Cai and J. Yang. "*Gekko reevesii.*" *The IUCN Red List of Threatened Species* (2021): e.T104717831A104718941.

[16] In 2022 an analysis of pygmy slow loris genetics showed the species to have diverged from other slow lorises between 4.9 and 21 million years ago, and that the divergence is now wide enough to warrant placing them in a separate genus, *Xanthonycticebus*. The suggested change to their taxonomy is new enough that it is not in common use, but future publications will likely increasingly favor *Xanthonycticebus* over *Nycticebus*.

Nekaris and Nijman. "A new genus name for pygmy lorises, *Xanthonycticebus* gen. nov. (Mammalia, primates)." *Zoosystematics and Evolution* 98 (2022): 87–92.

[17] Slow lorises gained attention on social media in part from videos of owners tickling their pet lorises' bellies. The lorises respond by raising their arms over their heads, an act often interpreted as a sign of enjoyment. In fact, lorises raise their arms as a defensive gesture. They activate their venom by combining their saliva with oil from glands located on their inner arms, and their painful bite can kill small animals and lead to anaphylactic shock—and potentially death—in humans. Pet traders pull or cut lorises' front teeth to render them harmless, a practice which often proves fatal due to blood loss or infection.

Researchers hypothesize that slow lorises' use of venom evolved as part of a suite of attributes that mimic cobras. Aside from venom, lorises have facial markings that resemble the spectacled cobra (*Naja naja*), especially when its arms are raised in defense. The small primates even move in a serpentine manner, and they hiss in close imitation of the snakes.

K Anne-Isola Nekaris et al. "Mad, bad and dangerous to know: the biochemistry, ecology and evolution of slow loris venom." *Journal of Venomous Animals and Toxins including Tropical Diseases* 19, 21 (2013).

[18] Qingyong Ni et al. "Distribution and Conservation Status of Slow Lorises in Indo-China," in *Evolution, Ecology and Conservation of Lorises and Pottos*, ed. K. A. I. Nekaris and Anne M. Burrows. Cambridge: Cambridge University Press, 2020, 326.

[19] Tan Bangjie. "The Status of Primates in China," *Primate Conservation* 5 (1985): 64.

[20] Ni et al. "Distribution and Conservation Status of Slow Lorises in Indo-China," 328.

[21] Ni et al. "Distribution and Conservation Status of Slow Lorises in Indo-China," 332–333.

[22] 全国强 等. "我国灵长目一种的新记录." 兽类学报 7 (1987): 158.

[23] Zhao et al. "Distribution and conservation status of Lorisinae primates in the middle and lower reaches of Nanxi River in southeastern Yunnan." *Acta Theriologica Sinica* 44 (2024): 85–93.

Coasts & Marine Waters

[1] The names of China's three major seas all closely match their English equivalents. The Yellow Sea is known as *Huáng Hǎi* (黄海) literally "yellow" and "sea." The East China Sea is *Dōng Hǎi* (东海), with *Dōng* meaning "east." The South China Sea is *Nán Hǎi* (南海), *Nán* predictably meaning "south."

[2] *Wōkòu* (倭寇) literally means "dwarf pirates" or "dwarf bandits." The word *Wō* (倭) can also mean "submissive" or "distant," and was the first known name applied to the Japanese. Whether it was at first meant as a pejorative is unknown, but today it is used as a slur common in the invective Chinese Japanophobes direct towards their neighbors and rivals across the East China Sea.

[3] The name for the Gulf of Tonkin derives from the Vietnamese name for Hanoi during the Lê dynasty, Đông Kinh or "Eastern Capital." Westerners used the name to refer to the northern half of modern Vietnam. In Chinese it is known as the Northern Gulf, *Běibù Wān* 北部湾.

[4] Zhao Ji et al. *The Natural History of China*. London: Collins, 1990, 109.

[5] For a thorough overview and history of China's expansive claims to the South China Sea, see Bill Hayton. *The South China Sea: The Struggle for Power in Asia*. New Haven: Yale University Press, 2014.

[6] Marks, *China: Its Environment and History*, 127.

[7] Marks, *China: Its Environment and History*, 127.

[8] Koxinga (or Coxinga), is also known by the Mandarin pronunciation of his given name Zheng Chenggong 鄭成功. "Koxinga" comes from the Hokkienese pronunciation of the title the Longwu Emperor (隆武帝, 1602–1646, r. 1645–1646) of the Southern Ming bestowed upon him, *Kok-sèng-iâ* 國姓爺, meaning "Lord of the Imperial Surname."

[9] The *li* is a traditional Chinese measure of distance, and its value has changed over the course of history. Today one *li* has been standardized to equal 500 m (1,640 ft).

[10] Robert B. Marks. *Tigers, Rice, Silk, and Silt: Environment and Economy in Late Imperial South China*. Cambridge: Cambridge University Press, 1998, 151–161.

[11] J. Y. Liu. "Status of Marine Biodiversity of the China Seas." *PLoS ONE* 8, e50719 (2013).

[12] Ting-ting Jiang et al. "Current status of coastal wetlands in China: Degradation, restoration, and future management." *Estuarine, Coastal and Shelf Science* 164 (2015): 265–275.

[13] Mark Barter. *Shorebirds of the Yellow Sea: Importance, threats and conservation status*. Canberra: Wetlands International, 2002, 88–89.

[14] Zhigao Sun et al. "China's coastal wetlands: Conservation history, implementation efforts, existing issues and strategies for future improvement." *Environment International* 79 (2015): 25–41.

Yellow Sea

[1] Guannan Wen et al. "Low diversity, little genetic structure but no inbreeding in a high-density island endemic pit-viper *Gloydius shedaoensis*." *Current Zoology* 68 (2022): 526–534.

[2] There are in fact no natural standing bodies of water on Shedao. The snakes rely instead on dew for much of their water, although now artificial pools have been installed around the island to provide a larger, more reliable supply.

[3] Richard Shine et al. "A review of 30 years of ecological research on the Shedao pitviper, *Gloydius shedaoensis*." *Herpetological Natural History* 9 (2002): 3.

[4] 李继宣, 栾永贵. 中国蛇岛. 北京: 中国环境科学出版社出版, 1990: 48–49.

[5] Shine et al., "A review of 30 years of ecological research," 10–11.

[6] Wen et al. "Low diversity, little genetic structure," 5.

[7] When the Qing dynasty still laid claim to northern Manchuria and its coasts, a second pinniped, the northern fur seal *Callorhinus ursinus*, could be said to have inhabited Chinese waters. The fur seals were prized not only for their fur, but especially for their penises, which were used as remedies for various maladies and to improve waning virility.

[8] Baengnyeong-do (백령도) is the westernmost point of the Republic of Korea, and sits just below the Northern Limit Line that demarcates South and North Korean waters.

[9] When the Kangxi Emperor stopped over at Mukden (Shenyang) during his 1682 tour of Manchuria, emissaries from the Korean Joseon court presented him a seal as tribute. Kangxi asked his Jesuit teacher and advisor, Ferdinand Verbiest (1623–1688), if Europeans knew of the peculiar "fish." After riders were sent back to Beijing to retrieve European natural history texts from the Jesuit libraries, Kangxi was reportedly delighted to find the illustrations and descriptions in the books matched the animal itself.

[10] Changman Won and Byoung-Ho Yoo. "Abundance, seasonal haul-out patterns and conservation of spotted seals Phoca largha along the coast of Bak-ryoung Island, South Korea." *Oryx* 38 (2004): 109.

[11] Wang Peilie. "Distribution, ecology and resource conservation of the Spotted Seal in the Huanghai and Bohai Seas." *Acta Oceanologica Sinica* 5 (1986): 126.

[12] Bian He. *Know Your Remedies: Pharmacy & Culture in Early Modern China.* Princeton: Princeton University Press, 2020, 162.

[13] Rev. Alexander Williamson. *Journeys in North China, Manchuria, and Eastern Mongolia; With Some Account of Corea, Vol. II.* London: Smith, Elder & Co., 1870, 74.

[14] *Manchuria: Land of Opportunities.* South Manchuria Railway Company. 1924, 27.

[15] Arthur de Carle Sowerby. *The Naturalist in Manchuria, Vols. II & III.* Tientsin: Tientsin Press, 1923, 77.

[16] Hua-Kun Yan et al. "Abundance, Habitat Conditions, and Conservation of the Largha Seal (*Phoca largha*) During the Past Half Century in the Bohai Sea, China." *Mammal Study* 43 (2018): 2.

[17] Won and Yoo, "Abundance, seasonal haul-out patterns and conservation of spotted seals," 111.

[18] P. L. Boveng et al. *Status Review of the Spotted Seal (Phoca largha).* NOAA Technical Memorandum NMFS-AFSC-200. Seattle: Alaska Fisheries Science Center, 2009, 25 & 79.

[19] Won and Yoo, "Abundance, seasonal haul-out patterns and conservation of spotted seals," 111.

[20] Wang, "Distribution, ecology and resource conservation of the Spotted Seal," 127.

[21] Boveng et al, *Status Review of the Spotted Seal (Phoca largha),* 59 & 75.

[22] Boveng et al, *Status Review of the Spotted Seal (Phoca largha),* 80.

[23] Zhang Xinyu, "As Dalian Saves Its Seals, Sea Cucumber Farmers Feel the Cost," *Sixth Tone,* February 15, 2022. https://www.sixthtone.com/news/1009640.

[24] Yan et al. "Abundance, Habitat Conditions, and Conservation of the Largha Seal," 6–7.

[25] Chris Hogg, "China struggles to recover from 'worst ever' oil spill," *BBC News,* July 30, 2010. https://www.bbc.com/news/world-asia-pacific-10819987.

26 "China needs zero tolerance for concealing major accidents," *People's Daily Online*, July 8, 2011. https://web.archive.org/web/20150201152400/http://en.people.cn/90001/90780/7433972.html.

27 Yan Hua-Kun et al. "Maritime construction site selection from the perspective of ecological protection: The relationship between the Dalian offshore airport and spotted seals (*Phoca largha*) in China based on the noise pollution." *Ocean and Coastal Management* 152 (2018): 145–153.

28 Zhang, "As Dalian Saves Its Seals, Sea Cucumber Farmers Feel the Cost."

29 Boveng et al, *Status Review of the Spotted Seal (Phoca largha)*, 110 & 119.

30 何强，"中国著名捕鲸之乡的故事——徐闻外罗渔埠，" 碧海银沙网讯，April 18, 2010. http://www.bbwfish.com/article.asp?artid=92542.

31 Rev. Alexander Williamson. *Journeys in North China, Manchuria, and Eastern Mongolia; With Some Account of Corea, Vol. II*. London: Smith, Elder & Co., 1870, 74.

32 Dairen is the Japanese pronunciation of the Chinese characters for Dalian 大连. Russia founded modern Dalian—as Dal'niy Дальний—in 1898. Japan had won control of the Liaodong Peninsula in 1895 at the close of the First Sino-Japanese War, but Russia, France, and Germany forced Japan to return the territory in an act known as the Triple Intervention. Russia then promptly bullied the Qing into signing over the peninsula, enraging Japan. Japan retook the Liaodong Peninsula during the of the Russo-Japanese War in 1905, and held onto Dalian and Port Arthur until its defeat in the Second World War.

As a member of the Entente Powers, Japan also took control of Qingdao from Germany during the First World War in late 1914; they returned the city to China in 1922 but maintained a heavy presence in the region until reoccupying the city in 1938 during the Second Sino-Japanese War. As in Dalian, they were finally expelled in 1945.

33 王丕烈. 中国鲸类. 北京: 化学工业出版社, 2011, 2–5.

34 王丕烈, 中国鲸类, 5–10.

35 王丕烈, 中国鲸类, 144–147.

36 David W. Weller et al. "The western gray whale: a review of past exploitation, current status and potential threats." *Journal of Cetacean Research and Management* 4 (2002): 7–12.

37 王丕烈, 中国鲸类, 130.

Wang Pi-lie and Lu Zhi-chuang. "Historical Records and Current Status of Western Gray Whale in China Waters." *Fisheries Science* 2 (2009): 767–771.

[38] Wang Xianyan et al. "Insights from a Gray Whale (*Eschrichtius robustus*) Bycaught in the Taiwan Strait off China in 2011." *Aquatic Mammals* 41 (2015): 327–332.

[39] J.G. Cooke et al. "*Eschrichtius robustus* (western subpopulation)." *The IUCN Red List of Threatened Species* (2018): e.T8099A50345475.

East China Sea

[1] Both the East Asian and Yangtze finless porpoises were earlier considered to be subspecies of the Indo-Pacific finless porpoise *Neophocaena phocaenoides*. Although their separation from *N. phocaenoides* is now broadly accepted, the question of whether to further split them remains to be settled. Most research continues to list them both as subspecies of narrow-ridged finless porpoise *N. asiaeorientalis*, but there is now a push to name the East Asian finless porpoise its own species, *N. sunameri*.

Zhou et al. "Population genomics of finless porpoises reveal an incipient cetacean species adapted to freshwater." *Nature Communications* 9, 1276 (2018).

[2] Thomas A. Jefferson and John Y. Wang. "Revision of the taxonomy of finless porpoises (genus *Neophocaena*): The existence of two species." *Journal of Marine Animals and Their Ecology* 4 (2011): 9–10.

[3] Zhou Kaiya, Stephen Leatherwood and Thomas A. Jefferson. "Records of Small Cetaceans in Chinese Waters: A Review." *Asian Marine Biology* 12 (1995): 133.

[4] 王丕烈, 中国鲸类, 375–376.

[5] Denghua Yin et al. "Gapless genome assembly of East Asian finless porpoise." *Scientific Data* 9, 765 (2022): 2.

[6] Zuo Tao et al. "Primary survey of finless porpoise population in the Bohai Sea." *Acta Theriologica Sinica* 38 (2018): 551–552.

[7] Li Yong-Tao et al. "The Population Density and Distribution of East Asian Finless Porpoise in Changdao Waters." *Chinese Journal of Zoology* 58 (2023): 658–668.

Yongtao Li et al. "Distribution and Abundance of the East Asian Finless Porpoise in the Coastal Waters of Shandong Peninsula, Yellow Sea, China." *Fishes* 8, 410 (2023).

[8] Jefferson and Wang, "Revision of the taxonomy of finless porpoises (genus *Neophocaena*)," 11–12.

[9] Thomas A. Jefferson et al. "Distribution and Abundance of Finless Porpoises in Hong Kong and Adjacent Waters of China." *The Raffles Bulletin of Zoology* suppl. 10 (2002): 43–55.

Thomas A. Jefferson and Jeffrey E. Moore. "Abundance and Trends of Indo-Pacific Finless Porpoises (*Neophocaena phocaenoides*) in Hong Kong Waters, 1996–2019." *Frontiers in Marine Science* 7, 574381 (2020).

[10] The Chinese crested tern has two names in Chinese. In the PRC its name is equivalent to the English (*Zhōnghuá fèngtóu yàn'ōu* 中华凤头燕鸥), while in Taiwan its name is black-billed crested tern (*Hēi zuǐduān fèngtóu yàn'ōu* 黑嘴端鳳頭燕鷗).

[11] Guoling Chen et al. "Long-term and extensive population decline drives elevated expression of genetic load in a critically endangered seabird." Preprint (2023).

[12] Chieh-Teh Liang, Shou-Hua Chang, and Woei-Horng Fang. "Little known Oriental bird: Discovery of a breeding colony of Chinese Crested Tern." *OBC Bulletin* 32 (2000): 18.

[13] The Matsu Islands are off of Fujian Province of the People's Republic of China, but are under the control of Taiwan.

[14] Liang, Chang, and Fang, "Little known Oriental bird," 18.

[15] Shuihua Chen et al. "A small population and severe threats: status of the Critically Endangered Chinese crested tern *Sterna bernsteini*." *Oryx* 43 (2009): 209–210.

[16] Chen et al., "A small population and severe threats," 211.

[17] Shuihua Chen et al. "Human harvest, climate change and their synergistic effects drove the Chinese Crested Tern to the brink of extinction." *Global Ecology and Conservation* 4 (2015): 140.

[18] S. H. Chen et al. "The breeding biology of Chinese Crested Terns in mixed species colonies in eastern China." *Bird Conservation International* 21 (2011): 266.

[19] BirdLife International. "*Thalasseus bernsteini*." *The IUCN Red List of Threatened Species* (2018): e.T22694585A131118818.

[20] Yiwei Liu et al. "Creating a conservation network: Restoration of the critically endangered Chinese crested tern using social attraction." *Biological Conservation* 248, 108694 (2020): 6.

[21] Song Se-Kyu et al. "First report and breeding record of the Chinese Crested Tern *Thalasseus bernsteini* on the Korean Peninsula." *Journal of Asia-Pacific Biodiversity* 10 (2017): 250–253.

Vladimir Dinets. "First Record of the Chinese Crested Tern *Thalasseus bernsteini* in Japan." *Journal of the Yamashina Institute for Ornithology* 50 (2019): 138–140.

[22] Liu et al. "Creating a conservation network," 7.

619

23 张辉, "中华凤头燕鸥保护成效显著, 种群数创新高——'神话之鸟' 全球种群数量突破220只," 福建日报, November 26, 2023. https://fjrb.fjdaily.com/pc/con/202311/26/content_323207.html.

24 BirdLife International. "*Calidris pygmaea.*" *The IUCN Red List of Threatened Species* (2021): e.T22693452A154738156.

25 P. S. Tomkovich et al. "First indications of a sharp population decline in the globally threatened Spoon-billed Sandpiper *Eurynorhynchus pygmeus.*" *Bird Conservation International* 12 (2002): 1–18.

26 Christoph Zöckler, Evgeny E. Syroechkovskiy and Philip W. Atkinson. "Rapid and continued population decline in the Spoon-billed Sandpiper *Eurynorhynchus pygmeus* indicates imminent extinction unless conservation action is taken." *Bird Conservation International* 20 (2010): 95–111.

27 BirdLife International, "*Calidris pygmaea.*"

28 Tom Bradfer-Lawrence et al. "Modelling the potential non-breeding distribution of Spoon-billed Sandpiper *Calidris pygmaea.*" *Bird Conservation International* 31 (2021): 169–184.

29 He-Bo Peng et al. "The intertidal wetlands of southern Jiangsu Province, China – globally important for Spoon-billed Sandpipers and other threatened waterbirds, but facing multiple serious threats." *Bird Conservation International* 27 (2017): 306.

30 Peter Crighton. "Bird mortality in fish nets at a significant stopover site of the Spoon-billed Sandpiper *Calidris pygmaea* in the Yellow Sea, China." *Stilt* 69-70 (2016): 74–76.

31 Christoph Zöckler, Pyae Phyo Aung and Sayam U. Chowdhury. "Summary of SBS winter counts 2021 and proportion of flagged Spoon-billed Sandpiper." *Spoon-billed Sandpiper Task Force News Bulletin* 24 (2021): 23–25.

Pyae Phyo Aung et al. "Gulf of Mottama SBS Survey January and February 2024." *Spoon-billed Sandpiper Task Force News Bulletin* 30 (2024): 9.

32 BirdLife International, "*Calidris pygmaea.*"

33 BirdLife International. "*Egretta eulophotes.*" *The IUCN Red List of Threatened Species* (2016): e.T22696977A93596047.

34 Hongying Xu et al. "Autumn migration routes of fledgling Chinese Egrets (*Egretta eulophotes*) in Northeast China and their implications for conservation." *Avian Research* 13, 100018 (2022).

35 BirdLife International, "*Egretta eulophotes.*"

[36] Yat-tung Yu and Chen Zhihong. "Dalmatian Pelican *Pelecanus crispus*: the largest waterbird in East Asia, and the rarest?" *BirdingASIA* 9 (2008): 62.

[37] Yu and Chen, "Dalmatian Pelican *Pelecanus crispus*," 63.

[38] "Below 150 individuals in East Asia Last chance for Dalmatian Pelican." *Hong Kong Bird Watching Society*. July 2019. https://cms.hkbws.org.hk/cms/en/hkbws/work/resarch/pelican.

[39] H. Q. Shi et al. "Status of the East Asian population of the Dalmatian Pelican *Pelecanus crispus*: the need for urgent conservation action." *Bird Conservation International* 18 (2008): 184–187.

[40] 焦盛武, 李豪, 胡利娟, "最新调查显示, 卷羽鹈鹕东亚种群数量突破150只," 中国科普网, January 26, 2024. http://www.kepu.gov.cn/news/2024-01/26/content_1757767.html.

[41] Yu and Chen, "Dalmatian Pelican *Pelecanus crispus*," 64–66.

[42] Shi et al., "Status of the East Asian population of the Dalmatian Pelican," 188–189.

[43] 焦, 李, 胡, "最新调查显示, 卷羽鹈鹕东亚种群数量突破150只."

[44] Zhijun Ma, Zijian Wang and Hongxiao Tang. "History of Red-crowned Crane *Grus japonensis* and its habitats in China." *Bird Conservation International* 8 (1998): 17.

[45] Qi-shan Wang, Hui Wang and Dong-Yu Hu. "Current status of the wintering population of the Red-crowned Crane in China," in *The Current Status and Issues of the Red-crowned Crane*, ed. Kimiya Koga, Dongyu Hu, and Kunikazu Momose. Kushiro: Tancho Protection Group, 2008, 55.

[46] Ma, Wang and Tang, "History of Red-crowned Crane," 17.

[47] Wang, Wang and Hu, "Current status of the wintering population," 55–56.

[48] Liying Su. "Challenges for Red-crowned Crane conservation in China," in *The Current Status and Issues of the Red-crowned Crane*, ed. Kimiya Koga, Dongyu Hu, and Kunikazu Momose. Kushiro: Tancho Protection Group, 2008, 66–67.

[49] BirdLife International. "*Grus japonensis*." *The IUCN Red List of Threatened Species* (2021): e.T22692167A175614850.

[50] Daqing Zhou et al. "Habitat changes in the most important stopover sites for the endangered red-crowned crane in China: a large-scale study." *Environmental Science and Pollution Research* 28 (2021): 54719–54727.

[51] BirdLife International, "*Grus japonensis*."

[52] "世界の今冬のタンチョウ総数カウント結果がでました," タンチョウ保護研究グループ Red-crowned Crane Conservancy, May 11, 2022. http://www6.marimo.or.jp/tancho1213/news20220511.html.

"今冬の世界のタンチョウ生息数がまとまりました," タンチョウ保護研究グループ Red-crowned Crane Conservancy, July 10, 2024. http://www6.marimo.or.jp/tancho1213/news20240710.html.

[53] Over the winter of 2019–2020, 1,900 red-crowned cranes wintered in Japan and another 1,669 in Korea.

South China Sea

[1] Jinzhong Fu. "Conservation, Management and Farming of Crocodiles in China," in *Crocodiles. Proceedings of the 2nd Regional (Eastern Asia, Oceania and Australasia) Meeting of the IUCN SSC Crocodile Specialist Group.* Gland: IUCN, 1994.

[2] Masaya Iijima et al. "An intermediate crocodylian linking two extant gharials from the Bronze Age of China and its human-induced extinction." *Proceedings of the Royal Society B* 289, 20220085 (2022).

[3] Simon Kin-Fung Chan et al. "A Comprehensive Overview of the Population and Conservation Status of Sea Turtles in China." *Chelonian Conservation and Biology* 6 (2007): 186–91.

[4] Edward H. Schafer. *The Vermilion Bird: T'ang Images of the South.* Berkeley: University of California Press, 1967, 215.

Although hawksbills and other sea turtles are no longer legal to use as medicinal ingredients, many texts continue to not only include entries on hawksbills, but also instructions to prepare their shells by using boiling hot vinegar to help scrape the scutes from the shells of live turtles.

[5] Chan et al., "A Comprehensive Overview," 187–91.

[6] 夏中荣, "时隔6年，惠东海龟湾再次发现"野海龟"归来产卵," 中国海龟湾, November 24, 2023. https://mp.weixin.qq.com/s/Iuu0_Kp2v1tnn5lrFJffgA.

[7] If you count Taiwan—as the Republic of China—separately from the People's Republic of China, there would be seven claimants active in the various South China Sea disputes.

[8] Chan et al., "A Comprehensive Overview," 186.

Ting Zhang et al. "Selection characteristics and utilization of nesting grounds by green sea turtles on Xisha Islands, South China Sea." *Global Ecology and Conservation* 54, e03091 (2024).

[9] Chan et al., "A Comprehensive Overview," 189.

[10] Liu Lin et al. "Sea turtle demand in China threatens the survival of wild populations." *iScience* 24, 102517 (2021): 1–3.

[11] Steller's sea cow *Hydrodamalis gigas*, a fifth member of the Sirenia and the dugong's closest genetic relative, was hunted to extinction within twenty-seven years of its discovery in 1741.

[12] Johan Nieuhof. *L'Ambassade de la Compagnie orientale des Provinces unies vers l'empereur de la Chine, ou Grand cam de Tartarie, faite par les Srs. Pierre de Goyer, & Jacob de Keyser*. Leiden: Jacob de Meurs, 1665, part 2, 100.

[13] Ellen M. Hines et al. "Dugongs in Asia," in *Sirenian Conservation: Issues and Strategies in Developing Countries*, ed. Ellen M. Hines et al. Gainsville: University Press of Florida, 2012, 71–72.

[14] Wang Peilie et al. "Survey on the resources status of dugong in Hainan Province, China." *Acta Theriologica Sinica 27* (2007): 71–73.

[15] Hines et al., "Dugongs in Asia," 71.

[16] Wang et al., "Survey on the resources status of dugong," 71–73.

[17] Mingli Lin et al. "Functional extinction of dugongs in China." *Royal Society Open Science* 9, 211994 (2022).

[18] Zhang Chun, "Will the dugong ever return to China?" *China Dialogue Ocean*, January 17, 2023. https://dialogue.earth/en/nature/will-the-dugong-ever-return-to-china/.

[19] Leszek Karczmarski, et al. "Humpback Dolphins in Hong Kong and the Pearl River Delta: Status, Threats and Conservation Challenges." *Advances in Marine Biology* 73 (2016): 31.

[20] Bingyao Chen et al. "Geographic variation in pigmentation patterns of Indo-Pacific humpback dolphins (*Sousa chinensis*) in Chinese waters." *Journal of Mammalogy* 99 (2018): 915–916.

[21] The dolphin's pink hue comes from blood flowing to their skin. This is a form of thermoregulation, releasing excess body heat into the surrounding waters to maintain a safe internal temperature.

[22] Karczmarski et al, "Humpback Dolphins in Hong Kong and the Pearl River Delta," 31.

[23] Wenzhi Lin et al. "Increased human occupation and agricultural development accelerates the population contraction of an estuarine delphinid." *Scientific Reports* 6, 35713 (2016): 6–8.

24 Mingming Liu, Mingli Lin and Songhai Li. "Population distribution, connectivity and differentiation of Indo-Pacific humpback dolphins in Chinese waters: Key baselines for improving conservation management." *Aquatic Conservation: Marine and Freshwater Ecosystems* 33 (2023): 411–415.

25 *Monitoring of Marine Mammals in Hong Kong Waters (2021–22): (Contract Ref.: AFCD/SQ/260/20/C) Final Report (1 April 2021 to 31 March 2022)*. Hong Kong Cetacean Research Project, 2022.

26 Peter (Pehr) Osbeck. *A Voyage to China and the East Indies, Vol. II*. London: Benjamin White, 1771, 27.

27 Thomas A. Jefferson and Samuel K. Hung. "A Review of the Status of the Indo-Pacific Humpback Dolphin (*Sousa chinensis*) in Chinese Waters." *Aquatic Mammals* 30 (2004): 153.

28 王丕烈, 中国鲸类, 290.

29 Bingyao Chen et al. "Survival rate and population size of Indo-Pacific humpback dolphins (*Sousa chinensis*) in Xiamen Bay, China." *Marine Mammal Science* 34 (2018): 1030.

30 Wenzhi Lin et al. "Indo-Pacific humpback dolphins face extirpation in Shantou waters." *Regional Studies in Marine Science* 77, 103641 (2024).

31 Cai Yiwen, "On a Fin and a Prayer: China's Disappearing White Dolphins," *Sixth Tone*, December 10, 2021. https://www.sixthtone.com/news/1009166.

32 Karczmarski et al, "Humpback Dolphins in Hong Kong and the Pearl River Delta," 29.

33 Thomas A. Jefferson, Elizabeth A. Becker and Shiang-Lin Huang. "Influences of natural and anthropogenic habitat variables on Indo-Pacific humpback dolphins *Sousa chinensis* in Hong Kong." *Endangered Species Research* 51 (2023): 155–157.

Stephen C.Y. Chan and Leszek Karczmarski. "Broad-scale impacts of coastal mega-infrastructure project on obligatory inshore delphinids: A cautionary tale from Hong Kong." *Science of the Total Environment* 920, 169753 (2024).

34 Karczmarski et al, "Humpback Dolphins in Hong Kong and the Pearl River Delta," 41 & 47.

35 Xue An et al. "Biosonar activity of the Indo-Pacific humpback dolphin (*Sousa chinensis*) near the tunnel section of the world's longest cross-sea bridge—the Hong Kong-Zhuhai-Macao Bridge—is negatively correlated with underwater noise." *Frontiers in Marine Science* 10, 1171709 (2023).

[36] John W. McManus. "Offshore Coral Reef Damage, Overfishing, and Paths to Peace in the South China Sea." *The International Journal of Marine and Coastal Law* 32 (2017): 203–206.

[37] Cui Liang et al. "Assessments of 14 Exploited Fish and Invertebrate Stocks in Chinese Waters Using the LBB Method." *Frontiers in Marine Science* 7, 314 (2020).

[38] Yvonne Sadovy and Wai Lung Cheung. "Near extinction of a highly fecund fish: the one that nearly got away." *Fish and Fisheries* 4 (2003): 87–90.

[39] M. Liu. "*Bahaba taipingensis.*" *The IUCN Red List of Threatened Species* (2020): e.T61334A130105307.

[40] Sadovy and Cheung, "Near extinction of a highly fecund fish," 87–90.

Another croaker species, the greater yellow croaker *Pseudosciaena crocea*, is valued for its flesh and not its swim bladder. Nonetheless, it, too, has been severely overfished since the 1980s.

[41] Lin Yan et al. "Early Growth and Developmental Characteristics of Chinese Bahaba (*Bahaba taipingensis*)." *Fishes* 9, 329 (2024): 1–2.

[42] M.Á. Cisneros-Mata et al. "*Totoaba macdonaldi.*" *The IUCN Red List of Threatened Species* (2021): e.T22003A2780880.

Daniel Shailer, "The Poachers Who Could Save Mexico's Vaquita," *Hakai Magazine*, September 24, 2024. https://hakaimagazine.com/features/the-poachers-who-could-save-mexicos-vaquita/.

The actual status of the totoaba population is uncertain. Research from the past several years suggests they are greater in number and are found more widely than previously believed. Whether they are in fact threatened with extinction, or even whether illegal fishing is particularly dangerous to their population, has become the subject of intense debate.

[43] Brooke Bessesen. *Vaquita: Science, Politics, and Crime in the Sea of Cortez.* Washington: Island Press, 2018.

[44] Jacqueline A. Robinson et al. "The critically endangered vaquita is not doomed to extinction by inbreeding depression." *Science* 376 (2022): 635–639.

"Vaquita Survey 2024 - Executive Summary," *Sea Shepherd*, June 11, 2024. https://seashepherd.org/2024/06/11/executive_summary/.

[45] Brian D. Smith et al. "Is the demand for fish swim bladders driving the extinction of globally endangered marine wildlife?" *Aquatic Conservation: Marine and Freshwater Ecosystems* 33 (2023): 1616.

[46] 洪水根. 中国鲎生物学研究. 厦门: 厦门大学出版社, 2011, 8–14.

47 Ming-Che Yang et al. "Phylogeography, Demographic History, and Reserves Network of Horseshoe Crab, Tachypleus tridentatus, in the South and East China Seaboards," in *Biology and Conservation of Horseshoe Crabs*, ed. John T. Tanacredi, Mark L. Botton and David T. Smith. Dordrecht: Springer, 2009, 163–182.

48 Zhou Wu et al. "Asian Horseshoe Crab Conservation: Knowledge, Attitudes, and Intentions of Local College Students in Northern Beibu Gulf, China," in *International Horseshoe Crab Conservation and Research Efforts: 2007-2020*, ed. John T. Tanacredi, Mark L. Botton, David T. Smith et al. Cham: Springer, 2022, 469–484.

49 Horseshoe crabs have blue blood. This is due to the blood's use of hemocyanin to carry oxygen, as opposed to the hemoglobin found in vertebrates. Whereas hemoglobin contains iron, hemocyanin contains copper, which lends the blood its blue hue.

50 D.R. Smith et al. *"Limulus polyphemus." The IUCN Red List of Threatened Species* (2016): e.T11987A80159830.

51 B. Akbar John et al. "A review on fisheries and conservation status of Asian horseshoe crabs." *Biodiversity and Conservation* (2018): 3573–3584.

52 Novitsky, Thomas J. "Economics of the Limulus/Tachypleus Amebocyte Lysate (LAL/TAL) Industry Relative to the Sustainability of Horseshoe Crabs Worldwide," in *International Horseshoe Crab Conservation and Research Efforts: 2007–2020*, ed. John T. Tanacredi, Mark L. Botton, David T. Smith et al. Cham: Springer, 2022, 352–354.

53 Chang Liu et al. "Research Progress and Prospect of Tachypleus Amebocyte Lysate in China," in *International Horseshoe Crab Conservation and Research Efforts: 2007–2020*, ed. John T. Tanacredi, Mark L. Botton, David T. Smith et al. Cham: Springer, 2022, 665.

54 Gao Baiyu, "Can new protections save China's horseshoe crabs?" *China Dialogue Ocean*, September 6, 2021. https://dialogue.earth/en/ocean/18403-can-new-protections-save-chinas-horseshoe-crabs/.

55 John et al., "A review on fisheries and conservation status of Asian horseshoe crabs," 3584.

56 Gao, "Can new protections save China's horseshoe crabs?"

57 ShaoHong Wu and WenJun Zhang. "Current status, crisis and conservation of coral reef ecosystems in China." *Proceedings of the International Academy of Ecology and Environmental Sciences* 2 (2012): 1–11.

58 黄晖 主编. 中国珊瑚礁状况报告: 2010–2019. 北京: 海洋出版社, 2021.

[59] Wu and Zhang, "Current status, crisis and conservation of coral reef ecosystems in China," 5.

[60] Terry P. Hughes and Hui Huang. "The Wicked Problem of China's Disappearing Coral Reefs." *Conservation Biology* 27 (2013): 266.

[61] Meixia Zhao et al. "Long-term Decline of a Fringing Coral Reef in the Northern South China Sea." *Journal of Coastal Research* 28 (2012): 1096.

[62] Gregory P. Asner, Roberta E. Martin and Joseph Mascaro. "Coral reef atoll assessment in the South China Sea using Planet Dove satellites." *Remote Sensing in Ecology and Conservation* 3 (2017): 57–65.

[63] KeFu Yu. "Coral reefs in the South China Sea: Their response to and records on past environmental changes." *Science China Earth Sciences* 55 (2012): 1217–1229.

[64] Li You, "Overheating Causes 'Severe' Coral Bleaching in Beibu Gulf," *Sixth Tone*, September 2, 2020. https://www.sixthtone.com/news/1006137.

Zhang Chun, "The parlous state of China's coral reefs," *China Dialogue Ocean*, March 4, 2021. https://dialogue.earth/en/ocean/16428-parlous-state-chinas-coral-reefs/.

[65] Hughes and Huang, "The Wicked Problem of China's Disappearing Coral Reefs," 265–266.

Conclusion

[1] Samuel T. Turvey er al. "Long-term archives reveal shifting extinction selectivity in China's postglacial mammal fauna." *Proceedings of the Royal Society B* 284, 20171979 (2017).

Xinru Wan et al. "Historical records reveal the distinctive associations of human disturbance and extreme climate change with local extinction of mammals." *Proceedings of the National Academy of Sciences* 116 (2019): 19001–19008.

[2] Erle C. Ellis. "Land Use and Ecological Change: A 12,000-Year History." *Annual Review of Environment and Resources* 46 (2021): 1–33.

[3] Madhav Gadgil and Ramachandra Guha. *This Fissured Land: An Ecological History of India*. Delhi: Oxford University Press, 1992.

Mahesh Rangarajan. *India's Wildlife History: An Introduction*. Delhi: Permanent Black, 2001.

[4] Prerna Singh Bindra. *The Vanishing: India's Wildlife Crisis*. Gurgaon: Viking, 2017.

[5] Peter Matthiessen. *Wildlife in America: Revised, Updated Edition*. New York: Viking, 1987.

David S. Wilcove. *The Condor's Shadow: The Loss and Recovery of Wildlife in America*. New York: Anchor Books, 2000.

[6] Stefanie Deinet et al. *Wildlife Comeback in Europe: The Recovery of Selected Mammal and Bird Species*. London: Zoological Society of London, 2013.

Sophie E. H. Ledger et al. *Wildlife Comeback in Europe: Opportunities and Challenges for Species Recovery*. London: Zoological Society of London, 2022.

[7] Boris Komarov. *The Destruction of Nature in the Soviet Union*. London: Pluto Press, 1980.

DJ Peterson. *Troubled Lands: The Legacy of Soviet Environmental Destruction*. Boulder: Westview Press. 1993.

[8] Craig Loehle and Willis Eschenbach. "Historical bird and terrestrial mammal extinction rates and causes." *Diversity and Distributions* 18 (2012): 84–91. Jamie R. Wood et al. "Island extinctions: processes, patterns, and potential for ecosystem restoration." *Environmental Conservation* 44 (2017): 348–358.

[9] Friederike C. Bolam et al. "How many bird and mammal extinctions has recent conservation action prevented?" *Conservation Letters* 14, e12762 (2020).

[10] Dan Liang et al. "Assessing the illegal hunting of native wildlife in China." *Nature* (2023).

[11] Katrin Fielder. "Rumble in the Eco-Jungle: China's Green Non-Governmental Organizations." *Education About Asia* 15 (2010): 23–27.

[12] Smiley Wang, "Environmental protection in China: international NGOs play crucial role," *China Development Brief*, October 16, 2023. https://chinadevelopmentbrief.org/reports/environmental-protection-in-china-international-ngos-play-crucial-role/.

[13] Lin Yang, "China to Limit Access to Largest Academic Database," *Voice of America*, March 30, 2023. https://www.voanews.com/a/china-to-limit-access-to-largest-academic-database-/7029581.html.

"Why China's government is hushing up court rulings," *The Economist*, January 15, 2024. https://www.economist.com/china/2024/01/15/why-chinas-government-is-hushing-up-court-rulings.

BIBLIOGRAPHY

Books & Book Chapters

Adams, Arthur. *Travels of a Naturalist in Japan and Manchuria*. London: Hurst and Blackett, 1870.

Adams, Douglas and Mark Carwardine. *Last Chance to See*. New York: Harmony Books, 1991.

Allen, Glover M. *The Mammals of China and Mongolia, Part 1*. New York: The American Museum of Natural History, 1938.

———. *The Mammals of China and Mongolia, Part 2*. New York: The American Museum of Natural History, 1940.

Allsen, Thomas T. *The Royal Hunt in Eurasian History*. Philadelphia: University of Pennsylvania Press, 2006.

Anderson, E.N. *Food and Environment in Early and Medieval China*. Philadelphia: University of Pennsylvania Press, 2014.

Andrews, Roy Chapman. *Across Mongolian Plains*. New York: D. Appleton & Company, 1921.

Andrews, Roy Chapman, Walther Granger, Clifford H. Pope, Nels C. Nelson, G. M. Allen, R. C. Andrews, C. P. Berkey et al. *The New Conquest of Central Asia: A Narrative of the Explorations of the Central Asiatic Expeditions in Mongolia and China, 1921–1930*. New York: American Museum of Natural History, 1932.

Baikov, N. *Big Game Hunting in Manchuria*. London: Hutchinson & Co, 1936.

Baker, Ian. *The Heart of the World: A Journey to the Last Secret Place*. New York: Penguin Press, 2004.

Barrett, Timothy H. and Mark Strange. "Walking by Itself: The Singular History of the Chinese Cat," in *Animals through Chinese History: Earliest Times to 1911*, edited by Roel Sterckx, Martina Siebert and Dagmar Schäfer, 84–98. Cambridge: Cambridge University Press, 2019.

Barter, Mark. *Shorebirds of the Yellow Sea: Importance, threats and conservation status*. Canberra: Wetlands International, 2002. https://www.wetlands.org/publications/shorebirds-of-the-yellow-sea-importance-threats-and-conservation-status/.

Beebe, William. *A Monograph of the Pheasants, Vol. IV*. London: H. F. & G. Witherby, 1922.

Bello, David A. *Across Forest, Steppe, and Mountain: Environment, Identity, and Empire in Qing China's Borderlands*. Cambridge: Cambridge University Press, 2015.

———. "Rival Empires on the Hunt for Sable and People in Seventeenth-Century Manchuria," in *Empire and Environment in the Making of Manchuria*, edited by Norman Smith, 53–79. Vancouver: UBC Press, 2017.

Berger, Joel. *Extreme Conservation: Life at the Edges of the World*. Chicago: University of Chicago Press, 2018.

Bessac, Frank Bagnall and Susanne Leppmann Bessac, with Joan Orielle Bessac Steelquist. *Death on the Chang Tang; 1950: The Education of an Anthropologist*. Missoula: University of Montana Printing and Graphic Services, 2006.

Bessesen, Brooke. *Vaquita: Science, Politics, and Crime in the Sea of Cortez*. Washington: Island Press, 2018.

Bian He. *Know Your Remedies: Pharmacy & Culture in Early Modern China*. Princeton: Princeton University Press, 2020.

Bindra, Prerna Singh. *The Vanishing: India's Wildlife Crisis*. Gurgaon: Viking, 2017.

Blakiston, Thomas W. *Five Months on the Yang-Tsze; with a Narrative of the Exploration of its Upper Waters, and Notices of the Present Rebellions in China*. London: John Murray, 1862.

Bouman, Inge and Jan. "The History of Przewalski's Horse," in *Przewalski's Horse: The History and Biology of an Endangered Species*, edited by Lee Boyd and Katherine A. Houpt, 5–38. Albany: State University of New York Press, 1994.

Bouman, Inge, Jan Bouman and Lee Boyd. "Reintroduction," in *Przewalski's Horse: The History and Biology of an Endangered Species*, edited by Lee Boyd and Katherine A. Houpt, 255–263. Albany: State University of New York Press, 1994.

Boveng, P. L., J. L. Bengtson, T. W. Buckley, M. F. Cameron, S. P. Dahle, B. P. Kelly, B. A. Megrey et al. *Status Review of the Spotted Seal (Phoca largha)*. NOAA Technical Memorandum NMFS-AFSC-200. Seattle: Alaska Fisheries Science Center, 2009. https://repository.library.noaa.gov/view/noaa/3671.

Bower, Hamilton. *Diary of a Journey Across Tibet*. London: Rivington, Percival and Co., 1894.

Boyd, Olivia. "The birth of Chinese environmentalism: key campaigns," in *China and the Environment: The Green Revolution*, edited by Sam Geall, 46–49. New York: Zed Books, 2013.

Caldwell, Harry R. *Blue Tiger*. New York: Abingdon Press, 1924.

Caldwell, John C. *China Coast Family*. Chicago: Henry Regnery Company, 1953.

Carruthers, Douglas. *Unknown Mongolia: A Record of Travel and Exploration in North-West Mongolia and Dzungaria, Vol. II*. London: Hutchinson & Co., 1914.

Chadwick, Douglas. *Tracking Gobi Grizzlies: Surviving Beyond the Back of Beyond*. Ventura: Patagonia, 2017.

Challender, Daniel W.S., Sarah Heinrich, Chris R. Shepherd and Lydia K.D. Katsis. "International trade and trafficking in pangolins, 1900–2019," in *Pangolins: Science, Society and Conservation*, edited by Daniel W.S. Challender, Helen C. Nash and Carly Waterman 259–276. London: Academic Press, 2020.

Chapman, G. P. and Y. Z. Wang. *The Plant Life of China*. Berlin: Springer, 2002.

Chapman, Jan. *The Art of Rhinoceros Horn Carving in China*. London: Christie's Books, 1999.

Chee, Liz P.Y. *Mao's Bestiary: Medicinal Animals and Modern China*. Durham: Duke University Press, 2021.

Chen D., X. Duan, S. Liu and W. Shi. "Status and Management of Fishery Resources of the Yangtze River," in *Proceedings of the Second International Symposium on the Management of Large Rivers for Fisheries, Volume 1*, edited by Robin L. Welcomme and T. Petr, 173–182. Bangkok: FAO-RAP, 2004.

Church, Percy W. *Chinese Turkestan with Caravan and Rifle*. London: Rivingtons, 1901.

Clark, Leonard. *The Marching Wind*. London: Hutchinson & Co., 1954.

———. *A Wanderer Till I Die*. New York: Funk & Wagnalls, 1937.

Clark, Robert Sterling and Arthur de Carle Sowerby. *Through Shên-Kan: The Account of the Clark Expedition in North China, 1908–09*. London: T. Fisher Unwin, 1912.

Coggins, Chris. "King of the Hundred Beasts: A Long View of Tigers in Southern China," in *Tigers of the World: The Science, Politics, and Conservation of Panthera tigris, 2nd Ed*, edited by Ronald L. Tilson and Philip J. Nyhus, 431–438. Amsterdam: Academic Press, 2010.

———. *The Tiger and the Pangolin: Nature, Culture, and Conservation in China*. Honolulu: University of Hawai'i Press, 2003.

Crane, Peter. *Ginkgo: The Tree That Time Forgot*. New Haven: Yale University Press, 2013.

Croke, Vicki Constantine. *The Lady and the Panda: The True Adventures of the First American Explorer to Bring Back China's Most Exotic Animal*. New York: Random House, 2005.

Cunningham, Alexander. *Ladák, Physical, Statistical, and Historical; With Notices of the Surrounding Countries*. London: Wm. H. Allen and Co., 1854.

Curtin, Philip D. *Cross-Cultural Trade in World History*. Cambridge: Cambridge University Press, 1984.

David, Armand. *Natural History of North China with Notices of that of the South, West and North-east, and of Mongolia & Thibet, compiled chiefly from the travels of Père Armand David*. Shanghai: Da Costa & Co., 1873.

Deasy, H. H. P. *In Tibet and Chinese Turkestan: Being the Record of Three Years' Exploration*. London: T. Fisher Unwin, 1901.

Deinet, Stefanie, Christina Ieronymidou, Louise McRae, Ian J. Burfield, Ruud P. Foppen, Ben Collen and Monika Böhm. *Wildlife Comeback in Europe: The Recovery of Selected Mammal and Bird Species*. London: Zoological Society of London, 2013.

Du Halde, Jean-Baptiste. *The General History of China: Containing a Geographical, Historical, Chronological, Political and Physical Description of the Empire of China, Chinese-Tartary, Corea and Thibet, Vol. 4, 2nd ed.* London: John Watts, 1739.

Economy, Elizabeth C. *The River Runs Black: The Environmental Challenge to China's Future.* Ithaca: Cornell University Press, 2004.

Ekvall, Robert B. *Fields on the Hoof: Nexus of Tibetan Nomadic Pastoralism.* New York: Holt, Rinehart and Winston, 1968.

Elvin, Mark. *The Retreat of the Elephants: An Environmental History of China.* New Haven: Yale University Press, 2004.

Fan Chengda. *Treatise of the Supervisor and Guardian of the Cinnamon Sea.* Translated by James M. Hargett. Seattle: University of Washington Press, 2010.

Fang Xiuqi, Yun Su, Zhudeng Wei and Jun Yin. "Social Impacts of Climate Change in Historical China," in *Socio-Environmental Dynamics along the Historical Silk Road*, edited by Jiang Emlyn Yang, Hans-Rudolf Bork, Xiuqi Fang and Stefan Mischke, 231–245. Cham: Springer Open, 2019.

Farrington, John D., Juan Li. "Climate Change Impacts on Snow Leopard Range," in *Snow Leopards: Biodiversity of the World: Conservation from Genes to Landscapes*, edited by Thomas McCarthy and David Mallon, 85–95. Boston: Academic Press, 2016.

Flad, Rowan. "Bronze, Jade, Gold, and Ivory: Valuable Objects in Ancient Sichuan," in *The Construction of Value in the Ancient World*, edited by John K. Papadopoulos and Gary Urton, 306–335. Los Angeles: Cotsen Institute of Archaeology Press, 2012.

Fleming, Robert L., Jr, Dorje Tsering and Liu Wulin. *Across the Tibetan Plateau: Ecosystems, Wildlife, and Conservation.* New York: W. W. Norton & Co., 2007.

Fu Jinzhong. "Conservation, Management and Farming of Crocodiles in China," in *Crocodiles. Proceedings of the 2nd Regional (Eastern Asia, Oceania and Australasia) Meeting of the IUCN SSC Crocodile Specialist Group.* Gland: IUCN, 1994. http://www.iucncsg.org/365_docs/attachments/protarea/Reg%20-17d4a33d.pdf.

Gadgil, Madhav and Ramachandra Guha. *This Fissured Land: An Ecological History of India.* Delhi: Oxford University Press, 1992.

Gamsa, Mark. *Manchuria: A Concise History.* London: I.B. Taurus, 2020.

Glatston, Angela R. "Red Pandas in Zoos Today; The History of the Current Captive Population," in *Red Panda: Biology and Conservation of the First Panda,* edited by Angela R. Glatston, 303–321. Boston: Academic Press, 2011.

Goldstein, Melvyn C. and Cynthia M. Beall. *Nomads of Western Tibet: The Survival of a Way of Life.* Berkeley: University of California Press, 1990.

Gong Jien and Richard B. Harris. "The Status of Bears in China," in *Understanding Asian Bears to Secure Their Future*, edited by Japan Bear Network, 96–101. Ibaraki: Japan Bear Network, 2006.

Gopinath, Ravindran, Riyaz Ahmed, Ashok Kumar and Aniruddha Mookerjee. *Beyond the Ban: A Census of Shahtoosh Workers in Jammu & Kashmir.* New Delhi: Wildlife Trust of India & International Fund for Animal Welfare, 2003.

Han Jianlin. "Wild yak (*Bos mutus* Przewalski, 1883)," in *Ecology, Evolution and Behaviour of Wild Cattle: Implications for Conservation*, edited by M. Melletti and J. Burton. Cambridge: Cambridge University Press, 2014. 194–215. https://doi.org/10.1017/CBO9781139568098.014.

Hare, John. *The Lost Camels of Tartary: A Quest into Forbidden China*. London: Little, Brown, 1998.

———. *Mysteries of the Gobi: Searching for Wild Camels and Lost Cities in the Heart of Asia*. London: I.B. Taurus, 2009.

Harkness, Ruth. *The Lady and the Panda: An Adventure*. New York: Carrick & Evans, 1938.

Harper, Francis. *Extinct and Vanishing Mammals of the Old World*. New York: American Committee for International Wild Life Protection (1945): 216–217.

Harris, James. *Safe Flyways for the Siberian Crane*. Baraboo: International Crane Foundation, 2009.

Harris, Richard B. *Wildlife Conservation in China: Preserving the Habitat of China's Wild West*. Armonk, NY: M.E. Sharpe, 2008.

Hathaway, Michael J. *Environmental Winds: Making the Global in Southwest China*. Berkeley: University of California Press, 2013.

———. *What a Mushroom Lives For: Matsutake and the Worlds They Make*. Princeton: Princeton University Press, 2022.

Hedin, Sven. *Adventures in Tibet*. London: Hurst and Blackett, 1904.

———. *Central Asia and Tibet: Towards the Holy City of Lassa, Volume I*. London: Hurst and Blackett, 1903.

———. *Scientific Results of a Journey in Central Asia 1899-1902, Vol. I The Tarim River*. Stockholm: Lithographic Institute of the General Staff of the Swedish Army, 1904.

———. *Scientific Results of a Journey in Central Asia 1899-1902, Vol. II Lop-Nor*. Stockholm: Lithographic Institute of the General Staff of the Swedish Army, 1905.

———. *Scientific Results of a Journey in Central Asia 1899-1902, Vol. III North and East Tibet*. Stockholm: Lithographic Institute of the General Staff of the Swedish Army, 1905.

———. *Through Asia*. London: Methuen, 1898.

———. *Trans-Himalaya: Discoveries and Adventures in Tibet, Vol. II*. London: Macmillan and Co., 1910.

———. *Trans-Himalaya: Discoveries and Adventures in Tibet, Vol. III*. London: Macmillan and Co., 1913.

Hines, Ellen M., Kanjana Adulyanukosol, Sombat Poochaviranon, Phay Somany, Leng Sam Ath, Nick Cox, Keith Symington et al. "Dugongs in Asia," in *Sirenian Conservation: Issues and Strategies in Developing Countries*, edited by Ellen M. Hines, John E. Reynolds III, Lemnuel V. Aragones, Antonio A. Mignucci-Giannoni and Miriam Marmontel, 58–76. Gainsville: University Press of Florida, 2012.

Hosie, Alexander. *Manchuria: Its People, Resources and Recent History*. London: Methuen & Co., 1901.

633

Huang Liangliang and Jianhua Li. "Status of Freshwater Fish Biodiversity in the Yangtze River Basin, China," in *Aquatic Biodiversity Conservation and Ecosystem Services*, edited by Shin-ichi Nakano, Tetsukazu Yahara and Tohru Nakashizuka, 13–30. Singapore: Springer, 2016.

Huber, Toni. "The chase and the Dharma: the legal protection of wild animals in premodern Tibet," in *Wildlife in Asia: Cultural Perspectives*, edited by John Knight, 36–55. London: RoutledgeCurzon, 2004.

Huc, M. *Travels in Tartary, Thibet and China During the Years 1844-5-6, Vol. II.* Chicago: Open Court, 1900.

Hughes, J. Donald. *Pan's Travail: Environmental Problems of the Ancient Greeks and Romans*. Baltimore: John Hopkins University Press, 1994.

Jackson, Rodney, Wang Z., Lu X. and Chen Y. "Snow Leopards in the Qomolangma Nature Preserve of the Tibet Autonomous Region," in *Proceedings of the Seventh International Snow Leopard Symposium* edited by J. Fox and J. Du, 85–95. Seattle: International Snow Leopard Trust, 1994.

James, H. E. M.. *The Long White Mountain or A Journey in Manchuria: With Some Account of the History People, Administration and Religion of that Country*. London: Longmans, Green, and Co., 1888.

Jardine, William. *The Naturalist's Library, Vol. XIV, Ornithology, Gallinaceous Birds*. Edinburgh: W. H. Lizars, 1845.

Jernigan, T. R. *Shooting in China*. Shanghai: Methodist Publishing House, 1908.

Jiang Guangshan, Hua Yan, Gu Jiayin, Qi Jinzhe, Ning Yao, Zhou Shaochun, Long Zexu et al. *Population and Habitat Dynamics of Amur Tigers and Their Targeted Management Strategies in China*. Beijing: Science Press, 2020.

Jiang Guangshun, Qi Jinzhe, Gu Jiayin, Chang You, Shi Quanta and Liu Peiqi. *Population and Habitat of Amur Leopard in China*. Beijing: Science Press, 2016.

Johnsgard, Paul A. *Cranes of the World*. Bloomington: Indiana University Press, 1983.

Kaczensky, Petra, Bayarbaatar Buuveibaatar, John C. Payne, Samantha Strindberg, Chris Walzer, Nyamsuren Batsaikhan, Sanjaa Bolortsetseg et al. *A Conservation Strategy for Khulan in Mongolia: Background and Key Considerations*. NINA Report 1889. Trondheim: Norwegian Institute for Nature Research, 2020. https://hdl.handle.net/11250/2688630.

Kemp, E. G. *The Face of China: Travels in East, North, Central and Western China*. New York: Duffield & Company, 1909.

Khalid, Adeeb. *Central Asia: A New History from the Imperial Conquests to the Present*. Princeton: Princeton University Press, 2021.

Kiefer, Michael. *Chasing the Panda: How an Unlikely Pair of Adventurers Won the Race to Capture the Mythical White Bear*. New York: Da Capo Press, 2002.

Kim, Seonmin. *Ginseng and Borderland: Territorial Boundaries and Political Relations between Qing China and Chosŏn Korea, 1636-1912*. Oakland: University of California Press, 2017.

Kinloch, Alexander. *Large Game Shooting in Thibet, the Himalayas, and Northern India*. Calcutta: Thacker, Spink and Co., 1885.

Komarov, Boris. *The Destruction of Nature in the Soviet Union*. London: Pluto Press, 1980.

Kram, Megan, Charles Bedford, Matthew Durnin, Yongmei Luo, Karlis Rokpelnis, Benjamin Roth, Nancy Smith et al. *Protecting China's Biodiversity: A Guide to Land Use, Land Tenure, and Land Protection Tools*. Beijing: The Nature Conservancy, 2012. https://www.nature.org/media/china/chinabook-wholebook-lowres.pdf.

Laird, Thomas. *Into Tibet: The CIA's First Atomic Spy and His Secret Expedition to Lhasa*. New York: Grove Press, 2002.

Lander, Brian. "Deforestation in Early China: How People Adapted to Wood Scarcity," in *The Cultivated Forest: People and Woodlands in Asian History*, edited by Ian M. Miller, Bradley Camp Davis, Brian Lander and John S. Lee, 1–19. Seattle: University of Washington Press, 2022

Lanning, George. *Wild Life in China or Chats on Chinese Birds and Beasts*. Shanghai: "The National Review" Office, 1911.

Laufer, Berthold. *Ivory in China*. Chicago: Field Museum of Natural History, 1925.

Ledger, Sophie E. H., Claire A. Rutherford, Charlotte Benham, Ian J. Burfield, Stefanie Deinet, Mark Eaton, Robin Freeman et al. *Wildlife Comeback in Europe: Opportunities and Challenges for Species Recovery*. London: Zoological Society of London, 2022.

Lee, Robert H. G. *The Manchurian Frontier in Ch'ing History*. Cambridge: Harvard University Press, 1970.

Li Fengshan. "Species Review: Black-necked Crane (*Grus nigricollis*)," in *Crane Conservation Strategy*, edited by Claire M. Mirande and James T. Harris, 301–311. Baraboo: International Crane Foundation, 2019.

Li Shizhen. *Ben Cao Gang Mu, Volume VIII: Clothes, Utensils, Worms, Insects, Amphibians, Animals with Scales, Animals with Shells*. Translated and annotated by Paul U. Unschuld. Oakland: University of California Press, 2021.

Liao Yanfa. "Snow leopard distribution, purchase locations and conservation in Qinghai Province, China," in *Proceedings of the Seventh International Snow Leopard Symposium* edited by J. Fox and J. Du, 65–72. Seattle: International Snow Leopard Trust, 1994.

Lin Hang. "Reindeer, Taiga, Ethnic Culture: State-Forced Resettlement and the Changing Human-Animal Interactions in the Aoluguya Ewenki Community," in *Human-Animal Interactions in Anthropocene Asia*, edited by Victor Teo, 93–110. London: Routledge, 2023.

Little, Archibald J. *Through the Yang-tse Gorges or Trade and Travel in Western China*, 3rd ed. London: Sampson Low, Marston & Company. 1898.

Liu Chang, Ximei Liu, Youji Wang, Jie Song, Jinfeng He, Zongguang Tai, Quangang Zhu and Menghong Hu. "Research Progress and Prospect of Tachypleus Amebocyte Lysate in China," in *International Horseshoe Crab Conservation and Research Efforts: 2007–2020*, edited by John T. Tanacredi, Mark L. Botton, David T. Smith et al, 661–668. Cham: Springer, 2022.

Liu Yanlin, Byron Weckworth, Juan Li, Lingyuan Xiao, Xiang Zhao, Zhi Lu. "China: The Tibetan Plateau, Sanjiangyuan Region," in *Snow Leopards: Biodiversity of the World: Conservation from Genes to Landscapes,* edited by Thomas McCarthy and David Mallon, 513–521. Boston: Academic Press, 2016.

Loeffler, Kati. "Management, Husbandry and Veterinary Medicine of Red Pandas Living ex situ in China," in *Red Panda: Biology and Conservation of the First Panda,* edited by Angela R. Glatston, 323–333. Boston: Academic Press, 2011.

Lohe, Adrienne. *Adriatic Sturgeon (Acipenser naccarii), European sturgeon (Acipenser sturio), Chinese sturgeon (Acipenser sinensis), Sakhalin sturgeon (Acipenser mikadoi), Kaluga sturgeon (Huso dauricus) 5-Year Review: Summary and Evaluation.* NOAA, 2021. https://repository.library.noaa.gov/view/noaa/30918.

López-Pujol, Jordi and Ming-Xun Ren. "China: A Hot Spot of Relict Plant Taxa," in *Biodiversity Hotspots,* edited by Vittore Rescigno and Savario Maletta, 123–137. New York: Nova Science Publishers, 2010.

Lorge, Peter. "The Great Ditch of China and the Song-Liao Border," in *Battlefronts Real and Imagined: War, Border, and Identity in the Chinese Middle Period,* edited by Don J. Wyatt, 59–74. New York: Palgrave Macmillan, 2008.

Loukashkin, A. S. "The Tarbagan or the Transbaikalian Marmot and its Economic Value." in *Extrait des comptes rendus du XIIe Congrès International de Zoologie, Lisbonne 1935,* 2233–2293. Lisboa: Casa Portuguesa, 1937.

Lu Houji. "Habitat Availability and Prospects for Tigers in China," in *Tigers of the World: The Biology, Biopolitics, Management, and Conservation of an Endangered Species,* edited by Ronald L. Tilson and Ulysses S. Seal, 71–74. Park Ridge: Noyes Publications, 1987.

Lü Zhi and George B. Schaller. *Giant Pandas in the Wild.* New York; Aperture, 2002.

Lumpkin, Susan & John Seidensticker. *Smithsonian Book of Giant Pandas.* Smithsonian Institution Press, 2002.

MacKinnon, John. *Wild China.* London: New Holland, 1996.

Marks, Robert B. *China: Its Environment and History.* Lanham: Rowman & Littlefield. 2012.

———. *China: An Environmental History, 2nd ed.* Lanham: Rowman & Littlefield, 2017.

———. *Tigers, Rice, Silk, and Silt: Environment and Economy in Late Imperial South China.* Cambridge: Cambridge University Press, 1998.

Matthiessen, Peter. *The Birds of Heaven: Travels with Cranes.* New York: North Point Press, 2001.

———. *Wildlife in America: Revised, Updated Edition.* New York: Viking, 1987.

McCullough, Dale R., Zhi-Guang Jiang, and Chun-Wang Li. "Sika Deer in Mainland China," in *Sika Deer: Biology and Management of Native and Introduced Populations,* edited by Dale R. McCullough, Seiki Takatsuki and Koichi Kaji, 521–539. Tokyo: Springer, 2009.

McDougal, Charles. "The Man-Eating Tiger in Geographical and Historical Perspective," in *Tigers of the World: The Biology, Biopolitics, Management, and Conservation of an Endangered Species,* edited by Ronald L. Tilson and Ulysses S. Seal, 435–448. Park Ridge: Noyes Publications, 1987.

Menzies, Nicholas K. "Forestry," in *Science and Civilisation in China: Vol. 6, Part III, Biology and Biological Technology, Agro-Industries and Forestry,* edited by Joseph Needham, 540–667. Cambridge: Cambridge University Press, 1996.

Meyer, Dirk, Frank Momberg, Christian Matauschek, Patrick Oswald, Ngwe Lwin, Saw Some Aung, Yin Yang, Wen Xiao et al. *Conservation status of the Myanmar or black snub-nosed monkey Rhinopithecus strykeri.* Yangon: Fauna & Flora International, 2017.

Meyskens, Covell F.. *Mao's Third Front: The Militarization of Cold War China.* Cambridge: Cambridge University Press, 2020.

Miller, D.J. and Rodney Jackson. "Livestock and Snow Leopards: making room for competing users on the Tibetan plateau," in *Proceedings of the Seventh International Snow Leopard Symposium* edited by J. Fox and J. Du, 315–328. Seattle: International Snow Leopard Trust, 1994.

Miller, Ian M. *Fir and Empire: The Transformation of Forests in Early Modern China.* Seattle: University of Washington Press, 2020.

Mills, J. A. *Blood of the Tiger: A Story of Conspiracy, Greed, and the Battle to Save a Magnificent Species.* Boston: Beacon Press, 2015.

Milner-Gulland, E.J., P. Hughes, E. Bykova, B. Buuveibaatar, B. Chimeddorj et al. *The Sustainable Use of Saiga Antelopes: Perspectives and Prospects.* Saiga Conservation Alliance Report to the Bundesamt für Naturschutz and the UN Convention on Migratory Species. 2021. https://www.cms.int/en/document/sustainable-use-saiga-antelopes-perspectives-and-prospects-0.

Miquelle, Dale G., John M. Goodrich, Linda L. Kerley, Dimitri G, Pikunov, Yuri M. Dunishenko, Vladimir V. Aramiliev et al. "Science-based Conservation of Amur Tigers in the Russian Far East and Northeast China," in *Tigers of the World: The Science, Politics, and Conservation of Panthera tigris, 2nd Ed*, edited by Ronald L. Tilson and Philip J. Nyhus, 403–423. Amsterdam: Academic Press, 2010.

Miquelle, Dale G., Philip A. Stephens, Evgeny N. Smirnov, John M. Goodrich, Olga J. Zaumyslova and Alexander E. Myslenkov. "Tigers and Wolves in the Russian Far East: Competitive Exclusion, Functional Redundancy, and Conservation Implications," in *Large Carnivores and the Conservation of Biodiversity*, edited by Justina C. Ray, Kent H. Redford, Robert S. Steneck and Joel Berger, 179–207. Washington DC: Island Press, 2005.

Mirande, Claire M. and Elena I. Ilyashenko. "Species Review: Hooded Crane (*Grus monacha*)," in *Crane Conservation Strategy*, edited by Claire M. Mirande and James T. Harris, 313–321. Baraboo: International Crane Foundation, 2019.

———. "Species Review: Siberian Crane (*Leucogeranus leucogeranus*)," in *Crane Conservation Strategy*, edited by Claire M. Mirande and James T. Harris, 209–222. Baraboo: International Crane Foundation, 2019.

Mirande, Claire M., Nyambayar Batbayar, and James T. Harris. "Species Review: White-naped Crane (*Grus vipio*)," in *Crane Conservation Strategy*, edited by Claire M. Mirande and James T. Harris, 273–285. Baraboo: International Crane Foundation, 2019.

Mischke, Steffen, Chenglin Liu and Jiafu Zhang. "Lop Nur in NW China: Its Natural State, and a Long History of Human Impact," in *Large Asian Lakes in a Changing World: Natural State and Human Impact*, edited by Steffen Mischke, 207–233. Cham: Springer Nature, 2020.

Mishra, Charudutt, Stephen R. Redpath, Kulbhushansingh R. Suryawanshi. "Livestock Predation by Snow Leopards: Conflicts and the Search for Solutions," in *Snow Leopards: Biodiversity of the World: Conservation from Genes to Landscapes*, edited by Thomas McCarthy and David Mallon, 59–67. Boston: Academic Press, 2016.

Moffett, Lacy I. *Common Birds of the Yangtze Delta*. Shanghai, 1912.

Momose, Yulia S. and Kunikazi Momose. "Species Review: Red-crowned Crane (*Grus japonensis*)," in *Crane Conservation Strategy*, edited by Claire M. Mirande and James T. Harris, 245–259. Baraboo: International Crane Foundation, 2019.

Monitoring of Marine Mammals in Hong Kong Waters (2021–22): (Contract Ref.: AFCD/SQ/260/20/C) Final Report (1 April 2021 to 31 March 2022). Hong Kong Cetacean Research Project, 2022.

Moorcroft, William and George Trebeck. *Travels in the Himalayan Provinces of Hindustan and the Punjab; in Ladakh and Kashmir; in Peshawar, Kabul, Kunduz, and Bokhara from 1819 to 1825, Vol. I*. London: John Murray, 1841.

Morden, William J. *Across Asia's Snows and Deserts*. New York: G. P. Putnam's Sons, 1927.

Mostern, Ruth. *The Yellow River: A Natural and Unnatural History*. New Haven: Yale University Press, 2021.

Nappi, Carla. *The Monkey and the Inkpot: Natural History and Its Transformations in Early Modern China*. Cambridge: Harvard University Press, 2009.

National Research Council. *Grasslands and Grassland Sciences in Northern China*. Washington DC: National Academy Press, 1992. https://doi.org/10.17226/1942.

Ni Qingyong, Xin He, Yu Wang and Xiangyun Meng. "Distribution and Conservation Status of Slow Lorises in Indo-China," in *Evolution, Ecology and Conservation of Lorises and Pottos*, edited by K. A. I. Nekaris and Anne M. Burrows, 326–338. Cambridge: Cambridge University Press, 2020.

Nieuhof, Johan. *L'Ambassade de la Compagnie orientale des Provinces unies vers l'empereur de la Chine, ou Grand cam de Tartarie, faite par les Srs. Pierre de Goyer, & Jacob de Keyser*. Leiden: Jacob de Meurs, 1665.

Novitsky, Thomas J. "Economics of the Limulus/Tachypleus Amebocyte Lysate (LAL/TAL) Industry Relative to the Sustainability of Horseshoe Crabs Worldwide," in *International Horseshoe Crab Conservation and Research Efforts: 2007–2020*, edited by John T. Tanacredi, Mark L. Botton, David T. Smith et al, 351–368. Cham: Springer, 2022.

Nowell, Kristin, Juan Li, Mikhail Paltsyn and Rishi Kumar Sharma. *An Ounce of Prevention: Snow Leopard Crime Revisited*. Cambridge: TRAFFIC, 2016.

Osbeck, Peter (Pehr). *A Voyage to China and the East Indies, Vol. II*. London: Benjamin White, 1771.

Parry-Jones, Rob and Joyce Y. Wu. *Musk Deer Farming as a Conservation Tool in China*. Hong Kong: TRAFFIC East Asia, 2001.

Percival, William Spencer. *The Land of the Dragon: My Boating and Shooting Excursions to the Gorges of the Upper Yangtze*. London: Hurst and Blackett, 1889.

Peterson, DJ. *Troubled Lands: The Legacy of Soviet Environmental Destruction*. Boulder: Westview Press. 1993.

Pfälzner, Peter. "The Elephant Hunters of Bronze Age Syria," in *Cultures in Contact. From Mesopotamia to the Mediterranean in the Second Millennium B.C.*, edited by Joan Aruz, Sarah B. Graff and Yelena Rakic, 112–131. New York: Metropolitan Museum of Art, 2013. https://www.metmuseum.org/art/metpublications/Cultures_in_Contact_From_Mesopotamia_to_the_Mediterranean_in_the_Second_Millennium_BC.

Pietz, David A. *The Yellow River: The Problem of Water in Modern China*. Cambridge, Harvard University Press, 2015.

Pollard, Samuel. *In Unknown China: A Record of the Observations, Adventures and Experiences of a Pioneer Missionary During a Prolonged Sojourn Amongst the Wild and Unknown Nose Tribe of Western China*. London: Seeley, Service & Co., 1921.

Pope, Clifford. *China's Animal Frontier*. New York: Viking Press, 1940.

Pratt, A. E. *To the Snows of Tibet Through China*. London: Longmans, Green, and Co., 1892.

Prejevalsky, N. *From Kulja, Across the Tian Shan to Lob-Nor: Including Notices of the Lakes of Central Asia*. London: Sampson Low, Marston, Searle, & Rivington, 1879.

———. *Mongolia, the Tangut Country, and the Solitudes of Northern Tibet: Being a Narrative of Three Years' Travel in Eastern High Asia, Vol. I*. London: Sampson Low, Marston, Searle, & Rivington, 1876.

Rangarajan, Mahesh. *India's Wildlife History: An Introduction*. Delhi: Permanent Black, 2001.

Rawling, Cecil Godfrey. *The Great Plateau: Being an Account of Exploration in Central Tibet, 1903, and of the Gartok Expedition, 1904–1905*. London: Edward Arnold, 1905.

Reichenbach, Herman. "Zoological Gardens of China," in *Zoo and Aquarium History: Ancient Animal Collections to Conservation Centers, 2nd Edition*, edited by Vernon N. Kisling, Jr., 299–318. Boca Raton: CRC Press, 2022. https://doi.org/10.1201/9781003282488.

Reid, Donald G. and Jien Gong. "Giant Panda Conservation Action Plan," in *Bears: Status Survey and Conservation Action Plan*, edited by Christopher Servheen, Stephen Herrero and Bernard Peyton, 241–254. Gland: IUCN, 1999.

Robinson, David M. *Martial Spectacles of the Ming Court*. Cambridge: Harvard University Asia Center, 2013.

Rogaski, Ruth. *Knowing Manchuria: Environments, the Senses, and Natural Knowledge on an Asian Borderland*. Chicago: University of Chicago Press, 2022.

Roosevelt, Theodore and Kermit Roosevelt. *Trailing the Giant Panda*. New York: Charles Scribner's Sons, 1929.

Rowell, Galen. *Mountains of the Middle Kingdom: Exploring the High Peaks of China and Tibet*. San Francisco: Sierra Club Books, 1983.

Schafer, Edward H. *The Golden Peaches of Samarkand: A Study of T'ang Exotics*. Berkeley: University of California Press, 1963.

———. *Shore of Pearls*. Berkeley: University of California Press, 1970.

———. *The Vermilion Bird: T'ang Images of the South*. Berkeley: University of California Press, 1967.

Schaller, George B. *A Naturalist and Other Beasts: Tales from a Life in the Field*. San Francisco: Sierra Club Books, 2007.

———. *Into Wild Mongolia*. New Haven: Yale University Press, 2020.

———. *The Last Panda*. Chicago: University of Chicago Press, 1993.

———. *Tibet's Hidden Wilderness: Wildlife and Nomads of the Chang Tang Reserve*. New York: Harry N. Abrams, 1997.

———. *Tibet Wild: A Naturalist's Journey on the Roof of the World*. Washington, DC: Island Press, 2012.

———. *Wildlife of the Tibetan Steppe*. Chicago: Chicago University Press, 1998.

Schaller, George B., Hu Jinchu, Pan Wenshi and Zhu Jing. *The Giant Pandas of Wolong*. Chicago: University of Chicago Press, 1985.

Schlesinger, Jonathan. *A World Trimmed with Fur: Wild Things, Pristine Places, and the Natural Fringes of Qing Rule*. Stanford: Stanford University Press, 2017.

Shapiro, Judith. *Mao's War Against Nature: Politics and the Environment in Revolutionary China*. Cambridge: Cambridge University Press, 2001.

Shi Kun, Lingyun Xiao, Luciano Atzeni, Zhuoluo Lyu, Yixuan Liu, Jun Wang, Xuchang Liang et al. "Snow leopard status and conservation in China," in *Snow Leopards: Biodiversity of the World: Conservation from Genes to Landscapes, 2nd ed.*, edited by David Mallon and Tom McCarthy, 577–601. London: Academic Press, 2023.

Simons, Craig. *The Devouring Dragon: How China's Rise Threatens Our Natural World*. New York: St. Martin's Press, 2013.

Smil, Vaclav. *The Bad Earth: Environmental Degradation in China*. New York: M.E. Sharpe, 1984.

Smith, Andrew T. and Yan Xie, ed. *A Guide to the Mammals of China*. Princeton: Princeton University Press, 2008.

Songster, E. Elena. *Panda Nation: The Construction and Conservation of China's Modern Icon*. New York: Oxford University Press, 2018.

Sowerby, Arthur de Carle. *Fur and Feather in North China*. Tientsin: Tientsin Press, 1914.

———. *The Naturalist in Manchuria, Vols. II & III*. Tientsin: Tientsin Press, 1923.

———. *A Sportsman's Miscellany*. Tientsin: Tientsin Press, 1917.

Sterckx, Roel. *Ways of Heaven: An Introduction to Chinese Thought*. New York: Basic Books, 2019.

———. "Attitudes towards wildlife and the hunt in pre-Buddhist China," in *Wildlife in Asia: Cultural Perspectives*, edited by John Knight, 15–35. London: RoutledgeCurzon, 2004.

Su Liying. "Challenges for Red-crowned Crane conservation in China," in *The Current Status and Issues of the Red-crowned Crane*, edited by Kimiya Koga, Dongyu Hu, and Kunikazu Momose, 63–73. Kushiro: Tancho Protection Group, 2008.

Summers, William C. *The Great Manchurian Plague of 1910-1911: The Geopolitics of an Epidemic Disease*. New Haven: Yale University Press, 2012.

Sun Dun Yuan, Gong Yazhen, Lei Xiaoping, Qui Yang, John Sale, Craig Kirkpatrick, Jon Ballou and Ulysses Seal, editors. *CBSG Guizhou Snub-nosed Monkey Conservation and PHVA Workshop Report*. Apple Valley, MN: CBSG, 1999. https://cbsg.org/sites/cbsg.org/files/documents/GuizhouMonkeyPHVA_Final%20Report.pdf.

Sun Xiaoping. "'War against the Earth': Military Farming in Communist Manchuria, 1949–75," in *Empire and Environment in the Making of Manchuria*, edited by Norman Smith Vancouver: UBC Press, 2017 248–275.

Tang Xiyang. *Living Treasures: An Odyssey Through China's Extraordinary Nature Reserves*. New York: Bantam, 1987.

Thorbjarnarson, John and Xiaoming Wang. *The Chinese Alligator: Ecology, Behavior, Conservation, and Culture*. Baltimore: Johns Hopkins University Press, 2010.

Tilson, Ronald, Philip J. Nyhus, and Jeff R. Muntifering. "Yin and Yang of Tiger Conservation in China," in *Tigers of the World: The Science, Politics, and Conservation of Panthera tigris, 2nd Ed*, edited by Ronald L. Tilson and Philip J. Nyhus, 439–451. Amsterdam: Academic Press, 2010.

Trautman, Thomas R. *Elephants and Kings: An Environmental History*. Chicago: University of Chicago Press 2015.

Turvey, Samuel. *Witness to Extinction: How We Failed to Save the Yangtze River Dolphin*. New York: Oxford University Press, 2008.

van Gulik, R. H. *The Gibbon in China: An Essay in Chinese Animal Lore*. Leiden: E. J. Brill, 1967.

Wallace, Harold Frank. *The Big Game of Central and Western China: Being an Account of a Journey from Shanghai to London Overland Across the Gobi Desert*. London: John Murray, 1913.

Wang, Hua-Feng, Zhao-Shan Wang, Cynthia Ross Friedman and Jordi López-Pujol. "Conservation of the Cathay Silver Fir, *Cathaya argyrophylla*: a Chinese evergreen 'living fossil'," in *Evergreens: Types, Ecology and Conservation* edited by Adriano D. Bezerra and Tadeu S. Ferreira 121–134. New York: Nova Science Publishers, 2012.

Wang Qi-shan, Hui Wang and Dong-Yu Hu. "Current status of the wintering population of the Red-crowned Crane in China," in *The Current Status and Issues of the Red-crowned Crane*, edited by Kimiya Koga, Dongyu Hu, and Kunikazu Momose, 55–60. Kushiro: Tancho Protection Group, 2008.

Wang Sung, ed. *China Red Data Book of Endangered Animals: Mammalia*. Beijing: Science Press, 1998.

Wearn, O.R., R. Raghavan, P. Nguyen Minh, T. Nguyen Duc, H. Wu, Z. Zhang, H. Trinh Dinh, P. Fan and C. Ma. *Conservation Action Plan for the Cao Vit Gibbon (Nomascus nasutus) 2021–2030 with a Vision to 2050.* Fauna & Flora International – Vietnam Programme, Hanoi and IUCN SSC Conservation Planning Specialist Group, 2022. http://cpsg.org/content/cao-vit-gibbon-action-plan.

Wei Fuwen and Zejun Zhang. "Red Pandas in the Wild in China," in *Red Panda: Biology and Conservation of the First Panda,* edited by Angela R. Glatston, 375–391. Boston: Academic Press, 2011.

Wellby, M. S. *Through Unknown Tibet.* London: T. Fisher Unwin, 1898.

Wilcove, David S. *The Condor's Shadow: The Loss and Recovery of Wildlife in America.* New York: Anchor Books, 2000.

Willekes, Carolyn. *The Horse in the Ancient World: From Bucephalus to the Hippodrome.* London: I.B. Taurus, 2016.

Williamson, Rev. Alexander. *Journeys in North China, Manchuria, and Eastern Mongolia; With Some Account of Corea, Vols. I & II.* London: Smith, Elder & Co., 1870.

Wilson, Ernest Henry. *A Naturalist in Western China: With Vasculum, Camera, and Gun: Being Some Account of Eleven Year's Travel, Exploration, and Observation in the More Remote Parts of the Flowery Kingdom, Vol. II.* London: Methuen & Co., 1913.

Winchester, Simon. *The River at the Center of the World: A Journey Up the Yangtze & Back in Chinese Time.* New York: Picador, 1996.

Wong How Man. *Exploring the Yangtze: China's Longest River.* San Francisco: China Books & Periodicals, 1989.

Wong-Quincey, J. *Chinese Hunter.* New York: John Day, 1939.

Wright, Belinda and Ashok Kumar. *Fashioned for Extinction: An Exposé of the Shahtoosh Trade, Second Edition.* New Delhi: Wildlife Protection Society of India, 1998. http://www.wpsi-india.org/images/fashioned_for_extinction.pdf.

Wu Shibao, Nick Ching-Min Sun, Fuhua Zhang, Yishuang Yu, Gary Ades, Tulshi Laxmi Suwal and Zhigang Jiang. "Chinese pangolin *Manis pentadactyla* (Linnaeus, 1758)," in *Pangolins: Science, Society and Conservation,* edited by Daniel W.S. Challender, Helen C. Nash and Carly Waterman 49–70. London: Academic Press, 2020.

Wu Zhou, Shuyan Huang, Yijian Fu, Junfu He, Wenquan Zhen, Xiaoyong Xie, Chun-Chieh Wang et al. "Asian Horseshoe Crab Conservation: Knowledge, Attitudes, and Intentions of Local College Students in Northern Beibu Gulf, China," in *International Horseshoe Crab Conservation and Research Efforts: 2007-2020,* edited by John T. Tanacredi, Mark L. Botton, David T. Smith et al, 469–484. Cham: Springer, 2022.

Xie Yuanyuan. *Ecological Migrants: The Relocation of China's Ewenki Reindeer Herders.* New York: Berghahn, 2015.

Xing Shuang, Timothy C. Bonebrake, Wenda Cheng, Mingxia Zhang, Gary Ades, Debbie Shaw and Youlong Zhou. "Meat and medicine: historic and contemporary use in Asia," in *Pangolins: Science, Society and Conservation*, edited by Daniel W.S. Challender, Helen C. Nash and Carly Waterman 227–240. London: Academic Press, 2020.

Yang Ming-Che, Chang-Po Chen, Hwey-Lian Hsieh, Hui Huang, and Chaolun Allen Chen. "Phylogeography, Demographic History, and Reserves Network of Horseshoe Crab, Tachypleus tridentatus, in the South and East China Seaboards," in *Biology and Conservation of Horseshoe Crabs*, edited by John T. Tanacredi, Mark L. Botton and David T. Smith, 163–182. Dordrecht: Springer, 2009.

Zhang Mingxia and Jianguo Zhu. "Natural Forest Change in Hainan, China, 1991-2008 and Conservation Suggestions," in *Tropical Forests*, edited by Padmini Sudarshana, 297–304. London: Intech, 2012. https://doi.org/10.5772/34016.

Zhang Yanming. "The Biology and Ecology of Plateau Zokors (*Eospalax fontanierii*)," in *Subterranean Rodents: News from Underground*, edited by Sabine Begall, Hynek Burda and Cristian E. Schleich, 237–249. Berlin: Springer, 2007.

Zhao Ji, Zheng Guangmei, Wang Huadong and Xu Jialin. *The Natural History of China*. London: Collins, 1990.

Zheng Xinxian. "Animals as Wonders: Writing Commentaries on Monthly Ordinances in Qing China," in *Animals through Chinese History: Earliest Times to 1911*, edited by Roel Sterckx, Martina Siebert and Dagmar Schäfer, 217–232. Cambridge: Cambridge University Press, 2019.

Zhou Kaiya and Zhang Xingduan. *Baiji: The Yangtze River Dolphin and Other Endangered Animals of China*. Washington, D.C.: Stone Wall Press, 1991.

Zhu, Annah Lake. *Rosewood: Endangered Species Conservation and the Rise of Global China*. Cambridge: Harvard University Press, 2022.

Zou Hongfei and Dongyu Hu. "The status and conservation of the Red-crowned Crane in the breeding site in China," in *The Current Status and Issues of the Red-crowned Crane*, edited by Kimiya Koga, Dongyu Hu and Kunikazu Momose, 43–53 Kushiro: Tancho Protection Group, 2008.

毕俊怀 等. 中国蒙古野驴研究. 北京: 中国林业出版社, 2015.

初雯雯. "天寒地冻，你贴得一身好膘，我却酸了，" // 走！守护动物及其家园, 宋大昭, 黄巧雯 主编, 149–156. 上海: 上海科技教育出版社, 2020.

冯祚建, 王祖望. "中国古代对穿山甲的认识、利用及其种群现状与保护的研究，" // 中國古代動物學研究. 王祖望 主编, 冯祚建, 黄复生 副主编, 124–129. 北京: 科学出版社, 2019.

管开云, 郭忠仁 主编. 中国濒危动植物寻踪——植物卷. 北京: 北京出版社, 2019.

郭郛, 李约瑟, 成庆泰. 中国古代动物学史. 北京: 科学出版社, 1999.

黄乘明 主编. 濒危动物. 南京: 江苏凤凰科学技术出版社, 2014.

黄乘明, 周岐海, 李友邦. 黑叶猴的行为生态与保护生物学. 上海: 上海科学技术出版社, 2018.

黄晖 主编. 中国珊瑚礁状况报告: 2010–2019. 北京: 海洋出版社, 2021.

洪水根. 中国鲎生物学研究. 厦门: 厦门大学出版社, 2011.

胡献国 等. 东方珍宝: 冬虫夏草. 北京: 人民军医出版社, 2008.

姜雅风. 我的野生动物邻居. 上海: 上海科学技术出版社, 2020.

李继宣, 栾永贵. 中国蛇岛. 北京: 中国环境科学出版社出版, 1990.

李思忠. 黄河鱼类志. 青岛: 中国海洋大学出版社, 2017.

刘少英, 吴毅 主编. 中国兽类图鉴. 福州: 海峡书局, 2019.

马连义, 杨国美. 大丰麋鹿. 南京: 江苏人民出版社, 2016.

马鸣, 徐峰, 程芸, 等. 新疆雪豹. 北京: 科学出版社, 2013.

马逸清, 李晓民, 马国良, 李淑玲. 中国丹顶鹤. 哈尔滨: 东北林业大学出版社, 2019.

潘文石 等. 白头叶猴自然史. 北京: 北京大学出版社, 2016.

朴仁珠, 张明海. 貂熊. 哈尔滨: 东北林业大学出版社, 2000.

朴正吉. 密林寻踪: 野生动物观察笔记. 北京: 人民邮电出版社, 2021.

任林举. 虎啸——野生东北虎追踪与探秘. 北京: 北京十月文艺出版社, 2021.

寿振黄 主编. 中国经济动物誌——兽类. 北京: 科学出版社, 1962.

宋大昭. "曾经广布中国的豹，如今散落在哪里？" // 来！聆听大自然的呼唤. 宋大昭, 黄巧雯 主编, 12–18. 上海: 上海科技教育出版社, 2020.

———. "今天说说中国的豺，消逝和归来，" // 来！聆听大自然的呼唤. 宋大昭, 黄巧雯 主编, 64–69. 上海: 上海科技教育出版社, 2020.

宋延龄 主编. 动物与人. 南京: 江苏凤凰科学技术出版社, 2014.

孙戈. "最迷人的猫，却有最恐怖的层脸杀，" // 来！聆听大自然的呼唤. 宋大昭, 黄巧雯 主编, 109–118. 上海: 上海科技教育出版社, 2020.

孙海义. 东北虎. 哈尔滨: 东北林业大学出版社, 2011.

田秀华, 王进军 等. 东方白鹳. 哈尔滨: 东北林业大学出版社, 2011.

王丕烈. 中国鲸类. 北京: 化学工业出版社, 2011.

王正寰, 叶晓青. "第三极"的原住民: 藏狐. 上海: 上海科技教育出版社, 2015.

危起伟 等. 中华鲟保护生物学. 北京: 科学出版社, 2019.

文榕生. 中国珍稀野生动物分布变迁. 济南: 山东科学技术出版社, 2009.

———. 中国珍稀野生动物分布变迁 (续:) 二. 济南: 山东科学技术出版社, 2018.

———. 中国珍稀野生动物分布变迁 (续:) 中. 济南: 山东科学技术出版社, 2018.

———. 中国珍稀野生动物分布变迁 (续:) 下. 济南: 山东科学技术出版社, 2018.

吴家炎, 王伟. 中国白唇鹿. 北京: 中国林业出版社, 1999.

吴家炎, 王伟 等. 中国麝类. 北京: 中国林业出版社, 2006.

叶晓青, 杨帆. 密林隐士: 金毛羚牛. 上海: 上海科技教育出版社, 2016.

尹峰, 梦梦 主编. 药用濒危物种可持续利用与保护. 北京: 中国农业出版社, 2013.

于江. 悲情国宝: 白鱀豚生死全记录. 北京: 华龄出版社, 2012.

张立. 中国亚洲象保护研究. 北京: 科学出版社, 2018.

张洁. "中国境内亚洲象分布及变迁的社会因素研究." 博士学位论文, 陕西师范大学, 2014.

中国野生动物保护协会 编, 尹峰 梦梦 主编. 药用濒危物种可持续利用与保护. 北京: 中国农业出版社, 2013.

朱方. 历代诗文里的长江江豚. 南京: 江苏凤凰教育出版社, 2021.

Articles

Abdukadir, Ablimit and Urs Breitenmoser. "The Last Tigers of Xinjiang." *Cat News* 47 (2007): 26–27.

Abduriyim, Shamshidin, Azizjan Nabi and Mahmut Halik. "Low Genetic Diversity in the Goitered Gazelle *Gazella subgutturosa* (Güldenstädt, 1780) (Artiodactyla: Bovidae) in North-western China as Revealed by the Mitochondrial Cytochrome *b* Gene." *Acta Zoologica Bulgarica* 70 (2018): 211–218. http://www.acta-zoologica-bulgarica.eu/downloads/acta-zoologica-bulgarica/2018/70-2-211-218.pdf.

Alden, Maureen. "Lions in Paradise: Lion Similes in the Iliad and the Lion Cubs of IL. 18.318-22." *The Classical Quarterly* 55 (2005): 335–342. https://doi.org/10.1093/cq/bmi035.

Ale, S.B., S. Sathyakumar, D.M. Forsyth, X. Lingyun and Y.V. Bhatnagar. "*Hemitragus jemlahicus.*" *The IUCN Red List of Threatened Species* (2020): e.T9919A22152905. https://dx.doi.org/10.2305/IUCN.UK.2020-2.RLTS.T9919A22152905.en.

Allen, Glover M. "Zoological results of the second Dolan expedition to western China and eastern Tibet, 1934–1936. Part III: mammals." *Proceedings of the Academy of Natural Sciences of Philadelphia* 90 (1938): 261–294. https://www.jstor.org/stable/4064252.

Allinson, Tris. "Review of the global conservation status of the Asian Houbara Bustard *Chlamydotis macqueenii*." BirdLife International: Report to the Convention on Migratory Species Office – Abu Dhabi (2014). https://www.cms.int/en/document/review-global-conservation-status-asian-houbara-bustard-chlamydotis-macqueenii.

An Xue, Pengxiang Duan, Weilun Li, Jing Yuan, Yuwei Chen, Fei Fan, Xiaojun Deng et al. "Biosonar activity of the Indo-Pacific humpback dolphin (*Sousa chinensis*) near the tunnel section of the world's longest cross-sea bridge—the Hong Kong-Zhuhai-Macao Bridge—is negatively correlated with underwater noise." *Frontiers in Marine Science* 10, 1171709 (2023). https://doi.org/10.3389/fmars.2023.1171709.

Arora, David. "The Houses That Matsutake Built." *Economic Botany* 62 (2008): 278–290. https://doi.org/10.1007/s12231-008-9048-1.

Ashton, Peter and Hua Zhu. "The tropical-subtropical evergreen forest transition in East Asia: An exploration." *Plant Diversity* 42 (2020): 255–280. https://doi.org/10.1016/j.pld.2020.04.001.

Asner, Gregory P., Roberta E. Martin and Joseph Mascaro. "Coral reef atoll assessment in the South China Sea using Planet Dove satellites." *Remote Sensing in Ecology and Conservation* 3 (2017): 57–65. https://doi.org/10.1002/rse2.42.

Aung, Pyae Phyo, Ngwe Lwin, Tin Htun Aung, Thura Soe Min Htike, Carolyn Thompson, Christian Roos, Sa Myo Zaw et al. "Confirmation of Skywalker Hoolock Gibbon (*Hoolock tianxing*) in Myanmar Extends Known Geographic Range of an Endangered Primate." *International Journal of Primatology* (2024). https://doi.org/10.1007/s10764-024-00418-6.

Badingqiuying, Andrew T. Smith, Jesse Senko and Marcelino U. Siladan. "Plateau pika *Ochotona curzoniae* poisoning campaign reduces carnivore abundance in southern Qinghai, China." *Mammal Study* 41 (2016): 1–8. https://doi.org/10.3106/041.041.0102.

Bai Jiade, Yuanyuan Zhang, Zhenyu Zhong, Zhibin Cheng, Ming Cao and Yuping Meng. "The 35th anniversary of the reintroduction of Milu deer to China: History, population status, achievements and challenges." *Biodiversity Science* 29 (2021): 160–166. https://www.biodiversity-science.net/EN/Y2021/V29/I2/160. (Chinese with English abstract)

Baikov, N. A. (Байкова, Н. А.) "The Manchurian Tiger (Маньчжурский тигр)," *Manchuria Monitor* (*Вестник Маньчжурии*) (1925). Translated by Alex Shevlakov. archive.wikiwix.com/cache/index2.php?url=http://www.tigers.ru/books/baikov/he1.html.

Bain, Mark B. "The conservation status of large migratory cyprinids including *Aspiorhynchus laticeps* of Xinjiang China." *Journal of Applied Ichthyology* 27, suppl. 3 (2011): 80–85. https://dx.doi.org/10.1111/j.1439-0426.2011.01857.x.

Ban Xuan, Pengcheng Li, Jinming Wu and Hao Du. "The silver lining in rewilding the vanished sturgeon in the Yangtze River." *The Innovation Life* 2, 100070 (2024). https://doi.org/10.59717/j.xinn-life.2024.100070.

Bao Shengwang and Fan Yang. "Influences of Climate Change and Land Use Change on the Habitat Suitability of Bharal in the Sanjiangyuan District, China." *International Journal of Environmental Research and Public Health* 19, 17082 (2022). https://doi.org/10.3390/ijerph192417082.

Bao Weidong. "Eurasian lynx in China - present status and conservation challenges." *Cat News* sp. 5 (2010): 22–25. http://www.catsg.org/fileadmin/filesharing/3.Conservation_Center/3.2._Status_Reports/Eurasian_lynx/Weidong_2010_Eurasian_lynx_in_China_01.pdf.

Barclay, David, Ilya Smelansky, Emma Nygren and Anastasia Antonevich. "Legal status, utilisation, management and conservation of manul." *Cat News* sp. 13 (2019): 37–40. http://www.catsg.org/fileadmin/filesharing/5.Cat_News/5.3._Special_Issues/5.3.12_SI_13/Barclay_et_al_2019_Legal_status_utilisation_management_and_conservation_of_manul.pdf.

Barker, David G. and Tracy M. Barker. "The Distribution of the Burmese Python, *Python molurus bivittatus.*" *Bulletin of the Chicago Herpetological Society* 43 (2008): 33–38. https://chicagoherp.org/wp-content/uploads/bsk-pdf-manager/2019/12/433.pdf.

———. "The Distribution of the Burmese Python, *Python bivittatus*, in China." *Bulletin of the Chicago Herpetological Society* 45 (2010): 86–88. https://chicagoherp.org/wp-content/uploads/bsk-pdf-manager/2019/12/455.pdf.

Bar-On, Yinon M., Rob Phillips and Ron Milo. "The biomass distribution on Earth." *Proceedings of the National Academy of Sciences* 115 (2018): 6506–6511. https://doi.org/10.1073/pnas.1711842115.

Bello, David. "The Cultured Nature of Imperial Foraging in Manchuria." *Late Imperial China* 31 (2010): 1–33. https://muse.jhu.edu/article/408284.

Bettelheim, Matthew P. "Swinhoe's Softshell Turtle (*Rafetus swinhoei*): The Legendary Sword Lake Turtle of Hoan Kiem Lake." *Bibliotheca Herpetologica* 10 (2012): 4–20. http://www.ishbh.com/2012/08/bibliotheca-herpetologica-101.html.

BirdLife International. "*Anser cygnoid.*" *The IUCN Red List of Threatened Species* (2023): e.T22679869A228564177. https://dx.doi.org/10.2305/IUCN.UK.2023-1.RLTS.T22679869A228564177.en.

———. "*Arborophila ardens.*" *The IUCN Red List of Threatened Species* (2016): e.T22679063A92802107. http://dx.doi.org/10.2305/IUCN.UK.2016-3.RLTS.T22679063A92802107.en.

———. "*Calidris pygmaea.*" *The IUCN Red List of Threatened Species* (2021): e.T22693452A154738156. https://dx.doi.org/10.2305/IUCN.UK.2021-3.RLTS.T22693452A154738156.en.

———. "*Ciconia boyciana.*" *The IUCN Red List of Threatened Species* (2018): e.T22697695A131942061. http://dx.doi.org/10.2305/IUCN.UK.2018-2.RLTS.T22697695A131942061.en.

———. "*Egretta eulophotes.*" *The IUCN Red List of Threatened Species* (2016): e.T22696977A93596047. http://dx.doi.org/10.2305/IUCN.UK.2016-3.RLTS.T22696977A93596047.en.

———. "*Emberiza aureola.*" *The IUCN Red List of Threatened Species* (2017): e.T22720966A119335690. http://dx.doi.org/10.2305/IUCN.UK.2017-3.RLTS.T22720966A119335690.en.

———. "*Gorsachius magnificus.*" *The IUCN Red List of Threatened Species* (2017): e.T22697232A117359084. http://dx.doi.org/10.2305/IUCN.UK.2017-3.RLTS.T22697232A117359084.en.

———. "*Grus japonensis.*" *The IUCN Red List of Threatened Species* (2021): e.T22692167A175614850. https://dx.doi.org/10.2305/IUCN.UK.2021-3.RLTS.T22692167A175614850.en.

———. "*Leucogeranus leucogeranus.*" *The IUCN Red List of Threatened Species* (2018): e.T22692053A134180990. https://dx.doi.org/10.2305/IUCN.UK.2018-2.RLTS.T22692053A134180990.en.

———. "*Lophophorus lhuysii.*" *The IUCN Red List of Threatened Species* (2022): e.T22679192A219003994. https://dx.doi.org/10.2305/IUCN.UK.2022-2.RLTS.T22679192A219003994.en.

———. "*Otis tarda.*" *The IUCN Red List of Threatened Species* (2023): e.T22691900A226280431. https://dx.doi.org/10.2305/IUCN.UK.2023-1.RLTS.T22691900A226280431.en..

———. "*Polyplectron katsumatae.*" *The IUCN Red List of Threatened Species* (2022): e.T22734897A207341783. https://dx.doi.org/10.2305/IUCN.UK.2022-2.RLTS.T22734897A207341783.en.

———. "*Thalasseus bernsteini.*" *The IUCN Red List of Threatened Species* (2018): e.T22694585A131118818. http://dx.doi.org/10.2305/IUCN.UK.2018-2.RLTS.T22694585A131118818.en.

Bleisch, B., W. Brockelman, R.J. Timmins, T. Nadler, S. Thun, J. Das and L. Yongcheng. "*Trachypithecus phayrei*." *The IUCN Red List of Threatened Species* (2020): e.T22040A17960739. https://dx.dci.org/10.2305/IUCN.UK.2020-2.RLTS.T22040A17960739.en.

Bleisch, W., L. Yongcheng and M. Richardson. "*Rhinopithecus brelichi*." *The IUCN Red List of Threatened Species* (2008): e.T19595A8985249. http://dx.doi.org/10.2305/IUCN.UK.2008.RLTS.T19595A8985249.en.

Bolam, Friederike C., Louise Mair, Marco Angelico, Thomas M. Brooks, Mark Burgman, Claudia Hermes, Michael Hoffmann et al. "How many bird and mammal extinctions has recent conservation action prevented?" *Conservation Letters* 14, e12762 (2020). https://doi.org/10.1111/conl.12762.

Boonratana, R., M. Chalise, S. Htun, and R.J. Timmins. "*Macaca assamensis*." *The IUCN Red List of Threatened Species* (2020): e.T12549A17950189. https://dx.doi.org/10.2305/IUCN.UK.2020-2.RLTS.T12549A17950189.en.

Bradfer-Lawrence, Tom, Alison E. Beresford, Guy Q. A. Anderson, Pyae Phyo Aung, Qing Chang, Sayam U. Chowdhury, Nigel A. Clark et al. "Modelling the potential non-breeding distribution of Spoon-billed Sandpiper *Calidris pygmaea*." *Bird Conservation International* 31 (2021): 169–184. https://doi.org/10.1017/S0959270920000398.

Bragina, E., S. Kim, O. Zaumyslova, Y.-S. Park, and W. Lee. "*Naemorhedus caudatus*." *The IUCN Red List of Threatened Species* (2020): e.T14295A22150540. https://dx.doi.org/10.2305/IUCN.UK.2020-2.RLTS.T14295A22150540.en.

Brockelman, W. and T. Geissmann. "*Hylobates lar*." *The IUCN Red List of Threatened Species* (2008): e.T10548A3199623. http://dx.doi.org/10.2305/IUCN.UK.2008.RLTS.T10548A3199623.en.

Brook, S.M., Donnithorne-Tait, D., Lorenzini, R., Lovari, S., Masseti, M., Pereladova, O., Ahmad, K. and Thakur, M. "*Cervus hanglu*." *The IUCN Red List of Threatened Species* (2017): e.T4261A120733024. https://doi.org/10.2305/IUCN.UK.2017-3.RLTS.T4261A120733024.en.

Browne, Robert, Zhenghuan Wang, Sumio Okada, Dale McGinnity, Qinghau Luo, Yuki Taguchi and Douglas Kilpatrick. "The Sustainable Management of Giant Salamanders (Cryptobranchoidea)." Review (2020). https://ag.purdue.edu/department/extension/hellbender/_docs/browne-et-al-2020-sustainable-management-of-giant-salamanders.pdf.

Brunson, Katherine and Brian Lander. "Deer and Humans in the Early Farming Communities of the Yellow River Valley: A Symbiotic Relationship." *Human Ecology* 51 (2023): 609–625. https://doi.org/10.1007/s10745-023-00432-x.

Bryant, Jessica V. "Developing a conservation evidence-base for the Critically Endangered Hainan gibbon (*Nomascus hainanus*)." Doctoral thesis, University College London. 2014. https://discovery.ucl.ac.uk/id/eprint/1434514.

Buskirk, Steven W., Ma Yiqing and Xu Li. "Sables (*Martes zibellina*) in managed forest of northern China." *Small Carnivore Conservation* 10 (1994): 12. https://smallcarnivoreconservation.com/index.php/sccg/issue/view/340/112.

Buzzard, P. and J. Berger. *"Bos mutus."* *The IUCN Red List of Threatened Species* (2016): e.T2892A101293528. http://dx.doi.org/10.2305/IUCN.UK.2016-2.RLTS.T2892A101293528.en.

Buzzard, Paul J., How Man Wong and Huibin Zhang. "Population increase at a calving ground of the Endangered Tibetan antelope *Pantholops hodgsonii* in Xinjiang, China." *Oryx* 46 (2012): 266–268. https://doi.org/10.1017/S0030605311001657.

Buzzard, Paul J., Hui Bin Zhang, Dong Hua Xü and How Man Wong. "A globally important wild yak *Bos mutus* population in the Arjinshan Nature Reserve, Xinjiang, China." *Oryx* 44 (2010): 577–580. https://doi.org/10.1017/S0030605310000591.

Caffrey, Patrick J. "Transforming the Forests of a Counterfeit Nation: Japan's 'Manchu Nation' in Northeast China." *Environmental History* 18 (2013): 309–332. https://doi.org/10.1093/envhis/emt004.

Cai Zhenyuan, Jingjie Zhang, Pengfei Song and Tongzuo Zhang. "Protecting Przewalski's gazelle." *Oryx* 56 (2022): 652–653. https://doi.org/10.1017/S0030605322000849.

Callaghan, Christopher B. "The Cathay Silver Fir: Its Discovery and Journey Out of China." *Arnoldia* 66 (2009): 15–25. https://assetbank.arboretum.harvard.edu/assetbank-aahu/action/directLinkImage?assetId=25451.

Campos-Arceiz, Ahimsa, J. Antonio de la Torre, Ke Wei, Xiaoyu O. Wu, Yufei Zhu, Mingxu Zhao, Shu Chen et al. "The return of the elephants: How two groups of dispersing elephants attracted the attention of billions and what can we learn from their behavior." *Conservation Letters* 14, e12836 (2021). https://doi.org/10.1111/conl.12836.

Cao Lei, Mark Barter and Gang Lei. "New Anatidae population estimates for eastern China: Implications for current flyway estimates." *Biological Conservation* 141 (2008): 2301–2309. https://doi.org/10.1016/j.biocon.2008.06.022.

Chai Jing, Chen-Qi Lu, Mu-Rong Yi, Nian-Hua Dai, Xiao-Dong Weng, Ming-Xiao Di, Yong Peng et al. "Discovery of a wild, genetically pure Chinese giant salamander creates new conservation opportunities." *Zoological Research* 43 (2022): 469–480. https://doi.org/10.24272/j.issn.2095-8137.2022.101.

Chan Bosco Pui Lok, Tan Xue-feng and Tan Wu-jing. "Rediscovery of the critically endangered eastern black-crested gibbon *Nomascus nasutus* (Hylobatidae) in China, with preliminary notes on population size, ecology and conservation status." *Asian Primates Journal* 1 (2008): 17–25. http://static1.1.sqspcdn.com/static/f/1200343/18198072/1337026342967/APJ1.1.nasutus.pdf?token=Pc0%2F1NR9P34SxoFXFrDRTNQHlr0%3D.

Chan, Simon Kin-Fung, I-Jiunn Cheng, Ting Zhou, Hua-Jie Wang, He-Xiang Gu, and Xiao-Jun Song. "A Comprehensive Overview of the Population and Conservation Status of Sea Turtles in China." *Chelonian Conservation and Biology* 6 (2007): 185–198. https://doi.org/10.2744/1071-8443(2007)6%5B185:ACOOTP%5D2.0.CO;2.

Chan, Stephen C.Y. and Leszek Karczmarski. "Broad-scale impacts of coastal mega-infrastructure project on obligatory inshore delphinids: A cautionary tale from Hong Kong." *Science of the Total Environment* 920, 169753 (2024). https://doi.org/10.1016/j.scitotenv.2023.169753.

Chang, Zong Fei, Mao Fang Luo, Zhi Jin Liu, Jing Yuan Yang, Zuo Fu Xiang, Ming Li and Linda Vigilant. "Human influence on the population decline and loss of genetic diversity in a small and isolated population of Sichuan snub-nosed monkeys (*Rhinopithecus roxellana*)." *Genetica* 140 (2012):105–114. https://doi.org/10.1007/s10709-012-9662-9.

Chatterjee, H.J., J.S.Y. Tse and S.T. Turvey. "Using Ecological Niche Modelling to Predict Spatial and Temporal Distribution Patterns in Chinese Gibbons: Lessons from the Present and the Past." *Folia Primatologica* 83 (2012): 85–99. http://dx.doi.org/10.1159%2F000342696.

Chen Bingyao, Huili Gao, Thomas A. Jefferson, Yi Lu, Lin Wang, Shanshan Li, Hui Wang et al. "Survival rate and population size of Indo-Pacific humpback dolphins (*Sousa chinensis*) in Xiamen Bay, China." *Marine Mammal Science* 34 (2018): 1018–1033. https://doi.org/10.1111/mms.12510.

Chen Bingyao, Thomas A Jefferson, Lin Wang, Huili Gao, Hongke Zhang, Yu Zhou, Xinrong Xu and Guang Yang. "Geographic variation in pigmentation patterns of Indo-Pacific humpback dolphins (*Sousa chinensis*) in Chinese waters." *Journal of Mammalogy* 99 (2018): 915–922. https://doi.org/10.1093/jmammal/gyy068.

Chen Fahu, Jifeng Zhang, Jianbao Liu, Xianyong Cao, Juzhi Hou, Liping Zhu, Xiangke Xu et al. "Climate change, vegetation history, and landscape responses on the Tibetan Plateau during the Holocene: A comprehensive review." *Quaternary Science Reviews* 243, 106444 (2020). https://doi.org/10.1016/j.quascirev.2020.106444.

Chen Guoling, Chenqing Zheng, Lanhui Peng, Jia Yang, Feng Dong, Yiwei Lu, Siyu Wang et al. "Long-term and extensive population decline drives elevated expression of genetic load in a critically endangered seabird." Preprint (2023). https://doi.org/10.21203/rs.3.rs-2960319/v1.

Chen Hao, Wanchang Zhang, Huiran Gao and Ning Nie. "Climate Change and Anthropogenic Impacts on Wetland and Agriculture in the Songnen and Sanjiang Plain, Northeast China." *Remote Sensing* 10, 356 (2018). https://doi.org/10.3390/rs10030356.

Chen Jiajia, Zhen Pu, Zhonghong Huang, Fengqin Yu, Jianjun Zhang, Donghua Xu, Junquan Xu et al. "Global distribution and number of overwintering black-necked crane (*Grus nigricollis*)." *Biodiversity Science* 31, 22400 (2023). https://www.biodiversity-science.net/EN/10.17520/biods.2022400. (Chinese with English abstract)

Chen Jiu-Yi, Nasendelger, Sun Quan-Hui, Zhang Li-Jia, Tang Ji-Rong, Lang Jian-Min, Liu Tong et al. "Amur Tiger and Prey in Jilin Hunchun National Nature Reserve, China." *Chinese Journal of Zoology* 46 (2011): 46–52. http://dwxzz.ioz.ac.cn/ch/reader/view_abstract.aspx?file_no=20110206. (Chinese with English abstract)

Chen Min, Aorui Pu, Xin He, Endi Zhang, Youzhong Ding, Tianhou Wang, Youming Cai, Enle Pei and Xiao Yuan. "Chinese Water Deer (*Hydropotes inermis*) Reintroduction in Nanhui, Shanghai, China." *Pakistan Journal of Zoology* 47 (2015): 1499–1501. https://www.zsp.com.pk/pdf47/1499-1501%20(38)%20.pdf.

Chen Shuihua, Shou-hua Chang, Yang Liu, Simba Chan, Zhongyong Fan, Cangsong Chen, Chung-wei Yen and Dongsheng Guo. "A small population and severe threats: status of the Critically Endangered Chinese crested tern *Sterna bernsteini*." *Oryx* 43 (2009): 209–212. https://doi.org/10.1017/S0030605308001142.

Chen S. H., Z. Y. Fan, C. S. Chen and Y. W. Lu. "The breeding biology of Chinese Crested Terns in mixed species colonies in eastern China." *Bird Conservation International* 21 (2011): 266–273. https://doi.org/10.1017/S0959270910000547.

Chen Shuihua, Zhongyong Fan, Daniel D. Roby, Yiwei Lu, Cangsong Chen, Qin Huang, Lijing Cheng and Jiang Zhu. "Human harvest, climate change and their synergistic effects drove the Chinese Crested Tern to the brink of extinction." *Global Ecology and Conservation* 4 (2015): 137–145. https://doi.org/10.1016/j.gecco.2015.06.006.

Chen Y. and H. Tang. "Desertification in north China: background, anthropogenic impacts and failures in combating it." *Land Degradation & Development* 16 (2005): 367–376. https://doi.org/10.1002/ldr.667.

Chen Yaning, Zhaoxia Ye and Yanjun Shen. "Desiccation of the Tarim River, Xinjiang, China, and mitigation strategy." *Quaternary International* 244 (2011): 264–271. https://doi.org/10.1016/j.quaint.2011.01.039.

Chen Ying, Nianfan Ding, Yakuan Sun, Chiwei Xiao, Kun Shi and David Dudgeon. "Is there scope for growth? Mapping habitat suitability for Asian elephant (*Elephas maximus*) across its range in China." *Global Ecology and Conservation* 47, e02665 (2023). https://doi.org/10.1016/j.gecco.2023.e02665.

Chen Yuan, Chi Ma, Li Yang, Zhenhua Guan, Xuelong Jiang and Pengfei Fan. "Asymmetric competition between sympatric endangered primates affects their population recovery." *Biological Conservation* 248, 108558 (2020). https://doi.org/10.1016/j.biocon.2020.108558.

Chen, Yuan Julian. "Frontier, Fortification, and Forestation: Defensive Woodland on the Song–Liao Border in the Long Eleventh Century." *Journal of Chinese History* 2, sp. 2 (2018): 313–334. https://doi.org/10.1017/jch.2018.7.

Chen Yulong, Zhongdong Wang, Guangwei Zhang, Wei Fan, Yuanqing Tao, Xue He, Sihai Zhao et al. "Genetic characterization of four wild species of Chinese marmots using microsatellite markers." *Biologia* 67 (2012): 1013–1017. https://doi.org/10.2478/s11756-012-0088-8.

Cheng Lei, Dan Song, Xiaoli Yu, Xue Du and Tangbin Huo. "Endangered Schizothoracin Fish in the Tarim River Basin Are Threatened by Introgressive Hybridization." *Biology* 11, 981 (2022). https://doi.org/10.3390/biology11070981.

Cheng Lei, Lizhi Zhou, Chao Yu, Zhenhua Wei and Chunhua Li. "Flexible nest site selection of the endangered Oriental Storks (*Ciconia boyciana*): Trade-off from adaptive strategies." *Avian Research* 14, 100088 (2023). https://doi.org/10.1016/j.avrs.2023.100088.

Chestin, Igor E., Mikhail Yu. Paltsyn, Olga B. Pereladova, Liza V. Iegorova and James P. Gibbs. "Tiger re-establishment potential to former Caspian tiger (*Panthera tigris virgata*) range in Central Asia." *Biological Conservation* 205 (2017): 42–51. https://doi.org/10.1016/j.biocon.2016.11.014.

Chetry, D., R. Boonratana, J. Das, Y. Long, S. Htun and R.J. Timmins. "*Macaca arctoides.*" *The IUCN Red List of Threatened Species* (2020): e.T12548A185202632. https://dx.doi.org/10.2305/IUCN.UK.2020-3.RLTS.T12548A185202632.en.

Chia Ning. "The Solon Sable Tribute, Hunters of Inner Asia and Dynastic Elites at the Imperial Centre." *Inner Asia* 20 (2018): 26–63. https://doi.org/10.1163/22105018-12340098.

"China's Biodiversity Conservation Strategy and Action Plan (2023-2030)." *Ministry of Ecology and Environment of the People's Republic of China.* January 2024. https://chinadevelopmentbrief.org/publications/chinas-biodiversity-conservation-strategy-and-action-plan-2023-2030/.

Christenhusz, Maarten J. M. and Christine Battle. "1051. *Cathaya argyrophylla* Chun & Kuang." *Curtis's Botanical Magazine* 40 (2023): 3–14. https://doi.org/10.1111/curt.12490.

Chu Hongjun and Zhigang Jiang. "Distribution and conservation of the Sino-Mongolian beaver *Castor fiber birulai* in China." *Oryx* 43 (2009): 197–202. https://doi.org/10.1017/S0030605308002056.

Chu Juan. "Protecting the Habitats of Endangered Species Through Environmental Public Interest Litigation in China: Lessons Learned from Peafowl Versus the Dam." *Journal of Environmental Law* 35 (2023): 455–466. https://doi.org/10.1093/jel/eqad031.

Chu Kwei-ling and William S. Cooper. "An Ecological Reconnaissance in the Native Home of *Metasequoia glyptostroboides.*" *Ecology* 31 (1950): 260–278. https://doi.org/10.2307/1932391.

Cisneros-Mata, M.Á., C. True, L.M. Enriquez-Paredes, Y. Sadovy and M. Liu. "*Totoaba macdonaldi.*" *The IUCN Red List of Threatened Species* (2021): e.T22003A2780880. https://dx.doi.org/10.2305/IUCN.UK.2021-2.RLTS.T22003A2780880.en.

Cohen. John. "Anywhere but here." *Science* 377 (2022): 805–809. https://www.science.org/content/article/pandemic-start-anywhere-but-here-argue-papers-chinese-scientists-echoing-party-line.

Collar, N. J., H. S. Baral, N. Batbayar, G. S. Bhardwaj, N. Brahma, R. J. Burnside, A. U. Choudhury et al. "Averting the extinction of bustards in Asia." *Forktail* 33 (2017): 1–26. https://www.orientalbirdclub.org/forktail33.

Cooke, J.G., B.L. Taylor, R. Reeves and R.L. Brownell Jr. "*Eschrichtius robustus* (western subpopulation)." *The IUCN Red List of Threatened Species* (2018): e.T8099A50345475. http://dx.doi.org/10.2305/IUCN.UK.2018-2.RLTS. T8099A50345475.en.

Crees, Jennifer J., Chris Carbone, Robert S. Sommer, Norbert Benecke and Samuel T. Turvey. "Millennial-scale faunal record reveals differential resilience of European large mammals to human impacts across the Holocene." *Proceedings of the Royal Society B* 283, 20152152 (2016). http://dx.doi.org/10.1098/rspb.2015.2152.

Crighton, Peter. "Bird mortality in fish nets at a significant stopover site of the Spoon-billed Sandpiper *Calidris pygmaea* in the Yellow Sea, China." *Stilt* 69-70 (2016): 74–76. https://awsg.org.au/wp-content/uploads/2020/11/Stilt-69-70.pdf#page=76.

Cui Liang-Wei, Ying-Chun Li, Chi Ma, Matthew B. Scott, Jin-Fa Li, Xiao-Yang He, Dong-Hui Li et al. "Distribution and conservation status of Shortridge's capped langurs *Trachypithecus shortridgei* in China." *Oryx* 50 (2016): 732–741. https://doi.org/10.1017/S0030605315000319.

Cui Shaopeng, Daiqiang Chen, Jinyu Wang, Jizhou Sun, Hongjun Chu, Chunwang Li and Zhigang Jiang. "Camera-trapping survey on mammals and birds in the Kanas River Valley of Altai Mountains, Xinjiang, China." *Biodiversity Science* 28 (2020): 435–441. https://www.biodiversity-science.net/EN/10.17520/biods.2020184. (Chinese with English abstract)

Cui Shaopeng, E. J. Milner-Gulland, Navinder J. Singh, Hongjun Chu, Chunwang Li, Jing Chen and Zhigang Jiang. "Historical range, extirpation and prospects for reintroduction of saigas in China." *Scientific Reports* 7, 44200 (2017). https://doi.org/10.1038/srep44200.

Cunningham, A.B., J.A. Brinckmann, S.-J. Pei, P. Luo, U. Schippmann, X. Long and Y.-F. Bi. "High altitude species, high profits: can the trade in wild harvested *Fritillaria cirrhosa* (Liliaceae) be sustained?" *Journal of Ethnopharmacology* 223 (2018): 142–151. https://doi.org/10.1016/j.jep.2018.05.004.

Cunningham, A.B. and Xingchao Long. "Linking resource supplies and price drivers: Lessons from Traditional Chinese Medicine (TCM) price volatility and change, 2002–2017." *Journal of Ethnopharmacology* 229 (2019): 205–214. https://doi.org/10.1016/j.jep.2018.10.010.

Cunningham, Andrew A., Samuel T. Turvey, Feng Zhou, Helen M. R. Meredith, Wei Guan, Xinglian Liu, Changming Sun, Zhongqian Wang and Minyao Wu. "Development of the Chinese giant salamander *Andrias davidianus* farming industry in Shaanxi Province, China: conservation threats and opportunities." *Oryx* 50 (2016): 265–273. https://doi.org/10.1017/S0030605314000842.

Çakırlar, Canan and Salina Ikram. "'When elephants battle, the grass suffers.' Power, ivory and the Syrian elephant." *Levant* 48 (2016): 167–183. https://doi.org/10.1080/00758914.2016.1198068.

Dai Qiang, Wang Yuezhao, and Liang Gang. "Conservation Status of Chinese Giant Salamander (*Andrias davidianus*)." Report. Chinese Academy of Sciences, Chengdu (2009). https://www.research-gate.net/publication/242711582_Conservation_Status_of_Chinese_Giant_Salamander_Andrias_davidianus.

Dai Yunchuan, Charlotte E. Hacker, Yuguang Zhang, Wenwen Li, Yu Zhang, Haodong Liu, Jingjie Zhang et al. "Identifying climate refugia and its potential impact on Tibetan brown bear (*Ursus arctos pruinosus*) in Sanjiangyuan National Park, China." *Ecology and Evolution* 9 (2019): 13278–13293. https://doi.org/10.1002/ece3.5780.

Dai Yunchuan, Xue Yadong, Cheng Yifan, Zhang Yuguang, Zhang Liushuan, Zhang Yu, Luo Ping and Li Diqiang. "The human-bear conflicts and herder attitudes and knowledge in the Yangtze River Zone of Sanjiangyuan National Park." *Acta Ecologica Sinica* 39 (2019): 8245–8253. http://dx.doi.org/10.5846/stxb201904270867. (Chinese with Englsih abstract)

Dai Yunchuan, Yi Li, Yadong Xue, Charlotte E. Hacker, Chunyan Li, Babar Zahoor, Yang Liu et al. "Mitigation Strategies for Human–Tibetan Brown Bear (*Ursus arctos pruinosus*) Conflicts in the Hinterland of the Qinghai-Tibetan Plateau." *Animals* 12, 1422 (2022). https://doi.org/10.3390/ani12111422.

David, Armand. "Extrait d'une lettre de même, datée de la principauté Thibétaine (indépendante), de Mou-pin, le 21 mars 1869." *Nouvelles archives du Muséum d'histoire naturelle de Paris, Bulletin* 5 (1869): 11–13.

D'Cruze, Neil, Joanna Toole, Katharine Mansell and Jan Schmidt-Burbach. "What is the true cost of the world's most expensive coffee?" *Oryx* 48 (2014): 170–171. https://doi.org/10.1017/S0030605313001531.

Deng Zeshuai, Xin Xia, Mu Zhang, Xiangying Chen, Xiangyun Ding, Bing Zhang, Guoxing Deng and Daode Yang. "Predicting the Spatial Distribution of the Mangshan Pit Viper (*Protobothrops mangshanensis*) under Climate Change Scenarios Using MaxEnt Modeling." *Forests* 15, 723 (2024). https://doi.org/10.3390/f15040723.

Dhendup, Tashi, Bikram Shrestha, Neeraj Mahar, Shekhar Kolipaka, Ganga Ram Regmi and Rodney Jackson. "Distribution and status of the manul in the Himalayas and China." *Cat News* sp. 13 (2019): 31–36. http://www.catsg.org/fileadmin/filesharing/5.Cat_News/5.3._Special_Issues/5.3.12_SI_13/Dhendup_et_al_2019_Distributtion_and_status_of_manul_in_the_Himalayas_and_China.pdf.

Di Dario, F. "*Tenualosa reevesii*." *The IUCN Red List of Threatened Species* (2018): e.T166910A143829403. https://dx.doi.org/10.2305/IUCN.UK.2018-2.RLTS.T166910A143829403.en.

Diao Yixin, Qianqian Zhao, Yue Weng, Zixin Huang, Yiqian Wu, Bojian Gu, Qing Zhao and Fang Wang. "Predicting current and future species distribution of the raccoon dog (*Nyctereutes procyonoides*) in Shanghai, China." *Landscape and Urban Planning* 228, 104581 (2022). https://doi.org/10.1016/j.landurbplan.2022.104581.

Dinets, Vladimir. "First Record of the Chinese Crested Tern *Thalasseus bernsteini* in Japan." *Journal of the Yamashina Institute for Ornithology* 50 (2019): 138–140. https://doi.org/10.3312/jyio.50.138.

Ding Chenchen, Jiu Liu, Chunwang Li and Zhigang Jiang. "Probable extirpation of the hog deer from China: implications for conservation." *Oryx* 56 (2022): 360–366. https://doi.org/10.1017/S0030605321000016.

Ding Chenchen, Yiming Hu, Chunwang Li and Zhigang Jiang. "Distribution and habitat suitability assessment of the gaur *Bos gaurus* in China." *Biodiversity Science* 26 (2018): 951–961. https://www.biodiversity-science.net/EN/Y2018/V26/I9/951. (Chinese with English abstract)

Dou Hongliang, Guangshun Jiang, Philip Stott, Renzhu Piao. "Climate change impacts population dynamics and distribution shift of moose (*Alces alces*) in Heilongjiang Province of China." *Ecological Research* 28 (2013): 625–632. https://doi.org/10.1007/s11284-013-1054-9.

Dou Huashan, Zhang Honghai, Wu Muren and Gui Manquan. "Wolf Predation on Livestock around the Dalai Lake National Nature Reserve, Inner Mongolia," in *Proceedings of the International Conference for the 20th anniversary of the DIPA*, 21–25. Ulaanbaatar: Wildlife Conservation Society Mongolia, 2014.

Du Cong-cong, Zhao Jing, Chu Hong-jun, Liu Yuan-chao, Duan Xiao-aan and Chen Gang. "Research on genetic diversities of Asiatic beaver (*Castor fiber birulai*) on mtDNA D-loop HV-I in Xinjiang, China." *Journal of Shandong University (Natural Science)* 51 (2016): 19–28. https://doi.org/10.6040/j.issn.1671-9352.0.2015.458. (Chinese with English abstract)

Du Linyao, Minmin Ma, Yiwen Lu, Jiajia Dong and Guanghui Dong. "How Did Human Activity and Climate Change Influence Animal Exploitation During 7500–2000 BP in the Yellow River Valley, China?" *Frontiers in Ecology and Evolution* 8 (2020). https://doi.org/10.3389/fevo.2020.00161.

Du Yu-Rong, Song-Chang Guo, Zhao-Feng Wang, Hai-sing Ci, Zhen-Yuan Cai, Qian Zhang, Jian-Ping Su and Jian-Qian Liu. "Demographic history of the Tibetan antelope *Pantholops hodgsoni* (chiru)." *Journal of Systematics and Evolution* 48 (2010): 490–496. https://doi.org/10.1111/j.1759-6831.2010.00095.x.

Duan Fei, Shuyi Zhu, Yuan Wang, Dazhao Song, Xiaoli Shen and Sheng Li. "Distribution of the Asiatic golden cat (*Catopuma temminckii*) and variations in its coat morphology in China." *Ecology and Evolution* 14, e10900 (2024). https://doi.org/10.1002/ece3.10900.

Dubost, Gérard, Florence Charron, Aurélie Courcoul and Aurélie Rodier. "The Chinese water deer, *Hydropotes inermis* —A fast-growing and productive ruminant." *Mammalian Biology* 76 (2011): 190–195. https://doi.org/10.1016/j.mambio.2010.04.001.

Duckworth, J.W. and J. MacKinnon. "*Naemorhedus goral.*" *The IUCN Red List of Threatened Species* (2008): e.T14296A4430073. http://dx.doi.org/10.2305/IUCN.UK.2008.RLTS.T14296A4430073.en.

Dwyer, Nancy C., Mary Anne Bishop, Jim S. Harkness, and Zhang Yao Zhong. "Black-necked cranes nesting in Tibet Autonomous Region, China," in *Proceedings of the Sixth North American Crane Workshop, Oct. 3-5, 1991, Regina, Sask.*, edited by D. W. Stahlecker 75–80. Grand Island, NE.: North American Crane Working Group, 1992. https://digitalcommons.unl.edu/nacwgproc/254/.

Ellis, Erle C. "Land Use and Ecological Change: A 12,000-Year History." *Annual Review of Environment and Resources* 46 (2021): 1–33. https://doi.org/10.1146/annurev-environ-012220-010822.

Ellis, S. and B. Talukdar. "*Dicerorhinus sumatrensis*." *The IUCN Red List of Threatened Species* (2020): e.T6553A18493355. https://dx.doi.org/10.2305/IUCN.UK.2020-2.RLTS.T6553A18493355.en.

Fan Ka-wai. "Climate change and Chinese history: a review of trends, topics, and methods." *WIREs Climate Change* 6 (2015): 225–238. https://doi.org/10.1002/wcc.331.

Fan Peng-Fei, Han-Lan Fei and Ai-Dong Luo. "Ecological extinction of the Critically Endangered northern white-cheeked gibbon *Nomascus leucogenys* in China." *Oryx* 48 (2013): 52–55. https://doi.org/10.1017/S0030605312001305.

Fan Peng-Fei and Huai-Sen Ai. "Conservation status of the eastern hoolock gibbon (*Hoolock leuconedys*) in China." *Gibbon Journal* 6 (2011): 22–25. http://www.gibbonconservation.org/07_publications/journal/gibbon_journal_6.pdf.

Fan Peng-Fei and Huo Sheng. "The northern white-cheeked gibbon (*Nomascus leucogenys*) is on the edge of extinction in China." *Gibbon Journal* 5 (2009): 44–52. http://www.gibbonconservation.org/07_publications/journal/gibbon_journal_5.pdf.

Fan Peng-Fei, Lu Zhang, Li Yang, Xia Huang, Kai-Chong Shi, Guo-Qing Liu and Chun-Hua Wang. "Population recovery of the critically endangered western black crested gibbon (Nomascus concolor) in Mt. Wuliang, Yunnan, China." *Zoological Research* 43 (2022): 180–183. https://doi.org/10.24272/j.issn.2095-8137.2021.390.

F. Pengfei, M.H. Nguyen, P. Phiaphalath, C. Roos, C.N.Z. Coudrat and B.M. Rawson. "*Nomascus concolor*." *The IUCN Red List of Threatened Species* (2020): e.T39775A17968556. https://dx.doi.org/10.2305/IUCN.UK.2020-2.RLTS.T39775A17968556.en.

Fan Yukun, Li Wang, Tao Su, Qinying Lan. "Spring drought as a possible cause for disappearance of native *Metasequoia* in Yunnan Province, China: Evidence from seed germination and seedling growth." *Global Ecology and Conservation* 22, e00912 (2020). https://doi.org/10.1016/j.gecco.2020.e00912.

Farjon, A. "*Metasequoia glyptostroboides*." *The IUCN Red List of Threatened Species* (2013): e.T32317A2814244. http://dx.doi.org/10.2305/IUCN.UK.2013-1.RLTS.T32317A2814244.en.

Fedosenko, Alexander K. and David A. Blank. "*Capra sibirica*." *Mammalian Species* 675 (2001): 1–13. https://doi.org/10.2307/0.675.1.

Feijó, Anderson, Yanqun Wang, Jian Sun, Feihong Li, Zhixin Wen, Deyan Ge, Lin Xia and Qisen Yang. "Research trends on bats in China: A twenty-first century review." *Mammalian Biology* 98 (2019): 163–172. https://doi.org/10.1016/j.mambio.2019.09.002.

Fellowes, John R., Chan Bosco Pui Lok, Zhou Jiang, Chen Shenghua, Yang Shibin and Ng Sai Chit. "Current status of the Hainan gibbon (*Nomascus hainanus*): progress of population monitoring and other priory actions." *Asian Primates Journal* 1 (2008). http://static1.1.sqspcdn.com/static/f/1200343/18198289/1337026355490/APJ1.1.hainanus.pdf?token=Q%2Ba3NhLS8sM9bF1d8seWpkrvykg%3D.

Fellowes, John R., Zhou Fang, Lee Kwok Shing, Billy C.H. Hau, Michael W. N. Lau, Vicky W.Y. Lam, Llewellyn Young and Heinz Hafner. "Status update on White-eared Night Heron *Gorsachius magnificus* in South China." *Bird Conservation International* 11 (2001): 101–111. https://doi.org/10.1017/S0959270901000193.

Feng Hui, Lu Wang, Fangjun Cao, Ji Ma, Jie Tang, Chengli Feng and Zhijian Su. "Forest musk deer (*Moschus berezovskii*) in China: research and protection." *Journal of Vertebrate Biology* 72, 22067 (2023). https://doi.org/10.25225/jvb.22067.

Fielder, Katrin. "Rumble in the Eco-Jungle: China's Green Non-Governmental Organizations." *Education About Asia* 15 (2010): 23–27. https://www.asianstudies.org/publications/eaa/archives/rumble-in-the-eco-jungle-chinas-green-non-governmental-organizations/.

Gao Linqiang and Chunrong Mi. "Double jeopardy: global change and interspecies competition threaten Siberian cranes." *PeerJ* 12, e17029 (2024). http://dx.doi.org/10.7717/peerj.17029.

Gao Shuaishuai, Hu Yang, Shao Changliang, Jiang Liwei, Zhang Yuguang, Su Zhizhu, Wu Bo and Li Jia. "Vulnerability assessment of suitable habitats for *Equus hemionus* in the Kalamaili National Park under climate change." *Acta Theriologica Sinica* 44 (2024): 287–296. https://www.mammal.cn/EN/10.16829/j.slxb.150846. (Chinese with English abstract)

Gao XingYi, Olivier Combreau, JianFang Qiao, WeiKang Yang, Jun Yao and KeFen Xu. "Distribution and migration of houbara bustard (*Chlamydotis undulata*) in China." *Journal of Arid Land* 1 (2009): 74–79. http://jal.xjegi.com/CN/10.3724/SP.J.1227.00074.

Gao Yong, Cao Guangjing, Chen Yongbo and Chang Jianbo. "A Review on Conservation Issue in Chinese Paddlefish, Psephurus Glasius." *Advances in Water Resources and Hydraulic Engineering* (2009): 2279–2284. https://doi.org/10.1007/978-3-540-89465-0_391.

Garshelis, D. and R. Steinmetz. "*Ursus thibetanus* (amended version of 2016 assessment)." *The IUCN Red List of Threatened Species* (2020): e.T22824A166528664. https://dx.doi.org/10.2305/IUCN.UK.2020-3.RLTS.T22824A166528664.en.

Geissmann, T., La Quang Trung, Trinh Dinh Hoang, Vu Dinh Thong, Dang Ngoc Can and Pham Duc Tien. "Rarest ape species rediscovered in Vietnam." *Asian Primates* 8 (2003): 8–9. http://www.primate-sg.org/storage/PDF/AS8.3-4.pdf.

Geissmann, Thomas, Ngwe Lwin, Saw Some Aung, Thet Naing Aung, Zin Myo Zung, Tony Htin Hla, Mark Grindley and Frank Momberg. "A New Species of Snub-Nosed Monkey, Genus *Rhinopithecus* Milne-Edwards, 1872 (Primates, Colobinae), From Northern Kachin State, Northeastern Myanmar." *American Journal of Primatology* 73 (2011): 96–107. https://doi.org/10.1002/ajp.20894.

Geissmann, Thomas, Frank Momberg and Tony Whitten. "*Rhinopithecus strykeri*." *The IUCN Red List of Threatened Species* (2012): e.T13508501A13508504. https://dx.doi.org/10.2305/IUCN.UK.2020-2.RLTS.T13508501A17943490.en.

Geissmann, T. and W. Bleisch. "*Nomascus hainanus*." *The IUCN Red List of Threatened Species* (2020): e.T41643A17969392. https://dx.doi.org/10.2305/IUCN.UK.2020-2.RLTS.T41643A17969392.en.

Gong Minghao, Shiliang Pang, Zhongyan Gao, Wanyu Wen, Ling Zhang, Gang Liu, Huixin Li et al. "The Path Forward: Conservation of Climate Change-Affected Breeding Habitat of Red-crowned Cranes near Zhalong Reserve, China." *Pakistan Journal of Zoology* 53 (2021): 733–742. https://dx.doi.org/10.17582/journal.pjz/20181205011224.

Gong Shi-Ping, Dao-de Yang, Yuan-hui Chen, Michael Lau and Fu-min Wang. "Population status, distribution and conservation needs of the Endangered Mangshan pit viper *Protobothrops mangshanensis* of China." *Oryx* 47 (2013): 122–127. https://doi.org/10.1017/S0030605311001037.

Gong Yan-An, Xu Jing-Cheng, Huang Song, Huang Ru-Yi, Li Jia-Qi, Jiang Yong-Qiang, Yang Dian-Cheng et al. "A New Species of the Giant Salamander of the Genus *Andrias* from Qimeng [*sic*], Anhui, China (Amphibia: Cryptorchiidae)." *Chinese Journal of Zoology* 58 (2023): 651–657. http://dwxzz.ioz.ac.cn/ch/reader/view_abstract.aspx?file_no=20230502. (Chinese with English abstract)

Gowlett, J. A. J.. "The discovery of fire by humans: a long and convoluted process." *Philosophical Transactions of the Royal Society B* 371, 20150164 (2016). http://dx.doi.org/10.1098/rstb.2015.0164.

Gray, T., J. Borah, C.N.Z. Coudrat, Y. Ghimirey, A. Giordano, E. Greenspan, W. Petersen, S. Rostro-García, M. Sharif and W. Wai-Ming. "*Neofelis nebulosa*." *The IUCN Red List of Threatened Species* (2021) e.T14519A198843258. https://dx.doi.org/10.2305/IUCN.UK.2021-2.RLTS.T14519A198843258.en.

Gray, T.N.E., S.M. Brook, W.J. McShea, S. Mahood, M.K. Ranjitsingh, A. Miyunt, S.A. Hussain and R. Timmins. "*Rucervus eldii*." *The IUCN Red List of Threatened Species* (2015): e.T4265A22166803. http://dx.doi.org/10.2305/IUCN.UK.2015-2.RLTS.T4265A22166803 en.

Gray, Thomas N. E., Romica Grosu and Chum Sokkheng. "Unexpected discovery in the Cardamom Rainforest Landscape, Cambodia: a White-eared Night Heron *Gorsachius magnificus* in Botum Sakor National Park." *BirdingASIA* 32 (2019): 12–14. https://www.orientalbirdclub.org/birdingasia-32.

Grueter, Cyril C., Xuelong Jiang, Roger Konrad, Pengfei Fan, Zhenhua Guan & Thomas Geissmann. "Are *Hylobates lar* Extirpated from China?" *International Journal of Primatology* 30 (2009): 553–567. https://doi.org/10.1007/s10764-009-9360-3.

Guo Yanlong, Xin Li, Zefang Zhao, Haiyan Wei, Bei Gao and Wei Gu. "Prediction of the potential geographic distribution of the ectomycorrhizal mushroom *Tricholoma matsutake* under multiple climate change scenarios." *Scientific Reports* 7, 46221 (2017). https://doi.org/10.1038/srep46221.

Guo Yanqing, Ren Baoping, Dai Qiang, Zhou Jun, Paul A. Garber and Zhou Jiang. "Habitat estimates reveal that there are fewer than 400 Guizhou snub-nosed monkeys, *Rhinopithecus brelichi*, remaining in the wild." *Global Ecology and Conservation* 24, e01181 (2020). https://doi.org/10.1016/j.gecco.2020.e01181.

Hale, Lauren J., Kun Shi, Tania C. Gilbert, Kelvin S.-H. Peh and Philip Riordan. "Social structure and demography of a remnant Asian elephant *Elephas maximus* population and the implications for survival." *Oryx* 55 (2021): 473–478. https://doi.org/10.1017/S0030605319000504.

Halley, Duncan J., Alexander P. Saveljev and Frank Rosell. "Population and distribution of beavers *Castor fiber* and *Castor canadensis* in Eurasia." *Mammal Review* 51 (2021): 1–24. https://doi.org/10.1111/mam.12216.

Han Sicheng, Daowei Lu, Yuchen Han, Ruohan Li, Jing Yang, Ge Sun, Lu Yang et al. "Distribution of leopard cats in the nearest mountains to urban Beijing and its affecting environmental factors." *Biodiversity Science* 32, 24138 (2024). https://www.biodiversity-science.net/CN/10.17520/biods.2024138. (Chinese with English abstract)

Han Yi, Wenjing Xu, Jiajia Liu, Xinqiao Zhang, Kexiong Wang, Ding Wang and Zhigang Mei. "Ecological impacts of unsustainable sand mining: urgent lessons learned from a critically endangered freshwater cetacean." *Proceedings of the Royal Society B* 290, 20221786 (2023). https://doi.org/10.1098/rspb.2022.1786.

Harding, Lee E. and Lian-Xian Han. "*Rhinopithecus bieti* (Primates: Cercopithecidae)." *Mammalian Species* 50 (2018): 148–165. https://doi.org/10.1093/mspecies/sey016.

Hare, John. "The wild Bactrian camel *Camelus bactrianus ferus* in China: the need for urgent action." *Oryx* 31 (1997): 45–48. https://doi.org/10.1046/j.1365-3008.1997.d01-2.x.

———. "*Camelus ferus*." *The IUCN Red List of Threatened Species* (2008): e.T63543A12689285. https://dx.doi.org/10.2305/IUCN.UK.2008.RLTS.T63543A12689285.en.

Harper, Donald. "The Cultural History of the Giant Panda (*Ailuropoda melanoleuca*) in Early China." *Early China* 35 (2013): 185–224. https://doi.org/10.1017/S0362502800000481.

Harris, James and Claire Mirande. "A global overview of cranes: status, threats and conservation priorities." *Chinese Birds* 4 (2013): 189–209. http://doi.org/10.5122/cbirds.2013.0025.

Harris, R.B. "*Cervus albirostris*." *The IUCN Red List of Threatened Species* (2015): e.T4256A61976756. https://dx.doi.org/10.2305/IUCN.UK.2015-2.RLTS. T4256A61976756.en.

———. "Rangeland degradation on the Qinghai-Tibetan plateau: A review of the evidence of its magnitude and causes." *Journal of Arid Environments* 74 (2010): 1–12. https://doi.org/10.1016/j.jaridenv.2009.06.014.

Harris, R.B. and J.W. Duckworth. "*Hydropotes inermis*." *The IUCN Red List of Threatened Species* (2015): e.T10329A22163569. https://dx.doi.org/10.2305/ IUCN.UK.2015-2.RLTS.T10329A22163569.en.

Harris, Richard B., Leah H. Samberg, Emily T. Yeh, Andrew T. Smith, Wang Wenying, Wang Junbang, Gaerrang, and Donald J. Bedunah. "Rangeland responses to pastoralists' grazing management on a Tibetan steppe grassland, Qinghai Province, China." *The Rangeland Journal* 38 (2016): 1–15. https://doi. org/10.1071/RJ15040.

Harris, Richard B., Wang Zhenghuan, Zhou Jiake and Liu Qunxiu. "Notes on the biology of the Tibetan fox." *Canid News* 11 (2008). https://www.canids.org/ canidnews/11/Biology_of_Tibetan_fox.pdf.

Harris, Richard B., Zhou Jiake, Ji Yinqiu, Zhang Xai, Yang Chunyan and Douglas W, Yu. "Evidence that the Tibetan fox is an obligate predator of the plateau pika: conservation implications." *Journal of Mammalogy* 95 (2014): 1207–1221. https://doi.org/10.1644/14-MAMM-A-021.

Hazitai, Ahebota, Han-Lan Fei, Chang-Yue Zhu, Ru-Xue Li, Li-Xiang Zhang and Peng-Fei Fan. "Cardamom (*Amomum tsaoko*) agroforest is important habitat for skywalker hoolock gibbon (*Hoolock tianxing*) in Mt. Gaoligong, Yunnan, China." *Global Ecology and Conservation* 54, e03129 (2024). https://doi.org/10.1016/j. gecco.2024.e03129.

He Jinsheng, Lin Jie and Chen Weilie. "The current status of endemic and endangered species *Davidia involucrata* and the preserving strategies." *Chinese Biodiversity* 3 (1995): 213–221. https://www.biodiversity-science.net/CN/ 10.17520/biods.1995036. (Chinese with English abstract)

He, J. "Globalised forest-products: commodification of the matsutake mushroom in Tibetan villages, Yunnan, Southwest China." *International Forestry Review* 12 (2010): 27–37. https://doi.org/10.1505/ifor.12.1.27.

He Jun. "Harvest and trade of caterpillar mushroom (*Ophiocordyceps sinensis*) and the implications for sustainable use in the Tibet Region of Southwest China." *Journal of Ethnopharmacology* 221 (2018): 86–90. https://doi.org/10.1016/j. jep.2018.04.022.

He Xingcheng, Fu Qiang, Wu Yongjie, Wang Bin, Chen Xue and Ran Jianghong. "Population structure and activity rhythm of sambar deer (*Rusa unicolor*)." *Acta Theriologica Sinica* 39 (2019): 134–141. http://www.mammal.cn/EN/ 10.16829/j.slxb.150195. (Chinese with English abstract)

Heim, Wieland, Simba Chan, Norbert Hölzel, Pavel Ktitorov, Alexander Mischenko and Johannes Kamp. "East Asian buntings: Ongoing illegal trade and encouraging conservation responses." *Conservation Science and Practice* 3, e405 (2021). https://doi.org/10.1111/csp2.405.

Heller, Natasha. "Why Has the Rhinoceros Come from the West? An Excursus into the Religious, Literary, and Environmental History of the Tang Dynasty." *Journal of the American Oriental Society* 131 (2011): 353–370. https://www.jstor.org/stable/41380706.

Hemmer, Helmut. "*Uncia uncia.*" *Mammalian Species* 20 (1972): 1–5. https://doi.org/10.2307/3503882.

Hodgson, B. H. "Notice of the Mammals of Tibet, with Descriptions and Plates of some new Species." *Journal of the Asiatic Society of Bengal* 11 (1842): 275–289.

Hopping, Kelly A., Stephen M. Chignell and Eric F. Lambin. "The demise of caterpillar fungus in the Himalayan region due to climate change and overharvesting." *Proceedings of the National Academy of Sciences* 115 (2018): 11489–11494. https://doi.org/10.1073/pnas.1811591115.

Hoy, Charles M. "The 'White-Flag' Dolphin of the Tung Ting Lake." *The China Journal of Science & Arts* 1 (1923): 154–157.

Hu Gang, Xin Dong, Yi Wei, Ying Zhu, Xihuan Duan. "Evidence for a decline of François' langur *Trachypithecus francoisi* in Fusui Nature Reserve, south-west Guangxi, China." *Oryx* 38 (2004): 48–54. https://doi.org/10.1017/S0030605304000080.

Hu, H. H. and Cheng Hsueh Chi-ju. "Reminiscences of Collecting the Type Specimens of *Metasequoia glyptostroboides.*" *Arnoldia* 45 (1985): 10–18. https://assetbank.arboretum.harvard.edu/assetbank-aahu/action/directLinkImage?assetId=24877.

Hu Jing-Yang, Zi-Qian Hao, Laurent Frantz, Shi-Fang Wu, Wu Chen, Yun-Fang Jiang, Hong Wu et al. "Genomic consequences of population decline in critically endangered pangolins and their demographic histories." *National Science Review* 7 (2020): 798–814. https://doi.org/10.1093/nsr/nwaa031.

Hu Junhua and Yang Liu. "Unveiling the Conservation Biogeography of a Data-Deficient Endangered Bird Species under Climate Change." *PLoS ONE* 9, e84529 (2014). https://doi.org/10.1371/journal.pone.0084529.

Hu Junhua and Zhigang Jiang. "Climate Change Hastens the Conservation Urgency of an Endangered Ungulate." *PLoS ONE* 6, e22873 (2011). https://doi.org/10.1371/journal.pone.0022873.

Hu Junhua, Zhigang Jiang and David P. Mallon. "Metapopulation viability of a globally endangered gazelle on the Northeast Qinghai–Tibetan Plateau." *Biological Conservation* 166 (2013): 23–32. https://doi.org/10.1016/j.biocon.2013.06.011.

Hu Wenqiang, Hongjiao Wang, Xueyou Li and Xuelong Jiang. "New records of the white-cheeked macaque provide range extension for the endangered primate in Gaoligong Mountains." *Primates* 65 (2024): 15–19. https://doi.org/10.1007/s10329-023-01096-3.

Hu Yibo, Arjun Thapa, Huizhong Fan, Tianxiao Ma, Qi Wu, Shuai Ma, Dongling Zhang et al. "Genomic evidence for two phylogenetic species and long-term population bottlenecks in red pandas." *Science Advances* 6, eaax5751 (2020). https://doi.org/10.1126/sciadv.aax5751.

Hu Yi-Ming, Zhi-Xin Zhou, Zhi-Wen Huang, Ming Li, Zhi-Gang Jiang, Jian-Pu Wu, Wu-Lin Liu et al. "A new record of the capped langur (*Trachypithecus pileatus*) in China." *Zoological Research* 38 (2017): 203–205. https://doi.org/10.24272/j.issn.2095-8137.2017.038.

Hu Yisi, Yibo Hu, Wenliang Zhou and Fuwen Wei. "Conservation Genomics and Metagenomics of Giant and Red Pandas in the Wild." *Annual Review of Animal Biosciences* 12 (2024): 69–89. https://doi.org/10.1146/annurev-animal-021022-054730.

Huang C. M., H. Yu, Z. J. Wu, Y. B. Li, F. W. Wei and M. H. Gong. "Population and conservation strategies for the Chinese crocodile lizard (*Shinisaurus crocodilurus*) in China." *Animal Biodiversity and Conservation* 31 (2008): 63–70. http://abc.museucienciesjournals.cat/volume-31-2-2008-abc/population-and-conservation-strategies-for-the-chinese-crocodile-lizard-shinisaurus-crocodilurus-in-china-2/?lang=en.

Huang Cheng, Li Xueyou and Jiang Xuelong. "Confirmation of the continued occurrence of Binturong *Arctictis binturong* in China." *Small Carnivore Conservation* 55 (2015): 59–63. https://smallcarnivoreconservation.com/index.php/sccg/issue/view/237/66.

Huang Chengming, Fuwen Wei, Ming Li, Guoqiang Quan and Hanhua Li. "Current status and conservation of white-headed langur (*Trachypithecus leucocephalus*) in China." *Biological Conservation* 104 (2002): 221–225. https://doi.org/10.1016/S0006-3207(01)00168-9.

Huang Chengming, Youbang Li, Qihai Zhou, Yongxin Feng, Zhi Chen, Hai Yu and Zhengjun Wu. "Karst Habitat Fragmentation and the Conservation of the White-headed Langur (*Trachypithecus leucocephalus*) in China." *Primate Conservation* 23 (2008): 133–139. https://doi.org/10.1896/052.023.0116.

Huang G., R. Sreekar, N. Velho, R. T. Corlett, R.C. Quan and K. W. Tomlinson. "Combining camera-trap surveys and hunter interviews to determine the status of mammals in protected rainforests and rubber plantations of Menglun, Xishuangbanna, SW China." *Animal Conservation* 23 (2020): 689–699. https://doi.org/10.1111/acv.12588.

Huang Jie, Zhigang Mei, Mao Chen, Yi Han, Xinqiao Zhang, Jeffrey E. Moore, Xiujiang Zhao et al. "Population survey showing hope for population recovery of the critically endangered Yangtze finless porpoise." *Biological Conservation* 241, 108315 (2020). https://doi.org/10.1016/j.biocon.2019.108315.

Huang Zhenli and Haiying Li. "Dams trigger exponential population declines of migratory fish." *Science Advances* 10, eadi6580 (2024). https://doi.org/10.1126/sciadv.adi6580.

Huffman, B. and R. Harris. "*Pseudois nayaur ssp. schaeferi*." *The IUCN Red List of Threatened Species* (2014): e.T18535A64313668. http://dx.doi.org/10.2305/IUCN.UK.2014-3.RLTS.T18535A64313668.en.

Hughes, Joelene, Justine Alexander, Kun Shi and Philip Riordan. "Confirmation of threatened white-lipped deer (*Przewalskium albirostris*) in Gansu and Sichuan, China, and their overlap with livestock." *Mammalia* 79 (2015): 241–244. https://doi.org/10.1515/mammalia-2014-0038.

Hughes, Terry P. and Hui Huang. "The Wicked Problem of China's Disappearing Coral Reefs." *Conservation Biology* 27 (2013): 261–269. https://doi.org/10.1111/j.1523-1739.2012.01957.x.

Iijima Masaya, Yu Qiao, Wenbin Lin, Youjie Peng, Minoru Yoneda and Jun Liu. "An intermediate crocodylian linking two extant gharials from the Bronze Age of China and its human-induced extinction." *Proceedings of the Royal Society B* 289, 20220085 (2022). https://doi.org/10.1098/rspb.2022.0085.

IUCN SSC Amphibian Specialist Group. "*Leptobrachium boringii.*" *The IUCN Red List of Threatened Species (*2020): e.T57625A63865231. https://dx.doi.org/10.2305/IUCN.UK.2020-2.RLTS.T57625A63865231.en.

IUCN SSC Antelope Specialist Group. "*Procapra picticaudata.*" *The IUCN Red List of Threatened Species* (2016): e.T18231A115142581. http://dx.doi.org/10.2305/IUCN.UK.2016-3.RLTS.T18231A50192968.en.

IUCN SSC-ASAP (Asian Species Action Partnership) and IUCN SSC Tortoise and Freshwater Turtle Specialist Group (TFTSG). "Conservation of *Rafetus swinhoei.*" Workshop Report (2014). https://web.archive.org/web/20240115155041/http://www.speciesonthebrink.org/wp-content/uploads/2015/12/Rafetus-report_draft_23SEPT.pdf.

Jefferson, Thomas A., Elizabeth A. Becker and Shiang-Lin Huang. "Influences of natural and anthropogenic habitat variables on Indo-Pacific humpback dolphins *Sousa chinensis* in Hong Kong." *Endangered Species Research* 51 (2023): 143–160. https://doi.org/10.3354/esr01249.

Jefferson, Thomas A. and Jeffrey E. Moore. "Abundance and Trends of Indo-Pacific Finless Porpoises (*Neophocaena phocaenoides*) in Hong Kong Waters, 1996–2019." *Frontiers in Marine Science* 7, 574381 (2020). https://doi.org/10.3389/fmars.2020.574381.

Jefferson, Thomas A. and John Y. Wang. "Revision of the taxonomy of finless porpoises (genus *Neophocaena*): The existence of two species." *Journal of Marine Animals and Their Ecology* 4 (2011): 3–16. https://web.archive.org/web/20201017170346/http://www.oers.ca/journal/volume4/issue1/Jefferson_Galley.pdf.

Jefferson, Thomas A. and Samuel K. Hung. "A Review of the Status of the Indo-Pacific Humpback Dolphin (*Sousa chinensis*) in Chinese Waters." *Aquatic Mammals* 30 (2004): 149–158. http://dx.doi.org/10.1578/AM.30.1.2004.149.

Jefferson, Thomas A., Samuel K. Hung, Lawman Law, Mientje Torey and Nick Tregenza. "Distribution and Abundance of Finless Porpoises in Hong Kong and Adjacent Waters of China." *The Raffles Bulletin of Zoology* suppl. 10 (2002): 43–55. https://lkcnhm.nus.edu.sg/wp-content/uploads/sites/10/2020/12/s10rbz043-055.pdf.

Ji Shengnan, Yanpeng Zhu, Shaopeng Cui, Huaiqing Deng and Chunwang Li. "The road home for Przewalski's horse in China." *Oryx* 56 (2022): 652. https://doi.org/10.1017/S0030605322000758.

Jiang Ting-ting, Jin-fen Pan, Xin-Ming Pu, Bo Wang and Jing-Jin Pan. "Current status of coastal wetlands in China: Degradation, restoration, and future management." *Estuarine, Coastal and Shelf Science* 164 (2015): 265–275. http://dx.doi.org/10.1016/j.ecss.2015.07.046.

Jiang Xuelong, Zhonghua Luo, Shiyuan Zhao, Rongzhong Li and Changming Liu. "Status and distribution pattern of black crested gibbon (*Nomascus concolor jingdongensis*) in Wuliang Mountains, Yunnan, China: implication for conservation." *Primates* 47 (2006): 264–271. https://doi.org/10.1007/s10329-005-0175-3.

Jiang Z. and R.B. Harris. "*Elaphurus davidianus*" *The IUCN Red List of Threatened Species* (2016): e.T7121A22159785. https://dx.doi.org/10.2305/IUCN.UK.2016-2.RLTS.T7121A22159785.en.

Jiang Zhigang, Chunwang Li and Chenchen Ding. "The roaming wild Asian elephants of Yunnan, China, pose a challenge to conservation." *Oryx* 55 (2021): 650–651. https://doi.org/10.1017/S0030605321000879.

Jiang Zhigang, David Mallon, Marc Foggen, Chunwang Li, Shaopeng Cui, Yan Zeng and Xiaoge Ping. "A Case of Reintroducing Saiga Highlights the Conservation Needs of Migratory Species." *Preprints* 2020020375 (2020). https://www.preprints.org/manuscript/202002.0375/v2.

Jin Xinyao, Hui Zi Chua, Keyi Wang, Nan Li, Wenke Zheng, Wentai Pang, Fengwen Yang, Bo Pang et al. "Evidence for the medicinal value of Squama Manitis (pangolin scale): A systematic review." *Integrative Medicine Research* 10, 100486 (2021). https://doi.org/10.1016/j.imr.2020.100486.

Jin Yongchao, Weiyao Kong, Hong Yan, Guangdao Dao, Ting Liu, Qiongfang Ma, Xinhai Li, Hongfei Zou and Minghai Zhang. "Multi-Scale Spatial Prediction of Wild Boar Damage Risk in Hunchun: A Key Tiger Range in China." *Animals* 11, 1012 (2021). https://doi.org/10.3390/ani11041012.

Jiu Yujie, Jianwei Zhou, Siwei Yang, Bin Chu, Huimin Zhu, Bo Zhang, Qiangen Fang et el. "Plant diversity is closely related to the density of zokor mounds in three alpine rangelands on the Tibetan Plateau." *PeerJ* 7, e6921 (2019). https://doi.org/10.7717/peerj.6921.

John, B. Akbar, B. R. Nelson, Hassan I. Sheikh, S. G. Cheung, Yusli Wardiatno, Bisnu Prasad Dash, Keiji Tsuchiya et al. "A review on fisheries and conservation status of Asian horseshoe crabs." *Biodiversity and Conservation* (2018): 3573–3598. https://doi.org/10.1007/s10531-018-1633-8.

Ju Yan, Huamiao Liu, Min Rong, Ranran Zhang, Yimeng Dong, Yongna Zhou and Xiumei Xing. "Genetic diversity and population genetic structure of the only population of Aoluguya Reindeer (*Rangifer tarandus*) in China." *Mitochondrial DNA Part A* (2018). https://doi.org/10.1080/24701394.2018.1448081.

Jutzeler, Eva, Wu Zhigang, Liu Weishi and Urs Breitenmoser. "Leopard." *Cat News* sp. 5 (2010): 30–33. http://www.catsg.org/fileadmin/filesharing/5.Cat_News/5.3._Special_Issues/5.3.5._SI_5/Jutzeler_et_al_2010_Leopard.pdf.

Jutzeler, Eva, Xie Yan and Kristina Vogt. "The smaller felids of China: Pallas's cat *Otocolobus manul*." *Cat News* sp. 5 (2010): 37–39. http://www.catsg.org/fileadmin/filesharing/3.Conservation_Center/3.2._Status_Reports/Manul/Jutzeler_et_al_2010_Pallas_cat_in_China.pdf.

Kaczensky, P., B. Lkhagvasuren, O.Pereladova, M. Hemami and A. Bouskila. "*Equus hemionus* (amended version of 2015 assessment)." *The IUCN Red List of Threatened Species* (2020): e.T7951A166520460. https://dx.doi.org/10.2305/IUCN.UK.2020-1.RLTS.T7951A166520460.en.

Kamler, J.F., N. Songsasen, K. Jenks, A. Srivathsa, L. Sheng and K. Kunkel. "*Cuon alpinus*." *The IUCN Red List of Threatened Species* (2015): e.T5953A72477893. http://dx.doi.org/10.2305/IUCN.UK.2015-4.RLTS.T5953A72477893.en.

Kamp, Johannes, Steffen Oppel, Alexandr A. Ananin, Yurii A. Durnev, Sergey N. Gashev, Norbert Hölzel, Alexandr L. Mishchenko et al. "Global population collapse in a superabundant migratory bird and illegal trapping in China." *Conservation Biology* 29 (2015): 1684–1694. https://doi.org/10.1111/cobi.12537.

Kang Aili, Yan Xie, Jirong Tang, Eric W. Sanderson, Joshua R. Ginsberg and Endi Zhang. "Historic distribution and recent loss of tigers in China." *Integrative Zoology* 5 (2010): 335–341. https://doi.org/10.1111/j.1749-4877.2010.00221.x.

Kang Dongwei and Junqing Li. "Giant panda protection: challenges and hopes." *Environmental Science and Pollution Research* 26 (2019): 18001–18002. https://doi.org/10.1007/s11356-019-05404-7.

Kaplan, Jed O., Kristen M. Krumhardt and Niklaus Zimmermann. "The prehistoric and preindustrial deforestation of Europe." *Quaternary Science Reviews* 28 (2009): 3016–3034. https://doi.org/10.1016/j.quascirev.2009.09.028.

Karczmarski, Leszek, Shiang-Lin Huang, Carmen K.M. Or, Duan Gui, Stephen C.Y. Chan, Wenzhi Lin, Lindsay Porter et al. "Humpback Dolphins in Hong Kong and the Pearl River Delta: Status, Threats and Conservation Challenges." *Advances in Marine Biology* 73 (2016): 27–64. https://doi.org/10.1016/bs.amb.2015.09.003.

Kerley, Graham I. H., Mariska te Beest, Joris P. G. M. Cromsigt, Daniel Pauly and Susanne Shultz. "The Protected Area Paradox and refugee species: The giant panda and baselines shifted towards conserving species in marginal habitats." *Conservation Science and Practice* 2, e203 (2020). https://doi.org/10.1111/csp2.203.

Kong Dejun, Fei Wu, Pengfei Shan, Jianyun Gao, Dao Yan, Weixiong Luo and Xiaojun Yang. "Status and distribution changes of the endangered Green Peafowl (*Pavo muticus*) in China over the past three decades (1990s–2017)." *Avian Research* 9 (2018). https://doi.org/10.1186/s40657-018-0110-0.

Koshelev, V. N., G. Ruban and A. Shmigirilov. "Spawning migrations and reproductive parameters of the kaluga sturgeon, *Huso dauricus* (Georgi, 1775), and Amur sturgeon, *Acipenser schrenckii* (Brandt, 1869)." *Journal of Applied Ichthyology* 30 (2014): 1125–1132. https://doi.org/10.1111/jai.12549.

Koshelev, V., A. Shmigirilov and G. Ruban. "Current status of feeding stocks of the kaluga sturgeon *Huso dauricus* Georgi, 1775, and Amur sturgeon *Acipenser schrenckii* Brandt, 1889, in Russian waters." *Journal of Applied Ichthyology* 30 (2014): 1310–1318. https://doi.org/10.1111/jai.12606.

Koshelev, V. N., O. Yu. Vilkova and D. V. Kotsyuk. "Modern Data on the Distribution, Abundance and Qualitative Structure of the Populations of the Kaluga *Huso dauricus* and the Amur Sturgeon *Acipenser schrenckii* (Acipenseridae) in the Amur River and the Amur Estuary." *Journal of Ichthyology* 62 (2022): 1394–1403. https://doi.org/10.1134/S0032945222070037.

Krause, Johannes, Tina Unger, Aline Noçon, Anna-Sapfo Malaspinas, Sergios-Orestis Kolokotronis, Mathias Stiller, Leopoldo Soibelzon et al. "Mitochondrial genomes reveal an explosive radiation of extinct and extant bears near the Miocene-Pliocene boundary." *BMC Evolutionary Biology*. 8 (2008). http://www.biomedcentral.com/1471-2148/8/220.

Krykhtin, Mikhail L. and Victor G. Svirskii. "Endemic sturgeons of the Amur River: kaluga, *Huso dauricus*, and Amur sturgeon, *Acipenser schrenckii*." *Environmental Biology of Fishes* 48 (1997): 231–239. https://doi.org/10.1023/A:1007358027263.

Laguardia, Alice, Jan F. Kamler, Sheng Li, Chengcheng Zhang, Zhefeng Zhou and Kun Shi. "The current distribution and status of leopards *Panthera pardus* in China." *Oryx* 51 (2015): 153–159. https://doi.org/10.1017/S0030605315000988.

Lai Chien Hsun and Andrew T. Smith. "Keystone status of plateau pikas (*Ochotona curzoniae*): effect of control on biodiversity of native birds." *Biodiversity and Conservation* 12 (2003): 1901–1912. https://doi.org/10.1023/A:1024161409110.

Lambert, Joseph P., Xiaozheng Zhang, Kun Shi and Philip Riordan. "The pikas of China: a review of current research priorities and challenges for conservation." *Integrative Zoology* 18 (2023): 110–128. https://doi.org/10.1111/1749-4877.12615.

Lan Zige, Zhangwen Su, Meng Guo, Ernesto C Alvarado, Futao Gun, Haiqing Hu and Guangyu Wang. "Are Climate Factors Driving the Contemporary Wildfire Occurrence in China?" *Forests* 12, 392 (2021). https://doi.org/10.3390/f12040392.

Lander, Brian. "Birds and beasts were many: the ecology and climate of the Guanzhong basin in the pre-imperial period." *Early China* 43 (2020): 207–245. https://doi.org/10.1017/eac.2020.10.

———. "From Wetland to Farmland: How Humans Transformed the Central Yangzi Basin." *Asia Major* 35 (2022): 1–31. https://www1.ihp.sinica.edu.tw/storage/publish5L/03_Asia_v35.1,_Lander,_IHP_COLOR.pdf.

Lander, Brian and Katherine Brunson. "The Sumatran rhinoceros was extirpated from mainland East Asia by hunting and habitat loss." *Current Biology* 28 (2018): R252–R253. https://doi.org/10.1016/j.cub.2018.02.012.

———. "Wild Mammals of Ancient North China." *Journal of Chinese History* 2, sp. 2 (2018): 291–312. https://doi.org/10.1017/jch.2017.45.

Le, Minh Duc and Peter Pritchard. "Genetic variability of the critically endangered softshell turtle Rafetus swinhoei: A preliminary report." *Proceedings of the First Vietnamese National Symposium on Reptiles and Amphibians* (2009): 84–92. https://iucn-tftsg.org/wp-content/uploads/file/Articles/Le_and_Pritchard_2009.pdf.

Lei Juncheng, She Wang, Junwei Wang and Jun Wu. "Potential effects of future climate change on suitable habitat of *Muntiacus crinifrons*, an endangered and endemic species in China." *Biodiversity Science* 24 (2016): 1390–1399. https://doi.org/10.17520/biods.2016152. (Chinese with English abstract)

Leipe C., T. Long, E. A. Sergusheva, M. Wagner and P. E. Tarasov. "Discontinuous spread of millet agriculture in eastern Asia and prehistoric population dynamics." *Science Advances* 5, eaax6225 (2019). http://doi.org/10.1126/sciadv.aax6225.

Leng Xiaoqian, Hao Du, Wei Xiong, Peilin Cheng, Jiang Luo and Jinming Wu. "Successful Ultrasonography-Assisted Artificial Reproduction of Critically Endangered Sichuan taimen (*Hucho bleekeri*)." *Fishes* 8, 152 (2023). https://doi.org/10.3390/fishes8030152.

Leslie, David M., Jr. "*Procapra picticaudata* (Artiodactyla: Bovidae)." *Mammalian Species* 42, 861 (2010): 138–148. https://doi.org/10.1644/861.1.

———. "*Przewalskium albirostre* (Artiodactyla: Cervidae)." *Mammalian Species* 42, 849 (2010): 7–18. https://doi.org/10.1644/849.1.

Leslie, David M., Jr., Colin P. Groves and Alexei V. Abramov. "*Procapra przewalskii* (Artiodactyla: Bovidae)." *Mammalian Species* 42, 860 (2010): 124–137. https://doi.org/10.1644/860.1.

Leslie, David M. Jr., Dana N. Lee, and Richard W. Dolman. "*Elaphodus cephalophus* (Artiodactyla: Cervidae)." *Mammalian Species* 45, 904 (2013): 80–91. https://doi.org/10.1644/904.1.

Leslie, David M., Jr. and George B. Schaller. "*Bos grunniens* and *Bos mutus* (Artiodactyla: Bovidae)." *Mammalian Species* 836 (2009): 1–17. https://doi.org/10.1644/836.1.

———. "*Pantholops hodgsonii* (Artiodactyla: Bovidae)." *Mammalian Species* 817 (2008): 1–13. https://doi.org/10.1644/817.1.

Li Bao-Guo, He Zhang, Ming Li, Xue-Long Jiang, Peng-Fei Fan, Jiang Zhou, Song-Tao Guo et al. "Achievements and challenges of primate conservation in China." *Zoological Research: Diversity and Conservation* 1 (2024): 66–74. http://zrdc.ac.cn/en/article/doi/10.24272/j.issn.2097-3772.2023.298.

Li Cheng, Chao Zhao and Peng-Fei Fan. "White-Cheeked Macaque (*Macaca leucogenys*): A New Macaque Species From Modog, Southeastern Tibet." *American Journal of Primatology* 77 (2015): 753–766. https://doi.org/10.1002/ajp.22394.

Li Fagen and Nianhe Xia. "Population structure and genetic diversity of an endangered species, *Glyptostrobus pensilis* (Cupressaceae)." *Botanical Bulletin of Academia Sinica* 46 (2005): 155–162. https://ejournal.sinica.edu.tw/bbas/content/2005/2/Bot462-09.html.

Li Fei, Xi Zheng, Xue-Long Jiang, Bosco Pui Lok Chan. "Rediscovery of the sun bear (*Helarctos malayanus*) in Yingjiang County, Yunnan Province, China." *Zoological Research* 38 (2017): 206–207. https://doi.org/10.24272/j.issn.2095-8137.2017.044.

Li Genhui, Qin Zhongyi, Lu Lixiong, Gao Wenjun, Luo Wenfu, Li Han, Li Yuwu et al. "Population size and distribution of western black crested gibbon (*Nomascus concolor*) in Ailao Mountain, Chuxiong Prefecture, Yunnan Province." *Acta Theriologica Sinica* 43 (2023): 513–522. http://www.mammal.cn/EN/10.16829/j.slxb.150749. (Chinese with English abstract)

Li Hongmei, T. Mitchel Aide, Youxin Ma, Wen Jun Liu and Min Cao. "Demand for rubber is causing the loss of high diversity rain forest in SW China." *Biodiversity and Conservation* 16 (2007): 1731–1745. https://doi.org/10.1007/s10531-006-9052-7.

Li Juan, Dajun Wang, Hang Yin, Duojie Zhaxi, Zhala Jiagong, George B. Schaller, Charudutt Mishra et al. "Role of Tibetan Buddhist Monasteries in Snow Leopard Conservation." *Conservation Biology* 28 (2014): 87–94. https://doi.org/10.1111/cobi.12135.

Li Juan, Hang Yin, Dajun Wang, Zhala Jiagong and Zhi Lu. "Human-snow leopard conflicts in the Sanjiangyuan Region of the Tibetan Plateau." *Biological Conservation* 166 (2013): 118–123. https://doi.org/10.1016/j.biocon.2013.06.024.

Li Juan, Lingyun Xiao and Zhi Lu. "Challenges of snow leopard conservation in China." *Science China Life Sciences* 59 (2016): 637–639. https://doi.org/10.1007/s11427-016-5067-9.

Li Juan, Thomas M. McCarthy, Hao Wang, Byron V. Weckworth, George B. Schaller, Charudutt Mishra, Zhi Lu and Steven R. Beissinger. "Climate refugia of snow leopards in High Asia." *Biological Conservation* 203 (2016): 188–196. https://doi.org/10.1016/j.biocon.2016.09.026.

Li Juan and Zhi Lu. "Snow leopard poaching and trade in China 2000–2013." *Biological Conservation* 176 (2014): 207–211. https://doi.org/10.1016/j.biocon.2014.05.025.

Li Junyi, Hao Du, Jinming Wu, Hui Zhang, Li Shen and Qiwei Wei. "Foundation and Prospects of Wild Population Reconstruction of *Acipenser dabryanus*." *Fishes* 6, 55 (2021). https://doi.org/10.3390/fishes6040055.

Li Qiyue, Geying Lai and Adam Thomas Devlin. "A review on the driving forces of water decline and its impacts on the environment in Poyang Lake, China." *Journal of Water and Climate Change* 12 (2021): 1370–1391. https://doi.org/10.2166/wcc.2020.216.

Li Qiyue, Geying Lai, Ying Liu, Adam Thomas Devlin, Shupin Zhan and Shang Wang. "Assessing the impact of the proposed Poyang lake hydraulic project on the Yangtze finless porpoise and its calves." *Ecological Indicators* 129, 107873 (2021). https://doi.org/10.1016/j.ecolind.2021.107873.

Li Sheng, William J. McShea, Dajun Wang, Xiaodong Gu, Xiaofeng Zhang, Li Zhang & Xiaoli Shen. "Retreat of large carnivores across the giant panda distribution range." *Nature Ecology & Evolution* 4 (2020): 1327–1331. https://doi.org/10.1038/s41559-020-1260-0.

Li Wenwen, Yang Yu, Peng Liu, Ruchun Tang, Yinchuan Dai, Li Li and Li Zhang. "Identifying climate refugia and its potential impact on small population of Asian elephant (*Elephas maximus*) in China." *Global Ecology and Conservation* 19, e00664 (2019). https://doi.org/10.1016/j.gecco.2019.e00664.

Li Wenxiu and Erica von Essen. "Guarding crops from monkey troops: farmer-monkey interaction near a nature reserve in Guangxi, China." *Environmental Sociology* 7 (2021): 12–24. https://doi.org/10.1080/23251042.2020.1811004.

Li Xiao, Qing Liu, Wenjia Li, Quanping Li, Zhengming Qian, Xingzhong Liu and Caihong Dong. "A breakthrough in the artificial cultivation of Chinese cordyceps on a large-scale and its impact on science, the economy, and industry." *Critical Reviews in Biotechnology* 39 (2019): 181–191. https://doi.org/10.1080/07388551.2018.1531820.

Li Xinming, Bochi Wang, Jing Zhang, Geoffrey W. H. Davison and Nan Wang. "Conflict between cultural development and wildlife conservation: A potential threat to Reeves's pheasant (*Syrmaticus reevesii*)." *Conservation Letters* 17, e12995 (2024). https://doi.org/10.1111/conl.12995.

Li Xinrui, Dafu Ru, Paul A. Garber, Qihai Zhou, Ming Li and Xumao Zhao. "Climate change and human activities promoted speciation of two endangered langurs (François' langur and white-headed langur)." *Global Ecology and Conservation* 38, e02185 (2022). https://doi.org/10.1016/j.gecco.2022.e02185.

Li Xue-You, Wen-Qiang Hu, Hong-Jiao Wang, Xue-Long Jiang. "Tiger reappearance in Medog highlights the conservation values of the region for this apex predator." *Zoological Research* 44 (2023): 747–749. https://dx.doi.org/10.24272/j.issn.2095-8137.2023.178.

Li Xueyou, William V. Bleisch, Xinwu Liu and Xuelong Jiang. "Camera-trap surveys reveal high diversity of mammals and pheasants in Medog, Tibet." *Oryx* 55 (2021): 177–180. https://doi.org/10.1017/S0030605319001467.

Li Yilin, Xinhai Li, Zitan Song and Changqing Ding. "Determining the distribution loss of brown eared-pheasant (*Crossoptilon mantchuricum*) using historical data and potential distribution estimates." *PeerJ* 4:e2556 (2016). https://doi.org/10.7717/peerj.2556.

Li Ying, Jee Hyun Kim, Hailong Li, Yuxi Peng, Min Chen, Weihong Zhu, Puneet Pandey et al. "Northward Range Expansion of Water Deer in Northeast Asia: Direct Evidence and Management Implications." *Animals* 12, 1392 (2022). https://doi.org/10.3390/ani12111392.

Li Yong-Tao, Yu Guo-Xu, Cheng Zhao-Long, Zuo Tao, Niu Ming-Xiang and Wang Jun. "The Population Density and Distribution of East Asian Finless Porpoise in Changdao Waters." *Chinese Journal of Zoology* 58 (2023): 658–668. http://dwxzz.ioz.ac.cn/ch/reader/view_abstract.aspx?file_no=20230504. (Chinese with English abstract)

Li Yongtao, Zhaolong Cheng, Tao Zuo, Mingxiang Niu, Ruisheng Chen and Jun Wang. "Distribution and Abundance of the East Asian Finless Porpoise in the Coastal Waters of Shandong Peninsula, Yellow Sea, China." *Fishes* 8, 410 (2023): https://doi.org/10.3390/fishes8080410.

Li Youbang, Chengming Huang, Ping Ding, Zheng Tang and Chris Wood. "Dramatic decline of François' langur *Trachypithecus francoisi* in Guangxi Province, China." *Oryx* 41 (2007): 38–43. https://doi.org/10.1017/S0030605307001500.

Li Yuehui, Nana Li, Long Chen, Yueyuan Li, Zapping Xiong and Yuanman Hu. "Estimating Abundance of Siberian Roe Deer Using Fecal-DNA Capture-Mark-Recapture in Northeast China." *Animals* 10, 1135 (2020). https://doi.org/10.3390/ani10071135.

Liang Chieh-Teh, Shou-Hua Chang, and Woei-horng Fang. "Little known Oriental bird: Discovery of a breeding colony of Chinese Crested Tern." *OBC Bulletin* 32 (2000): 18. https://sawfish-kazoo-6w4a.squarespace.com/chinese-cr-tern.

Liang Cui, Weiwei Xian, Shude Liu and Daniel Pauly. "Assessments of 14 Exploited Fish and Invertebrate Stocks in Chinese Waters Using the LBB Method." *Frontiers in Marine Science* 7, 314 (2020). https://doi.org/10.3389/fmars.2020.00314.

Liang Dan, Xingli Giam, Sifan Hu, Liang Ma and David S. Wilcove. "Assessing the illegal hunting of native wildlife in China." *Nature* (2023). https://doi.org/10.1038/s41586-023-06625-0.

Liang Wei, Wang Jicaho, Su Wenba, Wang Wenyi, Li Shining, Shi Haitao. "Surveys of the Hainan partridge *Arborophila ardens* on Hainan Island, China." *International Galliformes Symposium 2004*. 174–178. https://www.researchgate.net/publication/273130432_Surveys_of_the_Hainan_partridge_Arborophila_ardens_on_Hainan_Island_China.

Liang Wei and Zhengwang Zhang. "Hainan Peacock Pheasant (*Polyplectron katsumatae*): an endangered and rare tropical forest bird." *Chinese Birds* 2 (2011): 111–116. https://doi.org/10.5122/cbirds.2011.0017.

Lin Liu, Songhai Li, Min Chen, James F. Parham, and Haitao Shi. "Sea turtle demand in China threatens the survival of wild populations." *iScience* 24, 102517 (2021). https://doi.org/10.1016/j.isci.2021.102517.

Lin Mingli, Samuel T. Turvey, Chouting Han, Xiaoyu Huang, Antonios D. Mazaris, Mingming Liu, Heidi Ma et al. "Functional extinction of dugongs in China." *Royal Society Open Science* 9, 211994 (2022). https://doi.org/10.1098/rsos.211994.

Lin Wenzhi, Leszek Karczmarski, Jia Xia, Xiyang Zhang, Xinjian Yu and Yuping Wu. "Increased human occupation and agricultural development accelerates the population contraction of an estuarine delphinid." *Scientific Reports* 6, 35713 (2016). https://doi.org/10.1038/srep35713.

Lin Wenzhi, Ruiqiang Zheng, Shiyao Xu and Songhai Li. "Indo-Pacific humpback dolphins face extirpation in Shantou waters." *Regional Studies in Marine Science* 77, 103641 (2024). https://doi.org/10.1016/j.rsma.2024.103641.

Ling Zhang. "Ponds, Paddies and Frontier Defence: Environmental and Economic Changes in Northern Hebei in Northern Song China (960–1127)." *The Medieval History Journal* 14 (2011): 21–43. https://doi.org/10.1177/097194581001400102.

Littledale, George R. "A Journey across Central Asia." *The Geographical Journal* 3 (1894): 445–472. https://doi.org/10.2307/1773580.

Liu Gang, Xiaolong Hu, Aaron B. A. Shafer, Minghao Gong, Morigen Han, Changjiang Yu, Jingying Zhou et al. "Genetic structure and population history of wintering Asian Great Bustard (*Otis tarda dybowskii*) in China: implications for conservation." *Journal of Ornithology* 158 (2017): 761–772. https://doi.org/10.1007/s10336-017-1448-5.

Liu Guioqi, Xueli Lu, Zhao Liu, Zhi Xie, Xuming Qi, Jiang Zhou, Xiaojiang Hong et al. "The Critically Endangered Hainan Gibbon (*Nomascus hainanus*) Population Increases but not at the Maximum Possible Rate." *International Journal of Primatology* (2022). https://doi.org/10.1007/s10764-022-00309-8.

Liu J. Y. "Status of Marine Biodiversity of the China Seas." *PLoS ONE* 8, e50719 (2013). https://doi.org/10.1371/journal.pone.0050719.

Liu Jianyu, Huang Jian, Xiao Lingyun and Feng Jie. "Research Progress and Threat Analysis on Asiatic Golden Cat (*Catopuma temminckii* Vigors and Horsfield)." *Journal of Sichuan Forestry Science and Technology* 41 (2020): 137–146. https://doi.org/10.12172/202006170001. (Chinese with English abstract)

Liu Jie, Ruo-Yan Jiang, Guang-Fu Zhang. "Number and distribution of large old ginkgos in east China: Implications for regional conservation." *Nature Conservation* 42 (2020): 71–87. https://doi.org/10.3897/natureconservation.42.59284.

Liu Ke, Liu Yanlin and Li Sheng. "The current distribution and prediction of suitable habitat of Eurasian lynx (*Lynx lynx*) in China." *Acta Theriologica Sinica* 43 (2023): 652–663. http://www.mammal.cn/EN/10.16829/j.slxb.150801. (Chinese with English abstract)

Liu, M. "*Bahaba taipingensis*." *The IUCN Red List of Threatened Species* (2020): e.T61334A130105307. https://dx.doi.org/10.2305/IUCN.UK.2020-2.RLTS.T61334A130105307.en.

Liu Mingming, Mingli Lin and Songhai Li. "Population distribution, connectivity and differentiation of Indo-Pacific humpback dolphins in Chinese waters: Key baselines for improving conservation management." *Aquatic Conservation: Marine and Freshwater Ecosystems* 33 (2023): 409–422. https://doi.org/10.1002/aqc.3930.

Liu Peng, Hui Wen, Franziska K. Harich, Changhuan He, Lanxin Wang, Xianming Guo, Jianwei Zhao et al. "Conflict between conservation and development: cash forest encroachment in Asian elephant distributions." *Scientific Reports* 7, 6404 (2017). https://doi.org/10.1038/s41598-017-06751-6.

Liu Tian, Zhigang Jiang, Wei Wang, Guangyao Wang, Xiangrong Song, Aichun Xu and Chunlin Li. "Changes in habitat suitability and population size of the endangered Przewalski's gazelle." *Global Ecology and Conservation* 43, e02465 (2023). https://doi.org/10.1016/j.gecco.2023.e02465.

672

Liu Xu, Ma Ming, Xu Fujun, Xiong Jiawu, Zhu Shibing, Cui Shaopeng, Jiang Zhigang et al. "A preliminary study of wolverine in Altay, Xinjiang." *Acta Theriologica Sinica* 38 (2018): 519–524. http://www.mammal.cn/CN/10.16829/j.slxb.150161. (Chinese with English abstract)

Liu Xu and Roller Ma Ming. "Swans killed by poison in China." *Swan News,* 13 (2017): 26–31. http://www.swansg.org/wp-content/uploads/2017/11/Swan-News-13-October-2017-low-res892.pdf#page=26.

Liu Yiwei, Daniel D. Roby, Zhongyong Fan, Simba Chan, Donald E. Lyons, Chung-Hang Hong, Siyu Wang et al. "Creating a conservation network: Restoration of the critically endangered Chinese crested tern using social attraction." *Biological Conservation* 248, 108694 (2020). https://doi.org/10.1016/j.biocon.2020.108694.

Liu Yue-Chen, Xin Sun, Carlos Driscoll, Dale G. Miquelle, Xiao Xu, Paolo Martell, Olga Uphyrkina et al. "Genome-Wide Evolutionary Analysis of Natural History and Adaptation in the World's Tigers." *Current Biology* 28 (2018): 3840–3849. https://doi.org/10.1016/j.cub.2018.09.019.

Liu Zhi-Cheng, Peng Cen, Jian-Kun Sun, Fu- Hua Zhang, Amna Mahmood, Chen Lei and Shi-Bao Wu. "Chinese pangolins (*Manis pentadactyla*) are not functionally extinct in Chinese Mainland." *Zoological Research: Diversity and Conservation* 1 (2024): 79–81. http://zrdc.ac.cn/en/article/doi/10.24272/j.issn.2097-3772.2023.297.

Loehle, Craig and Willis Eschenbach. "Historical bird and terrestrial mammal extinction rates and causes." *Diversity and Distributions* 18 (2012): 84–91. https://doi.org/10.1111/j.1472-4642.2011.00856.x.

Londei, Tiziano. "About the geographic distribution of the Xinjiang Ground Jay (*Podoces biddulphi*)." *Chinese Birds* 4 (2013):184–186. https://doi.org/10.5122/cbirds.2013.0011.

Long Yongcheng, Frank Momberg, Jian Ma, Yue Wang, Yongmei Luo, Haishu Li, Guiliang Yang and Ming Li. "*Rhinopithecus strykeri* found in China!" *American Journal of Primatology* 74 (2012): 871–873. https://doi.org/10.1002/ajp.22041.

Long Yongcheng, Craig R. Kirkpatrick, Zhongtai and Xiaolin. "Report on the Distribution, Population, and Ecology of the Yunnan Snub-nosed Monkey (*Rhinopithecus bieti*)." *Primates* 35 (1994): 241–250. https://doi.org/10.1007/BF02382060.

Long Y. & M. Richardson. "*Rhinopithecus roxellana*." *The IUCN Red List of Threatened Species* (2020): e.T19596A17943886. https://dx.doi.org/10.2305/IUCN.UK.2021-1.RLTS.T19596A196491153.en.

Lou Dongqi, Yu Zhou, Kun Yang, Xiuyue Zhang, Yongbai Chen, Chong Li, Hua Li and Zhaobin Song. "Low genetic diversity in broodstocks of endangered Chinese sucker, *Myxocyprinus asiaticus*: implications for artificial propagation and conservation." *ZooKeys* 792 (2018): 117–132. https://doi.org/10.3897/zookeys.792.23785.

Lu Shunqing, Xiaotong Du, and Steven G. Platt. "Continued reintroduction of captive-bred Chinese alligators in Anhui National Chinese Alligator Reserve, Anhui Province, China." *Crocodile Specialist Group Newsletter* 40 (2021): 23–25. http://www.iucncsg.org/365_docs/attachments/protarea/09d0e0a5c4a731abd0e33be60944bfd3.pdf.

Lu Tie, Haiying Bao and Tolgor Bau. "Genetic diversity and population structure of endemic mushroom *Leucocalocybe mongolica* in Mongolian Plateau uncovered by EST-SSR markers." *Biotechnology & Biotechnological Equipment* 32 (2018): 1195–1204. https://doi.org/10.1080/13102818.2018.1510743.

Luo Jinhong, Tinglei Jiang, Guanjun Lu, Lei Wang, Jing Wang and Jiang Feng. "Bat conservation in China: should protection of subterranean habitats be a priority?" *Oryx* 47 (2013): 526–531. https://doi.org/10.1017/S0030605311001505.

Luo, S.-J., S. Han, D. Song, S. Li, Y. Liu, B. He, M. Zhang and N. Yamaguchi. "*Felis bieti.*" *The IUCN Red List of Threatened Species* (2022): e.T8539A213200674. https://dx.doi.org/10.2305/IUCN.UK.2022-1.RLTS.T8539A213200674.en.

Luo Shu-jin. "The status of the tiger in China. *Cat News* sp. 5 (2010): 10–13. http://www.catsg.org/fileadmin/filesharing/5.Cat_News/5.3._Special_Issues/5.3.5._SI_5/Luo_Shu-Jin_2010_Status_of_the_tiger_in_China.pdf.

Luo Zhenhua, Bingwan Liu, Songtao Liu, Zhigang Jiang and Richard S. Halbrook. "Influences of Human and Livestock Density on Winter Habitat Selection of Mongolian Gazelle (*Procapra gutturosa*)." *Zoological Science* 31 (2014): 20–30. http://dx.doi.org/10.2108/zsj.31.20.

Lwin, K., T. Neang, S. Phimmachak, B. Stuart, W. Thaksintham, G. Wogan, P. Danaisawat et al. "*Gekko gecko.*" *The IUCN Red List of Threatened Species* (2019): e.T195309A2378260. http://dx.doi.org/10.2305/IUCN.UK.2019-1.RLTS.T195309A2378260.en.

Ma Chang-yong, Hoang Trinh-Dinh, Van-Truong Nguyen, Trong-Dat Le, Van-Dung Le, Huu-Oanh Le, Jiang Yang et al. "Transboundary conservation of the last remaining population of the cao vit gibbon *Nomascus nasutus*." *Oryx* 54 (2020): 776–783. https://doi.org/10.1017/S0030605318001576.

Ma Chi, Zhonghua Luo, Changming Liu, Joseph D. Orkin, Wen Xiao and Pengfei Fan. "Population and Conservation Status of Indochinese Gray Langurs (*Trachypithecus crepusculus*) in the Wuliang Mountains, Jingdong, Yunnan, China." *International Journal of Primatology* 36 (2015): 749–763. https://doi.org/10.1007/s10764-015-9852-2.

Ma Liming, Xinhai Li, Tianqing Zhai, Yazu Zhang, Kai Song, Marcel Holyoak and Yuehua Sun. "Changes in the Habitat Preference of Crested Ibis (*Nipponia nippon*) during a Period of Rapid Population Increase." *Animals* 11, 2626 (2021). https://doi.org/10.3390/ani11092626.

Ma Ming. "Status of the Xinjiang Ground Jay: population, breeding ecology and conservation." *Chinese Birds* 2 (2011): 59–62. https://doi.org/10.5122/cbirds.2011.0007.

Ma Ting, Zhuo Zheng, Meiling Man, Yuxiang Dong, Jie Li and Kangyou Huang. "Holocene fire and forest histories in relation to climate change and agriculture development in southeastern China." *Quaternary International* 488 (2018): 30–40. https://doi.org/10.1016/j.quaint.2017.07.035.

Ma Yuan-Ye. "Yunnan snub-nosed monkey research of the Kunming Institute of Zoology, Chinese Academy of Sciences." *Zoological Research* 37 (2016): 189–190. http://www.zoores.ac.cn/en/article/doi/10.13918/j.issn.2095-8137.2016.4.189.

Ma Zhijun, Zijian Wang and Hongxiao Tang. "History of Red-crowned Crane *Grus japonensis* and its habitats in China." *Bird Conservation International* 8 (1998): 11–18. https://doi.org/10.1017/S0959270900003592.

Ma Zhiyu, Zaixin He, Yiqing Wang, Dazhao Song, Fan Xia, Shiming Cui, Hongxin Su et al. "An update on the current distribution and key habitats of the clouded leopard (*Neofelis nebulosa*) populations in China." *Biodiversity Science* 30, 22349 (2022): 1–15. https://www.biodiversity-science.net/EN/10.17520/biods.2022349. (Chinese with English abstract)

Macdonald, David W., Helen M. Bothwell, Żaneta Kaszta, Eric Ash, Gilmoore Bolongon, Dawn Burnham, Özgün Emre Can et al. "Multi-scale habitat modelling identifies spatial conservation priorities for mainland clouded leopards (*Neofelis nebulosa*)." *Diversity and Distributions* 25 (2019): 1639–1654. https://doi.org/10.1111/ddi.12967.

Mahmut, Halik, Masatsugu Suzuki, Sumiya Ganzorig, Aniwar Timur, Ablimit Abdukadir and Noriyuki Ohtaishi. "The present status of the Tarim red deer in Xinjiang, China." *Biosphere Conservation* 4 (2002): 79–86. https://www.researchgate.net/publication/313058425_The_present_status_of_the_Tarim_red_deer_in_Xinjiang_China.

Manolis, Charlie, Matthew Shirley, Pablo Siroski, Paolo Martelli, Marisa Tellez, Alexander Meurer and Mark Merchant. "CSG Visit to China, August 2016." IUCN-SSC Crocodile Specialist Group (2016). http://www.iucncsg.org/365_docs/attachments/protarea/fae0dd371b38fbcadca29ea8c62d03a6.pdf.

Marr, Melissa M., Kevin Hopkins, Benjamin Tapley, Amaël Borzée, Zhiqiang Liang, Andrew A. Cunningham, Fang Yan et al. "What's in a name? Using species delimitation to inform conservation practice for Chinese giant salamanders (*Andrias* spp.)." *Evolutionary Journal of the Linnean Society* Accepted manuscript, kzae007 (2024). https://doi.org/10.1093/evolinnean/kzae007.

McCarthy, T., D. Mallon, R. Jackson, P. Zahler and K. McCarthy. "*Panthera uncia*." *The IUCN Red List of Threatened Species* (2017): e.T22732A50664030. http://dx.doi.org/10.2305/IUCN.UK.2017-2.RLTS.T22732A50664030.en.

McGowan, P. J. K., J. W. Duckworth, Wen Xianji, B. Van Balen, Yang Xiaojun, Mohd, Khan Momin Khan, Siti Hawa Yatim et al. "A review of the status of the Green Peafowl *Pavo muticus* and recommendations for future action." *Bird Conservation International* 8 (1998): 331–348. https://doi.org/10.1017/S0959270900002100.

McManus, John W. "Offshore Coral Reef Damage, Overfishing, and Paths to Peace in the South China Sea." *The International Journal of Marine and Coastal Law* 32 (2017): 199–237. https://doi.org/10.1163/15718085-12341433.

Meng Xiuxiang, Achyut Aryal, Alice Tait, David Raubenhiemer, Jian Wu, Zhong Ma, Yan Sheng et al. "Population trends, distribution and conservation status of semi-domesticated reindeer (*Rangifer tarandus*) in China." *Journal for Nature Conservation* 22 (2014): 539–546. https://doi.org/10.1016/j.jnc.2014.08.008.

Merrill, E. D. "Metasequoia, another 'living fossil'." *Arnoldia* 8 (1948): 1–8. https://assetbank.arboretum.harvard.edu/assetbank-aahu/action/directLinkImage?assetId=24198.

Mi Chunrong, Huettmann Falk and Yumin Guo. "Climate envelope predictions indicate an enlarged suitable wintering distribution for Great Bustards (*Otis tarda dybowskii*) in China for the 21st century." *PeerJ* 4:e1630 (2016). https://doi.org/10.7717/peerj.1630.

Miller, Daniel J., Richard B. Harris and Gui-Quan Cai. "Wild yaks and their conservation on the Tibetan Plateau," in *Proceedings of the 1st International Congress on Yak* edited by R. Zhang, J. Han and J. Wu Gansu Agricultural University, Lanzhou, China 1994. 27–34. https://www.researchgate.net/publication/303249652_Wild_yaks_and_their_conservation_on_the_Tibetan_plateau.

Miller, Ian Matthew. "Roots and Branches: Woodland Institutions in South China, 800-1600." Doctoral dissertation, Harvard University. 2015. http://nrs.harvard.edu/urn-3:HUL.InstRepos:17467396.

———. "The Yangzi River and the Environmental History of South China." *Oxford Research Encyclopedia of Asian History* (2021). https://doi.org/10.1093/acrefore/9780190277727.013.161.

Milne-Edwards, Alphonse. "Note sue quelques mammifères du Thibet Oriental." *Annales des sciences naturelles*, 13 (1870).

Milner-Gulland, E.J. and Badamjavin Lhagvasuren. "Population dynamics of the Mongolian gazelle *Procapra gutturosa*: an historical analysis." *Journal of Applied Ecology* 35 (1998): 240–251. https://doi.org/10.1046/j.1365-2664.1998.00293.x.

Mittermeier, Russell A., Janette Wallis, Anthony B. Rylands, Jörg U. Ganzhorn, John F. Oates, Elizabeth A. Williamson, Erwin Palacios et al. "Primates in Peril: The World's 25 Most Endangered Primates 2008–2010." *Primate Conservation* 24 (2009): 1–57. https://doi.org/10.1896/052.024.0101.

Mori, Emiliano, Luca Nerva and Sandro Lovari. "Reclassification of the serows and gorals: the end of a neverending story?" *Mammal Review* 40 (2019): 256–262. https://doi.org/10.1111/mam.12154.

Nadler, T., L.K. Quyet, H. Covert and Y. Long. "*Trachypithecus francoisi*." *The IUCN Red List of Threatened Species* (2020): e.T39853A17958817. https://dx.doi.org/10.2305/IUCN.UK.2020-3.RLTS.T39853A17958817.en.

Nei Xuan-hua. "The Distribution and Transition of Rhinoceros Sinensis in the Perspective of Environmental History." *Journal of Wenshan University* 28 (2015): 68–73. http://www.rhinoresourcecenter.com/pdf_files/143/1438138099.pdf. (Chinese with English abstract)

Nguyen, T.Q., B. Cai and J. Yang. "*Gekko reevesii*." *The IUCN Red List of Threatened Species* (2021): e.T104717831A104718941. https://dx.doi.org/10.2305/IUCN.UK.2021-2.RLTS.T104717831A104718941.en.

Nguyen, T.Q., P. Hamilton and T. Ziegler. "*Shinisaurus crocodilurus.*" *The IUCN Red List of Threatened Species* (2014): e.T57287221A57287235. http://dx.doi.org/10.2305/IUCN.UK.2014-1.RLTS.T57287221A57287235.en.

Ni Qing-yong and Ma Shi-lai. "Population and Distribution of the Black Crested Gibbons in Southern and Southeastern Yunnan." *Zoological Research* 27 (2006): 34–40. https://www.zoores.ac.cn/en/article/id/2532.

Nie Chuanping. "The distribution and retreat of wild elephants in Ling Nan area during the Tang and Song dynasties." *Journal of Chinese Historical Geography* 33 (2018): 70–78. (Chinese with English abstract)

Nijhawan, S. "*Naemorhedus baileyi*". *The IUCN Red List of Threatened Species* (2020): e.T14294A179947455. https://dx.doi.org/10.2305/IUCN.UK.2020-3.RLTS.T14294A179947455.en.

Nishikawa Kanto, Masafumi Matsui, Natsuhiko Yoshikawa, Atsushi Tominaga, Koshiro Eto, Ibuki Fukuyama, Kazumi Fukutani et al. "Discovery of ex situ individuals of *Andrias sligoi*, an extremely endangered species and one of the largest amphibians worldwide." *Scientific Reports* 14, 2575 (2024). https://doi.org/10.1038/s41598-024-52907-6.

Niu Kefeng, Andie Ang, Zhi Xiao and Marco Gamba. "Is Yuan in China's Three Gorges a Gibbon or a Langur?" *International Journal of Primatology* (2022). https://doi.org/10.1007/s10764-022-00302-1.

Niu Yang, Martin Stevens and Hang Sun. "Commercial Harvesting Has Driven the Evolution of Camouflage in an Alpine Plant." *Current Biology* 31 (2021): 446–449. https://doi.org/10.1016/j.cub.2020.10.078.

Nyambayar, B., H. Mix and K. Tsytsulina. "*Moschus moschiferus.*" *The IUCN Red List of Threatened Species* (2015): e.T13897A61977573. https://dx.doi.org/10.2305/IUCN.UK.2015-2.RLTS.T13897A61977573.en.

Pan Ruling et al. "A New Conservation Strategy for China—A Model Starting With Primates." *American Journal of Primatology* 78 (2016): 1137–1148. https://doi.org/10.1002/ajp.22577.

Peng Jianjun, Zhigang Jiang and Jinchu Hu. "Status and conservation of giant panda (*Ailuropoda melanoleuca*): a review." *Folia Zoologica* 50 (2001): 81–88. https://www.researchgate.net/publication/260794984_Status_and_conservation_of_giant_panda_Ailuropoda_melanoleuca_A_review.

Pei Pengzu, Wang Liang, Shao Yaping, Shi Cunhai, Yang Yongwei and Bao Xinkang. "Re-introduced Przewalski's horses's breeding success and population viability analysis in Anxi National Nature Reserve." *Acta Theriologica Sinica* 38 (2018): 128–138. http://www.mammal.cn/CN/10.16829/j.slxb.150117. (Chinese with English abstract)

Peng He-Bo, Guy Q. A. Anderson, Qing Cheng, Chi-Yeung Choi, Sayam U. Chowdhury, Nigel A. Clark, Xiaojing Gan et al. "The intertidal wetlands of southern Jiangsu Province, China – globally important for Spoon-billed Sandpipers and other threatened waterbirds, but facing multiple serious threats." *Bird Conservation International* 27 (2017): 305–322. https://doi.org/10.1017/S0959270917000223.

Pham Thong Van, Olivier Le Duc, Cédric Bordes, Benjamin Leprince, Charlotte Ducotterd, Tomas Zuklin, Vinh Luu Quang et al. "Female wanted for the world's rarest turtle: prioritizing areas where *Rafetus swinhoei* may persist in the wild." *Oryx* 56 (2022): 396–403. https://doi.org/10.1017/S0030605320000721.

Phan, T.D., S. Nijhawan, S. Li, and L. Xiao. "*Capricornis sumatraensis*." *The IUCN Red List of Threatened Species* (2020): e.T162916735A162916910. https://dx.doi.org/10.2305/IUCN.UK.2020-2.RLTS.T162916735A162916910.en.

Phyo, Aung Pyae, Thura Soe Min Htike, Saw Moses, Gideon Dun, Ye Min Aung, Nyan Lin, Shein Thu Lwin et al. "Gulf of Mottama SBS Survey January and February 2024." *Spoon-billed Sandpiper Task Force News Bulletin* 30 (2024): 9–12. https://eaaflyway.net/wp-content/uploads/2024/06/240529-SBS-Newsletter-No-30-20240528-2.pdf.

Piao Zheng-Ji, Piao Long-Guo, Wang Zhuo-Cong, Luo Yu-Mei, Wang Chao and Sui Ya-Chen. "Population Size Variation of Black Bear (*Ursus thibetanus*) and Brown Bear (*U. arctos*) between 1986 to 2010 in the Changbai Mountain Nature Reserve, China." *Chinese Journal of Zoology* 47 (2012): 66–72. http://dwxzz.ioz.ac.cn/ch/reader/view_abstract.aspx?file_no=20120310. (Chinese with English abstract)

Pierson, Todd W., Yan Fang, Wang Yunyu and Theodore Papenfuss. "A survey for the Chinese giant salamander (*Andrias davidianus*; Blanchard, 1871) in the Qinghai Province." *Amphibian & Reptile Conservation* 8 (2014): 1–6. http://amphibian-reptile-conservation.org/pdfs/Volume/Vol_8_no_1/ARC_8_1_%5BGen_Sec%5D_1-6_e74_low_res.pdf.

Pikunov, Dmitry G. "Population and Habitat of the Amur Tiger in the Russian Far East." *Achievements in the Life Sciences* 8 (2014): 145–149. http://dx.doi.org/10.1016/j.als.2015.04.004.

Pilgrim, John D., David F. Walsh, Tran Thanh Tu, Nguyen Duc Tu, Jonathan C. Eames and Le Manh Hung. "The Endangered White-eared Night Heron *Gorsachius magnificus* in Vietnam: status, distribution, ecology and threats." *Forktail* 25 (2009): 142–146. https://static1.squarespace.com/static/5c1a9e03f407b482a158da87/t/5c2100c8032be4789673c0c7/1545666765164/Pilgrim-White-earedNight-Heron.pdf.

Ping Xiaoge, Chunwang Li, Chunlin Li, Songhua Tang, Hongxia Fang, Shaopeng Cui, Jing Chen et al. "The distribution, population and conservation status of Przewalski's gazelle, *Procapra przewalskii*." *Biodiversity Science* 26 (2018): 177–184. https://www.biodiversity-science.net/CN/10.17520/biods.2017152. (Chinese with English abstract)

Poirier, Frank E. "The Golden Monkey in the People's Republic of China." *Primate Conservation* 3 (1983): 31–32. http://www.primate-sg.org/storage/PDF/PC3.pdf.

Qi Jinzhe, Jiayin Gu, Yao Ning, Dale G. Miquelle, Marcel Holyoak, Dusu Wen, Xin Liang et al. "Integrated assessments call for establishing a sustainable meta-population of Amur tigers in northeast Asia." *Biological Conservation* 261 (2021): 109250. https://doi.org/10.1016/j.biocon.2021.109250.

Qian Shenhua, Cindy Q. Tang, Sirong Yi, Liang Zhao, Kun Song and Yongchuan Yang. "Conservation and development in conflict: regeneration of wild *Davidia involucrata* (Nyssaceae) communities weakened by bamboo management in south-central China." *Oryx* 52 (2018): 442–451. https://doi.org/10.1017/S003060531700045X.

Qian Shenhua, Yongchuan Yang, Cindy Q. Tang, Arata Momohara, Sirong Yi and Masahiko Ohsawa. "Effective conservation measures are needed for wild *Cathaya argyrophylla* populations in China: Insights from the population structure and regeneration characteristics." *Forest Ecology and Management* 361 (2016): 358–367. https://doi.org/10.1016/j.foreco.2015.11.041.

Qiao Y., X. Tang, S. Brosse and J. Chang. "Chinese Sturgeon (*Acipenser sinensis*) in the Yangtze River: a hydroacoustic assessment of fish location and abundance on the last spawning ground." *Journal of Applied Ichthyology* 22 (2006): 140–144. https://doi.org/10.1111/j.1439-0426.2007.00942.x.

Qin Aili, Kun Jin, Munkh-Erdene Batsaikhan, Javkhlan Nyamjav, Guangliang Li, Jia Li, Yadong Xue et al. "Predicting the current and future suitable habitats of the main dietary plants of the Gobi Bear using MaxEnt modeling." *Global Ecology and Conservation* 22, e01032 (2020). https://doi.org/10.1016/j.gecco.2020.e01032.

Qin Yiyuan, Philip J. Nyhus, Courtney L. Larson, Charles J.W. Carroll, Jeff Muntifering, Thomas D. Dahmer, Lu Jun and Ronald L. Tilson. "An assessment of South China tiger reintroduction potential in Hupingshan and Houhe National Nature Reserves, China." *Biological Conservation* 182 (2015): 72–86. https://doi.org/10.1016/j.biocon.2014.10.036.

Qiu Mingjiang. "Preserving Tigers in Southeast Tibet." Research proposal. 1996. http://www.catsg.org/catsglib/pdfs/Qiu_1996_Preserving_tigers_in_southeast_Tibet.pdf.

Qiu Mingjiang, Zhang Ming and Liu Wulin. "A preliminary study on the Bengal tiger (*Panthera tigris tigris*) in Namcha Barwa, Southeastern Tibet." *Acta Theriologica Sinica* 17 (1997): 1–7. http://www.mammal.cn/EN/Y1997/V17/I1/1. (Chinese with English abstract)

Reid, Donald G., Hu Jinchu, Dong Say, Wang Wei and Huang Yan. "Giant Panda *Ailuropoda melanoleuca* behaviour and carrying capacity following a bamboo die-off." *Biological Conservation* 49 (1989): 85–104.

Rieger, Ingo. "Tail Functions in Ounces, *Uncia uncia*." *International Pedigree Book of Snow Leopards*, Panthera uncia 4 (1984): 85–97. https://www.researchgate.net/publication/282847948_Tail_Function_in_Ounces_Uncia_uncia.

Riordan, Philip, Jun Wang, Kun Shi, Hongyan Fu, Zhu Dabuxilike, Kebiao Zhu and Xiaohu Wang. "New evidence of dhole *Cuon alpinus* populations in north-west China." *Oryx* 49 (2015): 203–204. https://doi.org/10.1017/S0030605315000046.

Roberts, N., R. M. Fyfe, J. Woodbridge, M.-J. Gaillard, B. A. S. Davis, J. O. Kaplan, L. Marquee et al. "Europe's lost forests: a pollen-based synthesis for the last 11,000 years." *Scientific Reports* 8, 716 (2018). https://doi.org/10.1038/s41598-017-18646-7.

Robinson, Jacqueline A., Christopher C. Kyriazis, Sergio F. Nigenda-Morales, Annabel C. Beichman, Lorenzo Rojas-Bracho, Kelly M. Robertson, Michael C. Fontaine et al. "The critically endangered vaquita is not doomed to extinction by inbreeding depression." *Science* 376 (2022): 635–639. https://doi.org/10.1126/science.abm1742.

Roborovsky, V. I. "The central Asian expedition of Captain Roborovsky and Lieut. Kozloff." *The Geographical Journal* 8 (1896): 161–173. https://doi.org/10.2307/1773618.

Roos, Christian, Kristofer M. Helgen, Roberto Portela Miguez, Naw May Lay Thant, Ngwe Lwin, Aung Ko Lin, Aung Lin et al. "Mitogenomic phylogeny of the Asian colobine genus *Trachypithecus* with special focus on *Trachypithecus phayrei* (Blyth, 1847) and description of a new species." *Zoological Research* 41 (2020): 656–669. https://doi.org/10.24272/j.issn.2095-8137.2020.254.

Ross, Steven. "Providing an ecological basis for the conservation of the Pallas's cat (*Otocolobus manul*)." Doctoral thesis, University of Bristol. 2009. https://research-information.bris.ac.uk/en/studentTheses/providing-an-ecological-basis-for-the-conservation-of-the-pallass.

Ross, Steven, Ehsan M. Moqanaki, Anna Barashkova, Tashi Dhendup, Ilya Smelansky, Sergey Naidenko, Anastasia Antonevich and Gustaf Samelius. "Past, present and future threats and conservation needs of Pallas's cats." *Cat News* sp. 13 (2019): 46–51. http://www.catsg.org/fileadmin/filesharing/5.Cat_News/5.3._Special_Issues/5.3.12_SI_13/Ross_et_al_2019_Threats_and_conservation_needs_of_Pallas%27s_cats.pdf.

Sadi, Saeed H., Nathan Goldberg, Josh Beck, Sayam U. Chowdhury, Dipta K. Das, James A. Eaton, Ross Gallardy et al. "White-eared Night Heron *Gorsachius magnificus* records in the Bangladesh Sundarbans: A new species for the country." *Indian BIRDS* 19 (2023): 50–52. https://indianbirds.in/pdfs/IB_19_2_SadiETAL_WhiteearedNightHeron.pdf.

Sadovy, Yvonne and Wai Lung Cheung. "Near extinction of a highly fecund fish: the one that nearly got away." *Fish and Fisheries* 4 (2003): 86–99. https://doi.org/10.1046/j.1467-2979.2003.00104.x.

Sand, Susan. "The Dawn Redwood: East and west cooperated to save this living fossil from extinction." *American Horticulturist* 71 (1992): 40–44. https://ahsgardening.org/wp-content/pdfs/Deciduous_Conifers_web_special.pdf.

Sanderson, Jim, Yin Yufeng and Drubgyal Naktsang. "Of the only endemic cat species in China. The Chinese mountain cat — *Felis bieti*." *Cat News* sp. 5 (2010): 18–21. http://www.catsg.org/fileadmin/filesharing/5.Cat_News/5.3._Special_Issues/5.3.5._SI_5/Sanderson_et_al_2010_The_Chinese_Mountain_cat.pdf.

Sanft, Charles. "Environment and Law in Early Imperial China (Third Century BCE–First Century CE): Qin and Han Statutes Concerning Natural Resources." *Environmental History* 15 (2010): 701–721. https://doi.org/10.1093/envhis/emq088.

Santiapillai, Charles, Zhu Xiang, Dong Yong Hua and Sheng Qin Zhong. "Distribution of Elephant in Xishuangbanna Dai Autonomous Prefecture, China." *Gajah* 12 (1994): 34–45. https://www.asesg.org/PDFfiles/Gajah/12-34-Santiapillai.pdf.

Schafer, Edward H. "Brief Note: The Chinese Dhole." *Asia Major* 4 (1991): 1–6. https://www2.ihp.sinica.edu.tw/file/1575xyynAgh.pdf.

———. "The Conservation of Nature under the T'ang Dynasty." *Journal of the Economic and Social History of the Orient* 5 (1962): 279–308. https://doi.org/10.2307/3596136.

———. "Hunting Parks and Animal Enclosures in Ancient China." Edward H. Schafer. *Journal of the Economic and Social History of the Orient* 11 (1968), 318–343. https://doi.org/10.2307/3596278.

———. "War Elephants in Ancient and Medieval China." *Oriens* 10 (1957): 289–291. http://www.jstor.org/stable/1579643?origin=JSTOR-pdf.

Schaller, George B., Li Hong, Talipu, Ren Junrang and Qiu Mingjiang. "The snow leopard in Xinjiang, China." *Oryx* 22 (1988): 197–204. https://doi.org/10.1017/S0030605300022328.

Schaller, George B. and Liu Wulin. "Distribution, Status, and Conservation of Wild Yak *Bos grunniens*." *Biological Conservation* 76 (1996): 1–8. https://doi.org/10.1016/0006-3207(96)85972-6.

Schaller, George B., Ren Junrang and Qui Mingjiang. "Status of the Snow Leopard *Panthera uncia* in Qinghai and Gansu Provinces, China." *Biological Conservation* 45 (1988): 179–194. https://doi.org/10.1016/0006-3207(88)90138-3.

Schlag, Juliane. "Living in decline – the dynamics of anthropogenic disturbances in the recent landcover history of Manchuria and its consequences for Northeast Asia." *Asian Geographer* 38 (2021): 179–196. https://doi.org/10.1080/10225706.2021.1952884.

Shafi, Shariq, Kamlesh K. Maurya, Pranav Chanchani, S. Chandrashekar, Amit Kumar, Gaurav Ojha and Alok Kumar. "Extraordinary discovery in Bihar, India: an apparent White-eared Night Heron *Gorsachius magnificus* in Valmiki Tiger Reserve." *BirdingASIA* 29 (2018): 9–10. https://www.orientalbirdclub.org/birdingasia-29.

Shah, N., A. St. Louis and Q. Qureshi. "*Equus kiang*." *The IUCN Red List of Threatened Species* (2015): e.T7953A45171635. http://dx.doi.org/10.2305/IUCN.UK.2015-4.RLTS.T7953A45171635.en.

Shao Mingqin, Jianying Wang, Hongxiu Ding and Fucheng Yang. "Response of Siberian Cranes (*Grus leucogeranus*) to Hydrological Changes and the Availability of Foraging Habitat at Various Water Levels in Poyang Lake." *Animals* 14, 234 (2024). https://doi.org/10.3390/ani14020234.

Sheeran, Lori K. and Frank E. Poirier. "The Black-crested Gibbon of China." *Primate Conservation* 11 (1990): 20–22. http://static1.1.sqspcdn.com/static/f/1200343/18197250/1337025414127/PC11.pdf?token=d0WhWB7SISqwoMNZ8N%2F%2FJ8qBLh8%3D.

Shen L, X-Y Chen, X Zhang, Y-Y Li, C-X Fu and Y-X Qiu. "Genetic variation of *Ginkgo biloba* L. (Ginkgoaceae) based on cpDNA PCR-RFLPs: inference of glacial refugia." *Heredity* 94 (2005): 396–401. https://doi.org/10.1038/sj. hdy.6800616.

Shen Yu. "Earthworms in Traditional Chinese Medicine: (Oligochaeta: Lumbricidae, Megascolecidae)." *Zoology in the Middle East* 51 (2010): 171–173. https://doi. org/10.1080/09397140.2010.10638470.

Shen Yubin. "Pneumonic Plagues, Environmental Changes, and the International Fur Trade: The Retreat of Tarbagan Marmots from Northwest Manchuria, 1900s–30s." *Frontiers of History in China* 14 (2019): 291–322. https://brill.com/ view/journals/fhic/14/3/article-p291_2.xml.

Shi, H. Q., L. Cao, M. A. Barter and N. F. Liu. "Status of the East Asian population of the Dalmatian Pelican *Pelecanus crispus*: the need for urgent conservation action." *Bird Conservation International* 18 (2008): 181–193. https://doi.org/ 10.1017/S0959270908000178.

Shine, Richard, Li-Xin Sun, Ermi Zhao and Xavier Bonnet. "A review of 30 years of ecological research on the Shedao pitviper, *Gloydius shedaoensis*." *Herpetological Natural History* 9 (2002): 1–14. https://www.researchgate.net/publication/ 278808990.

Smith, Andrew T., Badingqiuying, Maxwell C. Wilson and Brigitte W. Hogan. "Functional-trait ecology of the plateau pika *Ochotona curzoniae* in the Qinghai–Tibetan Plateau ecosystem." *Integrative Zoology* 14 (2019): 87–103. https://doi. org/10.1111/1749-4877.12300.

Smith, Andrew T. and J. Marc Foggin. "The plateau pika (*Ochotona curzoniae*) is a keystone species for biodiversity on the Tibetan plateau." *Animal Conservation* 2 (1999): 235–240. https://doi.org/10.1111/j.1469-1795.1999.tb00069.x.

Smith, A.T. and C.H. Johnston. "*Eospalax fontanierii*." *The IUCN Red List of Threatened Species* (2016): e.T14118A115120816. http://dx.doi.org/10.2305/ IUCN.UK.2016-3.RLTS.T14118A22277700.en.

Smith, Brian D., Elisabeth Fahrni Mansur, Mohammad Shamsuddoha and G. M. Masum Billah. "Is the demand for fish swim bladders driving the extinction of globally endangered marine wildlife?" *Aquatic Conservation: Marine and Freshwater Ecosystems* 33 (2023): 1615–1620. https://doi.org/10.1002/aqc.4025.

Smith, D.R., M.A. Beekey, H.J. Brockmann, T.L. King, M.J. Millard and J.A. Zaldívar-Rae. "*Limulus polyphemus*." *The IUCN Red List of Threatened Species* (2016): e.T11987A80159830. https://dx.doi.org/10.2305/IUCN.UK.2016-1. RLTS.T11987A80159830.en.

Smith, Felisa A., Emma A. Elliott Smith, Carson P. Hedberg, S. Kathleen Lyons, Melissa I. Pardi and Catalina P. Tomé. "After the mammoths: The ecological legacy of late Pleistocene megafauna extinctions." *Cambridge Prisms: Extinction* 1, e9 (2023). https://doi.org/10.1017/ext.2023.6.

Smith, William Lord. "The Cave Tiger of Amoy: The Story of a Hunt for a Man-eating Tiger that Lived in a Rocky Den Back of Amoy." *Natural History* 28 (1928): 430–438.

Sokolov, Vladimir E. and Anna A. Lushchekina. "*Procapra gutturosa.*" *Mammalian Species* 571 (1997): 1–5. https://doi.org/10.1644/0.571.1.

Song Se-Kyu, Seok Won Lee, Yun Kyung Lee, Sang Yeon Lee, Chang Hoe Kim, Seung Se Chou, Hyun Chul Shin et al. "First report and breeding record of the Chinese Crested Tern *Thalasseus bernsteini* on the Korean Peninsula." *Journal of Asia-Pacific Biodiversity* 10 (2017): 250–253. https://doi.org/10.1016/j.japb.2017.04.005.

Song, Y.-L., A.T. Smith and J. MacKinnon. "*Budorcas taxicolor.*" *The IUCN Red List of Threatened Species* (2008): e.T3160A9643719. http://dx.doi.org/10.2305/IUCN.UK.2008.RLTS.T3160A9643719.en.

Sowerby, Arthur de Carle. "The giant salamander of China." *The China Journal of Science & Arts* 1 (1923): 253–256.

———. "The Tiger in China." *The China Journal* 18 (1933): 94–101.

St-Louis, Antoine and Steeve D. Côté. "*Equus kiang* (Perissodactyla: Equidae)." *Mammalian Species* 835 (2008): 1–11. https://doi.org/10.1644/835.1.

Stuart, B., T.Q. Nguyen, N. Thy, L. Grismer, T. Chan-Ard, D. Iskandar, E. Golynsky and M.W.N. Lau. "*Python bivittatus.*" *The IUCN Red List of Threatened Species* (2012): e.T193451A151341916. http://dx.doi.org/10.2305/IUCN.UK.2012-1.RLTS.T193451A151341916.en.

Su Canxia, Chu Wenwen, Bahatibieke Pielizhati, Jiang Xiaoheng, Chen Yanqiu, Huang Wenpu, Ma Chi and Chu Hongjun. "Potential distribution changes of *Castor fiber birulai* under climate changes in the upper reaches of the Ulungur River, Xinjiang." *Arid Zone Research* 41 (2024): 509–520. http://azr.xjegi.com/EN/10.13866/j.azr.2024.03.15. (Chinese with English abstract)

Su Kaiwen, Jie Yang, Lin Lin, Yilei Hou and Yali Wen. "Balancing human–bear coexistence with biodiversity conservation." *Human Dimensions of Wildlife* (2021). https://doi.org/10.1080/10871209.2021.2013996.

Sun Yiwen, Tiejun Wang, Andrew K. Skidmore, Qi Wang and Changqing Ding. "Decline of traditional rice farming constrains the recovery of the endangered Asian crested ibis (*Nipponia nippon*)." *Ambio* 44 (2015): 803–814. https://doi.org/10.1007/s13280-015-0649-5.

Sun Zhigao, Wenguang Sun, Chuan Tong, Congsheng Zeng, Xiang Yu and Xiaojie Mou. "China's coastal wetlands: Conservation history, implementation efforts, existing issues and strategies for future improvement." *Environment International* 79 (2015): 25–41. http://dx.doi.org/10.1016/j.envint.2015.02.017.

Sun Zhonglou, Hui Wang, Wenliang Zhou, Wenbo Shi, Weiquan Zhu and Baowei Zhang. "How rivers and historical climate oscillations impact on genetic structure in Chinese Muntjac (*Muntiacus reevesi*)?" *Diversity and Distributions* 25 (2019): 116–128. https://doi.org/10.1111/ddi.12833.

Sun Zhonglou, Pablo Orozco-terWengel, Guozao Chen, Ruolei Sun, Lu Sun, Hui Wang, Wenbo Shi and Baowei Zhang. "Spatial dynamics of Chinese Muntjac related to past and future climate fluctuations." *Current Zoology* 67 (2021): 361–370. https://doi.org/10.1093/cz/zoaa080.

Sun Zhonglou, Tao Pan, Hui Wang, Mujia Pang and Baowei Zhang. "Yangtze River, an insignificant genetic boundary in tufted deer (*Elaphodus cephalophus*): the evidence from a first population genetics study." *PeerJ* 4, e2654 (2016). https://doi.org/10.7717/peerj.2654.

Svenning, Jens-Christian, Rhys T. Lemoine, Juraj Bergman, Robert Buitenwerf, Elizabeth Le Roux, Erick Lundgren, Ninad Mungi and Rasmus Ø Pedersen. "The late-Quaternary megafauna extinctions: Patterns, causes, ecological consequences and implications for ecosystem management in the Anthropocene." *Cambridge Prisms: Extinction* 2, e5 (2024). https://doi.org/10.1017/ext.2024.4.

Swaisgood, R., D. Wang and F. Wei. "*Ailuropoda melanoleuca*." *The IUCN Red List of Threatened Species* (2016): e.T712A121745669. https://dx.doi.org/10.2305/IUCN.UK.2016-2.RLTS.T712A45033386.en.

Swinhoe, Robert. "On Chinese Deer, with the Description of an apparently new Species." *Proceedings of the Zoological Society of London* (1873): 572–576.

———. "On the Mammals of Hainan." *Proceedings of the Zoological Society of London* (1870): 224–239.

Tan Bangjie. "The Status of Felids in China." *Proceedings from the Cat Specialist Group meeting in Kanha National Park.* (1984): 34–48. https://savemanul.org/download/the-status-of-felids-in-china/.

———. "The Status of Primates in China." *Primate Conservation* 5 (1985): 63–81. http://static1.1.sqspcdn.com/static/f/1200343/18197325/1337025509150/PC5.pdf?token=0h1J2jGUBzWtCLmAqSszVp%2BIVFw%3D.

———. "Conservation and economic importance of the mustelids and viverrids in China." *Mustelid & Viverrid Conservation* 1 (1989): 5–6. https://smallcarnivoreconservation.com/index.php/sccg/issue/view/350/121.

Tang, Cindy Q., Yi-Fei Dong, Sonia Herrando-Moraira, Tetsuya Matsui, Haruka Ohashi, Long-Yuan He, Katsuhiro Nakao et al. "Potential effects of climate change on geographic distribution of the Tertiary relict tree species *Davidia involucrata* in China." *Science Reports* 7, 43822 (2017). https://doi.org/10.1038/srep43822.

Tang, Cindy Q., Yongchuan Yang, Arata Momohara, Huan-Chong Wang, Hong Truong Luu, Shuaifeng Li, Kun Song et al. "Forest characteristics and population structure of *Glyptostrobus pensilis*, a globally endangered relict species of southeastern China." *Plant Diversity* 41 (2019): 237–249. https://doi.org/10.1016/j.pld.2019.06.007.

Tang, Cindy Q., Yongchuan Yang, Masahiko Ohsawa, Arata Momohara, Masatoshi Hara, Shaolin Cheng and Shenghou Fan. "Population structure of relict *Metasequoia glyptostroboides* and its habitat fragmentation and degradation in south-central China." *Biological Conservation* 144 (2011): 279–289. https://doi.org/10.1016/j.biocon.2010.09.003.

Tang, Cindy Q., Yongchuan Yang, Masahiko Ohsawa, Si-Rong Yi, Arata Momohara, Wen-Hua Su, Huan-Chong Wang et al. "Evidence for the persistence of wild *Ginkgo biloba* (Ginkgoaceae) population in the Dalou Mountains, southwestern China." *American Journal of Botany* 99 (2012): 1408–1414. https://dx.doi.org/10.3732/ajb.1200168.

Tang Haiming, Qiuting Chen and Min Chen. "Free-ranging dogs threaten reintroduced Chinese water deer." *Deer Specialist Group News* 35 (2024): 3–11. https://www.deerspecialistgroup.org/newsletters/dsgnews35-2/.

Tang Junfeng and Xuzhe Zhao. "Forecasting the combined effects of future climate and land use change on the suitable habitat of *Davidia involucrata* Baill." *Ecology and Evolution* 12, e9023 (2022). https://doi.org/10.1002/ece3.9023.

Tapley, Benjamin, Samuel T. Turvey, Shu Chen, Gang Wei, Feng Xie, Jian Yang, Zhiqiang Liang, et al. "Range-wide decline of Chinese giant salamanders Andrias spp. from suitable habitat." *Oryx* 55 (2021): 373–381. https://doi.org/10.1017/S0030605320000411.

Teichroew, Jonathan L., Jianchu Xu, Antje Ahrends, Zachary Y. Huang, Ken Tan, Zhenghua Xie. "Is China's unparalleled and understudied bee diversity at risk?" *Biological Conservation* 210, Part B (2017): 19–28. https://doi.org/10.1016/j.biocon.2016.05.023.

Thapa, Arjun, Yibo Hu, and Fuwen Wei. "The Endangered Red Panda (*Ailurus fulgens*): Ecology and Conservation Approaches Across the Entire Range." *Biological Conservation* 220, (2018): 112–121. https://doi.org/10.1016/j.biocon.2018.02.014.

Thomas, Nancy R. "A Lion's Eye View of the Greek Bronze Age." *Aegaeum* 37 (2014): 375–389.

Thomas, Oldfield. "Exhibition of a skin and description of a new species of monkey. *Rhinopithecus brelichi*." *Proceedings of the Zoological Society of London* (1903): 224–225.

Tilson, Ronald, Hu Defu, Jeff Muntifering and Philip J. Nyhus. "Dramatic decline of wild South China tigers *Panthera tigris amoyensis*: field survey of priority tiger reserves." *Oryx* 38 (2004): 40–47. https://doi.org/10.1017/S0030605304000079.

Tilson, Ronald, Kathy Traylor-Holzer and Qiu Ming Jiang. "The decline and impending extinction of the South China tiger." *Oryx* 31 (1997): 243–252. https://doi.org/10.1046/j.1365-3008.1997.d01-123.x.

Timmins, J and B. Chan. "*Muntiacus reevesi*." *The IUCN Red List of Threatened Species* (2016): e.T42191A22166608. http://dx.doi.org/10.2305/IUCN.UK.2016-2.RLTS.T42191A22166608.en.

Timmins, R. and B. Chan. "*Muntiacus crinifrons*." *The IUCN Red List of Threatened Species* (2016): e.T13924A22160753. http://dx.doi.org/10.2305/IUCN.UK.2016-1.RLTS.T13924A22160753.en.

Tisdell, Clem and Zhu Xiang. "Protected Areas, Agricultural Pests and Economic Damage: Conflicts with Elephants and Pests in Yunnan." *Environmentalist* 18 (1998): 109–118. https://doi.org/10.1023/A:1006674425017.

Tomkovich, P. S., E. E. Syroechkovski, Jr., E. G. Lappo and C. Zöckler. "First indications of a sharp population decline in the globally threatened Spoon-billed Sandpiper *Eurynorhynchus pygmeus*." *Bird Conservation International* 12 (2002): 1–18. https://doi.org/10.1017/S0959270902002010.

Tourenq, Christophe, Olivier Combreau, Mark Lawrence, Serguei B Pole, Andrew Spalton, Gao Xinji, Mohammed Al Baidani and Frédéric Launay. "Alarming houbara bustard population trends in Asia." *Biological Conservation* 121 (2005): 1–8. https://doi.org/10.1016/j.biocon.2004.03.031.

Tsahar, Ella, Ido Izhaki, Simcha Lev-Yadun and Guy Bar-Oz. "Distribution and Extinction of Ungulates during the Holocene of the Southern Levant." *PLoS ONE* 4, e5316 (2009). https://doi.org/10.1371/journal.pone.0005316.

Tulgat, R. and George B. Schaller. "Status and distribution of wild Bactrian camels *Camelus bactrianus ferus*." *Biological Conservation* 62 (1992): 11–19. https://doi.org/10.1016/0006-3207(92)91147-K.

Turghan, Mardan Aghabey, Paul Jason Buzzard and Roller Maming. "Current Status of Black-Necked Crane Grus Nigricollis in Southern Xinjiang China: Conservation Implications." *Wetlands* Preprint (2021) https://doi.org/10.21203/rs.3.rs-180720/v1.

Turvey, Samuel T., Heidi Ma, Tonglei Zhou, Tiantian Teng, Chuyue Yu, Lucy J. Archer, Xiaodong Rao et al. "Local ecological knowledge and regional sighting histories of Hainan Peacock-pheasant *Polyplectron katsumatae*: pessimism or optimism for a threatened island endemic?" *Bird Conservation International* 33, e25 (2023). https://doi.org/10.1017/S095927092200020X.

Turvey, Samuel T., Ian Barnes, Melissa Marr and Selina Brace. "Imperial trophy or island relict? A new extinction paradigm for Père David's deer: a Chinese conservation icon." *Royal Society Open Science* 4, 171096 (2017). https://doi.org/10.1098/rsos.171096.

Turvey, Samuel T., Jennifer J. Crees, Zhipeng Li, Jon Bielby and Jing Yuan. "Long-term archives reveal shifting extinction selectivity in China's postglacial mammal fauna." *Proceedings of the Royal Society B* 284, 20171979 (2017). http://dx.doi.org/10.1098/rspb.2017.1979.

Turvey, Samuel T., Kristoffer Bruun, Alejandra Ortiz, James Hansford, Songmei Hu, Yan Ding, Tianen Zhang and Helen J. Chatterjee. "New genus of extinct Holocene gibbon associated with humans in Imperial China." *Science* 360 (2018): 1346–1349. http://doi.org/10.1126/science.aao4903.

Turvey, Samuel T., Melissa M. Marr, Ian Barnes, Selina Brace, Benjamin Tapley, Robert W. Murphy, Ermi Zhao, Andrew A. Cunningham. "Historical museum collections clarify the evolutionary history of cryptic species radiation in the world's largest amphibians." *Ecology and Evolution* 9 (2019): 10070–10084. https://doi.org/10.1002/ece3.5257.

Turvey, Samuel T., Shu Chen, Benjamin Tapley, Zhiqiang Liang, Gang Wei, Jian Yang, Jie Wang et al. "From dirty to delicacy? Changing exploitation in China threatens the world's largest amphibians." *People and Nature* 3 (2021): 446–456. https://doi.org/10.1002/pan3.10185.

U.S. Fish and Wildlife Service. "Endangered and Threatened Wildlife and Plants; Listing the Yangtze Sturgeon as an Endangered Species." *Federal Register* 86 (April 26, 2021). https://www.federalregister.gov/documents/2021/04/26/2021-08466/endangered-and-threatened-wildlife-and-plants-listing-the-yangtze-sturgeon-as-an-endangered-species.

Vitekere, K., K. Tulizo, M. Zaman, H. Karanja, Y. Hua and G. Jiang. "Insights on the North China leopard (*Panthera padres japonensis* Gray, 1862): challenges in distribution, population status, threats, and implications for conservation." *The Journal of Animal & Plant Sciences* 31 (2021): 1–18. https://doi.org/10.36899/JAPS.2021.1.0187.

Wallace, H. Frank. "The Chinese Takin and Its Pursuit." *The Badminton Magazine of Sports and Pastimes* 36 (1913): 90–97.

Wan Xinru, Guangshun Jiang, Chuan Yan, Fangliang He, Rongsheng Wen, Jiayin Gu, Xinhai Li et al. "Historical records reveal the distinctive associations of human disturbance and extreme climate change with local extinction of mammals." *Proceedings of the National Academy of Sciences* 116 (2019): 19001–19008. www.pnas.org/cgi/doi/10.1073/pnas.1818019116.

Wan Yaqiong, Luanxin Li, Jiang Zhou, Yue Ma, Yanjiang Zhang, Yan Liu, Jiaqi Li and Wei Liu. "Predicting the potential distribution change of the endangered Francois' langur (*Trachypithecus francoisi*) across its entire range in China under climate change." *Ecology and Evolution* 14, e11684 (2024). https://doi.org/10.1002/ece3.11684.

Wang Chao, Zeng Jianwen, Li Changming and Liu Dongping. "A New Bird Distribution and Breeding Record in Shaanxi Province—White-eared Night Heron (*Gorsachius magnificus*)." *Terrestrial Ecosystem and Conservation* 2 (2022): 87–89. http://dx.doi.org/10.12356/j.2096-8884.2022-0033. (Chinese with English abstract)

Wang Chengliang, Xiaowei Wang, Xiaoguang Qi, Songtao Guo, Haitao Zhao, Wei Wei and Baoguo Li. "Influence of Human Activities on the Historical and Current Distribution of Sichuan Snub-Nosed Monkeys in the Qinling Mountains, China." *Folia Primatologica* 85 (2014): 343–357. https://doi.org/10.1159/000368398.

Wang Ding. "Population Status, Threats and Conservation of the Yangtze Finless Porpoise." *Chinese Science Bulletin* 54 (2009): 3473–3484. https://doi.org/10.1007/s11434-009-0522-7.

Wang Dongdong, Xiong Chen, Atanas G. Atanasov, Xiao Yi and Shu Wang. "Plant Resource Availability of Medicinal *Fritillaria* Species in Traditional Producing Regions in Qinghai-Tibet Plateau." *Frontiers in Pharmacology* 8, 502 (2017). https://doi.org/10.3389/fphar.2017.00502.

Wang Fang, Qing Zhao William J. McShea, Melissa Songer, Qiongyu Huang, Xiaofeng Zhang and Lingguo Zhou. "Incorporating biotic interactions reveals potential climate tolerance of giant pandas." *Conservation Letters* 11, e12592 (2018). https://doi.org/10.1111/conl.12592.

Wang Haijun, Puze Wang, Xu Zhao, Wenxia Zhang, Jing Li, Chi Xu and Ping Xie. "What triggered the Asian elephant's northward migration across southwestern Yunnan?" *The Innovation* 2, 100142 (2021). https://doi.org/10.1016/j.xinn.2021.100142.

Wang Ming, Meiying Yan, Huifang Xu, Weili Liang, Biao Kan, Bojian Zheng, Honglin Chen et al. "SARS-CoV Infection in a Restaurant from Palm Civet." *Emerging Infectious Diseases* 11 (2005): 1860-1865. https://doi.org/10.3201/eid1112.041293.

Wang Muyang, Manuel Antonio González, Weikang Yang, Peter Neuhaus, Beatriz Blanco-Fontao and Kathreen E. Ruckstuhl. "The Probable Strong Decline of the Great Bustard *Otis tarda tarda* Population in North-Western China." *Ardeola* 65 (2018): 291–297. https://doi.org/10.13157/arla.65.2.2018.sc2.

Wang Muyang and Weikang Yang. "The diminishing status of the Great Bustard *Otis tarda tarda* in Xinjiang province, north-west China." *Sandgrouse* 44 (2022): 96–100. http://eurasianbustardalliance.org/wp-content/uploads/2022/09/Wang-Yang-The-diminishing-status-of-the-Great-Bustard-in-Xinjiang-province-north-west-China.pdf.

Wang Pan, Bin Feng, Li Zhang, Xueyang Fan, Zhuo Tang, Xin Dong, Jindong Zhang et al. "Assessment of habitat suitability and connectivity across the potential distribution landscape of the sambar (*Rusa unicolor*) in Southwest China." *Frontiers in Conservation Science* 3, 909072 (2023). https://doi.org/10.3389/fcosc.2022.909072.

Wang Peilie. "Distribution, ecology and resource conservation of the Spotted Seal in the Huanghai and Bohai Seas." *Acta Oceanologica Sinica* 5 (1986): 126–133. http://aos.manuscripts.cn/article/id/19860115.

Wang Peilie, Han Jiabo, Ma Zhiqiang, Wang Nianbin. "Survey on the resources status of dugong in Hainan Province, China." *Acta Theriologica Sinica* 27 (2007): 68–73. http://www.mammal.cn/CN/Y2007/V27/I1/68. (Chinese with English abstract)

Wang Pi-lie and Lu Zhi-chuang. "Historical Records and Current Status of Western Gray Whale in China Waters." *Fisheries Science* 2 (2009): 767–771. http://www.shchkx.com/EN/Y2009/V28/I12/767. (Chinese with English abstract)

Wang Tianxiang, Wenting Li, Hongxia Cui, Yunrui Song, Changing Liu, Qing Yan and Yaoxing Wu. "Predicting the Potential Habitat Distribution of Relict Plant *Davidia involucrata* in China Based on the MaxEnt Model." *Forests* 15, 272 (2024). https://doi.org/10.3390/f15020272.

Wang Xianyan, Xu Min, Wu Fuxing, David W. Weller, Miao Xing, Aimee R. Lang and Zhu Qian. "Insights from a Gray Whale (*Eschrichtius robustus*) Bycaught in the Taiwan Strait off China in 2011." *Aquatic Mammals* 41 (2015): 327–332. http://dx.doi.org/10.1578/AM.41.3.2015.327.

Wang Xiaoming, Helin Sheng, Junghui Bi and Ming Li. "Recent history and status of the Mongolian gazelle in Inner Mongolia, China." *Oryx* 31 (1997): 120–126. https://doi.org/10.1046/j.1365-3008.1997.d01-100.x.

Wang Xiao-ming, Ke-jia Zhang, Zheng-huan Wang, You-zhong Ding, Wei Wu and Song Huang. "The decline of the Chinese giant salamander *Andrias davidianus* and implications for its conservation." *Oryx* 38 (2004): 197–202. https://doi.org/10.1017/S0030605304000341.

Wang Xin, Anthony D. Fox, Peihao Cong, Mark Barter and Lei Cao. "Changes in the distribution and abundance of wintering Lesser White-fronted Geese *Anser erythropus* in eastern China." *Bird Conservation International* 22 (2012): 128–134. https://doi.org/10.1017/S095927091100030X.

Wang Xin, Mark Barter, Lei Dao, Jinyu Lei and Anthony D. Fox. "Serious contractions in wintering distribution and decline in abundance of Baer's Pochard *Aythya baeri*." *Bird Conservation International* 22 (2012): 121–127. https://doi.org/10.1017/S0959270912000024.

Wang, Y. and R. Harris. "*Moschus berezovskii*." *The IUCN Red List of Threatened Species* (2015): e.T13894A103431781. http://dx.doi.org/10.2305/IUCN.UK.2015-4.RLTS.T13894A61976926.en.

Wang, Y. and R.B. Harris. "*Moschus anhuiensis*." *The IUCN Red List of Threatened Species* (2015): e.T136643A61979276. http://dx.doi.org/10.2305/IUCN.UK.2015-4.RLTS.T136643A61979276.en.

Wang Yamin and Jianbo Chang. "Status and conservation of sturgeons in Amur River, China: A review based on surveys since the year 2000." *Journal of Applied Ichthyology* 22, s1 (2006): 44–52. https://doi.org/10.1111/j.1439-0426.2007.00928.x.

Wang Yifu, Nigel Leader-Williams and Samuel T. Turvey. "Exploitation Histories of Pangolins and Endemic Pheasants on Hainan Island, China: Baselines and Shifting Social Norms." *Frontiers in Ecology and Evolution* 9, 608057 (2021). https://doi.org/10.3389/fevo.2021.608057.

Wang Yifu, Samuel T. Turvey and Nigel Leader-Williams. "Knowledge and attitudes about the use of pangolin scale products in Traditional Chinese Medicine (TCM) within China." *People and Nature* 2 (2020): 903–912. https://doi.org/10.1002/pan3.10150.

Wang Yuan, Liu Wulin, Liu Feng, Li Sheng, Zhu Xuelin, Jiang Zhigang, Feng Limin and Li Bingzhang. "Investigation on the population of wild Bengal tiger (*Panthera tigris tigris*) in Medog, Tibet." *Acta Theriologica Sinica* 39 (2019): 504–513. http://www.mammal.cn/EN/10.16829/j.slxb.150265. (Chinese with English abstract)

Wang Zhongwei, Jianfeng Zhou, Yuzhen Ye, Qiwei Wei and Qingjiang Wu. "Genetic structure and low-genetic diversity suggesting the necessity for conservation of the Chinese longsnout catfish, *Leiocassis longirostris* (Pisces: Bagriidae)." *Environmental Biology of Fishes* 75 (2006): 455–463. https://doi.org/10.1007/s10641-006-0035-z.

Wang Zongming, Kaishan Song, Wenhong Ma, Chunying Ren, Bai Zhang, Dianwei Liu, Jing Ming Chen and Changchun Song. "Loss and Fragmentation of Marshes in the Sanjiang Plain, Northeast China, 1954–2005." *Wetlands* 31 (2011): 945–954. https://doi.org/10.1007/s13157-011-0209-0.

Wearn, Oliver R., Hoang Trinh-Dinh, Chang-Yong Ma, Quyet Khac Le, Phuong Nguyen, Tuan Van Hoang, Chuyen Van Luong et al. "Vocal fingerprinting reveals a substantially smaller global population of the Critically Endangered cao vit gibbon (*Nomascus nasutus*) than previously thought." *Scientific Reports* 14, 416 (2024). https://doi.org/10.1038/s41598-023-50838-2.

Wei Chunyue, Huaiqing Chen, Zhengyi Dong, Xiang Zhao, Zhi Lu, Xiangying Shi, and Xuesong Han. "By their foes and by their kins — endemic Chinese mountain cats are threatened by domestic dogs and cats." *Authorea* Preprint (2023). https://doi.org/10.22541/au.169685367.72461484/v1.

Wei Qiwei. "*Acipenser dabryanus*." *The IUCN Red List of Threatened Species* (2022): e.T231A61462199. https://dx.doi.org/10.2305/IUCN.UK.2022-1.RLTS.T231A61462199.en.

———. "*Psephurus gladius*." *The IUCN Red List of Threatened Species* (2022): e.T18428A146104283. https://dx.doi.org/10.2305/IUCN.UK.2022-1.RLTS.T18428A146104283.en.

Wei Qiwei, Fu'en Ke, Jueming Zhang, Ping Zhuang, Junde Luo, Rueqiong Zhou and Wenhua Yang. "Biology, fisheries, and conservation of sturgeons and paddlefish in China." *Environmental Biology of Fishes* 48 (1997): 241–255. https://doi.org/10.1023/A:1007395612241.

Wei Yanqiang, Liang Zhang, Jinniu Wang, Wenwen Wang, Naudiyal Niyati, Yanlong Guo and Xufeng Wang. "Chinese caterpillar fungus (*Ophiocordyceps sinensis*) in China: Current distribution, trading, and futures under climate change and overexploitation." *Science of the Total Environment* 755, 142548 (2021). https://doi.org/10.1016/j.scitotenv.2020.142548.

Wei Zhen-Hua, Yan-Kuo Li, Peng Xu, Fa-Wen Qian, Ji-Hong Shan, Xiao-bin Tu. "Patterns of change in the population and spatial distribution of oriental white storks (*Ciconia boyciana*) wintering in Poyang Lake." *Zoological Research* 37 (2016): 338–346. https://www.zoores.ac.cn/en/article/id/3768.

Weller, David W., Alexander M. Burdin, Bernd Würsig, Barbara L. Taylor and Robert L. Brownell, Jr. "The western gray whale: a review of past exploitation, current status and potential threats." *Journal of Cetacean Research and Management* 4 (2002): 7–12. https://digitalcommons.unl.edu/usdeptcommercepub/96/.

Wen Guannan, Long Jin, Yayong Wu, Xiaoping Wang, Jinzhong Fu and Yin Qi. "Low diversity, little genetic structure but no inbreeding in a high-density island endemic pit-viper *Gloydius shedaoensis*." *Current Zoology* 68 (2022): 526–534. https://doi.org/10.1093/cz/zoab084.

Wen Lijia, Wang Lanhua, Ding Hongan, Li Jianzhi and Guo Yumin. "Using unmanned aerial vehicle for a population and wintering distribution survey of Siberian crane (*leucogeranus* [sic] *leucogeranus*)." *Acta Ecologica Sinica* 43 (2024): 7693–7700. https://www.ecologica.cn/stxb/article/abstract/stxb202205041234. (Chinese with English abstract)

Werhahn, Geraldine, Helen Senn, Jennifer Kaden, Jyoti Joshi, Susmita Bhattarai, Naresh Kusi, Claudio Sillero-Zubiri and David W. Macdonald. "Phylogenetic evidence for the ancient Himalayan wolf: towards a clarification of its taxonomic status based on genetic sampling from western Nepal." *Royal Society Open Science* 4 (2017). https://doi.org/10.1098/rsos.170186.

Werhahn, Geraldine, Helen Senn, Muhammad Ghazali, Dibesh Karmacharya, Adarsh Man Sherchan, Jyoti Joshi, Naresh Kusi et al. "The unique genetic adaptation of the Himalayan wolf to high-altitudes and consequences for conservation." *Global Ecology and Conservation* 16, e00455 (2018). https://doi.org/10.1016/j.gecco.2018.e00455.

Werhahn, Geraldine, Naresh Kusi, Xiaoyu Li, Cheng Chen, Lu Zhi, Raquel Lázaro Martín, Claudio Sillero-Zubiri and David W. Macdonald. "Himalayan wolf foraging ecology and the importance of wild prey." *Global Ecology and Conservation* 20, e00780 (2019). https://doi.org/10.1016/j.gecco.2019.e00780.

Winkler, Daniel. "Caterpillar Fungus (*Ophiocordyceps sinensis*) Production and Sustainability on the Tibetan Plateau and in the Himalayas." *Asian Medicine* 5 (2009): 291–316. https://doi.org/10.1163/157342109X568829.

———. "Forest use and implications of the 1998 logging ban in the Tibetan Prefectures of Sichuan: Case study on forestry, reforestation and NTFP in Litang County, Ganzi Tap, China." *Informatore Botanico Italiano* 35, Suppl. 1 (2003): 116–125. https://www.societabotanicaitaliana.it/SBI/IBI%2035%20S1%202003/05-131%20Procedings%20International%20Conference%20on%20Forest%20Ecosystems.pdf#page=112.

———. "Steps towards Sustainable Harvest of Yartsa Gunbu (Caterpillar Fungus, *Ophiocordyceps sinensis*)." *Proceedings of the 7th International Medicinal Mushroom Conference, Beijing, August 26-29* (2013): 635–644. https://www.mushroaming.com/sites/default/files/blog_images/Winkler%20Caterpillar%20fungus%20sustainability%20IMMC7%202013.pdf.

———. "*Yartsa Gunbu* (*Cordyceps sinensis*) and the Fungal Commodification of Tibet's Rural Economy." *Economic Botany* 62 (2008): 291–305. https://doi.org/10.1007/s12231-008-9038-3.

Won Changman and Byoung-Ho Yoo. "Abundance, seasonal haul-out patterns and conservation of spotted seals Phoca largha along the coast of Bak-ryoung Island, South Korea." *Oryx* 38 (2004): 109–112. https://doi.org/10.1017/S0030605304000171.

Wong, Michelle H.G., Yanni Mo and Bosco Pui Lok Chan. "Past, present and future of the globally endangered Eld's deer (*Rucervus eldii*) on Hainan Island, China." *Global Ecology and Conservation* 26, e01505 (2021). https://doi.org/10.1016/j.gecco.2021.e01505.

Wood, Jamie R., Josep A. Alcover, Tim M. Blackburn, Pere Bover, Richard P. Duncan, Julian P. Hume, Julien Louys et al. "Island extinctions: processes, patterns, and potential for ecosystem restoration." *Environmental Conservation* 44 (2017): 348–358. https://doi.org/10.1017/S037689291700039X.

Worthy, Fiona R. and J. Marc Foggin. "Conflicts between local villagers and Tibetan brown bears threaten conservation of bears in a remote region of the Tibetan Plateau." *Human–Wildlife Conflicts* 2 (2008): 200–205. https://digitalcommons.unl.edu/hwi/59/.

Wu J. M., Q. W. Wei, H. Du, C. Y. Wang and H. Zhang. "Initial evaluation of the release programme for Dabry's sturgeon (*Acipenser dabryanus* Duméril, 1868) in the upper Yangtze River." *Journal of Applied Ichthyology* 30 (2014): 1423–1427. https://doi.org/10.1111/jai.12597.

Wu Jianguo. "Risk and Uncertainty of Losing Suitable Habitat Areas Under Climate Change Scenarios: A Case Study for 109 Gymnosperm Species in China." *Environmental Management* 65 (2020): 517–533. https://doi.org/10.1007/s00267-020-01262-z.

Wu Lan and Hao Wang. "Poisoning the pika: must protection of grasslands be at the expense of biodiversity?" *Science China Life Sciences* 60 (2017): 545–547. https://doi.org/10.1007/s11427-016-0222-0.

Wu Lan, Yuyu Wang, Xunqiang Mo, Qian Wei, Chaohong Ma, Hao Wang, Terry Townshend et al. "Shifted to the South, Shifted to the North, but No Expansion: Potential Suitable Habitat Distribution Shift and Conservation Gap of the Critically Endangered Baer's Pochard (*Aythya baeri*)." *Remote Sensing* 14, 2171 (2022). https://doi.org/10.3390/rs14092171.

Wu ShaoHong and WenJun Zhang. "Current status, crisis and conservation of coral reef ecosystems in China." *Proceedings of the International Academy of Ecology and Environmental Sciences* 2 (2012): 1–11. http://www.iaees.org/publications/journals/piaees/articles/2012-2(1)/current-status-crisis-and-conservation-of-coral-reef-ecosystems.pdf.

Wu Shibao and Ma Guangzhi. "The Status and Conservation of Pangolins in China." *TRAFFIC East Asia Newsletter* 4 (2005): 1–5. https://www.pangolinsg.org/wp-content/uploads/sites/4/2016/06/Wu-and-Ma-2007-The-status-and-conservation-of-pangolins-in-China_TRAFFIC-East-Asia-Newsletter.pdf. (Chinese with English abstract)

Wu Shi-Bao, Ma Guang-Zhi, Tang Mei, Chen Hai and Liu Nai-Fa. "The status and conservation strategy of pangolin resource in China." *Journal of Natural Resources* 17 (2002): 174–180. https://doi.org/10.11849/zrzyxb.2002.02.008. (Chinese with English abstract)

Wu Tong, Xinming Lian, Hongqi Li, Dong Wang, Jiaping Chen, Ziyan Miao and Tongzuo Zhang. "Adaptation of migratory Tibetan antelope to infrastructure development." *Ecosystem Health and Sustainability* 7, 1910077 (2021). https://doi.org/10.1080/20964129.2021.1910077.

Wu Wen, Yuehui Li, Yuanman Hu, Long Chen, Due Li, Zeming Li, Zhiwen Nie and Tan Chen. "Suitable winter habitat for *Cervus elaphus* on the southern slope of the Lesser Xing'an Mountains." *Biodiversity Science* 24 (2016): 20–29. https://www.biodiversity-science.net/CN/Y2016/V24/I1/20. (Chinese with English abstract)

Wu Xiaotong, Xingxiang Zhang, Zhengyao Jin, Yanbo Song, Fengshi Luan and Xinming Xue. "Strontium isotope analysis of Yangtze alligator remains from Late Neolithic North China." *Archaeological and Anthropological Sciences* 11 (2019) 1049–1058. https://doi.org/10.1007/s12520-017-0589-z.

Xia Canjun, Jie Cao, Hefan Zhang, Xingyi Gao, Weikang Yang and David Blank. "Reintroduction of Przewalski's horse (*Equus ferus przewalskii*) in Xinjiang, China: The status and experience." *Biological Conservation* 177 (2014): 142–147. https://doi.org/10.1016/j.biocon.2014.06.021.

Xia Lin, Qisen Yang, Zengchao Li, Yonghua Wu and Zuojian Feng. "The effect of the Qinghai-Tibet railway on the migration of Tibetan antelope *Pantholops hodgsonii* in Hoh-xil National Nature Reserve, China." *Oryx* 41 (2007): 352–357. https://doi.org/10.1017/S0030605307000116.

Xiang Zuo-Fu, Sheng Huo, Lin Wang, Liang-Wei Cui, Wen Xiao, Rui-Chang Quan and Zhong Tai. "Distribution, status and conservation of the black-and-white snub-nosed monkey *Rhinopithecus bieti* in Tibet." *Oryx* 41 (2007): 525–531. https://doi.org/10.1017/S0030605307012124.

Xiang Zuo-Fu, Shuai-Guo Nie, Xiao-Ping Lei, Zong-Fei Chang, Fu-Wen Wei and Ming Li. "Current status and conservation of the gray snub-nosed monkey *Rhinopithecus brelichi* (Colobinae) in Guizhou, China." *Biological Conservation* 142 (2009): 469–476. https://doi.org/10.1016/j.biocon.2008.11.019.

Xu Ai-Chun, Jiang Zhi-Gang, Li Chun-Wang, Cai Ping. "Food habits and hunting patterns of Tibetan brown bear during warm seasons in Kekexili region on Qinghai-Tibetan Plateau." *Zoological Research* 31 (2010): 670–674. https://zoores.ac.cn/en/article/doi/10.3724/SP.J.1141.2010.06670. (Chinese with English abstract)

Xu Hongfa, Zheng Xiangzhong and Lu Houji. "Impact of human activities and habitat changes on distribution of Chinese water deer along the coast area in northern Jiangsu." *Acta Theriologica Sinica* 13 (1998): 161–167. http://www.mammal.cn/CN/Y1998/V18/I3/161. (Chinese with English abstract)

Xu Hongying, Zeyu Yang, Dongping Liu, Ru Jia, Lixia Chen, Boshi Liang, Zhengwang Zhang and Guogang Zhang. "Autumn migration routes of fledgling Chinese Egrets (*Egretta eulophotes*) in Northeast China and their implications for conservation." *Avian Research* 13, 100018 (2022). https://doi.org/10.1016/j.avrs.2022.100018.

Xu Wenjing, Qiongyu Huang, Jared Stabach, Hoshino Buho and Peter Leimgruber. "Railway underpass location affects migration distance in Tibetan antelope (*Pantholops hodgsonii*)." *PLoS ONE* 14, e0211798 (2019). https://doi.org/10.1371/journal.pone.0211798.

Xu Wenru, Hong S. He, Todd J. Hawbaker, Zhiliang Zhu and Paul D. Henne. "Estimating burn severity and carbon emissions from a historic megafire in boreal forests of China." *Science of the Total Environment* 716, 136534 (2020). https://doi.org/10.1016/j.scitotenv.2020.136534.

Xu Wenxuan, Canjun Xia, Jie Lin, Weikang Yang, David A. Blank, Jianfang Qiao and Wei Liu. "Diet of *Gazella subgutturosa* (Güldenstaedt, 1780) and food overlap with domestic sheep in Xinjiang, China." *Folia Zoologica* 61 (2012): 54–60. https://doi.org/10.25225/fozo.v61.i1.a9.2012.

Xu Wenxuan, Wei Liu, Wei Ma, Muyang Wang, Feng Xu, Weikang Yang, Chris Walzer and Petra Kaczensky. "Current status and future challenges for khulan (*Equus hemionus*) conservation in China." *Global Ecology and Conservation* 37, e02156 (2022). https://doi.org/10.1016/j.gecco.2022.e02156.

Xu Xu, Xianguo Lu, Qiang Wang, Chunyue Liu, Changchun Song, Haitao Wang, Guodong Wang, Bo Liu, Keji Sun and Haifeng Zheng. "Exploring conservation strategies for oriental white stork fledglings (*Ciconia boyciana*) across the breeding wetland landscape: Hints from tracking movement patterns." *Global Ecology and Conservation* 26, e01531 (2021). https://doi.org/10.1016/j.gecco.2021.e01531.

Xu Yanda, Fen Li, Cui Xu, Shanghua Luo, Shijun Chao, Yang Guo, Chengcheng Liu and Linbo Zhang. "Quantitative assessment of the ecological impact of Chinese cordyceps collection in the typical production areas." *Écoscience* 22 (2015): 167–175. https://doi.org/10.1080/11956860.2016.1181516.

Xu Yu, Biao Yang and Liang Dou. "Local villagers' perceptions of wolves in Jiuzhaigou County, western China." *PeerJ* 3, e982 (2015). https://doi.org/10.7717/peerj.982.

Xue Dayuan, Zhang Yuanyuan, Cheng Zhibin, Zhong Zhenyu, Cao Ming, Fu Mengdi, Bai Jiade and Yuan Xuejiao. "Père David's Deer (*Elaphurus davidianus*) in China: Population Dynamics and Challenges." *Journal of Resources and Ecology* 13 (2022): 41–50. https://www.jorae.cn/EN/10.5814/j.issn.1674-764x.2022.01.005.

Xue Yadong, Diqiang Li, Wenfa Xiao, Yuguang Zhang, Bin Feng and Heng Jia. "Records of the dhole (*Cuon alpinus*) in an arid region of the Altun Mountains in western China." *European Journal of Wildlife Research* 61 (2015): 903–907. https://doi.org/10.1007/s10344-015-0947-z.

Xue Yadong, Jia Li and Diqiang Li. "The wild camel (*Camelus ferus*) in China: Current status and conservation implications." *Journal for Nature Conservation* 60, 125979 (2021). https://doi.org/10.1016/j.jnc.2021.125979.

Xue Yadong, Jia Li, Yu Zhang, Diqiang Li, Lei Yuan, Yun Cheng, Shaochuang Liu and Charlotte E. Hacker. "Assessing the vulnerability and adaptation strategies of wild camel to climate change in the Kumtag Desert of China." *Global Ecology and Conservation* 29, e01725 (2021). https://doi.org/10.1016/j.gecco.2021.e01725.

Yan Fang, Jingcai Lü, Baolin Zhang, Zhiyong Yuan, Haipeng Zhao, Song Huang, Gang Wei et al. "The Chinese giant salamander exemplifies the hidden extinction of cryptic species." *Current Biology* 28 (2018): R581–R598. https://doi.org/10.1016/j.cub.2018.04.004.

Yan Hua-Kun, Nuo Wang, Nuan Wu and Wan-ni Lin. "Abundance, Habitat Conditions, and Conservation of the Largha Seal (*Phoca largha*) During the Past Half Century in the Bohai Sea, China." *Mammal Study* 43 (2018): 1–9. https://doi.org/10.3106/ms2017-0027.

———. "Maritime construction site selection from the perspective of ecological protection: The relationship between the Dalian offshore airport and spotted seals (*Phoca largha*) in China based on the noise pollution." *Ocean and Coastal Management* 152 (2018): 145–153. https://doi.org/10.1016/j.ocecoaman.2017.11.024.

Yan Lin, Yuanhao Ren, Tongxi Ai, Jianshe Shi, Junjie Wang, Kuoqiu Yan and Keji Jiang. "Early Growth and Developmental Characteristics of Chinese Bahaba (*Bahaba taipingensis*)." *Fishes* 9, 329 (2024). https://doi.org/10.3390/fishes9080329.

Yan Mingxiao, Bojian Gu, Mingxia Zhang, Wei Wang, Rui-Chang Quan, Jiaqi Li and Lin Wang. "The Range Contraction and Future Conservation of Green Peafowl (*Pavo muticus*) in China." *Sustainability* 13, 11723 (2021). https://doi.org/10.3390/su132111723.

Yang Fan, Quanqin Shao and Zhigang Jiang "A Population Census of Large Herbivores Based on UAV and Its Effects on Grazing Pressure in the Yellow-River-Source National Park, China." *International Journal of Environmental Research and Public Health* 16, 4402 (2019). https://doi.org/10.3390/ijerph16224402.

Yang Guangmei, Caichun Peng, Xiongwei Yang, Qunyi Guo and Haijun Su. "Habitat suitability and crop damage risk caused by wild boar in Guizhou Plateau, China." *Journal of Wildlife Management* 88, e22542 (2024). https://doi.org/10.1002/jwmg.22542.

Yang Haile, Li Shen, Yongfeng He, Huiwu Tian, Lei Gao, Jinming Wu, Zhigang Mei et al. "Status of aquatic organisms resources and their environments in Yangtze River system (2017–2021)." *Aquaculture and Fisheries* 9 (2024): 833–850. https://doi.org/10.1016/j.aaf.2023.06.004.

Yang Jian-Huan, Xiang-Yuan Huang, Shen-Heng Jin and Bosco Pui Lok Chan. "Filling a longstanding knowledge gap: Population size and conservation status of the Endangered Gaoligong hoolock Gibbon (*Hoolock tianxing*) in Houqiao Town, Yunnan." *Global Ecology and Conservation* 24, e01347 (2020). https://doi.org/10.1016/j.gecco.2020.e01347.

Yang Jing, Guo-Fen Zhu, Jian Jiang, Chang-Lin Xiang, Fu-Li Gao, Wei-Dong Bao. "Non-invasive genetic analysis indicates low population connectivity in vulnerable Chinese gorals: concerns for segregated population management." *Zoological Research* 40 (2019): 439-448. http://dx.doi.org/10.24272/j.issn.2095-8137.2019.058.

Yang Li, Mujiao Huang, Rui Zhang, Lv Jiang, Yueheng Ren, Zhe Jiang, Wei Zhang and Xiaofeng Luan. "Reconstructing the historical distribution of the Amur Leopard (*Panthera pardus orientalis*) in Northeast China based on historical records." *ZooKeys* 592 (2016): 143–153. https://doi.org/10.3897/zookeys.592.6912.

Yang Li, Rui Zhang, Hairui Duo, Wei Zhang, Zhe Jiang, Yueheng Ren, Jiang Lv et al. "Historical Distribution of Lynx (*Lynx lynx*) in Northeast China on the Basis of Historical Records." *Russian Journal of Ecology* 48 (2017): 569–575. https://doi.org/10.1134/S1067413617060133.

Yang Liuyang, Jiangnan Ling, Lilei Lu, Dongsheng Zang, Yunzhen Zhu, Song Zhang, Yongkang Zhou et al. "Identification of suitable habitats and priority conservation areas under climate change scenarios for the Chinese alligator (*Alligator sinensis*)." *Ecology and Evolution* 14, e11477 (2024). https://doi.org/10.1002/ece3.11477.

Yang Qisen, Xiuxiang Meng, Lin Xia and Zuojian Feng. "Conservation status and causes of decline of musk deer (*Moschus* spp.) in China." *Biological Conservation* 109 (2003): 333–342. https://doi.org/10.1016/S0006-3207(02)00159-3.

Yang Shangchen, Tianming Lan, Yi Zhang, Qing Wang, Haimeng Li, Nicolas Dussex, Sunil Kumar Sahu et al. "Genomic investigation of the Chinese alligator reveals wild-extinct genetic diversity and genomic consequences of their continuous decline." *Molecular Ecology Resources* 23 (2023): 294–311. https://doi.org/10.1111/1755-0998.13702.

Yang Xuefei, Jun He, Chun Li, Jianzhong Ma, Yongping Yang and Jianchu Xu. "Matsutake Trade in Yunnan Province, China: An Overview." *Economic Botany* 62 (2008): 269–277. https://doi.org/10.1007/s12231-008-9019-6.

Yang Yin, Aung Ko Lin, Paul A. Garber, Zhipang Huang, Yinping Tian, Alison Behie, Frank Momberg et al. "The 10th anniversary of the scientific description of the black snub-nosed monkey (*Rhinopithecus strykeri*): It is time to initiate a set of new management strategies to save this critically endangered primate from extinction." *American Journal of Primatology* 84, e23372 (2022). https://doi.org/10.1002/ajp.23372.

Ye Xiulin, Paul A. Garber, Ming Li and Xumao Zhao. "Climate and anthropogenic activities threaten two langur species irrespective of their range size." *Diversity and Distributions* 30, e13841 (2024). https://doi.org/10.1111/ddi.13841.

Yeh, Emily T., Leah H. Samberg, Gaerrang, Emily Volkmar and Richard B. Harris. "Pastoralist Decision-Making on the Tibetan Plateau." *Human Ecology* 45 (2017): 333–343. https://doi.org/10.1007/s10745-017-9891-8.

Yi Murong, Ping Lu, Yong Peng, Yong Tang, Jiuheng Xu, Haoping Yin, Luyang Zhang et al. "Population status and habitat of critically endangered Jiangxi giant salamander (*Andrias jiangxiensis*)." *Biodiversity Science* 32, 24145 (2024). https://www.biodiversity-science.net/EN/10.17520/biods.2024145. (Chinese with English abstract)

Yin Denghua, Chunhai Chen, Danqing Lin, Jialu Zhang, Congping Ying, Yan Liu, Wang Liu et al. "Gapless genome assembly of East Asian finless porpoise." *Scientific Data* 9, 765 (2022). https://doi.org/10.1038/s41597-022-01868-4.

Yin Yufeng, Drubgyal, Achu, Lu Zhi and Jim Sanderson. "First Photographs in Nature of the Chinese Mountain Cat." *Cat News* 47 (2007): 6–7.

Yongdan, Lobsang. "Precious Skin: The Rise and Fall of the Otter Fur Trade in Tibet." *Inner Asia* 20 (2018): 177–198. https://doi.org/10.1163/22105018-12340106.

Yu Dupao, Li Zhou, Wangming Zhou, Hong Ding, Qingwei Wang, Yue Wang, Xiaoqing Wu and Limin Dai. "Forest Management in Northeast China: History, Problems, and Challenges." *Environmental Management* 48 (2011): 1122–1135. https://doi.org/10.1007/s00267-011-9633-4.

Yu He, Shiya Song, Jiazi Liu, Sheng Li, Lu Zhang, Dajun Wang and Shu-Jin Luo. "Effects of the Qinghai-Tibet Railway on the Landscape Genetics of the Endangered Przewalski's Gazelle (*Procapra przewalskii*)." *Scientific Reports* 7, 17983 (2017). https://doi.org/10.1038/s41598-017-18163-7.

Yu He, Yue-Ting Xing, Hao Meng, Bing He, Wen-Jing Li, Xin-Zhang Qi, Jian-You Zhao et al. "Genomic evidence for the Chinese mountain cat as a wildcat conspecific (*Felis silvestris bieti*) and its introgression to domestic cats." *Science Advances* 7, eabg0221 (2021). https://doi.org/10.1126/sciadv.abg0221.

Yu KeFu. "Coral reefs in the South China Sea: Their response to and records on past environmental changes." *Science China Earth Sciences* 55 (2012): 1217–1229. https://doi.org/10.1007/s11430-012-4449-5.

Yu Si-Yu, Zhang Zhao, He Wei, Yang Yong-Xin, Zhang Zheng-Yi, Wang Na, Wang Xiao-Dan et al. "The Status of Red Deer Population in the Southern Part of the Greater Khingan Mountains in Inner Mongolia." *Chinese Journal of Zoology* 57 (2022): 759–765. http://dwxzz.ioz.ac.cn/ch/reader/view_abstract.aspx?file_no=22021. (Chinese with English abstract)

Yu Yang, Gang He, Da-Yong Li, Xu-Mao Zhao, Jiang Chang, Xue-Cong Liu, Zuo-Fu Xiang et al. "Climate change challenges extinction risk, and successful conservation experiences for a threatened primate species in China: Golden snub-nosed monkey (*Rhinopithecus roxellana*)." *Zoological Research* 43 (2022): 940–944. https://doi.org/10.24272/j.issn.2095-8137.2022.198.

Yu Yat-tung and Chen Zhihong. "Dalmatian Pelican *Pelecanus crispus*: the largest waterbird in East Asia, and the rarest?" *BiraingASIA* 9 (2008): 62–66. https://www.researchgate.net/profile/Yat_Tung_Yu/publication/281076398_Dalmatian_Pelican_Pelicanus_crispus_the_largest_waterbird_in_East_Asia_and_the_rarest/links/55d3e83a08aec1b0429f3fe3/Dalmatian-Pelican-Pelicanus-crispus-the-largest-waterbird-in-East-Asia-and-the-rarest.pdf.

Zeng Zhi-Gao, Wen-Qin Zhong, Yan-Ling Song, Jun-Sheng Li and Feng Guo. "Group size, composition and stability of golden takin in Shaanxi Foping Nature Reserve, China." *Folia Zoologica*. 51 (2002): 289–298.

Zeng Zhi-Gao, Yan-Ling Song, Jun-Sheng Li, L.-Wei Teng, Qiong Zhang and Feng Guo. "Distribution, status and conservation of Hainan Eld's deer (*Cervus eldi hainanus*) in China." *Folia Zoologica* 54 (2005): 249–257. https://www.ivb.cz/wp-content/uploads/54_249-257.pdf.

Zhang Chao, Yuwei Fan, Minhao Chen, Wancai Xia, Jiadong Wang, Zhenjie Zhan, Wenlong Wang et al. "Identification of Conservation Priority Areas and a Protection Network for the Siberian Musk Deer (*Moschus moschiferus* L.) in Northeast China." *Animals* 12, 260 (2022). https://doi.org/10.3390/ani12030260.

Zhang Chi and Hsiao-chun Hung. "The emergence of agriculture in southern China." *Antiquity* 84 (2010): 11–25. https://doi.org/10.1017/S0003598X00099737.

Zhang Fuhua, Shibao Wu and Peng Cen. "The past, present and future of the pangolin in Mainland China." *Global Ecology and Conservation* 33, e01995 (2022). https://doi.org/10.1016/j.gecco.2021.e01995.

Zhang Hui, Ivan Jarić, David L. Roberts, Yongfeng He, Hao Du, Jinming Wu, Chengyou Wang and Qiwei Wei. "Extinction of one of the world's largest freshwater fishes: Lessons for conserving the endangered Yangtze fauna." *Science of the Total Environment* 710, 136242 (2020). https://doi.org/10.1016/j.scitotenv.2019.136242.

Zhang Jingjie, Feng Jiang, Guangying Li, Wen Qin, Tong Wu, Feng Xu, Yuansheng Hou, Pengfei Song et al. "The four antelope species on the Qinghai-Tibet plateau face habitat loss and redistribution to higher latitudes under climate change." *Ecological Indicators* 123 (2021): 107337. https://doi.org/10.1016/j.ecolind.2021.107337.

Zhang Jinlong and Gunter A. Fischer. "Reconsideration of the native range of the Chinese Swamp Cypress (*Glyptostrobus pensilis*) based on new insights from historic, remnant and planted populations." *Global Ecology and Conservation* 32, e01927 (2021). https://doi.org/10.1016/j.gecco.2021.e01927.

Zhang Le, Tianming Lan, Chuyu Lin, Wenyuan Fu, Yaohua Yuan, Kaixiong Lin, Haimeng Li et al. "Chromosome-scale genomes reveal genomic consequences of inbreeding in the South China tiger: A comparative study with the Amur tiger." *Molecular Ecology Resources* 23 (2023): 330–347. https://doi.org/10.1111/1755-0998.13669.

Zhang Li. "Current Status of Asian Elephants in China." *Gajah* 35 (2011): 43-46. https://www.asesg.org/PDFfiles/2012/35-43-Zhang.pdf.

Zhang Li, Lichao Ma and Limin Feng. "New challenges facing traditional nature reserves: Asian elephant (*Elephas maximus*) conservation in China." *Integrative Zoology* 1 (2006): 179–187. https://doi.org/10.1111/j.1749-4877.2006.00031.x.

Zhang Li, Lu Dong, Liu Lin, Limin Feng, Fan Yan, Lanxin Wang, Xianming Guo, Aidong Luo. "Asian Elephants in China: Estimating Population Size and Evaluating Habitat Suitability." *PLoS ONE* 10, e0124834 (2015). https://doi.org/10.1371/journal.pone.0124834.

Zhang Libiao, Guangjian Zhu, Gareth Jones and Shuyi Zhang. "Conservation of bats in China: problems and recommendations." *Oryx* 43 (2009): 179–182. https://doi.org/10.1017/S0030605309432022.

Zhang Lu and Fan Pengfei. "Conservation status of otters in China and a discussion on restoring otter populations in the Pearl River Delta." *Acta Theriologica Sinica* 40 (2020): 71–80. http://www.mammal.cn/CN/10.16829/j.slxb.150345. (Chinese with English abstract)

Zhang Lu, Jiazi Liu, Dajun Wang, George B. Schaller, Yonglin Wu, Richard B. Harris, Kejia Zhang and Zhi Lü. "Distribution and population status of Przewalski's gazelle, Procapra przewalskii (Cetartiodactyla, Bovidae)." *Mammalia* 77 (2013): 31–40. https://doi.org/10.1515/mammalia-2012-0002.

Zhang Lu, Jiazi Liu, Dajun Wang, Hao Wang, Yonglin Wu & Zhi Lü. "Fencing for conservation? —The impacts of fencing on grasslands and the endangered Przewalski's gazelle on the Tibetan Plateau." *Science China Life Sciences* 61 (2016): 1593–1595. https://doi.org/10.1007/s11427-016-5096-4.

Zhang Lu, Jiazi Liu, Yonglin Wu, Jianxing Cheng, Yanlin Liu. "Influence of Fencing on Przewalski's Gazelle, Qinghai Province, China." Report. 2010. https://www.conservationleadershipprogramme.org/project/fencing-przewalskis-gazelle-china/.

Zhang Rui, Li Yang, Lin Ai, Qiuyuan Yang, Minhao Chen, Jingxi Li, Lei Yang and Xiaofeng Luan. "Geographic characteristics of sable (*Martes zibellina*) distribution over time in Northeast China." *Ecology and Evolution* 7 (2017): 4016–4023. https://doi.org/10.1002/ece3.2983.

Zhang Ting, Chenglong Zhang, Yunteng Liu, Yupei Li, Yangfei Yu, Jichao Wang, Liu Lin and Hai-Tao Shi. "Selection characteristics and utilization of nesting grounds by green sea turtles on Xisha Islands, South China Sea." *Global Ecology and Conservation* 54, e03091 (2024). https://doi.org/10.1016/j.gecco.2024.e03091.

Zhang Wei, Jiang Zhe, Gong Huzhong and Luan Xiaofeng. "Effects of climate change on the potential habitat of *Alces alces cameloides,* an endangered species in Northeastern China." *Acta Ecologica Sinica* 36 (2016): 1815–1823. http://dx.doi.org/10.5846/stxb201409161838. (Chinese with English abstract)

Zhang Xiao-Li, Facundo Alvarez, Martin J. Whiting, Xu-Dong Qin, Ze-Ning Chen and Zheng-Jun Wu. "Climate Change and Dispersal Ability Jointly Affects the Future Distribution of Crocodile Lizards." *Animals* 12, 2731 (2022). https://doi.org/10.3390/ani12202731.

Zhang Yaze, Yanwei Zheng, Qinghua Gong, Shuqing Fu, Cong Chen, Yongjie Tang, Xiao Zhang et al. "Human Impacts on Holocene Vegetation and Wetland Degradation in the Lower Pearl River, Southern China." *Land* 13, 530 (2024). https://doi.org/10.3390/land13040530.

Zhang Yongquan, Peixian Luan, Guangming Ren, Guo Hu and Jiasheng Yin. "Estimating the inbreeding level and genetic relatedness in an isolated population of critically endangered Sichuan taimen (*Hucho Bleekeri*) using genome-wide SNP markers." *Ecology and Evolution* 10 (2020): 1390–1400. https://doi.org/10.1002/ece3.5994.

Zhang Yu, Céline Clauzel, Jia Li, Yadong Xue, Yuguang Zhang, Gongsheng Wu, Patrick Giraudoux, Li Li and Diqiang Li. "Identifying refugia and corridors under climate change conditions for the Sichuan snub-nosed monkey (*Rhinopithecus roxellana*) in Hubei Province, China." *Ecology and Evolution* 9 (2019): 1680–1690. https://doi.org/10.1002/ece3.4815.

Zhang Yuguang, Yuhong Zhong, Yanyun Hong, Yadong Xue, Diqiang Li, Chengran Zhou and Shanlin Liu. "RAD-Seq data advance captive-based conservation of wild bactrian camels (*Camelus ferus*)." *Conservation Genetics* 20 (2019): 817–824. https://doi.org/10.1007/s10592-019-01173-5.

Zhang Zhixin, Stefano Mammola, Zhiqiang Liang, César Capinha, Qiwei Wei, Yuanan Wu, Jin Zhou and Chongrui Wang. "Future climate change will severely reduce habitat suitability of the Critically Endangered Chinese giant salamander." *Freshwater Biology* 65 (2020): 1–10. https://doi.org/10.1111/fwb.13483.

Zhao Jiale, Weiwei Shao, Yalei Li, Haozhan Chen, Zhihua Lin and Li Wei. "Potential impact of climate change on the distribution of *Capricornis milneedwardsii*, a vulnerable mammal in China." *Ecology and Evolution* 14, e11582 (2024). https://doi.org/10.1002/ece3.11582.

Zhao Kairui, Liao Linhong, Xie Lei, Du Yating, Dong Pengmei, Xie Meng and Ni Qingyong. "Distribution and conservation status of Lorisinae primates in the middle and lower reaches of Nanxi River in southeastern Yunnan." *Acta Theriologica Sinica* 44 (2024): 85–93. http://www.mammal.cn/EN/10.16829/j.slxb.150859. (Chinese with English abstract)

Zhao Meixia, Kefu Yu, Qiaomin Zhang, Qi Shi and Gilbert J. Price. "Long-term Decline of a Fringing Coral Reef in the Northern South China Sea." *Journal of Coastal Research* 28 (2012): 1088–1099. http://dx.doi.org/10.2112/JCOASTRES-D-10-00172.1.

Zhao Qikun. "Status of the Yunnan Snub-nosed Monkey." *Primate Conservation* 9 (1988): 131–134. http://www.primate-sg.org/storage/pdf/Primate%20Conservation%209%201988_Part2.pdf.

Zhao Shancen, Pingping Zheng, Shanshan Dong, Xiangjiang Zhan, Qi Wu, Xiaosen Guo, Yibo Hu et al. "Whole-genome sequencing of giant pandas provides insights into demographic history and local adaptation." *Nature Genetics* 45 (2013): 67–71. https://doi.org/10.1038/ng.2494.

Zhao Xiujiang, Jay Barlow, Barbara L. Taylor, Robert L. Pitman, Kexiong Wang, Zhuo Wei, Brent S. Stewart et al. "Abundance and Conservation Status of the Yangtze Finless Porpoise in the Yangtze River, China." *Biological Conservation* 141 (2008): 3006–3018. https://doi.org/10.1016/j.biocon.2008.09.005.

Zhao Xumao, Baoping Ren, Dayong Li, Zuofu Xiang, Paul A. Garber and Ming Li. "Effects of habitat fragmentation and human disturbance on the population dynamics of the Yunnan snub-nosed monkey from 1994 to 2016." *PeerJ* 7, e6633 (2019). https://doi.org/10.7717/peerj.6633.

Zhao Xumao, Baoping Ren, Paul A. Garber, Xinhai Li and Ming Li . "Impacts of human activity and climate change on the distribution of snub-nosed monkeys in China during the past 2000 years." *Diversity and Distributions* 24 (2018): 92–102. https://doi.org/10.1111/ddi.12657.

Zheng Chenqing, Qing Chen, Michelle Hang Gi Wong, Nick Marx, Thananh Khotpathoom, Hesheng Wang, Feng Yang et al. "Whole-Genome Analyses Reveal the Distinct Taxonomic Status of the Hainan Population of Endangered *Rucervus eldii* and Its Conservation Implications." *Evolutionary Applications* 17, e70010 (2024). https://doi.org/10.1111/eva.70010.

Zheng Zhuo, Ting Ma, Patrick Roberts, Zhen Li, Yuanfu Yum, Huanhuan Peng, Kangyou Huang et al. "Anthropogenic impacts on Late Holocene land-cover change and floristic biodiversity loss in tropical southeastern Asia." *Proceedings of the National Academy of Sciences* 118, e2022210118 (2021). https://doi.org/10.1073/pnas.2022210118.

Zhong T., L. Xiao, R.C. Kirkpatrick and Y.C. Long. "A Brief Report on Yunnan Snub-Nosed Monkeys, *Rhinopithecus (R.) lieti*, at Bamei in Northern Yunnan Province, China." *Primate Conservation* 18 (1998): 76–80. http://www.primate-sg.org/storage/PDF/PC18.pdf.

Zhou Chunfa, Jiliang Xu and Zhengwang Zhang. "Dramatic decline of the Vulnerable Reeves's pheasant *Syrmaticus reevesii*, endemic to central China." *Oryx* 49 (2015): 529–534. https://doi.org/10.1017/S0030605313000914.

Zhou Daqing, Haonan Zhang, Xingshuo Zhang, Wenwen Zhang, Tingting Zhang and Changhu Lu. "Habitat changes in the most important stopover sites for the endangered red-crowned crane in China: a large-scale study." *Environmental Science and Pollution Research* 28 (2021): 54719–54727. https://doi.org/10.1007/s11356-021-14488-z.

Zhou Jiang, Fuwen Wei, Ming Li, Jianfeng Zhang, Deli Wang and Ruliang Pan. "Hainan Black-crested Gibbon Is Headed For Extinction." *International Journal of Primatology* 26 (2005): 453–465. https://doi.org/10.1007/s10764-005-2933-x.

Zhou Kaiya, Stephen Leatherwood, and Thomas A. Jefferson. "Records of Small Cetaceans in Chinese Waters: A Review." *Asian Marine Biology* 12 (1995): 119–139.

Zhou Qihai and Huang Chengming. "Advances in ecological research on the limestone langurs in China." *Acta Theriologica Sinica* 41 (2021): 59–70. https://www.mammal.cn/CN/10.16829/j.slxb.150422. (Chinese with English abstract)

Zhou Xuming, Fengming Sun, Shixia Xu, Guangyi Fan, Kangli Zhu, Xin Liu, Yuan Chen et al. "Baiji genomes reveal low genetic variability and new insights into secondary aquatic adaptations." *Nature Communications* 4, 2708 (2013). https://doi.org/10.1038/ncomms3708.

Zhou Xuming, Xuanmin Guang, Di Sun, Shixia Xu, Mingzhou Li, Inge Seim, Wencai Jie et al. "Population genomics of finless porpoises reveal an incipient cetacean species adapted to freshwater." *Nature Communications* 9, 1276 (2018). https://doi.org/10.1038/s41467-018-03722-x.

Zhou Yijun, Xiuxiang Meng, Jinchao Feng, Qisen Yang, Zuojian Feng, Lin Xia and Luděk Bartoš. "Review of the distribution, status and conservation of musk deer in China." *Folia Zoologica* 53 (2004): 129–140. https://www.ivb.cz/wp-content/uploads/53_129-140.pdf.

Zhu Hua. "The Tropical Forests of Southern China and Conservation of Biodiversity." *The Botanical Review* 83 (2017): 87–105. https://doi.org/10.1007/s12229-017-9177-2.

Zhu Shibing, Shifang Zhang and Minghai Zhang. "Update on the status of wolverines in China." *Journal of Forestry Research* 28 (2017): 425–429. https://doi.org/10.1007/s11676-016-0310-6.

Zhuang Ping, Fu'en Ke, Qiwei Wei, Xuefu He and Yuji Cen. "Biology and life history of Dabry's sturgeon, *Acipenser dabryanus*, in the Yangtze River." *Environmental Biology of Fishes* 48 (1997): 257–264. https://doi.org/10.1023/A:1007399729080.

Zhuravlev, Yuri N, Olga G Koren, Galina D Reunova, Tamara I Muzarok, Tatiyana Yu Gorpenchenko, Irina L Kats and Yuliya A Khrolenko. "*Panax ginseng* natural populations: their past, current state and perspectives." *Acta Pharmacologica Sinica* 29 (2008): 1127–1136. https://doi.org/10.1111/j.1745-7254.2008.00866.x.

Zöckler, Christoph, Evgeny E. Syroechkovskiy and Philip W. Atkinson. "Rapid and continued population decline in the Spoon-billed Sandpiper *Eurynorhynchus pygmeus* indicates imminent extinction unless conservation action is taken." *Bird Conservation International* 20 (2010): 95–111. https://doi.org/10.1017/S0959270910000316.

Zöckler, Christoph, Pyae Phyo Aung and Sayam U. Chowdhury. "Summary of SBS winter counts 2021 and proportion of flagged Spoon-billed Sandpiper." *Spoon-billed Sandpiper Task Force News Bulletin* 24 (2021): 23–25. https://eaaflyway.net/wp-content/uploads/2021/05/SBS-Newsletter-No-24-May-2021-web.pdf.

Zuo Tao, Sun Jianqiang, She Yongqiang, Wang Jun. "Primary survey of finless porpoise population in the Bohai Sea." *Acta Theriologica Sinica* 38 (2018): 551–561. http://www.mammal.cn/EN/10.16829/j.slxb.150147. (Chinese with English abstract)

白德凤, 陈颖, 李俊松, 陶庆, 王利繁, 飘优, 时坤. "西双版纳尚勇自然保护区哺乳动物物种多样性." 生物多样性 26 (2018): 75–78. https://doi.org/10.17520/biods.2017223.

曹克清, 陈彬. "关于野生麋鹿绝灭原因的再探讨." 四川动物 1 (1990): 41–42.

杜浩, 李罗新, 危起伟, 张书环, 王成友, 孙庆亮, 杨晓鸽, 李雷. "濒危物种川陕哲罗鲑在汉江上游太白河再发现." 动物学杂志 49 (2014): 414. http://dwxzz.ioz.ac.cn/ch/reader/view_abstract.aspx?file_no=13239.

何晓瑞. "我国特有种滇螈的绝灭及其原因分析." 四川动物 (1998): 58–60.

嘉楠. "海獭: 水中灵鼬, 亦盗亦友." 博物 180 (2018): 38–43.

蒋志刚, 孙吉周, 崔绍朋, 陈代强, 张履冰, 李春旺, 汤宋华, 初红军. "分布在新疆阿尔泰山的欧亚驼鹿." 动物学杂志 49 (2014): 303–304. http://dwxzz.ioz.ac.cn/ch/reader/view_abstract.aspx?file_no=14083.

罗树毅, 徐芳英. "鳄蜥 '守株待兔' 的捕猎者." 森林与人类 381 (2022): 80–91.

马合木提·哈里克, 李新平, 阿布都外力, 黄人鑫, 金刚, 排孜都拉. "新疆阿尔泰山驼鹿的初步考察." 兽类学报 15 (1995): 159. http://www.mammal.cn/CN/Y1995/V15/I2/159.

全国强, 靳景玉, 黄金声, 周玉富. "我国灵长目一种的新记录." 兽类学报 7 (1987): 158. http://www.mammal.cn/CN/Y1987/V7/I2/158.

谭邦杰. "野生动物的灭种和保种." 自然杂志 2 (1979): 425–430.

曾治高, 宋延龄. "秦岭羚牛的生态与保护对策." 生物学通报 43 (2008): 1–3.

张洁. 中国境内亚洲象分布及变迁的社会因素研究. 陕西师范大学 博士学位论文. 2014.

郑生武, 高行宜. "中国野驴的现状、分布区的历史变迁原因探讨." 生物多样性 8 (2000): 81–87.

中国水獭调查与保护报告编辑组. 2019中国水獭调查与保护报告 (2019). http://www.shanshui.org/wp-content/uploads/2020/02/20200224074256676.pdf.

INDEX